THE UNIVERSAL
STANDARD
ENCYCLOPEDIA

THE THREE-COLOR PROCESS. *Separate engravings of the colors yellow, red, and blue, are combined to reproduce the painting "Jeanne Samary," by Pierre Auguste Renoir, in full color.*

THE UNIVERSAL STANDARD ENCYCLOPEDIA

VOLUME 13

IDAHO—JEWEL CAVE

An abridgment of The New Funk & Wagnalls Encyclopedia
prepared under the editorial direction of
JOSEPH LAFFAN MORSE, Sc.B., LL.B.
Editor in Chief

UNICORN PUBLISHERS, INC., NEW YORK

UNIVERSAL STANDARD ENCYCLOPEDIA
Copyright 1954
By WILFRED FUNK, INC.

NEW FUNK & WAGNALLS ENCYCLOPEDIA
Copyright 1949, 1950, 1951, 1952 and 1953
By FUNK & WAGNALLS COMPANY

FUNK & WAGNALLS NEW STANDARD ENCYCLOPEDIA
Copyright 1931, 1934, 1935, 1937, 1942, 1943, 1944,
1945, 1946, 1947, 1948 and 1949
By FUNK & WAGNALLS COMPANY

Printed in the United States of America
ALL RIGHTS RESERVED

Copyright Under the Articles of the Copyright Convention
of the Pan-American Republics and the United States

A E D

THE UNIVERSAL
STANDARD
ENCYCLOPEDIA

LIST OF ABBREVIATIONS USED

abbr., abbreviated
A.D., Anno Domini
alt., altitude
A.M., ante meridiem
anc., ancient
approx., approximately
Ar., Arabic
AS., Anglo-Saxon
A.S.S.R., Autonomous Soviet Socialist Republic
at.no., atomic number
at.wt., atomic weight
b., born
B.C., before Christ
b.p., boiling point
B.T.U., British Thermal Unit
Bulg., Bulgarian
C., centigrade, syn. Celsius
cent., century
Chin., Chinese
cm., centimeter
Co., County
colloq., colloquial
cu., cubic
Czech., Czechoslovakian
d., died
Dan., Danish
Du., Dutch
E., east, easterly, eastern
ed., edition
e.g., for example
Egypt., Egyptian
Eng., English
est., estimated
et seq., and following
F., Fahrenheit
fl., flourished
fr., from
Fr., French
ft., foot

Gael., Gaelic
Gen., General
Ger., German
Gr., Greek
Heb., Hebrew
Hind., Hindustani
Hon., Honorable
h.p., horsepower
hr., hour
Hung., Hungarian
I., Island
i.e., that is
in., inch
Ind., Indian
Ir., Irish
It., Italian
Jr., junior
kg., kilogram
km., kilometer
lat., latitude
Lat., Latin
lb., pound
lit., literally
long., longitude
m., mile
M., Middle
min., minute
M.L., Medieval Latin
mm., millimeter
mod., modern
m.p., melting point
M.P., Member of Parliament
m.p.h., miles per hour
Mt., Mount, Mountain
N., north, northerly, northern
N.T., New Testament
OE., Old English
OF., Old French
OHG., Old High German
ON., Old Norse

ONF., Old Norman French
O.T., Old Testament
oz., ounce
Phil., Philippine
P.M., post meridiem
Pol., Polish
pop., population
Port., Portuguese
prelim., preliminary
pron., pronounced
q.v., which see
R., River
rev., revised, revision
Rev., Reverend
Rom., Romanian
Russ., Russian
S., south, southerly, southern
sec., second
Skr., Sanskrit
Sp., Spanish
sp.gr., specific gravity
sq., square
S.S.R., Soviet Socialist Republic
Sum., Sumerian
Sw., Swedish
syn., synonym
temp., temperature
trans., translation, translated
Turk., Turkish
U.K., United Kingdom
U.N., United Nations
U.S., United States
U.S.A., United States of America
U.S.S.R., Union of Soviet Socialist Republics
var., variety
W., west, westerly, western
yd., yard

Note.—The official abbreviations for the States of the Union are used throughout. For academic degrees, see article DEGREE, ACADEMIC. Other abbreviations or contractions are self-explanatory.

IDAHO (*continued from previous volume*)
Hydroelectric installations in the State have an output capacity of 641,000 kilowatts. According to reliable estimates, undeveloped water power amounts to more than 8,676,000 kilowatts, a total exceeded only by the State of Washington.

Idaho ranks twenty-seventh among the States in production of minerals; it is first in the production of zinc, antimony, and silver, second in the production of lead, and third in the production of phosphate rock. Gold, copper, cadmium, tungsten, limestone, building stone, and clay are also mined in the State. In a recent year mineral output included about 16,095,000 troy ounces of silver, 7000 tons of antimony ore, 88,000 tons of zinc, 100,000 tons of lead, 4,282,000 tons of sand and gravel, 79,650 troy ounces of gold, and 2000 tons of copper. The value of minerals produced in that year was approximately $79,077,000.

Idaho contains numerous summer and winter resorts, and extensive areas, including the National Forests, are available for recreational purposes, particularly camping, fishing, and hunting. Bear, moose, deer, elk, antelope, cougar, wildcat, mountain sheep, and other varieties of big game abound in the forested regions; the mountain streams and lakes are well stocked with trout, black bass, salmon, and other game fish. In the s. central part of the State are excellent facilities for winter sports. Sun Valley, an all-year skiing center in the Sawtooth Mts., is one of the leading vacation resorts in the United States. A small section of Yellowstone National Park is situated in Idaho, and the State maintains eleven State parks, among them Heyburn State Park, with an area of 7838 acres. Additional scenic attractions include Shoshone Falls (q.v.), a Snake R. waterfall 210 ft. in height; the Grand Canyon of the Snake R., the deepest gorge (5500 ft.) in North America; and Craters of the Moon National Monument (q.v.), containing over fifty extinct volcanic craters and other volcanic formations.

The Union Pacific Railroad operates an elaborate network of lines in S.E., s., and w. central Idaho, and the N. section of the State is served by a number of railroads, notably the Northern Pacific, the Great Northern, and the Chicago, Milwaukee, St. Paul, and Pacific, but due to the mountainous terrain other sections have not been penetrated by railroad carriers. Main-track mileage in the State totals about 2800. Shallow-draft vessels operate between the Pacific Ocean and Lewiston via the Columbia R., the Celilo Canal, and the Snake R. Idaho has about 40,600 m. of roads, including about 4750 m. of State highways. There are about 150 airports, 82 of which are municipal.

Attendance at the public schools of the State is compulsory for all children between the ages of eight and eighteen. In a recent year there were over 4200 public elementary and secondary instructors teaching nearly 115,000 pupils in over 1100 schools. State institutions of higher education include the University of Idaho (see IDAHO, UNIVERSITY OF), Albion Normal School at Albion, North Idaho College of Education at Lewiston, the Deaf and Blind School at Gooding, and the Industrial Training School at St. Anthony. Private institutions of higher learning include Boise Junior College at Boise, College of Idaho at Caldwell, Northern Idaho Junior College at Coeur d'Alene, Northwest Nazarene College at Nampa, and Ricks Junior College at Rexburg.

Idaho is governed by a constitution adopted in 1889. Executive authority is vested in a governor and a lieutenant-governor, elected for four-year terms, and in a secretary of state, auditor, treasurer, attorney general, superintendent of public instruction, inspector of mines, and certain other appointed officials. Legislative authority is vested in a general assembly consisting of a senate of forty-four members, and a house of representatives of fifty-nine members. The members of both houses are elected for two-year terms. Judicial power is vested in a supreme court, district courts, probate courts, and various minor courts. The State is divided into forty-four counties, and is represented in the Congress of the United States by two senators and two representatives. The minimum voting age is twenty-one years.

History. The region occupied by present-day Idaho was originally part of the Oregon (q.v.) Country, a vast tract claimed during the first quarter of the 19th century by the United States, Great Britain, Spain, and Russia. The first white explorers of the region were the Americans Meriwether Lewis and

Neil F. Blair; Ida. State Bd. of Publicity

RANCHING AND FARMING IN IDAHO

Above: Sheep in corral in Hell's Canyon on the Snake River. Right: Herders eating lunch at old fashioned chuck wagon. Below: Mechanical sugar-beet harvester.

George Rogers Clark in 1805 and 1806 (see LEWIS AND CLARK EXPEDITION). David Thompson and Finan McDonald, fur traders for the British North-West Company, entered Idaho in 1809 and constructed a trading post on Lake Pend Oreille. In 1810 the American Missouri Fur Company established a trading post on a branch of the Snake R.; the next year John Jacob Astor, head of the American Fur Co., sent an expedition to the Idaho region. See OREGON TRAIL. The British assumed complete control of the Idaho region during the War of 1812, but in 1818 Great Britain and the United States adopted an agreement providing for joint occupation. Spain and Russia relinquished their claims to the Oregon Country in 1819 and 1824 respectively. American trading activity in Idaho was resumed with the construction (1834) of Fort Hall, near the site of present-day Pocatello. In 1836 an American Protestant missionary founded a school for Indians near the junction of the Snake and Clearwater rivers. A Roman Catholic mission was established in N.W. Idaho in 1842.

British and American commercial rivalry in the Oregon Country was resolved when, in 1846, Great Britain and the United States concluded a treaty recognizing American jurisdiction over the entire region s. of the 49th parallel. Two years later the Idaho region was made part of newly organized Oregon Territory; the section N. of lat. 46°N. was attached to Washington Territory in 1853.

Large-scale immigration to Idaho began in 1861, following the discovery of gold on a tributary of the Clearwater R. The influx of prospectors and settlers was accelerated by additional gold discoveries in 1862. On March 3, 1863, the United States government constituted the region consisting of present-day Idaho, Wyoming, and Montana, and parts of South Dakota, North Dakota, and Nebraska, as Idaho Territory. With the formation of Montana Territory (1864) and Wyoming Territory (1868), Idaho acquired its present boundaries.

The Territorial economy expanded steadily during the 1870's and 1880's. Livestock raising became a major industry, railroads were constructed, and new, rich mineral deposits were discovered. On several occasions between 1870 and 1880 various Indian tribes, resentful of encroachments on their ancestral domains, went on the warpath in Idaho Territory. Federal troops suppressed the uprisings, and the Indians were ultimately confined to reservations.

In 1883 the Territorial legislature, alarmed over the influx of Mormons into southern Idaho, enacted a law depriving professed polygamists of the right to vote. The law was sustained by the United States Supreme Court. In 1893, when the heads of the Mormon church rejected polygamy as an essential element of their creed, the anti-Mormon restrictions were removed, and Mormons not having more than one wife were admitted to the ballot. Meanwhile (July 3, 1890) Idaho had become the 43rd State of the Union.

From May to September, 1892, during a strike of miners at Coeur d'Alene, serious clashes took place between union and non-union workers. Federal troops were sent to the scene of disturbance, and military law was proclaimed. The strike was called off, but dissatisfaction persisted among the mine workers; new outbreaks occurred in April, 1899, necessitating again the use of United States troops. The bitter feeling engendered during subsequent attempts to organize the mine workers culminated (Dec. 30, 1905) in the assassination of ex-Governor Frank Steunenberg by a union organizer.

In 1910 the Coeur d'Alene region of Idaho was swept by disastrous forest fires. Several towns were almost entirely destroyed and many lives were lost.

Idaho has tended to favor the Democratic Party in national politics since the election of 1928. The electorate gave a majority of votes to the Democratic candidate Franklin Delano Roosevelt in 1932, 1936, 1940, and 1944. In the presidential election of 1948 the Democratic nominee Harry S. Truman received 107,370 votes; his Republican opponent Thomas E. Dewey received 101,-514 votes. The Republicans carried the State in the 1952 election. Their candidate General Dwight David Eisenhower received 180,707 votes. Adlai Ewing Stevenson received 95,081 votes.

IDAHO STATE COLLEGE, a coeducational institution of higher learning, at Pocatello, Idaho, established as the southern branch of the University of Idaho in 1901, and reconstituted as a separate organization by the State legislature in 1947. The college offers two-year junior-college courses in science, liberal arts, nursing, and business administration, and four-year courses in the liberal arts and pharmacy. It is a State-controlled institution, charging no tuition to Idaho residents. In a recent year the faculty numbered about 140, and almost 1700 students were enrolled.

IDAHO, UNIVERSITY OF, a coeducational institution of higher learning, founded in 1889 and opened in 1892 at Moscow, Idaho. The university offers courses in the liberal arts and in science, agriculture, engineering and mining engineering, pedagogy, forestry, business administration, and law, leading to bachelors' and masters' degrees. It is a State-controlled institution, charging no tuition to Idaho residents. Its endowment is over $5.5 million, and in a recent year the faculty numbered about 215 and the student body over 3040.

IDEA, a term used both popularly and in philosophy to denote a mental image or concept. Many philosophers have used the term in special senses. Plato regarded ideas as eternal archetypes or forms which existed only in the consciousness of God. To Aristotle ideas were eternal forms which caused the existence of real objects. Bishop Berkeley regarded ideas as the equivalent of perceptions, and David Hume defined ideas as mental representations, made up of memory and mental processes, as distinct from the impressions given by the senses. By ideas Immanuel Kant meant the highest concepts of reason which regulated all thought processes but could not be verified by experience. Georg Wilhelm Friedrich Hegel called ideas the final product or embodiment of reason. See articles on philosophers mentioned.

IDEALISM, in philosophy, a term applied to various systems of thought in which all nature and experience are explained in terms of *ideas,* or products of the intellect, contrasted with those systems based on materialism, realism, or determinism (qq.v.). The ancient Greek philosopher Plato conceived of a world of unchanging ideas as the only reality. Medieval realism postulated a similar world in its concept of *universals.* Modern idealism differs from the classical form in that it does not place ideal reality outside and transcendent to the world of experience, but rather places it in the consciousness of man. The 18th-century English philosopher George Berkeley developed the view that the objective or natural world had its existence in the consciousness of individuals. Immanuel Kant, in his *critical idealism,* held matter to be dependent for its existence on the sensation experience of the individual, but also maintained the existence of an unknowable Being-in-Itself; in the idealistic philosophical systems of Johann Fichte, Friedrich Schelling, and Georg Wilhelm Hegel the existence of such a Being

was denied. During the 19th century the development of the physical sciences, aided by the trend to naturalism and materialism, caused a decline in the popularity of idealism which lasted well into the 20th century.

IDES. See CALENDAR.

IDIOCY. See MENTAL DEFICIENCY.

IDOCRASE. See VESUVIANITE.

IDOLATRY, worship of a material image which is held to be the abode of a superhuman personality. The practice is common among primitive peoples, and was also a characteristic of such great civilizations as the Egyptian, Chaldean, Indian, Greek, and Roman. Worship of idols appears to be a phase of religious evolution natural to man at a certain stage of culture. The earlier stages are nature worship (q.v.), the adoration of personified objects, and animism (q.v.) or belief in spirits embodied in material things. Associated with idols, which are the object of public worship, are personal or domestic fetishes (see FETISHISM), for private veneration. Worship of the dead may also lead to idolatry by the same transitions as the worship of spirits. The elemental idea that after death the spirit continues in the body or in some relic gave rise to the practice of placing a statue of the dead man in or beside his grave. Influences exerted by the Babylonian and Egyptian cultures led the nations of Palestine to adopt symbolical representations of the gods until the teachings of the Hebrew prophets forced their abandonment. Islam forbids the making of a representation of any living thing, whether it is intended to be worshiped or not. Christian veneration of sacred images was at various times in history confounded with idolatry; see IMAGE WORSHIP.

IDUMÆA or **IDUMEA.** See EDOM.

IDYL or **IDYLL** (Gr. *eidyllion,* "little form or image"), originally, a short descriptive poem of a rural or pastoral character. The term originated with the Greek grammarians of the Alexandrian Age (q.v.), who used it with special reference .to the bucolic poems of Bion, Moschus, and Theocritus (qq.v.). The ten extant *Idyls* of Theocritus, some of which deal in realistic and elegiac, as well as in descriptive, terms with Sicilian country life, set the pattern for idyllic poetry of ancient times. From the 4th century A.D. until the end of the Middle Ages the classical meaning of the term was almost wholly lost, and short descriptive poems on a great variety of subjects were called idyls. The revival of classical forms of art and literature during the Renaissance gave the term new currency in its original sense; and it was applied to Latin and Greek imitations of Theocritus and Vergil (q.v.) and to pastoral poems in modern languages by such writers as the Italian, Torquato Tasso, and the Frenchman, Pierre de Ronsard (qq.v.). It continued to be used in its original sense until the second half of the 19th century, when the popularity of two works, *Idylles Héroiques* (1858) by Pierre Richard de Laprade (1812-83), and *Idylls of the King* (1859) by Alfred, Lord Tennyson (q.v.), led to the extension of the term as a title for lyrical and narrative poems. At the present time the term idyl is usually applied to any simple description, in poetry or prose, of rustic life and pastoral scenes.

IFNI, a Spanish colonial possession, situated on the N.W. coast of Africa, about 800 miles S.W. of Tetuán and about 50 miles N.E. of Rio de Oro. All of the land frontiers of Ifni adjoin French Morocco. The territory was ceded to Spain by the Moroccan government in 1860. However, Spanish occupation of Ifni did not begin until 1934. Area, 741 sq.m.; pop. (1951 est.) 44,000.

IFUGAO, a tribe of Malay origin living in a subprovince of the same name in Mountain Province, Luzon. They are of medium height, strong and well built, with dark brown skins and straight hair. The clothing of both sexes is scanty; they are usually elaborately tattooed, and use ear, neck, arm, and leg ornaments. The Ifugao are skilled agriculturists, their chief crop being rice, which is grown on terraced and irrigated mountainsides originally ill-adapted for agriculture. They are also excellent metalworkers and woodcarvers. Head-hunting was common before their Christianization, and head-hunting forays still occur occasionally when the tribe is not held in check; the skulls of enemies are placed on a shelf beside the entrance to a building. See PHILIPPINES, REPUBLIC OF THE.

IGNATIUS BEAN. See SAINT-IGNATIUS'S-BEAN.

IGNATIUS OF ANTIOCH, SAINT (fl. 100 A.D.), early Christian prelate and martyr, one of the Apostolic Fathers. He is also known as Theophoros (Gr., "God-bearer"), and from this name arose the legend that he was the child whom Jesus took in His arms and blessed (Mark 9). According to early Christian writers he was a disciple of St. John, and second bishop of Antioch. During the reign of the Emperor Trajan he was condemned to be killed by wild beasts in the arena, and was sent from Antioch to Rome for execution. Seven of his letters, written on this journey, are extant; they are important for their revelation of the teaching of the early Church and for their confirmation of the continuity of Apostolic doctrines. His feast is celebrated on February 1.

IGNATIUS OF LOYOLA, SAINT. See LOYOLA.

IGNITION, the act of initiating combustion (q.v.) of a substance by raising its temperature to the point at which combustion occurs. The ignition temperature of various substances which are used as fuels or otherwise usefully burned varies within wide limits. Yellow phosphorus, which is employed in the manufacture of matches, ignites at 93°F. (34°C.), and carbon monoxide, which is produced by the burning of most solid and liquid fuels, ignites at about 1250°F. (677°C.).

Primitive peoples use the frictional heat of such devices as the fire stick and fire bow to raise the temperature of timber and obtain a flame. In matches the frictional heat generated by striking the match is sufficient to cause ignition. Sparks obtained by striking flint and steel together and the concentration of the sun's heat rays by means of a lens have also been employed to induce ignition. In most types of modern guns and wartime explosive shells and bombs the ignition of the main charge is produced by the heat generated by a primer set off by the impact of a firing pin. The heating of a wire with the passage of an electric current is used to ignite explosive charges for blasting, and high-voltage electric sparks ignite the explosive mixture in the cylinders of gasoline engines. In Diesel engines ignition is obtained by compressing air to a small volume, thus causing a temperature rise which ignites the fuel charge; see INTERNAL COMBUSTION ENGINE. See also DETONATION; DETONATOR.

IGNORANCE OF THE LAW, common form of the legal maxim *ignorantia legis neminen excusat* ("ignorance of the law excuses no one"). As established by court decisions in the United States, the sense of the maxim is that the assertion by a defendant that he was ignorant of the law when he violated it does not excuse him from the civil or criminal consequences of

Ewing Galloway
Igorot man of the Philippine Islands

his acts. The maxim gives expression to an important principle of public policy; to permit a person who has committed a crime to escape the penalties of his wrongdoing by the plea he did not know his act was a crime would be subversive of criminal justice. On the other hand, the rule does not mean that a person must know all the legal consequences of his acts, as it is unreasonable to presume that every person is fully conversant with the law; he is presumed to know only its broad, general aspects. Ignorance of the legal rights of private individuals, e.g., the existence of an easement (q.v.) in favor of a certain person, is regarded as ignorance of fact, not of law, and is generally a valid answer to a criminal charge or civil action, entitling a person to relief from the consequences of his acts. However, some Federal and State statutes declare certain acts to be criminal irrespective of a person's knowledge or ignorance of material facts.

IGOROT (Igorot, "mountain people"), one of the savage tribes of N. central Luzon, Philippine Islands. The name "Igorot" is sometimes loosely applied to any of the Indonesian or proto-Malayan peoples of the mountains of N. Luzon, but the Igorot proper are of Indonesian origin and live only in the Bontok, Benguet, Amburayan, and Lepanto subprovinces. With the exception of the Bontok Igorot (q.v.) subtribe, their culture has been little modified by contact with white men, and the Igorot display considerable cultural homogeneity. All are agricultural, depending almost entirely upon their crops for subsistence. Like the Ifugao (q.v.), they construct irrigated mountain terraces for the cultivation of rice. Their houses, which are grouped in villages, have grass roofs which overhang wooden side walls, and are generally built in two stories of one room each. The Igorot are strong and well-built, though the inhabitants of Bontok are somewhat larger and more aggressive than those of Benguet and Lepanto. Until their Christianization by white missionaries, the Bontok Igorot were fierce warriors, and practiced head-hunting; even in recent years their isolation from and resistance to the civilization of Luzon's centers of settlement have tended to maintain their primitive culture patterns. The Benguet Igorot and Lepanto Igorot, on the other hand, have become adjusted to the rule of white men, and many of them are now engaged in mining and working gold and copper. During World War II the Igorot fiercely resisted the Japanese occupation, and played an important part in the guerilla warfare on the island. See PHILIPPINE ISLANDS.

IGUANIDAE, family of thick-tongued New World lizards, similar to the lizards of the Old World family Agamidae, and differing from the latter chiefly in having the teeth solidly joined with the inner edge of the jaw instead of having them joined with the jaw bone at its occluding margin. The family includes the basilisks and horned toads (qq.v.), and the American chameleons of the genus Anolis; the larger lizards of this family are commonly called iguanas.

Iguanas, which attain a length of about six feet, have characteristically compressed bodies, surmounted from the neck to the base of the tail by a row of leathery spines. The long powerful tail is usually somewhat flattened. Iguanas have distinct eyelids, large external eardrums, and conspicuous throat pouches. Each limb has five free toes ending in sharp claws. Iguanas feed on fruit and vegetation, and on small rodents, birds, and birds' eggs. Their habitats vary among the species; some are arboreal, some semiaquatic, and some terrestrial.

Iguana iguana, the common iguana, is abundant throughout tropical America. The male is gray with light-red spines; it is barred on the sides with black, and has broad black circles ringing its tail. The female is generally brown. This species is arboreal and is valued as food; both the flesh and eggs are eaten. The rhinoceros iguana, *Metopoceros cornutus,* a terrestrial species found in Haiti and Puerto Rico, is so called because of three horny projections on its forehead. It is dark brown and vicious, capable of doing much damage with its powerful jaws and tail. Two iguanas are confined to the Galapagos Islands (q.v.); one of these, the marine iguana, *Amblyrhynchus cristatus,* lives on beaches and dives into the water for the seaweed which constitutes its diet.

The name iguana is sometimes applied to the monitor lizards (q.v.) of the Old World.

IGUANODON, a genus of large, herbivorous, ornithischian dinosaurs (q.v.) which were common in Europe, especially England and Belgium, during Jurassic and Lower Cretaceous times. These dinosaurs, which attained a length of over 30 ft., had long, narrow heads and birdlike beaks; the jaws were provided with teeth resembling those of modern lizards in the family Iguanidae (q.v.), whence the technical name of these beasts. The front limbs, each bearing four well-developed digits and one rudimentary digit, were much shorter than the heavy, three-toed hind limbs. The tail was heavy, and flattened along its posterior half for swimming. The bones of the reptile's skeleton were hollow. *Iguanodon* walked on its hind legs, and sat on the tripod formed by the hind legs and tail.

Iguanodon is the type genus of the family Iguanodontidae, of which *I. mantelli,* about 18 ft. long, is the best-known species. A similar genus, *Claosaurus,* has been unearthed in North American remains of Upper Cretaceous times.

IGUASSÚ FALLS or **IGUAZÚ FALLS,** a famous cataract lying partly in Brazil and partly in Argentina, in central South America, about twelve miles from the mouth of the Iguassú River. The crest of the falls is approximately $2\frac{1}{2}$ m. wide and 200 ft. high; the water falls partly in a large double drop and partly in a series of cataracts. In the dry season there are two crescents, each 800 yards wide; in the wet season the two merge into one vast fall about 4000 yards wide.

Though their location in a virgin tropical forest makes the Iguassú Falls difficult to reach, they are a famous scenic feature of the region, and have been compared with Niagara Falls and the Victoria Falls on the Zambezi River.

IJSSEL LAKE or **IJSSELMEER.** See ZUIDER ZEE.

IKHNATON, AKHENATEN, AKHENATON, or **AKHNATON,** also known as AMENHOTEP IV, son of Amenhotep III (q.v.) and Tiy, pharaoh of Egypt from about 1375 to 1358 B.C. He was the last important ruler of the XVIIIth dynasty; see EGYPT: *History.* Ikhnaton is notable in history as the first to establish a religion based on the concept of monotheism (q.v.). It is believed that the Hebrew prophets' idea of a universal God, preached seven or eight centuries later in a land which Ikhnaton once ruled, was derived in part from his cult of Aton, or Aten, the sun-god or "solar disk", which he believed to be a universal, omnipresent spirit and the sole creator of the universe. After he had established the new religion, sometimes referred to as "solar monotheism", the pharaoh, who had been crowned Amenhotep IV, changed his name to Ikhnaton, meaning "Aton is satisfied". He ordered the obliteration of all traces of the polytheistic religion of his ancestors, even to

Rhinoceros iguana, of the Iguanidae family

the extent of expunging references to the plural word "gods" on all monuments throughout Egypt; and he fought bitterly against the powerful priests who attempted to maintain the worship of the state god Amon (q.v.). This religious revolution had a profound effect on Egyptian artists, who thenceforth turned from the ritualistic forms to which they had been confined to the representation of nature as evidence of the all-embracing power of Aton, the sun; see EGYPTIAN ARCHITECTURE AND ART. A new religious literature, containing hymns that closely parallel some of the later Hebrew psalms, also came into being.

ÎLE DE FRANCE. See MAURITIUS.

ÎLE DE FRANCE, or ISLE OF FRANCE, former province of France, centering about Paris, its capital, and comprising the territory now occupied by the departments of Seine, Seine-et-Oise, Seine-et-Marne, Aisne, and Oise. During the medieval period Île de France was part of the territory held by the Capet (q.v.) family, which became the royal family of France in 987, when Hugh Capet was elected to the kingship.

ÎLE DE LA RÉUNION. See RÉUNION, ÎLE DE LA.

ILES, FRANCIS (1893-), pen name of the English detective-story writer Anthony Berkeley Cox, a London businessman in private life. His first detective-story novel was *The Layton Court Mystery* (1925), at first published anonymously but later reprinted under the pseudonym Anthony Berkeley. The numerous works written under the latter name, especially *The Second Shot* (1930), are not only examples of the complicated puzzle type of mystery, but also show the careful development of psychological elements on which are based the series written under the name Francis Iles. The first detective novel to appear under the pseudonym Iles was *Malice Aforethought* (1931), describing chronologically the events leading up to the murder, with emphasis on psychological suspense. Iles' work had considerable effect on turning the emphasis of detective fiction during the 1930's away from the puzzle form and toward those novels of suspense which became popular in the 1940's. His best-known work of this type is *Before the Fact* (1932), which was made into the motion picture *Suspicion* (1941).

ILEUM. See INTESTINE.

ILEX, name given to plants having leaves which produce slender, spinelike extensions of the veins at the edges of the leaves. Holly,

inkberry, and winterberry (qq.v.) belong to the genus *Ilex,* and many other plants which have hollylike leaves are given the species name *ilicifolia* ("holly leaf"). The holm or holly oak, *Quercus ilex,* of s. Europe is sometimes called the ilex; see OAK.

ILFORD, municipal borough of Essex County, England, situated on the Roding R., 7 m. by rail E.N.E. of London. It is chiefly a residential suburb and contains part of the Becontree housing development, a project of the London County council. The buildings of the 12th-century leper hospital of St. Mary and St. Thomas have been converted into almshouses and a chapel. Ilford, comprising Greater and Little Ilford, was incorporated in 1926. Factories making photographic supplies and paper are located at Greater Ilford, on the E. bank of the Roding. Pop. (1951) 184,707.

ILI, a river of Central Asia, rising in N.W. Sinkiang, China, and flowing in a westerly direction to Iliysk, U.S.S.R., and thence northwestward into Lake Balkhash. In its early course the Ili is known as the Tekez. Much of the terrain it traverses is a fertile valley, containing numerous populous villages and well-stocked pastures. The delta of the Ili extends approximately 115 m. from Lake Balkhash. The river is generally shallow, but navigation is possible for about 280 miles E. of Illiysk during the rainy season. The total length of the Ili is 900 m.

ILIAD, an epic poem by the Greek poet Homer (q.v.), recounting the siege and destruction of Troy during the Trojan War (q.v.), about 1200 B.C. It is regarded by literary historians as the first great poetic work in Greek literature (q.v.), and has been esteemed for generations as one of the supreme masterpieces of world literature. Especially noteworthy in the *Iliad* are the heroic action, the dramatic emotional crises engendered by the clashing personalities of the principal characters, and the imaginative beauty of the language. Exactly when the *Iliad* was composed is unknown; the time of composition is believed by some literary historians to be the tenth century A.D.; see HOMERIC QUESTION. The first written text appeared during the late 6th century B.C. in Athens, where it was recited at the annual festival of Panathenæa (q.v.) by professional rhapsodists. The text as it exists today dates from a version prepared about 150 B.C. in Alexandria, and is divided into twenty-four books.

The Homeric narrative begins in the tenth

year of a siege undertaken by the Greeks to recover Helen, the beautiful wife of King Menelaus of Sparta, who has eloped with Paris, son of King Priam of Troy, taking much treasure with her. The siege stalemated. The dramatic action begins to unfold when Agamemnon, King of Mycenæ, brother of Menelaus, and commander of the Greek forces takes away a captive girl, Briseis, from Achilles, king of the Myrmidons, and chief warrior of the Greeks. A feud results, and Achilles refuses to take part in battle, preferring to sulk in his tent. His mother, the goddess Thetis, exacts a promise from Zeus, father of the gods, to punish the Greeks for her son's unhappiness. Zeus sends a dream to beguile Agamemnon into opening a pitched battle with the Trojans, for which the Greek armies are unprepared. Paris and Menelaus clash on the battlefield in personal combat; Aphrodite, goddess of love and beauty, saves Paris, her favorite, from harm. The goddess of wisdom Athena, siding with the Greeks, persuades the Lycian leader and Trojan ally, Pandarus, to inflict a wound on Menelaus by dishonorable means. Thus Agamemnon's wrath is roused, and the Greek chieftain gathers his men and the armies prepare for battle.

In the ensuing encounters, first the Greeks and then the Trojans are victorious. Heroes from each side are pitted against one another in single combat. Following the seemingly decisive intervention of Athena on the Greek side, Hector, son of King Priam, and the outstanding Trojan hero, decides to enter the battle. He bids farewell to his wife Andromache and to his child and, going forth from Troy, challenges all the Greeks. Ajax, greatest Greek hero after Achilles, is chosen by lot to fight the Trojan prince; the outcome is indecisive. Despairing of an early victory, the Trojan, Antenor, urges his brothers-in-arms to return Helen and her treasure, and sue for peace; Paris, however, refuses to give up Helen, although he offers to restore, and even add to, the treasure. The Greeks refuse the offer, but agree to a truce for the burial of the dead.

Zeus, fulfilling his promise to Thetis, commands the gods not to favor either side, and goes to Mt. Ida to watch over the battles; notwithstanding Zeus' command Poseidon, god of the sea, Hera, wife of Zeus, and Athena attempt to aid the Greeks, but are sternly warned by Zeus against doing so. The Trojans then camp on the battlefield, seriously menacing the Greeks. Aga-

memnon sends Odysseus, King of Ithaca and one of the Greek chieftains, and Ajax and Achilles' old tutor Phoenix to Achilles. In Agamemnon's name the emissaries propose to return Briseis to Achilles and offer other bribes to induce him to enter the battle. Achilles refuses, declaring he will return to Greece. After scoring a minor victory by a surprise attack on one of the Trojan camps, Agamemnon enters the battle himself, and is wounded. Odysseus and the brave Argolian prince Diomedes, among other Greek heroes, are also wounded. On seeing a wounded Greek pass his tent, Achilles sends his best friend, Patroclus, to see what is transpiring on the field of battle. Nestor, king of Pylos and wise counselor of the Greeks, tells Patroclus that Achilles should either take part in the fighting or dispatch Patroclus with the Myrmidons, or the Greeks will be defeated.

The fighting takes a desperate turn, with the Trojans attacking the wall which the Greeks have built to protect their ships. Despite the vigorous Greek defense, Hector breaks one of the gates, and the Trojan warriors rush in. Poseidon secretly encourages the Greeks to fight, and their resistance prevents a sweeping Trojan victory. Hera then persuades Zeus to leave his watch on Mt. Ida and go to sleep, giving Poseidon and other gods an opportunity to aid the Greeks. When Zeus awakes, Poseidon is restrained; the god Apollo abets Hector and the Trojans are temporarily victorious. Achilles again refuses to fight, but gives his armor and chariot, drawn by two immortal horses, to Patroclus, bidding him drive the Trojans back, but not to venture beyond the walls. Patroclus kills the Lycian prince Sarpedon, and pursues the Trojans until he is stopped by the sun-god Apollo. Hector then kills Patroclus, and strips Achilles' armor from his body. A battle follows for possession of the body, which is finally recovered by Menelaus. The hero Antilochus, Nestor's son, bears the news to Achilles, who, grief-stricken, and blaming himself for his friend's death, calls on his mother Thetis for new armor, that he may venture forth and kill Hector.

Thetis begs Hephæstus, smithy of the gods, for a new set of armor for her son. As the Trojans advance in an effort to recover Patroclus' body, Achilles affrights them with his war cry. He summons his Myrmidons, and enters the battle to avenge his friend. As the battle gains in intensity,

Achilles drives the Trojans armies back into Ilium; some Trojans are forced into the river Xanthus beside the city. A great battle ensues beside the river, which becomes choked with the bodies of the dead. The Trojans hurriedly seek refuge within their city, except for Hector, who stays outside the walls, despite the pleadings of his parents and wife. Achilles pursues Hector three times around the city walls. Apollo deserts Hector, and when both Hector and Achilles drop their spears, Athena sends Achilles' spear back to him, enabling him to kill Hector. In a passion of revenge Achilles then drags Hector's corpse behind his chariot, while Hector's family laments his death on the city walls.

While Hector's body lies unburied in the Greek camp, Achilles and the Greeks bury Patroclus with great honors and funeral games, and also sacrifice twelve noble Trojan youths previously taken by Achilles. Each day Achilles drags Hector's body around Patroclus's grave; Apollo preserves Hector's body from decay. Thetis urges Achilles to return Hector's body to his family for burial, lest he invoke the wrath of the gods. The old king Priam, prompted by Zeus, goes by night to Achilles to beg for his son's body, taking with him a chariot of gold to offer Achilles. Moved by the old king's pleas, and remembering his own father, Achilles relents, and at dawn Priam takes his son's body to Troy. There Andromache and Hecuba lament their loss, and great solemn funeral games take place, concluding the narrative.

ILIUM or **ILION.** See TROY.

ILLECEBRACEAE. See KNOTWEED.

ILLE-ET-VILAINE, a maritime department of N.W. France, bordering the English Channel and the Bay of St. Michel on the N. The principal rivers are the Vilaine and the Ille, for which the department is named. Rennes (q.v.) is the capital, and Saint-Malo and Saint-Servan-sur-Mer are the principal seaports. The chief sources of wealth are agricultural enterprises, notably dairying, horticulture, and stock raising. Productive mineral deposits of lead, granite, and slate are located in the department. Manufacturing industries are boatbuilding, tanning, smelting, and the production of pottery, leather goods, sailcloth, rope, paper, and furniture. Fishing and the tourist trade also are important. Area, 2697 sq.m.; pop. (1952 est.) 603,000.

ILLICIUM. See ANISE.

ILLINOIS, a confederacy of North American Indian tribes of Algonquian stock, originally occupying the region comprising the present State of Illinois and parts of Missouri, Iowa, and Wisconsin. The entire group consisted of the related tribes of the Cahokia, Kaskaskia, Michigamea, Moingwena, Peoria, and Tamaroa. Many of them have left a record of their existence in the form of place names throughout Illinois.

The Illinois Indians are tall and well built. Very little is known about their primitive culture, which seems to have resembled that of the Miami and Shawnee (qq.v.) Indians. Polygamy was apparently practiced. The Illinois were timid and often unsuccessful in intertribal warfare and easily driven from their villages by invading tribes such as the Sioux, Fox, and Iroquois. At the time of their earliest contact with white men their dead were not buried, but wrapped in skins and fastened to trees; the skeletons, however, were apparently buried later.

The Illinois conducted friendly negotiations with the French explorer Robert de La Salle (q.v.) from 1670 to 1682 and subsequently with French traders. Through these traders and the influence of Trappist monks, the tribes were held loyal to the French in the French wars with the neighboring tribes and afterward with the English. After the end of the American Revolution the United States had great difficulty in subduing them, though the tribes had already been greatly weakened by struggles with the Iroquois in the 17th century and with the tribes around the Great Lakes in the 18th century. However, their numbers continued to decrease, and in 1883, when survivors of only the Kaskaskia and Peoria tribes remained, they sold all the lands they still held in the State of Illinois, and moved west of the Mississippi R. At the present time less than two hundred Illinois Indians are still alive, concentrated in the N.E. part of Oklahoma.

ILLINOIS, one of the East North Central States of the United States, bounded on the N. by Wisconsin, on the E. by Lake Michigan and Indiana, on the S.E. and S. by the Ohio R., which separates it from Kentucky, and on the S.W. and W. by the Mississippi R., which separates it from Missouri and Iowa. It ranks as the twenty-third State of the Union in area, the fourth (1950) in population, and the eighth in order of admission after the thirteen original States, having been admitted on Dec. 3, 1818. Springfield (q.v.), fifth-largest city of the State, is the State capital. The largest city is Chicago (q.v.), outranked in population only by New York among U. S. cities. In descending order of population (1950), other cities with over 50,000 inhabitants are Peoria, Rockford, East St. Louis, Evanston, Cicero, Decatur, Oak Park, Joliet, Berwyn, and Aurora. The distance between the northernmost and southernmost points in the State is approximately 380 m.; the distance between the easternmost and westernmost points is 205 m. The area of the State is 56,400 sq.m., including 453 sq.m. of inland water surface; pop. (1950) 8,712,176.

The terrain, an extension of the Great Plains, is generally level; extensive glaciation of the region occurred during the Pleistocene epoch, creating smooth till plains. The general slope is from N.E. to S.S.W. Charles Mound (1241 ft. above sea level), the highest point, is situated in the N.W. corner of the State. The lowest point, at the junction of the Mississippi and the Ohio rivers, in the southernmost extremity of the State, is 279 ft. above sea level. Illinois has an approximate mean elevation of 600 ft. The N. quarter, consisting largely of morainic hills and ridges and unglaciated areas, has an elevation of over 700 ft.; the central half, composed of glacial drift plains, lies between 500 and 700 ft. above sea level; and the S. quarter, composed primarily of the valley floors of the larger rivers, has an elevation of less than 500 ft. Extending across the S. quarter between the Mississippi and Ohio rivers is an unglaciated region with elevations up to 1065 ft.

Illinois contains considerably over 400 rivers, more than two thirds of which belong to the drainage basin of the Mississippi R.; the remaining rivers are tributaries of either the Ohio R. or the Wabash R., which forms part of the Illinois-Indiana boundary. The largest river situated wholly within the State is the Illinois R., an affluent of the Mississippi. Other important rivers are the Kankakee, one of the headstreams of the Illinois; the Sangamon, an affluent of the Illinois; the Rock and the Kaskaskia, affluents of the Mississippi; and the Embarras and Little Wabash, affluents of the Wabash.

The climate of Illinois is characterized by frequent and occasionally sudden changes of weather. Cold waves invade all parts of Illinois during winter months, and high temperatures prevail in all sections during the summer months. The mean temperature for July ranges from about 70°F. in the extreme N.E. to about 80°F. in the extreme S.W. The mean for January ranges from about 20°F. in the

Illinois Development Council

Illinois State Capitol in Springfield

N. to about 30°F. in the S. In the vicinity of Chicago the mean January temperature is about 22°F. and the mean July temperature is about 73°F. The maximum and minimum temperatures recorded in the Chicago area are 105°F. and −23°F. The mean annual precipitation of Illinois is about 35 inches.

Illinois maintains forty-two State Parks which cover a total of 40,000 acres and three State forests which cover 10,280 acres, in addition to extensive community forests. These parks and forests, distributed throughout the State, preserve many diversified types of scenery, including sand dunes, stands of virgin timber, river gorges, and lakes, and many contain ancient Indian mounds, and relics of the early history of Illinois, including forts, houses, and other buildings constructed by the early pioneers of the region. Among State parks providing accommodations for vacationists are Apple River Canyon State Park (157 acres) near Stockton, Buffalo Rock State Park (43 acres) near Ottawa, Cahokia Mounds State Park (145 acres) near East St. Louis, Chain O'Lakes State Park (4500 acres) near Fox Lake, Fort Chartres State Park (20 acres near Prairie du Rocher, Gebhard Woods State Park (30 acres) near Morris, Giant City State Park (1163 acres) near Carbondale, Lincoln Log Cabin State Park (86 acres) near Charleston, Père Marquette State Park (5180 acres) near Grafton, Starved Rock State Park (1443 acres) near Utica, and White Pines Forest State Park (315 acres) near Oregon. Trout, carp, catfish, pike, and bass are some of the many species of fish indigenous to the streams and lakes of Illinois. The State game preserves are well stocked with ring-necked pheasants, ducks, geese, and rabbits.

Illinois is one of the ranking agricultural and manufacturing States of the United States. In a recent year farms in the State numbered over 195,250. These farms occupied approximately 30,980,000 acres and had a value of nearly $5,395,000,000. About 35 percent of the farms and 42 percent of the farm lands were operated by tenant farmers. The State ranks second (after Iowa) in the Union in the production of corn and it ranks among the first five in the production of oats; in a recent year the corn harvest totaled almost 491,900,000 bu. and the oats harvest totaled over 133,500,000 bu. Illinois is the chief soy bean-producing State, with a recent annual yield of about 94,600,000 bu. Other leading crops are hay, wheat, barley, rye, and potatoes. Livestock raising and dairying are major agricultural enterprises. In a recent year the livestock population included about 6,850,000 hogs, 3,287,000 cattle (including 971,000 milch cows), 683,000 sheep, 177,000 horses, and 17,000 mules. The wool clip in the same year totaled almost 1870 tons. Cash receipts from the sale of crops, livestock, and livestock products in a recent year amounted to over $2,017,580,000, a total exceeded in only three other States (California, Iowa, and Texas); farm income from Federal government subsidies was more than $10,600,000.

According to a recent official survey Illinois contains about 16,000 manufacturing establishments employing over 1,154,000 production workers. The manufactures produced in these establishments in a recent year were valued at about $7,930,000,000 plus the cost of materials, supplies, fuel, and contract work; the aggregate value added by manufacture was exceeded only in New York and Pennsylvania. Iron and steel making, meat packing, petroleum refining, and the manufacture of tractors are the principal industries. Other important industries are the manufacture of electrical machinery, automobiles, railroad cars, blast furnaces, cement, printed matter, and clothing.

In value of output, Illinois is one of the leading mineral-producing States of the Union. Bituminous coal fields in the State cover an area of about 35,000 sq.m., and in a recent year there were over 300 coal mines in operation. Production of bituminous coal in that year totaled about 54,870,000 tons, an output exceeded only in West Virginia, Pennsylvania, and Kentucky. Other mineral fuels include petroleum (about 58,210,000 barrels

in a recent year), natural gasoline, and natural gas. The State leads the Union in the production of fluorspar and is second in the production of tripoli. Among other mineral products are sand and gravel, sandstone, limestone, and zinc. In a recent year the mineral output of the State was valued at about $489,-900,000.

Illinois is traversed by an extensive network of transportation facilities, including fifty railroad systems with an aggregate of over 15,700 m. of main-track lines. Inland waterways, notably the Illinois Waterway (q.v.) providing a shallow-draft route between Lake Michigan and the Mississippi R., have a total length of about 4000 m. Excluding roads within urban areas, the highway system consists of almost 125,000 m. of roads, of which 104,000 are rural. The State has nearly 170 government-approved airports, about 40 of which are municipally controlled. There are, in addition, over 400 private airports located in Illinois.

Attendance at the public schools of Illinois is compulsory, throughout the entire school year, for children between the ages of seven and sixteen. The public elementary and secondary schools in the State recently numbered over 11,000, with about 46,000 teachers and an enrollment of over 1,100,000 pupils. In the State are 98 institutions of higher education, 38 of which are universities and colleges, 9 of which are teachers' colleges, and 35 of which are professional schools. Among the outstanding universities and colleges are the University of Illinois (see ILLINOIS, UNIVERSITY OF), at Urbana; University of Chicago, at Chicago; Northwestern University, at Evanston; Illinois Wesleyan University, at Bloomington; Loyola University, at Chicago; James Milliken University, at Decatur; Knox College, at Galesburg; North-Central College, at Naperville; De Paul University, at Chicago; Illinois College, at Jacksonville; MacMurray College, at Jacksonville; Rockford College, at Rockford; Augustana College, at Rock Island; and Monmouth College, at Monmouth.

Illinois is governed according to the constitution of 1870. By the terms of this document, executive authority is vested in a governor and lieutenant governor, elected for four-year terms, and a secretary of state, attorney-general, auditor, treasurer, and certain other appointed officials. Legislative authority is vested in a general assembly consisting of a senate of fifty-one members and of a house of representatives of one

ILLINOIS
RESOURCES AND PRODUCTS
Scale of Miles
0 5 10 20 30 40 50 60
Copyright by C.S. HAMMOND & Co., N.Y.

hundred fifty-three members. Members of the senate are elected for four-year terms, and members of the house of representatives are eleected for two-year terms. Legislative sessions are held biennially. Judicial power of the State is vested in a supreme court, consisting of seven members, circuit courts, consisting of three members, appellate courts, county courts, probate courts, and such courts as may be created by law and for cities and incorporated towns. The State is divided into 102 counties. It is represented in the Congress of the United States by two senators and by twenty-six representatives. The minimum voting age in Illinois is twenty-one years.

History. The first white men to traverse the Illinois region were probably the Canadian explorer Louis Jolliet and the French Jesuit missionary Jacques Marquette. En route (1673) to Lake Michigan from their exploratory voyage on the upper reaches of the Mississippi R., they ascended the river subsequently called Illinois (after the Indian confederacy inhabiting the region). Marquette established a mission on the site of present-day Kaskaskia in 1675. In 1679 the French explorer Robert de La Salle built Fort Crèvecœur at the foot of what is now called Peoria Lake, an expansion of the Illinois R. The first permanent French settlement was established about 1720 at Kaskaskia, then an Indian town. Meanwhile (1712) all of the region s. of the Illinois R. had been included in the French province of Louisiana. The French maintained friendly relations with the Illinois Indians, but made no serious attempts to colonize the region. Intermarriage between French and Indians was common, and ties of friendship were established which lasted after the power of France in the area had ended.

The region was ceded to the British in 1763 under the terms of the Treaty of Paris, concluding the French and Indian War; however, as a result of a rebellion led by the Indian chief Pontiac, two years elapsed before the British assumed effective control. In general, conditions remained unaltered after the British occupation but a number of prominent French settlers fled to St. Louis, Natchez, and other Mississippi Valley towns. Virginians began to move into the Illinois region about 1769. In 1774 the British government attached the region to the province of Quebec.

In 1778, during the American Revolution, a force of Virginians under the frontier leader George Rogers Clark invaded the region and captured the British garrisons at Cahokia and Kaskaskia. All the territory N. of the Ohio R. was annexed by Virginia the same year. By the terms of the peace treaty ending the Revolutionary War jurisdiction over the Illinois and adjacent regions passed to the government of the United States. Virginia ceded its claims to the region in 1784. Massachusetts and Connecticut, with colonial charters authorizing unlimited expansion to the west, gave up their rights in the following year, and in 1787 the region became a part of Northwest Territory (q.v.). In 1800 the U.S. government partitioned Northwest Territory, constituting a large area, including the Illinois region, as Indiana Territory. Illinois Territory, consisting of almost the entire region occupied by the present-day State, most of the region now included in Wisconsin, and part of the region forming present-day Minnesota, was organized on Feb. 3, 1809. The population of the Territory increased substantially during the next few years. Resentful of the consequent encroachments on their ancestral lands, the Indians supported the British in the War of 1812. On August 15, 1812, a group of soldiers and settlers were ambushed, with many casualties, while attempting to evacuate Fort Dearborn (on the site of present-day Chicago).

The present boundaries of Illinois were established on December 3, 1818, when it became the twenty-first State of the Union; the remainder of the Territory was attached to Michigan Territory. Many Illinois settlers had emigrated from the South, and as a result there was considerable proslavery sentiment in the newly organized State. In 1823 the proslavery majority in the legislature adopted a proposal providing for a convention to amend the constitution. Legalization of slavery was the implicit (but not the expressed) intent of the proposal. Referred to the electorate, it was defeated (1824) by a decisive vote. The murder of the abolitionist leader Elijah P. Lovejoy at Alton in 1837, however, showed the persistence of a strong proslavery sentiment. Meanwhile (1832) about 500 Indians, led by the Sac chief Black Hawk, had conducted a bitter but futile war against the Whites in northern Illinois. The Indians were expelled from the State after their defeat. Large numbers of immigrants from the New England and Middle Atlantic States arrived in northern Illinois in the ensuing period, and the process of economic development was accelerated. The Illinois and

Chi. Assoc. of Comm. & Ind.; Ill. Dev. Coun.
Above: Aerial view of Chicago, on the shore of Lake Michigan, Illinois. Right: Cattle in a stockyard in Chicago, center of the Illinois meat-packing industry.

Michigan Canal (q.v.) was begun in 1836; other public improvements were instituted, but the heavy expenditures nearly forced the State into bankruptcy.

In 1840 the Mormons (q.v.), who had migrated from Missouri and had founded Nauvoo, began to figure in the politics of Illinois. Acting as a unit, they succeeded in obtaining exclusive privileges from the legislature. Their religious practices and special privileges aroused hostility. In June, 1844 Joseph Smith, founder of the religion, was imprisoned at Carthage on charges of treason. Soon after his arrest Smith was removed from jail by a mob and lynched. The Mormons left the State in 1846.

With the influx of settlers from the northern States, the antislavery movement became increasingly potent in Illinois during the decade preceding the outbreak of the Civil War. The Democratic Party was defeated by an antislavery coalition in the elections of 1854, and in 1856 the coalition merged, forming the Illinois branch of the Republican Party. In the historic contest (1858) for the U.S. Senatorship between the Democratic candidate Stephen Arnold Douglas and the Republican candidate Abraham Lincoln, the Democrats carried the State, although only by a narrow margin. Lincoln won the Illinois electoral vote in the Presidential election of 1860.

At the outbreak of the Civil War Illinois produced three fifths of all the grain exported to Europe and was the second State in the Union in railway mileage. During the war the State furnished its quota of troops, sending almost 260,000 men into Federal service.

Beginning in 1862, the Democratic Party consistently opposed the war, and the pro-Confederate Knights of the Golden Circle (q.v.) subsequently won widespread support in the State.

The war and postwar periods were marked by steady expansion of the State economy. In October, 1871, a fire devastated a large part of Chicago, leaving 100,000 people homeless. The loss to the city was estimated at nearly $300,000,000. Relations between labor and management have often been stormy in Illinois. Unusually bitter strikes occurred in 1885–86. See HAYMARKET SQUARE RIOT. In 1894 a strike of the employees of the Pullman Car Company developed into a general strike of railway men. Traffic in Illinois was almost suspended, and in June lawlessness broke out. Interference with the United States mails led to the intervention of the Federal government. Chicago was occupied by the Federal troops; the strike leaders were arrested and sentenced to short terms of imprisonment for contempt of court.

In national politics the State of Illinois was consistently Republican after 1860 with the exception of 1892, when it voted for Grover Cleveland, and 1912, when its vote was in favor of Woodrow Wilson. From 1916 until 1928 it continued to vote Republican; however, from 1932 until 1948 it voted Democratic. In the 1948 presidential election 1,987,754 ballots were cast for the Democratic incumbent Harry S. Truman and 1,949,834 ballots were cast for Thomas E. Dewey, the Republican candidate. The State returned to the Republican fold in 1952. General Dwight David Eisenhower, the Republican candidate, received 2,457,327 votes. His Democratic opponent Adlai Ewing Stevenson, who was then governor of Illinois, received 2,013,920 votes.

ILLINOIS AND MICHIGAN CANAL, a canal about 100 m. long connecting Lake Michigan with the navigable waters of the Illinois River. In conjunction with the Welland Canal (q.v.), which connects lakes Erie and Ontario, it affords vessels of limited size passage from the Gulf of Mexico to the Gulf of St. Lawrence. The canal was first planned in 1825; construction was begun in 1836 and, after an interruption from 1841 to 1845 due to lack of funds, completed in 1848. The water at La Salle, Ill., where the canal meets the Illinois River, is 145 ft. lower than at Lake Michigan, and the descent is accomplished by means of seventeen locks varying in lift from 3½ to 10 ft.

The locks are 110 ft. long and 18 ft. wide, giving passage to boats of about 150 tons.

ILLINOIS INSTITUTE OF TECHNOLOGY, a coeducational institution of higher education, situated in Chicago, Ill. It was formed in 1941 by the consolidation of Armour Institute of Technology, founded in 1892, and Lewis Institute, founded in 1895. The Institute offers courses in chemical, civil, electrical, industrial, and mechanical engineering, biology and chemistry, business administration, public service, and home economics, leading to bachelor's, master's, and doctor's degrees. The institution, which is privately controlled, benefits from an endowment of over $2,500,000. In a recent year the faculty numbered about 200 and the student body over 6900.

ILLINOIS RIVER, the most important tributary of the upper Mississippi river, traversing the State of Illinois from a point about 45 miles s.w. of Chicago to a point on the Mississippi about 18 miles above Alton. It is formed by the union of the Des Plaines and Kankakee rivers in Grundy Co., Ill., and flows in a generally s.w. direction for a total distance of about 435 miles. The drainage area of the river is 29,013 sq.m., of which 24,726 sq.m. lie in Illinois and the remainder in Indiana and Wisconsin. The Illinois is broad and deep, and navigable by steamboats for about 250 m., from its mouth to the city of La Salle, Ill. From this point passage to Lake Michigan is afforded by the Illinois and Michigan Canal (q.v.), thus completing uninterrupted water communication between the Great Lakes and the Mississippi R. The Illinois has a large number of tributaries, the most important being the Fox and Sangamon rivers. The chief cities on its banks are Ottawa and Peoria, Ill.

ILLINOIS STATE NORMAL UNIVERSITY, a coeducational institution of higher education, founded in 1857 at Normal, Ill., to train teachers for the State schools. The university grants degrees of bachelor and master of education. It is State controlled, and is largely supported by appropriations voted in the State legislature. In a recent year the faculty numbered over 140 and the student body about 2210.

ILLINOIS, UNIVERSITY OF, a coeducational institution of higher education, founded in 1867 as Illinois Industrial University and given its present name in 1885. The principal site of the university is at Urbana, but it also maintains branches at Chicago and Galesburg. The university offers courses leading to bachelor's degrees for architectural, ceramic, chemical, civil, electrical, mechanical, mining, and metallurgical engineers, and for engineer-physicists; and also bachelor's degrees in the liberal arts and science, business administration, law, fine arts, music, and pharmacy. Master's degrees are granted in music, architecture, education, science, and fine arts; and doctor's degrees are granted in medicine, law, education, and dentistry. The colleges of medicine, dentistry, and pharmacy are situated in Chicago. The University, which is State controlled, benefits from an endowment of nearly $3,180,000, and in a recent year the faculty numbered about 3840 and the student body more than 22,000; the libraries contain a total of over 2,475,000 volumes.

ILLINOIS WATERWAY, system of rivers and canals of Illinois, about 325 m. in length. Connecting the Great Lakes with the Mississippi R., it extends from Lake Michigan at Chicago to Grafton, Ill. Sections of the waterway include the Chicago R., the Sanitary and Ship Canal, the Des Plaines R., and the Illinois R., an affluent of the Mississippi R. The toll-free waterway is operated by the U.S. Army Corps of Engineers. It facilitates transportation for shipments of coal, grain, steel products, petroleum, limestone, and other bulk cargoes. Recreational areas developed along the route of the waterway include the Illinois and Starved Rock State parks near La Salle and Pere Marquette State Park at Grafton.

ILLINOIS WESLEYAN UNIVERSITY, a coeducational institution of higher education founded in 1850 at Bloomington, Ill. The university offers instruction in the liberal arts, fine arts, music, and nursing, leading to bachelor's degrees, and courses in music leading to a master's degree. The institution, which is controlled by the Methodist Church, benefits from an endowment of almost $1,500,-000. In a recent year the faculty numbered over 45 and the student body nearly 750.

ILLUMINATED MANUSCRIPTS, manuscripts embellished with figures, letters, and illustrations, done in color and often, in addition, with varying thicknesses of gold or silver. Manuscript illumination was practiced in antiquity, became a major art in Byzantine times, flourished in Europe in the Middle Ages, and declined during the Renaissance. Following the invention of printing by movable type illumination became a minor art, limited in application and

cherished by bibliophiles and art lovers.

The embellishments employed in manuscript illumination varied at different periods and in different countries. The most common embellishment was a large initial letter at the beginning of a book, chapter, or paragraph. Others took the form of marginal drawings, borders, designs, or pictorial representations occupying an entire page or inset into the text. Among notable surviving examples of illuminated manuscripts of antiquity are the Egyptian papyri, called *Book of the Dead* (q.v.). Highly esteemed are two manuscripts in the Vatican, of the works of the Latin poet Vergil (q.v.), one dating from the 4th century A.D., and the other, entitled *Codex Romanus,* dating from the 5th or 6th century. Another noted illuminated manuscript in the Vatican is a calendar of the lives of the Saints, dating from the reign of the Byzantine Emperor Basil II. One of the most celebrated of all illuminated manuscripts is that of the Gospels, called *Book of Kells,* in Trinity College, Dublin. Regarded as a remarkable work of Carolingian times, is the manuscript called the *Utrecht Psalter,* in the Utrecht University Library, the Netherlands. Among the numerous manuscripts of the Gothic period in France are the psalters embellished in the 13th century for King Louis IX, in the Bibliothèque Nationale, Paris. A 15th-century manuscript of note was the lavishly decorated prayer book, called *Très Riches Heures du Duc de Berry,* in the Musée Condé, Chantilly. Art historians consider as a masterpiece of the age of the Renaissance, the 15th-century manuscript of the prayer book known as the *Book of Hours of Bona of Savoy,* in the British Museum, London. A modern master of the art of illuminating manuscripts is the Polish artist Arthur Szyk.

ILLUSION, a distorted or abnormal perception. The word is used in psychology in two principal senses. **1.** In abnormal psychology, the term denotes misinterpretation of the contents of perception, arising from such disorders as an abnormal irritability of the sensory centers of the brain cortex. Such illusions, which are usually based upon habits, attitudes, suggestions, and unconscious motivations, are sometimes called *active illusions.* Typical examples are subjective enhancements of the intensity of a stimulus, as when a gentle knocking at a door is taken for thunder, and falsifications of perception in terms related to a mental disorder or emotional predicament, as when

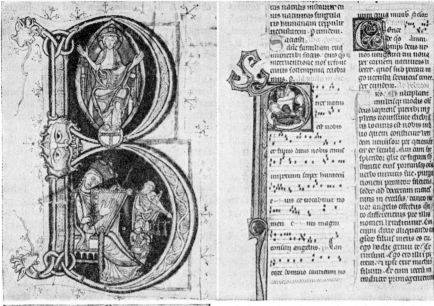

ILLUMINATED MANUSCRIPTS

Above, left: Ornamental letter in a 12th-century Latin manuscript containing commentaries on Biblical psalms. Above: A page from a 14th-century missal of the Abbey of Saint Denis, France. Left: Corner of page from the French "Lancelot du Lac," 13th century.

shipwrecked sailors see the mirage of a boat. Sane people of imaginative disposition are liable to illusion, particularly at times of mental stress or overwork; in general, however, intense and recurrent active illusions are characteristic of delirious or disoriented phases of mental illness. See PSYCHOLOGY, ABNORMAL. Compare HALLUCINATION. **2.** In physiological psychology, the term "illusion" denotes perversion of the contents of perception due to structural or functional peculiarities of the perceptual apparatus. Such illusions, which are natural and necessary rather than abnormal, are sometimes known as *passive illusions*. The most important of these "normal" illusions are those of touch and sight. The latter, which are typified by the apparent convergence of parallel lines and by the persistence of vision which gives continuity to motion pictures, have been closely studied by psychologists and physiologists. A large body of simple geometrical figures, termed collectively *geometrical optical illusions*, has been devised to demonstrate and test illusions in visual perception.

ILLUSTRATION, in books and other publications, the use of pictures to explain or enhance the text. From antiquity to the invention of printing by movable type in the 15th century, books were written and illustrated by hand; see ILLUMINATED MANUSCRIPTS. The first books printed from movable type were illustrated with pictures reproduced from engraved wood blocks, which were set with the type. After printing, the engravings were often colored by hand. Illustrations in several colors and in different shades of the same color were made in the 16th century; the method employed was to color a number of engraved wood blocks, each with a different hue or shade, and then to stamp them in succession on the page to be illustrated. Drawings by such noted painters as Raphael and Titian (qq.v.)

ILLUSTRATION 4551 ILLUSTRATION

were reproduced in this way. Illustrations printed from engraved or etched copper and steel plates were known as early as the 15th century; see ENGRAVING. By the end of the 16th century this process of illustration had gradually become more common than the wood-block method. 17th-century books, particularly historical and topographical works, were often illustrated with copper engravings. Among the best illustrations of this type were those executed by the German engraver Matthäus Merian. From about 1650 to 1750 the frontispieces and the title pages of most books were illustrated with elaborate copper engravings. In the 18th century the art of engraving illustrations on wood blocks was revived by Thomas Bewick (q.v.). The poet and artist William Blake (q.v.) also worked in this medium, which was widely employed until the end of the 19th century.

In the 19th century, when books, magazines, and newspapers began to be made on a mass scale, pictures were reproduced from wood engravings, engravings or etchings on metal, and also from lithograph stones; the latter method was invented about 1796 (see

ILLUSTRATION. *Top, left: Copper engraving illustrating an early edition of Cervantes' "Don Quixote." Top, right: Title page of 17th-century edition of "Dictionary of the French Academy." Bottom, left: Gargantua, illustration by Gustave Doré for "The Works of Rabelais." Bottom, right: White-line wood engraving by the illustrator Thomas Bewick.*

The sea dog, a woodcut illustrating "Dyalogue des Créatures", a 15th-century manuscript

LITHOGRAPHY). Original drawings for the illustrations were made by such noted artists as Joseph Mallard Turner and George Cruikshank in England, Gustave Doré in France, and Winslow Homer (qq.v.) in the United States. At the end of the 19th century, the method of reproducing illustrations by photoengraving, an inexpensive mechanical process, generally superseded earlier methods. Today most illustrations in publications are printed from photoengraved plates.

ILLYRIA, an ancient country of indefinite extent, comprising the eastern coast of the Adriatic Sea N. of Greece, a part of the N. Adriatic coast, and the hinterland of both coasts. The northern boundary was probably formed by the two rivers now called the Sava and Danube, the eastern boundary by the South Morava R., and the southern boundary by a line north of the site of the present city of Tirana, Albania. The Adriatic formed the western boundary. The inhabitants of Illyria spoke an Indo-European language from which the Albanian language (see ALBANIA) is probably derived. Herodotus and other Greek historians characterized the Illyrians as barbarians, but evidences of a progressive development in the neolithic civilization of the Illyrians have been discovered in present-day Bosnia and Dalmatia, and in Croatia and Slavonia. The colonization of the Illyrian coast by the Greeks probably began late in the 7th or early in the 6th century B.C., their chief settlements being Epidamnus and Salona, now Durazzo and Spalato respectively; Greek pottery and inscriptions dating from 600 B.C. have been discovered at Salona. Greek influence was restricted to the coastal cities and was superseded after the 3rd century B.C. by Roman civilization.

Until the appearance of the Romans, the Illyrians appear to have been engaged in constant warfare among themselves and with neighboring peoples; they often engaged in battle with the early Macedonian kings. Early in the 4th century B.C. however, under the threat of an invasion by the Celts (see CELTIC PEOPLES AND LANGUAGES) and other peoples, the Illyrians united as a kingdom for common defense. Late in the century they were defeated by Philip II of Macedon and part of their country was annexed. Their later history until the Roman conquest is one of piratical raids against Italian and Greek coastal cities and attacks on commerce in the Adriatic. The Greek colonies called upon Rome for help, with the result that, after two Illyrian wars, in 229 and 219 B.C., the Romans subjugated the Illyrians and took part of their territory. The Illyrian kingdom, however, retained considerable power until 180 B.C., when the Dalmatians declared their independence of Illyria. The Romans conquered and annexed Illyria in 168 B.C., but the Dalmatians successfully defended themselves against Roman invasions for the next 165 years; they were completely subdued in 9 A.D. by the Emperor Tiberius Claudius Nero Cæsar, who united Dalmatia, Iapydia, and Liburnia into the administrative province of Illyricum, comprising an area less than that of the former kingdom of Illyria. Under the Romans the Illyrians flourished; and from the Illyrian peasantry rose a number of Rome's outstanding soldier-emperors, including Aurelianus, Claudius, Diocletian, and Maximian (qq.v.).

In the reign of the Emperor Diocletian, Illyricum was included in the prefecture of Illyricum, one of the four subdivisions into which the Roman empire was divided, and comprising the greater part of the Balkan peninsula. From 285 A.D., when the empire was divided into the Western Roman Empire and the Eastern Roman Empire, until 379 A.D., the prefecture remained part of the western empire. In the latter year a part of the prefecture, called Eastern Illyricum, and separated from the remaining part, called Western Illyricum, by a line of demarcation between Latin-speaking and Greek-speaking peoples, was included in the Eastern Roman Empire. Eastern Illyricum comprised the entire Balkan peninsula south of the Danube R.

After attacks in 441 and 447 by the Huns, the entire region comprising ancient Illyria was invaded in the 6th century by Slavonic tribes who formed permanent settlements there. Between the beginning and the middle of the 7th century the Croats and Serbs occupied Illyria; see CROATIA AND SLAVONIA; DALMATIA. The Croats settled in the western, and the Serbs in the eastern, part of the country, with the result that the Croats came under the influence of Italian civilization and the Roman Catholic Church, and the Serbs were influenced by Byzantium and the Greek Orthodox Church. In time the Illyrians were absorbed, becoming entirely Serbo-Croatian in language and culture; the coastal city-states, however, clung to their independence for many years. A few Illyrian tribes who preserved their independence in the Albanian mountains are thought to be the ancestors of the Albanian people.

ILMENITE, TITANIC IRON ORE, or **MENACCANITE,** a mineral composed of ferrous titanate, $FeTiO_3$. It occurs massive and as rhombohedral, tabular crystals, frequently enveloped in crystalline metamorphic rocks and as an accessory mineral in igneous rocks. It is found in large quantities in the Ilmen Mountains, U.S.S.R., from which the name is derived, in parts of Norway, and in the United States in Connecticut, Washington, and New York. Ilmenite is a black, opaque mineral with a metallic or submetallic luster. It has a hardness ranging from $5\frac{1}{2}$ to 6, and specific gravity of 4.7. It becomes magnetic upon heating. Ilmenite is a valuable natural resource, being the chief source of titanium (q.v.) in the United States.

ILOILO, capital of a province of the same name, Panay Island, the Philippines. The province is watered by several rivers, notably the Jalaur and the Jaro, and is traversed by some of the finest roads in the Philippines. Forests of hardwood trees are extensive, and the province contains iron deposits and stone quarries. Sugar refining, textile manufacturing, the raising of livestock, farming, lumbering, and quarrying are the principal industries. The chief agricultural products are sugar cane, tobacco, fruits, rice, corn, and coconuts. The capital, located on Iloilo Strait, about 65 m. by rail s.w. of Cápiz, is an important manufacturing center and seaport. Its harbor is protected by Guimaras Island, which lies across the strait from the city. Sugar, rice, and tobacco are exported. The leading manufactures include vinegar and coconut oil. Area of province, 2048 sq.m.; pop. (1948 prelim.) 816,382. Pop. of municipality (1948 prelim.) 110,122.

ILOKANO, or ILOCANO, one of the most important of the civilized tribes of the Philippine Islands (q.v.). They form almost the entire Christianized population of the Ilocos Norte, Ilocos Sur, and La Union provinces of Luzon, and have migrated in large numbers to colonize other parts of the island. At the present time they number about one million, with the greatest concentration living along the west and northwest coasts. When the Spaniards arrived in the Philippines, the Ilokanos possessed a flourishing indigenous culture, many traces of which still remain, and a developed alphabet and literature. They were soon converted to Christianity, and adopted many of the customs of their conquerors. The language of the Ilokanos is a Malayan speech with a large number of local varieties and dialects. The most developed of these dialects, in which the most extensive literature is written, is that of the extreme northwest.

ILONGOT, a primitive pagan Malayan people with Negrito admixtures living around the headwaters of the Rio Grande de Cagayan in northern Luzon. The group now numbers about 3000, and is among the wildest and least known in the Philippine Islands. Head-hunting is widely practiced among them, and a man who has taken many heads is held in high esteem. Other positions of honor may be gained by those reputed to have magical power. However, social organization is in general of the simplest kind, and no positions of authority exist in matters of daily life or government. The Ilongots have no villages; they live in scattered dwellings along the mountainsides close to the clearings in which they raise rice, corn, millet, and sweet potatoes. To these products are added such game and fish as they are able to procure by the use of primitive traps and weapons. See PHILIPPINE ISLANDS.

ILORIN or **ILLORIN,** name of a province and its capital, s.w. Northern Provinces, Nigeria. The province is inhabited principally by the Yoruba people. Agriculture is the chief occupation, and rice, cotton, peppers, and kola nuts are raised. Forest products include rubber, shea butter, and palm oil. The capital, situated 160 m. by rail N.N.E. of Lagos, is a center for trade. It was founded in the late 18th century and soon became a capital of a Yoruba kingdom. In 1900, when the province of Ilorin was placed under British control, the town of Ilorin was made capital of the province. Pottery, leather goods, and other handicraft wares are made in the capital. Area of province, 18,095 sq.m.; pop., about 538,000. Pop. of town (1948 est.) 53,000.

IMAGE DISSECTOR. See TELEVISION.

IMAGE WORSHIP or **VENERATION OF IMAGES,** the use in worship of representations of sacred persons or things and the exhibition of reverence toward them. For the first four centuries of the history of the Christian Church, the fear of introducing the pagan practice of idolatry (q.v.) deterred the use of images in churches. Their use became popular, however, in the next three centuries, and abuses arose which evoked condemnation by the bishops of the Western Church and gave rise to the controversy over Iconoclasm (q.v.) in the Eastern Church. At the second Council of Nice in 787, the doctrine of the Church concerning the veneration of images was carefully defined. This doctrine, still held by the Roman Catholic and Orthodox churches, declared that veneration, not adoration, might be shown toward sacred images, but only in a relative manner, that is, addressed not to the image itself, but, through it, to the original person or object it represented.

At the Reformation, the Protestants generally rejected the use of images in worship, and stigmatized the practice as idolatrous. Martin Luther, however, while condemning the actual worship of images, permitted their use in churches as simple incentives to devotion, regarding them as *adiaphora,* or indifferent things, the presence of which might be permitted.

IMAGINARY NUMBERS, the product of any real number and the square root of minus one, $\sqrt{-1}$, usually represented in mathematics by the letter i, and occasionally by the letter j. The number 1 has two square roots: $+1$ and -1; thus the equation $x^2 - 1 = 0$ has two solutions: $x = 1$ and $x = -1$. But the equation $x^2 + 1 = 0$ has no real solution, and its only solutions are the two imaginary numbers i and $-i$.

Every quadratic equation (an equation of the form $ax^2 + bx = c$, where a, b, and c are real numbers) has two and only two solutions, both expressible in terms of real, imaginary, or complex numbers (a complex number is the sum of a real number and an imaginary number). By about 1600, mathematicians had shown that the solutions of any cubic or quartic equations (equations containing x^3 or x^4 respectively) could also be obtained in terms of complex numbers. About 1800 the German mathematician Karl

Friedrich Gauss showed that every algebraic equation (an equation setting any number equal to the sum of a finite number of terms of the form ax^n, where a is a real, imaginary, or complex number, and n is a positive integer) has a solution in terms of complex numbers.

The solutions of many types of transcendental (nonalgebraic) equations can also be expressed in terms of complex or imaginary numbers. For example, the logarithms of positive numbers greater than 1 are positive real numbers, and the logarithms of positive numbers less than one are negative real numbers; the logarithms of positive numbers thus exhaust the real numbers, and leave no real solution for the equation $x = \log(-1)$. In other words, the logarithm of a negative number is imaginary. The German mathematician Leonhard Euler (who introduced the symbol $i = \sqrt{-1}$) showed early in the 18th century that the solutions to all such equations could also be expressed in terms of imaginary or complex numbers. Euler also introduced imaginary numbers into the solution of trigonometric equations; he proved, for example, that $e^{ix} = \cos x + i \sin x$, where $\cos x$ and $\sin x$ are trigonometric functions.

The concept of imaginary numbers has also been extended to geometry. For example, a line and a circle drawn in the same plane theoretically intersect at two points; if a circle and a line are drawn so that they do not intersect, then these two points are imaginary. By the techniques of analytical geometry, the co-ordinates of these two points may be easily found as the solutions of the simultaneous equations of the circle and line; these two solutions are in the form of complex numbers.

The importance of imaginary numbers lies in their generalization of the solution of mathematical equations by the addition of a single new symbol and concept; no further degree of "imaginariness" need be introduced. For example, the equation $x = \sqrt{-i}$ has two solutions in terms of complex numbers: $x = \dfrac{1}{\sqrt{2}} - \dfrac{i}{\sqrt{2}}$ and $x = \dfrac{i}{\sqrt{2}} - \dfrac{1}{\sqrt{2}}$. Moreover, complex numbers obey all of the ordinary rules of arithmetic and algebra, and do not introduce any inconsistencies or paradoxes.

IMAGINATION, the conscious mental evocation of ideas or images of objects, events, relations, attributes, or processes which the subject has not experienced or perceived.

In this common meaning, imagination may be contrasted with memory (q.v.), which consists in the mental evocation of previous experience. Perception, memory, and imagination are essentially similar mental processes, particularly when their content consists of sensory images; memory and imagination were at one time grouped together under the name of imagination to include the processes of both reviving (or "recollecting") and creating mental images. Psychologists still occasionally distinguish between *passive* or *reproductive imagination,* which consists in having mental images which were originally perceived by the senses, and *active, constructive,* or *creative imagination,* by which future or hypothetical events or objects, unrelated or insecurely related to past and present reality, are produced (or "imaged") in the mind.

When an imagined and a real perception are simultaneous, the imagined perception may be confused with or even mistaken for the true perception. Colored hearing and synesthesia (qq.v.), which permit of objective study and measurement, are examples of this phenomenon; the events and objects apparently perceived in dreams (see DREAMING), are examples of nonverifiable and nonrepeatable exercises of imagination. In all such psychological events, imagination takes over the functions of perception. The most extreme examples of such confusion are the hallucinations (q.v.) suffered by the victims of any of several mental disorders. An opposite error, in which a genuine perception is assumed by the individual to be an imagined one, also exists, though more rarely, and can be induced in the laboratory under experimental conditions. In one well-known experiment, subjects are asked to imagine a scene or object on a screen upon which, unknown to them, the same scene or object is being dimly projected. The visual stimulus thus provided is almost invariably taken to be a product of pure imagination, even when it does not correspond exactly with the subject's own imagined perception.

IMAGISM, the name given to the esthetic movement founded in England and the United States early in the 20th century by a group of poets, including Richard Aldington, D(avid) H(erbert) Lawrence, Amy Lowell, Ezra Pound (qq.v.), and John Gould Fletcher. These poets issued manifestoes and wrote articles embodying their theories. The imagists placed primary reliance on the use of verbal images as a means of poetic expression, and stressed the use of the language of common speech, of meticulous precision in the choice of words, and of complete freedom in the choice of subject matter. Most of the imagist poets wrote in free verse (q.v.). Notable among collections of imagist poetry are *Des Imagistes: An Anthology* (1914), compiled by Ezra Pound; and the three anthologies compiled by Amy Lowell, all under the title *Some Imagist Poets* (1915, 1916, 1917).

IMBECILITY. See MENTAL DEFICIENCY.

IMHOFF TANK. See SEWAGE.

IMHOTEP, or IMOUTHES (fl. 2980-50 B.C.), Egyptian physician, architect, and statesman, chief advisor to King Zoser (q.v.) of the IIId Dynasty. Imhotep built the Step Pyramid, oldest of the known Egyptian pyramids, for Zoser. His fame as a physician and scholar grew through the centuries until, at the end of the New Kingdom (see EGYPT: *The New Kingdom*), he was deified and worshiped as the god of learning. The Greeks identified Imhotep with Æsculapius (q.v.), the god of medicine and the son of Apollo.

IMITATION, in biology. See MIMICRY.

IMMACULATE CONCEPTION, in Roman Catholic theology, the dogma holding that, from the first instant of its creation, the soul of the Virgin Mary was free from original sin; this doctrine is not to be confused with that of Virgin Birth (q.v.). In spite of divergent opinions on the part of various theologians from time to time, the Church has been consistent in maintaining the dogma of the Immaculate Conception; a festival under that title was celebrated in the Greek Orthodox Church as early as the 5th century, and in the Western Church from the 7th century. In the 14th century the Scottish theologian John Duns Scotus (q.v.) maintained the doctrine, and it was declared an article of faith by the Council of Basel (1431-43) and the Council of Trent (1545-63). Finally Pope Pius IX issued a solemn decree on December 8, 1854, declaring the doctrine to be a dogma essential for the belief of the universal church. The feast of the Immaculate Conception is celebrated on December 8. Under this title the Virgin Mary is invoked as the patroness of the United States of America, the United States of Brazil, Portugal, and Corsica, and has been portrayed in art, notably by the painters Bartolommeo Carducci, Hans Holbein the

Younger, Bartolomé Esteban Murillo, Guido Reni, José Riberra, and Lucca Signorelli.

IMMANENCE, in philosophy and theology, the idea that the intelligent and creative force or being which governs the universe pervades the universe. Immanence is a fundamental doctrine of pantheism (q.v.), and is opposite in meaning to transcendence, in which the intelligent and creative force or being is distinct from the universe. In pantheistic systems of thought, for example, all physical objects in the universe are pervaded with the infinite Divine presence; in Judæo-Christian religions, God is infinite, but transcends (i.e., figuratively, rises above) the universe which He created; see GOD. Some theologians consider immanence and transcendence to be compatible when immanence is defined as activity or causality the effects of which remain within the active agent, and when transcendence is defined as activity of causality the effects of which go beyond the active agent and affect other agents.

IMMERMANN, KARL (1796-1840), German writer, born in Magdeburg and educated at the University of Halle. In 1834 he became manager of the Düsseldorf Theater, at which he carried out a notable series of experiments in dramaturgy, later described in his book *Düsseldorfer Anfänge* (1840). In his other writings, Immermann was at first an exponent of the romantic school, but he later became a realist and a supporter of the revolutionary literary movements of his time; see GERMAN LITERATURE. Among his works are the historical tragedies *Das Trauerspiel in Tirol* (1827) and *Alexis* (1832); the mystical peom *Merlin* (1831), generally regarded as his finest work; and the novels *Die Epigonen* (3 vols., 1836) and *Münchhausen* (4 vols., 1838-39), the latter of which contains a celebrated idyllic portrait of village life *Der Oberhof*.

IMMIGRATION, the transfer of residence from one country to another, regarded from the standpoint of the country in which the new residence is taken. From time immemorial, immigration has been an important factor in the diffusion of culture. In modern times, the first great immigration was the colonizing movement of the 16th and 17th centuries, which introduced essential features of western European civilization to the New World. Sporadic population movements from the Far East to other continents took place in the 15th and 17th centuries. With respect to the number of persons involved, im-migration, on a world scale, reached a peak in the 19th and 20th centuries. For a comprehensive, historical, and more detailed account of the movement of populations, see MIGRATION. In this article only immigration to the United States is discussed.

The original settlers of the territory comprising the United States were immigrants from western Europe. The first great influx of immigrants to the United States began early in the 19th century, when large numbers of Europeans sought to escape the economic distress resulting from the French Revolutionary and Napoleonic Wars, and to avail themselves of opportunities for a better life in the New World. Subsequently, other wars, political oppression, and economic depressions caused large numbers of Europeans to seek peace, freedom, and security in the United States. Between 1820 and 1850 most of the immigrants came from Great Britain, Ireland, Germany, and the Scandinavian countries. In the second half of the 19th century, the proportion of immigrants from northern and western Europe rapidly declined; in the period from 1890 to 1910 less than one-third of the total number of immigrants came from those regions; the remainder came chiefly from southern and eastern Europe, with nationals of Austria, Hungary, Italy, and Russia alone constituting more than one-half of the total immigration for the period. Until World War I, immigration had generally increased in volume annually. From 1905 to 1914 an average of more than a million aliens entered the United States every year. Following the outbreak of the war, the volume declined sharply, and the annual average from 1915 to 1918 was little more than 250,000. In 1921 the number again rose; 800,000 immigrants were admitted. Thereafter the number of immigrants admitted to the United States was determined by the President in accordance with Congressional enactments.

Legislation Regulating Immigration to the United States. The first measure restricting immigration enacted by Congress was a law in 1862 forbidding American vessels to transport Chinese immigrants to the United States; twenty years later Congress passed the Chinese Exclusion Act excluding Chinese immigrants. In 1875, 1882, and 1892, acts passed by Congress provided for the examination of immigrants and for the exclusion from the United States of convicts, polygamists, prostitutes, persons suffering from loathsome or contagious diseases, and persons liable to become public charges. The Alien Contract Labor Laws of 1885, 1887, 1888, and 1891 prohibited the immigration to the United States of persons entering the country to work under contracts made previous to their arrival; professional actors, artists, singers, lecturers, educators, ministers, and personal and domestic servants were exempt from this provision. Alien skilled laborers, under these laws, were permitted to enter the United States to work in new industries. A diplomatic agreement made in 1907 by the U.S. and Japanese governments, called a *gentleman's agreement,* provided that the Japanese government would not issue passports to Japanese laborers intending to enter the United States; and under the terms of this agreement, the U.S. government refrained from the enactment of laws excluding Japanese immigrants; in 1924 Congress enacted legislation under which immigration to the United States by Japanese was prohibited.

In 1917 Congress passed a new immigration law which has since continued in effect as the basic immigration statute of the United States. By the terms of this statute, aliens unable to meet minimum mental, moral, physical, and economic standards as defined in the law are excluded from the country. After World War I, a marked increase in immigration for impoverished European countries gave rise to a widespread demand in the United States for further restrictive legislation. In 1921 a Congressional enactment provided for a quota system for immigrants, whereby the number of aliens of any nationality admitted to the United States in a year could not exceed three percent of the number of foreign-born residents of that nationality living in the United States in 1910. By its terms, the law applied to nationals of Europe, the Near East, Africa, Australia, New Zealand, Asiatic Russia, and to certain islands in the Atlantic and Pacific oceans distant from the mainland of the Western Hemisphere. Immigrants who had been living for one year in the Western Hemisphere were not subject to the quota; later, this time limit was increased to five years. In 1924 the basic immigration quota was fixed in a law which superseded the act of 1921. The later law provided for annual immigration quotas for all countries from which aliens might be admitted. Again, aliens fulfilling residence requirements stipulated in the law were exempted from the quotas. Alien wives and children of U.S.

citizens are exempt from the quotas, as are, under certain conditions, alien husbands of U.S. citizens. Under the new quota system, visas permitting immigration are issued in foreign countries by the U.S. Consular Service.

In 1941 Congress passed an act providing for the refusal of visas to aliens whose presence in the United States would endanger the public safety. Immigration legislation passed after 1941 includes a Congressional act of 1943, repealing the laws barring Chinese persons from entering the United States, and allowing their admission to the country in accordance with an annual quota. A Federal law passed in 1945 authorized for a limited time the admission to the United States, without regard to quota, and physical and other standards, the wives and children of citizens serving in, or honorably discharged from, the armed forces of the United States during World War II.

A Federal law of 1946 authorized the admission to the United States under annual quota of persons of races indigenous to India. Legislation was enacted by Congress in 1948 to permit the immigration before July 1, 1950 of 202,000 European displaced persons, i.e., persons driven from their homes in the years preceding World War II as a result of political or racial persecution, and those forcibly transported from their homes during World War II; the number admitted was to be deducted from subsequent annual quotas for the various nationalities.

The Immigration and Nationalization Act of 1952 codified and amended most of the laws relating to immigration. It raised quotas slightly and ended racial bars, but retained a quota system based on place of national origin. See also DEPORTATION.

NUMBER OF IMMIGRANTS TO THE UNITED STATES

1821-30	143,439
1831-40	599,125
1841-50	1,713,251
1851-60	2,598,214
1861-70	2,314,824
1871-80	2,812,191
1881-90	5,246,613
1891-1900	3,687,564
1901-10	8,795,386
1911-20	5,735,811
1921-30	4,107,209
1931-40	528,431
1941-50	1,035,039

IMMIGRATION AND NATURALIZATION SERVICE, an agency of the U.S. Department of Justice, created by Congressional enactment in 1891. It was originally an agency of the U.S. Department of Labor, and was transferred to the Department of Justice in 1940. The service is empowered to administer the Federal laws relating to the admission, exclusion, and deportation of aliens, and to the naturalization of aliens lawfully residing in the United States. It investigates the qualifications of applicants for citizenship, and provides the public schools of the country with textbooks and other materials required for the schooling of candidates for citizenship. Agents of the service patrol the borders of the United States to prevent the illegal entry of aliens. In accordance with the Alien Registration Act of 1940, the service also registers and fingerprints all aliens residing in the United States.

The service is vested with exclusive authority to conduct hearings for the purpose of determining whether undesirable aliens shall be deported. The power of the courts to review its decisions has been greatly limited by Congressional enactment. After World War II, the service was engaged, in co-operation with the Federal Bureau of Investigation, in an intensive drive to deport aliens accused of conducting subversive activities, or charged with illegal entry into the United States. See DEPORTATION.

IMMORTALITY, endless existence of the soul or ego of the individual after personal death. This doctrine is part of the religion of all civilized peoples, but in different cultures takes various forms, ranging from ultimate extinction of the ego to complete survival of the soul and resurrection of the body. In Hinduism, the goal is absorption into the Universal Spirit, and the Buddhist doctrine promises a *nirvana* of complete extinction of the personality. In the ancient Egyptian religion, the abode of the immortals was definitely described, and entrance to immortal life was dependent upon the result of a divine examination of the merits of the life of the individual. Early Greek religion promised a shadowy continuation of life on earth in Hades; later the concept became crystallized in the *Apology* and *Phædo* of Socrates. In the Christian and Mohammedan religions, as in Judaism, the immortality promised is primarily of the spirit; both religions differ from Judaism in that after the resurrection of the body and a general judgment of the entire human race, the body is to be reunited with the spirit to experience the reward or punishment awarded by the judgment. In Jewish eschatology the resurrection will take place at the advent of the Messiah, and the reunion of body and spirit will endure only for the Messianic Age, after which the spirit will return to heaven. See JUDGMENT, FINAL; ESCHATOLOGY.

IMMORTELLE. See EVERLASTINGS.

IMMUNITY, the effective resistance of a living organism to the effects of a poison, or to infection with a bacterial, fungus, or virus disease, to which it is *susceptible*. Lack of susceptibility to specific diseases, known as *natural immunity,* is often a characteristic of a species or race; for example, man is susceptible to infantile paralysis whereas cattle are not, and cattle are susceptible to Johne's disease whereas man is not. The term "immunity" is commonly restricted to resistance by members of a species to diseases to which other members of the same species are susceptible.

Two factors creating immunity are present in an animal body: *phagocytes* (q.v.), wandering tissue cells which engulf any pathogenic microorganisms which they come upon in the body; and *antibodies,* protein-containing chemical substances produced in the body to combat specific disease organisms or poisons.

Immunity caused by the presence of specific antibodies may be *congenital,* i.e., passed on to the child from the mother through the placenta, or *acquired,* i.e., contracted by an individual by inoculation, by vaccination (q.v.), or by recovery from an attack of the disease. Acquired immunity may be *active,* produced by antibody production in the body cells of the immune individual, or *passive,* acquired by transfusion with the antibody-containing serum of an immune person. All these forms of immunity attenuate with time; the speed with which they do so depends on such factors as the virulence of the attack which caused the immunity (if active), or on the strength of the injected antibodies (if passive).

The science of immunology (the study of immunity in animals) dates from the late 18th century when Edward Jenner (q.v.) discovered that immunity to smallpox could be given to an individual by vaccination. Louis Pasteur (q.v.), who developed a method for conferring immunity against hydrophobia, attempted to explain the phenomena of immunity in his *exhaustion theory,* postulated in 1880. This theory states that the body contains limited amounts of specific nutritive substance which can be used by a disease organism, and that once an organism has exhausted this nutritive substance the body is immune. In 1889 Pierre P. E. Roux (q.v.) found that a toxin was produced in diphtheria. In 1890 Emil Adolph von Behring (q.v.) discovered the diphtheria antitoxin (q.v.) as a result of his work in injecting serum taken from a person immune to the disease into nonimmune persons. This work led to a theory of immunity advocated by Hans Buchner known as the *humoral theory.* Buchner hypothesized that blood plasma and serum contain microbe-killing substances which can be passed from one individual to another. Another theory proposed somewhat later, known as the *antitoxin theory,* states that toxins (q.v.) produced by bacteria during disease give rise to antitoxins, or neutralizing substances, in the serum of an ill person. Both the humoral and antitoxin theories, though not fully explaining immunity, have practical applications. A recent explanation of immunity phenomena is contained in the *side-chain theory* proposed by Paul Ehrlich (q.v.). According to this theory the cells of the body are regarded as chemical units with dynamic side chains, or groups of chemical elements, which change in structure to combine with molecules of poison or of bacterial protein. The structure change is stimulated by the bacterial protein or poison in the body. When overstimulated, the cells produce more specific side chains than are necessary to combine with all the poisons in the body, and the excess side chains break loose into the circulating blood. After they have broken loose these side chains can no longer change in structure and can combine only with the toxin which caused their production. Free side chains, or *antibodies* as they are commonly called, are found in the serum or plasma after disease and remain there for some time. They are capable of combining with and neutralizing toxins of the same disease in the original individual in which they were produced and in other individuals of the same species to which an immune individual's serum is transfused. In allergy (q.v.) and in anaphylaxis antibodies are produced in a similar manner, but cause heightened susceptibility to the stimulus rather than increased resistance.

The study of immunity has led to the development of several new sciences: *immunochemistry,* the study of the chemical problems involved in immunity; *crop immunity,* the study of immunity in plants; and *serology,* the branch of medical science dealing with the reactions between antibodies and the organisms or poisons, known as *antigens,* which stimulate their production. Techniques for the diagnosis of diseases such as typhoid fever, syphilis, amebic dysentery, and undulant fever have been developed through serology, and the study of blood grouping and blood incompatibilities (see TRANSFUSION OF BLOOD) are included in this science. See also BORDET, JULES.

IMMUNITY, in law, a general term meaning exemption from liability. Its most frequent usage occurs in criminal law in connection with exemption from compulsory self-incrimination. The 5th Amendment to the U.S. Constitution provides that no person "shall be compelled in any criminal case to be witness against himself". This provision is applicable to persons charged with crime, and to witnesses in a criminal case; defendants and witnesses may refuse to furnish evidence incriminating themselves. They, however, can waive immunity voluntarily. U.S. congressmen and the members of the national legislatures of a number of other countries enjoy a limited privilege of immunity from arrest, and only while in attendance at legislative sessions; see CONGRESS OF THE UNITED STATES. The term "immunity" is also used in international law in connection with extraterritoriality (q.v.), as, for example, diplomatic immunity, the exempting of diplomats from liability under the laws of the countries to which they are accredited.

IMPANEL or **EMPANEL.** See PANEL.

IMPATIENS. See BALSAM.

IMPEACHMENT, in the United States and England, a proceeding by a legislature for the removal from office of a public official charged with misconduct in office. Impeachment comprises both the act of formulating the accusation and the resulting trial of the charges; it is frequently but erroneously construed to mean only the removal from office of an accused public official. An impeachment trial may result either in an acquittal or in a verdict of guilty. In the latter case the impeached official is removed from office; if the charges against him warrant such action, he is also remanded to the proper authorities for trial before a court. In the law of evidence, impeachment signifies the act of an attorney in the course of a trial, of attacking the credibility of a witness called by him to testify in behalf of his client.

In England the House of Lords exercised the exclusive right of impeachment of public officials from the earliest days of Parliament until 1376. In that year the House of Commons began to initiate by resolution impeachment proceedings which were then tried by the House of Lords. Among notable instances of impeachment in English history was that involving the colonial administrator and soldier Warren Hastings (q.v.) in 1788. In recent years in England the proceeding of impeachment has rarely been invoked.

In the United States the Federal Constitution, in Article I, Section 3, provides for the impeachment of Federal public officials and gives explicit directions for conducting impeachments. See CONSTITUTION OF THE UNITED STATES. The House initiates impeachment proceedings by resolution, and appoints a number of its members to act as managers in prosecuting the impeachment before the Senate, which acts as a court to try the impeachment. The Vice President, who presides over the Senate, also presides at impeachment trials, except in the case of an impeachment of the President, when the Chief Justice of the U.S. Supreme Court presides. A two-thirds majority vote of the Senators present at an impeachment trial is necessary to secure conviction. Most impeachment proceedings in U.S. history have involved Federal judges; acquittals have been more numerous than convictions. The most notable of all impeachments in the United States was that of President Andrew Johnson in 1868 on charges of defying the authority of the Congress and of violating Federal law. He was acquitted. Impeachment procedure in the States is modeled on that of the Federal Constitution, and has been infrequently invoked.

IMPERIALISM, a national policy directed to the creation or expansion of an empire i.e., rule by one nation over other nations and colonial areas. Imperialism has been an important factor in world history since remote antiquity. Among the motives impelling rulers and governments to adopt imperialist policies, the following have been outstanding: greed for wealth; ambition for power; the need to acquire strategic advantages against existing or potential enemies; religious fervor to convert unbelievers and suppress heretics; and the need to control distant markets and raw materials essential to domestic prosperity. In former times imperialism took the form of a superstate, or empire, in which diverse national units and territories were subjected to a central governmental authority. Historians have distinguished two major divergent factors in such empires, namely, coercion and exploitation of subject peoples, and an ideal of human brotherhood in which a single authority establishes justice and peace under a rule of equality and rational law. Every important empire in ancient history was affected by both elements, and the idea of a universal community had important progressive effects even when it was propagated to disguise political oppression and economic exploitation.

One of the most notable of all empires was the Chinese Empire, beginning in 2205 B.C., under the Hsia dynasty, in a small portion of what is now northern China, and ending under the Manchu dynasty in 1912 A.D. During the course of forty centuries many areas were annexed and many peoples were absorbed to form a more or less homogeneous culture. (See CHINA: *History*.) The most extensive early Western empire was founded upon the conquests of Alexander the Great (q.v.) in the 4th century B.C., and was an attempt to combine the then known world into a cosmopolitan community with a common culture, free trade, and equality among peoples. The Roman Empire (27 B.C.-476 A.D.) united all the lands bordering the Mediterranean Sea and reached as far east as the Caspian Sea and as far north as Britain. It was based upon military conquest and yielded great wealth in booty, tribute, and slaves; it was also marked by the widespread extension of Roman citizenship to other peoples within the Empire, thereby making them the political equals of their conquerors; other basic aspects of the Empire included free trade between all parts of the Empire, and a system of law which laid the foundations of later European jurisprudence; see ROMAN LAW; CIVIL LAW.

The secular power of imperial Rome and its ideal of a world union of peoples governed according to established principles of law were originally represented in the person of the god-emperor. After the Empire collapsed under the barbarian onslaughts, the Christian Church, in the name of religious ideals, replaced Rome as the exponent of the ideal of a universal community. Although European secular society remained fragmented and virtually stagnant throughout the early Middle Ages, local rulers considered themselves bound in the community of Christendom; the Holy Roman Empire (q.v.), encompassing German Austrian, and Italian principalities, preserved a formal, if weak, expression of that Christian community until early in the 19th century.

The growth of nation-states during the later Middle Ages led to the development of a new type of imperialism, following the discovery, conquest, and colonization of vast territories in the New World, Africa, and Asia. See COLONY; EXPLORATION. The new imperialism differed from ancient imperialism chiefly in that it was primarily a result of economic pressures; and there was little, if any, attempt by the European colonial powers to grant their colonies political equality. In its first stage, exemplified by the Spanish Empire (see SPAIN: *History*) the new imperialism was primarily concerned with plundering subject areas of gold. This process often was ruthless and destructive, as in the destruction of Aztec civilization in Mexico by the Spanish conquistadors. In its second stage, the new imperialism, as exemplified by the British Empire during the period following the Industrial Revolution (q.v.), consisted essentially of the acquisition of sources of raw materials and markets for the export of manufactured goods. At the beginning of the 19th century, Napoleon I attempted to expand the French Empire within Europe. He revived the prospect of a universal society through the annexation of areas contiguous to France and having related cultures; and he propagated the Code Napoleon (q.v.) and a number of the equalitarian political ideas of the French Revolution (q.v.). His attempt failed, largely as a result of opposition from France's great capitalist and colonial rival, England; in the second half of the century, French imperialist policy centered on the acquisition of territory in Africa.

During the 19th century, virtually all of Africa and most of Asia were colonized by rival European powers. Even China, though nominally independent, was penetrated by nations seeking markets for trade and investment, and was forced to cede control of many of her ports (see TREATY PORTS) and to make other concessions to the great powers of the world. The competition for markets and raw materials increased in intensity following the unification of Italy (1870) and Germany (1871) and their subsequent bids for empires of their own; see ITALY: *History*; GERMANY: *History*. The resulting tensions had much to do with the precipitation of World War I. Friction in international affairs decreased for a period following the dismemberment of the German Empire and the partial dismemberment of the Italian colonial realm at the end of the war; but it soon increased, with the rise of Japanese imperialism in the Far East (see JAPAN: *History*) and with the revival of Italian and German imperialism under the fascist regimes of Benito Mussolini and Adolph Hitler, respectively, which contributed to the outbreak of World War II. See EUROPE: *History*.

While the development of nationalism has been a factor favoring the growth of imperialism on the part of some countries, it has also been an opposing force in subject regions. Significant examples of the latter process were the revolutions against British and Spanish imperialism in the New World, where the populations were European in origin and were intensely hostile to oppression and exploitation. In later years, especially after World War I, the continually rising tide of nationalism affected countries such as India, whose populations are predominantly native in origin. The revolt of colonial peoples against foreign rule continued after World War II, notably on the part of the Indonesians; see INDIA: *History;* INDONESIA: *History*. In general, the period following the end of World War II was marked by a series of nationalist uprisings and movements which significantly reduced the extent of the colonial empires established in the 19th and early part of the 20th centuries. But as this older imperialism waned, a new form of imperialism became manifest.

As the Soviet Union emerged from World War II as a world political and economic power second in strength and influence only to the United States, it made use of military, political, and economic means to build an empire of a new type, exceeding in extent the empire of the Czars. Soviet imperialism resembled older types of imperialism with respect to the annexation by the Soviet Union of territory in Europe and Asia to which the Soviet government had neither historically nor ethnically justifiable claims. But Soviet imperialism differed from all other types of imperialism in the variety and character of the techniques and instruments employed by the Soviet government to accomplish its purposes. The chief of these weapons was the use of communist parties to subvert the governments of a number of countries in eastern and central Europe, an to establish "people's democratic republics" with social systems identical with or akin to that of the Soviet Union and with governments acquiescent to the wishes of the Soviet government.

IMPERIAL MOTH, a large American moth, *Eacles imperialis,* in the family Citheroniidae. It attains a length of over 1½ in. and a wingspread of over 5 in. Its color is sulfur yellow marked with purplish brown. The olive-colored, woolly larva, which is about 3 in. long when fully grown, feeds on the leaves of various trees, especially the hickory.

IMPERIAL VALLEY, the name of a valley embracing about 4000 sq.m. of Imperial County in S.E. California, extending s. into Lower California, Mexico. The valley lies between Salton Sea (q.v.) on the N., the Chocolate Mountains on the E., and the Cuyamaca range on the W., and is slightly more than 100 miles E. of San Diego. The entire valley is well below sea level, and was formerly an arid desert, but is now one of the most prolific agricultural areas in the world as the result of irrigation by waters of the Colorado R. The first water was brought in through the Imperial Canal in 1902; the All-American Canal (q.v.) was completed in 1940. The most important crops are carrots, flax, alfalfa, citrus fruits, lettuce, cabbage, and a wide variety of fruits and vegetables; cotton is the principal crop in the Mexican portion of the valley. Cattle and sheep from many States are brought to Imperial Valley for fattening before slaughter. Much of the manual labor is performed by migratory Mexicans and Negroes. The principal business and shipping centers are El Centro, Brawley, Calexico (qq.v.), Holtville (pop. in 1950, 2472), self-styled "Carrot Capital of the United States," and Mexicali (q.v.) in Lower California.

IMPEYAN PHEASANT. See MONAL.

IMPLEMENTS, AGRICULTURAL, devices used to perform operations necessary for the growing of crops. Since prehistoric times, when cultivation of plants was first undertaken by primitive farmers, man has found the use of implements necessary. Primitive implements were pointed objects used for digging and keeping soil loosened, and sharp, knifelike objects used for cutting the ripened crop. Modifications of these early implements led to the development of small hand tools, still used in small-scale gardening, such as the spade, hoe, rake, trowel, and scythe, and larger implements drawn by humans, animals, or simple machines, such as plows and larger rakes and hoes. See AGRICULTURE: *History.*

A large proportion of the earth's arable land is still tilled by primitive tribes or nations (see separate articles on tribes and nations), or by other farmers operating under conditions which do not permit use of expensive machinery. Use of modern agricultural implements has developed most extensively in the U.S. and Canada.

Modern large agricultural implements, adapted to large-scale farming methods, are usually operated by motor-driven prime movers. The principal prime mover of modern agriculture is the tractor (q.v.), which provides locomotion for other implements and can furnish power for operation of component parts of implements by means of power belts. Small implements, such as portable irrigators, are often powered by individual motors.

Implements for Growing Crops. Many types of implements have been developed for breaking ground, planting, tilling, weeding, fertilizing, and combatting pests. Ground is broken by plows to prepare the seedbed. Early plows consisted of a bladelike plowshare which broke the soil, and a curved moldboard, against which the soil was lifted, turned, and pulverized. Modern tractor plows are usually equipped with three or more plowshares and can break a wide area of ground at a single sweep; see PLOW.

Planting of many cereal crops is still accomplished by broadcasting seed. Machines for broadcasting usually consist of a long seedbox mounted on wheels and equipped with an agitator to disperse the seed. Broadcasted seeds are not always covered by a uniform or sufficient depth of soil, and so seeding is usually done with drills, which produce continuous furrows of uniform depth as seedbeds. The rate of sowing is adjustable in modern drills, but specialized implements, called *lister planters,* are necessary for sowing crops, such as corn, which are planted in widely separated hills. The lister planter has a special feed device which picks up separate grains or small quantities of grain for distribution to each hill.

Fertilizer is usually distributed shortly before seeding time. Manure and other consolidated fertilizers are distributed primarily from *manure spreaders,* which are wagons equipped with a conveyor belt to carry the

International Harvester Co.; The Esso Marketer; Standard Oil Co. (N.J.)

MODERN AGRICULTURAL IMPLEMENTS

Top: Left, three-furrow plow; right, cotton planter. Middle: Left, cultivator; right, insecticide sprayer. Bottom: Left, hay loader; right, combine harvesting cereal grain.

fertilizer to the rear of the wagon, where it is disintegrated and strewn on the ground by a beater attachment. Artificial manures are commonly distributed, along with seeds, by drills.

Tillage and weeding are accomplished primarily by rollers, cultivators (qq.v.), and harrows. The harrow is used to smooth plowed land, to cover seeds and fertilizers distributed by drills, and to uproot weeds. *Rotary harrows* are similar to plows, but have rapidly revolving blades or hooked tines instead of plowshares. *Disk harrows,* which have curved, sharp-edged steel disks, are used on exceptionally hard, dry, or sticky ground. The roller is used to break clods in the soil, consolidate the soil, and smooth its surface. The resulting topsoil has a relatively uniform texture, which affords better aeration and water-holding capacity. Cultivators, such as hoes, are used after crops have begun growing, to destroy weeds and loosen and aerate the soil. A flame weeder, which produces a hot-air-blast flame, can destroy weeds on as many as 50 acres a day.

Large-scale use of insecticide sprays in agriculture has been impeded, in the past, by difficulties encountered in supplying running water, used to dilute spray compounds, to the fields. During the 1940's, however, a blower was developed which is powered by a fan driven at 4000 revolutions per minute, forcing air through a 3½-inch flexible hose at about 160 miles per hour. The blower atomizes liquid so thoroughly that it is possible to treat an acre of field crops with as little as 1 to 3 gallons of liquid insecticide.

Implements for Harvesting Crops. Machinery used for harvesting differs with the crop. Implements commonly called "harvesters" are intended for harvesting of cereal crops only. Most cereal crops are now usually harvested by means of a *combine,* which is equipped to remove the fruiting heads, beat off the grain kernels, and clean the grain while moving through the fields. The cleaned grain is accumulated in an attached grain tank until removed.

Corn harvesting formerly included several stages; the ears were picked and husked by a corn picker and the standing stalks were cut and tied into bundles by a binder. The stalks used for ensilage were then chopped into smaller pieces and elevated into a silo by an ensilage cutter. The modern two-row corn harvester combines most of these operations in a single machine. The harvester cuts the stalks and passes them butt-

end first into the machine. The ears are picked, husked, and dumped into a wagon, and the stalks are shredded.

Hay harvesting cannot be combined in a single operation because of the necessity of drying after cutting. Hay is first cut close to the ground with a mower (q.v.) After drying, the hay is gathered by pickup implements. The *pickup baler* lifts the hay to a conveyor which carries it to a baling chamber, in which it is cut to uniform length and compressed into bales. The machine can bale as much as 6 tons an hour, making bales up to 85 pounds in weight. The *pickup chopper* chops field-cured hay from windrows, and standing green hay for silage. It can also be adjusted to chop row crops such as corn and sorghum. In harvesting grass silage, the machine is provided with a cutter bar and a special reel for picking up mowed material.

Specialized machinery is used to harvest large crops of underground plants such as potatoes and sugar beets. Many types of cotton pickers have been developed, most of them of doubtful practicality. The most efficient mechanical cotton pickers are equipped with rotating barbed spindles which pick the cotton from the plant. Not all cotton gathered by mechanical pickers is in prime condition because all bolls in a single field do not ripen simultaneously, but the machines pick cotton forty to fifty times as fast as the average hand picker.

Practical Significance. Use of agricultural implements usually reduces the amount of human labor necessary for raising crops; in the U.S. during the period 1927 to 1947, for example, the average amount of labor required to grow cereal crops dropped twenty to forty percent because of increased use of farm machinery. Such use has also made cultivation of large-scale crops possible in many areas where the labor force is small. During a harvest season, for example, a large crop of a plant which must be reaped by hand within a single day would require a large labor force which on other days would be idle; use of machinery has made such rapid harvests possible with a minimum of human labor.

IMPORTS AND EXPORTS. See FOREIGN TRADE.

IMPRESSIONISM, the name given to the art movement which took place in French painting in the last quarter of the 19th century. The painters who founded the movement included Claude Monet, Auguste Renoir, Camille Pissarro, Edgar Degas, Paul

"L'Inondation," an Impressionist painting by Alfred Sisley

Cézanne, and Alfred Sisley (qq.v.). They rejected both the Neo-Greek classicism which was the dominant force in the art academies, and the story-telling or anecdotal type of painting which prevailed at exhibits of the Salon in Paris. The Impressionists sought inspiration in nature, and painted almost wholly out-of-doors; their subject matter included a great variety of landscapes, scenes of streets, parks, gardens, and seasides, and such figure compositions as boating parties. They revolutionized the role of color in painting, using the primaries (red, yellow, and blue) as well as the intermediaries (orange, green, and purple) in the purest form possible, often placing separate spots of pure color on the canvas, rather than a single area of mixed color, so that a greater brilliance and luminosity resulted; for instance, a red tone placed next to a blue tone merges with it into a resultant purple if viewed at a slight distance. They discovered a range of blue and purple tones in shadows, whereas brown or black had been the previous tones used. Through their experiments with pure color they eventually achieved a palette of the richest and most vibrant hues,

which influenced all subsequent painting.

Among the important formative influences on the work of the Impressionist painters were the lyrical landscape art of Jean Baptiste Camille Corot, the stolid realism of Gustave Courbet, and the vivid painting of everyday subjects in the work of Édouard Manet (qq.v.), all French contemporaries. The works of the two great English landscape painters John Constable and Joseph Mallard William Turner (qq.v.), which were seen by Monet and Pissarro during a visit to England in 1871, displayed a mastery of light and texture that also influenced the Impressionists. Their discovery of some Japanese wood-block prints that had been brought to Paris in 1867 had a decided effect on the new painters, particularly Degas and Monet, who were impressed by the deft use of line and decorative simplicity found in the prints.

The group's first joint exhibition took place in Paris in 1877. The works were ridiculed alike by a press and public long accustomed to sentimental realism, and the term "Impressionism" was used derisively in connection with a painting by Monet entitled

"Sunrise—An Impression". Vague as the term was, the painters nevertheless accepted it as a word underlining the common element in their efforts. That which distinguished the Impressionists from other painters was the treatment of a subject in terms of tone and not of the subject itself. Although the public ridiculed the group, the collector-painter Caillebotte and the art dealer Durand-Ruel befriended them and gave them encouragement; the group struggled on, painting despite poverty, scorn, and neglect. They held seven more large group exhibits, the last taking place in 1886.

By this time, however, they had lost their common goal, each painter developing his own particular sensations in his art. Monet registered the fugitive aspects of nature in his series of haystack pictures, each version painted at a different time of day. Pissarro subdued his palette, concentrating on broad city vistas for his subjects. Sisley emphasized the most intimate, carefree effects of landscape. Renoir began to create his grand, sensuous nudes. Degas, who had never shared his friends' preoccupation with color and light, composed intricately-woven patterns based on ballet and racecourse scenes, and nudes emerging from their baths. Cézanne, working in solitude, devoted his entire attention to the solidifying of planes in his still lifes and landscapes, imposing on nature a monumental structure which was to wield so large an influence on the succeeding generation of painters.

The role of Impressionism in the history of modern art cannot be overestimated. Besides the painters mentioned, the movement helped develop the art of Eugène Henri Paul Gauguin, Vincent van Gogh, Georges Seurat, Pierre Bonnard, and other key figures in modern painting. It opened up entirely new horizons in art, particularly in the realm of color and texture.

IMPRESSIONISM, in music, term applied to the school of composers of the late 19th and early 20th century, led by the French composer Claude Achille Debussy (q.v.). Influenced by the paintings of the French impressionists Claude Monet, Édouard Manet, and Pierre Auguste Renoir, and by the poetry of Paul Verlaine, Charles Baudelaire, and Stéphane Mallarmé (qq.v.), musical impressionism emphasized tonal color rather than formal structures such as the sonata and the symphony. Debussy, an active critic as well as a composer, viewed impressionism as a reaction to both the formal emphasis of such composers as Wolfgang Amadeus Mozart and Ludwig van Beethoven, and the sentimentalism of romantic composers such as Robert Schumann. In pursuit of this goal, Debussy developed a combination of both new and ancient devices in his music. On one hand he used complex, hitherto unexploited intervals of the ninth and higher; on the other hand he returned to the parallel fourth and fifth intervals of the medieval church modes. These technical features were fully developed in Debussy's early work, *Afternoon of a Faun* (1893), based upon a poem by Mallarmé.

Debussy's innovations had been anticipated to some extent in the work of Édouard Lalo and Alexis Emmanuel Chabrier (qq.v.), and his own work was followed in France by that of Maurice Ravel (q.v.). Other French composers of the impressionist school were Paul Dukas and Albert Roussel (qq.v.). Outside of France various aspects of Debussy's style were imitated by a number of composers. His piano pieces exhibited a new range of tone colors and new techniques of performance based largely upon the sensitive use of the pedals. Debussy's orchestration influenced such composers as the Englishman Frederick Delius and the American Charles Martin Loeffler (qq.v.).

By the beginning of World War I, the overrefinement and technical limitations of impressionism provoked adverse criticism from composers and critics. A new group of anti-romantic French composers, the Six, including Debussy's friend Erik Satie (q.v.), satirized the impressionist style in such compositions as Satie's piano suite, *Three Pieces in the Shape of a Pear*. Eventually impressionism, conceived by Debussy as the negation of romanticism, came to be regarded by musical historians as the final period in romantic music.

IMPRESSMENT, in English history, the arbitrary seizure of individuals for the military service of the state. It was practiced from the 12th to the 19th centuries. Originally it was initiated because of the failure of voluntary enlistment to furnish the necessary men for service abroad. Bodies of armed men, called press gangs, seized boys and men chiefly in seaport towns, and conveyed them forcibly to naval vessels. During the revolutionary struggles of the 17th century, Oliver Cromwell's New Model Army was raised largely by impressment. In the course of the 18th century several acts of Parliament sanctioned the impressment, or pressing, of vagrants and idle or disorderly persons. In 1779 the use of impressment for the army was discontinued. The pressing of sailors from American vessels by the British who claimed that the impressed sailors were British subjects, and the right of search which this involved was an important factor leading to the War of 1812. Impressment for the British navy was discontinued after the conclusion of the Napoleonic Wars in 1815. In later times the British government secured adequate military forces through voluntary enlistment. In wartime it resorted to conscription, which differs from impressment in that it imposes uniform and definite obligations either on the entire British population or on large and defined classes of the community.

IMPROVISATION, the art of simultaneously creating and performing music. Among all primitive peoples musical composition consists of improvised passages subsequently memorized; folk music is thus built by a constant process of creation, memorization, and alteration through defective memory and new creation. True improvisation, the completely spontaneous creation of new musical ideas, is rare, inasmuch as even the most untutored musician is influenced by music he has heard or played before himself. The famous improvisatory performances by 18th-century master composers, and those of the jazz (q.v.) virtuosi of today, depend in large part upon previous creation remembered rather than upon spontaneous creation. Such 18th-century composers as George Frederick Handel, Wolfgang Amadeus Mozart, and Ludwig van Beethoven were renowned during their own time as improvisers; actually many of the elements of their improvisations had previously been planned or were variations on earlier compositions. Johann Sebastian Bach, while visiting the Emperor Frederick the Great at Potsdam in 1747, extemporized a fugue on a theme written by that ruler; the fugue later became Bach's *Musical Offering.*

The history of formal music reflects a constant struggle between the improvisationalists and the composers who objected to changes in their work being made by performers. The plain songs were the traditional Church songs written down, and when the desire of the singers to embellish these by means of counterpoint (q.v.) became too great, efforts were made to establish rules of improvisation, such as the famous edict of Pope John XXII (1322).

In the 17th century, the opera and the sonata were the two forms most frequently used for improvisation within a composition. At the cadence (or close) of an aria, a singer was expected to show his skill in improvised embellishing figures; Arcangelo Corelli's sonatas were often written as mere sketches of what was required for a complete musical performance. During the 17th and 18th centuries, accompaniment was largely left to the improvising skill of the harpsichordist. Handel rebuked his singers for attempting to alter his music, and Bach adopted the expedient of making instrumental accompaniments so complex that neither singer nor instrumentalist dared depart from the text. By the end of the 18th century, improvisation was regularly used only in the cadenzas of opera and concerto, in which the singer or player was allowed to improvise within certain limits. Even here, however, notation took command and when Johannes Brahms' *Violin Concerto* was published (1879) his friend Joseph Joachim wrote cadenzas to be played with the work.

From the 19th century on, improvisation as an element of formal music steadily decreased in importance. The essential reason for this change was the growth of Romantic music, with its large orchestras, scoring complexities, and disregard for the details of form, all of which made improvisation extremely difficult. The conductor thus inherited the liberty of improvisation formerly enjoyed by the soloist, and the traditional conflict between soloist and composer changed to one between conductor and composer; the latter conflict continues today. Along with the reaction to Romantic music and the large, flamboyant scores of such composers as Richard Strauss, signs exist today of a return to interest in improvisation contained within a composition. Igor Stravinsky, Arnold Schönberg, and other modern composers, perhaps influenced by jazz, but also by the use of smaller orchestras and performing groups, are making cautious use of improvisation. The classical tradition of improvisation still continues among the organists, who first combined it with notated instrumental music on a grand scale. Marcel Dupré and other well-known organists practice the art, which is included in the Paris Conservatory curriculum. Improvisation is extensively used in jazz and may also still be heard in such religious music as the common church voluntary.

INARCHING. See GRAFTING.

INARTICULATA. See BRACHIOPODA.

INCAS, a group of South American Indian tribes of Quechuan stock (see QUECHUAS), who established their capital at Cuzco in Peru in the 12th century, and gradually extended their dominion from Quito to the borders of Chile. At the time of the earliest Spanish expeditions to Peru in the 16th century, their empire had become the most powerful and highly developed Indian state in the history of South America. See PERU: *History*.

INCENDIARISM. See ARSON.

INCENSE, material, such as fragrant gums and spices, which produces a fragrant smoke when burned, or the smoke itself. The ingredients are usually combinations of frankincense, benzoin, styrax, and cascarilla bark (qq.v.) in various proportions. Other substances often used in incense include aloes wood, balsam, bdellium, camphor, cinnamon, civet, cloves, dragon's blood, elemi, musk, myrrh, saffron, sandalwood, and star anise. The burning of incense has been a feature of sacrificial religious ceremonies since ancient times; one of the earliest representations of incense offering is an inscribed tablet, placed on the Sphinx at Giza, Egypt, in about 1533 B.C. Incense was used by the ancient Romans, both in religious ceremonies and on various state occasions. The use of incense is still carried on in the practice of most Oriental religions, but in the Western world is almost entirely restricted to the ceremonies of the Roman Catholic and Orthodox Eastern churches. Burning of incense is permitted in the Anglican Church, but not as a ceremonial part of the service.

INCENSE CEDAR, common name of softwood trees of the genus *Libocedrus,* belonging to the Pine family. The genus, which contains about eight species, is native to w. United States, Mexico, Chile, China, Japan, New Caledonia, and New Zealand. The decurrent-leaved incense cedar, *L. decurrens,* is a valuable timber tree, native to high mountains of Oregon, Nevada, California, and Lower California, which grows as much as 150 feet in height. It has cinnamon-red bark and slender branches which bear shining, cypresslike leaves. The durable, fragrant wood is used for lumber, telephone poles, and fence posts. Chilean incense cedar, *L. chilensis,* is a smaller, similar species. Both species are extensively planted for ornament in temperate regions of the United States.

INCHŎN. See CHEMULPHO.

INCHWORM. See GEOMETERS.

INCOME TAX, in tax law, a tax upon the income of individuals, business firms, estates, and other taxpayers, levied by a government. Income taxes are levied in most countries and are the largest source of the income of the governments of many countries. As a general rule, income-tax systems provide for a graduated tax structure, with a greater rate of tax on large incomes than on small ones. This type of tax structure is based on the theory that the larger the income of an individual, the greater the proportion of his income he can afford to pay in taxes. In other respects, differences in the income-tax systems of the countries of the world may be noted. Thus, the tax structure of Great Britain differs from that of the United States in two important particulars. Income in the British tax system does not include capital gains, i.e., profits from the sale of such capital assets as securities or buildings; and taxes on income from investments are deducted from dividends and interest before payment to investors.

The income tax is a relatively modern development. The earliest instances of a general income tax were those levied in France in 1793, in England in 1798, in Switzerland in 1840, in Austria in 1849, and in Italy in 1864; an income tax levied in the United States in 1862 was abandoned ten years later. In 1894 the Congress of the United States adopted an income tax on individuals and business firms at a rate of two percent; this levy was declared unconstitutional by the U.S. Supreme Court in 1895. On February 25, 1913, when the Sixteenth Amendment to the U.S. Constitution went into effect, Congress was invested with the power "to lay and collect taxes on income from whatever source derived, without regard to any census or enumeration". A law providing for a tax on incomes was incorporated in the Tariff Act of October 3, 1913. Under this law the tax on corporate income was fixed at one percent. The tax on individuals was set at one percent for single persons with annual incomes over $3000 and for married persons with incomes over $4000, and a surtax, ranging from one to six percent, was imposed on incomes over $20,000. Since that date individual and corporate income-tax rates have been sharply increased. Probably the two most significant developments with regard to Federal income taxes in recent years were the institution in 1938 of a special surtax on corporate income to be assessed by the U.S. Treasury, when in its judgment corporations make unreasonable accumulations of their earnings, and the adoption in 1943 of the Current Payment Tax providing a system of collecting income taxes at source on current wage income.

Under Federal statutes in the U.S. an individual is required to file an income-tax return if his gross income is greater than the statutory minimum. For Federal tax purposes, the term "gross income" includes salaries, wages, and other compensation for personal or professional services; gains from trade, business, and dealings in property and securities; interest, dividends, and rent; and "income from any other source". The return must be filed with the Collector of Internal Revenue for the district in which the legal residence or principal place of business of the taxpayer is situated. Every corporation subject to taxation, regardless of the amount of its income, is required to file a return. Most income-tax returns are due on March 15 of the year following the close of the calendar year for which they are made. Returns made on the basis of a fiscal year are due on the 15th day of the third month following the close of the fiscal year. An employer must withhold from the wages of employees the tax due on such wages and pay such taxes to the Federal Treasury. The withheld tax is credited against the employee's tax liability as computed on his final return, and a refund is made by the Treasury to the employee in case of excess withholdings. A declaration of estimated annual income-tax liability must be filed by individuals whose tax, as met by withholding from wages, will, presumably, be less than the total tax due; payment of that part of the tax unsatisfied by withholdings, may be paid in quarterly installments.

Thirty-two States also levy on incomes. The rate varies from State to State and is considerably lower than the Federal income-tax rate. The annual amount paid in State income taxes by a taxpayer may be credited by him in computing his Federal income-tax return in the following year as a deduction from gross income.

The importance of the income tax in the fiscal affairs of the U.S. government may be seen from the fact that in a recent year the total collection from that source amounted to about $33.5 billion, or about 50 percent of all Federal budget receipts. Income taxes collected by the individual States were much less in total and comprised a smaller percentage of the revenue of the States.

INCONNU (Fr., "unknown"), common name of a large migratory food fish, *Stenodus mackenzii,* in the Salmon family, so called because it is intermediate in characteristics between whitefish and salmon; the fish comprises a genus by itself. It averages about 10 lbs. in weight, and ascends into all rivers of arctic America, especially the Mackenzie River (q.v.), whence arises another common name, "Mackenzie River salmon".

INCUBATION (Lat. *incubare,* "to sit upon"), or BROODING, the warming of birds' eggs during development of the embryo and before the hatching, or emergence, of the young. In most species of birds the requisite heat (about 40°C. or 104°F.) is supplied by the female parent; in some of the passerine birds the male and female alternately sit on the eggs, while in others the male alone is responsible for incubation. Some birds, such as ostriches, allow their eggs to be incubated by the heat of the sun. Others, such as the megapodes, build nests of decaying vegetable matter; heat generated by the plants in the process of decay incubates the eggs.

The incubation period of hummingbirds is about 12 days; that of canaries, 15 to 18 days; that of the raven and common fowl, 21 days; that of the turkey, 30 days; and that of the swan, 40 to 45 days.

The term "incubation" is also applied to the period during which the developing young of any animal are supplied with heat, natural or artificial, and to the process whereby microorganisms are kept at temperatures favorable to their growth. In medicine the term incubation is used for the period between the time a person comes in contact with an infectious disease and the time the first symptoms appear. See articles on individual animals named above; see also INCUBATOR. For incubation of snakes' eggs, see COLD-BLOODED ANIMALS.

INCUBATOR, an apparatus or specially constructed chamber for maintaining living organisms at a constant external temperature.

In poultry raising, incubators, or brooders, are used for the artificial incubation (q.v.) of eggs and for warming the young chicks immediately after hatching. Brooders are kept at 90° F. to 100° F. (32° C. to 38° C.) for the first week after the eggs are laid, with gradually lowered temperatures thereafter; the temperature is kept constant by means of a thermostat (q.v.) in most modern, elec-

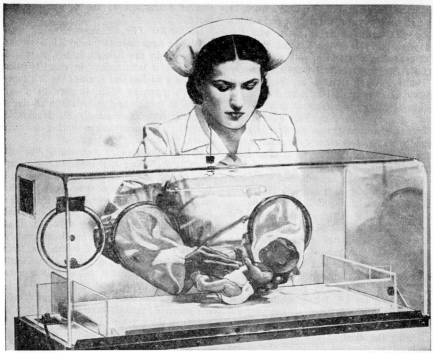

Air Shields, Inc.

*Nurse demonstrating use of incubator for premature babies. Incubator receives air from out-
side the hospital, and baby is handled through holes protected by sleeves*

trically heated brooders. Moist fresh air is
continuously circulated through the brooder.
See POULTRY.

In bacteriology incubators are rectangular
boxes usually kept at 68° F. (20° C.) for the
culture of bacteria which do not cause disease,
and at human-body temperature (98.6° F. or
37° C.) for the growth of disease-causing
bacteria. Bacteriological incubators have a
double door on the front side and double
walls containing water on all the other sides.
The water is heated by gas or electricity and
maintained at constant temperature by a
thermostat.

The term incubator is also applied to a device used to keep a prematurely born child
warm. The child is usually kept at 88° F. to
90° F. (31° C. to 32° C.) in a closed, well-
ventilated chamber; the entering air is hu-
midified and usually filtered.

INCUNABULA (Lat., "cradle," "origin"),
in bibliography, a collective term denoting
books printed before the year 1500. The study
of incunabula is important as a source of information regarding the early development

of the art of typography. Included among the
approximately 35,000 existing collections of
incunabula are volumes published by the
German printer Johann Gutenberg, and others by the English printer William Caxton
(qq.v.). Important collections of incunabula
are housed in the British Museum, London;
the Bibliothèque Nationale, Paris; the Royal
Library, Munich; the Pierpont Morgan Library, New York City; and the Library of
Congress, Washington, D.C.

INDEPENDENCE, county seat of Jackson
Co., Mo., situated 3 miles s. of the Missouri
R., and 10 miles E. of Kansas City, of which
it is a residential suburb. Independence is a
manufacturing and commercial center, serviced by three railway systems. The principal
industries are the manufacture of steel, cement, aluminum, stoves, flour, lumber, harvester combines, and petroleum products.
Among notable buildings of the city are the
oldest court house w. of the Mississippi R.,
built in 1827, and the home of Harry S. Truman, thirty-third President of the U.S. Independence was founded and made the county

seat in 1827. From 1831 to 1844 it was the starting point for covered-wagon caravans heading westward on the Santa Fe and Oregon trails. A group of Mormons under Joseph Smith, founder of the Mormon Church, established (1831) a settlement, called New Jerusalem near Independence, but they were driven out in 1833. The gold rush of 1849 brought a new influx of people into Independence, and it was chartered as a city in the same year. Pop. (1950) 36,963.

INDEPENDENCE DAY, in the United States, an annual holiday commemorating the adoption by the Continental Congress on July 4, 1776, of the Declaration of Independence. The anniversary of this event is celebrated as a legal holiday in all States of the Union.

INDEPENDENCE HALL, a historical structure in Philadelphia, Pa., erected between 1732 and 1741. The building, situated on Chestnut Street, was constructed as the State House for the colony of Pennsylvania. From 1775 to 1781 it was the meeting place of the Continental Congress. George Washington was appointed commander in chief of the Continental Army there in 1775. The Declaration of Independence was adopted in the east room of the building on July 4, 1776, and four days later the famous Liberty Bell (q.v.), then in the tower of the hall, was rung to acclaim its adoption. In 1787 the Constitutional Convention which framed the Constitution of the United States met in Independence Hall. From 1789 to 1800 the hall was the seat of the United States Supreme Court. Independence Hall was restored in 1898 and is maintained as a historical museum. In addition to the Liberty Bell, which hangs in the rear hall of the first floor, the building contains the original desk and chair used by the signers of the Declaration of Independence.

INDEPENDENT ORDER OF ODD FELLOWS, a secret, fraternal benefit society, organized in England in the 18th century, and introduced into the United States in 1806. See FRATERNAL ORDERS. The exact origin of the Order is not known. A number of Odd Fellows lodges existed in England in 1780; these were united as the Patriotic Order shortly thereafter. The Patriotic Order eventually became the Independent Order of Odd Fellows, Manchester Unity, and the principal fraternal order of England.

The first Odd Fellows lodge in the United States was founded in New York City and was not affiliated with the Order in England.

The Odd Fellows subsequently expanded into several States, and in 1825 the Grand Lodge of the United States was formed as the governing body for lodges in New York, Pennsylvania, Maryland, and Massachusetts. The Grand Lodge was chartered by the Manchester Unity in the following year, and maintained its affiliation until 1842, when it separated from the English organization. Until 1852, membership in the American order was restricted to men, but in that year the Rebekah degree of membership, open to both sexes, was established. During the latter half of the 19th century the American order established branches in all the States of the United States and in numerous foreign countries, including Canada, Mexico, Australia, Germany, Switzerland, Czechoslovakia, Denmark, Norway, Sweden, and Poland.

The Order maintains homes for the aged, the poor, and for widows and orphans in several States of the United States, and provides its members with financial aid in cases of sickness or death. National headquarters of the Order are situated in Baltimore, Md. In a recent year, the total membership was about 1,500,000.

INDEPENDENT TREASURY, name given to the system of keeping and disbursing the public money without the intermediary action of State or national banks. It was adopted in the United States by the Act of 1846 which provided that the public revenues should be held, until actually paid out, in the vaults of the Treasury at Washington or in the sev-

Penna. Dept. of Commerce Photo
Independence Hall in Philadelphia

eral subtreasuries in the larger cities created by the act. Prior to this date the government receipts had been deposited in banks. The Independent Treasury System was modified from time to time, but it was not capable of keeping pace with the growth of business in the United States and had far outlived its usefulness at the time the Federal Reserve System (q.v.) was adopted in 1914.

INDETERMINACY PRINCIPLE. See UN-CERTAINTY PRINCIPLE.

INDETERMINATE EQUATION, an equation which has an infinite number of solutions, and which cannot therefore be uniquely solved. Such equations become soluble in the ordinary sense only when additional restrictions are put on the problem; the commonest such restriction is that the solutions must be expressed in integers.

A simple example of this type of problem is the following: in what ways can change be given for a half dollar in nickels and quarters? Algebraically this reduces to the equation $5x + 25y = 50$. This equation has an infinite number of solutions if fractional solutions are admissible, but the phrasing of the problem prohibits such solutions, since a third of a nickel, for example, is meaningless. With this restriction it is apparent that there are three and only three solutions: ten nickels and no quarters; five nickels and one quarter; or no nickels and two quarters. Some such problems have no solutions; an example of such a problem is the following: in what ways can change be given for 37 cents in nickels and quarters.

In more complex problems, the solution or solutions are not apparent, and an extensive algebra has been developed to elaborate the solutions. The simplest such problems, which can be expressed in the form of a linear algebraic equation in two unknowns (of which the above equation is an example) can all be solved by a method developed by the ancient Greek mathematicians Diophantus and Euclid; the solutions (if any exist) can be determined by finding the largest common divisors of the numbers by which x and y are multiplied in the equation (for example, in the above equation, the numbers are 5 and 25, and their largest common divisor is 5). If this largest common divisor divides the number on the right-hand side of the equation (as 5 divides 50) the equation has one or more integral solutions.

Some further simple examples of indeterminate problems are given in the article DIOPHANTINE ANALYSIS. Many of the greatest mathematicians, such as Karl Friedrich Gauss, spent much time developing integer solutions of exceedingly complex indeterminate equations.

INDEX, CEPHALIC, one of the basic measures of the skull used by anthropometrists in classifying the dimensions and proportions characteristic of the various races of mankind and of the various species of ancient man. It is defined as one hundred times the ratio of the width of the head to its length. When measurements are made directly on a skull, this figure is known as the *cranial index*. Craniologists distinguish three basic classifications of skulls based upon cranial and cephalic indices: the *dolichocephalic* (long skulls); the *mesocephalic* (medium skulls); and the *brachycephalic* (broad skulls).

Indices derived from proportions of other parts of the human body or skeleton are also used for the same purposes as the head and skull indices. Among the parts upon which classifications according to indices have been set up are the face, nose, eyes, teeth, jaws, and pelvis. See RACES OF MANKIND.

INDEX OF PROHIBITED BOOKS, in the Roman Catholic Church, a catalogue, published by papal authority, of books which have been found to contain doctrines contrary to faith or morals, and which, as a consequence, Catholics are forbidden to read. The first such Index was published by Pope Paul IV in 1557, and the responsibility of examining books and maintaining the Index was given to the Inquisition. It was transferred by Pope Sixtus V about 1590 to a separate Congregation of the Index, which was merged with the Holy Office (q.v.) by Pope Benedict XV in 1917.

INDIA, in physical geography, a subcontinent of Asia, extending southward approximately from 37° N. latitude to 8°5′ N. latitude and westward from 97°30′ E. longitude to 61° E. longitude. In political geography, the subcontinent, formerly composed of British India (q.v.), 562 princely states (see INDIA, NATIVE STATES OF), Portuguese India, and French India (qq.v.), now comprises the two last-named entities, and the sovereign states of India and Pakistan, established by partition of British India on August 15, 1947. (For data regarding the respective boundaries, administrative divisions, forms of government, histories, and other pertinent aspects of the newly organized states, see INDIA, UNION OF; PAKISTAN.)

The subcontinent of India is bounded on the N.W. by Afghanistan; on the N. by

Afghanistan, China, Nepal, and Bhutan; on the E. by Burma and the Bay of Bengal; on the S. by the Gulf of Mannar (which separates it from Ceylon) and the Indian Ocean; and on the W. by the Arabian Sea and Iran. As constituted prior to the establishment of the Union of India and Pakistan, British India was divided into eleven major provinces and several minor provinces. In the order of size, the major provinces were Madras, United Provinces, Punjab, Central Provinces and Berar, Bengal, Bombay, Bihar, Assam, Baluchistan, and Orissa. The largest of the minor provinces was North-West Frontier Province. Of the foregoing, each of which is the subject of a separate article, Baluchistan, North-West Frontier Province, Sind, and parts of Bengal, Punjab, and Assam are included in Pakistan. The other provinces and the remainder of the partitioned provinces, known respectively as West Bengal, Punjab, and Assam, are administrative divisions of the Union of India.

The Indian princely states, semi-autonomous realms formerly subject to varying degrees of control by the British crown, were grouped, prior to partition, into twenty-three major units and agencies. Listed alphabetically, these states and agencies were Assam, Baluchistan, Baroda, Bengal, Central India, Chhattisgarh, Cochin, Deccan and Kolhapur, Gujarat, Gwalior, Hyderabad, Kashmir and Feudatories, Madras, Mysore, North-West Frontier Province, Orissa, Punjab, Punjab Hill, Rajputana, Sikkim, Travancore, United Provinces, and Western India. Following partition, a large majority of the feudatories acceded, either as units or as confederations, to the Union of India; with certain exceptions, the remainder joined Pakistan. The Indian government granted the acceding states limited autonomy in domestic affairs and assumed the residual responsibilities, including control of foreign affairs and the military forces. In some instances, serious jurisdictional disputes regarding certain states developed between India and Pakistan. The most serious of these disputes arose over Kashmir.

Excluding French India and Portuguese India, which have a combined area of about 1735 sq.m., but including the Laccadive, Andaman, and Nicobar (qq.v.) islands, Pakistan, and the Union of India, the subcontinent has an area of 1,634,377 sq.m. Of this total, an area of 715,964 sq.m. was occupied by the former feudatory states; the remainder was occupied by British India. The population (1951 est.), excluding that of French and Por-

tuguese India, is 432,672,000. British India had a population (1941) of 295,808,722; the population (1941) of the feudatory states was 93,189,233.

Physical Features. The subcontinental character of India is determined by its natural isolation from the rest of Asia. More than half of the subcontinent is a vast triangular peninsula, projecting nearly 1000 m. southward from the mainland into the Indian Ocean. On the N., E., and W., the frontiers of the Indian mainland are fringed or traversed by the ranges, spurs, and foothills of two great mountain systems. The Himalayas (q.v.), the greatest of these systems and the highest uplift on earth, extend for a distance of nearly 1600 m. along the northern borders of India. Offshoots of the Himalayas, which project in a mighty semicircle from the extreme N.E. of India through Bhutan and Nepal northwestward into the Kashmir region, protect the Indo-Burmese frontier. Numerous summits of the main chain attain elevations over 20,000 feet within India. Mt. Everest (29,141 ft.) the loftiest peak known to man, is situated on the boundary between Nepal and Tibet. Among the outstanding summits within India proper are Godwin Austen (28,-250 ft.), which ranks second to Mt. Everest; Nanga Parbat (26,620 ft.); Nanda Devi (25,-645 ft.); Kamet (25,547 ft.); Rakapushi (25,-550); and Haramosh (24,270 ft.). Most of these peaks are in Kashmir. Overland travel across the Himalayas is confined to a number of defiles, including Karokoram, Muztagh, and Changchenno passes.

The second great mountain system of India, the Hindu Kush (q.v.), extends from the W. extremity of the Himalayas along the entire N.W. and W. frontier. Most of the western region of the Indian mainland is occupied by the spurs and ranges of this chain, which also dominates E. Afghanistan. Tirach Mir (25,-420 ft.), in Chitral, is the highest peak in the Hindu Kush system, and the chain has a number of other peaks over 20,000 feet. The Sulaiman Mountains, one of the chief ranges of the system, lies completely within India. Kaisargarh (11,316 ft.) is the highest summit. Other notable ranges of the Hindu Kush system are the Safed Koh Mountains, with an extreme elevation of 15,620 feet, and the Kirthar Mountains, about 7000 feet in elevation. Khyber Pass (q.v.), the principal overland route between Afghanistan and N.W. India, is situated in the Safed Koh range.

The distinguishing physiographical features of the peninsular portion of India are a tableland or plateau, sometimes called the Deccan (q.v.), and two mountain ranges, known as Eastern Ghats and Western Ghats (see GHATS), which are respectively contiguous to the E. and W. boundaries of the Deccan. A number of ranges, known collectively as the Vindhya Hills (q.v.), delineate the N. limits of the peninsular tableland. Elevations in the plateau region generally range between 1000 and 3000 feet, but outcroppings as high as 4000 feet occur. The Western Ghats, a bold escarpment overlooking the Arabian Sea (see MALABAR COAST), has a general elevation of about 3000 feet. Dodabetta Peak (8760 ft.), situated near Calicut, is the highest summit of the Western Ghats. Between the Eastern Ghats, which averages about 1500 feet in elevation, and the Bay of Bengal is a narrow coastal plain (see COROMANDEL COAST). Three of the principal rivers of the Deccan, namely the Godavari, the Kistna, and the Cauvery (qq.v.), course through gaps in the Eastern Ghats, traverse the coastal plain, and empty into the Bay of Bengal. The Narbada R. (q.v.), the only important westerly flowing stream of the Deccan, skirts the s. slopes of the Vindhya Hills and empties into the Gulf of Cambay (see CAMBAY, GULF OF).

The major portion of the Indian mainland, i.e., the region N. of the Vindhya Hills, w. and s. of the Himalayas, and E. of the Hindu Kush, consists largely of the broad plains surrounding the major river systems of the subcontinent. Because of the abundance of water and alluvial soil, this generally level belt of lowlands is the most fertile region of India. The region is consequently the most densely populated section of the subcontinent and is the traditional cradle of Indian civilization. All of the great river systems traversing the plains region originate on the slopes of the Himalayas. With its numerous tributaries, which drain the s. slopes of the Himalayas, the Ganges R. (q.v.) forms the most extensive river system of India, flowing across the subcontinent in a generally southeasterly direction for a distance of more than 1500 m. and emptying into the Bay of Bengal. The N.E. portion of the plains region is watered by the Brahmaputra R. (q.v.) and its affluents, a system that originates on the N. slopes of the Himalayas and enters the subcontinent at the E. extremity of the main chain. Like the Ganges, the Brahmaputra, which has a total length, in Tibet and India, of about 1800 m., empties into the Bay of Bengal. The third great river system of India is that of the Indus R. (q.v.). From its sources, relatively near those of the Brahmaputra, the Indus flows N.W. across Kashmir, passes between the W. and N. extremities respectively of the Himalayas and the Hindu Kush, and courses generally southward to the Arabian Sea, covering a distance of about 2000 m. The principal tributaries of the Indus are the Sutlej, Ravi, and Chenab (qq.v.). East of the Indus R. is the Indian or Thar Desert, the most arid portion of the Indian lowlands. The hydrography of India includes very few lakes.

Excluding the Gulf of Cambay, the Gulf of Cutch (see CUTCH, GULF OF), and the Great Rann of Cutch (see CUTCH), all of which are shallow arms of the Arabian Sea, the principal indentations of the coast of India are the great river deltas, mainly the deltas of the Brahmaputra and the Ganges. In consequence, India has very few harbors that are accessible to ocean-going vessels. The chief harbors are those of Calcutta, Bombay, and Karachi (qq.v.).

Geology. Differences in geological structure account for the major physiographic divisions of the subcontinent. The main system of the Himalayas consists largely of crystalline strata, including gneisses, schists, and igneous rock of the Archean age, which reveal the effects of upheaval and folding during the great crustal movement that elevated the ranges in the late Tertiary period. In the s. offshoots of the Himalayas, the most prominent formation comprises Tertiary sandstones, conglomerates, and clays, in disturbed positions. These strata, known as the Siwalik formation, are enormously developed and contain a remarkable assemblage of fossil mammals. The Deccan tableland, especially in the N. and W., is formed mainly of basalt, which probably poured out of vast fissures during the late Cretaceous and early Eocene periods. Known as the Deccan trap, the basaltic deposits occupy an area of about 250,000 sq.m. and attain a vertical thickness of several thousand feet. Among interesting deposits of more recent origin in the Deccan plateau is laterite. The Vindhya Mountains have a gneissic axis, with Paleozoic sediments on the flanks. To the s. and E. of this range are the formations, known as the Gondwana System, consisting mainly of shales, clays, sandstones, and seams of coal. The fossil flora and fauna of these formations are more nearly allied to the forms of South Africa than to those of Eurasia. In the view of some authorities, this circumstance adds weight to the theory that s.E. India was linked to the African continent at a remote epoch in geologic time. The Indo-

Canadian Pacific Railways

Above: Sanganeer Gate, an entrance to the city of Jaipur in central India. Right: A Hindu yogi, a member of the largest religious sect in India.

Gangetic plain, the third great geological and physiographical division of the subcontinent, is coextensive with the Himalayan foredeep. In the course of eons of geologic time, alluvial deposits from the Himalayas displaced the sea from this immense depression. The depth of the alluvium of the Indo-Gangetic plain has never been determined. According to authoritative estimates, the base of the depression may be 40,000 feet below the surface.

Climate. Because of the peninsularity, unusual topography, and geographical position of the subcontinent, its climatic conditions are remarkably diversified, both on a seasonal and regional basis. The diversity ranges from tropical to temperate zonal extremes, with the temperature extremes confined largely to the slopes of the Himalayas. Except in the elevated regions, the remainder of India has a uniformly tropical climate. Seasonal variations, resulting from the southwest and northeast monsoons, profoundly influence such climatic factors as temperature, humidity, and precipitation throughout the subcontinent. For general purposes, the seasons of India may

be classified as rainy and dry. The rainy season, which extends from June to November, is the season of the southwest monsoon, a moisture-laden wind blowing off the Indian Ocean and the Arabian Sea. Beginning early in June on the w. coast of the peninsula, the southwest monsoon gradually embraces almost the entire subcontinent. However, various physiographic features, such as the axial directions of the river valleys, often determine in many parts of India the quarter from which the wind blows during the monsoons. During the rainy period, precipitation attains great proportions, often more than 125 inches, along the slopes of the Western Ghats. In the N.E. section of the subcontinent, particularly in the Khasi Hills, the annual rainfall occasionally exceeds 500 inches. Mean annual precipitation along the S. slopes of the Himalayas is about 60 inches. In certain areas, including the interior of the peninsular tableland, the Indian Desert, and a broad belt in N. central India, precipitation ranges between 15 and 20 inches annually. Protracted delay in the arrival of the southwest monsoon or failure of the winds to deposit sufficient rain occurs occasionally, causing severe droughts and famines in the subcontinent. In normal circumstances, the power of the monsoon begins to diminish in September.

During the initial phase of the dry season, the period of the northeast monsoon, cool weather prevails over most of the mainland portion of India, with temperatures in some sections averaging more than 25° F. lower than on the peninsula. The cool season, extending from early in December through February, is usually accompanied by extremely dry weather, although severe storms, attended by slight precipitation on the Indo-Gangetic plain and heavy snowfalls in the Himalayas, sometimes traverse the subcontinental mainland. The hot season, beginning about the middle of March and extending until the onset of the southwest monsoon, reaches its most oppressive stage during May, when temperatures up to 125° F. are commonly recorded in central India. In the vicinity of Calcutta, the mean annual temperature is about 79° F. The mean annual temperature in the w. central coastal region of the peninsula is about 82° F. In the vicinity of Madras temperatures range from about 76° F. to 92° F., with an annual mean of about 84° F.

Flora and Fauna. The vegetation of the subcontinent is characterized by wide regional variations, with climatic factors the chief qualitative and quantitative determinants. In the Indus plains, a region of general aridity, the flora is sparse and largely herbaceous. Various thorny species, including representatives of the genera *Capparis* (caper) and *Zizyphus* (jujube) are common. Bamboo occurs in some areas, and among the few varieties of trees is the palm. The Gangetic plain, which has more abundant supplies of moisture, supports many types of plant life. Vegetation is especially luxuriant in the Ganges and Brahmaputra deltas. The mangrove and the sal, a hardwood timber tree, flourish in the deltaic region of the Gangetic plain. Many varieties of arctic flora are found on the higher slopes of the Himalayas. The lower levels of the chain support numerous families of subtropical plant life, notably the Orchidaceae, and are densely forested. Coniferous spe-

cies, including cedar and pine, predominate in the N.W. portion of the Himalayas region. To the E., the S. slopes of the Himalayas abound with tropical and subtropical types of vegetation. An especially noteworthy genus is the *Rhododendron.* Among the predominant trees are the oak and magnolia. The Malabar coast of the Indian peninsula and the slopes of the Western Ghats, areas of excessive rainfall, are thickly wooded. Evergreens, bamboo, and several varieties of valuable timber trees, including teak, predominate in this region. Extensive tracts of impenetrable jungle occur in the swampy lowlands and along the lower elevations of ths Western Ghats. The vegetation of the peninsular plateau is less luxuriant, but dense thickets of bamboo, palm, and deciduous trees are scattered throughout the Deccan. In the S. central area are valuable stands of sandalwood.

The forests, plains, hills, and mountains of the subcontinent are inhabited by a wide variety of animal life. The tiger and panther are common in many sections of India, and the Deccan has, in addition, the cheetah. Among other species of the cat family are the snow leopard, the jungle cat, and the clouded leopard. The elephant is found along the N.E. slopes of the Himalayas and in the remote forests of the Deccan. Other large quadrupeds indigenous to India include the rhinoceros, gaur, black bear, wolf, jackal, dhole, wild buffalo, wild hog, and several species of ape, antelope, and deer. Various species of wild goat and sheep abound in the Himalayas and other mountainous areas. The ibex and the serow, which is related to the chamois, are also among the mountain fauna. The pygmy hog, bandicoot rat, and tree mouse are typical of the smaller quadrupeds. Venomous reptiles, including the cobra, the daboia, and the saltwater snakes, are especially numerous. The reptilian fauna also includes the crocodile. Among noteworthy examples of the tropical bird life of the subcontinent are the parrot, peacock, kingfisher, and heron. The pheasant, quail, partridge, plover, duck, and widgeon also figure prominently in the Indian ornithology. There are a number of predatory species, such as eagles, vultures, peregrines, and several types of hawk. The rivers and coastal waters of India teem with fish, including many edible varieties.

Natural Resources. With about two thirds of the total population dependent on agrarian enterprises for their livelihood, the land is the chief source of wealth of India. About 280,000,000 acres, more than a third of the

British Information Services

Left: Procession of elephants in Mysore, India, carrying empty thrones in honor of the deceased predecessors of the maharaja of Mysore. Right: Bengali teacher and a student.

total area of the subcontinent, are cultivable. Mainly because of the protracted dry season, facilities for irrigation are a traditional and significant feature of the Indian countryside. Approximately a fifth of the cultivable land of the subcontinent is irrigated. The principal areas dependent on artificial water supplies, which are furnished by means of reservoirs, dams, barrages, canals, and wells, are in the Punjabs, Uttar Pradesh, Madras, Sind, and Bihar. Another important resource of India is the forests, which total nearly 100,000 sq.m. in area and yield a considerable annual volume of valuable timber, particularly teak, sal, sandalwood, and pine. The subcontinent has a wide variety of mineral deposits, including coal, petroleum, salt, saltpeter, mica, graphite ilmenite, chromite, magnesite, monazite, diamonds, zircons, sapphires, and ores of gold, silver, copper, iron, manganese, and tungsten. Of these, the most important in terms of value are coal, manganese, gold, petroleum, salt, iron, mica, and copper.

Ethnology. See INDIAN PEOPLES.

Religion. See INDIAN RELIGIONS.

Languages. See INDIAN LANGUAGES.

History. The following account of the history of India is necessarily limited in scope. Definitive detail, chiefly of interest to the professional scholar, is deliberately omitted, and only the highlights and major turning points of Indian history are stressed. For sup-plementary information regarding the history and civilization of the subcontinent, the reader is referred to the following articles, in addition to those already cited: BRAHMA; BRAH-MANISM; BUDDHISM; CASTE; DRAMA: *Drama of India;* DRAVIDIANS; EAST INDIA COMPANY; HINDUISM; INDIAN ART AND ARCHITECTURE; INDIAN LITERATURE; INDIAN MUTINY; IN-DIAN MYTHOLOGY; JAINS; MOHAMMEDANISM; PARSEES; SANSKRIT LANGUAGE; SANSKRIT LIT-ERATURE; SIKHS; and YOGA. The attention of the reader is also directed to the biographical sketches of many of the Indian rulers, administrators, and leaders mentioned in the context of this article.

Because the Indians of remote antiquity left no written records of their social, cultural, and political activities, historians are obliged to rely almost exclusively on archeological discoveries for an understanding of the earliest civilization on the subcontinent. Evidence exists that, possibly during the Neolithic period of the Stone Age, the aboriginal inhabitants of the subcontinent were dispersed and partially assimilated by invading Dravidian tribesmen, who probably came from the w. On the basis of recent archeological discoveries in the Indus valley, the civilization subsequently developed by the Dravidians equaled and possibly surpassed in splendor the civilizations of ancient Mesopotamia and Egypt. About the middle of the

3d millennium B.C., Dravidian India was subjected to the first of a sustained series of invasions by tribes of the Indo-European linguistic stock. These tribes, of uncertain racial origin but usually referred to as Indo-Aryans, entered the subcontinent through the mountain passes along the N.W. frontier and gradually occupied most of the territory N. of the Vindhya Mountains and w. of the Jumna R. Many of the Dravidians fled to the N. and into the Indian peninsula, regions where the Dravidian linguistic stock is still numerous. The remnants of the Dravidian people and, in the view of some authorities, much of their culture, was absorbed by the Indo-Aryans.

Obscurity surrounds Indo-Aryan political history for many centuries after the conquest of the Dravidians, but the Veda (q.v.), a collection of sacred writings dating from about 1200 B.C., contains considerable data regarding Indo-Aryan social practices, religious beliefs, and cultural attainments. As depicted in some of the Vedic hymns, the civilization that emerged during the early centuries of Indo-Aryan dominance on the subcontinent was notable in several respects. Tribal political organs functioned according to democratic principles, the social status of women compared favorably to that of men, and the institution of marriage was regarded as sacred. In various arts and sciences, including livestock raising, metal handicrafts, carpentry, boatbuilding, and military science, the Indo-Aryans reached a high degree of perfection. The Vedic hymns composed during this and later periods also depict the emergence and crystallization of the great social-religious system known as Hinduism. With respect to political developments, virtually all that is known with certainty is that the Indo-Aryans, in the course of the 1st millennium B.C., established sixteen autonomous states in the region bounded by the Himalayas, the s. reaches of the Ganges, the Vindhya Mountains, and the Indus valley. Of these states, comprising both republics and kingdoms, the most important was Kosala, a kingdom situated in the region occupied by modern Oudh. Other important kingdoms were Avanti, Vamsas, and Magadha. The last-named kingdom, which occupied the territory of modern Bihar, became, about the middle of the 6th century B.C., the dominant state of India. During the reign (582–554 B.C.) of its first great king Bimbisara, Gautama Buddha and Vardhamāna Jnatiputra Mahavira, the respective founders of Buddhism and Jainism, preached and taught in Magadha.

Late in 327 B.C., Alexander the Great led an expedition across the Hindu Kush into N. India. The Macedonian king won a number of victories during his march into India, climaxing the first phase of his campaign by defeating the native King Porus near the Hydaspes R. (now the Jhelum). In the course of the next two years, Alexander achieved sovereignty over a large section of N.W. and central India. The political effects of the Greek invasion were relatively insignificant, mainly because of the internal strife that arose in Macedonia after Alexander's death (323 B.C.); but the art, sculpture, and science of the Greeks figured with increasing importance thereafter in the development of Indian culture.

Macedonian overlordship in India was destroyed when, in 322 B.C., a native leader named Chandragupta, who became known to the Greeks as Sandrocottus, fomented a successful rebellion and seized control of Magadha. Within the next decade Chandragupta, founder of the Maurya dynasty of Indian kings, extended his sovereignty over most of the subcontinental mainland. The military power of the Indian empire caused Seleucus I Nicator, a former general of Alexander's army and the founder of the Seleucid Empire, to abandon plans for the invasion of India and to arrange an alliance with the Maurya ruler. Concluded in 302 B.C., the alliance was consolidated by Chandragupta's marriage to the Seleucid ruler's daughter. As one result of the close political union between the two empires, the Greek cultural influence became even more widespread in N. India. The Maurya dynasty endured until about 185 B.C. During the reign of Asoka (273–232 B.C.), its greatest sovereign, Buddhism became the dominant religion of the empire. Of the dynasties that appeared in the period immediately following the downfall of the Mauryas, the Sunga endured longest, ruling more than a century. The chief event of this period, extending approximately from 184 B.C. to 72 B.C., was the persecution and decline of Buddhism in India and the triumph of Brahmanism. In consequence of this victory of the Brahmin priests of Hinduism, the caste system became deeply ingrained in the Indian social structure, creating great obstacles to the national unification of the Indian peoples.

An extensive section of w. India had been occupied meanwhile (about 100 B.C.) by invading Sakas (Scythians), then in retreat before the Yuechi (q.v.) of central Asia. Pushing southward, the Yuechi subsequently settled in N.W. India, where Kadphises, one of their kings, founded, about 40 A.D., the Kushan dynasty. A large part of N. India shortly fell under the sway of the Kushan kings. One of the early Yuechi monarchs established diplomatic and commercial relations with the Roman Empire. The rulers of the native Andhra dynasty, which came into control of the former Sunga dominions about 27 B.C., and endured for about 460 years, made repeated attempts to expel the Sakas. These attempts ended in failure, and about 236 A.D. the Sakas attained complete sovereignty over W. India. In 225 A.D., shortly before the fall of the Andhra dynasty, the Yuechi realm also disintegrated. The ensuing century was a period of political confusion throughout most of India.

In 320 A.D. a Magadha raja named Chandragupta, who had completed the conquest of neighboring territories, founded a new imperial regime and the Gupta dynasty. His grandson Chandragupta II vastly expanded the realm, subjugating all of the subcontinent N. of the Narbada R. Under the rulers of the Gupta dynasty, which reigned for 160 years, Indian culture reached new heights. The period was one of sustained peace, steady economic advance, and intellectual accomplishment, particularly in art, music, and literature (see KALIDASA). Equally important, Hinduism, long in a state of decline, experienced a robust renaissance through absorption of some of the features of Buddhism. Toward the close of the 5th century, Hunnish invaders, often referred to as the White Huns, pushed into India from central Asia. The Gupta empire broke up under the blows of these marauders, whose supremacy went unchallenged for nearly a century. Foreign military reverses, notably at the hands of the Turks about 565 A.D., finally undermined the Hunnish power in India. Among the contemporary descendants of the Huns who remained on the subcontinent are certain tribal groups of modern Rajputana. Another powerful kingdom was founded in N. India, in 606, by Harsha, the last Hindu monarch of consequence in Indian national history. During his reign, which lasted until 647, Harsha secured control of almost the entire mainland and assayed, without success, the conquest of the Deccan. Harsha's dominions disintegrated into a multiplicity of warring petty states and principalities following his death. This anarchic state of affairs, which had also been generally characteristic for many centuries of the situation on the peninsula, prevailed throughout India until the beginning of the 11th century.

As the prolonged period of internal strife in India drew to a close, a new power, solidly united under Mohammedanism, had arisen in western Asia. The new power was Khurasan, originally a Samanid province, which had been transformed (997) into an independent kingdom by Mahmud of Ghazni. A capable warrior, whose sovereignty over Khurasan had been recognized by the caliph of Baghdad, Mahmud launched, in 1000, the first of seventeen consecutive expeditions across the Afghan frontier into India. These incursions were marked by frequent victories over the disunited Indians, and by 1025 Mahmud had sacked many W. Indian cities, including fabulously wealthy Somnath (q.v.), and had made the Punjab region into a dependency. The most successful of the Moslem rulers after Mahmud was Mohammed of Ghor, whose reign began in 1173. Regarded by most historians as the real founder of Mohammedan power in India, he initiated his campaigns of conquest in 1175 and, in the course of the next three decades, subjugated all of the Indo-Gangetic plain w. of Benares. On the death (1206) of Mohammed of Ghor, Kutb-ud-din, his viceroy of Delhi and a former slave, proclaimed himself king (sultan). The Slave Dynasty founded by Kutb-ud-din, its only outstanding ruler, endured until 1288. Another capable Mohammedan, Ala-ud-din, second of the succeeding Khilji dynasty, consolidated the Indian realm and plundered and conquered the Deccan. Before the end of his reign in 1315, the Mongols began to infiltrate the N. frontiers of the Moslem dominions in India. Mohammed Tughlak, the last Delhi sultan of importance, completely alienated both the Moslems and the subject Hindus by his cruelty and religious fanaticism. As a result, the empire was torn by revolutionary strife, and some of the provinces, notably Bengal, seceded. The internal turmoil increased after Tughlak's death (1351); when, in 1398, the Mongol conqueror Tamerlane led his armies into India, he met little organized resistance. Climaxing his victorious invasion, Tamerlane sacked and destroyed Delhi and massacred its inhabitants. The Mongol conqueror withdrew from India shortly after the sack of Delhi, leaving the remnants of the empire to Mahmud Tughlak, the last of the Tughlak dynasty. Mahmud was succeeded, in 1414, by the first of the Sayyids, a dynasty that was later driven from power by Bahlol, founder of the Lodi line of kings. The Lodi dynasty, generally weak and ineffectual, was terminated in 1526. In that year Baber, a descendant of Tamerlane and the founder of the great Mogul dynasty, climaxed a series of raids into India by defeating the Lodi army. Baber shortly occupied Agra, the Lodi capital, and proclaimed himself emperor of the Mohammedan dominions. Within four years of his initial victory, Baber controlled a large part of the Indian mainland.

Akbar, the grandson of Baber, was the greatest sovereign of the Mogul Empire. During his reign, which extended from 1556 to 1605, he subdued rebellious princes in various regions, including Punjab, Rajputana, and Gujarat. He added Bengal to his realm in 1576, conquered Kashmir between 1586 and 1592, and annexed Sind in 1592. Between 1598 and 1601 he subjugated a number of the Moslem kingdoms of the Deccan. In the administration of his vast dominions, Akbar revealed remarkable organizational ability. He secured the allegiance of hundreds of feudatory rulers, promoted trade, introduced an equable system of taxation, and encouraged religious tolerance. The Mogul Empire attained its peak of cultural splendor under the rule of Shah Jahan, Akbar's grandson. His reign (1628–58) coincided with the golden age of Indian Saracenic architecture, best exemplified by the Taj Mahal (q.v.). Shah Jahan was driven from the throne in 1658 by his son Aurangzeb, who took the title of Alamgir ("Conqueror of the World"). Treacherous and aggressive, Aurangzeb murdered his three brothers and waged a series of wars against the autonomous kingdoms of India, sapping the moral and material strength of the empire. During his campaigns in the Deccan, the Mahrattas or Marathas (q.v.), a Scytho-Dravidian people, inflicted numerous defeats on the imperial armies. The stability of Aurangzeb's regime was further undermined as a result of popular antagonism to the religious bigotry which he fostered. In the course of his reign, which ended (1707) with his death in exile, the Sikhist faith obtained a strong foothold in India.

In the half century following the death of Aurangzeb, the Mogul Empire ceased to exist as an effective state. The political chaos of the period was marked by a rapid decline of centralized authority, by the creation of numerous petty kingdoms and principalities by Moslem and Hindu adventurers, and by the formation of large independent states by the governors of the imperial provinces. Among the first of the large independent states to emerge was Hyderabad, established in 1712. The tottering Mogul regime suffered a disastrous blow when, in 1739, the Persian king Nadir Shah led an army into India and plundered Delhi. Among the loot seized by the invaders, the sixth Moslem force to overrun India, was the mammoth Kohinoor diamond and the fabulous Peacock Throne, of solid gold inlaid with precious stones. According to some estimates, the value of the booty taken from Delhi by Nadir Shah approximated more than $120,000,000. The Persian king soon withdrew from India, but in 1756 Delhi was again captured by Ahmad Shah, the Amir of Afghanistan, who had previously seized Punjab. In 1760, the Marathas and the Sikhs joined forces against Ahmad Shah's armies. The ensuing battle, fought at Panipat on January 7, 1761, resulted in complete victory for the invaders. In 1764, following the withdrawal of the latter from India, the Mogul emperor regained his throne. His authority, like that of the emperors who followed him, was purely nominal, however. With the defeat of the Marathas and the Sikhs, the possibility of reunification of the Indian peoples into a strong national state had vanished. India, long the arena of bitter colonial rivalry among the maritime powers of Europe, fell increasingly thereafter under the domination of Great Britain.

Because of Moslem control of the trade arteries between the Mediterranean and India, various European monarchs had begun to dream of a new route to the Far East long before Baber founded the Mogul Empire. The Portuguese devoted remarkable zeal and initiative to the search for such a route, and in 1497–98, Vasco da Gama, one of the royal navigators, led an expedition around the Cape of Good Hope and across the Indian Ocean. On May 19, 1498, da Gama sailed into the harbor of Calicut, on the Malabar coast of the Deccan, opening a new era of Indian history. Establishing friendly relations with the dominant kingdom of the Deccan, the Portuguese secured a monopoly of Indian maritime trade and maintained it for a century. The Portuguese monopoly was broken early in the 17th century by the United East India Company of the Netherlands, an amalgamation of private Dutch commercial firms brought together under the auspices of the Dutch government. During the initial period of Dutch activity in the Far East, the British entered the race for Far Eastern markets, functioning, like the Dutch, through a private

British Information Services

A busy thoroughfare in the city of Bombay, India

firm known subsequently as the British East India Company. Company negotiations with the Mogul emperor Jahangir Shah were successful, and in December, 1612, the British founded their first trading post at Surat, on the Gulf of Cambay. On the 29th of the preceding month, a Portuguese fleet had attacked a number of British vessels in the Gulf of Cambay, and the British had triumphed in the ensuing battle. During the next decade the Portuguese were defeated in several additional naval engagements by the British, who thereafter encountered little opposition in India from that quarter. The Dutch, already entrenched in the Malay Archipelago, also endeavored to drive the British out of India, but were themselves eliminated as a serious competitive force before the end of the 17th century. Meanwhile, the British steadily expanded their sphere of influence and operations. They secured a foothold in Orissa in 1633, founded Madras in 1639, obtained trading privileges in Bengal in 1651, acquired Bombay from Portugal in 1661, arranged a commercial treaty with the Maratha ruler Sivaji in 1674, and established Calcutta in 1690. Native opposition to the last-named move, begun in 1686, was forcibly suppressed.

During the first half of the 18th century, the French, who had begun to operate in India about 1675, emerged as a serious threat to the growing power and prosperity of the British East India Company. The friction between the French and British reached an acute stage in 1746, when a French fleet seized Madras. This action, a phase of the War of the Austrian Succession (1740–48), and the subsequent fighting in India ended in a stalemate, and in 1748 the French returned Madras to the British. Within three years the smoldering feud between the European rivals again flared into armed conflict. Robert Clive (q.v.), an employee of the British East India Company, won distinction and victory in this phase of the struggle, essentially a fight for control of Hyderabad and the Carnatic (q.v.). The final stage of the contest between the French and British for dominance in India developed as an extension of the Seven Years' War (q.v.) in Europe. In the course (1756–63) of the hostilities, which involved large contingents of native partisans, the British won several decisive victories, effectively demolishing French plans for political control of the subcontinent. The climactic events of the war were the seizure of Calcutta by Bengalese insurgents (see BLACK HOLE) and Clive's victory at Plassey (see PLASSEY, BATTLE OF). By the terms of the general peace settlement following the Seven Years' War, French territory in India was reduced to a few trading posts.

As a result of its victories, the East India Company had acquired strategic political and territorial positions in Bengal, the most populous province of India, and in important areas of the Deccan. Consolidation and extension of these gains characterized the subsequent policy of the Company, which retained its status as a private commercial firm until 1773. In that year the East India Company became, under the provisions of Parliamentary legislation, a semi-official agency of the British government. The application of British policy in India was tremendously facilitated by the disintegration of centralized authority following the catastrophe suffered by the Marathas and Sikhs at Panipat in 1761. In the pursuit of their objectives, the British relied primarily on superior military power; but bribery, extortion, and political manipulation of the native chieftains were frequently and successfully employed (see HASTINGS, WARREN). Disunity among the various Indian kingdoms and principalities paved the way for eventual British subjugation of the entire subcontinent and contiguous regions, notably Burma. At sporadic intervals, individual Indian states and groupings of states fiercely, but vainly, resisted the exploitation, brutality, and territorial seizures of the Company. The chief centers of armed resistance to British rule included, at various times, a Maratha confederacy, Mysore, Sind, and Punjab. In 1845, the Sikhs of the last-named region attacked British positions, starting a war that proved costly to both sides. The Sikhs were defeated in 1846, but two years later they again engaged the British in sanguinary fighting. In one battle, fought at Chillianwalla, the Sikhs inflicted nearly 2500 casualties on the British. The latter won a decisive victory on February 21, 1849, however, and the Sikhs capitulated.

Annexation of Punjab by the East India Company followed. During the next few years James Andrew Broun Ramsay, Earl of Dalhousie, then governor general of the Company in India, annexed, on the death of the native rulers, Satara, Jaitpur, Sambalpur, Jhansi, and Nagpur. Ramsay's annexationist policy engendered profound hostility among the Indian nobility and peoples. In many material respects India benefited from various improvements and reforms introduced by Ramsay's administration. Railways, bridges, roads, and irrigation systems were constructed. A telegraph and postal service was established. Restrictions were imposed on suttee, slave trading, and other ancient practices. However, these innovations and reforms aroused little enthusiasm among the Indian people, many of whom regarded the modernization of their country with fear and distrust. In 1856 Ramsay annexed Oudh, an act that added immeasurably to the popular discontent. As the unrest in India mounted, a large-scale conspiratorial movement spread among the sepoys, the native troops employed by the British East India Company. A general uprising, known in history both as the Indian Mutiny (q.v.) and as the Sepoy Mutiny or Rebellion, began at Meerut, a town near Delhi, on May 10, 1857. Rallying around the banner of Bahadur Shah II, titular emperor of the moribund Mogul Empire, the mutineers quickly occupied Delhi and other strategic centers, massacred hundreds of Europeans, and, on June 30, laid siege to the British Residency at Lucknow (see LUCKNOW, BATTLE OF). Lucknow was relieved in November, and reinforcements of British troops and loyal sepoys were rushed to the disaffected areas. Fighting continued throughout the remainder of 1857 and into 1859, but by June, 1858, the chief rebel strongholds had fallen. In the same year, the judicial authorities of the East India Company convicted Bahadur Shah II on charges of rebellion and sentenced him to life imprisonment, thus closing the final chapter of Mogul history. As one major result of the Indian Mutiny, the British Parliament in 1858 enacted legislation, termed the Act for the Better Government of India, which transferred the administration of India from the East India Company to the British crown.

Many of the abuses prevalent in India during the rule of the East India Company were eradicated after the British government assumed control of Indian affairs. Important fiscal, governmental, juridical, educational, and social reforms were instituted, and the system of public works inaugurated by Ramsay was vastly extended. However, the British government had inherited numerous difficult problems, including the impoverished condition of the masses of the Indian people, popular resentment over the colonial status of the country, and a growing spirit of nationalism. Frequent disastrous famines, beginning with the Orissa famine of 1866, which took the lives of 1,500,000 persons, contributed substantially to political unrest. In 1877 the British government, then headed by Prime Minister Benjamin Disraeli, proclaimed Queen Victoria Empress of India.

In the closing years of the 19th and during the first decade of the 20th century, the

Canad. Pacif. Rys.; Govt. of India Info. Ser.

HANDCRAFT INDUSTRY IN INDIA

Above: Adults and children weaving a rug on a hand loom. Right: A boy of Madhya Pradesh, Indian Union, combing wool, for making blankets, with pair of steel-bristled pads.

social and political ferment in India spread widely. Occidental political doctrines and methods were introduced by Hindus who had studied in British and American universities. Under the stimulus of vigorous propaganda campaigns in the native press, mass meetings, and secret political organizations, Indian nationalism began seriously to threaten the British position in India. A number of associations, dedicated to the struggle against British rule, had been created in the decades following the Indian Mutiny. Of these, the most influential was the Indian National Congress, founded in 1885. This organization, which enlisted the support of many prominent Hindus and Mohammedans, gradually heightened the political consciousness of the Indian masses and accelerated the trend toward national unification. On the cultural level, the celebrated Indian poet and educator Rabindranath Tagore (q.v.) made enduring contributions to the cause of Indian unity.

The National Congress drew inspiration and encouragement from the Japanese victory in the Russo-Japanese War (1904–05), a practical demonstration of the latent power of the Oriental peoples. Hostile manifestations against British rule became more and more

frequent, particularly in Bengal. The more radical nationalists resorted to assassination, bombings, and other acts of terrorism. Retaliatory measures by the colonial authorities were countered by a popular boycott (*Swadeshi*) of British goods. Condemning most of the nationalist activities as seditious, the British government adopted a special criminal code in order to deal with the situation. Among other measures, this code provided for trial without jury for persons accused of treason, and for deportation or summary imprisonment for agitators. These repressive

British Info.; Can. Pac. Railways

CULTIVATING RICE IN INDIA

Top: Flooded fields where rice, India's leading crop, is grown. Left: Carrying straw for mulching of rice. Above: Tilling soil before planting.

steps were followed in 1909 by the India Councils Act, which introduced a limited degree of self-government in India. Dissatisfied with this concession to Indian demands for independence, the nationalist movement continued to gain headway.

A new and disruptive current had meanwhile been introduced into the movement for national unification with the formation, in 1906, of the Moslem League. Established with the encouragement of the British government and supported chiefly by those Mohammedans who, for reasons of self-interest, loyalty to Great Britain, or Islamic national-

ism, were hostile to the objectives of the National Congress, the League succeeded in diverting significant numbers of the Indian Moslem youth and intelligentsia from the independence struggle. However, many outstanding Mohammedans, including the influential journalist Abul Kalam Azad, registered disapproval of League policy, resigned from the organization, and joined the National Congress.

Following the outbreak of World War I, large numbers of the Indian people, including both Hindus and Moslems, rallied to the British cause. More than 1,200,000 Indians participated in the British war effort, giving valiant and loyal service in all theaters of the conflict. The nationalist movement, generally quiescent during the first two years of the war, resumed the campaign for fundamental political reforms in the fall of 1916. The campaign was initiated by a joint declaration of minimum demands by the Indian National Congress and by the Moslem League, which had been forced to abandon its pro-British policy after Turkey, a Moslem country, entered the war on the side of the Central Powers. There followed a policy pronouncement from the British government in August, 1917, promising an increase of ". . . the association of Indians in every branch of the administration and the gradual development of self-governing institutions with a view to the progressive realization of responsible government in India . . .".

Political strife became intense in India after World War I. In reply to the upsurge of nationalist activity, the British government obtained passage of legislation, known as the Rowlatt Acts, which suspended civil rights and provided for martial law in areas disturbed by riots and uprisings. Passage of the Rowlatt Acts precipitated a wave of violence and disorder in many parts of India. In this period of turmoil, Mohandas K. Gandhi, Hindu social and religious reformer and ascetic, called on the Indian people to meet British repression with passive resistance (*Satyagraha*). The protest movement reached insurrectionary proportions on April 13, 1919, proclaimed by Gandhi as a day of national mourning. In Amritsar, Punjab, city authorities, unable to cope with the aroused citizenry, appealed to the military for aid. The troops dispersed a huge assembly of people, freely using their firearms and causing about 1600 casualties. In consequence of the Amritsar massacre, the anti-British movement in India reached new levels of intensity. The outstanding feature of this stage of the struggle was Gandhi's policy of non-co-operation, instituted in 1920. Among other things, the policy called for the boycott of British commodities, courts, and educational institutions, for non-co-operation in political life, and for the renunciation of British titles held by Indians. The non-co-operation movement was often attended by violence, despite Gandhi's admonitions against the use of force. Combined with parliamentary methods of struggle, the movement proved to be a remarkably effective weapon in the fight for Indian freedom. In the view of British officialdom,

Gandhi's activities constituted sedition, and the Indian leader was periodically imprisoned or interned in the course of the next two decades. Gandhi, known among the Indian people as *Mahatma* (Skr., "great-souled"), nonetheless figured decisively in the political history of India during this period. (For an account of his career, which included practical leadership of the Indian National Congress as well as moral and spiritual guidance of the Indian people, see GANDHI, MOHANDAS KARAMCHAND.)

Between 1922, the year of Gandhi's initial imprisonment for sedition, and 1942, when he was placed in custody for the last time, the fight for Indian independence was marked by serious setbacks, including the renewal of dissension between Moslems and Hindus, and by many victories. The tide of Indian nationalism, having acquired momentum steadily since Gandhi's first arrest, attained a climactic stage in the spring of 1930. On March 12 of that year, following British rejection of demands for dominion status for India, Gandhi announced that he would lead a mass violation of the government salt monopoly. The violation was accomplished, after a long march to the Gulf of Cambay, by boiling sea water to produce salt. Similar actions occurred throughout India, and on May 5 Gandhi was again jailed by the British authorities. Riots and demonstrations developed immediately in Calcutta, Delhi, and other centers. Trains were stoned, telegraph wires were cut, and various government officials were assassinated. Striving to cope with these and later disorders, the government carried out wholesale arrests, and by November about

Woman of Bengal, India, playing a vina

British Information Services

FACTORIES IN INDIA. *Left: Welder in an iron and steel works. Right: In a cotton mill.*

27,000 Indian nationalists had been sentenced to prison terms.

Finally, in March, 1931, the British government arranged a truce with Gandhi, who had been released in the preceding January along with Jawaharlal Nehru (q.v.), his closest associate and the secretary of the Indian National Congress, and other political prisoners. Meanwhile, the Moslem League, professing fears of Hindu domination, had advanced demands for special privileges in the proposed dominion government. In the course of the resultant controversy, bitter Hindu-Moslem rioting ravaged many communities of India. Adding to the misery and suffering occasioned by these outbursts, the world economic crisis, which had begun in 1929, completely disrupted the economy of India during the early 1930's. Falling demand on the world markets for Indian products, industrial and agricultural stagnation, mass unemployment, and widespread starvation aggravated an already desperate political situation.

In 1935, following a series of conferences in London between British and Indian lead-

ers, legislation known as the Government of India Act received the approval of the British Parliament. The legislation provided for the establishment of autonomous legislative bodies in the provinces of British India, for the creation of a central government representative of the provinces and princely states, and for the protection of Moslem minorities. In addition, the Act provided for a bicameral national legislature and an executive arm under the control of the British government. Largely influenced by Gandhi, the Indian people approved the measure, which was scheduled to become effective in 1937. However, many members of the National Congress insisted on full independence for India, and in 1936, Nehru, then president of the Congress, denounced the proposed new constitution as a charter of slavery. In the elections, held early in 1937, for the provincial legislatures, the National Congress party won absolute majorities in six of the eleven assemblies and pluralities in three others. The new constitution became operative on April 1, 1937.

On the provincial level, few difficulties developed in the application of the Government of India Act. The plan for federation proved unworkable for a variety of reasons, including the reluctance of the Indian princes to cooperate with the radicals of the National Congress party, reciprocal hostility on the part of the latter, and Moslem claims that the Hindus would have excessive influence in the national legislature. As an alternative, the Moslem League, then headed by Mohammed Ali Jinnah (q.v.), advocated the creation of an independent Moslem state (Pakistan). This proposal met violent Hindu opposition. Further complicating the Indian political situation, Subhas Chandra Bose (q.v.), an extreme nationalist, was elected to the presidency of the Indian National Congress early in 1939. Within a few months the Congress rejected his policies, however, and he resigned.

On the outbreak of World War II the viceroy of India, Victor Alexander John Hope, Marquis of Linlithgow, declared war on Germany in the name of India. This step, taken in accordance with the constitution of 1937 but without prior consultation with Indian leaders, alienated Gandhi and important sections of the National Congress. Influential groupings of the National Congress, supporting Gandhi's position, intensified the campaign for immediate self-government, naming self-government as their price for co-operation in the war effort. At the end of October, 1939, the ministries of eight provinces resigned in protest against the adamant attitude of the British. The civil-disobedience campaign was resumed by the National Congress in October, 1940. Meanwhile, the Moslem League, many of the princely states, and certain members of the National Congress had endorsed the British war effort. The subsequent contributions of India to the struggle against the Axis powers were extensive. Indian troops at home and on the fronts numbered about 1,500,000 before the termination of hostilities, and Indian expenditures totaled approximately $12,000,000,000.

In December, 1941, the British authorities in India released the various Congress leaders who had been placed under arrest in 1940. A new wave of anti-British agitation followed, and in March, 1942, the government of the United Kingdom dispatched Sir Richard Stafford Cripps, then lord privy seal, to India with proposals designed to satisfy nationalist demands. These proposals contained the promise of full independence for India after World War II and called for the estab-

lishment of an interim Indian government in which the United Kingdom would retain control of national defense and foreign affairs. Because the leaders of both the National Congress and the Moslem League had basic objections to various sections of the proposed program, the Cripps mission ended in failure. The civil disobedience movement was again resumed in August, 1942. Gandhi, Nehru, and thousands of their supporters were rounded up and imprisoned, and the National Congress was outlawed. Encouraged by Indian disunity and with the help of Bose, who had organized a "provisional Indian government" in Burma, the Japanese promptly intensified military operations along the Burmese-Indian frontier. The Japanese invasion of India began along a 200-mile front in March, 1944. After a number of initial successes, the invaders were gradually forced back into Burma by Anglo-Indian troops. India later became a charter member of the United Nations.

The British government released Gandhi from jail on May 6, 1944. In the meantime, the Indian leader had modified most of his views regarding the nature of the war and the Cripps program, and in September, 1944, he and the Moslem leader Jinnah began discussions on mutual differences. Chiefly because of Jinnah's insistence on demarcation of the Pakistani frontiers prior to the formation of an interim government, the discussions ended in failure.

In June, 1945, India became a charter member of the United Nations. In the same month Nehru was released from jail and shortly thereafter the government of the United Kingdom issued a White Paper on the Indian question. The proposals contained in the White Paper closely resembled those of the Cripps program. Another deadlock developed, and during the second half of 1945 a new wave of anti-British riots and outbursts swept over India. Three representatives of the British government, including Cripps, made another attempt to negotiate an agreement with Indian leaders in the spring of 1946. Although the Moslem League temporarily withdrew its demands for the partition of India along religious lines, insuperable differences developed with respect to the character of an interim government. The negotiations were fruitless, and on June 29 the British viceroy Sir Archibald Percival Wavell announced the formation of an emergency "caretaker" government. An interim executive council, headed by Nehru, and representative of all major political groupings except the

Moslem League, replaced this government on September 2. In the next month, the Moslem League agreed to participate in the new government. However, communal strife between Moslems and Hindus increased in various parts of India.

By the end of 1946, the Indian political situation verged on anarchy. The British Prime Minister Clement R. Attlee announced on February 20, 1947, that his government would relinquish power in India not later than June 30, 1948. According to Attlee's announcement, the move would be made regardless of whether or not the political factions of India agreed on a constitution before that time. Political tension mounted in India after Attlee's statement, creating grave possibilities of a disastrous Hindu-Moslem civil war. After consultations with Indian leaders, Lord Louis Mountbatten, who succeeded Wavell as viceroy on March 22, recommended immediate partition of India to the British government as the only means of averting catastrophe. A bill incorporating Mountbatten's recommendations was introduced into the British Parliament on July 4. Termed the Indian Independence Act, the bill obtained speedy and unanimous approval in both houses of Parliament. Besides providing for the partition of India into independent Hindu and Moslem states and granting these states the right to remain in or withdraw from the British Commonwealth of Nations, the legislation established procedures for the determination of boundaries in certain disputed areas, particularly Bengal, Punjab, and the North-West Frontier Province. On August 15, 1947, officially designated Indian Independence Day, the British government transferred its authority to the constituent assemblies of the respective states. For accounts of subsequent developments, see INDIA, UNION OF; PAKISTAN.

INDIA, FRENCH. See FRENCH INDIA.

INDIA INK. See INK.

INDIA, MUSIC OF. The earliest music of India is traced to the Vedic rituals, about 2000–1000 B.C. The Vedic chant consisted of a simple liturgical melody of two or three tones within the range of a tetrachord (q.v.). This archaic type, sung to the hymns of the *Rig-Veda* was superseded about 400 B.C. by a seven-note scale within a range of an interval of a sixth. The modern system of Indian scales was first expounded in the comprehensive treatise of Bharata (about 500 A.D.), *Natya-Sastra*. The range of the seven-note scale was expanded from a sixth to an oc-

tave. The seven steps of the Indian scale are called *shadja, rsabha, gandhara, madhyama* ("middle"), *panchama* ("fifth"), *dhaivata,* and *nisada,* and are usually abbreviated to *sa, ri, ga, ma, pa, dha,* and *ni;* these steps roughly correspond to the Occidental intervals C-D-E-F-G-A-B. Instead of musical notation the Indian musicians use the musical syllables. The two most important *gramas* or scales are the *sagrama* (the scale formed on *sa*) and the *magrama* (the scale based on *ma*). Although these scales consist of seven intervals, the octave contains twenty-two intervals, which are called *sruti.*

The basis of Indian music is the *raga,* which means "mood" or "color". The *raga* has been compared to Occidental modes, but it is actually more of a melodic pattern. The *ragas* may consist of five, six, or seven tones, and are usually based on the two scales *sagrama* and *magrama.* The amount of *ragas* possible has been estimated to be high in the thousands, but each *raga* has its own special connotation. There are *ragas* which are used only in association with a specific season, day, or hour or a special ceremony; other *ragas* express moods.

The rhythm of Indian music is based on a pattern, called *tala,* which is repeated over and over again. The singer is usually accompanied by a drone of one or two tamburi (an Oriental four-stringed lute), by hand-beaten drums, by a *vina* (a guitarlike instrument with a bamboo finger board and a pair of gourd resonators), and by a violin.

The form of an Indian musical piece is usually in two parts: the introduction (*alapa*), in which the singer improvises upon the *raga* that is used; and the *raga* proper, which has various forms, usually based upon the verse used. Very often this latter part resembles the Western rondo form, in that episodes are introduced between verses.

INDIANA, one of the East North Central States of the United States, bounded on the N. by Michigan and Lake Michigan, on the E. by Ohio, on the S.E. and S. by the Ohio R., which separates it from Kentucky, and on the W. by Illinois. It ranks as the thirty-seventh State of the Union in area, the twelfth (1950) in population, and the sixth in order of admission after the thirteen original States, having been admitted on Dec. 11, 1816. Indianapolis (q.v.) is the State capital and largest city. In descending order of population (1950), other cities with over 50,000 inhabitants are Gary, Fort Wayne, Evansville, South Bend, Hammond, Terre Haute, Muncie,

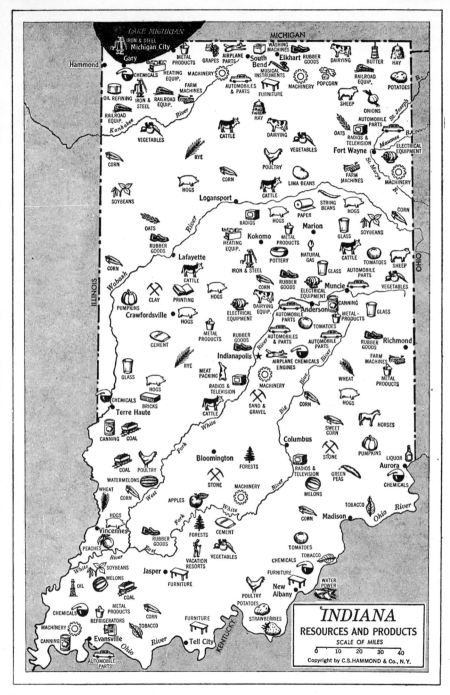

INDIANA
RESOURCES AND PRODUCTS
SCALE OF MILES
0   10   20   30   40
Copyright by C.S.HAMMOND & Co., N.Y.

and East Chicago (qq.v.). The distance between the northernmost and southernmost points in the State is about 265 m.; the distance between the easternmost and westernmost points is about 160 m. The area of the State is 36,291 sq.m., including 86 sq.m. of inland water surface; pop. (1950) 3,934,224.

Indiana may be divided into two physiographic provinces, namely a region of glaciated, rolling plains and a region of low, forested uplands. The uplands extend from the E. central section southwestward across the southern third of the State. Greensfork Top (1240 ft.), the highest point in Indiana, is situated in the E. central uplands, geologically an extension of the Appalachian highlands. The upland terrain is generally characterized by a complex system of valleys, ridges, and knobs. Mineral springs and limestone caverns are numerous in the s. part of the region. Wyandotte Cave (q.v.) is one of the largest caverns in the world. The plains region, occupying the remainder of the State, is traversed by massive marginal moraines which form belts of drift hills, especially in Kosciusko, Whitley, Noble, DeKalb, Lagrange, Steuben, and St. Joseph counties. In the valleys formed by these hills are upward of a thousand small lakes, of which Wawasee Lake in Kosciusko Co. is the largest. The shore of Lake Michigan is bordered by a belt of sand hills with elevations up to 300 ft. above sea level. In the central area, demarcated on the s. by marginal moraines extending through Vigo, Parke, Putnam, Morgan, Johnson, Bartholomew, Decatur, Fayette, Wayne, and Franklin counties, is the most fertile part of the State. The terrain in this region is underlaid by glacial clay, from 100 to 300 ft. deep, and is broken only by shallow valleys and low moraine ridges. Indiana has an approximate mean elevation of 700 ft.; its lowest point, in the extreme s.w., is about 320 ft. above sea level.

The Wabash R., the largest river wholly within Indiana, drains over two thirds of the State and forms part of the Indiana-Illinois boundary. Among the principal tributaries of the Wabash are the Tippecanoe, White, and Patoka rivers. Tributaries of the Ohio include the Blue R. and a number of smaller streams. The Kankakee R. traverses the N.W. section of the State, and in the N.E. the St. Joseph's and the St. Mary's unite at Fort Wayne to form the Maumee R.

Climatic conditions are relatively mild. The mean annual temperature varies from 49° F. in the N. to 54°F. in the s. Indianapolis, situated near the geographic center of the State, has an average temperature in January of 29°F. and in July of 76.4°F. The highest and lowest temperatures of record in the same city are 106°F. and —25°F. Annual precipitation varies from 36 inches in the N. to 42 inches in the s. The mean annual precipitation in Indianapolis is 39.77 inches.

Indiana has sixteen State parks totaling 43,161 acres, fourteen State forests totaling 96,161 acres, and seventeen community forests totaling 2514 acres. These areas, distributed throughout the State, preserve many types of scenery, including sand dunes, virgin forests, river gorges, caves, and lakes. Noteworthy among the parks and forests, many of which contain accommodations for vacationists and a wide variety of recreational facilities, are Yellowstone State Forest (about 20,000 acres), in Brown Co.; Clark State Forest (17,000 acres), near Scottsburg; Harrison State Forest (15,500 acres), near Corydon; Morgan-Monroe State Forest (15,200 acres), near Martinsville; Tippecanoe River State Park (6233 acres), near Winamac; Indiana Dunes State Park (2221 acres), near Michigan City; and Clifty Falls State Park (618 acres), near Madison. The State maintains thirteen fish hatcheries, which supply millions of fish annually to the lakes and streams. Quail, pheasants, wild turkeys, ducks, and rabbits abound in the State game preserves.

Indiana is one of the ten leading manufacturing States of the Union. According to a recent official survey the State contains about 5400 industrial establishments employing over 457,500 production workers. The manufactures produced in these establishments in a recent year were valued at over $3,000,000,000 plus the cost of materials, supplies, fuel, and contract work. Indiana ranks third (after Pennsylvania and Ohio) in the manufacture of iron and steel. This industry and various other basic industries, including petroleum refining and the manufacture of iron and steel products, are largely concentrated in the Calumet area (bordering Lake Michigan), one of the world's major industrial regions. Among other manufactures produced in the State as a whole are railway cars, engines, automobiles and automotive parts, machine-shop and foundry products, refrigerators, agricultural implements, electrical machinery and equipment, watches and clocks, household furniture, prefabricated houses, cement, brick and tile, glass, meat products, flour, canned vegetables and fruits,

Acme; Indiana Dept. of Comm. & Pub. Rel.

Above: Picking corn with a mechanical harvester on large farm near Kokomo, Indiana. Right: The George Rogers Clark Memorial in Vincennes, southwestern Indiana.

cheese and other dairy products, and soap.

Indiana is also one of the ten leading agricultural States. Its farms recently numbered nearly 167,000. These farms occupied more than 19,659,000 acres, about 85 percent of the total area of the State, and had a value of approximately $2,691,000,000. About 19 percent of the farms and about 29 percent of the farmlands are operated by tenant farmers. The average farm acreage is 118 acres. Indiana is second in the Union (after California) in the production of tomatoes for processing and second (after Illinois) in the production of soy beans; in a recent year the harvests of these crops totaled respectively about 588,000 tons and 36,450,000 bu. The corn harvest in that year was almost 242,000,-000 bu., an output exceeded only in Iowa, Illinois, and Nebraska. Other leading crops, with approximate average annual output, include oats, 48,000,000 bu.; wheat, 29,800,000 bu.; potatoes, 4,300,000 bu.; barley, 1,100,-000 bu.; hay, 2,500,000 tons; apples, 1,300,000 bu.; peaches, 450,000 bu.; and tobacco, 5970 tons. Approximately 2,900,000 watermelons are grown in Indiana in a typical year, and the State is the chief source in the United States for spearmint and peppermint oils. The livestock population of the State recently included over 4,980,000 hogs, almost 1,900,000 cattle, about 387,000 sheep, and 82,000 horses. In a recent year the wool clip amounted to over 1300 tons. Cash receipts from the sale of crops, livestock, and livestock products in a recent year totaled nearly $981,000,000; farm income from Federal government subsidies was about $5,700,000.

Bituminous coal, the most important mineral resource of the State, is obtained from both shaft and strip mines. The coal fields cover an area of 6500 sq.m., mainly in the s.w. portion of the State. Coal output in a recent year totaled over 19,950,000 tons. About four fifths of the building limestone used in the United States is quarried in Indiana, and the State has nearly 3500 producing oil wells with an annual output of more than 10,000,000 barrels. Other important mineral resources include cement gravel, clays, mineral waters, and natural gas. The value of mineral production in a recent year was almost $167,000,000.

Indiana is served by extensive networks of railroad systems, motor-truck lines, and inland-water carriers. Main-track railroad mileage in the State totals almost 6700 m. Excluding roads within urban areas, the highway system consists of almost 83,000 m. of roads; more than 73,000 m. are surfaced, about 9500 m. are maintained by the State, and about 73,000 m. are locally maintained. There are about 150 airports, and the State is served by seven major air lines.

Attendance at the public schools of Indiana is compulsory, during the entire school year, for children between the ages of seven and sixteen. Public elementary and secondary schools in the State recently numbered over 3400, with a total enrollment of about 627,500 pupils, taught by nearly 23,000 teachers. The State contains 38 institutions of higher learning, 25 of which are colleges and universities, 8 are professional schools, 2 are teachers colleges, and 3 are junior colleges. Among the outstanding universities are Indiana University (q.v.) at Bloomington, De Pauw University (q.v.) at Greencastle, University of Notre Dame (see NOTRE DAME, UNIVERSITY OF) at Notre Dame, Purdue University (q.v.) at Lafayette, Butler College at Indianapolis, Evansville College at Evansville, Franklin College at Franklin, Goshen College at Goshen, Hanover College at Hanover, and St. Mary's College at Notre Dame.

Indiana is governed according to the constitution of 1851, which replaced the original State constitution of 1816. By the terms of this document, executive authority is vested in a governor and lieutenant governor, elected for four-year terms, and a secretary of state, attorney general, auditor, treasurer, superintendent of public instruction, and certain other officials. Legislative authority is vested in a general assembly consisting of a senate of 50 members and a house of representatives of 100 members. Members of both houses are elected for two-year terms. Legislative sessions are held biennially. Judicial power is vested in a supreme court, consisting of five members elected for six-year terms; an appellate court consisting of six members elected for four-year terms; and a system of circuit courts with judges elected for six-year terms. The State is divided into 92 counties.

It is represented in the Congress of the United States by two senators and by eleven representatives. The minimum voting age in Indiana is twenty-one years.

History. In pre-Columbian times the region occupied by present-day Indiana was inhabited by the Indian people known as Mound Builders (q.v.); various types of earthworks, the distinctive feature of their civilization, are extant within the State. The Miamis, an Algonquian confederation, inhabited the region when it was first visited (probably in the 1670's) by white men, pioneering fur traders and missionaries from New France (Canada). The first European (of whom there is record) to traverse any part of the Indiana region was the French explorer Robert de La Salle.

Several trading and military posts were established in the region by the French. About 1731 the French-Canadian explorer François Marie Bissot, Sieur de Vincennes (1700–36) constructed a fort on the site of present-day Vincennes. With the arrival (about 1735) of a group of French emigrants this outpost, subsequently named in honor of its founder, became the first permanent settlement in Indiana.

Great Britain acquired the Indiana region, along with most of the other French possessions in North America, under the provisions of the Treaty of Paris (1763), the peace agreement concluding the French and Indian War, but fourteen years elapsed before the British assumed control of Vincennes. The British government attached the region to the province of Quebec in 1774. In 1778, during the American Revolutionary War, Vincennes was captured by troops of a Virginian expeditionary force. Though the British soon regained the town, it was recaptured (February, 1779) by a force under the frontier leader George Rogers Clark, head of the expedition. All of the territory N. of the Ohio R. was annexed by Virginia and constituted as "Illinois County". Clarksville (now a suburb of Jeffersonville), the first settlement established in the Indiana region by U.S. citizens, was founded in 1784.

By the terms of the treaty (1783) concluding the Revolutionary War, Illinois County and the rest of what was then the Northwest were ceded by Great Britain to the United States. In 1787, after Virginia and other States had relinquished their territorial claims in the region, it was included in the newly organized Northwest Territory (q.v.).

The Algonquians of the Indiana section of

the Territory conducted a relentless struggle in defense of their ancestral lands during the post-Revolutionary period; they were finally defeated (1794) and forced to sue for peace by Federal troops under General Anthony Wayne. Fort Wayne was constructed the same year. Many emigrants settled in the region after the termination of hostilities.

In 1800 the U.S. government partitioned Northwest Territory, constituting an extensive area, including the Indiana region, as Indiana Territory. The first Territorial governor, William Henry Harrison, later ninth President of the United States, negotiated a number of favorable land treaties with the Indians during the next few years. A large part of Indiana Territory was organized as Michigan Territory in 1805, and in 1809, when Illinois Territory was created, the present-day boundaries of Indiana were delineated.

Meanwhile the Shawnee chief Tecumseh had begun the organization of an Indian confederacy to resist further U.S. encroachments on the tribal domains N. of the Ohio R. This challenge to the consolidation of Indiana Territory was met successfully when, on November 7, 1811, American forces under Governor Harrison defeated a numerically superior army commanded by Tecumseh's brother Tenskwatawa (see TIPPECANOE, BATTLE OF). Some of the Indiana tribes resumed hostilities during the War of 1812, but they were quickly subdued. Virtually all of the survivors were forced westward during the quarter century following the war.

A large majority of the immigrants into Indiana came from the South, and before 1816, despite statutory prohibitions, repeated attempts were made to legalize slavery in the Territory. Antislavery sentiment prevailed at the first State constitutional convention, held in 1816; however, a law prohibiting Negroes and mulattoes from immigrating into the State remained in force until after the Civil War.

The growth of the State in wealth and population was accelerated by the construction of the National Road (see CUMBERLAND ROAD) and the Wabash and Erie canals (qq.v.). Wild speculation in lands and railroads led to general bankruptcy in 1837; but after 1846, when a compromise with the public creditors was effected, the economic and financial condition of the State improved steadily. Under the leadership of Governor Oliver Perry Morton, Indiana contributed substantially to the Union cause during the Civil War, furnishing over 200,000 men to the armed forces. The State legislature, then controlled by the Democratic Party, consistently opposed the war, and the pro-Confederate Knights of the Golden Circle (q.v.) won numerous adherents in many localities. Expanding transportation facilities and the discovery and exploitation of mineral resources, particularly coal, provided the basis for steady agricultural and industrial growth during the half century following the Civil War.

In national politics the Indiana electorate supported the Presidential candidates of the Democratic Party in all except two elections up to 1860. The Whig Presidential candidate William Henry Harrison carried the State in 1836 and 1840. From 1860 to 1872 Indiana voted Republican in Presidential elections; in the period ending in 1928 the State electoral vote was won by the Republicans on ten occasions and by the Democrats on four occasions. The Democrats were victorious in the elections of 1932 and 1936; in the next three Presidential elections the Republicans carried the State. In the 1952 Presidential election the Republican candidate Dwight David Eisenhower received 1,136,259 votes; his Democratic opponent Adlai Ewing Stevenson received 801,530 votes.

INDIAN AFFAIRS, BUREAU OF, an agency incorporated into the Department of the Interior in 1849, which, in accordance with various treaties and subsequent acts of Congress, serves certain Indians who have retained membership in their tribes or who own property under Federal jurisdiction. Such Indians comprise a great majority of the 340,-000 Indians in continental U.S., and of the 35,000 Indians, Eskimos, and Aleuts in Alaska. In a recent year nearly 57,000,000 acres of Indian lands were under the jurisdiction of the Bureau, of which about 38,600,000 were owned by individual tribes; about 16,500,000 were allotted to individual tribes but held in trust for them by the U.S. government; and about 863,000 were owned by the government. None of these lands are subject to Federal, State, or local taxes; however, the Indians living on them are subject to certain taxes, including the Federal income tax.

The main objective of the Bureau of Indian Affairs in this century has been to foster the political, economic, and cultural development of the Indians under its jurisdiction. It has been aided toward this end by acts of Congress and by independent administrative decisions made within the Bureau which subse-

Indiana Dept. of Comm. & Public Relations
Soldiers and Sailors Monument in Indianapolis, the capital of Indiana

quently received the support of Congress.

The first recent major advance made in the status of the Indian was accomplished by an act of June 2, 1924, in which Congress declared all Indians born within the territorial limits of the U.S. to be citizens (prior to this time about two thirds of the Indian population had already attained citizenship). Economic development was furthered by the Indian Reorganization Act of 1934, which has been termed the Indian's Magna Charta. Any tribe which votes to accept this act may adopt a constitution governing its own members and incorporate for the purposes of obtaining Federal loans and carrying on business enterprises. Under this law, about 150 Indian communities have adopted constitutions and established tribal machinery for self-government, and about 100 communities have incorporated for business purposes. The principal sources of income, with the exception of royalties from oil, gas, and minerals in a few areas, have been in livestock, fishing, timber, and crops. Arts and crafts furnish a supplementary income, and the Indian Arts and Crafts Board, established by Congress in the Department of the Interior in 1936, works with the Bureau of Indian Affairs to aid Indian craftsmen in marketing their merchandise at a fair price.

Measures such as these have not yet wholly succeeded in achieving economic and political independence for the Indians, and certain tribes, such as the Navaho, are subject to great poverty and to more or less complete dependence upon government subsidies. Under the new economic policy, however, some amelioration of their condition may be expected; at the present time the Indian properties are being improved with irrigational structures, roads, bridges, timber and mining operations, hunting and fishing, and wildlife conservation, all managed co-operatively by the Indian tribes and the Bureau of Indian Affairs.

The cultural status of the Indians is also being improved. In areas in which the majority of the Indians still speak their native tongues, Indian service schools carry on instruction in both the native language and English, using bilingual texts published by the government. Full religious liberty, protecting the ancient beliefs of the Indians, was granted by Commissioner of Indian Affairs John Collier on January 15, 1934. According to his administrative ruling, any representative of a native Indian religion is accorded the same privileges as a Christian missionary or a representative of any other religion.

INDIANAPOLIS, port of entry, county seat of Marion Co., and capital of Indiana, on the White R., near the geographical center of the State. Indianapolis is the largest city in the State, and the largest city in the Union not situated on navigable water. It is an important railway center, with service by seven trunk-line systems, and contains extensive railroad shops. Among other transportation facilities are five airports. The city lies in the midst of the corn and wheat belts, and adjacent to large coal fields and extensive deposits of building stone and marl. Because of its excellent transportation facilities and central location, affording accessibility to populous markets in all directions, the city is a leading commercial and manufacturing center. It is one of the principal corn, soybean, livestock, and wheat markets of the United States. Industrial establishments in Indianapolis include numerous grain elevators, meat-packing plants, chemical plants, and plants producing automobiles, automobile parts and accessories, automobile bodies, truck bodies, airplane engines, road machinery, radio-broadcasting equipment, theater sound equipment, transmission chains, refrigerators, automatic stokers, electrical equipment, malleable castings, lenses, furniture, home appliances, saws, shoe polish, veneers, phonograph records, paper products, canned foods, gloves, clothing, hosiery, and poultry remedies.

Indianapolis is the site of Butler University, the schools of medicine and dentistry of Indiana University (qq.v.), Indiana Central College (United Brethren), established in 1902, Indianapolis College of Pharmacy, Indiana Law School, the Benjamin Harrison Law School, the Arthur Jordan Conservatory of Music, and the John Herron Art School. Among the State institutions in the city are the State schools for the deaf and blind, the Central Hospital for the Insane, and the Indiana Prison for Women. The last-named institution, established in 1873, was the first prison of its kind in the U.S. Indianapolis is an episcopal see of the Roman Catholic, Episcopal, and Methodist churches, and the site of the national headquarters of the American Legion. Three daily newspapers are published in Indianapolis, namely the *News,* the *Star,* and the *Times.* The Indianapolis Symphony Orchestra was founded in 1930.

Indianapolis possesses a number of noteworthy structures. The State Capitol, built in 1878 of Indiana limestone, contains, in addition to the State governmental offices, the Indiana State Museum, with geological and historical exhibits. Opposite the Capitol is the Indiana State Library and Historical Building, which has a collection of more than 33,-000 works dealing with Indiana. The Soldiers and Sailors Monument, a 285-foot structure surmounted by a huge statue popularly called Miss Indiana, stands in a circular park from which the four main avenues of the city radiate. An elevator operates to the top of the monument, which affords a panoramic view of the city and its environs. Nearby is the World War I Memorial Plaza, occupying five city blocks and containing several public buildings. Other places of interest in and near the city are the Scottish Rite Cathedral, containing a carillon of 63 bells, the Carmelite Monastery, the home of Benjamin Harrison, 23rd President of the U.S., the home of the American poet James Whitcomb Riley, and the Indianapolis Motor Speedway, where a 500-mile automobile race is held annually. The city is also the site of a State Fish Hatchery and the State Fair Grounds. Indianapolis

maintains 33 municipal parks, with a total area of more than 3000 acres, and facilities for golf, swimming, and other forms of recreation. Fort Benjamin Harrison, a large United States Army post, is situated 10 miles N.E. of the city.

A settlement was established on the site of Indianapolis in 1820. In the same year the location was chosen as the site of the future capital of Indiana and named Indianapolis. The town was laid out in 1821 from plans by Major Pierre Charles L'Enfant, the designer of Washington, D.C. In 1825 it became the seat of the State government. It was incorporated as a town in 1832 and chartered as a city in 1847, the year that marked the arrival of the first railroad. Indianapolis developed slowly until the Civil War, but thereafter its growth was rapid. Area, 54.15 sq.m.; pop. (1950) 427,173.

INDIAN ART AND ARCHITECTURE, that work produced in India from about the 3rd millennium B.C. to modern times. Its earliest expression was in brick buildings which were undoubtedly contemporary with buildings of wooden construction. The wooden structures disappeared but were succeeded and imitated in stone buildings, and these have survived. In subsequent centuries, along with the development of elaborate building styles, a profusion of art forms developed, expressed in sculpture, painting, jewelry, pottery, metal work, and textiles. As in other cultures, religion provided one of the strongest demands for the production of buildings and works of art. The arts of India were spread throughout the Far East with the diffusion of Buddhism, and exercised a strong influence on the arts of China, Japan, Burma, Siam, Cambodia, and Java. Buddhism and Hinduism with their various offshoots were dominant in India until Mohammedanism became powerful from the 11th to the 18th century. With Mohammedanism, which forbids representation of the human figure, geometrical patterns became the commonest form of decoration in all the arts.

Architecture. The oldest remains, buildings of burnt brick found at Mohenjo-Daro and Harappa, date from 3300 B.C. and later. The subsequent Vedic period, which precedes the beginning of the well-known or historical styles, is represented by burial mounds at Lauriya-Nandangarh and rock-cut tombs in Malabar. The historical styles begin about 250 B.C. in the time of Asoka, the Indian monarch who made Buddhism the state religion. Accordingly, the monuments of this time were

British Information Services

INDIAN ART. *Left: "Alexander the Great," by Huzuri, Rajput court painter. Right: Stucco image of Maitreya, a Buddhist divinity, dating from about the 3rd or 4th centuries.*

built for Buddhist purposes. Characteristic Buddhist constructions were the *tope* or stupa, a memorial mound encased in masonry, with a superstructure at the top, corridors around the base, and four entrances marked by gateways; the *dagoba*, a relic shrine, said to be the ancestral form of the pagoda; the *lat*, a stone edict pillar, generally monumental; the *chaitya*, a hall of worship in basilican form; and the *vihara*, a monastery. Chaityas and viharas were often hewn out of the living rock. Architectural details such as capitals and moldings show influence from Near Eastern and Greek sources. Notable examples of early rock-cut monuments are the temple at Karli (about 100 B.C.) with its elaborate sculptured façade and tunnel-vaulted nave, and temples and monasteries at Ajanta and Ellora.

Buddhism waned from the 5th century on, as Hinduism and Jainism grew dominant. The Jain and Hindu styles overlapped and produced the elaborate all-over patterns carved in bands that became the distinguishing feature of Indian architecture. The Jains often built on a gigantic scale, a marked feature being pointed domes constructed of level courses of corbelled stones. Extensive remains have been discovered on hilltops far removed from one another at Parasnath in Bengal, Abu in Rajputana, and Satranj in Kathiawar. Small temples were congregated in great num-

ber on hilltops. One of the earlier groups is on Mount Abu. Typical of Jaina commemorative towers is the richly ornamented, nine-story Jaya Sthamba.

The Hindu style is closely related to the Jain style. It is divided into three general categories: northern, from 600 to the present; central, from 1000 to 1300; and southern, or Dravidian, from 1350 to 1750. In all three periods the style is marked by great ornateness and the use of pyramidal roofs. Spirelike domes terminate in delicate finials. Other features include the elaborate, grand-scale *gopuras* or gates, and the *choultries* or ceremonial halls. Among the most famous examples of the style are the temples in the south at Tiravalur, Tanjore, and Ramasvaram; temples in the north at Barolli and Benares; and the Black Pagoda of Kannaruc.

Indo-Saracenic style, dating from the 11th century to the present, is divided into two phases, the Pathan and the Mogul. Examples of the earlier Pathan style in stone occur at Ahmedabad, and in brick at Gaur in Bengal. They are closely allied to Hindu models, but are simpler, and lack sculptures of human figures, which were banned by Moslem religious belief. The dome, the arch, and the minaret are constant features of the style. The dome at Bijapur in the Dekkan is a famous monument of the period. The Mogul phase of the

Indo-Saracenic style, from the 16th to the 18th century, developed to a high degree the use of luxurious materials such as marble. The culminating example of the style, the Taj Mahal (1631–45) was encased entirely in this material inlaid with precious and parti-colored stones. Other renowned examples are the Pearl Mosque at Agra, the palace fortresses at Agra and Delhi, and the Jaina mosques at Delhi and Lahore.

Building in India since the 18th century has either carried on the indigenous historical forms or has been patterned after European models introduced by the English. Innumerable examples of Western styles of the 18th, 19th, and 20th centuries may be seen in public buildings, factories, hotels, and houses. There are also examples of the adaptation of local tradition to modern requirements, as in the railroad station at Alwar.

Sculpture. The earliest prehistoric work was produced in stone, clay, ivory, copper, and gold. Examples of the 3rd millennium B.C. from the Indus valley, found among the remains of the burnt-brick buildings of Mohenjo-Daro, include alabaster and marble figures, terra-cotta figurines of nude goddesses, terra-cotta and faïence representations of animals, a copper model of a cart, and numerous square seals of ivory or faïence showing animals and pictographs. The similarity of these objects to Mesopotamian work in subject matter and stylized form indicates an interrelationship of the two cultures and a possible common ancestry. In Vedic and later times, from the 2nd millennium to the 3rd century B.C., connections with Near Eastern culture are not evident. An example of the earlier phase of this period is a 9th-century B.C. gold figurine of a goddess found at Lauriya-Nandangarh. Later, from 600 B.C. to historical times, common examples include finely polished and ornamented stone disks, and coins representing many kinds of animals and religious symbols.

With the rise of Buddhism in the 3rd century B.C., and the development of a monumental architecture in stone, stone sculpture both in relief and in the round became an important architectural adjunct. Buddha himself was not shown in early Indian art; he was represented by symbols and scenes from his life. Among other common subjects for representation were Buddhist deities and edi-

INDIAN ARCHITECTURE. *Below: The tope, Sarnath, near Benares, India. Right: Gate to the Great Temple, Hindu shrine at Ramasvaram.* British Information Services; Ewing Galloway

fying legends. At this time and subsequently throughout the history of Indian sculpture, figures and design were arranged in extensive and intricately related compositions. Monuments of the period include the animal capitals of King Asoka's sandstone edict pillars, and the marble railings that surround the Buddhist stupas at Barhut, where the reliefs seem to be compressed between the surface plane and the background plane, and at Sanchi, where the reliefs suggest the delicacy and detail of ivory carving. Later elaborate examples occur at Ellora, Kanheri, and Ajanta.

An important school of sculpture developed at Mathura from the 2nd century B.C. to the 6th century A.D. Remains of the earlier work of this school show a close relationship to the style of the sculpture at Bharhut. Later, in the 1st and 2nd centuries A.D., the school discarded the old symbols of Buddha and represented him by actual figures. This innovation was carried on through subsequent phases of Indian sculpture, although at Gandhara and Amaravati the symbols were retained until much later.

In the northwest of India, which was anciently called Gandhara and now includes Afghanistan and part of the Punjab, a Greco-Buddhist school of sculpture arose which combined the influence of Greek forms and Buddhist subject matter; it reached the peak of its production in the 2nd century A.D. Although it greatly influenced sculptural work in central Asia and even in China, Korea, and Japan, it did not have a major effect in the rest of India.

The Gupta period from 320 to about 600 A.D. produced Buddhas characterized by clearly defined lines and refined contours. The drapery of the figure was diaphanous and clung to the body as if wet. Occasionally the figures were made on a great scale, as in the colossal copper example from Sultanganj, which weighs more than a ton.

From the 7th to the 9th century a number of schools flourished; they include the highly architectural style of the Pallavas, exemplified by the work at Kancipuram; the Rastrakuta style, of which the best-preserved examples are a colossal temple relief and the three-headed bust of Siva at Elephanta; and the Kashmir style, which shows some Greco-Buddhist influence in the remains at Vijrabror, and more indigenous forms in figures of Hindu gods found at Vantipor.

From the 9th century to the consolidation of Moslem power at the end of the 12th century, Indian sculpture became linear, the forms appearing to be sharply outlined rather than voluminous. More than previously, it was applied as a decoration, subordinate to its architectural setting. It was intricate and elaborate in detail, and was characterized by complicated, many-armed figures drawn from the pantheon of Hindu and Jaina gods, which replaced the earlier simple figures of Buddhist gods. Emphasis on virtuosity in technical skill also added to the multiplication of involved forms.

At this time the three distinct areas of production in sculpture were the north and east, Rajputana, and the south-central and western regions. In the north and east, one of the main schools was centered in Bihar and Bengal under the Pala dynasty from 750 to 1200. A notable source for sculpture was the monastery and university of Nalanda in Bihar. Black slate was a common medium, and the themes, at first still Buddhist, gradually became more and more Hindu. Another northeastern school, in Orissa, produced typically Hindu work, including the monumental elephants and horses and erotic friezes at the Sun Temple in Konarak. In Rajputana the local style was exemplified in the hard sandstone temple of Khajuraho, which was literally covered with Hindu sculptures. The south-central and western regions produced notable works at Mysore, Halebid, Belur, and other places. The temples were embellished with richly sculptured, many-tiered friezes, pillars, and brackets carved in fine-grained dark stone.

After the Moslems became dominant, the established traditions of Indian sculpture were still continued by the Hindus and Jains, and the Mohammedans also adopted many of the native patterns as ornament. The traditions have persisted until the present day, and, especially in the south, copper images and stone sculpture are made by craftsmen carrying on the style and techniques of previous centuries.

Painting. Remains of Indian painting prior to 100 A.D. have survived in two localities. The remarkable frescoes of the Ajanta caves (q.v.) cover the period from 50 to 642 A.D. The earlier paintings of the Ajanta caves represented figures of indigenous types, having noble bearing and depicted with strong sensuality. In the Jogimara cave at Orissa, there is painting of two periods, 1st century B.C. and medieval; the later work is of poor quality, and almost obscures the earlier work, which sometimes reveals figures drawn with great vigor.

The Gupta period (320-600) established

the classical phase of Indian art, at once serene and energetic, spiritual and voluptuous. Art was the explicit medium of stating spiritual conceptions. A special kind of painting depicted the reward of good and evil deeds in the world, and was executed on scrolls. Painting of the Gupta period has been preserved in three of the Ajanta caves. Represented are numerous Buddhas, sleeping women, and love scenes. Another group of Buddhist wall-paintings were found at Bagh Baqu, over the Afghanistan border, in what is now Iran. These show that the artists had a complete command of representing any human posture. The drawing was stated in firm outline and the quality of the painting varied from sublime to grotesque effects. The whole spirit was one of emphatic, passionate force. The paintings in the first and second Ajanta caves date from the early 7th century and can hardly be distinguished in style from those of the Gupta period. Represented are bacchanalian scenes of the type that recurs in Buddhist art from the early Kusana period onward. There are remains of frescoes at Ellora (late 8th century). Such subjects as a rider upon a horned lion and many pairs of figures floating among clouds anticipate characteristic themes of the later Indian medieval style.

The only surviving documents of the Pala school (750–1200) are the illustrations in the two palm-leaf manuscripts in the Cambridge University library, in England, one dating from the beginning and the other from the middle of the 11th century, and containing, in all, fifty-one miniatures. All the illustrations represent Buddhist divinities or scenes from the life of Buddha, evidently replicas of traditional compositions. The work is that of accomplished craftsmen.

One example of an illustrated *Kalpa Sutra,* or manual of religious ceremonial, on palm leaf, is known, dated equivalent to 1237 A.D. and now at Patan. The variety of scenes represented affords valuable information on the contemporary manners, customs, and dress of the Gujarati culture; Gujarati painting was a continuation of the early west Indian style, the frescoes of Ellora representing an intermediate stage of development.

Rajput painting represents the art of Rajputana, Bundelkhand, and the Punjab Himalayas. The known examples, ranging from the latter part of the 16th into the 19th century, fall into two main groups, the Rajput and Mogul styles. The flat, decorative patterns and bright colors of these Indian manuscript paintings are similar to Persian miniatures, though not as varied and subtle in color. Mogul painting reflects an interest that is exclusively in persons and events, even to the signing of the work by the painters, at least a hundred of whose names are known; it is essentially an art of portraiture and chronicle, and is traditional, dramatic, and eclectic. Rajput painting is essentially a refined and lyrical folk art, and has been extensively used to illustrate medieval Hindu literature.

Jewelry, Pottery, and Textiles. Of all the minor arts in India, jewelry is the most universally interesting and beautiful. The techniques of filigree and granular work, which disappeared in Europe after the fall of the Roman Empire and were not again used until their introduction by the Moors in the 15th century, were never lost in India. The special pre-eminence of the best Indian pottery has always been the strict subordination of color and ornament to form, and the conventionalizing and repetition of natural forms in the decoration. Unglazed pottery has been made throughout India; decorative pottery for commercial purposes, painted, gilded, and glazed, is made in special varieties in different provinces. Exquisite color tones and combinations are found in the glazed tiles which came into fashion with the Mohammedan conquest after the 11th century. Among the branches of artistic metal work, that of the arms and equipment of the great chieftains is prominent.

Kashmir is the home of richly colored woolen shawls; Surat produces silk prints; and sumptuous brocades come from Ahmedabad, Benares, and Murshidabad. India has long been famous for its silk and cotton textiles, printed and embroidered as well as loom-figured.

INDIA, NATIVE STATES OF, prior to the partition of India (q.v.) into the Union of India (see INDIA, UNION OF) and Pakistan (q.v.), a designation sometimes applied to the Indian princely states. These had semi-autonomous regimes under varying degrees of control by the British government; they numbered 562 on August 15, 1947, when Indian independence was established. Under the terms of the Indian Independence Act, the enactment of the British Parliament which provided for the partition of British India (q.v.), the rulers of the native states were left free to determine the political future of their realms, i.e., whether to accede to Pakistan or to the Union of India. A number of the states, with Moslem majorities, acceded to Pakistan, either as independent sovereign states or by amalgamation with existing provinces. The vast majority of the states, those with predominantly Hindu populations, acceded to the Union of India by merger, in most instances, with the democratic states of the Union. In other instances, confederations of princely states, grouped on a regional basis, were absorbed as separate political units by the Union, as were a number of the larger states. In the case of the larger states, the acceding regimes surrendered control of foreign affairs, defense, and communications in exchange for a degree of autonomy in domestic matters. A number of disputes developed with respect to certain of the feudatories. For an account of the most serious of these disputes, see INDIA, UNION OF: *History;* PAKISTAN: *History;* HYDERABAD; KASHMIR. As constituted prior to partition, the native states of India were grouped for administrative purposes into twenty-three agencies and units: Assam, Baluchistan, Baroda, Bengal, Central India, Chhattisgarh, Cochin, Deccan and Kolhapur, Gujarat, Gwalior, Hyderabad, Kashmir and Feudatories, Madras, Mysore, North-West Frontier Province, Orissa, Punjab, Punjab Hill, Rajputana, Sikkim, Travancore, United Provinces, and Western India. Combined area of native states, 715,964 sq.m.; pop. (1941) 93,189,233.

INDIANA UNIVERSITY, a coeducational State institution of higher learning, opened in 1824 as the Indiana Seminary, at Bloomington, Ind. It was renamed the Indiana College in 1827, and became a university in 1838. Enrollment was open only to men until 1867, when women were also admitted. In addition to the main establishment at Bloomington, the university maintains a large branch at Indianapolis, and extension centers in several other cities. Courses are offered in liberal arts, fine arts, sciences, medicine, dentistry, nursing, law, business administration, physical education, and social service; baccalaureate, master's, and doctoral degrees are conferred. By arrangement made by Indiana University with Purdue University, law students who require a background in engineering may study for three years at Purdue and then for three years at Indiana, earning the degrees of Bachelor of Science in Engineering Law and Bachelor of Law. In a recent year, the faculty of Indiana University consisted of about 1080 persons, and more than 17,500 students were enrolled.

 INDIAN BEAN. See CATALPA.

 INDIAN CAUCASUS. See HINDU KUSH.

INDIAN CRESS. See TROPAEOLUM.

INDIAN CURRANT. See SNOWBERRY.

INDIAN FIG. See BANYAN.

INDIAN HEMP. See HEMP; DOGBANE.

INDIAN LANGUAGES, the languages of the Indian subcontinent. According to an official linguistic survey completed in 1937, the number of languages and dialects spoken in India totals 203. Two major families of languages, the Indo-European and Dravidian, represent the speech of about ninety-six percent of the population. More than a quarter of a billion people speak languages belonging to the Sanskritic group of the Indic branch of the Indo-European family (see INDO-IRANIAN LANGUAGES). In point of time, this group of languages covers a period extending from at least 1000 B.C. to the present day, a history which is often divided into three main divisions: (1) *Old Indian,* comprising the earliest Vedic dialect and the dead tongue, Sanskrit (q.v.); (2) *Middle Indian,* which embraces Prakrit and Pali (q.v.); and (3) *New Indian,* comprising the modern Sanskritic languages of the northern and central parts of the peninsula. In the order of importance, these modern languages include Western Hindi (q.v.) and the related Hindustani (q.v.) dialects (which have become the lingua franca of northern India); Bengali; Bihari and the related Bhojpuri, Magahi, and Maithili dialects; Panjabi; Marathi and the related Konkani dialect; Rajasthani; Gujarati and the related Bhili dialect; Oriya; Eastern Hindi and its related dialects; Sindhi; and Assamese. Another group of the Indic branch, Dardic, also embraces several Indian languages, notably Shina and Kafiri.

The Dravidian (q.v.) languages, confined mainly to the southern section of the peninsula, are spoken by about 67,000,000 people. The four main literary languages of s. India, Telugu, Tamil, Kanarese, and Malayalam, are members of this family, as are a large number of dialects spoken by the central Indian hill tribes.

Kherwari, a branch of the Munda division of the Austroasiatic family of languages, is spoken by approximately 4,000,000 inhabitants of central India. An outlying group of languages, belonging to the Indo-Chinese family, is spoken in a large number of dialects and languages by about 13,000,000 people living around or outside the borders of India from Tibet to Burma.

 INDIAN LITERATURE. See SANSKRIT LITERATURE.

INDIAN-MEAL MOTH. See ENTOMOLOGY, ECONOMIC.

INDIAN MUTINY or **SEPOY MUTINY,** a rebellion against British authority in India, extending from May, 1857, to July, 1859. Begun as an uprising of the native troops (sepoys) in the Bengal army of the East India Company (q.v.), the rebellion climaxed a protracted period of popular unrest. The general hostility to British rule had been aggravated by a variety of factors, including systematic annexation of Indian territory by the East India Company and the failure of British civil and military officials to respect Hindu and Moslem religious customs. Of primary importance among immediate causes of the outbreak was the discovery by the sepoys that the cartridges used in the muzzle-loading Enfield rifle were greased with tallow and lard, respectively taboo among the Hindus and Moslems. Inasmuch as the sepoys had to remove the greased Minie ball (bullet) from the cartridge casing with their teeth in order to load the rifle, they became profoundly resentful. Agitation against the cartridges spread throughout the army, and several mutinous incidents occurred at scattered military stations.

In February, 1857, the troops of a native battalion at Berhampur refused to load their rifles. The battalion was disbanded. On May 10, 1857, the native garrison at Meerut, a station near Delhi, mutinied in protest against the imprisonment of several comrades who had refused to touch cartridges. The mutineers killed their officers, liberated the imprisoned soldiers and massacred most of the Europeans in the vicinity. Following the action at Meerut, the mutineers advanced on Delhi. Their arival early the next morning precipitated a general uprising in the city. The local sepoys murdered their officers and, with the help of native civilians, slaughtered all Europeans and Christians within the city. Rallying around the banner of Bahadur Shah II, titular emperor of the moribund Mogul Empire, natives throughout the whole of the Bengal Presidency joined the revolt. British-trained troops of the larger native states, the discontented inhabitants of annexed territories, and other large sections of the population also joined the rebellion.

One of the principal leaders of the insurrection was Nana Sahib, whose claims as the adopted son of Baji Rao II, last Peshwa of Poona, had not been recognized by the British authorities. At the end of June, General Sir Hugh Wheeler, commander of the military station at Cawnpore, was forced to surrender, with about 450 men and 330 women and children, to Nana Sahib. Despite Sahib's promise of safe conduct by boat to Allahabad, all of the male captives were immediately massacred. The women and children were killed on July 15, when Sahib learned of the approach of Sir Henry Havelock from Allahabad with a relieving force. The next day Havelock defeated the mutineers and entered Cawnpore. The British Residency at Lucknow (see LUCKNOW, BATTLE OF), which had been besieged since June 30, was relieved by Sir Colin Campbell on Nov. 17. Meanwhile, in September, Delhi had been retaken by British and loyal native troops. By June, 1858, no city or fortress of any importance remained in the hands of the mutineers, although savage fighting continued in various regions into 1859. The capture and execution of the able rebel leader, Tantia Topi, a Maratha Brahman, in April, 1859, marked the end of effective native resistance. Bahadur Shah II, the last of the Moguls, had been convicted in 1858 by the judicial authorities of the East India Company on charges of rebellion and sentenced to life imprisonment. The immediate consequence of the mutiny was the transfer of governmental authority in India from the East India Company to the British crown. See INDIA: *History*.

INDIAN MYTHOLOGY. The myths of India, as exemplified in the ancient hymns of the *Vedas* (q.v.), the oldest sacred writings of the Hindus (see HINDUISM), represent an earlier stage of mythological thought than that found in any other literary remains of the Indo-European peoples. Myths abound in the *Rig-Veda*, the most ancient and most important of the four Vedic compilations. These myths are the outgrowth of personifications of the powers of nature. Among the chief divinities of the earlier Hindu pantheon are Agni, god of the sacrificial altar fire; Indra, god of the thunderbolt and the rain, and the rewarder of faithful men; Marut, a god of the storm; Mitra, a god of the sun; Soma, god of the intoxicating beverage made from the East Indian soma vine; Surya, another god of the sun; Ushas, goddess of the dawn; Vayu, god of the wind; and Yama, a deified mortal, the first of the race of men to die, and therefore made ruler and judge of the deceased. In later Hindu mythology the deities of the old order are gradually supplanted by the great *Trimurti,* or triad, composed of Brahma (the Creator), Vishnu (the Preserver), and Siva (the Destroyer). Also occupying the later pantheon are several subordinate divinities, godlings, or demigods, such as Ganesa, the elephant-headed god of prudence; Karttikeya or Skanda, god of war; Kubera, god of wealth; Durga (the implacable one), a malignant goddess, one of the multiple identities of Devi, the mother of the universe; Lakshmi, goddess of beauty and affluence; and Sarasvati, goddess of speech, music, and learning. Parallels along etymological lines have been drawn between the mythological figures of India and those of the Greek and Roman pantheons. Thus the Sanskrit *Dyaus pitr* (Heaven father) is the Greek *Zeus pater,* and the Latin *Jupiter,* a corruption (apparently through elision) of the Greek form. See SANSKRIT LITERATURE; INDIAN RELIGIONS; and separate articles on most of the individual deities.

INDIAN OCEAN, the vast body of salt water bounded on the w. by Africa, on the N. by Asia, and on the E. by Australia and the Australasian islands. A Southern, or Antarctic, Ocean is no longer recognized, since the existence of an antarctic land mass has been established. There is, therefore, no natural line of demarcation to separate the Indian from the Atlantic Ocean. A line about 2500 miles long on the twentieth meridian E. of Greenwich, connecting Cape Agulhas at the southern end of Africa and the Antarctic Continent, is generally taken to be the boundary which separates the Indian from the Atlantic Ocean. The total area of the ocean is about 28,000,000 sq.m. The Indian Ocean narrows toward the north, and is divided by the Indian peninsula into the Bay of Bengal on the east and the Arabian Sea on the west; the latter sends two arms northward, the Persian Gulf and the Red Sea. The mean depth of the water is about 13,800 ft., or slightly greater than that of the Atlantic; the greatest depth thus far ascertained is 22,968 ft. at latitude 10° 15′S, longitude 108° 5′E. In general, the greatest depths are in the northeastern part, where about 50,000 sq.m. of the ocean floor lie at a depth of over 18,000 ft.

From Africa the Indian Ocean receives the waters of the Limpopo and Zambezi rivers, and from Asia those of the Irrawaddy, Brahmaputra, Ganges, Indus, and Shatt al Arab rivers. It contains numerous islands, chiefly in the northern and western regions; of these Madagascar and Ceylon are the only ones of considerable magnitude. As a rule, the winds over the Indian Ocean are gentle, with frequent protracted calms; hurricanes occur occasionally (see MONSOONS).

INDIAN PAINTBRUSH. See PAINTED CUP.

INDIAN PEOPLES, the prehistoric and historic peoples of the Indian subcontinent, including both indigenous (e.g., pre-Dravidian) and invading (e.g., Indo-Aryan) races. The exact origins of these peoples are in most cases impossible to determine, but ethnologists and archeologists have traced successive waves of invasion and assimilation, some of which occurred in comparatively recent, historical times, and a classification of no less than eight distinct surviving racial strains has been set up for modern India.

Modern Races of India. The eight types listed below represent both pure races and hybrid results of centuries of intermarriage. In some cases, such as Dravidian (q.v.), a single name is used to cover peoples of diverse cultures and languages; in each case, the racial names are used to distinguish distinct somatological types. These types, with the areas in modern India where they are chiefly found, are as follows. (1) The aboriginal inhabitants, often called pre-Dravidian, represented by short, platyrrhinian Negroid peoples now found in scattered primitive tribes of the hills and jungles, such as the Santals and Irulas (qq.v.). (2) The Dravidians, now occupying the southern part of the subcontinent from Ceylon to the valley of

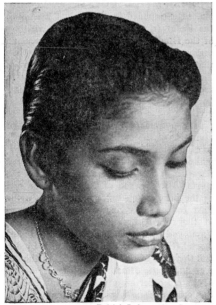

British Information Services

Aryo-Dravidian girl of India

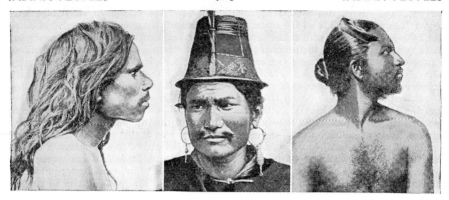

INDIAN PEOPLES. *From left to right: Pre-Dravidian; Mongoloid; Dravidian.*

the Ganges River. (3) The Indo-Aryans, now found mainly in Kashmir, with smaller populations in Rajputana and the Punjab. (4) The Hindustani-speaking peoples of the Ganges River valley, sometimes called Aryo-Dravidians, and consisting of mixtures of pure Dravidian strains with those of Indo-Aryan colonists to the west. (5) The hybrid peoples resulting from mixtures of Dravidians with Scythian strains from the north, sometimes called Scytho-Dravidian, and living east of the Indus River as far south as the western part of Bombay. (6) The Turko-Iranian peoples of the northwest, representing a mixture of peoples of s.w. Asia and Asia Minor, and living west of the Indus River in the regions around the northwest frontier. (7) The Mongoloid peoples of the northeast, stemming from China and Tibet, and living in Burma, Assam, and on the foothills of the eastern Himalayas. (8) Mixtures of these Mongoloid peoples with Dravidians and, among the upper classes, with some Indo-Aryan elements, represented typically by the Bengalis, and often called Mongolo-Dravidians.

Invasions and Settlements in India. The anthropological history of India includes a number of successive invasions and acculturations of disparate races. The pre-Dravidian aborigines, consisting of essentially Negroid peoples with occasional mixtures of Negrito and primitive Malayan strains, were invaded in prehistoric times by the Dravidians, who entered India from western Asia through Baluchistan and eventually made their way far to the south. Another, more limited prehistoric invasion was made at the northeastern frontiers by Mongoloid races, who, except for the mixtures called Mongolo-Dravidian, have remained in the area in which they entered

India. At a much later though still prehistoric period, when these infiltrations were substantially completed, another series of invading waves began to pour through the northwest passes. The first of these waves, which began about 2000 B.C., brought the Indo-Aryans to India, and established the eastern division of the Indo-European languages on Indian soil (see INDO-EUROPEANS). The next invasions occurred during historical times, when the Greeks under Alexander the Great penetrated as far as the Indus River. Subsequently Bactrian invasions had their effect in the northwest, and Scythian invasions in the northeast, and finally, from about 1000 to 1400 A.D., Mohammedan invasions resulted in Moslem domination of the west and northwest and the establishment of many dynasties in the principalities of those regions. More or less constant influences were those of the Pathans in the northwest and of the Indo-Chinese peoples in the northeast. Malayan elements were also present in the south; and a somewhat isolated group of Persian stock, the Parsis (q.v.), were of importance around Bombay. In the recent historical period, the dominant classes have been affected and infiltrated by the Dutch, Portuguese, French, and British, while on the other hand, the modern demand for coolie labor has caused mass emigrations to regions such as Madagascar, the West Indies, and Africa.

Relative Status of the Indian Peoples. At the earliest period to which historical records extend, the dominant peoples of India have been Hindu of the Indo-Aryan stock. The Indo-Aryans never overcame the land by mere force of numbers, however, and their influence upon the pre-Hindu population was less racial than social and religious (see HIN-

DUISM). The complicated system of caste (q.v.) is largely the result of the contact of the Indo-Aryan invaders with earlier populations (e.g., Dravidian) of the peninsula, and of the efforts of the conquering race to preserve its purity. The Dravidians, including the more or less civilized Kodagu, or Koorgs, and tribes such as those of the Nilgiri Hills, central India, and parts of Bengal, are the next most important peoples. These tribes display diverse levels of culture, from the jungle-dwelling Kurumbas (q.v.) to the highly civilized Tamils (q.v.), who have extended their influence to the north of Ceylon. Another important group is the Kolarian (q.v.) people of the Orissa-Bengal country and further inland. Finally, at the bottom of this scale, are such peoples as the Veddas of Ceylon, who are among the most primitive peoples now existing.

INDIAN PIPE, common name of *Monotropa uniflora,* a leafless herb belonging to the Heath family. It is native to deep, dark woods of North America and Asia. The plant grows 2 to 12 inches in height, and has a smooth stem which is usually white, but is occasionally flesh-colored or deep red. The flower, which appears in summer, has a calyx of bractlike scales, a corolla of scalelike petals, eight to ten awl-shaped stamens, and a solitary pistil; the flower is also usually white in color. The fruit is an ovoid, loculicidal capsule containing many minute seeds. Indian pipe is one of the very few flowering plants which lack chlorophyll and are consequently unable to manufacture their own food by the process of photosynthesis (q.v.). The plant obtains its organic nourishment by saprophytic dependence on rotting vegetable matter or by parasitic dependence on the roots of trees.

INDIAN RELIGIONS. From the earliest times India has been a land of numerous religions. The majority of the Indian people, approximately 85% of the entire population, acknowledge Hinduism and Brahmanism (qq.v.) as their faith. Prior to the partition of the Indian subcontinent into the dominions of India and Pakistan (qq.v.), Mohammedanism (q.v.), introduced into India in the 11th century A.D., was the second-largest religious grouping of the country. Among other notable Indian religions are Sikhism, Jainism (qq.v.), and Parsiism. Christians number about 6,000,000.

The major religious development of India falls into five general periods. The first is the Vedic era (see VEDA), in which the earliest religious ideas of the Aryan Hindus were formulated; the second is the period of classical Brahmanism, the ethical and metaphysical system expounded by an organized priesthood and set forth in the religious scriptures called *Brahmanas* and in the philosophical treatises known as *Upanishads;* the third is the period of the two great religious reforms, Buddhism (q.v.) and Jainism, both of which represented a reaction against decadent Brahmanism; the fourth period is that of Brahmanic counter-reform and a revitalized Hinduism, a broader and more catholic faith which sprang from the schismatic reform movements; and finally, the period of the multiplication of popular sects within the framework of the new Hinduism. The *Rig-Veda,* containing over a thousand hymns and prayers, and the *Atharva-Veda,* devoted to ritualistic spells, charms, and maledictions, represent the literature of the earliest period; the *Yajur-Veda,* comprising liturgical incantations and ceremonial formulas, is nearer to the second religious phase, that of sacerdotal Brahmanism; the sacred scriptures of the Buddhistic and Jainistic reformations are written respectively in Pali (q.v.) and Prakrit; and the great Sanskrit epic poems, the *Mahabharata* and the *Ramayana,* exemplify both the purer Brahmanic stage and the later sectarianism. For these sectarian tendencies the chief sources of information are the *puranas* (q.v.), treatises dealing with physical, astronomical, and theological questions, and the *tantras,* sacred scriptures containing demonic lore.

The chronology of the aforementioned periods cannot be established with any exactitude. In general, however, it is assumed that the Vedic period extended from remote antiquity down to about 1000 B.C., or a number of centuries thereafter, merging into the Brahmanic age, which closed perhaps around 500 B.C. The age of Buddhism ranged from approximately 500 B.C. to 500 A.D., and the age of epic Hinduism covered roughly the same centuries. The era of Brahmanic counterreforms and of sectarianism ran from 500 to 1500, and since that time unifying tendencies have been increasingly operative. See INDIAN MYTHOLOGY; SANSKRIT LITERATURE.

INDIAN RESERVATIONS, in the U.S., tracts of land reserved from settlement and held in trust for Indian occupants. Such tracts are usually the residue of tribal claims after conquest or purchase. The practice of settling Indians on reservations, which provide them with homes and with lands for cultivation and at the same time keep them under the control of the government, was begun as early as the colonial period in American history; in 1786 this practice was confirmed as a national policy when the government set aside certain lands and guaranteed the titles of the Indians to them. These transactions were made by treaty, thus recognizing to some extent the independence of the Indian tribes; control over the Indians was subsequently extended by conquest, and the procedure for establishing reservations was simplified from time to time, finally being placed in the hands of the President, who now has the power of making allotments of land for reservations by executive order. All dealings with the Indians themselves are under the immediate control of Congress, and the administration of the reservations is delegated to the Office of Indian Affairs (see INDIAN AFFAIRS, OFFICE OF), an agency of the Department of the Interior. See also AMERICAN INDIANS.

INDIAN RICE. See WILD RICE.

INDIANS, AMERICAN. See AMERICAN INDIANS.

INDIAN TERRITORY, a former Territory of the United States, now included in the State of Oklahoma. Originally a part of the Louisiana Purchase, the Territory was set apart by an Act of Congress in 1829 for the use of Indians living E. of the Mississippi R. Through a treaty negotiated in 1834, the U.S. allocated the Territory to the Five Civilized Nations, i.e., the Cherokee, Chickasaw, Choctaw, Creek, and Seminole Indian tribes. The tribal authority of these tribes was guaranteed under the provisions of the treaty. By the provisions of treaties subsequently negotiated with the Five Civilized Nations by the U.S., other Indian tribes were admitted to the Territory. Meanwhile, the unoccupied w. portion of the Territory was settled by white Americans. Another unoccupied tract was purchased from the Indians by the Federal government in 1889, and opened to homesteaders. In 1890, the U.S. government authorized the establishment of Oklahoma Territory, which comprised the lands of the w. portion. As then delimited, Indian Territory covered an area of about 31,246 sq.m. The Dawes Commission, appointed by Congress in 1893 for the purpose of terminating the tribal ownership of lands in Indian Territory, secured the necessary agreements with the Five Civilized Nations, and by 1905 arrangements had been completed for the transfer of lands to individual Indian ownership. Other Congressional enactments gradually extended the authority of the U.S. government in Indian territory. On Nov. 16, 1907, Indian and Oklahoma territories were admitted to the Union as the State of Oklahoma. See OKLAHOMA.

INDIAN TOBACCO. See LOBELIA.

INDIA, PORTUGUESE. See PORTUGUESE INDIA.

INDIA, UNION OF or **BHARAT,** republic of Asia, situated in the subcontinent of India (q.v.) and comprising, with Pakistan (q.v.), the territories formerly included in British India (q.v.) and the Native States of India (see INDIA, NATIVE STATES OF). Under the provisions of the Indian Independence Act, an enactment of the British Parliament which became effective on August 15, 1947, India and Pakistan were established as independent dominions of the British Commonwealth of Nations, with the right to withdraw from or remain within the Commonwealth. The Indian government, by the terms of a declaration issued jointly by the eight members of the British Commonwealth of Nations on April 28, 1949, elected to retain its membership in the Commonwealth of Nations. Unlike the other members of the Commonwealth, however, the Union is a sovereign republic, with symbolic rather than formal allegiance to the British crown.

The new states or India and Pakistan were created along religious lines, with areas inhabited predominantly by Hindus being allocated to India and areas inhabited predominantly by Moslems being allocated to Pakistan. Inasmuch as the overwhelming majority of the population of the Indian subcontinent are Hindus, partition resulted in the inclusion within the Union of India of most of the 562 princely states in existence prior to August 15, 1947, of a majority of the British provinces, and of parts of three of the remaining provinces. The status of certain of the princely states, notably Kashmir (q.v.), was in dispute or subject to international adjudication following partition.

Excluding Kashmir, which, with other disputed areas, is dealt with in the *History* section of this article, the Union of India consists, in physical geography, of the entire Indian peninsula except Portuguese India and French India (qq.v.) and of large portions of the central, N. central, and N.E. mainland.

The Union of India is composed of ten "Part A" States, eight "Part B" States, ten "Part C" States, a "Part D" Territory, and a Protectorate. Each of the Part A States consists primarily of a former province or part of a province of British India; certain of these States include varying numbers of former princely states; and each is administered by a governor who is an appointee of the Union government. The Part A States are Andhra, Assam, Bihar, Bombay, Madhya Pradesh, Madras, Orissa, Punjab, Uttar Pradesh, and West Bengal.

Each of the Part B States consists of either a former princely state of major size or a union of former princely states. Nominal executive authority in the Part B States is vested in a *rajpramukh*, an hereditary prince, but actual power is exercised by a cabinet responsible to the State legislature. The Part B States are Hyderabad, Jammu and Kashmir (claimed by Pakistan), Madhya Bharat, Mysore, Patiala and East Punjab States Union, Rajasthan Union, Saurashtra Union, and Travancore-Cochin.

Each of the Part C States is a centrally administered area consisting of either a former chief commissionership of British India, or a small former princely state, or a group of former princely states. Executive authority in the Part C States is vested in a chief commissioner who is an appointee of the Union government. The Part C States are Ajmer, Bhopal, Bilaspur, Coorg, Delhi, Himachal Pradesh, Kutch, Manipur, Tripura, and Vindhya Pradesh.

The Part D Territory consists of the Andaman Islands and the Nicobar Islands. Executive authority is vested in a centrally appointed chief commissioner. The Protectorate is the princely state of Sikkim.

The capital of the Union of India is New Delhi and Bombay (qq.v.), a leading seaport, is the largest city in population (1951). The principal seaport and second-largest city in population is Calcutta (q.v.). Besides Bombay and Calcutta, the Union of India has ten cities with populations (1951) over 400,000. In descending order of size these cities are Madras, Hyderabad, Delhi, Ahmadabad, Bangalore, Kanpur, Poona, Lucknow, Nagpur, and Howrah. There are six cities with populations between 300,000 and 400,000, fourteen cities with populations between 200,000 and 300,000, and forty-one cities with populations between 100,000 and 200,000. The population (1951) of India, excluding the Part B State of Jammu and Kashmir and certain parts of Assam, is 356,829,485. Hindus comprise the vast majority of the population. The area of the Union, including Jammu and Kashmir, is 1,269,640.

Physical Features. See INDIA: *Physical Features.*

Climate. See INDIA: *Climate.*

Flora and Fauna. See INDIA; *Flora and Fauna.*

Natural Resources. The Union of India contains more than two thirds of the entire area of the subcontinent, including a major portion of the fertile Indo-Gangetic plain. Besides extensive cultivable regions, a comprehensive network of irrigation facilities, and valuable stands of timber, the Union contains most of the known mineral deposits of the subcontinent. See INDIA: *Natural Resources.*

Production and Industry. Agricultural enterprises are the chief source of wealth of the Indian Union. In terms of area sown, the leading crop is rice, the staple foodstuff of a large section of the Indian population. In a typical year more than 75,000,000 acres are planted to this crop, and the average annual yield is between 25 and 35 million tons. China is the only country producing a larger harvest. Wheat ranks next in importance to rice as a crop, the yield in a recent year being about 6,600,000 tons. Other crops grown in large volume for domestic consumption are millet, gram, lentils, corn, barley, and many types of fruits and vegetables. In terms of cash value, tea ranks high among crops produced mainly for export; India is second only to China in the production of this commodity. The yield of tea in a recent year was nearly 300,000 tons. In the production of cotton the country ranks third in the world, being surpassed only by the United States and the U.S.S.R. The cotton harvest totaled about 588,000 tons in a recent year. India ranks second in the world (after Pakistan) in the production of jute. The recent annual yield of this crop, grown chiefly in the Bengal region, was nearly 600,000 tons. Among other important crops are rubber, coffee, sugar cane, linseed, sesamum, rape, groundnuts, turmeric, castor seed, aniseed, ginger, pepper, cinchona, and the poppy.

The raising of livestock, particularly horned cattle, buffaloes, horses, and mules, is a central feature of the agricultural economy of India. In a recent year the Indian Union had about 150,000,000 cattle, considerably more than any other country in the world. These animals, like the buffaloes, horses, and mules, are utilized almost exclusively as beasts of burden, mainly because meat consumption, owing to religious or social scruples, is taboo among the Hindus. As a result of such factors as inadequate pasturage and water supplies, the breeds of cattle of India are generally inferior. The number of buffaloes, which are largely employed in the deltaic regions, recently totaled nearly 40,000,000. In the dry regions of Punjab and Rajasthan camels are the principal beasts of burden. The total of these animals is about 650,000. According to a recent census, the combined total of sheep and goats, raised mainly for wool, numbered almost 80,000,000. The combined total of horses, mules, donkeys, and ponies was over 2,500,000. There were about 3,650,000 hogs and the poultry population totaled nearly 60,000,000.

The weaving of cotton fabrics, which are absorbed mainly by the domestic market, is the leading manufacturing industry of India. In a recent year the number of cotton spindles and looms in operation throughout the subcontinent totaled about 11,000,000 and 194,-500 respectively. The output of cotton fabrics amounted to 30,500 tons; the production of cotton yarn totaled 652,000 tons. The manufacture of jute products ranks next in importance to cotton weaving. Other important industries are carpet weaving, tea processing, rice processing, cotton ginning, flour milling, printing, petroleum refining, sugar refining, and the manufacture of lumber, woolen and silk goods, leather, electrical equipment, tile and bricks, linseed and other vegetable oils, paper, iron, brass, tobacco products, and railway equipment. India is renowned for the quality of various handmade products, including wood carvings, pottery, and brass, copper, and silver objects.

Communications. The Indian Union has an extensive network of railway lines. In a recent year the mileage of these lines, almost all of which are publicly owned and operated, totaled about 34,000. Standard-gauge trackage comprised about 15,700 m. of the total. The remainder consisted of narrow-gauge trackage. More than 1,307,000,000 passengers were transported by the Indian railway system in a recent year, and the volume of freight carried in the same year totaled 92,349,000 tons. The highway system of India comprised about 249,000 m. of roads, including more than 90,000 m. of first-class routes. The major Indian ports, including Calcutta and Bombay, are reached by cargo carriers and passenger liners operating to all parts of the world. A comprehensive network of Indian-operated air routes provides connections among the major cities and towns of the country. International connections are maintained by a number of Indian and foreign air-transport services. India has a modern postal system, including about 30,000 permanent post offices; an extensive telegraph system, with more than 113,-500 m. of lines; and a telephone system, which maintains about 4200 exchanges and nearly 180,000 telephones.

Commerce. Because India is largely dependent on foreign markets for various commodities including manufactured goods, raw materials, and foodstuffs, its import trade is extensive. Exports of indigenous products also are considerable, but an unfavorable balance of trade is a traditional feature of the Indian economy. The United States is the principal source of exports to India and the leading market for Indian goods is the United Kingdom. Other countries maintaining large-scale commercial relations with India include Pakistan, Iran, France, Belgium, the Netherlands, Burma, and Australia. Among the chief products imported into India are raw cotton, grain and pulse, motor vehicles, metals, machinery, cotton manufactures, vegetable oils, chemicals, paints, drugs and medicines, dyes, instruments, hardware, spices, raw silk, tobacco, liquors, paper and pasteboard, fruits, vegetables, and other foodstuffs. The major exports include jute manufactures, raw jute, raw cotton, cotton goods, tea, hides, oilseeds, rice, lac, raw wool, manganese ore, other ores and metals, fruits and vegetables, and tobacco. Under normal conditions, between 8500 and 9000 vessels operating in the foreign trade enter and clear Indian ports annually.

Education. According to a recent estimate approximately 80 percent of the total population of the Indian Union is illiterate. However, educational facilities have been improved and expanded in recent years in accordance with a comprehensive program adopted in 1944 and subsequently accepted, for the most part, by the Indian government. Among other things, the program provides for the eventual establishment of universal, compulsory primary education. The school systems of the various States are under the direct control of the State governments, but there is a Union Ministry of Education, which assists the State systems, directs the systems of the Centrally Administered Areas, provides financial help for the nation's institutions of higher learning, and discharges various other responsibilities.

Educational facilities in the Indian Union consist of "recognized" institutions, i.e., schools with officially credited standards and courses of study, and "unrecognized" institutions, i.e., schools that fail to fulfill these conditions. The official educational system comprises three general categories of schools, namely nursery, elementary, and secondary. Separate schools for males and females are maintained at the secondary level of the system. Native vernaculars are employed exclusively for the purposes of elementary instruction, which extends over a period of four to six years. Secondary institutions are divided into middle and high schools. Middle-school instruction, extending over a period of two to four years, is given in the native vernacular; pupils may elect to study English. The high-school course of study varies from two to four years. English is a compulsory subject in these schools.

In a recent year the elementary schools in the Indian Union numbered about 207,000; the combined enrollment was about 17,402,-000. Secondary schools totaled nearly 20,000, with an aggregate enrollment of more than 4,700,000. In the same year the country had a total of 282 training and professional colleges with a combined enrollment of about 58,000. In addition there were 470 colleges of arts and sciences and 28 universities with an aggregate of about 277,000 students. "Unrecognized" institutions of all types recently numbered almost 9100 and had a combined enrollment of 372,000.

Ethnology. See INDIAN PEOPLES.

Religion. See INDIAN RELIGIONS.

Languages. See INDIAN LANGUAGES.

Government. The Union of India is governed according to the provisions of the constitution of 1950, a document containing various features of the constitutional systems of the United Kingdom, the United States, and other Western democracies. By the terms of the Indian organic law, which proclaims the state a "Sovereign Democratic Republic", the Union government is federal in structure and republican in character. Like the United States, India is a union of States, but its government is more highly centralized than the U.S. government, and States' rights are rigidly limited, particularly with respect to Part C States. The Indian constitution is distinguished by several innovations. For example, in a section designated "Directive Principles of State Policy", it provides a series of propositions for the guidance of governmental policy on matters relating to the welfare of the Indian people. The "Directive Principles", which cannot be enforced by the courts, include an injunction against ". . . the concentration of wealth and the means of production to the common detriment".

In the chapter dealing with fundamental liberties, a section closely patterned after the U.S. Bill of Rights, the Indian constitution outlaws untouchability, prohibits double jeopardy, *ex post facto* laws, and discriminatory treatment of individuals on the basis of sex, race, religion, or caste, and guarantees freedom of worship, equal treatment of all religious organizations by the state, and freedom of speech and peaceable assembly. The free-speech guarantee does not include the right to offend decency or morality or to endanger state security. The foregoing and other fundamental rights guaranteed by the constitution are enforceable in the courts.

The constitution vests legislative authority in the Indian Union in a bicameral Parliament consisting of the House of the People, which is composed of 500 members, and the Council of States, which is composed of 250 members. Members of the House of the People, the lower house, are elected by direct adult suffrage from constituencies with at least 500,000 and not more than 750,000 inhabitants. Members normally serve for five years, the statutory limit for the duration of the House, but the House may be dissolved following defeat of major legislation proposed by the executive branch of the government. All except twelve members of the Council of States are elected by the elected members of the State legislatures. The twelve exceptions are presidential appointees, usually notables prominent in the arts and sciences. The Council is a permanent body; the terms of one third of its members expire biennially. Legislation involving revenue and appropriations is beyond the competence of the Council, and its powers are otherwise limited, especially with respect to control over enactments of the lower house.

The chief executive of the Indian Union is the president. His role in the government is largely nominal and ceremonial, however, for actual executive power resides in a Council of Ministers responsible to the House of the People. The president is elected for a five-year term by an electoral college consisting of the elected members of the national and State legislatures. He is eligible to succeed himself. Balloting in the electoral college is highly complicated, each member having a voting strength proportional to the population of his constituency. If a presidential vacancy occurs as the result of death or disability, the electoral college convenes within six months and elects a new president. In the interim the functions of the office are discharged by the vice-president. This official, who serves as exofficio chairman of the Council of States, is elected by the national legislature in joint session.

Screen Traveler, from Gendreau

SCENES IN INDIA. *Top: View of Shri Lakshminarian, a Hindu temple in New Delhi, from the gardens. Bottom: Ceremony in the court of a native prince, in Bharatpur, Rajasthan Union.*

The Council of Ministers, or Cabinet, is headed by a prime minister. Each of its members is the head of an administrative department of the central government. Cabinet ministers who are not members of one of the houses of the national legislature may not hold office for more than six months. They may speak in either house, but can vote only in the house in which they hold membership. In most important respects the Indian cabinet system is identical with that of the United Kingdom (see UNITED KINGDOM: *Government*).

Judicial authority in the Indian Union is exercised through a system of national courts which administer the laws of both the Union and the States. All judges are appointees of the executive branch of the government, but their independence is guaranteed by various safeguards. Noteworthy among the latter is a provision requiring a two-thirds vote of the national legislature to effect removal from office. At the apex of the judicial system is the Supreme Court. This body, consisting of seven members, is the highest court of appeal and the final arbiter on constitutional questions. Next in authority below the Supreme Court are the Part A and Part B State High Courts. Subordinate courts include Judicial Commissionerships, which function in the Part C States, Courts of Sessions, which have jurisdiction in criminal cases, Courts of Magistrates, and various minor and special courts.

History. (For an account of early, modern, and pre-partition Indian history, see INDIA: *History*.) By the terms of the Indian Independence Act, governmental authority in the newly established Union of India was vested in the Constituent Assembly, originally an all-India body created for the purpose of drafting a constitution for the entire nation. The all-India Constituent Assembly, which held its first session in December, 1946, was boycotted by the delegates of the Moslem League, the major political organization of Moslem nationalists; the remaining delegates, who were chiefly representative of the Indian National Congress, the corresponding Hindu organization, formed the Constituent Assembly of the Indian Union.

After the transfer of power from the British government the Constituent Assembly assigned executive responsibility to a cabinet, with Jawaharlal Nehru, a veteran leader of the Indian independence movement, as premier. Lord Louis Mountbatten, the last viceroy of India, became governor general of the new dominion.

The termination of British paramountcy in India was greeted enthusiastically by Indians of every religious faith and political persuasion. On August 15, 1947, officially designated Indian Independence Day, celebration ceremonies were held in all parts of India and in Indian communities abroad. These ceremonies took place, however, against an ominous background of Hindu-Moslem and Sikh-Moslem antagonism, which was particularly acute in regions equally or almost equally shared by members of the different faiths. In anticipation of border disputes in such regions, notably Bengal and Punjab, a boundary commission with a neutral (British) chairman was established prior to partition. The recommendations of this commission occasioned little active disagreement with respect to the division of Bengal. In that region, largely because of the moderating influence of Mohandas Karamchand Gandhi (q.v.), the spiritual leader of the Indian masses and elder statesman of the independence movement, little communal strife developed. In the Punjab, where the line of demarcation brought nearly 2,000,000 Sikhs, traditionally anti-Moslem, under the jurisdiction of Pakistan, the decisions of the boundary commission precipitated bitter fighting. A mass exodus of Moslems from Union territory into Pakistan and of Sikhs and Hindus from Pakistan into Union territory took place. In the course of the initial migrations, which involved more than 4,000,000 persons in the month of September alone, convoys of refugees were frequently attacked and massacred by fanatical partisans. Coreligionists of the victims resorted to reprisals against minorities in other sections of the Union and Pakistan. Union and Pakistan authorities brought the strife under control during October, but the shift of populations in Punjab and other border areas continued until the end of the year. Relations between the two states grew worse when, on October 6, the armed forces of the Union surrounded Junagadh, a princely state on the Kathiawar Peninsula. This action was taken because the Nawab of Junagadh, a state with a large majority of Hindus, had previously announced that he would affiliate with Pakistan. The Union military subsequently assumed control of the state, pending a plebiscite.

Kashmir, a princely state inhabited predominantly by Moslems, became the next major source of friction between the Union and Pakistan. On October 24, 1947, Moslem insurgents, supported by invading coreligion-

Screen Traveler, from Gendreau

View of the post office from across lake of Dalhousee Square, in Calcutta

ists from the North-West Frontier Province, proclaimed establishment of a "Provisional Government of Kashmir". Sir Hari Singh, the Maharaja of Kashmir and a Hindu, announced, on October 27, the accession of Kashmir to the Union of India. Approving the Maharaja's decision and promising a plebiscite after the restoration of peace, the Union government immediately dispatched troops to Srinagar, the capital of Kashmir and a major objective of the insurgents. Hostilities quickly attained serious proportions, and on January 1, 1948, the Union government filed a formal complaint with the Security Council of the United Nations, accusing Pakistan of giving help to the Moslem insurgents.

Despite repeated attempts by the Security Council to obtain a truce in the troubled area, fighting continued throughout 1948. The peace-making efforts of the Security Council finally met with success when, on January 1, 1949, the Union and Pakistan governments accepted proposals for a plebiscite, under the auspices of the United Nations, on the political future of Kashmir. Cease-fire orders were issued by the two governments on the same day. Among other things, the plan of the United Nations provided for the withdrawal

of combat troops from the state, for the return of refugees desirous of participating in the plebiscite, and for a free and impartial vote under the direction of a "personality of high international standing". On March 21, 1949, the United Nations Secretary General Trygve Lie appointed Admiral Chester William Nimitz (q.v.), U.S. Navy (retired), as administrator of the Kashmir plebiscite, scheduled for later in 1949.

Meanwhile, both the Union of India and Pakistan had suffered the loss of their outstanding leaders, and the Union government had become embroiled in a major dispute with the Nizam of Hyderabad, Sir Mir Osman Ali Khan Bahadur. Mohandas Gandhi was assassinated by a Hindu fanatic on January 30, 1948, and Mohammed Ali Jinnah (q.v.), the founder of Pakistan, died in the following September. The tension between the Union government and Hyderabad, inhabited preponderantly by Hindus, resulted from the reluctance of the Nizam, a Moslem, to bring his state into the Union. Protracted negotiations for a peaceful solution of the dispute ended in failure, and on September 17 the Union forces captured Hyderabad, the capital city, ending the Nizam's resistance. The ruler subsequently signed instruments of accession

Wide World Photo

Premier Jawaharlal Nehru of Union of India

making Hyderabad part of the Union of India.

Although India and Pakistan agreed (July 1949) on a line demarcating their respective zones of occupation in Kashmir, the two nations were unable to reconcile basic differences on the terms of the proposed plebiscite. The deadlock was due to several factors, mainly Indian insistence that Pakistani troops be withdrawn from the disputed territory prior to the plebiscite and Pakistan's refusal to withdraw its troops unless the Indians also withdrew. Attempts by the United Nations to arrange a compromise solution met with systematic failure.

The Indian Constituent Assembly approved a constitution for the Union on November 26, 1949. Comprising a preamble, 395 articles, and 8 schedules, the document proved to be more voluminous than any body of organic law in existence. One of the constitution's features is a clause outlawing untouchability, the ancient practice of caste (q.v.) that condemned about 40,000,000 Hindus to social and economic degradation. The Gandhi disciple and All-India Congress leader Rajendra Prasad was elected first president of the republic on January 23, 1950. As provided by the constitution, the republic was formally proclaimed on January 26. The Constituent Assembly then reconstituted itself as a provisional Parliament, and Jawaharlal Nehru was elected prime minister.

During its first year as a republic India figured with growing importance in international affairs, particularly in the deliberations and activities of the United Nations. Prime Minister Nehru's government, adhering to policies developed in the prerepublican period, maintained a generally neutral position with respect to the so-called "cold war", the mounting ideological and political struggle between the Soviet bloc of states and the Western democracies. Indian determination to avoid entanglement with either of these power groupings became increasingly apparent following the outbreak (June 25) of war in Korea. On June 29 the Indian government approved the U.N. Security Council resolution (adopted two days previously) invoking military sanctions against North Korea. No Indian troops were committed to the U.N. cause, however, and beginning on July 13, when Prime Minister Nehru dispatched notes on the Korean situation to the United States and the Soviet Union, India sought repeatedly to restore peace in the Far East. In its initial attempts at mediation the Indian government suggested that admission of the Chinese People's Republic to the United Nations was prerequisite to a solution of the Far Eastern crisis. India adhered to this view, which was rejected by a majority of the Security Council, after Red China intervened (October) in the Korean fighting and despite sharp differences with the neighboring regime over Tibet. On October 26, after a Chinese Communist army invaded Tibet, the Indian government dispatched a note to Red China expressing "surprise and regret". The ensuing correspondence was marked by an Indian declaration that the attack on Tibet endangered the friendly relations prevailing between India and China and by a Chinese charge that the Indian government's views on Tibet were prompted by "foreign influences hostile to China". In December India and twelve other Far Eastern and Middle Eastern nations appealed unsuccessfully to Red China for a truce in Korea. The Indian delegation to the General Assembly of the U.N. voted (February 1, 1951) with the Soviet bloc and Burma against an American-sponsored resolution condemning Red China as an aggressor.

Outstanding among domestic events during the first year of republican rule was a series of natural disasters, notably an extended drought in southern India and severe earthquakes and floods in Assam. About six million tons of grain and other foodstuffs were lost, according to an official estimate made in November. During the resultant famine large sections of the population were forced to subsist on a daily ration of two ounces of rice. India appealed to the United States on December 16 for $200 million worth of food. On February 12, 1951, U.S. President Harry S. Truman asked Congress to enact legislation providing two million tons of grain for Indian relief. Considerable opposition to the request developed in Congress, chiefly because of Indian policy on the Korean war. Indian restrictions on the export of certain strategic materials also provoked Congressional opposition to the relief measure. On May 1 Prime Minister Nehru declared that India would refuse to accept relief "with political strings attached". In June the U.S. Congress approved a $190-million relief loan to be repaid on terms acceptable to the Indian government. The first shipment of the two million tons of U.S. wheat purchased with loan funds arrived in Bombay on Aug. 7. Meanwhile Prime Minister Nehru had announced (July 7) that the government must encourage birth control in order to cope with the problem of a rapidly growing population and a food supply rendered inadequate by primitive agricultural methods and frequent natural disasters. On July 10 the government promulgated a five-year national development plan providing for expenditures of $3.8 billion, largely on irrigation and hydroelectric projects.

In the field of foreign relations during 1951, India signed (February) an agreement with Pakistan providing for full resumption of trade and exchanged trade and cultural missions with Communist China. In July the American educator Frank P. Graham, who had been appointed the U.N. Security Council mediator for Kashmir, arrived in New Delhi. His subsequent attempts to arrange a plebiscite in Kashmir met with failure because of disagreement between India and Pakistan on demilitarization of the disputed area. In a foreign policy statement (Nov. 4) Prime Minister Nehru, denying charges of Indian "neutralism", explained that India agreed with the Western objective of curbing aggression, but differed on the question of methods.

On Jan. 5, 1952, the Union government signed a Point Four agreement with the United States. The agreement, which made available $50 million in U.S. funds, was later supplemented by accords under which the Indian government would provide an additional $86 million. With particular emphasis on community agricultural projects, the agreements made possible the largest rural-development program in the world.

The results of the first general elections in the Indian Union were announced on March 1. Based on universal suffrage, the balloting had begun in October, 1951, and ended in February, 1952. The Indian National Congress, the party in power, won 364 out of 489 contested seats in the national legislature and was victorious in all but two of the States. The newly constituted Electoral College elected President Rajendra Prasad to the presidency for a full five-year term on May 6. Prime Minister Nehru declared (May 22) that the Indian Communist Party was counterrevolutionary and that India would never go the way of the Soviet Union and Communist China to achieve its ends. On July 1 agrarian reform became effective with the transfer of 60 million acres in Uttar Pradesh State from absentee ownership to the tenants and laborers working the land.

On June 9, 1952, India, which had boycotted the 1951 Japanese peace conference, signed a bilateral peace treaty with Japan. Among the provisions was a waiver of all reparations claims. During September the Union government accepted famine-relief shipments of food from Communist China and the Soviet Union, but only after both countries agreed to Indian stipulations against possible "political strings". An Indian-sponsored compromise resolution on the repatriation of Korean prisoners of war was approved by the U.N. General Assembly on Dec. 4. The resolution subsequently was made the basis of the Korean truce agreement (See UNITED NATIONS: *The Korean War*). On Dec. 8 India rejected an Anglo-American suggestion proposing direct negotiations with Pakistan on Kashmir.

The Union received additional U.S. Point Four assistance on Feb. 9, 1953. Indian estimates of its foreign-aid needs for the next three years totaled $1.31 billion. On May 5 the national legislature granted the government power to control all means of production and distribution and regulate all commodity prices. A new Indian State, known as Andhra (pop. about 20,000,000), was established on Oct. 1. Formed out of the coastal area of Madras, it is populated by Telugu-speaking Dravidians. Andhra is the first Indian State to be constituted on a linguistic basis.

The Indian Union figured significantly in international developments during 1953. An Indian general was named chairman of the

Neutral Nations Repatriation Commission provided for by the Korean armistice agreement (July 27). In this position, during the period of so-called explanations to unrepatriated prisoners, he perpetuated the Indian policy of neutrality, provoking accusations of partiality from both the U.N. and Communist commands. The issue of Indian participation in the projected Korean peace conference was decided (Aug. 27) when the U.N. General Assembly voted down a British-backed resolution inviting India to the conference. Subsequently the U.S. secretary of state termed Indian exclusion from the proposed peace parley the "price" of neutrality. On Nov. 15 India, responding to reports that the United States planned to grant military aid to Pakistan and to establish air bases there, warned that effectuation of such plans would be regarded as an unfriendly act. In December the U.S. government denied seeking air bases in Pakistan and stated that any military aid to that country would be on the scale of assistance going to Iran. Indian-Pakistani talks on plebiscite arrangements for Kashmir were terminated (Dec. 26) over disagreement on the number and composition of troops to be stationed there during the voting.

INDICOLITE. See TOURMALINE.

INDICTION. See CHRONOLOGY.

INDICTMENT, in criminal law in the United States, England, and a number of other countries, a formal, written accusation of crime against a person, presented by a grand jury to a court, and upon which the accused person is subsequently tried. The essential requisites of a valid indictment are that it contain a statement of the time and place of the commission of the offense and the material facts charged against the accused, and that it be found "a true bill" and be signed by the foreman of the grand jury. See GRAND JURY. Some legal historians trace to the Saxons the origin of the institution of the grand jury with which the process of making accusations by indictment is inseparably connected. Other authorities ascribe the origin of the grand jury, and, therefore, of indictments, to statutory enactments made in England in 1164 A.D. and known as the Constitutions of Clarendon; see CLARENDON, CONSTITUTIONS OF.

As an integral part of the grand-jury system, the process of indictment has long been regarded as a guarantee against arbitrary prosecution for offenses against the state. The Fifth Amendment to the United States Constitution provides "that no person shall be held to answer for a capital or otherwise infamous crime, unless on a presentment or indictment of a grand jury". Many of the State constitutions contain a similar provision applying to prosecutions in the State courts. The penal codes of the States generally specify that individuals charged with felonies or grave misdemeanors can be brought to trial only upon an indictment.

INDIGO, a blue dye, $C_{16}H_{10}N_2O_2$, formerly obtained from various plants, particularly the indigo plant (q.v.), and now made synthetically. It is obtained by hydrolysis of the glycoside indican which is contained in the indigo plant and related plants. The structure of indigo and its first synthesis were elaborated by J. F. Adolf Baeyer (q.v.). In dyeing practice, indigo is reduced to colorless indigo white, which is soluble in alkali, and the cloth to be dyed is impregnated with the alkali solution of indigo white. Upon oxidation the dye is precipitated within the cloth as blue indigo. Indigo is the most important vat dye used today. See DYESTUFFS.

INDIGO BUNTING or **INDIGO BIRD,** a common finch, *Passerina cyanea,* of E. United States, found in summer as far N. as Nova Scotia and as far W. as the Great Plains. The bird winters in Central America. The male is a deep indigo blue with black wings and tail; the female is pale brown above and grayish white below. The indigo bunting, which is about 5½ in. long, frequents low bushes and is an indefatigable singer. See BUNTING.

INDIGO PLANT, common name applied to leguminous herbs and shrubs of the genus *Indigofera,* belonging to the family Papilionaceae. The genus, which contains about four hundred species, is native to tropical and subtropical regions all over the world. The plants have pinnately compound leaves, and bear irregular pink or purple flowers composed of five sepals, five petals, ten stamens, and a single pistil. The fruit is a sickle-shaped, short, compressed pod. The indigo plant contains the glycoside indican, which can be broken down by a fermentative process to form glucose, and the dyestuff indigo (q.v.). The most widely cultivated species of indigo plant are *I. anil,* native to tropical America, *I. tinctoria,* which is cultivated in India, and *I. argentea,* native to Arabia and parts of N. Africa. Plants of the genus were once extensively cultivated in the East and West Indies, but not since the development of synthetic indigo.

INDIGO SNAKE. See GOPHER SNAKE.

INDIUM, a metallic element, symbol In, atomic number 49, atomic weight 114.76. It was discovered spectroscopically in 1863 by the German chemists Theodor Richter and Ferdinand Reich. Indium ranks sixty-fourth in order of abundance of the elements in the earth's surface. It never occurs native, and is usually found as the sulfide, In_2S_3, in certain zinc blendes, and in tungsten, tin, and iron ores. Indium is a soft, silver-white, malleable, ductile metal with a specific gravity of 7.3, m.p. 155° C. (311° F.), b.p. 1450° C. (2642° F.). It resembles aluminum in chemical properties and forms mostly trivalent salts. It is used as an alloying agent with nonferrous metals; a thin surface layer of indium alloy is used on certain highly stressed bearings, such as aircraft-engine master-rod bearings.

INDIVIDUALISM, in political and economic theory, the doctrine, promulgated by such writers as the English philosopher Thomas Hobbes and the English economist Adam Smith (qq.v.), that society is an artificial device, existing only for the sake of its members as individuals, and properly judged only according to criteria set up by them as individuals. Individualism differs from socialist or collectivist theories not so much in setting a high value upon the well-being and free initiative of the individual, as in subordinating the demands of the community as a whole to individual welfare. An individualist does not necessarily subscribe to the ethical doctrine of egoism (q.v.); he may be guided in his political and economic thinking by motives of altruism (q.v.), holding that the end of social, political, and economic organization is the greatest good of the greatest number; what characterizes such an individualist is his conception of the "greatest number" as composed of independent units, and his opposition to the interference of the state with the happiness or freedom of these units.

In all the sciences which deal with man as a social being, individualistic tendencies or theories play a part. Practical distinctions between individualism and its antitheses (such as socialism) are, however, often difficult to make; the differences are usually differences of degree, and the terms are used loosely or with constant changes of meaning, and often with overtones of reproach or praise.

INDOCHINA, known also as FARTHER INDIA, the s.e. peninsula of Asia. In political geography, Indochina consists of the Union of Burma, an independent republic; the Associated States of Indochina, within the French Union; Siam, an independent monarchy; and

Indigo (Indigofera tinctoria)

the Federation of Malaya, a British protectorate. Each of the foregoing is the subject of a separate article.

INDOCHINA, ASSOCIATED STATES OF, formerly FEDERATION OF INDOCHINA, frequently FRENCH INDOCHINA, popularly INDOCHINA, group of three semiautonomous states within the French Union (q.v.), situated on the s.e. peninsula of Asia, and bounded on the N. by China, on the E. and s.e. by the South China Sea, on the s.w. by the Gulf of Thailand, and on the w. by Thailand (Siam). French Indochina consists of Cambodia and Laos, both constitutional monarchies, and of Viet-Nam, a unitary state nominally composed of Annam, Cochin China, and Tonkin provinces. Large sections of these provinces (in recent official styling known as Central Viet-Nam, South Viet-Nam, and North Viet-Nam respectively) are under the control of the anti-French, communist-led Republic of Viet-Nam. (For additional data on physical features, resources, industries, and histories, and for other information regarding the Associated States, see articles dealing with the separate entities; see also ANNAM, COCHIN CHINA, and TONKIN.) Area of Associated States, 285,794 sq.m.; pop. (1949 est.) 27,030,000.

The chief cities of French Indochina are Saigon (q.v.), capital of Viet-Nam and administrative center of Cochin China; Hanoi (q.v.), administrative center of Tonkin; Haiphong (q.v.), principal seaport of Tonkin; Hué (q.v.), administrative center of Annam; Pnom-Penh (q.v.), capital of Cambodia; and Vientiane (pop., about 14,000), capital of Laos.

Industry and Commerce. The principal industries of French Indochina are agriculture, fishing, and mining. Rice is the main crop, the southern part of Viet-Nam being one of the most important rice-growing regions in the world. The harvest in a recent year was about 6,000,000 tons. Other crops include rubber, sugar cane, tobacco, coffee, corn, raw silk, cotton, tea, kapok, medicinal plants, spices, and fruits. The forests, aggregating about 76,500,000 acres, yield tropical hardwoods and bamboo. Among the leading minerals are anthracite coal, bauxite, tungsten, phosphates, gold, zinc, tin, iron, manganese, salt, and cement gravel. In a recent year about 624,000 metric tons of coal were mined. Rice milling, cement making, and saw milling are the chief manufacturing industries; small-scale enterprises, mainly engaged in producing commodities for domestic consumption, include sugar refining, distilling, and the manufacture of silk and cotton textiles, soap, matches, and tobacco products. In the communist-occupied sections of Viet-Nam the manufacture of military equipment is an important industry.

Under the terms of an agreement signed in 1950, the Associated States perpetuated the customs union of 1887, an arrangement instituted by the French. The principal exports during a recent year in descending order of value were rubber, rice, corn, hides, fish, and dried vegetables; exports of rubber and rice totaled about 53,000 and 359,000 metric tons respectively. In descending order of value textiles, machinery, metals and metal products, motor vehicles, petroleum and petroleum products, and paper were recently the major imports. Exports during the year under review were valued at $135,800,000; imports were valued at $306,000,000. France, the other countries of the French Union, and the United States are the leading export markets; France supplies most of the imports.

Communications. The railroad systems of the Associated States have a combined length of almost 2100 m., but many sections of the systems were damaged or captured by the Viet-Nam republicans during hostilities with the French. Approximately 800 m. of maintrack lines were in operation in a recent year. In the same year surfaced highways aggre-

gating about 4200 m. in length were open to traffic in those sections of the Associated States not under communist occupation. Secondary roads, including roads in communist-held areas, totaled about 8700 m. There is an extensive network of inland waterways, notably about 3500 m. in Cochin China and nearly 900 m. in Cambodia; in addition the Mekong R., the largest river of French Indochina, is navigable s. of Luangprabang (pop. about 15,000), Laos. Domestic air lines link many of the cities and towns. Other communications facilities include about 18,000 m. of telephone lines and 3100 m. of telegraph lines.

People, Language, and Religion. Annamese, a Mongoloid people with a Chinese culture, comprise the overwhelming majority of the population of Viet-Nam, the most densely populated of the Associated States. Cambodia is inhabited mainly by Khmer, a people of uncertain racial origins. The principal ethnic group of Laos is Thai, who belong to the same racial and linguistic stock as the inhabitants of Thailand. Various remote areas of French Indochina are inhabited by aboriginal and Mongoloid tribes. Annamese, Khmer, and French are the predominant languages, and Buddhism is the predominant religion. About 4 percent of the population is Christian, chiefly Roman Catholic.

Government. Under the provisions of agreements concluded in 1949 between France and Cambodia, Laos, and Viet-Nam, each of the Associated States is a semiautonomous component of the French Union. Each of the three governments has nominal jurisdiction over internal affairs; foreign relations and national-defense matters are controlled by the French Union. The three states are linked by certain federal arrangements, including the customs union and a common fiscal policy. Co-ordination of federated services and administration of the foreign and defense policies of the French Union are the responsibility of a high commissioner and commander in chief. This official, an appointee of the French government, is assisted by eight counsellors and by three commissioners of the republic, his representatives in the respective states. Each of the states is entitled to representation in the National Assembly of France and in the High Council of the French Union.

History. French missionaries were active in Indochina as early as 1615. Beginning in 1772 the Annamese Empire, embracing most of the region included in the present-day Associated States, was torn by successive dynastic dis-

Ewing Galloway

Cambodian dancing girls in Pnom-Penh, the capital of Cambodia, Indochina

putes and civil wars. In 1787 the French missionary Pigneau de Behaine, Bishop of Adran, arranged a treaty between King Louis XVI and Prince Gia Long (d. 1820), deposed claimant to the Annamese throne; in exchange for guarantees of privileges in Annam France promised to aid Gia Long against his enemies. Partly in consequence of the French Revolution Gia Long received no effective help until 1798; in that year he ascended the throne of Annam. By 1801 he had added Tonkin and Cochin China to his dominions.

Gia Long's successors refused to continue the privileges granted to the French. During the first half of the 19th century Annamese kings relentlessly persecuted French missionaries and native converts to Christianity. In 1861 a French expeditionary force began a campaign to subdue Cochin China. The three eastern provinces of Cochin China were ceded to France in 1862, Cambodia soon afterward became a French protectorate, and the three western provinces of Cochin China were seized in 1867. The French subjugated part of Tonkin, including Hanoi, in 1873–74. Under the terms of a treaty concluded (1874) by France and the Annamese ruler, France relinquished Hanoi but obtained important concessions, especially recognition of its sovereignty over Cochin China. In 1883, following an insurrection in Tonkin, both Annam and Tonkin were placed under French protection by the provisions of another treaty imposed on the Annamese ruler. The Chinese government,

having protested vainly against French penetration of Tonkin, began (1883) to extend military aid to Indochinese guerrillas in that area. In June, 1884, by the Treaty of Hué, the Annamese ruler granted France the right to occupy any part of his realm. Friction between China and France over the Indochinese question culminated the same month in undeclared war. The hostilities, marked by French destruction of the Foochow arsenal and by a Chinese victory over French troops in N.E. Tonkin, were terminated on June 9, 1885, by the Treaty of Tientsin. China recognized the validity of the Treaty of Hué and France agreed to respect the Chinese-Tonkin frontier.

In 1887 the French government united Cochin China Colony with Annam-Tonkin and Cambodia for administrative purposes; both the Cambodian and Annamese rulers retained nominal authority in their respective realms, but actual governmental control was vested in a French governor general. The colony and protectorates were officially designated *Union Indo-Chinoise* (Indochinese Union). Indochinese insurgents continued to resist French rule for nearly a decade after the merger.

Laos and part of Luangprabang, kingdoms over which the Annamese crown claimed sovereignty, were taken forcibly from Siam by France in 1893 and made a protectorate within the Indochinese Union. In 1898 France obtained from China a 99-year lease of Kwangchowan, a coastal area on the Luichow Peninsula; this territory was attached to the Union for administrative purposes. The final territorial acquisitions of France in the Indochinese region were the remainder of Luangprabang, seized in 1904, and Battambang, a Cambodian town which had been ceded to Siam in 1809. Siam was forced to return the town to Cambodia in 1907.

After consolidating their power in Indochina the French initiated many administrative and juridical reforms. In addition railroads, highways, canals, and port facilities were extended, agriculture was modernized, and large areas were opened to exploitation. Dissatisfaction with French rule persisted, however, particularly among the Annamese. In 1930–31 a series of uprisings, supported by nationalists and communists, took place in Tonkin. The outbreaks were vigorously quelled, but the Annamese revolutionary movement continued to gain momentum.

French capitulation (June, 1940) to Germany in World War II had serious repercussions in Indochina. Shortly before its collapse France had been forced to yield important economic concessions to Japan, particularly prohibitions on Sino-Indochinese trade. Japanese military forces occupied strategic areas in Tonkin in September, 1940. Encouraged by Japan, Siam invaded the Indochinese Union in January, 1941. The French government, then a pro-Axis regime headed by Marshal Henri Philippe Pétain; accepted (March, 1941) a Japanese-mediated peace settlement; part of Cambodia and all of Laos w. of the Mekong R. were ceded to Siam.

By the terms of an agreement (July 29, 1941) between the Pétain and Japanese governments the Indochinese Union became virtually a Japanese protectorate. The agreement included provisions for Japanese occupation of numerous strategic areas. Japan subsequently invaded the Malay Peninsula from bases in the s. part of the Union.

The Indochinese government, abandoning traditional administrative procedures in favor of the highly centralized system prevailing in France, grew increasingly dictatorial as the war progressed. Its arbitrary methods and its subservience to Japan engendered profound discontent among the Indochinese, and as a consequence the nationalist movement gained broad popular support.

In August, 1944, following the liberation of most of German-occupied France by Allied armies, the Provisional Government of the French Republic voided the Indochinese governor general's "power to collaborate with Japan". This pronouncement had no tangible effect on the political situation in Indochina. On March 9, 1945, the Japanese government, striving to expand its "Co-Prosperity Sphere" in Asia, proclaimed the independence of the Indochinese Union. The governor general and other French authorities were placed under arrest, and French garrisons in various areas were disarmed. Later in March the French government announced that the Indochinese would be granted "virtual economic autonomy" and partial self-government after the defeat of Japan.

Kwangchowan was returned to China by France on August 18, 1945, shortly after the unconditional surrender of Japan. On August 22 the Allied powers divided the Indochinese Union into northern and southern occupation zones, to be held by Chinese and British troops respectively pending the arrival of French forces.

Viet Minh, an Indochinese coalition political party composed of nationalists and communists, forced the Annamese emperor Bao Dai (1913–   ) to abdicate on August 24; four days later Viet Minh proclaimed the establishment of the Republic of Viet-Nam, consisting of Annam, Tonkin, and Cochin China. The Russian-trained communist Ho Chi Minh (1891–   ), head of Viet Minh, was elected president of the republic. Bao Dai was appointed his "supreme adviser". Among major problems confronting the new government were economic chaos, severe floods in Tonkin, and famine throughout N. Viet-Nam. Deaths from starvation in this area totaled between 600,000 and 2,000,000 during 1945, according to reliable estimates.

Republican forces in N. Indochina obtained large quantities of Japanese military equipment. Thus strengthened and by virtue of the neutral policy of the Chinese occupation army, Viet-Nam soon won *de facto* control of Annam and Tonkin. In Cochin China the British occupation army, reinforced by commandeered Japanese military units, refused to recognize Viet-Nam authority. The British launched a vigorous offensive against the revolutionary regime. Within a few weeks Saigon and other parts of Cochin China were cleared of republican troops, and following the arrival (October, 1945) of French occupation contingents the campaign against Viet-Nam partisans in s. Indochina was intensified.

On January 6, 1946, Cambodia and France signed a *modus vivendi* which provided domestic autonomy for the protectorate pending the preparation and adoption of a definitive treaty. Parliamentary elections were held in Viet-Nam the same day. Viet Minh, basing its appeal to the electorate mainly on promises of national independence and agrarian reforms, won an overwhelming victory.

Protracted negotiations between Vietnamese and French leaders led to the adoption (March 6) of an armistice agreement recognizing Viet-Nam as a "free state having its own government, its parliament, its army, and its finances within the framework of the Indochinese Federation and the French Union" and providing for a referendum in Cochin China for the purpose of determining whether that colony should become an autonomous state or part of Viet-Nam. Under another provision of the agreement French troops were allowed to occupy positions in N. Viet-Nam. Cochin China was constituted an autonomous republic within the Indochinese Federation and the French Union on June 1.

The unilateral action of the French in Cochin China provoked deep hostility among Vietnamese extremists and impeded Franco-Viet-Nam negotiations (begun in Paris in July) to implement the March accord. In August, while the negotiations were still in progress, representatives of Laos, Luangprabang, and France signed a provisional agreement amalgamating the two protectorates and granting the new kingdom domestic autonomy within the framework of the Federation. A number of compromises were worked out at the Paris conference, concluded on September 15, but the negotiators were unable to reconcile differences over the proposed Cochin China referendum and the degree of autonomy to be exercised by Viet-Nam within the French Union.

During the autumn of 1946 clashes between Vietnamese extremists and French troops became increasingly frequent in N. Viet-Nam. Large-scale fighting began in Hanoi on December 20, and the French commander in chief in Tonkin assumed control of the government and decreed martial law. By the end of the year the war had spread throughout N. Viet-Nam and into Cochin China.

Sanguinary battles took place in many parts of Indochina during 1947. In the course of the fighting the French occupied all important Viet-Nam cities. Led by Ho Chi Minh and waging guerrilla warfare, the Vietnamese forces retained control of extensive nonurban areas. Toward the end of the year the French,

having tried repeatedly and fruitlessly to reach a settlement with Ho, began negotiations with Bao Dai, who had left Viet-Nam in the preceding July. With Bao Dai's consent and official encouragement, a group of the former emperor's associates established (May, 1948) a provisional pro-French government of Viet-Nam. In the absence of a definitive agreement with France Bao Dai refused to associate himself directly with the new regime; however, its leaders recognized his claims to sovereignty over Viet-Nam. On June 6 French and pro-French Vietnamese leaders approved a document defining Viet-Nam as an associated state within the French Union and guaranteeing the unity and independence of Viet-Nam. This document evoked little enthusiasm among the Annamese. Preparation of a definitive agreement began in France on January 16, 1949, with Bao Dai representing the provisional government. The agreement, signed on March 8, contained provisions for inclusion of Cochin China in Viet-Nam, for a semiautonomous Vietnamese government (see *Government,* above), and for extraterritorial rights for French nationals in Viet-Nam. On May 21 the French National Assembly approved legislation making Cochin China part of Viet-Nam. The new Vietnamese government, with Bao Dai as chief of state, was constituted on July 1. Laos and Cambodia were made associated states within the French Union under the respective treaties of July 19 and Nov. 8, 1949.

During the second half of 1949 Annamese apathy toward the Bao Dai government, failure of the French to subdue the Viet Minh guerrillas, and the formation (September) of the communist-led People's Republic of China considerably strengthened the political position of anti-French Viet-Nam. The total collapse (December) of Chinese Nationalist resistance on the mainland of China and the consequent establishment of common frontiers between communist China and anti-French Viet-Nam marked the beginning of a new phase of the war. In this phase, coinciding with a general intensification of the world-wide diplomatic and ideological struggle (the so-called cold war) between the Western democracies and the communist-led states, anti-French Viet-Nam received substantial material aid from the Chinese communist government. The latter established diplomatic relations with anti-French Viet-Nam on January 16, 1950. Ho's government was recognized by the Soviet Union on January 31 and by the Soviet satellite states in E.

French Embassy, Information Division

A girl of Indochina

Europe during the next few weeks. The United States, Great Britain, and various other democratic countries granted recognition to Cambodia, Laos, and the Bao Dai government in February.

On May 8, 1950, the U.S. government, responding to urgent official requests from France, instituted a military-aid program for the Associated States. The first shipment of military equipment reached Indochina on June 10. Following the outbreak (June 25) of the war in Korea the American military-aid program was steadily expanded. Viet Minh forces inflicted several costly defeats on the French in the closing months of the year, however. According to official figures released early in 1951, losses sustained by European French troops in Indochina then included 19,000 killed and missing.

On Jan. 17, 1951, French and pro-French Indochinese forces won a five-day battle N. of Hanoi, repulsing an army of 25,000 Viet Minh troops. Viet Minh abandoned conventional military tactics in the ensuing period; on April 17 Ho Chi Minh formally proclaiming the start of a "new war of attrition", ordered his army to resume guerrilla warfare against the French. In the meantime the Chinese government, by intervening (November, 1950) in the Korean war, had implicitly warned of similar action in Indochina. French reaction to this possibility included shipment of heavy reinforcements to Viet-Nam. By May, 1951, French military units in Indochina aggregated 391,000 troops. The French, speeding formation of a Viet-Nam army,

asked (September) the United States to provide military equipment for eight Vietnamese divisions.

Fierce fighting continued throughout 1952 and 1953, with neither side able to win a decisive victory. In the 1953 fighting a Viet Minh army invaded Laos, but subsequently withdrew. American aid to the war effort of France and the Associated States was substantially increased after President Dwight D. Eisenhower assumed office. By the close of 1953 French and U.S. expenditures in the eight-year war against the Viet Minh rebels aggregated about $8 billion.

INDOCHINESE LANGUAGES, a family of languages spoken throughout a large region extending from N. India in the west to Formosa in the east, and central Asia in the north to the Malay Peninsula in the south. The family is generally divided into two large subfamilies, the *Chinese-Siamese* and the *Tibeto-Burman*. The Chinese-Siamese subfamily is in turn divided into two main branches: the *Sinitic,* which comprises the language and group of dialects of China, and the *Tai* or *Shan,* which is still further subdivided into three groups containing the languages of Lower Burma, the Shan States, and Siam. The Tibeto-Burman subfamily, though comprising a greater number of individual languages than the Chinese-Siamese and spoken by a wider variety of ethnic groups, is more difficult to classify and actually covers a smaller population. Four main branches divided into about nine groups are recognized by most linguists; the provenance of the languages within these groups (of which about thirty have been studied and described by Western linguists) includes Indochina, Tibet and the Himalayan slopes, Assam, Burma, and eastern Bengal.

The entire Indochinese family is distinguished from the language families of the West by a combination of two main characteristics: isolating (or monosyllabic) character, and the use of tones. The entire family was at one time agglutinative, but with the passage of centuries it passed into a monosyllabic stage, though recrudescences and new adoptions of agglutination appear at the present time, particularly in the Tibeto-Burman subfamily. In such a language compound words do not occur; each (usually monosyllabic) word is in effect an ideal root, and expresses a discrete idea in sentences whose meanings and syntax are determined entirely by word order and the use of formally independent particles. Parts of speech (such as

nouns, verbs, and prepositions) are not differentiated. The disappearance of meaningful
prefixes from the languages led to their other
distinguishing peculiarity, the use of variations in tone or pitch to indicate differences
of meaning in words which are spelled and
pronounced identically. This characteristic
presents the major difficulty faced by West-
erners in acquiring an Eastern language; in
some extreme cases, such as the dialects of s.e.
China, as many as eight distinct tones may
be used in voicing what to Western ears is a
single word.

INDO-EUROPEAN LANGUAGES, also
called INDO-ARYAN and (especially by German
philologists) INDO-GERMANIC LANGUAGES, the
most important family of languages in the
world, embracing almost all of the languages
native to Europe together with a large number of the languages of western Asia and the
Indian peninsula. (The notable exceptions in
Europe are Albanian, Basque, Estonian, Finnish, and Hungarian.) Proof that these highly
diverse languages are members of a single family was accumulated during a period of about
fifty years around the turn of the 19th century. By 1800 a close relation between the
dead Indian language Sanskrit (q.v.) and the
languages of Europe had been demonstrated.
The extensive literature of India, which began earlier than that of any other Indo-European language, preserved characteristics of the
basic Indo-European forms and pointed to
the existence of a common parent language.
Hindu grammarians had systematically studied and classified the formative elements by
which changes in pronunciation occurred,
leading to the formation of distinct languages.
With the formulation of Grimm's Law (q.v.)
about 1820, linguistic scientists began to explain the development and ramifications of
the Indo-Europeans languages of Europe on
the basis of consonantal change, and later of
other types of phonetic change. Throughout
the 19th century, related comparative and historical studies of all the Indo-European
tongues conclusively established their lineage.
Progress was also made in the reconstruction
of their hypothetical common ancestor, usually called *proto-Indo-European,* and even in
the description, based almost entirely upon
philological evidence, of the late Stone Age
civilization in which this unrecorded language
was spoken (see INDO-EUROPEANS).

In general, the evolution of the Indo-European languages displays a progressive decay
of inflection (q.v.); thus, proto-Indo-European itself seems to have been a highly inflected language, as are two of the oldest dead
languages of the family, Sanskrit and ancient
Greek, while comparatively modern languages, such as French and English, have
moved toward an analytic stage. In classification, a basic line of division extending geographically from Scandinavia to Greece separates two well-defined groups of languages
usually called the *Western* or *Centum Division* and the *Eastern* or *Satem Division* (*centum* and *satem* being the words for one hundred in Latin and Avestan respectively). This
line is often taken as indicating the point of
cleavage in Europe from which dispersion occurred eastward and westward; it marks two
divergent lines of consonantal development
from primitive palatal gutturals, which became stops or mutes (such as the *k* in the
Latin pronunciation of *centum*) in the West
and spirants or sibilants (such as the *s* in
satem) in the East. Within these major divisions numerous subfamilies, branches, and
groups of languages may be demarcated, the
main outlines of which, along with the areas
in which they are or were spoken, are given
in the following table. Articles on most of
the terms in the table will be found in this
encyclopedia.

I. WESTERN OR CENTUM DIVISION

    A. Hellenic Subfamily
        1. Greek Branch (spoken in Greece
           and Asia Minor)
    B. Italic Subfamily
        1. Osco-Umbrian and Sabellian
           Branches (spoken in Italy)
        2. Latinian Branch
          a. Latin and the Romance Lan-
           guages (spoken in Italy, France,
           Spain, Portugal, and Romania)
    C. Celtic Subfamily (spoken in ancient
        Gaul, and until recent times in Corn-
        wall, Wales, Brittany, Ireland, and
        Scotland)
    D. Teutonic or Germanic Subfamily
        1. Eastern Branch (spoken in and
          around ancient Germany)
        2. North or Scandinavian Branch
          (spoken in Scandinavia)
        3. Western Branch
          a. High Group (spoken in Ger-
           many and Austria)
          b. Low Group (spoken in Ger-
           many, in n.w. European countries
           such as Belgium and Holland, and
           in England)

II. Eastern or Satem Division

A. Indo-Iranian or Aryan Subfamily
   1. Indic Branch (spoken in India)
   2. Iranian Branch
      a. Eastern Group (spoken in parts of s.w. Asia, such as Afghanistan and Baluchistan)
      b. Western Group (spoken in the Iranian plateau)
B. Thraco-Phrygian or Anatolic Subfamily (spoken in Armenia and ancient Phrygia)
C. Thraco-Illyrian (spoken in the Balkan peninsula)
D. Balto-Slavic
   1. Slavic or Slavonic Branch (spoken in Russia, and in Czechoslovakia, Poland, and Germany)
   2. Baltic or Lettic Branch (spoken in E. Prussia, Lithuania, and Latvia).

INDO-EUROPEANS, the peoples whose native tongues are the Indo-European languages (q.v.). The term is rarely extended to include natives of the New World and other regions where these peoples are now spoken, because these peoples are ethnically unrelated, and have adopted the languages in relatively recent times. All of the Indo-European tongues are probably derived from a single extinct and unknown parent language usually called *proto-Indo-European*. This language and the Indo-European people who spoke it have been extensively studied, principally through philological evidence. In recent times archeological research on such artifacts as prehistoric Indo-European pottery has added further information. Ethnological speculation has been carried on since the Indo-European problem was stated in the first half of the 19th century. One of the best-known of such speculative theories is the assertion (which was officially adopted by the Nazi government of Germany) that the tall, fair, blue-eyed, dolichocephalic "Aryan" of modern Germany and Scandinavia is the direct descendant and truest replica of the proto-Indo-European. Such theories have failed of validation, however, largely because of the complex mixture of modern European and Asiatic races.

The Indo-European community existed as a social unit during neolithic times, entered into the beginning of a primitive metal age based upon copper or bronze, and broke up in a series of migrations some time between 3000 and 2000 B.C. The region from which the Indo-European people spread was probably at some distance from the sea, ˀnd a temperate climate, and was fitted for both agricultural and pastoral life. This region was probably on the plains of central Europe, in the region extending from modern Lithuania to the steppes of Southern Russia. From there, the Indo-Europeans radiated to all parts of Europe and, through Asia Minor, to the western and s. central parts of Asia, apparently entering the Indian peninsula from the northwest.

The primitive Indo-European economy seems to have passed beyond a purely nomadic stage, mingling elements of sedentary agricultural and seminomadic pastoral pursuits, supplemented by spinning, weaving, hunting, and fishing. A large number of the Indo-Europeans were probably lake-dwellers, settled in villages organized along patrilineal lines with some sort of chief or king. Though nothing is known of their religion, words had been developed to describe both God and the soul, and certain purely ethical ideas apparently had currency.

INDO-IRANIAN LANGUAGES, the most important eastern or "satem" subfamily of the Indo-European languages (q.v.), the member languages of which are spoken chiefly in India and the Iranian plateau. The subfamily is generally divided into two branches, the *Indic,* which comprises the Sanskritic tongues of India and the Dard tongues of such areas as Chitral and Kafiristan, and the *Iranian,* which comprises an eastern group of languages spoken in such areas as Afghanistan and Baluchistan and a western group spoken on the Iranian plateau and in Kurdistan and Caucasia.

Although the vowel system of the Indo-Iranian languages is generally meager, their consonantal structure is extremely elaborate and well preserved, and is usually considered by linguistic scientists to reflect the characteristics of proto-Indo-European better than any of the other Indo-European languages. In inflection (q.v.), too, this subfamily is the most primitive and thus the most complex of all the Indo-European language divisions. Indo-Iranian is also noteworthy as the repository of the oldest extant literature in any of the Indo-European tongues. The most important dead language of the eastern Indo-European languages, Sanskrit (q.v.), is a member of the Indic branch.

INDONESIA, in political geography, the designation officially applied, after September 20, 1948, to the Netherlands Indies (q.v.). Prior to that time, when the change in nomenclature was embodied in an amendment to the constitution of the Kingdom of the Netherlands, the term was sometimes applied to the entire Malay Archipelago. See REPUBLIC OF INDONESIA.

INDONESIAN LANGUAGES, the most important subfamily of the Austronesian language family, spoken mainly in the Malay Peninsula and Archipelago. The subfamily is usually divided into two branches, the *Malayo-Javanese,* including Malay and Javanese groups, and the *Tagala,* comprising languages of the Philippine Islands, the Marianas and Palau islands, Formosa, Madagascar, and the areas around Indo-China, the Malay Peninsula, and the Mergui Archipelago.

Like all members of the Austronesian family, the Indonesian languages are agglutinative. In structure they are the most archaic of all the Austronesian languages, and philologists believe that the two related subfamilies which complete the entire group, Melanesian and Polynesian (qq.v.), are derived from Indonesian. The Indonesian tongues, moreover, display a more elaborate development than that of any others of the family; in a few of these tongues, notably Kavi (q.v.), the literary language of Java, important bodies of literature have been preserved.

INDONESIA, REPUBLIC OF. See REPUBLIC OF INDONESIA.

INDORE, city and summer capital of Madhya Bharat State, Union of India, situated near the junction of the Saraswati and Khan rivers, about 320 miles N.E. of Bombay. It is the commercial and transportation center of an agricultural region producing wheat, millet, corn, cotton, opium, and oilseed. The city contains factories engaged in the manufacture of cotton textiles, hosiery, chemicals, furniture, and metal products. Noteworthy features include several palaces, Daly College (a school for Indian princes), and the Institute of Plant Industry. Founded in 1715, the city rose to prominence under the rule of the Holkar dynasty. In 1818 it became the capital of the princely state of Indore, which merged with Madhya Bharat in 1948. Pop. (1951) 310,859.

INDRA, in early Hindu mythology, the supreme deity, ruler of the atmosphere, and god of thunderbolts and rain. In some 300 hymns of the *Vedas* (q.v.), the ancient sacred literature of the Hindus, Indra is praised as the god of battles; armed with the thunderbolt, and riding in a golden chariot drawn by golden and red horses, he goes forth to do battle with the demon Vritra who has imprisoned the rivers and rains, and with other enemies. In the Vedic hymns Indra is also described as the royal patron of the victorious Indo-Aryan conquerors of the Dravidian inhabitants of India. See INDIA: *History.*

In later Hindu mythology Indra, no longer the supreme deity, is described as one of the eight guardians of the world, called *Devas,* and wields his thunderbolt as before. He is conceived of as a sensuous deity who inhabits Svarga, a delightful paradise, where he is surrounded by musicians and nymphs, called the Gandharvas and Apsarasas, as well as by a host of worshipers. In a still later period, in that division of the Hindu scriptures known as the Purana (q.v.), Indra is subordinate to the supreme deities Vishnu, Brahma, and Siva (qq.v.). In modern Hinduism, Indra, as the god of rain, is often represented as riding the elephant Airavata, and as holding a thunderbolt and an elephant goad in his hand.

INDRE, department of central France, occupying land formerly included within the old provinces of Berry, Touraine, Orléanais, and Marche. It is drained by the Indre R. Agriculture is the principal occupation, and grains, fruits, and livestock are raised. In the N. part of Indre champagne is made. Among the industrial products of the region are woolens, ironware, paper, and felt hats. Châteauroux is the capital. Area, 2664 sq.m.; pop. (1952 est.) 258,000.

INDRE-ET-LOIRE, department of N. central France. The Loire and its tributaries the Cher, Vienne, and the Indre are the principal rivers. In the valley of the Loire are situated several famous châteaux, notably those at Aboise and at Tours (q.v.), the capital. The province is a fertile agricultural region, containing extensive orchards and vineyards. Cereal grains, hemp, vegetables, and sheep also are raised. Many wines are made in Indre-et-Loire. Among other important industries are tanning, the spinning and weaving of silk, and the manufacture of pottery and iron and lead wares. Area, 2377 sq.m.; pop. (1952 est.) 365,000.

INDUCTANCE, the property possessed by a varying electric current in a conductor of producing or "inducing" a current in a nearby conductor; see ELECTRICITY. Whenever an electric current flows through a conductor a magnetic field (see MAGNETISM) is created around the conductor, and whenever the lines of force of this field cut another conductor a current is induced in it. When the current flowing through a conductor is steady and unchanging (as in the case of direct current) the magnetic field about the conductor is stationary and does not induce a current in nearby stationary conductors. In the case of alternating current or a continuously varying direct current, however, when the current is constantly rising and falling, the magnetic field expands and contracts continuously and its lines of force cut neighboring conductors, inducing a current. In direct-current circuits the magnetic field about the circuit expands momentarily when the current is switched on and contracts when the current is switched off, creating brief surges of induced current in nearby conductors.

When the magnetic field about a conductor expands it cuts the original conductor and induces a current in it. This current, produced by *self-induction,* is opposite in direction to the original current and thereafter tends to limit the flow of the original current. Similarly, when current is switched off, the magnetic field contracts and tends to perpetuate the current by self-induction. Electrical self-induction is thus analogous to mechanical inertia. The property of self-induction is particularly valuable in alternating-current circuits, in which circuit elements designed to have high self-inductance can be used to regulate current flow.

The most common forms of inductive circuit elements are *coils* and *transformers.* A coil consists of a helically wound conductor in which the various parallel turns of the helix reinforce the magnetic field produced by other turns. In addition the field may be reinforced by the addition of a core within the helix made of iron or some other ferromagnetic material. Simple inductance coils of this kind are used as parts of resonant circuits (see RESONANCE) and also as chokes to limit the flow of alternating currents. Transformers consist of two or more coils wound concentrically or coaxially. An alternating current propagated in one coil induces a similar current of opposite polarity in the other coil or coils of the transformer. The voltage of the induced current varies according to the ratio between the number of turns of the primary and secondary coils. Thus if a voltage of 110 volts is applied to the primary of a transformer having 100 turns, the voltage induced in a secondary with 350 turns is 3.5 x 110 or 385 volts. Transformers are employed extensively in electric-power-supply systems and in most electronic devices such as radio and television sets.

INDUCTION. See INDUCTANCE.

INDUCTION, in logic, the process of reasoning from the particular to the general. It is the inverse process and complement of deduction (q.v.), the reasoning from the general to the particular; however, unlike deduction, which is sure, induction provides only a high degree of probability. The processes of deduction, proceeding from a given general law to a particular instance, are certain: for, if the law applies in all instances, it must apply in a particular instance. Induction, on the other hand, is valid only insofar as the number of instances of observation yields a probability greater than the desired certitude: for what is true in all observed instances may also, but less surely, be true in all unobserved instances.

The first description of inductive processes was given by the Greek philosopher Aristotle, who did little to develop them, being more concerned with the deductive method. The systematic development of the inductive method did not occur until the 17th century, when Francis Bacon (q.v.) advocated the formulation of general laws from the observation of many instances of particular action. In the 18th century the English empiricists, especially David Hume, further developed the inductive method, and in the 19th century John Stuart Mill laid down canons for its application. These philosophers postulated, as a basis of the method, a law of "the uniformity of nature", presuming a correspondence of cause and effect in identical circumstances. The existence of such a correspondence is not borne out by the observations of modern scientists, however; it has become evident that it is impossible to determine the totality of conditions surrounding an experiment, or to reproduce such conditions exactly from one instance to another. In certain sciences, such as those dealing with social phenomena and atomic action, the laws of cause and effect apply only in a statistical sense, and the processes of induction may be used only with corresponding modifications. In general, however, inductive reasoning may be applied to obtain results of any desired degree of accuracy, dependent upon the number of experiments considered and the care with which identity of conditions is maintained.

INDUCTION COIL. See INDUCTANCE.

INDULGENCE, in Roman Catholic theology, a remission of the temporal punishment, or expiation, for sin after absolution in the sacrament of Penance (q.v.). During the early years of the Church, severe penitential observances were required by all who had been guilty of a serious crime, especially apostasy, murder, or adultery. In time the Church gradually substituted for such canonical penances lesser works of devotion, such as specific prayers, fasts, or almsgivings, to which were attached indulgences equivalent to corresponding periods of canonical penance, or, in the case of *plenary* indulgences, to the entire temporal punishment. The Church bases its authority to grant indulgences on two doctrines: (1) that the merits of Christ were infinite, and form an inexhaustible treasury; and (2) that the Church has jurisdiction in dispensing these merits through the "power of the keys", or of binding and loosing, conferred by Christ (Matt. 16) on Peter and his successors.

INDUS, a river of India. It is formed by the confluence of Himalayan glacial streams in Tibet, flows N.W. across Kashmir, passing between the W. and N. extremities respectively of the Himalayas and the Hindu Kush, and then courses generally S. to the Arabian Sea, covering a distance of about 2000 m. The major tributaries of the Indus are the Sutlej, Ravi, and Chenab (qq.v.). The Indus enters the Punjab area 812 m. from its source, and at a point 48 m. further it becomes navigable as a result of its junction with the Kabul R. from Afghanistan. Entering the Sind it flows under the Lansdowne bridge at Sukkur and the Hyderabad-Kotri bridge before branching into the delta which covers an area of about 3000 sq.m. and extends for some 125 m. along the Arabian Sea. The Indus has some importance as an artery of traffic, and in addition provides irrigation for many millions of acres of the naturally arid lands of the Sind. See INDIA: *Physical Features.*

INDUSIUM. See LEAF.

INDUSTRIAL ARBITRATION. See ARBITRATION: *Industrial Arbitration.*

INDUSTRIAL EDUCATION. See TECHNICAL EDUCATION.

INDUSTRIAL MANAGEMENT, in business, a term used to describe the techniques of the efficient organization, planning, direction, and control of the operations of a business enterprise. In the theory of industrial management, organization has two principal aspects. One relates to the establishment of "lines of responsibility", drawn usually in the form of an "organization chart" which designates the executives of the business, from the president to the foreman or department head, and which also specifies the functions for which they are responsible; the other principal aspect of organization relates to the development of a staff of qualified executives. Planning has three principal aspects. One comprises the establishment of the broad basic policies of the enterprise with respect to production, sales, the purchase of equipment, materials, and supplies, and accounting. The second aspect of planning relates to the implementation of these policies in the form of departmental policies. The third is the establishment of standards of work in all departments of the enterprise. Direction is concerned primarily with supervision and guidance by the executives of those under their authority. In this connection a distinction is generally made between "top management", which is essentially administrative in nature, and "operative management", which is concerned with the direct execution of policy. Control comprises the use of records and reports to compare performance with the established standards for work.

Industrial management as defined above, is a recent development, dating from the latter part of the 19th century. A notable impetus to its evolution was the writings of the American engineer Frederick W. Taylor (q.v.), who developed techniques for analyzing the operations involved in production and for setting standards for a day's work. Early practitioners of his techniques, which became known as "the Taylor method", were concerned primarily with securing the maximum output at minimum cost through use of the piecework system of paying for the amount of work done rather than for the time consumed. In later years, the techniques originally devised by Taylor were adapted by industrialists to other phases of business, including the employment of qualified workers; and wage-incentive programs were devised, in part to replace, and in part to supplement, the piecework system.

INDUSTRIAL PSYCHOLOGY, the application of various psychological techniques to the selection and training of industrial workers and to the promotion of efficient working conditions and techniques. This field of applied psychology became of great importance during World War II when it was necessary to recruit and train a large group of new workers to meet the expanding demands of industry.

The selection of workers for particular jobs is essentially a problem of discovering the special aptitudes requisite for the job and of devising tests which will determine whether candidates have such aptitudes. The development of tests of this kind and the determination of their validity has long been a field of psychological research. See PSYCHOLOGICAL

TESTING; PSYCHOLOGY: *Perception, Imagination.*

The fundamental aim of the industrial psychologist is to find ways in which the effort required to do a particular job can be decreased. This attitude is entirely different from that of the so-called "efficiency expert" whose purpose is to increase production by any means whatsoever. Psychological techniques used to lessen the effort involved in a given job include a detailed study of the motions required to do the job, of the equipment used, and of the conditions under which the job is performed. These conditions include ventilation, heating, lighting, noise, and any other factor affecting the worker's comfort or morale. After such a study is made, the industrial psychologist can often determine that the job may be accomplished with less effort by changing the routine motions of the work itself, by changing or moving the tools, by improving the working conditions, or by a combination of several of these methods. Industrial psychologists also have made studies of the effects of fatigue on workers with the object of determining the length of working time that gives the greatest production. In some cases such studies have proved that total production on particular jobs could be increased by reducing the hours of work, since the workers' efficiency increased more than enough to offset the shortening of the work day.

INDUSTRIAL REVOLUTION, in economic history, a term designating specifically the rapid changes in methods of production and technology, which began to take place in England about 1760, and which resulted in the replacement of the domestic or putting-out system of manufacturing by the factory system; see FACTORIES AND THE FACTORY SYSTEM. The term was popularized in the 19th century by the British social economist Arnold Toynbee. By extension, it was also applied specifically to those periods in the history of other countries when they, too, experienced a development from manual to machine techniques of production. Thus the American industrial revolution, for example, is said to have occurred in the latter part of the 19th century (see UNITED STATES: *History*), and the German industrial revolution after 1870; see GERMANY: *History*. In a further extension of its meaning, "industrial revolution" signifies not only the industrial and technological changes denoted by the specific meanings of the term, but also the broad economic and social consequences which

resulted from these changes. As thus inclusively defined, the term is applicable to the experience of all the industrially developed countries of the world, and, ultimately, to all countries, and is therefore employed by some scholars in the sense of a world-wide tendency of social development.

Virtually all authorities agree that the experience of England in the period of its industrialization is characteristic of other countries. Two confluent sets of historic factors are believed to account for the Industrial Revolution. One set of factors comprised the opening of the Near East to trade with Europe after the Crusades (q.v.), and the later discovery of new lands in the Western Hemisphere and the Orient, which greatly stimulated commerce; both factors created demands which could be satisfied only by an enormous expansion of industry. The second broad historic influence was the Renaissance (q.v.) which upset age-old patterns of thought and gave rise to the scientific spirit of inquiry and experimentation necessary for the realization of the technological progress vital to the development of industry. In England in the latter part of the 18th century, these historic influences combined to constitute the dynamic cause of a social transformation unique in world history, and effected at a rate theretofore unparalleled in the life of any country. New scientific conceptions, notably those formulated by Isaac Newton (q.v.), spurred the invention of new devices which found immediate practical and profitable application in industry. Among the inventions which gave rise to the factory system were the steam engine (1769) by James Watt, the spinning jenny (1764) by James Hargreaves, and the power loom (1785) by Edmund Cartwright (qq.v.). As a result of these and a veritable host of other inventions, new and large-scale industries, with greater productive capacities than had been thought possible, became commonplace. Capital for the new industries was forthcoming in large part from the accumulated reserves and other assets of the trading companies; see EAST INDIA COMPANY.

Among important consequences of the Industrial Revolution were an enormous increase in productivity, a marked increase in population, the creation of large centers of production and complex systems of transportation (see CANALS: *History;* RAILROADS: *Development*) and communication (see TELEGRAPH), the development of a numerous urban working class which was ruthlessly exploited by employers, the occurrence of severe economic depressions of long duration (see DE-PRESSION), the evolution of the corporate form of business enterprise (see CORPORA-TION), and the stimulation of further scientific research and technological progress. As a consequence of all these changes England was transformed in a relatively few years from an agricultural country into an industrial nation. Its subsequent rise as the foremost economic, colonial, naval, and political power in the world, was the result primarily of the Industrial Revolution and would have been impossible without it; see ENGLAND: *History;* GREAT BRITAIN: *History;* COLONY; IMPERIAL-ISM.

INDUSTRIAL SCHOOLS. See TECHNICAL EDUCATION.

INDUSTRIAL WORKERS OF THE WORLD, an American industrial labor union, notable in U.S. labor history as an exponent of syndicalist doctrines (see SYNDICALISM) and for its former militant policy in the conduct of strikes. Its members are frequently referred to as "wobblies". From its formation in 1905 the IWW espoused the cause of a workers' society and advocated the Marxian theory of the class struggle between the working class and the capitalist class. After 1908 it consistently opposed every form of political action, including participation in elections. Formerly, the IWW practiced a policy of "direct action" in the conduct of strikes intended to win improvements in the conditions and wages of the workers it represented; it made use of violent tactics with the aim of forcing employers to grant its demands, and at first rejected the negotiation of wage agreements as an unprincipled compromise with its class enemies. Later it abandoned the policy of "direct action", and like other unions, negotiated collective-bargaining agreements.

The IWW was founded in Chicago by a convention of delegates from unions of workers in forty different trades or occupations. Among the unions which played the principal role in the establishment of the IWW were the Western Federation of Miners (now the International Union of Mine, Mill and Smelter Workers, CIO), the American Labor Union, and the Socialist Trade and Labor Alliance (composed of trade unions and socialist groups). The outstanding labor leaders at the founding convention included Eugene V. Debs, William Dudley Haywood (qq.v.), Daniel De Leon, and the militant leaders of the Western Federation of Miners, Vincent St. John and Charles H. Moyer. The aim of the IWW was to include in its membership the entire industrial population of the United States; this aim was projected in the phrase "one big union". The organizational plan of the IWW provided for seven departments: agriculture, mining, transportation, building, manufacturing, public service, and distribution of foodstuffs. Each department was subdivided into its various constituent industries, and these in turn were divided into their component trades or crafts. Thus, the manufacturing department was divided into textiles, leather, woodworking, metals and machinery, glass and pottery, paper mills, chemicals, rubber, brooms, and jewelry; and the textiles division was subdivided into thirty-eight trades, including weaving, spinning, garment making, and dyeing.

The IWW was at the peak of its strength in 1912 when its membership probably numbered about one hundred thousand. Its chief adherents were lumberjacks from the Northwest, migratory workers from the wheat fields of the central States, textile workers, miners and longshoremen. Between 1906 and 1917 the IWW carried out a number of strikes notable for violence of feeling and action on both sides. Among these strikes were the miners' strike at Goldfield, Nev. (1906–07), the textile workers' strike at Lawrence, Mass. (1912), and the silk workers' strike at Paterson, N.J. (1913). In connection with its strike and organizing activities, the IWW also conducted militant struggles in a number of States for the right of free speech for its organizers and agitators. The union was opposed to the entrance of the United States into World War I. Ninety-five of its leaders and hundreds of its members were convicted of draft evasion, of conspiracy to cripple the war effort by fomenting strikes in important war industries, and of other crimes, and were given heavy fines and long jail sentences. The losses sustained by wartime prosecution, by the subsequent action of several States, notably California and Washington, in prohibiting "criminal syndicalism", and by the action of many IWW members in joining the American Communist Party after its formation in 1919–21, caused a decline in the union's membership. Thereafter the IWW ceased to play a prominent part in the American labor movement.

INDY, PAUL MARIE THÉODORE VINCENT D' (1851–1931), French composer, teacher, and musicologist, born in Paris, and educated at the Paris Conservatory. He began the study of the piano at the age of eleven and in 1870 published his first compositions. Two years

Vincent d'Indy

later he became a pupil of César Franck (q.v.), studying organ and composition. D'Indy's reputation as a composer was established in 1886 with the performance of his "dramatic legend" *Le Chant de la Cloche,* which had won the "Prize of the City of Paris" the year before. In 1890 he became president of the Société Nationale de Musique, and from 1900 until his death he taught composition at the Schola Cantorum.

His compositions reveal the influence of his master César Franck, from whom he learned the principle of "cyclic form", i.e., the principle of using the same thematic material throughout all the movements of a composition. D'Indy's work is in general more complex and intellectual than that of Franck, a tendency counterbalanced in part by the influence upon it of impressions from nature and of folk song. He wrote three symphonies, of which the *Symphonie sur un Chant Montagnard Français* (1886) is now the most frequently performed, numerous orchestral suites and symphonic poems, and several choral works. Among his literary works are biographies of Beethoven (1906) and César Franck (1911).

INERT GASES, RARE GASES, or **NOBLE GASES,** term applied to a group of gaseous elements which are chemically inactive and form no chemical compounds. The group consists of argon, helium, krypton, neon, radon, and xenon (qq.v.). The atoms of the inert gases do not combine with each other to form polyatomic molecules as do the atoms of most other gaseous elements, but remain as separate atoms in the gas. With the exception of radon they are present in the atmosphere (q.v.) in measurable quantity.

INEZ DE CASTRO. See CASTRO, INEZ DE.

INFALLIBILITY, in theology, the doctrine that in matters of faith and morals the teaching of the Church is immune from error by divine dispensation. The Orthodox Church applies the doctrine to decisions of ecumenical councils; the Roman Catholic Church restricts its effects to certain acts of the pope. According to the definition of the Vatican Council in 1870, the doctrine applies only when: (1) the pope speaks *ex cathedra,* that is, in his official capacity as pastor and teacher; (2) he speaks with the manifest intention of binding the entire church to acceptance; and (3) the matter pertains to faith or morals. Two such *ex cathedra* pronouncements on doctrine have been made in the past hundred years: the definition of the dogma of the Immaculate Conception (q.v.), and the definition of infallibility itself.

INFANTICIDE, in criminal law, the killing of a newborn child by its parent or by another with the parent's consent. In most countries it is considered a form of murder. Infanticide was a widespread practice among most savage races. Among ancient peoples the principal cause for infanticide was a shortage of food. In China and India and other countries, for economic and religious reasons, infanticide of females was more common than that of males. Deformed infants of both sexes were destroyed in ancient Greece and Rome. In later times, the Christian church attempted to prevent infanticide by excommunicating women guilty of the practice. The Mohammedan Koran forbade infanticide. Infanticide, in modern times, has been regarded with universal horror. The subject of infanticide has formed a theme in many great works of literature throughout the ages, including the tragic play *Medea* by the ancient Greek dramatist Euripides.

INFANTILE PARALYSIS, or POLIOMYELITIS, infectious virus disease of the central nervous system, sometimes resulting in paralysis. The greatest incidence of the disease is in children between the ages of five and ten years, but persons of any age may be afflicted. The disease probably is a very ancient one but was not recognized as a separate entity until described in 1840 by Jacob von Heine. The presence of infantile paralysis was not recognized in the United States until 1894. Today evidence of it is found in all parts of the world but it is usually more prevalent in temperate zones.

The severity of the symptoms is variable; there are many more mild, unreported cases than cases correctly diagnosed and reported to health departments. Current research indicates that for every paralytic case of poliomyelitis there are at least 100 nonparalytic cases, most of which are not recognized as poliomyelitis. The virus may find entry to the body through one of several portals, the alimentary and respiratory tracts apparently being the most common. It then spreads along the nerve fibers to different parts of the central nervous system. The extent and character of the symptoms depend upon the site of involvement in the central nervous system and the number of nerve cells involved. Since nerve cells once destroyed are not replaced, permanent paralysis may ensue, but the largest percentage of cases with proper care recover with few, if any, permanent aftereffects. A similar form of paralysis occurring during and as an aftermath of this disease involves destruction of the respiratory centers, which control the movements of the diaphragm in breathing; victims of this form of paralysis are kept alive by an apparatus known as an "iron lung" (q.v.).

The incubation period of poliomyelitis ranges from about four to about eighteen days. The early symptoms are fatigue, headache, fever, vomiting, constipation, stiffness of the neck, or, less commonly, diarrhea and pain in the extremities. The inability to move parts of the body which may follow these early symptoms is, as a rule, due to paralysis from destruction of the anterior horn cells of the spinal cord. The virus commonly is excreted from the body in the stools for six to eight weeks, or sometimes longer, after onset. It may frequently be demonstrated in the throat, but only for a very short period very early in the illness.

Treatment is entirely symptomatic, there being no drug or serum with any specific effect. The Sister Kenny method (see KENNY, ELIZABETH) of intensive use of moist heat coupled with special physical therapy may relieve severe pain when present. Salicylates and aspirin are also effective in reducing pain, and antispasmodic drugs are administered to produce muscular relaxation. Secondary infections may be controlled by the use of aureomycin or sulfa drugs, and vitamin therapy is frequently employed. In the convalescent stage of the disease occupational therapy (q.v.) is used extensively.

The existence of many strains of the poliomyelitis virus vastly complicates immunization against the disease. At least three broad types of the virus have thus far been established; these are identified as the Brunhilde, Lansing, and Leon strains. The most hopeful development in the search for poliomyelitis control occurred late in 1953, when researchers at the University of California isolated for the first time two strains of the virus in pure form. Electron-microscope photographs revealed it to be a sphere-shaped particle with a diameter of about 1 millionth of an inch. An attack of poliomyelitis is generally believed to create lasting immunity to only one specific strain of the virus. Beginning in 1951 large scale field tests, involving the mass inoculation of children with gamma globulin were conducted in the United States; this substance, originally used as prophylactic against measles and hepatitis, is prepared from adult blood plasma, which, when collected from many donors, has been found to contain antibodies against all three types of poliomyelitis. Reports of the field trials, which were continued in 1952 and 1953, indicate that gamma globulin gives temporary protection for 5 to 6 weeks; if the disease does develop during this period its severity seems to be markedly reduced. According to some authorities no protection is afforded in the days immediately following inoculation.

An experimental vaccine containing the three known types of poliomyelitis virus was prepared in 1953, and in 1954 a program was launched to test it on 500,000 volunteer school children.

Since the founding by Franklin D. Roosevelt in 1938 of the National Foundation for Infantile Paralysis, research in this disease has received considerable financial support in the U.S. The Foundation has made new therapeutic techniques and equipment available to victims of the disease and has extended facilities for treatment, convalescence, and physiotherapy to many areas of the U.S., including Alaska, Hawaii, and Puerto Rico, which never before had such facilities.

INFANT MORTALITY. See VITAL STATISTICS.

INFANTRY, the largest and oldest branch of all armies, made up of soldiers who fight on foot, chiefly with small arms (q.v.). The infantry is the basic offensive force of the army; positions weakened by the combined efforts of the artillery and air force are taken by infantrymen. Modern infantry troops are often carried by truck or plane; special infantrymen are trained as *parachute troops* or *ski troops* for particular types of service. Tanks are included in modern infantry equipment. The largest individual operating unit of infantry in the U.S. Regular Army, without increments from other branches, is the regiment, under the command of a colonel. The regiment varies in size and composition; it regularly includes several special companies, such as Headquarters, Service, Antitank, Antiaircraft, and Medical companies. See ARMY SCHOOLS ; MILITARY ORGANIZATION.

INFELD, LEOPOLD (1898–), Polish-American physicist, born in Cracow, and educated at the University of Cracow. After serving as a lecturer at the University of Lemberg he was awarded a fellowship by the Rockefeller Foundation in 1934–35. In 1936 he was appointed a member of the Institute for Advanced Study at Princeton, N.J., at which he worked with Albert Einstein. He accepted a professorship at the University of Toronto in 1939. Infeld is known for his theoretical research in relativity and quantum theory. He wrote several books, for the layman as well as the scientist, including *The World in Modern Science* (1934), *The Evolution of Physics* (with Albert Einstein, 1938), *Quest* (1941), and *Albert Einstein* (1950).

INFINITE or **TRANSFINITE,** in mathematics, anything which goes on endlessly, or a number which is immeasurably and incalculably large. The concept of infinity first entered mathematics (as distinct from philosophy) with the development of the so-called infinitesimal calculus at the end of the 17th century. In the manipulations of the calculus, mathematicians employed infinitely small quantities called infinitesimals; see CALCULUS. The later development of the calculus, in which mathematicians eliminated the concept of infinitesimals and achieved the same results with the mathematically rigorous concept of limits, is typical of the modern mathematical attitude toward infinity. Since the use of infinity almost invariably leads to paradoxes and contradictions, mathematicians avoid such use whenever possible; for example, whereas mathematicians formerly stated that division of any number by zero yields infinity, modern mathematicians state that division by zero is a forbidden operation.

The development of a consistent theory of infinite numbers is due to the labors of the German mathematician Georg Cantor (q.v.), especially during the years 1882 and 1883. Cantor's theory resolved such paradoxes as are contained in the statements infinity plus one equals infinity or infinity times two equals infinity, which contradict the axiom that the whole cannot equal any of its parts. Cantor proposed that the entire series of integers, 1, 2, 3, ..., be considered a number, which he represented by the Hebrew letter aleph. He showed that any series which is denumerable or can be set in one-to-one correspondence to the aleph series (such as the even numbers 2, 4, 6 . . . .) is equal to it; but that there are other series which have a greater number of terms (such as the total number of fractions between 0 and 1) are equal to higher orders of infinities, which he represented by other letters.

The most important application of infinity to practical mathematics is in the summation of infinite series. The series $\frac{1}{2} + \frac{1}{4} + \frac{1}{8} \ldots$ can be easily shown to have the finite sum of 2. But the series $\frac{1}{2} + \frac{1}{3} + \frac{1}{4} \ldots$ has no finite sum. Mathematicians avoid stating that such a "divergent series" has a sum equal to infinity; they state instead: "it can be shown that the sum of this series is greater than any preassigned finite number if enough terms of the series are taken". See SERIES.

INFLATION, in economics, a sharp rise in the general level of commodity prices, resulting from a rapid increase in the supply of currency or credit (qq.v.) of a country without a corresponding increase in the volume of goods and services for sale. An inflation is called *temporary* when the upward movement of prices, sometimes called *price inflation,* is of relatively short duration and is followed by a decline to lower levels. The decline is called *deflation.* In economic theory, an inflation is said to be *permanent* when prices do not decline but are stabilized at the high levels reached during the period of inflation. Economists differ with regard to the relative influence of the many factors that cause inflation. Most authorities agree, however, that the principal causes are the following: excessive printing of paper money not backed by metallic reserves or not freely convertible into bullion, frequently described as *currency inflation;* and abnormal expansion of credit in connection with government expenditures to finance war or to combat economic crises, often called *credit inflation.*

Inflation, whether temporary or permanent, has serious economic and social consequences. Purchasing power is reduced, effecting a serious disruption of the economy, often so great as drastically to curtail production of essential items. The rise in prices is especially burdensome for individuals with relatively fixed incomes, such as civil-service employees or pensioners, whose incomes tend to rise at a much slower rate than do commodity prices. The value of the savings of all classes of the population also shrinks with a decline in the purchasing power of the currency.

Significant inflations among modern nations occurred for the first time in the latter part of the 18th century. In France during the French Revolution, the issue of assignats (q.v.) represented the first modern example of an unlimited issue of fiat currency, that is, currency without metallic backing. In England, during the period of the Napoleonic Wars, convertibility of pound notes into bullion was abandoned, and the accompanying excessive issue of paper currency resulted in a sharp increase in prices. The United States, during the Revolutionary War, experienced a sharp price inflation. Later, the need of the Federal government for money to prosecute the Civil War resulted in the issuance of inconvertible currency, called greenbacks (q.v.), and in a consequent doubling of wholesale prices. During the Civil War, the issue of fiat currency by the Confederacy also resulted in extraordinary price rises in the Southern States. Not until World War I, however, did inflation become widespread among all industrialized countries.

The experience of France and Germany during and after World War I is characteristic of the inflationary consequences of modern war. The French government called upon the central bank (Banque de France) to provide funds for war expenditures. A steep rise in prices and depreciation in the exchange value of the franc accompanied the resulting increase in currency circulation. The inflation that began thus during the war continued in the postwar period, until the currency was stabilized in 1926 at a level approximately ten percent of its prewar value. In Germany, convertibility of the reichsmark into bullion was suspended early in the war and the government resorted to the central bank (Reichsbank) to an increasing degree for funds for war financing. The resultant inflationary movement of prices and depreciation of the foreign-exchange value of the currency continued throughout the war and postwar periods. A virtually complete destruction of the value of the paper currency took place by 1923. The United States experienced a more moderate inflation during World War I and the early postwar period. The level of wholesale commodity prices in the United States increased by about 150 percent from 1913 to the middle of 1920. During the same period, the total money supply of the country—the total currency circulation and bank deposits —more than doubled.

World wide inflation developed again during World War II. To limit the inflationary rises, practically every belligerent country adopted drastic measures. Among methods used to combat inflation were control of production to insure an adequate supply of necessary articles, control of the prices of these and other articles, compulsory savings to limit competitive bidding for goods in black markets (q.v.), and high income and excess-profits taxes. Curbs on the extension of credit were also used. In the United States, price-control legislation enacted in March, 1942, was notably effective in limiting wartime price inflation; see PRICE CONTROL; CURRENCY; DEVALUATION. The U.S. Federal Reserve Board exercised its power to curtail the expansion of credit by member banks by increasing reserve requirements; and to restrain excessive speculation on the security markets by raising margin requirements; see FEDERAL RESERVE SYSTEM; STOCK EXCHANGE. A number of the wartime control measures were continued after World War II.

INFLECTION, the variations or changes which words undergo to indicate their relations with other words. Inflection is one of the main divisions of the subject matter of philology (q.v.). It includes conjugation, which comprises such distinctions as number, tense, person, mood, and voice; declension, which comprises such distinctions as number, case, and gender; and the inflections which indicate comparison. The characteristic features of inflection are internal change of words and the use of affixes which are fused to their roots, having no independent existence or significance. Such affixes distinguish inflectional languages from agglutinative ones, and the appearance of either agglutination or inflection distinguishes a language from the monosyllabic or isolating languages such as Chinese (see INDOCHINESE LANGUAGES).

Internal inflectional change is especially characteristic of the Semitic languages (q.v.), and the entire Indo-European language system is marked by more or less elaborate systems of inflections, one of the most complex of which appears to have been exhibited by proto-Indo-European. Most modern Indo-European languages display both internal inflectional change (as in English *ring, rang, rung*) and external affixes (as in English *spell, spelled* or *ox, oxen*), often simultaneous-

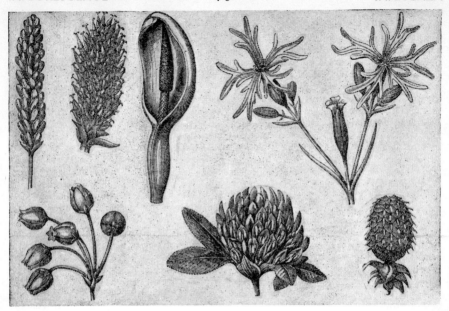

TYPES OF INFLORESCENCE. *Top, left to right: Spike; catkin, a scaly spike; spadix; cyme.*
Bottom, left to right: Simple umbel; head, or capitulum; strobile, a modified spike.

ly in a single word (as German *Männer* from
Mann or English *sold* from *sell*).

Languages which rely entirely or almost entirely upon inflection and agglutination to indicate word relations are called *synthetic;*
purely synthetic languages, however, are rarely found. In their development many Indo-
European languages, such as French and
English, have modified or dropped their inflections, passing into an *analytic* stage in
which old inflected forms are broken into
combinations of independent words. This decay or loss of inflectional forms is best typified, perhaps, in English; see GRAMMAR:
Distinctive Features of English Grammar.
Loss of inflection represents a loss of com-
pactness; some Latin sentences, for example,
more than double in wordage when translated
literally into English. On the other hand, this
evolution tends to simplify the grammatical
structure of a language (a Greek verb, for
example, may have as many as 249 different
forms, and a Sanskrit verb may have no less
than 891), and most linguistic scientists believe that development toward analytic speech
increases the flexibility of language.

INFLORESCENCE, term applied to flowers
arranged on a specialized extension of the
stem called a *floral axis.* A few flowering
plants, such as tulip and trillium, bear single
flower at the end of the floral axis; such flowers are termed *solitary.* The majority of flowering plants, however, bear more than one
flower on each floral axis. The inflorescence,
which includes the floral axis and the flowers
it bears, is classified according to type of
branching of the axis and arrangement of
flowers on the branches. A common feature
of most inflorescences is the production of
leaves called bracts, which may be simple
scales, larger leaflike structures, or petal-
like colored leaves. An aggregation of bracts,
usually in a whorl or rosette, is called an involucre. The three main types of inflorescences
are (1) *racemose inflorescences,* in which the
tip of the main floral axis does not bear a
flower, although its branches usually terminate in a flower; (2) *cymose inflorescences,*
in which the tips of both the main floral axis
and the branches are terminated by flowers;
and (3) *mixed inflorescences,* in which racemose and cymose characteristics are combined.

INFLUENZA or GRIPPE, an acute, infectious, and contagious respiratory disease
characterized by a sudden onset of extreme
weakness, and generally by catarrh of the
nasal and respiratory passages. The disease
may occur pandemically, epidemically, or
sporadically.

The cause of influenza was formerly

thought to be Pfeiffer's bacillus, *Hemophilus influenzae,* which commonly occurs in individuals affected with the disease, and which is the cause of so-called influenzal cerebro-spinal meningitis. In 1933 the cause of influenza was shown to be a filtrable virus. Two distinct types of virus, called "A" and "B" respectively, have been isolated as causing epidemic influenza, and several strains of each, varying in virulence, have been demonstrated. The variation in virulence probably results from the fact that the virus mutates rapidly. Infective particles of influenza virus seem to decay spontaneously; their half life (q.v.) was determined (1953) to be about 150 minutes.

Influenza is transmitted from person to person by spray from the mouth and nose, and occasionally by contact with objects which the lips or hands of an infected person have contaminated. The initial symptoms are headache, chill followed (in severe cases) by fever of 102° to 105° F. (39° to 40.5° C.), aching muscles and joints, and sometimes inflammation of the throat and lungs, and coughing. Dizziness and loss of appetite are common, and, as the disease develops, mental depression and neuritis often occur. The average incubation period of influenza is about one to two days; the average duration of uncomplicated cases is about three to four days.

Uncomplicated cases of influenza tend to recover with few residual symptoms; occasionally, in more severe cases, the disease may bring about chronic bronchitis and mental disorder. The mortality rate from uncomplicated influenza is negligible. The mortality rate from epidemic and pandemic influenza, which varies from seventeen to fifty percent, is known to be due to concomitant secondary infection with various bacteria, especially the pneumococcus which causes pneumonia. In such complicated cases, even when recovery occurs, there is usually a weakened resistance of the lungs to disease and often a residual neuritis.

In uncomplicated cases of influenza the patient is kept in bed until free from symptoms and until the temperature has been normal for three or four days. The patient is fed a high-caloric diet to restore energy, and large amounts of liquid. When the temperature remains over 100° F. (38° C.), the patient is kept on a purely liquid diet. Sedations are administered together with antibiotics to reduce the likelihood of complications.

Epidemics of influenza have been recognized in medical history from the 12th century on. Epidemics occur every two to three years, and most frequently attack children between the ages of five and nine, and adults between the ages of twenty-five and thirty-five. Children under one year of age and adults over forty seem to be most resistant to the disease. The first pandemic of influenza on record occurred in 1510 and subsequently spread over the whole of Europe. The most recent pandemics of the disease occurred in 1889 and in 1918 to 1919. The latter pandemic occurred in three distinct waves. The first wave began in May of 1918, and most of the cases were mild, with few complications and many recoveries. The second wave, occurring in the fall of 1918, was particularly severe, with many deaths. The third wave, ending in May of 1919, was somewhat less severe than the second, but also resulted in many deaths.

In order to prevent a recurrence of such a pandemic in World War II the U.S. Army Epidemiological Board developed a vaccine, a single injection of which was found to be effective in reducing the incidence of both influenza A and B for approximately three or four months after inoculation. Preparation of new vaccines is required frequently to include the varying strains of influenza virus encountered in different epidemics. The World Health Organization (q.v.) undertook (1952) a long-range program for the study and control of influenza to prevent future pandemics of the disease.

INFRARED, term applied to radiation which lies just beyond the limit of the red portion of the visible spectrum. The wave lengths of the infrared spectrum are longer than those of visible light and shorter than those of radio waves; they range between approximately eight ten-thousandths of a millimeter and four tenths of a millimeter. Infrared rays are detected by their thermal effect with such instruments as the bolometer. See RADIATION; SPECTRUM.

Infrared lamps are a useful means of applying heat energy. Large banks of such lamps are used in industry for many purposes, including drying paints and lacquers. Infrared radiation is used medically as a source of heat energy only where it is necessary to warm the superficial layers of the body, because infrared rays do not penetrate the skin.

Infrared photography is valuable in photographing distant objects obscured by atmospheric haze, because infrared radiation is not scattered by haze as is visible light. It is used in astronomy to detect nebulae and stars

Robert Ingersoll

invisible in ordinary light because of haze or because their radiation lies chiefly in the infrared region.

Among the infrared devices used during World War II were the sniperscope and snooperscope, with which a marksman could see his target in total visual darkness. Both instruments consist essentially of an infrared lamp that sends out a beam of infrared light, often referred to as "black" light, and a telescope receiver that picks up returned light from the object observed and converts it from invisible infrared light to a visible image. In the receiver, reflected rays picked up on the objective lens of the telescope are focused on an image tube. When the rays strike this tube electrons are released in direct proportion to the intensity of the rays. The released electrons are attracted to a positive plate and are accelerated as they pass through the tube to a fluorescent screen. They bombard the screen and produce a visible image. The action of each instrument is thus similar to the combined action of the image tube and picture tube of a television system.

The sniperscope is attached directly to a rifle, the infrared lamp being placed under the barrel and the telescope receiver over it. An electrical-supply unit containing a six-volt battery is carried on the user's back. The snooperscope is usually carried by hand; in one type, however, the infrared lamp is mounted on the front of a jeep or tank and the driver is equipped with special headgear with the receiving telescope attached to the visor.

INFUSORIA, class of Protozoa (one-celled animals) characterized by the presence of cilia (q.v.) throughout part of the life cycle, and by a mouth into which food is taken. Infusoria are found in any open accumulation of water, fresh or salt. The class is divided into two subclasses: Ciliata, in which the organism is free-swimming, equipped with cilia throughout its life; and Suctoria, in which the animal usually attaches itself in the adult stage to a solid object in the water. Suctorians have cilia when young, and lose them when fully developed; sucking tentacles take the place of cilia in the adult. *Paramecium* and *Vorticella* (qq.v.) are common ciliate genera; *Acineta* is a common suctorial genus.

INFUSORIAL EARTH. See DIATOMACEOUS EARTH.

INGE, WILLIAM RALPH (1860–1954), English theologian, born in Crayke, Yorkshire, and educated at Eton College, and at King's College, Cambridge University. After holding minor teaching posts he was made select preacher at Oxford and Cambridge, and subsequently, from 1907 to 1911, was professor of divinity at Oxford. He was dean of St. Paul's Cathedral, London, from 1911 to 1934. Because of his criticism of modern tendencies and his pessimistic outlook, he was called "the gloomy dean". He wrote *England* (1926), *Freedom, Love and Truth* (1936), *The Fall of the Idols* (1940), and *Diary of a Dean* (1950).

INGERSOLL, ROBERT GREEN (1833–99), American lawyer and agnostic, born in Dresden, N.Y. As a child he went to Illinois, and at the age of twenty-one was admitted to the bar. He recruited and was colonel of the 11th Illinois Cavalry at the beginning of the Civil War, but resigned his commission in 1863, after the Confederate forces, who had captured and paroled him, refused to exchange him and free him for active service. Ingersoll became a Republican after the war and was prominent in politics, particularly as a speaker. He was attorney general of Illinois from 1867 to 1869, but was unable to continue his political career because of opposition to his many lectures attacking the Bible and Christianity. These lectures, some of which were published as *The Gods, and Other Lectures* (1876), *Some Mistakes of Moses* (1879), and *Superstition* (1898), by causing open discussion of religious questions, had a profound influence on contemporary religious thought in the United States. After 1882 Ingersoll practiced law in New York City, and became noted as a trial lawyer.

INGLEWOOD, a city of Los Angeles Co., Calif., situated 10 miles s.w. of the city of Los Angeles. The Los Angeles Airport adjoins Inglewood, which is also served by three railroads. Among the principal industries are the manufacture of airplanes, microphones, enamelware, pottery, electric fixtures, and furniture; and the city contains several large chinchilla farms. Inglewood was founded in 1873 and incorporated as a city in 1908. Pop. (1950) 46,046.

INGOLDSBY, Thomas, pseudonym of Richard Harris Barham (q.v.).

INGRES, Jean Auguste Dominique (1780–1867), French portrait and historical painter, born in Montauban. He entered the studio of the great French classical painter Jacques Louis David at Paris in 1797, and won prizes in 1800 and 1801 for his paintings of scenes from Greek myths. From 1806 to 1820 he painted in Rome, where he developed his extraordinary gifts for drawing and design. He was greatly influenced by the work of Raphael, and his style has often been described as a combination of those of Raphael and David. While in Italy he made many pencil portraits which are distinguished for purity and economy of style. In 1820 he left Rome and went to Florence, returning to Paris in 1824.

At Paris he opened an atelier for students and became the recognized leader of the Classicist school as opposed to the new romantic movement led by Théodore Géricault and Eugène Delacroix. During this period Ingres painted the "Apotheosis of Homer" for one of the ceilings in the Louvre. In 1834 he accepted the directorship of the French Academy at Rome. At the end of his seven-year term as director he returned again to Paris, and was welcomed as one of France's most celebrated painters. His position was established, his works began to command high prices, and he was given the rank of commander of the Legion of Honor in 1845. In the Universal Exhibition of Paris in 1855 an entire salon was devoted to his works, and both he and his chief opponent in art, Delacroix, were awarded gold medals.

Ingres' most important work was in the field of portraiture, in which he displayed a keen sensitivity for personality and precise neoclassic linear style that was perfectly suited to portraiture. "Mme. Moitessier" at the National Gallery, London, and "The Vicomtesse d'Hanssonville" in the Frick Collection, New York City, are outstanding examples of his many studies of distinguished men and beautiful women. His portrait "M. Bertin" in the Louvre is considered one of the finest of the century. Ingres continued to paint vigorously in his old age, producing such works as his famous "Turkish Women at the Bath" (Louvre) in his 82nd year. A large number of his works are in the Louvre, Paris, and in the Montauban Museum, the latter devoted entirely to his work. There are fine portrait examples by him at the Metropolitan Museum of Art, New York City, at the National Gallery, Washington, D.C., and the Taft Museum, Cincinnati.

INHERITANCE, in biology. See Heredity.

INHERITANCE, in law, succession to the real and personal property of a decedent. Inheritance may be by will (q.v.) or, in the absence of a will, by operation of the statutes governing intestacy. The transfer of property by testate and intestate succession is of remote origin. The code promulgated by the Babylonian ruler Hammurabi (q.v.) in the 20th century b.c. made provision for both testate and intestate succession. In ancient Greece, wills were made at Athens in the time of the lawgiver Solon (q.v.), in the 6th century b.c. The ancient code of Roman law, called the Twelve Tables (q.v.), contained

"Mme. Rivière," painting by Jean Ingres

provisions for the disposition of testate and intestate property. In England, the introduction of the feudal system resulted in the elimination of the right to dispose of real property by will, and this disability continued until the reign of Henry VIII under whom the enactment of the Statute of Wills partially restored the right to dispose of real property by will. See HEIRS. Subsequently this right was entirely restored. In the United States, the statutes of most States provide for the inheritance of property by will, and for the succession to property in cases of intestacy. The statutes of some States provide that the successor to the real property of an intestate decedent may not also succeed to his personal property. Jurisdiction over decedents' estates is vested in the probate courts (q.v.). See INHERITANCE TAX.

INHERITANCE TAX, in United States law, a tax upon the transmission of the property of a decedent, imposed by the Federal and State governments. Inheritance taxes are usually imposed on the net estate of a decedent. The net estate represents the value of the estate at the time of death, less allowable deductions as provided by law. The value of the decedent's insurance policies is not deductible and is included in the estate. Gifts of real or personal property, made by a testator in contemplation of death, are considered under Federal and most State inheritance-tax laws as part of the decedent's estate. See GIFT. Under Federal law the principal deduction, called a marital deduction, applies to estates of married decedents and amounts to approximately half of the value of the estate after other deductions have been made. The latter include chiefly claims against the estate and administration expenses.

In computing the Federal inheritance tax on a decedent's estate, the law makes provision for the exemption from tax of the first $60,000 of the net estate.

INISFAIL (Ir. *inis,* "island"; *Lia-fáil,* "inauguration stone"), the poetic name for Ireland. According to legend, the stone used in the coronation ceremonies of the Irish monarchs at Tara was originally the stone on which the Biblical Jacob dreamed of the ladder to heaven. The Scots obtained possession of the Irish inauguration stone and installed it at Scone. Subsequently, during the reign of King Edward I, it was removed to Westminster Abbey, where it still rests under the coronation chair. Irish writers frequently allude to their homeland as the island of the Fáil.

INITIATIVE, in government, a procedure for the introduction of proposed legislation by means of petition, and for its enactment by popular vote. Two types of initiative are practiced, namely, *direct initiative* and *indirect initiative.* In the practice of direct initiative, a body of voters addresses to the government a petition containing a proposed law; if the petition contains the minimum number of valid signatures as prescribed by statute, the government must submit the proposed law directly to the electorate in the form of a referendum (q.v.). In the practice of indirect initiative, voters submit a petition containing a proposed law to the legislature, which must then consider it; if the law is rejected by the legislature, it must then be submitted to the electorate for a referendum vote. The first constitution of Georgia, adopted in 1777, reserved to the voters the exclusive right to propose amendments to the constitution of the State. The right to initiate all types of legislation was first granted to voters by South Dakota, in 1898. By a recent year more than twenty States had made legal provision for the right of initiative.

INJUNCTION, in the law of equity in England and the United States, generally an order or decree in equity requiring a defendant to refrain from committing a specific act, either in process or threatened, injurious to plaintiff. Injunctions are granted on the usual grounds for equitable actions, namely, that there is no adequate remedy at law, and that the act complained of is causing, or will cause, irreparable damage to plaintiff. Injunctions are generally preventive, restraining, or prohibitory in nature, but on the same grounds may be granted to compel a defendant to undertake an affirmative act, such as to destroy a wall which encroaches on plaintiff's property, or to restore the course of a stream which has been diverted from his property. Such affirmative orders or decrees are called *mandatory* injunctions.

Injunctions are classed as *temporary* or *permanent.* A permanent injunction is granted only after full hearing and adjudication of the case, and is usually so phrased as to enjoin defendant permanently from commission of the act complained of. When, however, plaintiff's right is clear, a court may on application of the plaintiff issue a temporary injunction, or injunction *pendente lite,* at the outset of the proceedings, to prevent defendant from committing an act during pendency of the proceedings which would cause irreparable injury to plaintiff, or which would render final adjudication ineffectual.

Because of the innumerable instances in which injunctions may be used to prevent or halt the commission of wrongs, it has become perhaps the most important remedy of an equitable nature. Injunctions are employed, for example, to abate nuisances, prevent the violation of contracts, to protect patent rights, and to stay proceedings in a court of law. A United States court may thereby restrain all creditors of a bankrupt from prosecuting actions against him in State courts, thus compelling creditors to bring before it all matters relating to the bankrupt's estate. Failure to obey an injunction is a contempt of court, punishable by fine, or imprisonment, or both.

In recent years, considerable controversy has attended the use of injunctions in labor disputes. The first important case involving the use of an injunction in such disputes occurred in 1894. In that year, during the strike of railroad workers in and around Chicago, Eugene Victor Debs (q.v.) and other labor leaders were enjoined by a U.S. District Court from interfering in any way with the railroads entering Chicago and from inducing railway employees to leave their jobs. The Clayton Act (q.v.), passed by Congress in 1914, limited the use of injunctions in labor disputes and provided, for the first time, for jury trials in certain cases arising from the violation of such injunctions. Subsequent court decisions extended the use of injunctions in labor disputes. Dissatisfaction with the situation resulting from these decisions, on the part of labor and its supporters, led to the enactment by Congress, in 1932, of the Norris-La Guardia Act, which restricted the issuance by the Federal courts of injunctions in labor disputes. The Management Labor Relations Act of 1947, known as the Taft-Hartley Act, invested the National Labor Relations Board with power to seek injunctions to delay for 80 days strikes threatening "national health or safety". Many States have statutes providing for the use of injunctions to limit picketing in labor disputes.

INK, any liquid or pasty pigmented substance used for writing, printing, or drawing. The composition and consistency of inks vary according to the purpose for which they are used. The more common types of ink include writing inks, drawing inks, duplicating inks, indelible inks, invisible or sympathetic inks, and printing inks. Many inks differ from paints only in the purposes for which they are used.

Writing Inks. The earliest writing inks were compounded of lampblack and a gum or glue and were mixed with water before use. Such inks, which are still used extensively in Asia, are called India inks and are virtually permanent because the carbon of the pigment is chemically inert and is not bleached or otherwise affected by sunlight. The disadvantage of India ink is that it is manufactured in the form of solid sticks or tablets which must be pulverized in water to form a suspension of the pigment. For this reason solid India ink has been largely supplanted in the western world by liquid inks. A certain amount of solid India ink is used by artists, but most draftsmen and artists prefer to employ a ready-mixed India ink in liquid form.

The most common kind of black ink is made by mixing an iron salt, usually ferrous sulfate, with a mixture of gallic acid and tannins (q.v.) in water. The iron combines with the gallic acid and tannins to form ferrous tannate. This compound has little color as applied to the surface of the paper, but as the ink dries the soluble ferrous tannate is oxidized by contact with the air and becomes insoluble ferric tannate, which is black in color. To aid the user in seeing the trace of the unoxidized ink, a dye, usually blue, is added to the liquid. Mineral acids are also sometimes added to the ink to prevent oxidization and clouding while the ink is in the bottle. Writing inks of other colors are usually water suspensions of natural or synthetic dyes plus gums. Special inks which contain wetting agents are manufactured for use in fountain pens. The addition of a wetting agent permits the ink to flow freely from the pen and to penetrate the paper speedily, so that such inks "dry" at once. The ink used in ball-point fountain pens is similar to printing inks (see below).

Ink Removers. Writing in the ordinary ferric tannate black ink can be eradicated by the application of oxalic acid, which reduces the ferric tannate to the colorless ferrous salt. The organic dyes of colored inks can be eradicated by a solution of sodium hypochlorite, which bleaches the dyes.

Duplicating Inks. Two general types of inks are used in office duplicating machines. Duplicators of the hectograph type employ an ink containing a large concentration of dye, together with glycerin. The stencil type of duplicating machine uses an ink that is a mixture of dyes and solid pigments in oil. The ink used in typewriter ribbons and rubber-stamp pads is composed of dyes in water with enough glycerin added to prevent the ink from drying on the ribbon or pad.

Special Purpose Inks. Indelible inks such as those used for laundry markings are often solutions of silver salts which are reduced to black metallic silver in the marked fabric by the action of heat, light, or chemical action. Other marking inks act on the principle of developed dyes; see DYEING.

Many substances have been employed as inks for secret writing. Usually these are substances such as milk or lemon juice which leave no visible mark when the writing is made but which can be developed (made visible) by heating. Other sympathetic inks are dilute water solutions of sulfuric acid, cobalt chloride, and salts of a number of heavy metals such as platinum. Inks of the first type can be permanently developed by heat; inks of the second type become visible when heated but again fade when recooled; inks of the third type become visible when exposed to ammonium sulfide fumes.

Printing Inks. Printing inks are more like paints than they are like writing inks, in that they consist of solid pigments mixed with an oil. The simplest form of black printing ink is made of carbon black in linseed oil. Colored inks are made of organic pigments, largely of synthetic origin, and some inorganic coloring materials. In many modern inks the oils used as vehicles are also semisynthetic. These oils have the advantage of drying faster than natural oils such as linseed oil, and make possible the high-speed printing of newspapers and magazines. One of the most spectacular of the quick-drying inks developed with a semisynthetic oil is the heat-drying ink used in printing many magazines. This ink is dried by passing the paper over a flame as it leaves the printing press, and permits the web of paper to flow through the press at a speed of 1000 ft. per minute. See PRINTING.

INKBERRY, common name of several evergreen shrubs of the genus *Ilex,* belonging to the Holly family, which produce black fruits. The common inkberry, *I. glabra,* native to sandy soils along the E. coast of North America, is a small shrub, growing 2 to 4 feet high. It bears small, four- to eight-parted, white or greenish flowers which produce small, black drupes. The southern inkberry, *I. lucida,* is a taller, similar shrub which is native to swamps of S.E. United States.

INKBLOT TEST. See PSYCHOLOGICAL TESTING.

INKY CAP. See FUNGI.

INLAND SEA (Jap. *Seto chi Umi* or *Seto no Uchi*), an arm of the Pacific Ocean, situated in Japan between the island of Honshu on the N. and the islands of Shikoku and Kyushu on the S. It is about 240 m. long and 8 to 40 m. wide. Many picturesque islands dot the surface of the sea, which is noted for its fisheries.

INMAN, HENRY (1801–46), American portrait, genre, and landscape painter, born in Utica, N.Y. He studied painting with John Wesley Jarvis in New York City. In 1832 he settled in Philadelphia, where he built a large practice as portrait painter. Among his sitters were such distinguished figures as Chief Justice John Marshall and John James Audubon. He was one of the founders of the National Academy of Design, and in 1834 he served as director of the Pennsylvania Academy of Fine Arts. He visited England in 1844–45, where he painted portraits of William Wordsworth, Thomas Babington Macaulay, and other prominent contemporaries. At the time of his death he was engaged in painting a series of historical pictures for the Capitol at Washington, D.C. Inman was one of the first to introduce the art of lithography into the United States. Among his works are a portrait of the Marquis de Lafayette, in the Capitol at Albany, N.Y.; a portrait of William Penn, in Independence Hall, Philadelphia; and several paintings in the Metropolitan Museum of Art, New York City.

INN (anc. *Ænus*), river of Switzerland, Austria, and Germany, rising in the Swiss canton of Grisons and flowing generally N.E. to the Danube R. From its source the Inn flows through the Swiss valley of the Engadine, enters Austria at Martinsbruck, and crosses the Tirol and Bavaria. The river joins the Danube at Passau. In the last part of its course of about 320 m., the Inn forms the boundary between Germany and Austria. Its chief tributary is the Salzach R.

INNATE IDEAS, certain ideas or concepts, such as those of right and wrong, which were supposed by some philosophers to exist in the mind from birth and not to be derived from experience. Innate ideas were important in the systems of many philosophers, including that of Immanuel Kant (q.v.), but have no place in most modern philosophies.

INNESS, GEORGE (1825–94), American landscape painter, born near Newburgh, N.Y. He studied for a brief period with Régus Gignoux in New York City, but soon became interested in the work of the new Hudson River School (q.v.), particularly that of Asher Brown Durand and Thomas Cole. Their style, traditional and detailed, influenced Inness' early work. The work of his middle period reflects his interest in the French openair Barbizon School (q.v.), in the work of the English painter John Constable, and in Italian art, though he retained his individuality both in subject matter and treatment. The charming "Hackensack Meadows" (1859, collection of the New York Public Library) exemplifies, in its more direct, colorful, and decorative treatment, Inness' departure from his earlier stilted Hudson River manner. His steady growth in breadth of treatment, his increasing feeling for mass over detail, and his fine mastery of space and atmosphere are revealed in the "Delaware Valley" (1865, Metropolitan Museum of Art, New York City). In 1878 Inness settled permanently in Montclair, N.J. The last years of his life were marked by widespread recognition and success. Many of the landscapes show a marked preference for the soft effects of early spring and the glowing russet hues of autumn. He was made a full member of the National Academy of Design in 1868. "Spring Blossoms" (Metropolitan Museum) is one of his finest paintings. His work is represented in over forty museums in the United States. The Art Institute of Chicago contains twenty-two examples, the most important single collection of his work.

INNOCENT, the name of thirteen popes and one antipope, the most important of whom are the following. **1.** INNOCENT I, SAINT (d. 417), Pope from 402 to 417, born in Albano, Italy. During his pontificate he confirmed the primacy of the bishops of Rome. His feast is celebrated July 28. **2.** INNOCENT III (fl. 1180), Antipope in 1179–80, born in Italy as Lando dei Frangipani. He was made antipope in opposition to Pope Alexander III by the followers of the deceased antipope Octavian. After four months, however, he was surrendered by his partisans, and was imprisoned in a monastery. **3.** INNOCENT III (1161–1216), Pope from 1198 to 1216, born in Anagni, Italy, as Giovanni Lotario de' Conti. He was educated at the universities of Paris, Rome, and Bologna, and was elected pope at the age of thirty-seven. During his pontificate the papacy reached the peak of its temporal power; see PAPAL STATES. Aided by the conflict between rival claimants to the throne of the Holy Roman Empire, he expelled the German nobles holding Italian fiefs under the Empire, and consolidated Italy under the papacy. He promoted the fourth Crusade (see CRUSADES), which captured Constantinople and thereby established the Latin Empire. In 1207 he proclaimed a crusade against the Albigenses (q.v.), after nearly ten years of attempting their conversion by peaceful means. In Germany he kept the Holy Roman Empire weak by supporting alternately the claims of the rival emperors Philip of Swabia and Otto IV. In 1213 he forced the submission of King John of England in the controversy over the appointment of Stephen Langton (q.v.) as archbishop of Canterbury. **4.** INNOCENT XI (1611–89), Pope from 1676 to 1689, born in Como as Benedetto Odescalchi. He engaged in a controversy with the French king Louis XIV over the royal prerogative in ecclesiastical appointments; the conflict resulted in the *Declaration of the French Clergy* (see GALLICANISM), a document which declared the virtual independence of the French clergy from the authority of the pope.

INNSBRUCK, capital of Tirol Province, Austria, located on the Inn R., about 80 m. by rail s. of Munich, Germany. In ancient times the site of the city was occupied by the Roman station of Veldidena. The Premonstratensian abbey of Wilten was established on the site in later times, but the town of Innsbruck is not mentioned in history until the 12th century. In 1420 it became the capital of Tirol and the site of a castle built by Archduke Frederick IV of Austria. The chief points of interest are the *Hofkirche,* a Franciscan church which dates from the period of the Italian Renaissance, and the University of Innsbruck, which was established in 1677. The city contains numerous structures, including the former imperial palace, dating from the 17th and 18th centuries. Innsbruck was an important tourist center before the enforced union of Austria with Nazi Germany in 1938. Following World War II, the city was incorporated within the French Zone of Occupation. Pop. (1951) 95,055.

İNÖNÜ, İSMET, assumed name of İSMET PAŞA (1884–), Turkish statesman, born in Izmir (formerly Smyrna), and educated at the Military Artillery College and the Military Academy of Istanbul. In World War I he commanded the Fourth Army Corps in operations against the Russians. In 1919–22 he was chief of staff to Kemal Atatürk (q.v.), leader of the campaign against Greek armies invading Turkey (see TURKEY: *History*). On two successive occasions he scored brilliant victories over the Greeks at İnönü, and in 1922 was made a lieutenant general. Later that year he became minister of foreign af-

Austrian State Tourist Dept.

Maria Theresa Street in Innsbruck, Austria

fairs, and in 1923 he signed the Treaty of Lausanne, formally ending the war between Turkey and the Allies. He was appointed the first prime minister of the Republic of Turkey in 1923 and served almost continuously until 1937, effecting a number of important reforms including the abolition of the Caliphate (see CALIPH) and the closing of the religious schools and monasteries. He adopted the name İnönü in 1934. Upon the death of Atatürk in 1938, he was unanimously elected president, and he served in that capacity until 1950.

INOSITOL. See VITAMIN.

INOUYE, MARQUIS KAORU or KAARU (1835–1915), Japanese statesman, born in Choshu. As an advocate of the assimilation of Occidental culture by the Japanese, he incurred the enmity of the reactionary feudal nobility,

and in 1863 was compelled to flee to England. Soon after his departure the Japanese fired on several foreign vessels passing through the strait of Shimonoseki, and Inouye returned to his native land with the intention of working to avert the danger of war; he was badly injured when a group of samurai (q.v.) ambushed him. He was foreign minister from 1881 to 1888, and negotiated several important revisions of the treaties then in force between Japan and a number of Western powers (see JAPAN: *History*). In 1885 he was elevated to the peerage with the title of count. He was sent as special commissioner to inaugurate reforms in Korea in 1895. During the Russo-Japanese War of 1904–05 he was adviser to the Japanese emperor, and in 1907 he was made a marquis.

INQUISITION, THE, a system of tribunals formerly existing in the Roman Catholic Church, for the discovery, repression, and punishment of heresy. After Christianity became the established religion of the Roman Empire, heresy was regarded as a crime against the civil as well as the canon law, and heretics were punished by the secular courts. No special ecclesiastical bodies for the investigation of heresy were established until the 13th century, when civil and ecclesiastical authorities became alarmed at the spread of the Cathari, Waldenses, and Albigenses, sects reputed to be dangerous to both church and state. An extraordinary commission was sent into the south of France by Pope Innocent III to aid the local authorities in checking the spread of the Albigensian heresy. The fourth Lateran Council in 1215 instructed bishops and magistrates to be especially vigilant against heresy, and a council held at Toulouse directed that in each parish the pastor and two or three reputable laymen (known afterward as "familiars") should examine and report to the bishop all instances of heresy found in the district.

The Inquisition (often called the *Roman Inquisition* to distinguish it from the *Spanish Inquisition;* see below) was established as an ecclesiastical tribunal in 1231, and its judges were generally chosen from members of the Dominican Order. Jurisdiction in matters of heresy was changed from the bishops to local tribunals of the Inquisition, and no appeal was possible except to the Holy See, and after 1542, to the Holy Office (q.v.) in Rome. When found guilty of heresy and contumacious or obstinate in his belief, the heretic was yielded to the civil courts for punishment. Judicial torture for eliciting evidence, then in common use in the civil courts, was authorized by Pope Innocent IV in 1252. As a means of reducing the great number of appeals to Rome, inquisitors general were appointed, first for Provence in 1263, and later for the other territories in central and southern Europe. In England the only occasion of a tribunal of the Inquisition was suppression of the Templars (see KNIGHTS TEMPLARS) in 1308.

The Spanish Inquisition was established by the Spanish rulers Ferdinand and Isabella in about 1480. All of its officials were appointed by the sovereigns, and were free of responsibility to the Church; its first and most notable inquisitor general was Tomás de Torquemada (q.v.). Its proceedings were motivated by politics as often as by religious beliefs, and were conducted with great severity, especially through the 16th century, not only in Spain but also in the Spanish colonies in the New World. In addition to heresy, such crimes as polygamy, seduction, smuggling, usury, and false personation were subject to its tribunals. For extracting information and confessions the Inquisition used the methods, now considered barbarous, which were in use in the secular courts of the time, and which included torturing of defendants and witnesses alike. Its severity was relaxed in the 17th century, and by 1770 royal authority was required for even an arrest. The Spanish Inquisition was finally abolished in 1834. Unlike the Roman Inquisition, under which capital sentences were extremely rare, the Spanish Inquisition frequently pronounced sentences of execution upon heretics; the exact number has been the subject of violent controversy, estimates by partisans ranging from less than four thousand to more than thirty thousand for the Spanish Inquisition's three and a half centuries of existence.

The functions of the Roman Inquisition are continued by the Congregation of the Holy Office, but, since the beginning of the 19th century, they have been chiefly concerned with heretical writings.

INSANITY. See PSYCHOLOGY, ABNORMAL.

INSECT, common name given to any animal of the class Insecta, belonging to the phylum Arthropoda. The term "Hexapoda", meaning six-legged, is also sometimes given to this class. According to the original systematic classification of animals made by the Swedish

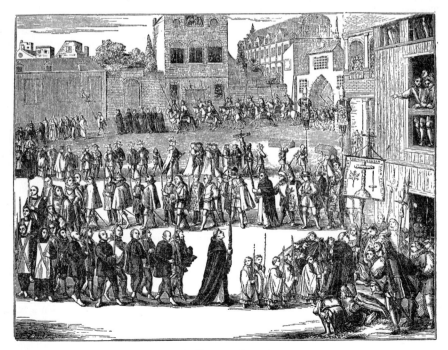

The Inquisition in Spain: an auto-da-fé procession, the ceremony which accompanied the pronouncement of judgment on heretics (from a 17th-century copper engraving)

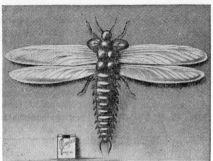

Mechanix Illustrated

Model of a Palaeodictyoptera, huge prehistoric insect. Cigarette package shows size.

naturalist Carolus Linnaeus in 1735, the term "Insecta" embraced the entire group of arthropods, but since the middle of the 18th century the word has been used to denote only the single class.

The insects are the largest class in the animal kingdom, outnumbering all other animals. At least 625,000 separate species have been described, and entomologists believe that as many or more remain to be discovered. The class is distributed throughout the world from the polar regions to the tropics and is found not only on land but also in fresh and salt water and even in such unlikely environments as salt lakes and hot springs. The insects reach their greatest number and variety, however, in the tropics. In size, the insects also exhibit a great variation. Some small parasitic insects are less than one hundreth of an inch in length when fully grown, and at least one fossilized species related to the modern dragon flies is known to have had a wingspread of more than 2 ft. The largest present-day insect known is *Palophus titan,* a stick insect (q.v.), which reaches a length of almost a foot. Insects are the most highly developed class of invertebrate animals. Not only are their structures more complex than those of other invertebrates (with the possible exception of some of the mollusks), but some insects such as the bees, ants, and termites have elaborate "social structures" in which the various forms of activity necessary for the feeding, shelter, and reproduction of the colony are divided among individuals especially adapted for the various activities. Another characteristic of most insects is that they achieve maturity by metamorphosis rather than by direct growth. In most species, the individual passes through at least two distinct and dissimilar stages before reaching its adult form.

In their living and feeding habits, the insects exhibit extreme variations. Nowhere is this more apparent than in the life cycle of various species. Thus the cicada or "seventeen-year locust" matures over a period as long as seventeen years; but the ordinary house-fly can reach maturity in about ten days, and certain parasitic wasps reach their mature form seven days after the eggs have been laid. In general the insects are very precisely adapted to the environments in which they live, and many species depend on a single variety of plant, usually feeding on one specific portion of the plant such as the leaves, stem, flowers, or roots. The relationship between insects and plants is frequently a necessary one for the growth and reproduction of the plant, as in the case of plants which depend on insects for pollination; see SYMBIOSIS. A number of insect species do not feed on living plants, but act as scavengers. Some of these species live on decaying vegetable matter, and others on ordure and the carcasses of animals. The activities of the scavenger insects hasten the decomposition of all kinds of dead organic material.

Certain insects also exhibit predation and parasitism, either feeding on other insects, or existing on or within the bodies of insect or other animal hosts. Parasitic insects are sometimes parasitic upon parasitic insects, and in a few instances, parasitic upon such secondary parasites, a phenomenon known as hyperparasitism. A few species of insects, while not strictly parasitic, live at the expense of other insects, with whom they associate closely. An example of this form of relationship is the wax moth which lives in the hives of bees and which feeds on the comb which the bees produce. In certain cases, the relation between two species is symbiotic. Thus ant colonies provide food for certain beetles which live with them, and in return consume fluids which the beetles secrete. See ENTOMOLOGY, ECONOMIC; ENTOMOLOGY, MEDICAL.

Social Insects. One of the most interesting forms of insect behavior is exhibited by the social insects, which, unlike the majority of insect species, live in organized groups. The social insects include about 800 species of wasps, 500 species of bees, the ants, and the termites. Characteristically an insect society is formed of a parent or parents and a large number of offspring. The individual members of the society are divided into groups, each having a specialized function, which often exhibit markedly different bodily structures. For discussion of the organization of typical insect societies, see articles on the insects mentioned above.

Anatomy. Although the superficial appearance of insects is extremely varied, certain characteristics of their anatomy are common to the entire class. All mature insects have bodies composed of three parts: head, thorax, and abdomen (the abdomen and thorax are not always differentiated in larvae). Each of these parts is composed of a number of segments. The insect's head carries a pair of antennae used for feeling, a pair of jaws or mandibles, and two pairs of auxiliary jaws or maxillae. All insects have exactly three pairs of legs, growing from the thorax, and many larvae have in addition several pairs of leg-like appendages called *struts*. In winged insects, the wings also grow from the thorax. The abdomen is devoid of legs, and in female insects contains egg-laying structures which may be modified into stings, saws, or drills for depositing the eggs in the bodies of plants or animals. The detailed anatomy of a generalized mature insect is given below.

Insects have an external rather than an internal skeleton; this exoskeleton is a tough integument formed by the hardening of the outer layer of skin through the formation of a chemical substance called chitin. The skin at the joints does not become chitinized and hence remains flexible.

Insects' heads are composed of six segments, but these segments are usually so grown together that they cannot be differentiated. The two antennae, which are usually attached to the anterior part of the head, are usually also made up of segments and may be jointed. In some insects the antennae bear organs of smell as well as organs of touch. The eyes of an insect are also situated on the head. The *mandibles* are large and heavy jaws on either side of the mouth which usually close horizontally, and which are used for grasping food as well as for crushing it. The inner jaws or *maxillae* are lighter in structure and are equipped with a pair of feelers or *palps*. The mouths of many insects are adapted for piercing and sucking rather than for biting.

The thorax of any insect is made up of three segments, called from front to back the *prothorax*, the *mesothorax*, and the *metathorax*. A pair of legs grows on each of these segments. The form of the legs varies, depending on their uses, but all insect legs are made up of five parts. Wings, usually four in number when present, arise from the mesothorax and the metathorax. The upper and lower membranes of the wings cover a net-work of chitinized tubes incorrectly called *veins* or *nerves*, which stiffen the wing. The pattern of the "veins" of insects' wings is characteristic in each species and is extensively used by entomologists as a basis for classification.

Insects' abdomens usually have ten or eleven clearly defined segments, but in some species more are present. In all cases the anal opening is located on the last segment and in some species, such as the May flies, a pair of feelers called *cerci* also appear on this segment. The sexual organs, including the egg-laying organ or *ovipositor*, arise from the eighth and ninth segments.

Respiration. Certain species of insects breathe through small openings in the skin, but in general the respiratory system of members of this class consists of a network of tubes or *tracheae* which carry air throughout the body to smaller tubelets or tracheoles with which all the organs of the body are supplied. In the tracheoles the oxygen from the air diffuses into the bloodstream and carbon dioxide from the blood diffuses into the air. The exterior openings of the tracheae are called *spiracles*. The spiracles are situated on the insect's sides and are usually twenty in number, four on the thorax and sixteen on the abdomen. Some water-breathing insects

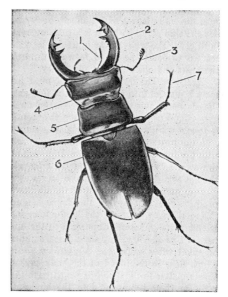

Anatomy of a male stag beetle. 1, maxillae; 2, mandibles; 3, antennae; 4, head; 5, thorax; 6, abdomen; 7, leg.

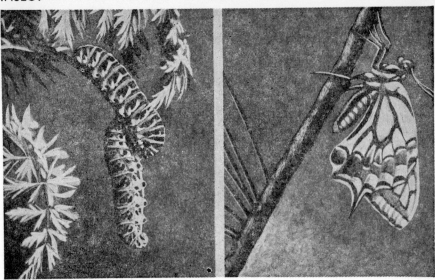

Metamorphosis of the swallowtail butterfly. Left: Caterpillars. Right: Adult.

are provided with gill-like structures within the tracheae.

Circulation. The circulatory system of insects is simple. The entire body cavity is filled with blood which is kept in circulation by means of a primitive heart. This heart, which runs the entire length of the insect's body under the skin along its back, is a tube, open at both ends. The walls of the heart can be contracted to force the blood forward through the heart and out into the body cavity.

Digestion. The digestive tract of most insects is divided into three parts: the fore-gut, the stomach, and the hind-gut. In the fore-gut, a food passage or gullet from the mouth is followed by a crop. Salivary glands empty into the gullet and their secretions are mixed with the food during mastication. Digestion of the food takes place chiefly in the crop, although this organ sometimes also serves as a storage space for food. Most of the digestive products are absorbed in the stomach, and the food waste passes to the hind-gut or intestine for elimination. Connected to the upper part of the hind-gut are a large number of small tubes called the *Malpighian tubes* which float in the blood of the body cavity. Waste matter in the blood passes through the walls of these tubes and into the hind-gut, from which it is eliminated from the insect's body.

Nervous System. The nervous system of insects centers around a nerve cord which runs

from the insect's head to its abdomen along the underside of its body. Typically the cord is equipped with a pair of *ganglia* or nerve centers for each segment of the body. The brain, which is located just above the insect's gullet, is made up of three ganglia fused into one. The brain receives the stimuli from the antennae and from the eyes.

The sense organs of insects consist of eyes, auditory organs, organs of touch, organs of smell, and organs of taste. Insect eyes are of two types. Each of the two compound eyes, which are usually situated directly behind the antennae, contains from 12 to 28,000 light-sensitive nerve endings grouped under a lens or cornea that is composed of an equal number of hexagonal prism-shaped facets. These facets only permit light that is parallel to their axes to reach the nerve endings, and thus build up an optical image that is a mosaic of the light impulses reaching the individual nerves. In addition many species have simple eyes or *ocelli* which are usually located between the compound eyes. Entomologists believe that the compound eye is adapted to the vision of swiftly moving objects, whereas the simple eyes or ocelli with which some insects are equipped are adapted to seeing close-by objects and fluctuations in light intensity. The ocellus has a simple lens overlying a series of light-sensitive nerve elements, all of which are connected by a single nerve to the brain.

The auditory organs of insects vary widely in structure and in some species are quite complex. In some grasshoppers, large auditory membranes are situated on either side of the first segment of the abdomen. Behind these membranes are spaces filled with fluid which transmit the sound impulses to nerve endings which project into the fluid. Other types of grasshoppers and crickets have auditory organs on their legs below the knees. These organs consist of air chambers which communicate with the outside air through slits in their walls and which are supplied with nerve endings. The organs of touch in insects resemble hairs and are located on various parts of the body and on the antennae.

Reproduction. The various species of insects exhibit an extreme variety in their modes of reproduction. In some insects such as the honeybee, the female or queen mates only once and produces thousands of fertilized eggs over a period of several years, although the male dies shortly after the mating. In other species, such as the May flies, both male and female insects have only a short span of life after mating. In a number of species of beetles, both males and females mate repeatedly, and in at least one species the eggs of the female are infertile until after several matings. In addition, various species of insects reproduce parthenogenetically, developing from unfertilized eggs. This form of reproduction occurs regularly in certain species, and occasionally or in alternate generations in others. In some gall wasps and sawflies, all reproduction is by parthenogenesis, and no sexual reproduction occurs. In the social bees and other related insects, male insects are always produced from unfertilized eggs. In certain moths, which exhibit sporadic parthenogenesis, both sexes are produced from unfertilized eggs. Among the aphids several successive generations of females may be produced parthenogenetically before the production of a generation of male and female insects which reproduces sexually.

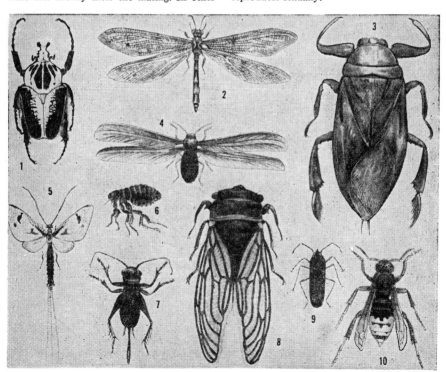

VARIOUS INSECTS OF THE SUBCLASS PTERYGOTA. *1, goliath beetle (order Coleoptera); 2, ant lion (Neuroptera); 3, giant water bug (Heteroptera); 4, termite (Isoptera); 5, May fly (Plectoptera); 6, flea (Siphonaptera); 7, cricket (Orthoptera); 8, cicada (Homoptera); 9, chinch bug (Heteroptera); 10, hornet (Hymenoptera).*

Certain flies occasionally reproduce by means of the method of paedogenesis, the production of eggs by immature forms, either larvae or pupae. The larvae of midges of the genus *Miastor* produce several generations of larval females, before producing male and female larvae which develop into adult insects and reproduce sexually.

The method of development of eggs also varies widely among the insects. Some insects are viviparous, and give birth to living young. In other species, the entire larval stage of development takes place within the mother's body, and the insect becomes a pupa at birth. Most insects' eggs, however, are deposited and hatch outside the body of the parent. The egg-laying habits of the different species vary. In many cases single eggs or masses of eggs are deposited on the plants on which the larvae will feed. A number of insects lay their eggs within the tissues of the food plant, and the eggs may give rise to swellings or galls on the leaves or stems of the plant.

Certain insects show a unique form of embryonic development in which more than one embryo is formed by a single egg. This process is known as polyembryony, and in some species more than 100 larvae are formed from a single egg by division within the egg.

Metamorphosis. One of the characteristics of the development of insects from birth to maturity is metamorphosis, the change through one or more distinctive immature body forms to the imago or adult body form. Metamorphosis of some kind occurs in most insects, though in a few species, such as the bristle-tails, the newborn insect is essentially dissimilar in form to the imago.

Entomologists recognize two basic forms of metamorphosis: complete and incomplete. In complete metamorphosis, the insect first assumes a larval form, an active immature form typified by the caterpillar; then changes to a pupa, a more or less dormant form, usually enclosed in a cocoon; and finally emerges as the adult insect or imago. In incomplete metamorphosis, the insect is born in a relatively mature form called a nymph, which resembles the imago but which lacks or has only partly-developed wings and reproductive apparatus. The nymph changes to the imago by a gradual process, and no pupal stage occurs. In the most primitive insects this process is almost continuous, but in most cases it is separated into several distinct stages, separated by *moulting* or *ecdysis* of the inelastic exoskeleton. A form of complete metamorphosis in which the insect larva undergoes one or more changes in form (usually to adapt it to a change in food supply) before becoming a pupa is called hypermetamorphosis. Hypermetamorphosis takes place in certain beetles and flies, and certain parasitic insects of the order Hymenoptera.

In a typical generalized example of metamorphosis, the larva is a caterpillar which can crawl in search of food and which has mouth parts adapted for feeding on leaves or grasses. As the larva grows, it sheds its skin from three to nine times. At the end of the larval period, the insect spins a cocoon about itself and enters the pupal stage. At this time the wings and other body structures of the mature insect first develop. During the pupal stage the insect is quiescent and does not eat, but its body gradually assumes the imago form. When the pupa is fully developed, it breaks open its cocoon and emerges as a complete adult insect, such as a moth or butterfly.

Classification. The class of insects is arranged in various ways by different naturalists. The following classification is representative. The whole class Insecta is divided into two subclasses: the Apterygota, primitive wingless insects; and the Pterygota, including the great bulk of insects, most of which have wings in the imago form.

The Apterygota are in turn subdivided into four orders: the Protura, a group of very tiny, blind insects; the Thysanura, which includes the silver fish; the Entotrophi, a small group which contains the largest of the Apterygota, an insect of the genus *Heterojapyx,* which is about 2 in. long; and the Collembola, which includes the springtails.

The Pterygota are divided into a total of 29 orders. These orders are: the Plectoptera, which includes the May flies; the Plecoptera, the stone flies; the Odonata, the dragonflies and damsel flies; the Grylloblattodea, a small wingless order; the Orthoptera, the katydids, crickets, and locusts; the Phasmatodea, the walking sticks; the Thysanoptera, the thrips; the Dermaptera, the earwigs; the Mantodea, the mantes; the Blattariae, the roaches; the Isoptera, the termites; the Embioidea, a small group of social insects living in tropical and subtropical regions; the Corrodentia, the book lice; the Mallophaga, the bird lice; the Zoraptera, of which only one termitelike species is known; the Anoplura, the true lice; the Homoptera, which includes the cicadas, the leaf hoppers, the plant lice, and the true scale insects; the Heteroptera, the true bugs; the Megaloptera, the alder flies and hellgrammites; the Raphidiodea, the snake flies; the Neuroptera, the ant lions and aphis lions; the Mecoptera, the scorpion flies; the Trichoptera, the caddis flies; the Lepidoptera, the butterflies and moths; the Diptera, mosquitoes, gnats, and true flies; the Siphonaptera, the fleas; the Coleoptera, the beetles; the Strepsiptera, a group of tiny insects parasitic on other insects such as wasps; and the Hymenoptera, including ants, bees, wasps, hornets, and ichneumon flies.

Fossil Insects. Because of their delicate structure, insects have left fewer fossil remains than have other classes of animals. The earliest fossils found have been in Devonian rocks, and represent primitive forms of wingless insects which lived more than 300 million years ago. The fossil records indicate that the class may have developed in a still earlier period. Among the more advanced orders of insects, the Diptera appeared in Jurassic times, the Hymenoptera in the Cretaceous period, and the Lepidoptera in the Oligocene epoch, contemporary with the great apes. See GEOLOGY, HISTORICAL.

INSECTICIDE, preparation or substance used to destroy insects and related animals sometimes called insects. Such related animals include mites, ticks, spiders, and various other invertebrates which bear a superficial resemblance to insects. The three principal types of insecticides are fumigants, stomach poisons, and contact poisons. Fumigants can be used against insects in an enclosed space, such as a greenhouse. Outdoor plants are sometimes covered with tents and fumigated. Stomach poisons are used to kill insects, such as beetles and caterpillars, which have chewing and biting mouth parts. Contact poisons are used to kill insects, such as bedbugs, which have piercing and sucking mouth parts, and which do not eat poisons (such as stomach poisons) which are placed on the surfaces of plants.

Since the beginning of World War II, a great many effective insecticides have been developed; older insecticides, however, are still in common use. The latter include such fumigants as hydrocyanic acid gas, nicotine, sulfur dioxide, and carbon bisulfide; such stomach poisons as lead arsenate, calcium arsenate, Paris green (q.v.) (copper aceto-arsenite), and hellebore (q.v.); and such contact poisons as nicotine, sulfur, and various oil emulsions and mixtures. The arsenical poisons and nicotine have a tendency to damage tender foliage and leave poisonous residues on the surfaces of treated plants. Oils may usu-

ally be used only when plants are in a dormant state. Insecticides used to combat infestation of humans include various oils and fats, such as kerosene, dilute carbolic acid, vaseline, or lard.

Two of the older insecticides, *pyrethrum* and *rotenone,* are in unabated use because they are only slightly toxic to humans. Pyrethrum consists of the powdered flowers of several species of chrysanthemum (q.v.), containing a volatile oil which acts as a contact poison. Pyrethrum is especially effective against cabbage loopers, cabbage webworms, cabbage worms, and bean or potato leafhoppers. Rotenone, which is a crystalline ketone, $C_{23}H_{22}O_6$, extracted from roots of *Derris* and *Jacquinia,* is effective both as a contact and stomach poison against the Mexican bean beetle, the pea weevil, the asparagus beetle, and several pests of cabbage, lettuce, cucumber, and potato.

The most widely known insecticide developed during World War II is *D.D.T.* (q.v.), an organic poison which has high toxicity for insects and relatively low toxicity for humans. It is effective against mosquitoes, lice, fleas, bedbugs, cockroaches, and many insect pests, particularly thrips, which attack growing plants. It has strong residual action when used in large quantities. D.D.T., which acts slowly, may be combined with pyrethrum, which acts rapidly, to provide a strong insecticide with lasting effect. The two insecticides, or D.D.T. alone, are frequently used as contents for aerosol (q.v.) bombs. Many less-publicized new insecticides, however, are more effective than D.D.T. in eradicating specific insect pests, or are still less toxic to humans. These insecticides include two compounds closely related to D.D.T.: its methoxy analogue, $C_{16}H_{15}Cl_3O_2$, and *T.D.E.,* tetrachlorodiphenyl-ethane (1,1-dichloro-2,2-*bis*-[p-chlorophenyl]-ethane), $C_{14}H_{10}Cl_4$. The two related compounds are less toxic to insects than D.D.T., but are proportionately more toxic to insects than to humans. *Benzene hexachloride,* $C_6H_6Cl_6$, which is prepared by the reaction of chlorine and benzene, is effective against boll weevils, grasshoppers, wireworms, and livestock lice and ticks. Its immediate effect is stronger than that of D.D.T., but it has no residual action. *Chlordane,* $C_{10}H_6Cl_8$, is more effective than D.D.T. against cockroaches and houseflies, but the effect is brief. It has been used successfully against ants, boll weevils, chiggers, fleas, mosquitoes, squash bugs, and ticks, and in large-scale eradication of grasshoppers. One of the most effective agents against aphids is *hexaethyl tetraphosphate,* which is approximately twice as toxic as nicotine. *Parathion,* which was developed in Germany, is very effective against mites which attack apple orchards, as well as a wide range of other pests. When used as a spray, Parathion retains its insecticidal properties for several weeks. *Cryolite* (sodium aluminum fluoride), Na_3AlF_6, is effective against vegetable pests, such as tomato pinworm and fruitworm, pepper weevil, and the potato flea beetle. Among the newer insecticides are toxaphene, malathon, and the two synthetic chlorinated hydrocarbons (q.v.), adrin and dieldrin. Various hydrocarbon insecticides were developed (1953) without chlorine, which is harmful to warm-blooded animals. One of this group was reported to be 100 times more deadly to the flour beetle than D.D.T.; another was said to equal D.D.T. in toxicity to mosquito larvae, though harmless to other species.

The tendency of flies to develop resistance to such insecticides as D.D.T., chlordane, and dieldrin, creates a serious problem in control of these pests. Chemically different insecticides are being investigated in laboratory tests on D.D.T.-resistant flies in an effort to discover some compound which will retain toxicity to flies for several generations.

Extensive development and testing of new insecticides is carried on by the Bureau of Entomology and Plant Quarantine of the U.S. Department of Agriculture, and by most State agricultural stations.

INSECTIVORA, an order of insect-eating mammals the members of which are distributed throughout every continent except Australia and South America. Several species subsist on vegetation and small invertebrates other than insects. The order includes the hedgehog, mole, shrew, solenodon, tenrec (qq.v.), and desman; only the common mole and common shrew are found in continental North America.

Insectivores are small animals with the snout projecting beyond the lower jaw. The body is usually covered with soft thick fur; in animals such as the hedgehog the fur is bristly. Five-clawed toes are present on each foot. The animals have glands which give off an offensive odor. They are chiefly terrestrial; the otter shrew, *Potamogale velox,* a w. African species, and the desman are aquatic. Insectivores are nocturnal in habit.

INSECTIVOROUS PLANTS. See CARNIVOROUS PLANTS.

INSEMINATION. See REPRODUCTION.

INSIGNIA, emblems or symbols used by armed forces, orders, and societies as marks of identification, rank, or honor. Modern insignia, derived from the heraldic devices (see HERALDRY) of the Middle Ages, first appeared in the 17th century when soldiers of the French Army wore brass plates bearing numbers indicative of the regiment to which the wearer belonged.

In the U.S. armed forces, insignia are distributed to indicate rank, specialty, branch of service, organization, wounds, length of service in a combat theater, total length of service, and accomplishments of the wearer. In World War II, officers' insignia of rank were small, designed to be visible only at short distances in order to avoid identification by enemy sharpshooters.

Insignia of the various branches of U.S. military service are shown in the accompanying illustrations. Officers' insignia of rank in the Air Force and the Marine Corps are identical with insignia designating corresponding ranks in the Army. However, general is the highest rank held in the Marine Corps. Warrant officers of the Marine Corps wear a gold bar with a vertical red stripe. Coast Guard insignia of rank are similar to those of the Navy.

INSOMNIA. See SLEEP.

INSPIRATION, in theology, divine guidance exerted upon sacred teachers and writers, preserving them from error and giving divine authority to the inspired work. Inspiration is characterized as *verbal* if the exact words are revealed, and the writer or speaker merely reproduces them in a mechanical manner; as *plenary,* if the faculties and vocabulary of the speaker or writer are allowed full function, but the divine guidance is such as to preclude all error; and as *moral,* when the divine influence affects only the moral or religious content of the message, without reference to the material and historical data in which the teaching is contained.

Before the Reformation, the doctrine of the Church on inspiration was not specifically defined. In the 17th century the German theologian Abraham Calov advanced the principle that nothing exists in Scripture which is not inspired; this principle was generally adopted as the Protestant doctrine. The Roman Catholic Church holds that the plenary inspiration of the original writing of the Scriptures does not necessarily apply in their copying and translation.

INSTALLMENT SELLING, in commerce in the United States, sales of merchandise, usu-

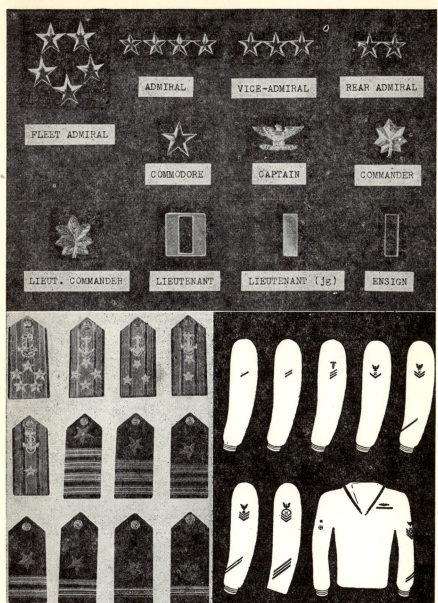

INSIGNIA OF THE U.S. NAVY. *Top: Pin-on miniature rank devices for officers. Bottom, left: Officers' epaulets. Top row, left to right, fleet admiral, admiral, vice-admiral, rear admiral; middle row, commodore, captain, commander, lieutenant commander; bottom row, lieutenant, lieutenant (j.g.), ensign, chief warrant officer. Bottom, right: Rating marks and specialty badges for enlisted men. Top row, seaman recruit, seaman apprentice, seaman, petty officer 3rd class, petty officer 2nd class; bottom row, petty officer 1st class, chief petty officer, front of blouse. Each forearm stripe shows 4 years of service.*

U.S. ARMY OFFICERS' INSIGNIA OF RANK

General of
the Army

General

Lieutenant General

Major General

Brigadier
General

Colonel

Lieutenant Colonel
(silver)

Major
(gold)

Captain

1st Lieutenant
(silver)

2nd Lieutenant
(gold)

Chief Warrant
Officer

Warrant Officer
(j.g.)

INSIGNIA OF ENLISTED GRADES

1st Sgt.

Master
Sgt.

Sgt. 1st
Class

Sergeant

Corporal

Private
1st Class

INSIGNIA FOR VARIOUS BRANCHES OF U.S. MILITARY SERVICE

| *Army* | *Navy* | *Marine Corps* | *Coast Guard* |

AIR FORCE INSIGNIA

Command Pilot   *Senior Pilot*   *Pilot*   *Navigator*

Aircraft Observer   *Flight Surgeon*   *Flight Nurse*   *Air Crew Member*

INSIGNIA OF AIR FORCE ENLISTED GRADES

Master Sgt.   *Tech. Sgt.*   *Staff Sgt.*   *Airman 1st Class*   *Airman 2nd Class*   *Airman 3rd Class*

INSIGNIA OF MARINE CORPS ENLISTED GRADES

Master Sgt.   *Tech. Sgt.*   *Staff Sgt.*   *Sergeant*   *Corporal*   *Private 1st Class*

INSIGNIA FOR VARIOUS BRANCHES OF U.S. MILITARY SERVICE

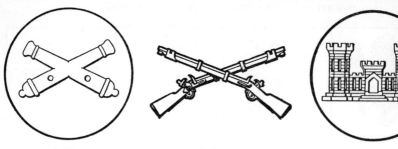

Artillery

Infantry

Corps of Engineers

Armor

Transportation Corps

Military Police

Ordnance Department

Quartermaster Corps

Signal Corps

Inspector General's Department

Judge Advocate General's Department

Medical Department

ally by retail dealers, in which possession of goods is transferred from a seller to a purchaser in consideration for an initial cash payment and a commitment to pay the balance of the purchase price in a series of subsequent, periodic cash payments. Title vests in the purchaser with the final payment; failure by the purchaser to meet the periodic payments entitles the seller to recover possession of the goods. Virtually every type of merchandise is marketed by installment selling; the principal commodities sold in this manner are automobiles, furniture, washing machines, refrigerators, radios, certain articles of clothing, and other durable consumers' goods.

A large proportion of installment sales are financed by enterprises, called finance companies, which specialize in this type of credit operation. These companies, about 1500 in number in a recent year, advance the entire purchase price of the article to the seller; they protect their interests by securing from the purchaser a series of promissory notes and, according to the laws of the various States, a conditional-sales contract between the finance company and the purchaser, a chattel mortgage on the goods, or other similar security device. Many commercial banks are empowered by law to engage in the financing of installment sales. In many cases, the seller finances the sale.

Retail installment selling became important in the United States during the prosperity years of the 1920's; many economists believe that the inflation of credit (see CREDIT; INFLATION) which resulted from installment selling during this period was a contributory factor to the onset of the economic crisis of 1929 and the ensuing depression in the 1930's. During World War II the Federal Reserve Board was vested with authority to regulate consumer-credit operations by determining the percentage of the purchase price to be paid initially on installment-plan purchases and by fixing the time limit for completing payment on them. This regulatory power of the Board was continued in the postwar period. In a recent year about 10 percent of all goods sold in the United States were marketed by installment sales, and the total unpaid balance on installment-plan sales was more than $18,600,000,000.

INSTINCT, nonspecific term for unlearned behavior which satisfies a basic need of an organism. The term instinct is generally restricted to those mental and emotional drives which cause an animal or human being to perform an act voluntarily; the term reflex (q.v.)

behavior, with which instinct is often confused, is generally restricted to uncontrollable physical responses to specific stimuli. The organization of instinctive responses involves widespread areas of the nervous system including the brain, whereas reflex responses often involve only a restricted portion of the nervous system, including the spinal cord but not the brain. Furthermore, although reflex behavior can be conditioned, instinctive behavior is more flexible in being more subject to immediate change in response to differing environmental conditions.

Scientists accept certain behavior patterns as being purely instinctual, though considerable controversy exists among them. Generally accepted among the instincts of humans and animals are the instinct of *self-preservation*, which includes behavior to satisfy hunger and thirst, and the *sex instinct*, which includes mating behavior. These instincts, though present at birth, are modified by learning after birth. A baby chick is able to peck for food upon emerging from the egg, but at first pecks inefficiently, often missing the insect or grain, until it has learned to co-ordinate its movements. Those birds or lower animals which participate in elaborate courtship ceremonies before mating perfect their courtship displays through experience even though their first attempts are instinctual. In certain birds, such as the blackbird, the mating song is instinctive; in others, such as the chaffinch, it must be learned from other members of the species. In man, instincts are modified by the culture; consequently, in various cultures, different behavioral patterns are employed to satisfy the same instinctive needs.

Beside the instincts of self-preservation and sex, many other instincts have been postulated. These include: the migratory instincts of birds and fishes; the nesting instinct of birds; and the maternal instinct of higher animals in general. The migratory "instinct" of some birds has been proven to be initiated chiefly by the indirect physiological response of the animals' gonads to a decrease in concentration of the actinic rays of the sun. Present researches are being conducted to determine whether or not other "instincts" may be due to physiological stimulation.

INSTITUTE OF ARTS AND LETTERS, NATIONAL, an American society of artists, writers, and musicians, founded by the American Social Science Association in 1898 to promote the development of, and interest in, literature and the fine arts in the United States. It is privately supported. The organization of the

Institute is modeled on the Institute of France (q.v.), and comprises three sections: art, music, and literature. Membership is limited to a total of 250 persons. The Institute grants awards to American artists, writers, and musicians who have performed outstanding work; organizes conferences of writers and artists; and brings representatives of foreign cultural institutions to the United States for purposes of international cultural exchange. Headquarters of the Institute are in New York City.

A subsidiary organization of the Institute is the American Academy of Arts and Letters, created in 1904 as an honorary association of fifty outstanding members of the Institute. The Academy elects its own members, among whom, in a recent year, were the novelists John Dos Passos, Sinclair Lewis, William Faulkner, and John Steinbeck; the poets Archibald MacLeish and Mark Van Doren; the painters John Sloan and Leon Kroll, and the composers Ernest Bloch and John Alden Carpenter.

INSTITUTE OF FRANCE, a group of five learned societies in France, each organized at a different time prior, with one exception, to the creation of the Institute itself in 1795; each society has for its purpose the fostering of some special branch or branches of work in literature, art, philosophy, or science. The Institute was organized during the French Revolution by the government known as the National Convention (see CONVENTION, NATIONAL). At the time, the Institute was comprised of only three societies, one devoted to physics and mathematics, one to the moral and political sciences, and one to literature and the fine arts. The five present sections of the Institute are as follows.

(1) The *Académie Française,* founded in 1635 for the purpose principally of preparing an authoritative dictionary of the French language. The first edition of the *Dictionnaire de l'Académie Française* was published in 1694; the eighth, in 1932–35. The Académie Française has forty members. (2) The *Académie des Inscriptions et Belles Lettres,* organized in 1663. Its purpose is the historical study of ancient inscriptions and documents, of numismatics, and of languages, both living and dead. This section of the Institute has forty members. (3) The *Académie des Sciences,* created in 1666. It promotes original work in the mathematical sciences, such as geometry and astronomy; and in the physical sciences, such as chemistry, botany, and anatomy. The Académie des Sciences numbers seventy-eight members. (4) The *Académie des Beaux-Arts,*

established in 1648 to encourage progress in the fine arts. It has forty members. (5) The *Académie des Sciences Morales et Politiques,* the only section organized at the same time as the Institute (1795). It consists of five divisions: philosophy, morals, legislation and jurisprudence, political economy, and history and geography. It has forty members.

The Institute in all has over two hundred members, each of whom receives a small annuity from the government of France, and about three hundred correspondents; many of the latter are foreigners. Each section of the Institute elects its own members, whenever a vacancy occurs. Since 1805 the Institute has held its meetings in the Palais de l'Institut, a columned and domed building in Paris on the Seine River at the Pont des Arts. The various sections of the Institute give many annual prizes, the money for which is usually supplied by rich benefactors, to nonmembers who do notable work in the intellectual fields covered by the societies.

INSTRUMENTALISM, in American philosophy, a variety of pragmatism (q.v.) developed at the University of Chicago by John Dewey (q.v.) and his colleagues. Thought is considered by instrumentalists to be a method of meeting difficulties, particularly such difficulties as arise when immediate, unreflective experience is interrupted by the failure of habitual or instinctive modes of reaction to cope with a new situation. According to the doctrine, thinking consists in the formulation of plans or patterns of both overt action and unexpressed responses or ideas; in each case, the goals of thought are a wider experience and a successful resolution of problems. In this view, ideas and knowledge are exclusively functional processes; that is, they are of significance only as they are instrumental in the development of experience. The realistic and experimental emphasis of instrumentalism has had a far-reaching effect on American thought; Dewey and his followers have applied it with conspicuous success in such fields as education and psychology. See EPISTEMOLOGY.

INSTRUMENTATION. See ORCHESTRATION.

INSULATION, any material which is a poor conductor of heat or electricity, and which is used to prevent unwanted thermal circulation or flow of electric currents.

Electric Insulation. The perfect insulator for electrical applications would be a material that is absolutely nonconducting, but such a material does not exist. The materials used as insulators, although they actually do conduct electricity, have a resistance to the flow of electric currents as much as 2,500,000,000-000,000,000,000,000 times that of such conductors as silver and copper, and are thus virtually nonconductors.

In ordinary electric wiring, rubber and rubber-impregnated cloth are commonly used as insulating sheathing for the wire itself. Very fine wire, such as that used for the winding of coils and transformers, is insulated with a thin sheathing of cotton or silk cloth or, sometimes, by a coat of enamel. Glass has excellent insulating qualities and is often employed for the insulators by which power lines are attached to the towers which support them. The internal insulation of electrical equipment is made of a number of substances, among them hard rubber, paper, mica, fiber, varnished cloth, various ceramics, and plastics. Most plastics and ceramics have good insulating properties. In certain types of equipment, such as the heavy transformers and circuit breakers in electrical distribution systems, oil is used as an insulator. When wires carrying high-frequency alternating current must be insulated, the dielectric (q.v.) properties of the insulator are often as important as the insulating properties.

Thermal Insulation. Materials which resist the circulation or flow of heat are widely employed both to keep heat confined and to exclude it. An example of the former use of thermal insulation is the asbestos sheathing often placed around steam and hot water pipes to prevent heat losses by radiation; an example of the latter use is the employment of thermal insulation in the walls of refrigerators.

Thermal insulating materials can be divided into two types: those materials which prevent heat conduction; and those materials which reduce radiation of heat. A vacuum is a perfect nonconductor of heat, but air is almost equally good if convection currents can be prevented. For the latter reason, most materials used for thermal insulation are porous and contain a large proportion of air-filled cavities. Such materials include asbestos, magnesium carbonate, cork, felt, cotton batting, rock wool, and diatomaceous earths. Spaces filled with air or partially evacuated also have excellent heat insulating qualities and advantage is taken of this fact in the manufacture of such building materials as hollow glass bricks, insulating glass (consisting of two bound sheets of plate glass with a small air space between), hollow earthenware tile, and partially hollow concrete tile.

Highly reflective surfaces such as those of polished metals prevent heat losses or heat absorption by radiation. Thin aluminum foil is therefore sometimes used as insulating material in the walls of houses, and metallic roofs are used to minimize the heating effect of the sun. The Dewar flask or thermos bottle (see article on CRYOGENICS) contains both a vacuum which prevents conduction of heat and highly polished surfaces which prevent radiation of heat.

The relative insulating values of various building and insulation materials are given approximately in the following table.

Marble	1	Oak	20
Sandstone	2	White pine	27
Limestone	4	Balsa	60
Glass	4	Fiber boards	60
Plaster	7	Cork board	66
Cinder concrete	10	Rock wool	77

INSULIN, a hormone which regulates the metabolism of carbohydrates in the body, produced in the islands of Langerhans in the pancreas (q.v.). A deficiency of insulin causes the condition known as diabetes (q.v.). For the biochemistry of insulin see SUGAR, METABOLISM OF. Insulin was first extracted from pancreatic tissue in 1921 by Frederick Grant Banting, Charles Herbert Best, and John James MacLeod (qq.v.), and was produced in sufficiently pure form to be injected in persons suffering from diabetes by the Canadian biochemist James Bertram Collip (q.v.).

Insulin is a water-soluble protein, which is stable in acid, but destroyed in alkaline solution. Like other proteins it is partially digested when administered orally, and for this reason, when used clinically, it must be injected. Normal pancreatic tissue is relatively rich in zinc, and crystalline preparations of the hormone contain zinc. In the treatment of diabetes, insulin is often combined with protamine, a simple protein; the combination is absorbed more slowly than insulin alone and the effects are more lasting. A preparation called protamine zinc insulin prolongs the effective action of insulin still further.

INSURANCE, in law and business, a contract, called an insurance policy, providing compensation by an insurer to an insured party, for loss resulting from death, illness, accident, theft, fire, flood, and other contingencies. The insurer is generally a private corporation, but may be a fraternal society (q.v.) or a government agency; see FEDERAL DEPOSIT INSURANCE CORPORATION. The consideration for the contract is usually the payment of a premium by the assured directly to the insurer in accordance with terms stipulated in the contract and subject to regulations established by statute. In workmen's-compensation (q.v.) insurance, the employer contracts with an insurance company to insure his employees and pays the consideration for the insurance contract. In the insurance of bank deposits, the Federal Deposit Insurance Corporation compensates depositors in cases of bank failure; the banks pay the FDIC an assessment based on their deposits.

As defined above, the term "insurance" does not include those forms of compensation collectively designated as social insurance and social security (qq.v.), and which include governmentally administered unemployment insurance, old-age pensions, and health insurance. Social insurance involves the insurance principle to the extent that benefit payments are made to insured persons, in consideration of payments previously made by the insured or their employers or both. It differs from the usual forms of insurance in several respects. The most important is the replacement of the contractual relationship among parties, characteristic of usual forms of insurance, by a statutory relationship between a government and the insured in social insurance.

In the United States the principal types of insurance are life insurance, fire insurance, marine insurance, workmen's compensation, health insurance (qq.v.), automobile, accident, burglary, and general-liability insurance. Among many other types are earthquake, rain, flood, hail, tornado, plate-glass, title, and credit insurance. Insurance in the United States is underwritten and policies issued by various types of enterprise. Mutual-insurance companies, the largest and most important type, are owned by their policyholders. Stock-insurance companies are corporations owned by their stockholders. Another common type is that modeled on the celebrated English insurance firm of Lloyd's (q.v.). In this type of insurance enterprise, a number of individuals combine to share the risks of insuring parties against business losses, and share the profit or loss in proportion to the risk assumed by each.

INSURANCE, HEALTH, a system of providing financial indemnity against loss of earning power resulting from the disability of the insured person by reason of sickness or accident, and against extraordinary expenses connected therewith. Such protection may be furnished by private insurers to individuals, singly or in groups, or by government as a form of social insurance to the entire population of a state; see article on SOCIAL INSURANCE.

The craft guilds of the Middle Ages paid benefits to their members in case of disability caused by illness; with the decline of the guilds no such protection was available to the workingman until the formation of mutual-aid societies, notably the friendly societies of Great Britain. Fraternal orders and trade unions also adopted the principle of paying stated benefits to their members incapacitated by illness. In the early decades of the 20th century, private insurance companies began to furnish such protection, usually in the form of accident and health insurance policies for individual persons and for groups. The benefits from such policies include payments amounting to a maximum of one half of the insured person's salary for periods of disability ranging from thirteen weeks to two years, and starting after a short waiting period of five to fourteen days. They also include reimbursement of expenses incurred in obtaining first aid in the case of accidents, and generally include hospitalization insurance (q.v.).

In contrast to the relatively small volume of insurance handled by strictly voluntary organizations, however, is the national health insurance made compulsory by law, and furnishing protection to large sections of the population. This protection may be administered by the same organizations which handle the voluntary insurance: the friendly societies, the mutual aid organizations, the fraternal orders, or mutual and stock insurance companies; the entire system, however, is controlled by the central government of the nation, which fixes rates of contribution by the worker and the employer, and the subsidy from the public treasury. The government also fixes the conditions of payment and rates of benefits paid.

The first nation to include health insurance in its program of social insurance was Germany, which under Bismarck in 1883 took advantage of the growing sentiment for expansion of the mutual-protection movement to make compulsory a health insurance supported by a state subsidy. Austria and Hungary followed German's lead before the turn of the century, then Norway and Serbia in 1909–10, and Great Britain and Russia in 1911. After the Bolshevik revolution of 1917 the U.S.S.R. introduced health insurance in

1923, and after the Socialist Labor government came into power in Great Britain after World War II the British system was extensively revised to include as beneficiaries all employed and the self-employed workers who had completed payment of 156 premium payments. In France compulsory health insurance was adopted in 1930; through a 5 or 6 percent payroll tax it finances benefits covering all wage earners to the extent of 80 percent of pharmacal and medical costs.

Since World War II, the extension of health insurance has been widespread. It is generally co-ordinated with the national programs of social security and social insurance, and with workmen's compensation (qq.v.). Several nations, notably Poland and Turkey, reimburse the worker for loss of wages to the extent of 70 to 75 percent of his earnings; others, including Australia and Turkey, supplement benefits paid for periods of sickness with invalid pensions paid to persons incapacitated beyond the ordinary period of sickness benefits.

In the United States, attempts to enact Federal legislation co-ordinating health insurance with the social-security program were unsuccessful from the passage of the Social Security Act in 1935. The question was the cause of much controversy, with the labor organizations the American Federation of Labor and the Congress of Industrial Organizations leading the fight in favor of adoption, and the American Medical Association leading the opposition. In spite of alternative proposals for a State-managed system, with State contributions matched by Federal funds, only three States, California, New Jersey, and Rhode Island, have adopted State systems of health insurance.

INTEGUMENT. See SKIN.

INTELLIGENCE, the capacity to learn or to understand. It is generally synonymous with intellect, but is usually differentiated from it in practice to emphasize ability or efficiency in dealing with concrete situations and in profiting intellectually from sensory experience. In psychology, intelligence is somewhat more narrowly defined as the capacity to acquire knowledge or understanding and to use it in novel situations. Such situations may be prepared under experimental conditions, and the success of a subject in adjusting his behavior to the total situation or in meeting the challenge of the specific situation may be studied and, to some extent, measured in quantitative terms. Psychologists believe that the capacities measured in testing or labora-

tory situations are also significant in everyday life, in which individuals analyze or apprehend new sensory and mental data so as to direct their actions toward desired goals. Psychologists still differ, however, as to a precise definition of the comprehensiveness and functions of intelligence; one school of thought considers it as a sum of specific abilities best displayed in specific situations. In the formulation of "intelligence tests", most psychologists tend to adopt an eclectic concept, according to which intelligence is treated as a general ability operating as a common factor in a wide variety of special aptitudes. It is observed and measured by techniques focused upon these aptitudes singly or in combination. See MENTAL DEFICIENCY; PSYCHOLOGICAL TESTING.

INTELLIGENCE, MILITARY, collective term for all agencies of a government engaged in obtaining and interpreting any information of military value, and in countering the efforts of hostile foreign powers to obtain similar information. Since 1885 the armed forces of the U.S. have maintained a distinct central intelligence department (see MILITARY ORGANIZATION); individual military units also maintain intelligence services for reconnaissance and for gathering specific, immediately applicable information while in the field. Military intelligence includes espionage (q.v.) agencies, agencies which register enemy aliens (see FEDERAL BUREAU OF INVESTIGATION), and propaganda agencies such as the branch of the State Department in charge of the "Voice of America" broadcasts to Europe. See NATIONAL SECURITY BOARD.

INTELLIGENCE TESTS. See PSYCHOLOGICAL TESTING.

INTER-AMERICAN HIGHWAY, the name given to that section of the All-American Highway (q.v.) extending between Laredo, Texas, and Panama City, Panama, for a distance of more than 3300 m. In 1941 the U.S. Army undertook to complete construction of the portion of the route through Central America to the Panama Canal Zone but relinquished the task to the U.S. Public Roads Administration in 1943 after building more than 900 m. of highway. The principal completed sections are between Laredo and Mexico City, from Guatemala City through the Republic of El Salvador to San Lorenzo, Honduras, and from David, Panama, to Panama City. See PAN-AMERICAN HIGHWAY.

INTERDICT, in the Roman Catholic Church, a penalty consisting in the withdrawal of the administration of the sacraments and of all public religious services. Interdicts are of three kinds: *local,* which affect a particular place; *personal,* which affect a person or persons; and *mixed,* which affect both a place and its inhabitants. In the medieval period (see EXCOMMUNICATION) it was used as an ordinary church censure. The most remarkable interdicts were those laid upon Scotland in 1180 by Pope Alexander III; on Poland by Pope Gregory VII, on the murder of Stanislaus at the altar; by Pope Innocent III on France in 1200; and on England under King John in 1208.

INTEREST, in economics, a term signifying money paid for the use of capital advanced in the form of a loan. Many economists consider interest as the reward for thrift, i.e., as the payment that must be made to lenders to encourage them to save and to make their savings available to others. Interest is usually paid only on the principal, that is, on the money loaned, and is called *simple interest.* In some cases, interest payments may be added to the principal, and interest is then paid on the new principal thus obtained; this procedure is called *compounding the interest,* and the interest so paid is called *compound interest.* The rate at which interest is paid is usually expressed as a percentage of the principal for a given period of time, usually a year. Thus, a loan of $100, carrying interest of 4 percent per annum, earns interest of $4 a year. The current, or market, rate of interest is determined by various factors, the most important being the relation between the supply of money and the demands of borrowers; see SUPPLY AND DEMAND. An increase in the supply of money available for investment, without a corresponding increase in the requirements of borrowers, tends to result in a declining interest rate; conversely, interest rates tend to rise when investment funds decrease without a corresponding decrease in demands by borrowers.

In ancient times and during the Middle Ages, the payment of interest for the use of money was generally condemned, and the taking of interest was considered immoral. The Christian Church approved interest on loans for business purposes, but adjudged as a sin, interest on loans made for the purchase of articles of consumption. With the development of modern commerce and industry and the increasing need for capital, the payment of interest was no longer condemned; but a maximum rate of interest was usually fixed by the state to prevent usury (q.v.). In the United States, the statutes of most States prescribe a legal rate of interest, the maximum

interest rate which lenders may charge borrowers. A lower rate may be established by agreement by parties to a loan; in the absence of such agreement, the legal rate prevails. When an interest rate in excess of the legal rate is charged, the transaction is considered usurious, and in some States the maker of such a loan is penalized by being prohibited from collecting either the principal or the interest; other States provide for forfeiture of the interest alone; and still others impose criminal penalties. A few States impose no penalty for usury. However, by statute in most States, an interest rate higher than the legal rate is allowed in contracts providing for small loans made by enterprises licensed as loan agencies or finance companies. The rate generally permitted in such contracts is $2\frac{1}{2}$ percent a month or 30 percent a year.

INTERFERENCE, a phenomenon associated with wave motion, caused by the superposition of two waves moving simultaneously in the same region. When two beams of monochromatic light (light of one wave length and consequently of one color) arrive simultaneously at the same source, an interference pattern of light and dark bands is produced. Wherever the waves of the two beams are in phase (the crest of one wave coinciding with the crest of the other) the light is intensified; where the waves are out of phase (the crests of the waves not coinciding or the crest of one wave coinciding with the trough of another) the light is reduced in intensity or completely extinguished. This intensificaton and reduction of illumination creates alternating bands of light and darkness which are called fringes. When white light, which is a composite of all the colors of the spectrum, is used instead of monochromatic light, each color produces its own interference fringes. The resulting brilliantly colored pattern of interference fringes is due to the combined effect of all the colors. The iridescent display of colors in thin films, such as soap bubbles and layers of gasoline floating on water, is an interference phenomenon. The colors are caused by the interference of the two beams of light reflected from the front and back surfaces of the film, respectively. See LIGHT. Compare DIFFRACTION.

The interference effect is also exhibited by sound and radio waves, the interaction of two waves of slightly different frequencies or phases producing alternate annulments and intensifications which form beats. In radio reception, "interference" is used somewhat loosely in reference to a number of ways in which an undesired signal may be received; two of these are related to superimposed waves: those caused by unintentional beat and by heterodyne. For example, two transmitters broadcasting at 1000 and at 1001 kilocycles will produce an audible difference-frequency, or beat, of 1000 cycles (1 kilocycle), which may be heard in a receiver as an audible whistling note; a heterodyne frequency which may also appear in reception could be produced by two transmitters broadcasting carrier signals of 550 and 600 kilocycles, which produce a sum-frequency of 1150 kilocycles interfering with a third transmitter broadcasting at this higher frequency. Other types of radio interference consist of noise picked up from power circuits, atmospheric disturbances (static), and signals introduced by inductance from a nearby wire communication circuit such as a telephone or telegraph.

INTERFEROMETER, an instrument which utilizes the phenomenon of interference of light waves for the measurement of wave lengths of light, of small distances, and of certain optical phenomena. Many forms of the instrument are used, but in each case two or more beams of light travel separate optical paths, determined by a system of mirrors and plates, and are finally united to form interference fringes; see INTERFERENCE. In one form of interferometer for measuring the wave length of monochromatic light, the apparatus is so arranged that a mirror in the path of one of the beams of light can be moved forward through a very small distance, which can be accurately measured, thus varying the optical path of one of the beams. Moving the mirror through a distance equal to one half of the wave length of the light causes a complete cycle of changes in the pattern of interference fringes. The wave length is calculated by measuring the number of cycles caused by moving the mirror through a measured distance. The standard meter in the C.G.S. (q.v.) system has been measured by the interferometer in terms of the wave length of monochromatic light produced in a lamp containing isotopically pure mercury vapor.

When the wave length of the light used is known, very small distances in the optical path can be measured by means of the interference patterns produced. The refractive indices of substances are also measured with the interferometer, the refractive index being calculated from the shift in interference fringes caused by the retardation of the beam.

The principle of the interferometer is also adapted for use in astronomy to measure the diameter of large stars, such as Betelgeuse (q.v.).

Michelson-Morley Experiment. The first and best-known form of interferometer is the one devised about 1887 by the American physicist Albert Michelson (q.v.) for the experiment he conducted with Edward Williams Morley. The Michelson-Morley experiment was designed to measure the absolute motion of the earth through the ether (q.v.) by means of the effect such a motion (if it existed) would have upon the velocity of light. If ether were a fixed medium through which the earth moved, it would be expected that light traveling a back-and-forth path parallel to the direction of the earth's motion through the ether would take a longer time to pass through a fixed distance than would light traveling a back-and-forth path at right angles to the direction of the earth's motion through the ether. The interferometer was arranged so that a ray of light was split into two rays which passed along two paths at right angles to each other; the rays were then reflected and recombined, producing interference fringes where the two beams met. The apparatus was mounted on a heavy block of stone supported by a disk of wood floating in a tank of mercury, an arrangement which allowed the apparatus to be rotated smoothly. If the hypothesis of the ether were correct, as the apparatus was rotated the two beams of light would interchange their roles (the one which traveled more rapidly in the first position would travel more slowly in the second position) and a shift of interference fringes would occur. Michelson and Morley failed to find such a shift. The experiment, which showed that the velocity of light is unaffected by the motion of the earth and that ether is not a material substance, conflicted with the nineteenth-century view of the physical universe and was a starting point for the theory of relativity (q.v.).

INTERIOR DECORATION, the term applied to the study and process of decorating and, especially furnishing the interior of buildings. Monumental interior decoration is concerned with the decorative treatment of the interiors of large public buildings, such as churches and city halls. Domestic interior decoration deals with the furnishings and decorative treatment of the rooms and other interior divisions, such as halls, of private residences. The present article is a historical survey of domestic interior decoration in Europe and America. For a more extended description of the furniture used in each historic period of interior decoration, see the various corresponding sections in the article FURNITURE.

Middle Ages (about 5th to 13th century). During medieval times the mass of people lived in hovels or huts that provided little but shelter; the nobility and their retainers lived in the castle (q.v.). The principal room of the castle was the great hall, which in early medieval days served for cooking, dining, and sleeping; until the use (beginning about the 12th century) of separate rooms for sleeping, all the retainers slept in the great hall, the women occupying a space enclosed by curtains. The great hall was of monumental proportions. Across the ceiling ran great wooden beams or trusses, which were often carved or painted. The floor, which was of stone, brick, or tile, was, in northern Europe, covered with rushes, straw, or leaves. During the time of the Crusades (q.v.) the use of Oriental rugs, brought from the Middle East, came into vogue for use on floors. The walls of the great hall were often hung with tapestries (see TAPESTRY). Need for insulation against heat and cold led to the plastering of the stone walls, and after plastering came into use the walls were often decorated with fresco paintings. The principal objects of furniture were tables, chairs, and large storage chests. The last-named articles were of particular importance; most of the possessions of the lord of the castle, and also those of his retainers, were stored in chests which could be removed expeditiously when abandonment of the castle was made necessary by military attack.

Late Middle Ages and Renaissance (13th to 17th century). Beginning with the 13th century a great change took place in the type of dwelling of the upper classes in Europe. The castle, which could not withstand the fire of the artillery in use in the 13th century, no longer served for military protection. In addition, the cessation of the constant feudal warfare of the Middle Ages (see FEUDALISM) and the establishment of comparatively peaceful conditions in Europe, together with the increase in wealth due to the growth of trade, led to a demand for homes more comfortable than the castle. The demand was answered by the creation of houses with many rooms for specialized purposes. The first such houses appeared in Italy in the 13th century. The rooms of this new type of dwelling were large and had high ceilings elaborately ornamented with painted decorations and with plaster moldings, usually in imitation of

or derived from ancient Greek and Roman styles. Both the decorations and furniture of the rooms were intended to enhance the effect of richness and magnificence given by the large dimensions of the room. In France, which speedily followed Italy in the development of the new type of house, a room was judged by the amount of ornament applied to ceilings and walls. Because the rooms served for display rather than comfort, little furniture was used in the French rooms of this period. With the exception of sideboards (*dressoirs*) and clothes presses (*armoires*), none of the French furniture of the early Renaissance was designed to be in harmony with the architectural features of the rooms. After 1400 the use of tapestries made in Arras, France, became general in northern Europe for wall coverings, to partition large rooms, to hang over windows and doors, and to enclose beds.

In England the principal type of house that succeeded the feudal castle was constructed half of timber and half of brick and stone, and with many rooms for specialized purposes; it came into general use among the nobility and well-to-do in the 16th century. Many of the features of the medieval castle survived in these houses of the Tudor and Elizabethan periods. The most important feature was the great hall, which, however, was no longer given its former extensive use. Other Gothic features in the 16th-century English house were the windows mullioned with small panes of glass, and the fireplaces with elaborate overmantels of stone or wood. The rooms were simple and dignified, with few articles of furniture and accessories. The walls had oak panels which were usually left undecorated, although occasionally they were carved and, less frequently, painted. Unpaneled or partially paneled walls were decorated with plaster moldings or hung with tapestries. Windows, doors, and the large four-poster beds of the period were draped with heavy velvets, damasks, and brocades.

The Seventeenth Century. France set the style for interior decoration for most of Europe from the 17th well into the 19th century. Two decorative styles predominated in 17th-century France: Louis XIII (known as "Louis Treize style") and Louis XIV ("Louis Quatorze"). The former style prevailed during approximately the first half of the century; it was a development of French Renaissance style which still retained some Gothic features, such as furniture that was angular and square-shaped. In the second half of the 17th

INTERIOR DECORATION

Top, left: A 15th-century Italian bedroom (from "Vision of St. Ursula," by Carpaccio).
Top, right: 16th-century English fireplace. Bottom: A bedroom of 17th-century England.

and the first two decades of the 18th century the Louis XIV style prevailed; it was characterized by solidity, magnificence, dignity, and a profusion of gold ornament. It possessed the classic quality of symmetry, but it was Baroque (q.v.) in its elaborateness and ostentation. Tapestries made in the Gobelin tapestry works in Paris came into extensive use in France and elsewhere during the 17th century.

In England during the early part of the 17th century an elaborate style known as the Jacobean was in vogue; it employed many elements of the styles of ancient Greece and Rome. During the Protectorate (1653–60) the tendency was toward greater simplicity in the design and decoration of rooms. The Restoration (1660) again brought into fashion a heavy and ostentatious style of decoration. After the accession of William and Mary (1689) decorative influences from the Netherlands restored simplicity to English interiors. The English rooms of the last decade of the century were designed for intimate and comfortable living. They were small, with low ceilings and many windows. Ceilings were unornamented; walls and floors were usually of wood. Oriental rugs were commonly used for the floors. Wallpaper, designed to resemble tapestry, became common in England toward the end of the century.

The Eighteenth Century. In France the early part of the 18th century was dominated by the Baroque style of Louis XIV. This was succeeded in the third decade of the century by the Rococo (q.v.) style of Louis XV ("Louis Quinze"), which was characterized principally by the elaborate use of curved lines. The rooms of the dwellings of the noble and rich generally had wall panels of carved wood. Unpaneled walls were in some cases painted in pastel colors, with forms taken from Chinese art or with representations of scenes from nature. A particular feature of the Louis XV room was its small marble mantel exquisitely carved with an elaborate curved design; above the mantel was a richly carved and painted overmantel with a mirror (*trumeau*). The draperies and upholstery used in the Louis XV style were fine-textured, and were patterned with designs having scrolls, ribbons, and flowers as motifs. Lighting fixtures, fireplace accessories, and hardware were of finely chased metal work. The floors were of wood arranged in marquetry patterns or in larger, geometric parquet designs. The use of Aubusson rugs, a type made of tapestry weave at Aubusson, France,

and of Savonnerie rugs was a feature of the Louis XV room.

In the last third of the 18th century the Louis XV style was succeeded by the Louis XVI ("Louis Seize"), which in contrast to the Louis XV was characterized by classical simplicity. Louis XVI furniture and decorations had straight lines and right angles; rooms were smaller and less formal, and became more specialized in use: the bedroom, boudoir, dining room, and library became distinct types. Special kinds of furniture were created to fill the needs of the intimate social life that marked the reign of Louis XVI; among them are the chaise longue, the type of sofa known as the *bergère,* and a type of small desk for writing social correspondence. The paneling of the walls of the Louis XVI room was less profusely carved than that of the Louis XV. In wall painting, scenes from nature gave way to designs that utilized elements from the decorations of classic times. Doors, windows, and marble mantels were of classic rectangular design. Ceilings were in most instances left unornamented; occasionally, when a more luxurious effect than usual was sought, ceilings were painted to represent sky and clouds.

In England also, the beginning of the 18th century was dominated by a Baroque style of interior decoration. This style was succeeded by the Georgian (see GEORGIAN ARCHITECTURE), which was contemporaneous with the Louis XVI style in France and, like that style, was characterized by classic simplicity. The principal designers of furniture in the Georgian period were the Adam brothers, Thomas Chippendale, George Hepplewhite, and Thomas Sheraton (qq.v.). In interior decoration the work of the Adam brothers was outstanding. They were primarily architects, but they also designed and decorated the interiors of the houses they built. The modern conception of interior decoration as part of the work of the architect was first put into practice by the Adam brothers. Adam interiors are characterized by formality, symmetry, a simplicity verging on coldness, and the use of details from ancient Greece and Rome and of broad surfaces of delicate color.

In America, up to the 18th century houses were designed primarily for shelter; comfort and beauty of appearance were secondary considerations. The New England interiors of the early 17th century were characterized by large fireplaces and small windows. More provisions for comfort marked the New England interiors of the late 17th century. The walls

Art Institute of Chicago

Model of a room in an American colonial house

were finished with rectangular wood panels of upright boards; the ceilings were beamed; and the fireplace, which took up most of one wall, was usually spanned with a heavy carved beam. The floors were constructed of wide boards; the use of small Turkey carpets for floors was general. In the 18th century the merchant class in the American colonies imported architectural style and furniture from England; the so-called Colonial style is a modification of English Georgian. Chippendale furniture served as a model for American cabinetmakers in Philadelphia and Newport; the Adam style of furniture and interior decoration influenced the work of the noted American architects John Bullfinch and Samuel McIntire; and the Sheraton style influenced the early work of the famous American cabinetmaker Duncan Phyfe (q.v.). American interiors of the 18th century were characterized by woodwork painted white, by the abundant use of pilasters, and cornices, by mantelpieces of carved wood, and by floors of wide boards. Imported wallpapers were in general use, as were damasks and satins for draperies. After the American Revolution there was a tendency to find ideas and materials elsewhere than in England; during this time a type of printed cotton or linen, known as *toiles-de-Jouy* and used chiefly for curtains, was imported from France.

Nineteenth and Twentieth Centuries. Early 19th-century interiors in Europe and America were decorated largely in the Empire style which dominated France during the Napoleonic era (1804–15). The Empire style of furniture was modeled on classic and Oriental styles and was characterized by long, curving lines and by the use of ornaments of ivory and brass. A modified form of this style was developed in America and was known as American Empire; its chief exponent was Duncan Phyfe.

In the last three decades of the 19th century and in the early part of the 20th century, two general schools of interior decoration prevailed in Europe and the United States. The traditional school treated each room in a house as a separate entity unrelated to any other room, and decorated it according to one particular historical style. The second school of interior decorators sought to break away from the copying of historical styles; it did not consist of any particular group of decorators but its principles were made manifest in the activities of various groups. One was the Arts and Crafts movement in England and America in the second half of the 19th century; it stressed simplicity in furniture and attempted to create interiors that had a relationship to the functions and the spirit of modern life. The creation of the "mission style" of furniture in the United States was an attempt to establish a native style independent of historical styles and adapted to modern use. Mission furniture is heavy, sturdy, and plain; it is dark in color and has straight lines and square sections.

After World War I the division became even sharper between the traditionalists among interior decorators, who devoted themselves to furnishing rooms with antiques

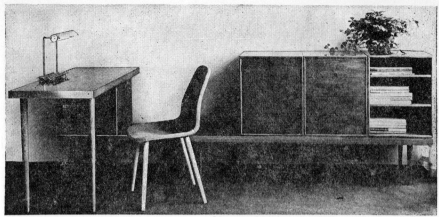

Museum of Modern Art, N.Y., and Saarinen & Eames

Section of a living room, an example of "modern" American interior decoration

or reproductions of them, and the modernists, whose aim was to originate new styles in keeping with 20th-century life. The modernists themselves were divided into several schools. One made use of traditional historical styles freely modified and adapted to the needs of contemporary life. The interiors created by this school were characterized by the use of pastel color schemes and rich textures for draperies and upholstery. Another group, influenced by the hectically dynamic spirit in social life of the so-called "Jazz Age", the decade following World War I, designed interiors that were characterized by violent color schemes and the use of Cubistic (see CUBISM) patterns. A third group of modernists, one of the most important of contemporary groups, insisted on interiors reflecting the functionalism that characterizes modern architecture (q.v.); this group utilized steel, aluminum, and plywood, among other materials, to make simple, practical furniture unlike that of any historical style, and known as "modern" furniture (see FURNITURE: *Modern Furniture*).

The practice, originated by the Adam brothers in the 18th century, in which the architect of a building concerns himself also with the interior decoration of the rooms of the structure has often been followed in the 20th century. It is the belief of many experts today that to obtain the best results in interior decoration either the architect must decorate the interiors of the house, or the interior decorator must have a knowledge of architecture sufficiently thorough to enable him to create interiors in keeping with the general architectural plan.

INTERIOR, DEPARTMENT OF THE, one of the ten executive departments of the Federal government of the United States, created by Congressional enactment in 1849. The Department is administered by a secretary, who is appointed by the President with the approval of the Senate, and who is a member of the Cabinet. The principal functions of the Department include the efficient utilization and conservation of natural resources; the management of public lands; flood control; the reclamation of arid lands; the conduct of geological surveys; the administration of Indian affairs; the management of national parks; and the administration of certain territorial and island possessions of the United States. In 1849, when the Department was established, most of the continental United States, with its vast natural resources, was unexplored. In the following years the Department assisted citizens to discover and exploit the nation's resources. During the latter half of the 19th century, concomitantly with the settlement of the West and the development of large-scale industry, the basic function of the Department was gradually changed to that of the conservation of the country's natural resources. At the same time, the size and functions of the Department were steadily extended, until it became one of the largest agencies of the government, with jurisdiction over territories many thousands of miles from the American mainland.

As originally constituted, the Department consisted of the Patent Office, the General Land Office, the Pension Office, and the Bureau of Indian Affairs. Of these, only the last-named has remained as a unit of the Department. The Patent Office was transferred to the Department of Commerce in 1925; the General Land Office was merged into the Bureau of Land Management, within the Department, in 1946. The functions of the Pension Office, which has been abolished, were assigned chiefly to the Veterans Administration (q.v.). The principal component units of the Department are the Bureau of Land Management, the Bureau of Reclamation, the Geological Survey, the Bureau of Mines, the Bureau of Indian Affairs, the National Park Service, the Fish and Wildlife Service, and the Office of Territories; see separate articles on these agencies. In a recent year, the expenditures of the Department totaled more than $575,000,000, almost two fifths of which was disbursed by the Bureau of Reclamation, and the Department employed more than 58,000 persons.

INTERJECTION, in grammar, one of the eight parts of speech, generally an ejaculatory word used to express sudden or powerful emotion, as "Ah!". When nouns, adjectives, or phrases are used in this manner, as "Goodness!", "Marvelous!", or "Great Scott!", they are commonly termed *exclamatory nouns, exclamatory adjectives,* and *exclamatory phrases,* respectively. When used as a part of a sentence, an interjection does not usually have grammatical connection with the other words of the sentence, as in the celebrated line from Shakespeare's play *Romeo and Juliet:* "O, Romeo, Romeo! wherefore art thou Romeo?".

INTERLAKEN, a village of Berne Canton, Switzerland, situated on the Aar R., between the lakes of Brienz and Thun. It is connected by steamer and rail with Thun. The village developed around the religious house of Austin Canons, which was founded in the early 12th century. A 12th-century castle houses the administrative offices of the canton. Interlaken is a popular summer resort, noted for the beauty of its surroundings. Nearby tourist attractions include the Jungfrau (q.v.), of which Interlaken commands a fine view. Pop., about 3000.

INTERLOCUTORY JUDGMENT. See JUDGMENT.

INTERMARRIAGE, nonspecific popular term for the marriage (q.v.) of individuals prohibited from marrying by social custom, tradition, or law. The most widespread legal taboo against intermarriage is that prohibiting incest; this taboo has considerable justification in scientific fact. Other taboos, with little such justification, present themselves in societies which practice endogamy (q.v.), or marriage within a specified social group, and exogamy (q.v.), or marriage outside of the group. In most States of the U.S., miscegenation (q.v.), marriage between white persons and members of the colored races, is legally prohibited. Many religious groups forbid their members to marry outside of the denomination or sect.

INTERMEZZO, originally, a light entertainment introduced between the acts of an opera, tragedy, or comedy to allow time for a change of scene, to give performers a rest, or to divert an audience during a serious work. Intermezzi consisting of hymns or carols were composed in the Middle Ages to be introduced between the scenes of Mysteries and Miracle Plays. In the 16th century, intermezzi in the form of madrigals, choruses, arias, and ballets began to appear between the scenes of secular Italian plays. At times these intermezzi took on plots of their own, so that the audience was presented with two alternating and distinct dramas. By the 18th century they had won such popularity that they were often produced independently, and were called *opera buffa* ("comic opera") in distinction from *opera seria* ("serious opera"). One of the most famous of these works was *La Serva Padrona* (1733) by the Italian composer Giovanni Battista Pergolesi, which was originally a true intermezzo, performed between the acts of another, longer work.

In the 19th century the intermezzo became an instrumental piece performed between acts of an opera and having no special connection with the opera itself. It indicated the passage of time in the opera's plot, and differed from the entr'acte (q.v.) in that the curtain was not lowered during its performance. The most famous example of this type is the *Intermezzo* from *Cavalleria Rusticana* by the Italian composer Pietro Mascagni (q.v.).

Another 19th-century development of the term was its application in purely instrumental music by such composers as Ludwig van Beethoven (q.v.) to a short movement between two longer movements. The term was further extended by such composers as Robert Schumann and Johannes Brahms (qq.v.) to denote small, independent piano pieces.

INTERNAL-COMBUSTION ENGINE, any type of prime mover which obtains mechanical energy directly from the expenditure of the heat energy of fuel burned in a combustion chamber which is an integral part of the engine. Only three types of internal-combustion engines are in general use, the *Otto-cycle* *engine,* the *Diesel engine,* and the *gas turbine,* although other types are theoretically possible. For discussion of the last-named type, see GAS TURBINE. The Otto-cycle engine is the familiar "gasoline engine" used in automobiles and airplanes; the Diesel, which operates on a different principle and usually uses oil as a fuel, is employed in electric-generating and marine-power plants and, to a limited extent, in trucks and busses. Diesel engines have also been used in aircraft. Both Otto-cycle and Diesel engines are manufactured in two-stroke and four-stroke cycle models.

Components of Engines. The essential parts of Otto-cycle and Diesel engines are the same. The *combustion chamber* consists of a *cylinder,* usually fixed, which is closed at one end and in which a close-fitting *piston* slides. The in-and-out motion of the piston varies the volume of the chamber between the inner face of the piston and the closed end of the cylinder. The outer face of the piston is attached to a crankshaft by a connecting rod. The purpose of the crankshaft is to transform the reciprocating motion of the piston into rotary motion. In multicylindered engines the crankshaft has one offset portion, called a *crankpin,* for each connecting rod, so that the power from each cylinder is applied to the crankshaft at the appropriate point in its rotation. Crankshafts are equipped with heavy flywheels and counterweights, which by their inertia minimize irregularity in the shaft's motion. The number of cylinders in an individual engine varies from one to as many as twenty-eight.

The fuel supply system of an internal-combustion engine consists of a *tank,* a *fuel pump,* and a device for vaporizing or atomizing the liquid fuel. In Otto-cycle engines this device is a carburetor (q.v.), and in Diesel engines some type of fuel injector is used. The vaporized fuel in most multicylindered engines is conveyed to the cylinders through a branched pipe called the *intake manifold* and, and many engines, a similar *exhaust manifold* is provided to carry off the gases produced by combustion. The fuel is admitted to each cylinder and the waste gases exhausted through mechanically operated *poppet valves* or *sleeve valves.* The valves are normally held closed by the pressure of springs and are opened at the proper time during the operating cycle by cams on a rotating *camshaft* which is geared to the crankshaft.

In all engines some means of igniting the fuel in the cylinder must be provided. The ignition of Diesel engines is described below.

The ignition system of Otto-cycle engines consists of a source of low-voltage, direct-current electricity which is connected to the primary of a transformer called an *ignition coil.* The current is interrupted many times a second by an automatic switch called the timer. The pulsations of the current in the primary induce a pulsating, high-voltage current in the secondary. The high-voltage current is led to each cylinder in turn by a rotary switch called the *distributor.* The actual ignition device is the *sparkplug,* an insulated conductor set in the wall or top of each cylinder. At the inner end of the sparkplug is a small gap between two wires. The high-voltage current arcs across this gap, yielding the "spark" which ignites the fuel mixture in the cylinder.

Because of the heat of combustion all engines must be equipped with some type of cooling system. Some aircraft engines, small stationary engines, and outboard motors for boats are cooled by air. In this system the outside surfaces of the cylinder are shaped in a series of radiating fins with a large area of metal to radiate heat from the cylinder. Other types of engines are water-cooled, and have their cylinders enclosed in an external water jacket. In automobiles, water is circulated through the jacket by means of a *water pump* and cooled by passing through the finned coils of a *radiator.* In marine engines sea water is used for cooling.

Unlike steam engines and turbines, internal-combustion engines develop no torque when starting and therefore provision must be made for turning the crankshaft so that the cycle of operation can begin. Automobile engines are normally started by means of an electric motor or *starter* which is geared to the crankshaft with a clutch which automatically disengages the motor after the engine has started. Small engines are sometimes started manually by turning the crankshaft with a crank or by pulling a rope wound several times around the flywheel. Methods of starting large engines include the *inertia starter,* which consists of a flywheel that is rotated by hand or by means of an electric motor until its kinetic energy is sufficient to turn the crankshaft, and the *explosive starter,* which employs the explosion of a blank cartridge to drive a turbine wheel that is coupled to the engine. The inertia and explosive starters are chiefly used to start airplane engines.

Otto-Cycle Engines. The ordinary Otto-cycle engine is a four-stroke engine; i.e., its pistons make four strokes, two toward the head (closed head) of the cylinder and two away from the head, in a complete power cycle. During the first stroke of the cycle, the piston moves away from the cylinder head while simultaneously the intake valve is opened. The motion of the piston during this stroke sucks a quantity of fuel mixture into the combustion chamber. During the next stroke the piston moves toward the cylinder head and compresses the fuel mixture in the combustion chamber. At the moment when the piston reaches the end of this stroke and the volume of the combustion chamber is at a minimum, the fuel mixture is ignited by the spark and burns, expanding and exerting a pressure on the piston, which is then driven away from the cylinder head in the third stroke. During the final stroke, the exhaust valve is open and the piston moves toward the cylinder head, driving the exhaust gases out of the combustion chamber and leaving the cylinder ready to repeat the cycle.

The efficiency of a modern Otto-cycle engine is limited by a number of factors, including losses by cooling and by friction. In general the efficiency of such engines is determined by the compression ratio of the engine. The compression ratio (the ratio between the maximum and minimum volumes of the combustion chamber) is usually about 7 to 1 or 8 to 1 in most modern Otto-cycle engines. Higher compression ratios, up to about 12 to 1, with a resulting increase of efficiency, are possible with the use of high-octane anti-knock fuels; see DETONATION. The efficiencies of good modern engines which work on the Otto cycle range between 20 and 25 percent (i.e., only this percentage of the heat energy of the fuel is transformed into mechanical energy).

Diesel Engines. Theoretically the Diesel cycle differs from the Otto cycle in that combustion takes place at constant volume rather than at constant pressure. Most Diesels are also four-stroke engines, but operate differently than the four-stroke Otto-cycle engines. The first or suction stroke draws air, but no fuel, into the combustion chamber through an intake valve. On the second or compression stroke the air is compressed to a small fraction of its former volume and is heated to approximately 800° F. (440° C.) by this compression. At the end of the compression stroke vaporized fuel is injected into the combustion chamber and burns instantly because of the high temperature of the air in the chamber. Some Diesels have auxiliary electrical ignition systems to ignite the fuel when the engine starts, and until it "warms up". This com-

bustion drives the piston back on the third or power stroke of the cycle. The fourth stroke, like that of the Otto-cycle engine, is an exhaust stroke.

The efficiency of the Diesel engine, which is in general governed by the same factors which control the efficiency of Otto-cycle engines, is inherently greater than that of any Otto-cycle engine and in actual engines approaches 40 percent. Diesels are in general slow-speed engines with crankshaft speeds of 100 to 750 revolutions per minute as compared to 2500 to 5000 revolutions for typical Otto-cycle engines. Some types of Diesel, however, have speeds up to 2000 revolutions. Because Diesels use compressions ratio of 14 to 1 or more, they are generally more heavily built than Otto-cycle engines, but this disadvantage is counterbalanced by their greater efficiency and the fact that they can be operated on inexpensive fuel oils.

Two-Stroke Engines. By suitable design it is possible to arrange to run either an Otto-cycle or Diesel as a two-stroke or two-cycle engine with a power stroke every other stroke of the piston instead of once every four strokes. The efficiency of such engines is less than that of four-stroke engines, and therefore the power of a two-stroke engine is always less than twice that of a four-stroke engine of comparable size.

The general principle of the two-stroke engine is to shorten the periods in which fuel is introduced to the combustion chamber and in which the spent gases are exhausted to a small fraction of the duration of a stroke instead of allowing each of these operations to occupy a full stroke. In the simplest type of two-stroke engine, the poppet valves are replaced by sleeve valves or ports (openings in the cylinder wall which are uncovered by the piston at the end of its outward travel). In the two-stroke cycle the fuel mixture or air is introduced through the intake port when the piston is fully withdrawn from the cylinder. The compression stroke follows and the charge is ignited when the piston reaches the end of this stroke. The piston then moves outward on the power stroke, uncovering the exhaust port and permitting the gases to escape from the combustion chamber.

For fuller discussion of automotive and aero engines, see AUTOMOBILE; AIRPLANE.

INTERNAL REVENUE SERVICE, formerly BUREAU OF INTERNAL REVENUE, agency of the U.S. Treasury Department, established in 1862, reorganized in 1953, and responsible for the enforcement of the internal-revenue laws. The agency is administered by the commissioner of internal revenue, who is appointed by the President with the advice and consent of the Senate. A highly decentralized agency, the Service consists of the Headquarters Organization, located in Washington, D.C., and the Field Organization, which functions in nine geographical areas known as Internal Revenue Regions. The Headquarters Organization includes the Office of the Commissioner, which supervises the assessment and collection of all taxes imposed by laws providing internal revenue; the Office of the Deputy Commissioner, which exercises executive leadership of the Service; the Office of the Assistant Commissioner (Administration), the top administrative branch of the Service; the Office of Assistant Commissioner (Inspection), which is responsible for ensuring proper ethics and standards of conduct among Service personnel, for the detection of irregularities and defalcations, and for the efficient operation of the Service; and the Office of the Chief Counsel, the legal division.

Each of the nine regions is headed by a regional commissioner. Assisting each of the latter are six assistant commissioners, who have respectively jurisdiction over administration, collection, audit, intelligence, alcohol and tobacco tax, and appellate activities. The Internal Revenue Regions are divided into varying numbers of Districts, each of which is administered by a director. There were recently 64 Offices of District Directors. Among the functions of these Offices are such duties as providing service to the public in the preparation of tax returns, collection of internal-revenue taxes, selling internal-revenue stamps, and ascertainment of delinquent and additional tax liability.

INTERNATIONAL BANK FOR RECONSTRUCTION AND DEVELOPMENT, a specialized agency of the United Nations, established in December, 1945, in accordance with the provisions of the Articles of Agreement, adopted in July, 1944, by representatives of the forty-four nations attending the international monetary conference held at Bretton Woods, N.H.; see BRETTON WOODS CONFERENCE. The Bank was created to promote the international flow of capital for productive purposes, to assist in financing the reconstruction of areas devastated during World War II, and to further the development of the resources of the member nations. The total authorized capital stock of the Bank was fixed at $10,000,000,000; of this amount, about $8,000,000,000 was subscribed during the first three years of the Bank's existence; $3,200,000,000 was subscribed by the United States. The Articles require the Bank to make short- and long-term loans solely on the basis of the economic needs of the applicants, and explicitly forbid interference by the Bank in the political affairs of member nations. The highest governing authority of the Bank, which has its principal office in Washington, D.C., is the Board of Directors, consisting of representatives appointed by the member nations. Voting power on the Board is apportioned in accordance with the number of shares subscribed by the members. By a recent year, loans totaling more than $1,590,766,000 had been made by the Bank.

INTERNATIONAL CHILDREN'S EMERGENCY FUND, an agency of the United Nations, established in December, 1946, to provide children and expectant and nursing mothers in war-devasted areas with food and other essentials needed to combat malnutrition and disease. In establishing the Fund, the General Assembly of the United Nations promulgated the following guiding principle. "Distribution will be on the basis of need, without discrimination because of race, creed, nationality status, or political belief." The operating principles of the Fund are formulated by the Economic and Social Council (q.v.), and its subsidiary, the Social Commission. The Fund is administered by an executive board and an executive director elected by the board members; the executive board consists of representatives of the member nations of the Social Commission and of eight other nations, who need not be U.N. members, named by the Economic and Social Council.

The fund is financed through contributions granted by governments, voluntary agencies, private individuals, and various other sources; and through the transfer to it of assets from the defunct United Nations Relief and Rehabilitation Administration (q.v.). To assist in financing the work of the agency, the Economic and Social Council in March, 1947, created the United Nations Appeal for Children, an agency charged with the task of carrying out a world-wide campaign for voluntary contributions from private citizens. In December, 1948, the Appeal was merged with the Fund; to that date it had obtained a total of $10,000,000. By a recent year contributions to the Fund totaled more than $185,000,000, of which the United States gave more than $100,000,000. In 1953, when the Fund became a permanent agency, its name was changed to U.N. Children's Fund, but the abbreviation U.N.I.C.E.F. was retained.

INTERNATIONAL COPYRIGHT. See COPYRIGHT.

INTERNATIONAL COURT OF JUSTICE, one of the principal organs of the United Nations, created in 1945 under an international treaty known as the Statute of the Court, and comprising an integral part of the United Nations Charter. The Court is empowered to deal with disputes arising among nations signatory to the Statute, but may exercise jurisdiction only when the dispute is referred to it by the nations concerned, and when the dispute involves matters stipulated in the Charter or in existing conventions or treaties. At the request of the Security Council or the General Assembly of the United Nations, the Court may also render advisory decisions on legal questions. The Court may base its decisions on the provisions of international treaties and conventions, the principles of international law, and judicial decisions previously rendered by the highest courts of the various nations.

The Court consists of fifteen judges, no two of whom may be citizens of the same country, elected by the Security Council and the General Assembly. Under the Statute the term of office of the judges was set at nine years, but in order to provide for regular changes in the composition of the Court, at the first election, held in 1946, five members were elected for three years, five for six years, and five for the full term of nine years. The Court sits at The Hague.

INTERNATIONAL DATE LINE, an irregular line drawn on the map of the Pacific Ocean, near, and in many places coincident with, the 180th meridian. It marks the place where navigators change their date one day on a transpacific voyage.

Any traveler circling the globe in a westward direction lengthens his day by one hour for every 15° of longitude traveled, because he is following the apparent motion of the sun; by the time he has traveled completely around the world he is one full day ahead, in calculated time, of the people who have remained at the place from which he started out. Going eastward, a traveler similarly arrives a day behind.

Close to the 180th meridian, nearly in the middle of the Pacific Ocean, a place chosen because of the virtual absence of land and of civilization in the region, navigators going westward drop a day from their calendars (for example, the day after

Aug. 6 would be Aug. 8), and navigators going eastward add a day to their calendars (for example, the day after Aug. 6 would be Aug. 6) in order to correct for this gain or loss of time. The date line is curved eastward around Siberia, westward around the Aleutian Islands, and eastward around the Fiji Islands and New Zealand to avoid crossing land. See TIME, STANDARD.

INTERNATIONAL LABOR ORGANIZATION, a specialized agency of the United Nations. It was originally established in 1919 as an autonomous agency of the League of Nations, and was brought into formal relationship with the United Nations in December, 1946. Sixty-six nations are represented in the I.L.O., which is charged with the task of contributing to the establishment of a universal and lasting peace through the improvement of labor conditions and living standards, and the promotion of economic and social stability on a world scale.

The I.L.O. consists of two main bodies, the International Labor Conference and the International Labor Office. The former is composed of four delegates from each of the member nations of the I.L.O.; of each group of four delegates, two represent government, one represents management, and the fourth, labor. The Conference meets annually to consider and formulate Conventions and Recommendations which are adopted by a two-thirds majority vote of the Conference. The Conventions consist of proposals relating to such matters as hours of labor, the protection of women and children in industry, the prevention of, and compensation of workers for, industrial accidents, colonial labor problems; and social-security problems. These proposals take effect within each member nation upon the ratification of the Convention by the individual nations. Countries which have ratified a Convention are required to furnish the I.L.O. with annual reports on the implementation of the Convention. Of the 103 Conventions adopted by the Conference since the establishment of the I.L.O., more than half were in force in various countries in a recent year. Unlike the Conventions, Recommendations are merely suggestions to be considered by the member governments. By a recent year the Conference had adopted 95 Recommendations; many had been implemented in various countries.

The International Labor Office, with headquarters at Geneva, Switzerland, is the permanent secretariat of the I.L.O. Its activities are carried on under the supervision of an executive body called the Governing Body and composed of sixteen representatives of government, eight management representatives, and eight labor representatives. The Office, which is a center of information and research on social and economic problems, publishes the monthly *International Labor Review,* the *Legislative Series* which contains the texts and translations of important labor and social legislation enacted in all countries, the *Year Book of Labor Statistics,* numerous reports for the Conference, and a variety of special reports and periodicals. It also published the *International Labor Code* (1951), containing a systematic arrangement of all Conventions and Recommendations formulated by the Conference since its formation.

INTERNATIONAL LADIES' GARMENT WORKERS' UNION, a semi-industrial union of American and Canadian needle-trades workers, constituting one of the largest affiliates of the American Federation of Labor (q.v.). This union, generally known as the ILGWU, is notable in U.S. labor history for the militancy with which its early organizational drives were conducted, for its pioneering work in the initiation of educational, health, and welfare programs for union members, and for its policy of collaboration with employers in the solution of problems confronting the women's garment industry.

The ILGWU was founded in New York City in June, 1900, at a meeting of eleven delegates representing about 2000 members of seven local unions in New York City, Newark, Philadelphia, and Baltimore. Three weeks after its formation, the ILGWU became an affiliate of the American Federation of Labor. Immediately after its establishment, the ILGWU launched a compaign to raise the wages of needle-trades workers, which, in some shops, were as low as five dollars for an eighty-hour work week; and to eliminate the requirement that workers pay for the use of needles, thread, and sewing and other machines. The first great advance occurred after a strike of the shirtwaist workers of New York City in 1909-10; this strike, known in labor history as the "Uprising of the 20,000", resulted in the establishment of a 52-hour work week in the needle trades in New York City, and in substantial wage increases. The "Uprising" was followed in 1910 by a strike known as the "Great Cloak Revolt" in New York

City. The "Revolt" was terminated by an agreement referred to as the "Protocol of Peace", providing for wage increases and other benefits for the needle-trades workers. This agreement was one of the earliest industry-wide collective-bargaining agreements ever negotiated by employers and workers in the United States. As a result of these and other strikes, the ILGWU was successful in eliminating the sweatshop system of exploiting workers in the women's-garment industry in New York and other cities; see SWEATING OR SWEATSHOP SYSTEM.

The ILGWU followed a policy of maintaining industrial peace and stability during World War I. In the 1920's it resumed its struggle to improve working conditions and to expand its membership. This period in the union's history was marked by an internecine struggle which arose when a Communist-led group of needle-trades workers attempted to gain control of the ILGWU, and succeeded in electing their candidates for office in a number of large locals. In 1926, a strike conducted by the garment workers of New York City, under the leadership of this faction, was defeated. The dissident faction then split from the ILGWU and formed the Needle Trades Industrial Union as a rival organization, which was dissolved several years later. Widespread unemployment caused by the economic crisis of 1929 and the ensuing depression led to a general decline in the membership of the ILGWU; this trend was subsequently reversed when union organization in the United States generally was facilitated by the New Deal (q.v.) policies of the Franklin D. Roosevelt administration.

The year 1932 was notable in the history of the ILGWU for the election of David Dubinsky (1892-   ) to the union presidency. Dubinsky, a Polish immigrant, had been a coat-and-suit cutter, a member of the General Executive Board and a vice-president of the ILGWU since 1922, and secretary-treasurer since 1929. Dubinsky was re-elected to the presidency at successive conventions. Under Dubinsky's leadership, the ILGWU rapidly expanded its membership from a total of 40,000 in 1932 to 225,000 in 1937. This rise in membership signalized a fundamental change in the composition of the ILGWU. Originally, the union had been composed chiefly of Jewish immigrants from eastern and southeastern Europe; after 1937 a majority of the membership was of Italian, Spanish, and Puerto Rican extraction.

In 1935 the ILGWU joined the Committee for Industrial Organization, a group of AFL unions united for the purpose of organizing the unorganized workers, especially those in the mass-production industries (steel, auto, rubber, and others). In 1938, when the member unions of this group set up the Congress of Industrial Organizations (q.v.) as an independent federation of labor, the ILGWU rejoined the AFL. During World War II, the ILGWU gave all possible aid to the U.S. war effort, avoiding strikes, helping to raise production levels, and participating in civilian-defense activities; its locals and individual members disbursed about $175,000,000 for purchases of U.S. Government War Bonds. After the war, the ILGWU renewed its organizing drives. By a recent year, it had succeeded in raising its membership to a total exceeding 400,000 workers in more than 8500 plants and shops.

The ILGWU also carries on a large-scale education and welfare program for its membership. The Education Department of the union disburses more than $200,000 annually for a wide range of educational and recreational activities. The Union Health Center, housed in a 26-story structure in New York City, provides low-cost medical care and handles more than 175,000 visits by union members each year. The ILGWU also maintains Unity House, a vacation resort founded in 1920 in the Pocono Mts., Pa., accommodating 1100 guests at moderate rates. The semi-monthly ILGWU periodical *Justice* has a circulation exceeding 300,000, and publishes monthly editions in Yiddish, Spanish, and Italian. The ILGWU also operates radio stations in Chattanooga, Tenn., Los Angeles, Calif., and New York City. These stations serve chiefly as media for the dissemination of news about labor-management relations, and of public-service programs. National headquarters of the ILGWU are situated in New York City.

INTERNATIONAL LANGUAGE. See UNIVERSAL LANGUAGE.

INTERNATIONAL LAW, the principles and rules of conduct which civilized states regard as obligatory upon them and hence observe in their relations with one another.

The need for some principles and rules for the conduct between independent states arises whenever such states develop relations with one another. Rules, especially concerning the treatment of foreign traders, travelers, and ambassadors, as well as the signing of and obedience to treaties, devel-

oped early in history. In antiquity, the Romans in their *jus gentium,* and the Greeks and the Jews also developed systems of international law.

The beginning of the modern system of international law coincided with the emergence of the concept of the "sovereign" state, and was stimulated by the revived interest in Roman law in the 16th century. Building largely on the work of previous legal scholars, Hugo Grotius (q.v.), sometimes called the founder of modern international law, wrote his celebrated *De Jure Belli ac Pacis Libri Tres* ("Three Books on the Law of War and Peace") in 1625. He based his system on the law of nature, or, as he called it, "natural justice". He also taught that the already existing customs governing relations between nations had the force of law and were generally binding, unless they were contrary to natural justice. His influence on the conduct of international affairs and the settlement of wars and other conflicts was very great. In quick succession during the 17th and early 18th centuries, other scholars, among them the Dutch jurist Cornelis van Bynkershoek, further developed the basic principles of international law. By the second half of the 19th century, the literature on the subject had reached vast proportions, and in 1873 the Institute of International Law was established to make a continuing study of the law. The Institute, later disbanded, was composed of the leading international lawyers of various nations, among whom the American David Dudley Field took an early and prominent part. Since the end of the 19th century, two developments have contributed decisively to the growth of international law: international conferences held for the purpose of drafting international conventions and clarifying and codifying specific subjects of concern to all nations; and the establishment and activities of international courts, the most important of which are the Permanent Court of Arbitration organized in 1899 and 1907, the Permanent Court of International Justice (functioning since 1922) and its successor, created under United Nations auspices, the International Court of Justice.

The body of international law stems from three main sources: treaties and international conventions; customs and customary usage; and the general principles of law and equity. Precedents, created by the decisions handed down by international and domestic courts, are also important for the interpretation and development of international law.

The present state system and, therefore, the present system of international law, is based on the concept of sovereign states. Hence, it is within the discretion of each state whether it wishes to participate in the negotiation of, or to sign, or to ratify, any international treaty. Likewise, each member state of an international agency, such as the United Nations, is free to ratify any convention adopted by that agency. However, once a state has ratified a treaty or convention, it is bound by it, and this act may have far-reaching consequences, i.e., may bind it in the future to a considerable extent. For example, all nations which joined the Permanent Court of International Justice undertook, under certain conditions, to submit disputes to it and to abide by its decisions. At that time, the United States finally decided against joining. But after World War II, the United States joined the International Court of Justice, and accepted, in essence, the same obligations it had previously refused to accept.

Treaties and conventions were, at first, restricted in their effects to these countries which ratified them. They are *particular,* and not *general* international law. Yet regulations and procedures contained in treaties and conventions have often developed into *general* customary usage, that is, have come to be considered binding even on those states which did not sign and ratify them. Otherwise, customs and customary usages become part of international law by continued acceptance on the part of the great majority of nations, even if they are not embodied in a written treaty instrument. "Generally accepted principles of law and justice" fall into the same category and are, in fact, difficult to distinguish from "customs" in many cases.

The Treaty of Westphalia, ending the Thirty Years' War in 1648, gave the first great impetus to the use of treaties as a source of international law. Although binding only upon its signatories, its principles soon began to govern the relations of all nations. Likewise, the Treaty of Utrecht (1713) set forth clearly the doctrine of the balance of power, i.e., that a "just equilibrium" be maintained among nations, to prevent one state or a coalition of states from dominating the others.

The Congress of Vienna (1814-15) which reorganized Europe after the downfall of Napoleon I, also contributed to the development of international law. For example, it established rules for diplomatic procedure and the treatment of ambassadors; such problems had created many disputes in former times. In 1856 a great forward step was taken when the signatories to the Treaty of Paris, ending the Crimean War, issued the "Declaration of Paris", formulating basic rules of maritime warfare, abolishing privateering, defining "contraband" and the rights of neutral ships, and setting up rules for "effective blockade". The Declaration was intended to be, and actually became, generally applicable, to nations other than its original signatories. In 1899 and 1907, the First and Second Peace Conference in The Hague resulted in agreements signed by many nations, on the pacific settlement of international disputes, on the adaptation to maritime warfare of the principles of the Geneva Convention of 1864, on the laws and customs of war on land, on the opening of hostilities, and other matters. In 1919, the Covenant of the League of Nations was signed, providing for the submission to the League Council of all disputes likely to lead to rupture of relations. The council under this covenant could issue decisions which were legally binding upon the member states. In 1928, the Kellogg Briand Pact was signed in Paris, making it obligatory upon nations to renounce war "as an instrument of policy". In 1929, a new and detailed convention concerning prisoners of war, and another improving the rules for treatment of sick and wounded soldiers, were signed in Geneva by many nations. Finally, in 1945, the Charter of the United Nations established an elaborate machinery for the growth of international law through international conventions, and for solving difficulties in international relations.

Treaties (also often called conventions, pacts, or agreements) have become the most important part of international law. Those treaties to which the U.S. is a party, form "the supreme law of the land", the Constitution of the United States declaring in Art. VI, Section 2: ". . . all Treaties made or which shall be made, under the authority of the United States, shall be the supreme law of the land; and the Judges in every State shall be bound thereby, any Thing in the Constitution or Laws of any State to the Contrary notwithstanding". Normally, every nation is expected to obey international law. Some states, e.g., Great Britain, have incorporated into their municipal law (q.v.)

the provision that international law shall be made part of the law of the land. Art. 1, Section 8 of the U.S. Constitution empowers Congress "to define and punish . . . Offenses against the Law of Nations".

It is true that a specific municipal statute of any country may conflict with a rule of international law; in such cases, the courts of that country may be expected to apply such statute. However, from the viewpoint of international law, this condition does not alter the fact that both the statute and the decision based on it are wrong. Hence, if the case were brought before an international court, or if redress is sought through diplomatic channels with reference to international law, the decision of the state court would be overruled. In cases involving international law, American courts tend to interpret American law in conformity with international law; such an attitude has consistently been urged by the U.S. Supreme Court. If each nation were free unilaterally to declare that it is no longer bound by international law, the result would be anarchy. A test was provided in the conduct of Nazi Germany. The Nuremberg Tribunals (see NUREMBERG TRIALS) held that the German government regulations ordering, for example, the killing of prisoners of war in contravention to the generally valid rules of warfare, were null and void, and persons responsible for issuing and executing such orders are criminally responsible for violations of international law. See GENOCIDE.

The Law of War, which was largely codified at the Hague Conferences of 1899 and 1907 and amplified in the Geneva Conventions of 1929, deals with such topics as: the prohibition of treacherous methods of warfare and the use of weapons causing unnecessary suffering, as, for example, dumdum bullets; prohibition of the use of poison gas; protection of "open" cities against bombardments (only defended places, and undefended places of military character may be bombarded by artillary or air forces); the rights and duties of prisoners of war, of wounded and sick enemies, of the civilians of occupied territory, of partisan fighters, of hostages, and of parliamentarians; the legal nature of armistices; the protection of the flag of truce; the protection of hospitals on land and of hospital ships; the prerogatives of humanitarian institutions such as the Red Cross; and the various and often complicated questions concerning the rights and duties of neutral states and their

citizens. The Geneva Conventions of 1929 also promulgated detailed rules concerning the care for sick and wounded soldiers by neutrals, and the treatment of combatants who cross into neutral territory.

The development of international law with respect to all these various topics has been uneven. There still exist many gaps and uncertainties. On the other hand, not only does the body of international law constantly grow through the conclusion of international treaties on the most widely varied subjects, but international law is created by the United Nations, principally by its "specialized agencies" which deal with questions in their respective fields on a world-wide or nearly world-wide scale: see UNITED NATIONS EDUCATIONAL, SCIENTIFIC AND CULTURAL ORGANIZATION (UNESCO); INTERNATIONAL LABOR ORGANIZATION; WORLD HEALTH ORGANIZATION; INTERNATIONAL BANK FOR RECONSTRUCTION AND DEVELOPMENT. See also POSTAL UNION. In connection with the settlement and prevention of international controversies, the establishment of the United Nations as a supreme international arbiter of disputes among nations, with power to enforce its decisions, initiated a new era in international law.

At the same time, while bilateral, multilateral, and regional treaties, as well as conventions adopted by international agencies, are increasing the bulk and body of international law, new problems arise. Need exists for constant interpretation, co-ordination, and sometimes reconciliation of these various sources of international law. It cannot be said that international law has developed to the degree of completeness and reliability to which domestic law has developed in the civilized countries. Yet the growing interdependence of states, the growing "internationalization" in the movement of persons, goods, and ideas, and the wish to prevent future wars, are important stimuli in the progress of international law.

INTERNATIONAL LAW, PRIVATE, that part of the law of a country which applies to cases involving foreign law. In the main, private international law is concerned with the following matters: (a) the decision by a court that it has or does not have jurisdiction in a case containing foreign elements, for example, the residence in a foreign country by the plaintiff or defendant, the fact that a judicial determination of the case has already been made in another country, or the fact that the case involves a contract made abroad or to be fulfilled abroad; (b) the decision by the court, after it has assumed jurisdiction, to apply the law of the country in which the court is situated or the law of the foreign country in which, for example, a judicial determination of the case may have already been made; (c) the determination by the court of the circumstances under which the decisions of the foreign tribunal are to be enforced by it; and (d) the determination by the court of the validity in the country in which it is situated of contracts, testaments, marriages, divorces, adoptions, legitimations of illegitimate children, and other acts other than court decisions, made in foreign countries and in accord with the laws of those countries.

These determinations are made by a court under statutes enacted by the national legislature of the country in which it is situated, and these statutes comprise an integral part of the law of that country. However, to the extent that these statutes provide for the enforcement of the laws of foreign countries, they partake of the nature of international law. Hence the designation "private international law". To the extent that they relate to the determination of the applicability of laws which, owing to their diverse national origins, may conflict, they are said to relate to the "conflict of law".

In general international practice, whenever the recognition of foreign laws or of foreign legal acts made under them would result in unconscionable injury, or is specifically prohibited by statute, or would contravene the public policy of a country, its courts do not grant such recognition. For example, U.S. courts refused to recognize decrees issued by the Nazi government of Germany just prior to World War II by which American-owned private property was confiscated and matured obligations of German companies held by citizens of the United States were repudiated.

The judgments of duly constituted courts are usually recognized and enforced in a foreign state, subject only to scrutiny as to irregularity, fraud, or lack of jurisdiction over parties or the cause of action. Foreign judgments of divorce will generally be accepted if one of the parties was domiciled in the foreign country in which the decree was granted. Certain courts in the United States refuse to set aside a foreign divorce, even if neither party was domiciled in the foreign state, if both parties submitted to the jurisdiction of the foreign court and

were duly granted divorce in accordance with the laws of the foreign state.

INTERNATIONAL MONETARY FUND, an agency of the United Nations, established in December, 1945, in accordance with the Articles of Agreement adopted in July, 1944, by representatives of forty-four nations attending the international monetary conference held at Bretton Woods, N.H.; see BRETTON WOODS CONFERENCE. The Fund was created primarily to promote international monetary co-operation, to establish stable exchange rates among the currencies of the member nations, to remove restrictions on foreign exchange, and by these means to promote international trade and a high level of employment throughout the world. The financial resources of the Fund are derived from contributions made by the member nations, partly in their own currency, and partly in United States dollars or in gold. In a recent year, the resources of the Fund totaled approximately $7,671,100,000, of which about $3,300,000,000 was in the form of United States dollars or in gold. In the first year of operations, the Fund helped to establish official values in foreign exchange for the currencies of thirty-two member nations. Between March, 1947, and May, 1948, the Fund sold to ten of its members foreign exchange amounting to about $606,000,000, for the purpose of enabling the recipient countries to make commodity purchases in the United States. Numerous official missions were sent by the Fund to member countries, to collect information and to furnish expert technical assistance and advice regarding monetary and fiscal problems.

INTERNATIONAL RED CROSS. See RED CROSS.

INTERNATIONAL REFUGEE ORGANIZATION, formerly, a specialized agency of the United Nations, operating under a constitution prepared by the U.N. Economic and Social Council and approved by the General Assembly in December, 1946. It was charged with identification, registration, and classification of refugees and displaced persons, i.e., persons who fled from their countries because of political or racial persecution during the years immediately prior to World War II, and those forced to evacuate their homes or forcibly transported from them during the war. The I.R.O. was also responsible for the care and assistance of such persons, for their legal and political protection; for the repatriation of those wishing to return to their homelands; and for the transportation to, and resettlement in, countries able and willing to receive them, of those refugees and displaced persons who do not wish to be repatriated. By the terms of its constitution, the I.R.O. was to become a United Nations agency when fifteen U.N. members had ratified the constitution and contributed at least 75 percent of the first annual operational budget of the I.R.O. totaling $151,060,500. In August, 1948, Denmark became the fifteenth nation to ratify the constitution, and in the following month the I.R.O. was duly constituted. Headquarters of the I.R.O. were situated in Geneva, Switzerland. Pending establishment of the I.R.O., the activities assigned to it were carried on after July 1, 1947, by a Preparatory Commission. In January, 1952, the I.R.O. was liquidated. During the period of its existence the agency effected the repatriation of 72,834 persons, and the resettlement, mainly in North and South America and Australia, of 1,038,750 persons. The Office of the U.N. High Commissioner for Refugees was established in 1951 to provide international protection for refugees after the dissolution of the I.R.O.

INTERNATIONAL TRADE. See FOREIGN TRADE.

INTERNATIONAL WORKINGMEN'S ASSOCIATION or **FIRST INTERNATIONAL,** the first society of workingmen to be organized on an international scale for the establishment of socialism throughout the world. It was founded in London in 1864, on the initiative of the revolutionary socialist Karl Marx and his associates. Those in attendance at the founding convention were chiefly trade unionists from England, France, Germany, Poland, and Italy. At this convention, Marx, in making the inaugural address, declared the goal of the International to be the amelioration of "the misery of the toiling masses" through the application of "the simple laws of morality and justice". At the congresses of the International, held annually after 1866 at Geneva, Lausanne, Brussels, and Basle successively, Marx gave expression to his theory of scientific socialism and expounded his program of international proletarian revolution; he won the support of the membership for this aim. These congresses urged such measures as the nationalization of the means of production and communication in each country, and advocated a general strike in any country embarking upon an imperialist war. The period from 1864 to 1870 was characterized by a notable increase in the size and scope of the membership of the International. Starting with an original membership of about 70,000, by 1870 the organization had attained a membership of approximately 450,000, with adherents in Belgium, Holland, Denmark, Switzerland, Austria-Hungary, Spain, and the United States, in addition to those countries represented at the founding convention. The organizational structure of the International was essentially loose and informal, comprising both representatives of trade unions, which officially supported but were not formally affiliated with the organization, and representatives of numerous political groups.

The decision of the leaders of the International to give full support to the revolutionary Commune of 1871 (q.v.), set up in Paris in the closing stages of the Franco-Prussian War, marked a turning point in the history of the International. As a result of this action, a number of the less radical members within the International, notably the English trade unionists, withdrew from the organization; the membership declined further when the French sections of the International were suppressed following the overthrow of the Commune. In 1872 the International was split when the protracted struggle between the adherents of Marx and those members who supported the anarchist principles of Michael Bakunin (q.v.), was brought to a culmination. With the expulsion of the Bakuninists late in 1873, the First International established its headquarters in New York City; three years later it was formally dissolved. The fundamental significance of the First International, in the view of many labor historians, lies in the fact that it was the first international organization to formulate and attempt to apply the doctrines of revolutionary socialism. These doctrines were later adopted by socialist and communist leaders in many countries; they were adopted particularly by the Second or Socialist and Labor International, and the Third (Communist) International (qq.v.).

INTERNODE. See STEM.

INTERSTATE COMMERCE ACT, a Federal law comprising a number of Congressional enactments providing for the regulation by the Federal government of interstate commerce. The first of these enactments, in 1887, entitled "An Act to Regulate Commerce", is frequently but erroneously called the Interstate Commerce Act. The law of 1887 required common carriers engaged in the transportation of passengers and property wholly by railroad or partly by rail and partly by water, to establish reasonable and just rates therefor. It prohibited agreements among these carriers to maintain uniform rates, and combinations by them to prevent the continuous carriage of freight from its point of origin to its destination. It required the carriers to publicize their rate schedules, and forbade changes of rates without due notice to the public. The penalty for violation of the act was a fine of not more than $5000, or imprisonment for two years, or both. The act also provided for the establishment of the Interstate Commerce Commission (q.v.) to administer the law. Notable among subsequent amending acts are the Elkins Act of 1903, prohibiting the railroads from granting secret rebates and from establishing discriminatory rates; the Hepburn Act of 1906, extending the jurisdiction of the Federal government over interstate commerce to include express companies, companies operating pipe lines transporting petroleum products, and companies operating sleeping cars on the railroads; and the Transportation Act of 1920, empowering the Commission to prescribe rates for common carriers in intrastate commerce when necessary to eliminate discrimination against carriers in interstate commerce.

In 1935 all the foregoing enactments and certain others were grouped together by Congress to form Part I of a new law entitled the Interstate Commerce Act; at the same time the Motor Carrier Act, extending Federal regulatory authority to motor carriers engaged in interstate commerce, was enacted as Part II of the Interstate Commerce Act. A further extension of Federal powers over interstate commerce was contained in the Transportation Act of 1940; a number of sections of this law, which vested the ICC with authority to regulate common carriers operating in interstate commerce in the coastal, intercoastal, and inland waters of the United States, were included as Part III of the Interstate Commerce Act. Part IV of the act, adopted by Congress in 1942, comprised regulations governing the operations of freight forwarders. As these various enactments enlarged the regulatory powers of the Federal government over interstate commerce, the jurisdiction of the ICC was correspondingly extended by the provisions of this legislation.

INTERSTATE COMMERCE COMMISSION, an independent agency of the U.S. government, created by the Act to Regulate Commerce, passed by Congress in 1887, and now known as the Interstate Commerce Act (q.v.). Authority for the creation of the Commission is contained in the U.S. Constitution, which explicitly vests Congress with the power "to regulate commerce . . . among the several States". The Commission, generally referred to as the ICC, is empowered to regulate common carriers (q.v.) and freight forwarders engaged in transporting passengers or property, respectively, in interstate commerce, or in foreign commerce insofar as it is carried on within the United States. Carriers engaged in transportation by rail or motor, or upon the coastal, intercoastal, and inland waters of the United States, freight forwarders employing the services of such carriers in the performance of contracts to transport property for the general public, and all pipe lines except those for the conveyance of water and natural gas come within the Commission's jurisdiction. Interstate air transportation, however, is regulated by the Civil Aeronautics Board (q.v.).

The ICC consists of eleven members appointed by the President with the consent of the Senate for terms of six years, and is directed by a chairman, elected by his fellow commissioners.

In regulating the operations of the carriers and forwarders, the ICC prescribes just, reasonable, and nondiscriminatory rates, establishes qualifications for certain types of employees, fixes the maximum hours of their work, and sets up safety standards. All proposed consolidations and mergers of the carriers and forwarders are subject to the approval of the Commission; in this connection, the Commission investigates alleged violations of the antitrust laws, and transmits its findings to the U.S. attorney general. The organization, operations, and property of the carriers and forwarders are described and analyzed in periodic and special statistical reports compiled and prepared by the Commission.

INTERVAL, in music, the relation between the pitches of two different notes sounded either successively (*melodic interval*) or simultaneously (*harmonic interval*). The foundations for the modern conception of intervals were laid by the Greek scientist Pythagoras in the 6th century B.C. He showed that if the frequency of a tone is taken as n, the frequencies of its octave, fifth, and third are $2n$, $3/2n$, and $5/4n$, respectively. Thus, the ratios of the intervals within an octave may be expressed by an improper fraction lying between 1 and 2. These relationships were cited by the Greek philosopher Plato in his famous exposition of the music of the spheres and the esthetic balance of ideas and action.

The Platonic attitude has persisted in theories of intervals and harmony to the present day. The idea that certain intervals such as the perfect third are "better" or "more harmonic" than others is gradually giving way, however, to the idea that the harmoniousness of intervals depends upon the musical context in which they are used. Many intervals formerly considered discordant are used freely in contemporary music, and composers continuously employ new intervals in the harmonies of modern music. In general the tendency has been to replace simple and perfect intervals with more complex intervals of the seventh and higher.

The utilization of intervals is limited to some extent by the mechanical adaptability of the ear. Technically, a string vibrates at different frequencies in sounding notes such as $D\#$ and Eb, but to most ears no difference is discernible. This lack of subtlety on the part of the ear, and the necessity, particularly in keyboard instruments, for a scale which repeats itself perfectly and permits transposition from one key to another, led to the use in modern music of the system of intervals known as equal temperament (q.v.). The tempered scale of intervals replaced the perfect interval relationships of the Pythagorean system with a system which is slightly out of tune in some intervals. The notes of such a scale are arrived at by dividing the octave into twelve arbitrarily equal semitones and subsequently determining intervals such as the second, third, and fourth.

INTERVENTION, in international law, the interference, particularly by armed force, in the domestic or foreign affairs of another state. The reasons advanced by various nations in justification of their intervention in the affairs of other states vary, but they most frequently include: rights under treaties, the need to protect nationals, and considerations of humanity. Because intervention in the affairs of another nation results usually in the impairment of the sovereignty of that nation, the United States, with certain notable exceptions, has followed a policy of non-intervention. In 1898, the United States interfered in Cuba on the grounds of humanity, protection of its nationals, injury to its commerce, and menace to its peace. In 1903, U.S. intervention in Panama was justified on the grounds of treaty rights, preservation of national rights and safety, and protection of civilization. In 1915, the U.S., ostensibly to protect life and property of its nationals, intervened in Haiti, and in 1926, for the same declared reason, intervened in Nicaragua.

Many instances of intervention may be cited from the history of other powers. Among these may be mentioned the invasion of Holland by the Prussians in 1787 to restore to his old position the Stadholder, who was a brother-in-law of the Prussian king; the intervention of Austria and Prussia in behalf of Louis XVI of France in 1791; the intervention of the Holy Alliance to thwart liberal movements and restore absolutism in Spain, Naples, Sicily, and Piedmont in the early 19th century; the intervention of France in Rome in 1849 to restore the temporal power of the pope; and the allied intervention in China in 1900 to quell the Boxer uprisings.

In international law today such intervention, accompanied by force, is considered illegal. However, other forms of intervention, which do not impair the sovereignty of a nation, are still frequently resorted to, including diplomatic intervention by protest to the offending nation, the granting or withdrawal of recognition, and the imposition of economic or financial sanctions designed to accomplish the correction of grievances.

The Charter of the United Nations expressly provides that "nothing contained in the present Charter shall authorize the United Nations to intervene in matters which are essentially within the domestic jurisdiction of any state, or shall require the members to submit such matters to settlement . . ." However, the United Nations may intervene in matters which are not essentially domestic affairs, and particularly where a threat to peace is shown to exist.

INTESTINE or BOWEL, the portion of the digestive tract between the stomach and anus of higher animals. The bowel of man is divided into two major sections: the *small intestine,* about twenty feet long, of major importance in digestion and absorption; and the *large intestine,* about five feet long, chiefly important in the absorption of water and in the excretion (q.v.) of solid waste material; see FECES.

The small intestine begins with the *duodenum,* which is attached to the pyloric end of the stomach; it continues through a middle portion, known as the *jejunum,* and

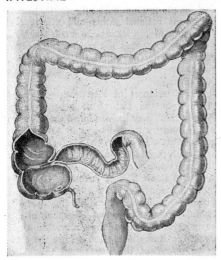

A drawing of the large intestine of man

a long terminal portion, known as the *ileum;* it terminates in the side of the first portion of the large intestine, the caecum. The small intestine lies within the center of the abdominal cavity, coiled upon itself. The horse-shoe-shaped duodenum surrounds the head of the pancreas; the pancreatic duct opens into the duodenum, as do ducts leading from the liver and gall bladder. The mucosa of the small intestine is depressed into tiny glandular pits, the *crypts of Lieberkühn,* which secrete intestinal digestive enzymes. Minute projecting portions of the intestinal mucosa, known as *villi,* absorb digested material. Each villus is a tube of epithelium (q.v.) surrounding a small central lymphatic, or *lacteal,* and containing many capillaries. Digested carbohydrates and proteins are transported by the capillaries to the portal vein which enters the liver; digested fats are absorbed into the lacteals and transported into the general blood stream through the lymphatic system. The lining of the intestine also elaborates a hormone, known as *secretin,* which stimulates the production of digestive enzymes in the pancreas.

The large intestine is divided into the *caecum, ascending colon, transverse colon, descending colon, sigmoid flexure,* and *rectum.* The caecum, located at the lower right-hand corner of the abdominal cavity, is a swollen sac which in herbivorous animals is very large. In man the importance of the caecum lies in two structures: the vestigial vermiform appendix (see APPENDICITIS)

which commonly becomes diseased; and the *ileocaecal valve,* a membranous structure between the caecum and the small intestine which prevents the passage of toxic waste products from the large bowel back into the small bowel. The ascending colon rises along the right side from the caecum to below the liver; the transverse colon runs across the body to the left side where the descending colon travels downward. The sigmoid flexure is the S-shaped portion of the large intestine where it enters the pelvic cavity. The rectum, about six inches long, is the almost straight terminal portion of the large bowel, closed at the exit, or anus, by a round muscle, the anal sphincter. The large intestine secretes no enzymes; it does secrete large amounts of mucus which lubricate the waste materials.

Food and waste materials are moved along the length of the intestine by rhythmic contractions of intestinal muscles; these contractions are collectively called *peristaltic movements.* The entire intestine is held in place by membranes known as *mesenteries.* See DIGESTION.

INTOLERABLE ACTS, in American colonial history, the name given to a series of laws passed by the British Parliament in March, 1774, as punitive measures against the colony of Massachusetts. The Intolerable Acts comprised an important factor contributing to the outbreak of the American Revolution (q.v.) two years later. Prior to the enactment of these measures, the American colonists had defied various British policies they considered repressive; they had resisted the Stamp Act (q.v.) in 1765, and in March, 1770, had openly shown their resentment of the quartering of British troops in Boston; see BOSTON MASSACRE. After the Boston Tea Party (q.v.) in December, 1773, King George III requested Parliament to enact measures punishing Massachusetts as an example to the other rebellious colonies. Under the Intolerable Acts, the colonists were held liable for the tea which had been destroyed, the port of Boston was closed to trade, town meetings were forbidden, public buildings were converted into barracks for British troops, and colonial courts were denied jurisdiction over British officials. The other American colonies united in sympathy with Massachusetts. Virginia set aside a day for prayer and fasting, and later proposed that the colonies meet to formulate joint action against the objectionable features of British rule. This proposal led to the calling of the first Continental Congress (q.v.), which met in Philadelphia, Pa., in the fall of 1774.

INTOXICATION, term used in medicine to designate poisoning by any agent, such as spirits, narcotics, bacterial toxins, or serum injections; see POISON.

Colloquially the term "intoxication" refers only to the condition of inadequate control of mind and body resulting from overconsumption of alcoholic beverages. Alcoholic intoxication, which is characterized by depressed function of the central nervous system, may be acute, subacute, or chronic. Acute alcoholic intoxication, which results from drinking a large quantity of alcohol in a short time, is characterized by profound insensibility soon after drinking, accompanied by difficult breathing, purpling of the face, frothing at the mouth, and weak pulse. The occurrence of acute alcoholic intoxication is rare because ingestion of a fatal or near-fatal dose of alcohol is normally followed by vomiting before the alcohol can be absorbed, but in many cases victims must be treated speedily and drastically to survive. Subacute alcoholic intoxication, sometimes called acute alcoholism, is the common type of drunkenness or *inebriation* which occurs in individuals who drink immoderate amounts of alcoholic beverages periodically; large amounts produce mild delirium, staggering, and loss of muscular power, followed by vomiting, depression, and tremor. Chronic alcoholic intoxication, resulting from long-continued use of excessive amounts of alcohol, leads to general depression of nerve centers; in habitual drinkers it may result in *delirium tremens* (q.v.), characterized by tremors, hallucinations, and fever. Many habitual drinkers are subject to an uncontrollable intermittent desire for alcohol, a condition called *dipsomania*.

INTRACOASTAL WATERWAYS, a canalized system of protected water routes in the United States, comprising the Atlantic and Gulf intracoastal waterways. It affords a channel for barges and other light-draft vessels extending for more than 2500 m. along the Atlantic and Gulf of Mexico coasts. The system, which utilizes rivers, bays, coastal sounds, and canals, provides a navigable channel with a minimum depth of 12 ft. throughout most of its length. Channels with a minimum depth of about 8 ft. have been dredged in the 370-mile section between Jacksonville and Miami, Fla., on the Atlantic Coast, and the 150-mile section on the Gulf Coast from Corpus Christi to Brownsville, Tex. The principal artificial channels in the system are the Cape Cod Canal (q.v.) and the Chesapeake and Delaware Canal.

INTUITION, in philosophy, a form of knowledge or of cognition independent of experience or reason. In the work of philosophers who lay stress on intuition, the intuitive faculty and intuitive knowledge are generally regarded as inherent qualities of the mind. The term has been used in different, sometimes opposing, senses by various writers and cannot be defined except with reference to its meaning in the writings of an individual philosopher. The concept of intuition apparently arose from two sources: the mathematical idea of an axiom (a self-evident proposition which needs no proof) and the mystical idea of revelation (truth which surpasses the power of the intellect).

Intuition was important in Greek philosophy (q.v.), particularly in the thinking of such philosophers as Pythagoras and his followers, who were trained in mathematics. The concept also had great significance in much of Christian philosophy as one of the basic ways in which human beings could know God. But the philosophers who relied most on the idea of intuition were Baruch Spinoza, Immanuel Kant, and Henri Bergson (qq.v.).

In Spinoza's philosophy, intuition is the highest form of knowledge, surpassing both empirical knowledge derived from the senses, and "scientific" knowledge derived from reasoning on the basis of experience. Intuitive knowledge, according to Spinoza, gives man the comprehension of an orderly and united universe and permits the mind to be a part of the Infinite Being.

Kant regarded intuition as the portion of a perception that is supplied by the mind itself. He divided perceptions or "phenomena" into two parts: the sensation caused by the external object perceived, and the "form", or the understanding of the perception in the mind, which results from intuition. Such apprehensions as space and time, he held, are types of pure intuition (*Anschauung*).

Bergson contrasted instinct with intelligence, and regarded intuition as the purest form of instinct. Intelligence, he believed, was adequate for the consideration of material things but could not deal with the fundamental nature of life or thought. He defined intuition as "instinct that has become disinterested, self-conscious, capable of reflecting upon its object and of enlarging it indefinitely." Intelligence, on the other hand, can only analyze, and the function of analysis is to produce what is relative in an object, rather than what is absolute, or individual. Only by intuition, he declared, can the absolute be comprehended.

A number of ethical philosophers, among them Spinoza, have been called *intuitionists* or *intuitionalists* because of their belief that man's sense of moral values is intuitive and immediate. This view contrasts with that of the empiricists who hold that moral values are a result of human experience, and that of the rationalists who believe that moral values can be determined by reason. See ETHICS.

INUNDATIONS. See FLOODS AND INUNDA-TIONS, NOTABLE.

INVALIDES, HÔTEL DES, an institution in Paris founded by Louis XVI in 1671 as a hospital for wounded French army veterans. It comprises an immense group of buildings symmetrically disposed and divided into many wings giving on courtyards. Originally the hospital accommodated 6000 men; later these accommodations were drastically curtailed. In 1861 Napoleon's body was placed in a tomb under the dome of the chapel occupying the central pavilion, and since then the Hôtel des Invalides has been one of the standard tourist sights in Paris. Housed in the Hôtel des Invalides are the living quarters and offices of the military governor of Paris and of the general in charge of the institution; and the Museum of the Army. The museum contains collections of arms, armor, flags, documents, models of fortifications, and military vehicles.

INVECTED. See HERALDRY.

INVENTION, process of producing new devices, objects, ideas, or procedures usable in accomplishing human objectives in ways which were formerly difficult or impossible. The process of invention is invariably preceded by one or more discoveries; a discovery may be *accidental,* such as a child's discovery that fire burns, or *induced,* such as the discovery that helium is the lightest of the inert gases and, therefore, best suited for use in inflating airships. In common usage the term "invention" is applied only to the production of new materials or operable devices, and the name "inventor" is applied to a person who has produced a new device or material. Less frequently, the term "invention" is applied to a new procedure; thus a person may be said to have invented a new game or a new system of accounting.

Under strict definition, however, anything produced by man which is new and unique is an invention; this definition was recognized by the German composer, Johann Sebastian Bach, who gave the title *Inventions* to a series of his short piano compositions. Similarly, an artist who produces an original painting, an author who writes an original book, a philosopher who introduces a new concept into a system of thought, an administrator who alters the procedure of the government of which he is a component, or a breeder who produces a new fruit variety, is an inventor just as much as a person who produces a new carburetor.

In most countries, certain classes of inventions are legally recognized, and their use temporarily restricted to the control of the inventor. In the U.S., any new and useful art, machine, manufacture, or material, or any new and useful improvement of these, may be protected by patent (q.v.); written material, music, paintings, sculpture, and photographs may be protected by copyright (q.v.). The protection afforded by this legal recognition is limited; in many cases, slight alterations in the device, material, or work of art may produce sufficient improvement or difference to afford legal justification for issuance of a new patent or copyright to the person who made the alteration. Patent and copyright laws do not provide coverage for all inventions. Many processes and ideas which do not have clear-cut characteristics, such as psychological concepts useful in advertising, cannot be legally protected.

Inventiveness is restricted to man and perhaps a few of the higher animals. Inventiveness implies a continued ability to adapt discoveries to use. Many lower animals have, at some time in the history of their species, acquired the ability to produce complicated devices, and have continued this ability from generation to generation. A spider's web, for example, is a complicated device used to trap other small animals for food; all members of a spider species produce webs of exactly the same pattern, and no two species produce identical patterns. The art of building is highly developed in the insect order Hymenoptera, which includes ants, bees, and wasps. Most birds build nests during the reproductive season. Dams constructed by beavers follow a pattern which, although simple, is almost perfect from the standpoint of structural design. All these examples, however, illustrate the perpetuation of complicated types of in-

Central pavilion of the Hôtel des Invalides

herited animal behavior by instinct, and furnish little evidence of intelligent understanding by the constructing animals of the structural principles involved. In man, on the other hand, the development of processes of construction is preceded and followed by development of the physical laws which made the construction possible. The never-ending succession of discovery followed by invention followed by further discovery, which results in continual development of new concepts, procedures, and devices, is characteristic of the inventiveness possessed by humans.

The earliest artifacts of primitive man show evidence of his inventiveness. The names of the great archeological ages, the Stone Age, the Bronze Age, and the Iron Age, are derived from the inventive use of stone and metal implements by man; see ARCHEOLOGY. Early stone implements were crude, but the protective and food-getting purposes they served were instrumental in sustaining the early progress of man's growing domination of the earth. Many of the most significant inventions of man were developed prior to the period covered by written history. These include the invention of crude tools, the development of speech, the cultivation of plants and domestication of animals, the development of building techniques, the ability to produce and control fire, the ability to make pottery, the development of simple political systems, and the invention of the wheel.

The period of recorded history began with the invention of writing, and writing as a means of mass communication became important with the invention of movable type in the 15th century. Invention proceeded steadily throughout the period of written history, but since the advent of printed books people all over the world have been able to obtain records of the discoveries of the past for use as a basis for further discoveries and inventions.

The present era of history, in which invention multiplies from year to year, making archaic many of the innovations of the preceding decade, is a development of the machine age aided by the new swiftness of communication and transportation. The machine age developed from a complex of inventions, of which the most important included the use of fossil fuels such as coal as sources of energy, the improvement of metallurgical processes (especially of steel and aluminum), the development of electricity and electronics, the invention of the internal-combustion engine, and the use of metal and cement in construction work. Current developments in the use of atomic energy promise to introduce a new age in the inventiveness of man.

Early inventors were usually isolated individuals dependent on other means of subsistence than the risky outcome of their endeavors. Most modern invention takes place in large research organizations supported by institutions of higher learning, governmental agencies, private industries, or privately endowed foundations. The impact of technological advances on society, in recent years, has made invention one of the most important single forces in determining the direction and pace of social progress.

TABLE OF MODERN INVENTIONS

Date	Invention	Inventor	Nationality
1590	Compound Microscope	Zacharias Janssen	Dutch
1593	Water Thermometer	Galileo Galilei	Italian
1608	Telescope	Hans Lippershey	Dutch
1642	Adding Machine	Blaise Pascal	French
1643	Barometer	Evangelista Torricelli	Italian
1656	Pendulum Clock	Christian Huygens	Dutch
1705	Atmospheric-pressure Steam Engine	Thomas Newcomen	English
1710	Pianoforte	Bartolommeo Cristofori	Italian
1714	Mercurial Thermometer	Gabriel Daniel Fahrenheit	German
1745	Leyden Jar (condenser)	E. G. von Kleist	German
1752	Lightning Rod	Benjamin Franklin	American
1758	Achromatic Lens	John Dolland	English
1764	Spinning Jenny	James Hargreaves	English
1765	Steam Engine	James Watt	Scottish

Date	Invention	Inventor	Nationality
1770	Automobile	Nicolas Joseph Cugnot	French
1776	Submarine Torpedo	David Bushnell	American
1780	Bifocal Lens	Benjamin Franklin	American
1783	Balloon	Joseph Michel Montgolfier and Jacques Étienne Montgolfier	French
1784	Threshing Machine	Andrew Meikle	Scottish
1785	Power Loom	Edmund Cartwright	English
1787	Steamboat	John Fitch	American
1793	Cotton Gin	Eli Whitney	American
1796	Lithography	Aloys Senefelder	German
1799	Fourdrinier Machine (paper-making)	Louis Robert	French
1800	Electric Battery	Count Alessandro Volta	Italian
1804	Screw Propeller	John Stevens	American
1805	Electroplating	Luigi Gasparo Brugnatelli	Italian
1810	Food Preservation (by sterilization and exclusion of air)	François Appert	French
1814	Railroad Locomotive	George Stephenson	English
1815	Safety Lamp	Sir Humphry Davy	English
1816	Kaleidoscope	Sir David Brewster	Scottish
1819	Stethoscope	René Théophile Hyacinthe Laënnec	French
1820	Galvanometer	Johann Salomo Christoph Schweigger	German
1821	Electric Motor	Michael Faraday	English
1822	Calculating Machine	Charles Babbage	English
1823	Electromagnet	William Sturgeon	English
1827	Friction Match	John Walker	English
1830	Sewing Machine	Barthélemy Thimonnier	French
1831	Phosphorus Match	Charles Sauria	French
1831	Reaper	Cyrus Hall McCormick	American
1831	Dynamo	Michael Faraday	English
1832	Telegraph	Samuel Finley Breese Morse	American
1835	Pistol (revolver)	Samuel Colt	American
1838	Stereoscope	Sir Charles Wheatstone	English
1839	Photography	Louis Jacques Mandé Daguerre and Joseph Nicéphore Niepce	French
1839	Vulcanized Rubber	Charles Goodyear	American
1840	Bicycle	Kirkpatrick MacMillan	Scottish
1845	Pneumatic Tire	Robert William Thompson	American
1846	Guncotton	Christian Friedrich	German
1846	Rotary Printing Press	Richard March Hoe	American
1849	Safety Pin	Walter Hunt	American
1849	Hydraulic Turbine	James Bicheno Francis	American
1850	Mercerized Cotton	John Mercer	English
1851	Breach-loading Rifle	Edward Maynard	American
1851	Ophthalmoscope	Hermann Ludwig Ferdinand von Helmholtz	German
1852	Elevator (with brake)	Elisha Graves Otis	American
1852	Gyroscope	Jean Bernard Léon Foucault	French
1855	Safety Matches	J. E. Lundstrom	Swedish
1855	Gas Burner	Robert Wilhelm Bunsen	German
1856	Bessemer Converter (steel)	Sir Henry Bessemer	English
1859	Spectroscope	Gustav Robert Kirchhoff and Robert Wilhelm Bunsen	German
1861	Electric Furnace	Wilhelm Siemens	English

Date	Invention	Inventor	Nationality
1861	Machine Gun	Richard Jordan Gatling	American
1861	Motion-picture Projector	Coleman Sellers	American
1866	Paper (from wood pulp, sulfite process)	Benjamin Chew Tilghman	American
1866	Self-projecting Torpedo	Robert Whitehead	English
1866	Dynamite	Alfred Bernhard Nobel	Swedish
1868	Typewriter	Carlos Glidden and Christopher Latham Sholes	American
1868	Air Brake	George Westinghouse	American
1868	Car Coupler	Eli Hamilton Janney	American
1870	Celluloid	John Wesley Hyatt	American
1874	Quadruplex Telegraph	Thomas Alva Edison	American
1876	Telephone	Alexander Graham Bell	American
1877	Gas Engine (four-cycle)	Nikolaus August Otto	German
1877	Talking Machine (phonograph)	Thomas Alva Edison	American
1877	Microphone	Emile Berliner	American
1877	Electric Welding	Elihu Thomson	American
1878	Incandescent Lamp	Thomas Alva Edison	American
1879	Automobile Engine (two-cycle)	Karl Benz	German
1879	Arc Lamp	Charles Francis Brush	American
1880	Cream Separator	Carl Gustav Patrik de Laval	Swedish
1880	Linotype	Ottmar Mergenthaler	American
1883	Rayon (nitrocellulose)	Sir Joseph W. Swan	English
1884	Rayon (nitrocellulose)	Comte Hilaire Bernigaud de Chardonnet	French
1884	Fountain Pen	Lewis Edson Waterman	American
1884	Steam Turbine	Sir Charles Algernon Parsons	English
1884-87	Electric Trolley Car	Charles Joseph Van Depoele	American
1885	Graphophone (phonograph)	Alexander Graham Bell and Charles Sumner Tainter	American
1885	A.C. Transformer	William Stanley	American
1887	Gramaphone (phonograph)	Emile Berliner	American
1887	Gas Mantle	Baron Carl Auer von Welsbach	Austrian
1887	Monotype	Tolbert Lanston	American
1888	Adding Machine (recording)	William Seward Burroughs	American
1888	Kodak	George Eastman	American
1890	Rayon (cuprammonium)	Louis Henri Despeissis	French
1891	Commercial Gas Engine	Levassor	French
1891	Gun Sight (telescopic)	Bradley Allen Fiske	American
1891	Synthetic Rubber	Sir William Tilden	English
1892	A.C. Motor	Nikola Tesla	American
1892	Color Photography	Frederick Eugene Ives	American
1892	Rayon (viscose)	Charles Frederick Cross	English
1892	Vacuum Bottle	Sir James Dewar	Scottish
1893	Diesel Engine	Rudolph Diesel	German
1893	Gasoline Automobile	Charles Edgar Duryea and J. Frank Duryea	American
1893	Halftone Engraving	Frederick Eugene Ives	American
1893	Motion-picture Machine	Thomas Alva Edison	American
1894	Even-keel Submarine	Simon Lake	American
1895	Rayon (acetate)	Charles F. Cross	English
1896	Experimental Airplane	Samuel Pierpont Langley	American
1896	Wireless Telegraph	Marchese Guglielmo Marconi	Italian
1898	Sensitized Photographic Paper	Leo Hendrik Baekeland	American

Date	Invention	Inventor	Nationality
1900	Rigid Dirigible Airship	Count Ferdinand von Zeppelin	German
1902	Radio Telephone	Valdemar Poulsen and Reginald Aubrey Fessenden	American
1903 (?)	Airplane	Karl Jatho	German
1903	Airplane	Wilbur Wright and Orville Wright	American
1905	Diode Radio Tube	Sir John Ambrose Fleming	English
1906	Gyrocompass	Herman Anschütz-Kämpfe	German
1907	Bakelite	Leo Hendrik Baekeland	American
1907	Radio Vacuum-tube Triode	Lee De Forest	American
1908	Sulfanilamide	P. Gelmo	German
1909	Silencer (firearm)	Hiram Percy Maxim	American
1910	Hydrogenation of Coal	Friedrich Bergius	German
1910	Gyroscope Compass and Stabilizer	Elmer Ambrose Sperry	American
1911	Hydroplane	Glenn Hammond Curtiss	American
1912	Mercury-vapor Lamp	Peter Cooper Hewitt	American
1913	Multigrid Electron Tube	Irving Langmuir	American
1913	Cracked Gasoline	William Meriam Burton	American
1913	Heterodyne Radio Receiver	Reginald Aubrey Fessenden	American
1914	Military Tank	Sir Ernest Dunlop Swinton	English
1916	Browning Gun (automatic rifle)	John Moses Browning	American
1916	Gas-filled Incandescent Lamp	Irving Langmuir	American
1916	X-ray Tube	William David Coolidge	American
1917	Automobile Self-Starter	Charles Kettering	American
1920	Autogiro	Juan de la Cierva	American
1922	Ethyl Gasoline	Thomas Midgley	American
1923	Television Iconoscope	Vladimir Kosma Zworykin	American
1926	Koroseal (synthetic rubber)	Waldo Lonsbury Semon	American
1926	Thiokol (synthetic rubber)	J. C. Patrick	American
1928	Penicillin	Sir Alexander Fleming	British
1930	High-octane Gasoline	Vladimir Nikolaevich Ipatieff	Russian
1930	Nylon (fiber-forming synthetic polyamides)	Wallace Hume Carothers	American
1930	Freon (low-boiling fluorine compounds)	Thomas Midgley and co-workers	American
1930	Neoprene (synthetic rubber)	Father Julius Arthur Nieuwland and Wallace Hume Carothers	American
1931	Cyclotron	Ernest Orlando Lawrence	American
1931	Differential Analyzer (calculating machine)	Vannevar Bush	American
1932	Phase Contrast Microscope	Fritz Zernike	Dutch
1933	Frequency Modulation	Edwin Howard Armstrong	American
1935	Buna (synthetic rubber)	German Scientists	
1935	Radiolocator (Radar)	Sir Robert Watson-Watt	British
1935	Cortisone	Edward C. Kendall	American
		Tadeusz Reichstein	Swiss
1935	Electron Microscope	German Scientists	
1935	Sulfanilamide	Gerhard Domagk	German
1938	Jet-propelled Airplane	Gianni Caproni	Italian
1941	Programmed Digital Calculator	Harvard University	American
1941	Turbo-jet-propelled Airplane	Frank Whittle	English
1944	V-2 (rocket-propelled bomb)	German Scientists	

Date	Invention	Inventor	Nationality
1945	Atomic Bomb	U.S. Government Scientists	American
1945	Streptomycin	Selman A. Waksman	American
1946	Electronic Numerical Integrator and Computer (ENIAC)	University of Pennsylvania	American
1947	Chloromycetin	Mildred Rebstock	American
1948	Scintillation Counter	Hartmut Kallmann	German
1948	Aureomycin	Benjamin M. Duggar and Chandra Bose SubbaRow	American
1948	Transistor	John Bardeen and Walter H(ouser) Brattain	American
1949	Neomycin	Selman A. Waksman	American
1950	Terramycin	Alexander Finlay and Associates	American
1952	Hydrogen Bomb	U.S. Government Scientists	American
1953	Electrocortin	Tadeusz Reichstein	Swiss

So much of recent invention takes place in large industrial, governmental or institutional laboratories that it is difficult to ascribe any single invention to a specific inventor. Researchers in modern laboratories are often members of a "project"; the planning is often the work of more than one person, and the actual development, including the solution of many practical problems almost invariably encountered in research, and the addition of various refinements, all of which contribute to making the invention unique and workable, are invariably the work of many individuals. The atomic bomb, for example, was developed during World War II under the guidance of a small group of leading scientists of many nationalities who directed a much larger group of scientists and technicians; most individuals in the latter group were unaware of the project's purpose.

INVERNESS, burgh, seaport, and county seat of Inverness-shire, Scotland, situated at the mouth of the Ness R., on Beauly Firth, and 118 m. by rail N. of Perth. It was a Pict stronghold in the 6th century and the site of the castle in which Macbeth reputedly murdered Duncan. The castle was razed in the 11th century by Malcolm III MacDuncan. Inverness was chartered a royal burgh by William the Lion about the beginning of the 13th century. Donald of the Isles burned the town in 1411, but it was later rebuilt. Among leading points of interest are the house in Bridge Street where Mary Stuart lived for a period, the county administrative offices, located in a castle built in 1835 on the site of Macbeth's Castle, and a museum containing Jacobean relics. Many tourists are attracted annually to Inverness to view its historic buildings and to visit the surrounding region, rich in Highland lore. Inverness is a market for the wool producers of the Highlands. Its industries include brewing, distilling, iron founding, milling, shipbuilding, and the manufacture of tweeds and machinery. Granite works and nurseries are also operated in Inverness. The port has a flourishing trade with the east-coast cities of Scotland and England. Population (1951) 28,115.

INVERNESS-SHIRE, the largest county of Scotland, bordered by the Atlantic Ocean on the w., and including several of the Outer and Inner Hebrides islands, notably Skye, Harris, and North and South Uist. The county has a mountainous terrain, comprising a part of the Highlands, and contains Ben Nevis (4406 ft.), the loftiest peak in the British Isles. Loch Ness, the largest body of fresh water in Great Britain, is in Invernessshire. There are numerous other lakes and many picturesque valleys, glens, and straths. Glen More, or the Great Glen, a fault which traverses the county from the s.w. to the N.E., is occupied by the Caledonian Canal and several lakes, including Loch Ness. The Spey, Ness, and Beauly are among the principal rivers. Inverness (q.v.), a royal burgh, is the county seat. Relics of the Stone Age have been found in Inverness-shire. During the Roman occupation of Britain, the region was inhabited by the Picts. After the 12th century the clan system was instituted in Inverness-shire, where it attained fuller development than in any other part of Scotland. Agriculture is carried on in some of the fertile glens and straths. Fishing, the grazing of sheep, and the quarrying of granite are the chief occupations. Area, 4211 sq.m.; pop. (1951) 84,924.

INVERSION, in music, the transposition of the low and high tones of either chords or melodies, known respectively as *harmonic inversion* and *melodic inversion*. In harmonic inversion the names of the notes of a chord remain the same, but the intervals between the notes are changed. A second becomes a seventh, a third a sixth, a fourth a fifth, and so on through the intervals; the sum of the original interval and the interval after inversion is always the figure nine. In melodic inversion the intervals remain the same as those of the original melody, but the notes are shifted upward or downward to produce a "mirror image" of the original. Melodic inversion was common in contrapuntal music until the middle of the 18th century, particularly in the canon and fugue (qq.v.) forms, and certain modern composers such as Arnold Schönberg (q.v.) have to some extent revived it. With the development of Romantic music, however, composers turned to harmonic inversion, especially for the introduction of inversions of complex chords.

INVERTEBRATA, a collective name for all the members of the animal kingdom except those in the phylum Chordata (q.v.); the name is applied because none of the animals except the chordates have vertebrae (backbones). All of the invertebrates are cold blooded. For animals with characteristics intermediate between invertebrates and vertebrates see ENTEROPNEUSTA; HEMICHORDATA. For classification of invertebrates see ZOOLOGY.

INVESTMENT TRUST, in finance, a corporation chartered to invest in other business enterprises funds raised through the sale of its own securities. Investment trusts are of two principal types, called *management trusts* and *fixed trusts*. Management trusts exercise virtually unlimited discretion in their choice of investments. Fixed trusts are restricted by their charters to specific types of investments. Both types of investment trust generally invest their funds in the securities of sound, established business enterprises, and purchasers of investment-trust securities are

thus offered the advantages resulting from diversification of investment and skilled management in the handling of investment funds.

INVIOLABILITY, in international law, immunity from the operation of its laws, extended by a country to the diplomatic representatives and rulers of other countries while within its territory, and to foreign warships and, in limited degree, merchant vessels while in its territorial waters. From earliest times envoys sent on diplomatic missions from one sovereign state to another have been held inviolate for the duration of their mission. The codification of international law and custom with respect to inviolability was undertaken for the first time, following the conclusion of the Napoleonic Wars, by the Congress of Vienna in 1814-15. Various treaties among nations subsequently negotiated, reaffirmed and extended the decisions of the Congress of Vienna. See DIPLOMACY; EXTRATERRITORIALITY.

INVOLUCRE. See INFLORESCENCE.

INVOLUTION. See EVOLUTION, in algebra.

IO, in Greek mythology, daughter of Inachus, king of Argos. She was loved by Zeus, father of the gods, who, to protect her from the jealousy of his wife Hera, changed her into a heifer. Hera obtained the heifer from Zeus and set Argus, a herdsman who had eyes all over his body, to watch her. Argus, however, was killed by Zeus' son Hermes. Hera then sent a gadfly to pursue Io, who wandered over the earth until she reached Egypt, where she was restored to her original form.

IODIC ACID. See CHLORIC, BROMIC, AND IODIC ACIDS.

IODINE, an element, symbol I, member of the halogens (q.v.), atomic number 53, atomic weight 126.92. It was first isolated in 1812 by B. Bourtois, a French manufacturer of saltpeter, and established as an element by Joseph Louis Gay-Lussac (q.v.) two years later. Iodine is a lustrous, blue-black, soft, crystalline solid, with a specific gravity of 4.93. When heated to moderate temperatures it sublimes, forming a violet vapor with an odor resembling that of chlorine. The vapor rapidly condenses to crystals on a cold surface. When heated in a closed vessel, iodine melts at 113°C. (235.4°F.); it boils at 183°C. (361.4°F.). It is soluble in alcohol, chloroform, and other organic reagents, but is only slightly soluble in pure water. It dissolves readily in an aqueous solution of potassium iodide.

Most of the iodine produced in the United States is obtained from oil-well brines in California. The beds of sodium nitrate (Chile saltpeter) on the west coast of South America contain iodine salts and are the best source of iodine in the world. Small amounts of iodine salts occur in sea water, and are absorbed by certain species of seaweed; the iodine is extracted from the ash of the seaweed in the form of sodium iodide. Iodine is a constituent of the hormone thyroxine (q.v.), thus playing an important role in body metabolism. It is found in the blood in small amounts (about four millionths of a gram per 100 c.c.) in the form of a complex organic compound called thyroglubulin, produced in the thyroid gland (q.v.).

Iodine is prepared by treating sodium iodate (obtained from saltpeter) with sodium bisulfite, by treating an iodide, such as potassium iodide, with chlorine, or by reacting potassium iodide and sulfuric acid in the presence of an oxidizing agent such as manganese dioxide.

Iodine is the least active chemically of the four common halogens, and is displaced from its compounds by each of the other halogens. It combines with hydrogen less readily than do the other halogens, forming hydrogen iodide (see HYDROCHLORIC ACID.) It combines directly with many nonmetals, including phosphorus (forming phosphorus triodide) and chlorine (forming iodine trichloride). The metallic salts are called iodides. When added to a solution of starch, iodine produces an intense blue color; this reaction with starch is frequently used as a test for detecting the presence of the element.

Iodine and its compounds are used in medicine. An alcoholic solution of iodine, called tincture of iodine, is used as an antiseptic. Iodoform, CHI_3, a yellow, crystalline compound, made by the reaction of iodine and alkali on alcohol or acetone, is used as an antiseptic and disinfectant, particularly for the treatment of burns. Compounds of iodine are administered in the treatment of cretinism and goiter (qq.v.). Iodized table salt (salt to which a small amount of an iodide has been added) is used in many regions where the natural iodine content of food is low, to prevent goiter and other malfunctioning of the thyroid glands. Silver iodide is one of the two important photosensitive compounds used in making photographic film. A solution of iodine and potassium iodide is the active ingredient in the biological tissue stain called Gram's stain (q.v.).

IODOFORM. See IODINE.

IO MOTH, a large American saturniid moth, *Automeris io,* known for its beautiful coloration. The adult female is about $1\frac{1}{4}$ in. long and has a wing span of about 3 in. Its body is greenish red; its forewings are lavender and red, each with a longitudinal, green, wavy marking; and its hind wings are red and yellow, each with a characteristic circular dark-purple marking, about $\frac{1}{2}$ in. in diameter, near the center. The male, which is slightly smaller, is chiefly yellow and has similar marks on its hind wings. The larva, about 2 in. long, is green, with two longitudinal stripes, one red and one white, on each side; it is covered with sharp spines which when stimulated cause the production of a stinging fluid. The larva feeds on various plants, especially corn.

ION, a particle formed by the gain or loss of one or more electrons by a neutral atom or group of atoms. An atom which loses an electron forms a positively charged ion or *cation;* an atom which gains an electron forms a negatively charged ion or *anion.* When sodium and chlorine combine to form sodium chloride each sodium atom loses an electron to a chlorine atom, forming sodium cations and chloride anions which are rigidly held together by their electrical charges. See ELECTROCHEMISTRY; ELECTROLYSIS; IONIZATION.

ION EXCHANGE, in chemistry, a method of removing small amounts of certain chemicals from a solution containing large amounts of other chemicals by passing the solution through porous solid materials, usually minerals of the zeolite (q.v.) group or specially prepared resins containing large, complex molecules. Certain ions in the solution replace ions or groups of ions in the resin or zeolite, from which they can then be eluted or washed out. By controlling the acidity, strength, and composition of the solution, and the nature of the resin, ions in solution are more or less selectively exchanged for the labile ions in the resin.

Hardness in water (q.v.) is removed by an ion-exchange method. The water is filtered through *Permutite,* an artificial zeolite, and the sodium in the zeolite replaces the undesirable calcium, magnesium, or iron ions in the water. When the zeolite is saturated with these metallic ions, it is washed with salt solution, which restores it to its original condition. During World War II, ion-exchange materials were included in the emergency equipment of members of the armed forces who might be stranded with no source of water other than salt water. With such material, a complex series of ion-exchange reactions is effected in the salts of the sea water; hydrogen ion is exchanged for sodium, and hydroxyl ion is exchanged for chloride, thus converting the salt water to virtually pure water and making it drinkable.

Ion-exchange methods have been used to great advantage in the hitherto almost impossible separation of the various rare-earth elements (q.v.). Hafnium (q.v.) has been separated from zirconium by ion-exchange methods to a greater extent than has ever been achieved with ordinary chemical separation methods. See ION.

Synthetic ion-exchange resins are employed extensively as filters and conditioners for automobile radiators and other cooling systems. They are also widely used in the pharmaceutical field as antacids for the treatment of peptic ulcers, as intestinal adsorbents for diarrhea control, and as sodium reduction agents in the treatment of migraine headache, heart disease, and dropsy. In other applications the resins are used for the removal of clot-producing calcium from whole blood in the preparation of blood plasma, and for the isolation of antibiotics, as in the manufacture of streptomycin.

IONIA, the ancient name of the district comprising the central portion of the w. coast of Asia Minor, together with the adjacent islands. The region received its name from the Ionians (q.v.), Greeks who came from the mainland of Greece after the Dorian invasion (see DORIANS). The area is mountainous, and includes three fertile valleys, watered by the rivers Cayster, Hermus (Gedis), and Mæander (Menderes). Ionia was extremely prosperous in ancient times, due to its flourishing agriculture and commerce. In the 7th and 6th centuries B.C. Ionia made important contributions to Greek art and literature, and particularly to philosophy (see IONIAN SCHOOL). Great cities grew up, of which Ephesus, Clazomenæ, Erythræ, Colophon, and Miletus were the most celebrated. Several cities, such as Miletus and Phocæa, became important commercial centers and sent out colonies to the w. Mediterranean Sea and northward to the Black Sea.

Common interests led the Ionian cities, twelve in number, to form a confederacy, within which each city remained autonomous. Smyrna, originally settled by the Æolian Greeks, was later occupied by colonists from Colophon and became an Ionian city. In the 6th century B.C. the cities of Ionia were involved in a series of wars with the kings of Lydia (q.v.), to whom they yielded a nominal submission. Ionia exercised a powerful influence upon Lydian culture, its own culture being influenced in turn by Lydia. In 546 B.C. the Ionians came under the sway of Persia, but revolted from Persian rule in 500 B.C., assisted by the Greek cities Athens and Eretria. The revolt was put down, but the participation of Athens and Eretria gave the Persians a pretext for declaring war upon Greece. With the defeat of Persia by the Greeks (479 B.C.) the Ionian cities became nominally free, but in reality were dependent upon Athens. Subsequently, Ionia reverted to Persian rule, then fell within the sphere of the Greco-Macedonian Empire founded by Alexander the Great, and was finally incorporated into the Roman Empire as a part of the province of Asia. See GREECE: *History of Ancient Greece.*

IONIAN ISLANDS, a group of islands in the Ionian and Mediterranean seas, w. of the Greek mainland, and comprising one of the six geographical divisions of Greece. The principal islands are Corfu (Gr. *Kerkyra*), Cephalonia (*Kephallenia*), Zante (*Zakynthos*), Cerigo (*Kythera*) (qq.v.), Ithaca (*Ithake*), Leukas, and Paxos. For administrative purposes, the islands of Corfu, Cephalonia, and Zante form the prefecture of the Ionian Islands. Largest and most important of the cities of the islands is Corfu (q.v.), capital of the island of the same name. The islands are largely mountainous and the climate is more temperate than that of the mainland. The chief products are olive oil, currants, and grain. Major industries are fishing, shipbuilding, and textile weaving. The great majority of the inhabitants belongs to the Greek Orthodox Church.

Anciently colonized by the Greeks, the islands later formed part of the Roman and Byzantine empires. They were held in part or in whole during their subsequent history by a succession of foreign countries. They were under the Venetian Republic from 1386 until taken by the French in 1797. In 1798 they were surrendered to the Russians and the Turks. From 1800 to 1807 they formed an independent state. In 1807 they reverted to the French who held them until 1814, when they became a British protectorate. British control lasted until 1864, the date of their incorporation into the Greek monarchy. Area of the Ionian Islands, 853 sq.m.; pop. (1951) 228,119.

IONIANS, one of the three important ethnic divisions of the ancient Greeks, the others being the Æolians and the Dorians (qq.v.). In Greek mythology, the eponymous ancestor of the Ionians was Ion, son of Xuthus and brother of Achæus (see HELLEN). The Ionians seem to have been one of the earliest Greek-speaking peoples from the N. to reach the mainland of Greece. They may, in fact, have been the very first, and were possibly the originators of Mycenæan culture (see GREECE: *History of Ancient Greece.*) The name *Iones,* or *Iavones,* was current in remote antiquity; *Javan,* a variant form, occurs in Genesis 10:2, and in Hebrew usage applies to the whole Greek race. In historical times the Ionians occupied Attica and parts of Eubœa, most of the islands of the Ægean Sea, and the narrow strip along the w. coast of Asia Minor known as Ionia (q.v.). The Ionian Greeks possessed greater artistic and literary ability than either the Æolians or Dorians, but they also had a less vigorous and hardy character, and exhibited tendencies toward luxurious living.

IONIAN SCHOOL, the name commonly assigned to the earliest school of Greek philosophy, which flourished in the 6th and 5th centuries B.C. in Ionia (q.v.) on the w. coast of Asia Minor. The principal philosophers of this school, Thales and Anaximander Miletus, Heraclitus of Ephesus, and Anaxagoras of Clazomenæ (qq.v.), laid the foundations of European speculative philosophy and metaphysics by their efforts to discover an ultimate, irreducible principle behind all natural phenomena. See GREEK PHILOSOPHY.

IONIAN SEA, an arm of the Mediterranean Sea, separating Greece and Albania from Italy and Sicily. It is connected with the Adriatic Sea to the north by the Strait of Otranto. It forms a deep indentation, the Gulf of Taranto, in the southern coast of Italy between the Calabrian and Otranto peninsulas, and a number of deep inlets on the Greek coast, including the Gulf of Corinth.

IONIUM, a radioactive isotope of thorium (q.v.) with atomic weight 230 and atomic number 90. It was discovered in 1907, and was at that time believed to be a new element.

IONIZATION, the formation of electrically-charged particles from atoms or molecules. Atoms are electrically neutral; the electrons which bear the negative charge are equal in number to the protons in the nucleus bearing the positive charge. When sodium combines with chlorine to form sodium chloride, each sodium atom transfers an electron to a chlorine atom, thus forming a sodium ion with a positive charge and a chloride ion with a negative charge. In a crystal of sodium chloride the strong electrostatic attraction between ions of opposite charge holds the ions firmly in place and close together. When sodium chloride is melted the ions tend to dissociate because of their thermal motion, and can move about freely. If two electrodes are placed in molten sodium chloride and an electric potential is applied, the sodium ions migrate to the negative electrode and the chloride ions migrate to the positive electrode, causing a current of electricity to flow. When sodium chloride is dissolved in water the ions are even more free to dissociate (because of the attraction between the ions and the solvent), and the solution is an excellent conductor of electricity. Solutions of most inorganic acids, bases, and salts conduct electricity and are called electrolytes; solutions of sugar, alcohol, glycerine, and most other organic substances are poor conductors of electricity and are called nonelectrolytes. Electrolytes which give strongly conducting solutions are called strong electrolytes (nitric acid, sodium chloride); electrolytes which give weakly conducting solutions are called weak electrolytes (mercuric chloride, acetic acid).

The Swedish chemist Svante Arrhenius (q.v.) was the first investigator to recognize that substances in solution are in the form of ions and not molecules, even when no electrical potential is applied. In 1887 he stated the hypothesis that when an electrolyte goes into solution it is only partly dissociated into separate ions, and that the amount of dissociation depends on the nature of the electrolyte and the concentration of the solution. Thus, according to the Arrhenius theory, when a given quantity of sodium chloride is dissolved in a large amount of water the ions dissociate to a greater degree than when the same quantity is dissolved in less water. However, a different theory of the dissociation of electrolytes, developed by the Dutch physicist Peter Debye (q.v.), has been generally accepted since 1923. The so-called Debye-Hückel theory assumes that electrolytes are completely dissociated in solution. However, the tendency of ions to migrate and thus conduct electricity is retarded by the electrostatic attraction between the oppositely charged ions and between the ions and the solvent. As the concentration of the solution is increased this retarding effect is increased. Thus, according to this theory, a fixed amount of sodium chloride is a better conductor when dissolved in a large amount of water than when dissolved in a smaller amount, because the ions are further apart and exert less attraction upon each other and upon the solvent molecules. The ions are not infinitely free to migrate, however. The dielectric constant of the solvent (see DIELECTRIC) is also an important factor in the conductance of a solution; ionization is most marked in a solvent such as water, which has a high dielectric constant. See ATOM AND ATOMIC THEORY; ELECTROCHEMISTRY.

Ionization occurs also in gases. When a rapidly moving particle, such as an electron, an alpha particle, or a quantum of radiant energy, collides with a gas atom, an electron is ejected from the atom, leaving a charged ion. The ions render the gas conductive; see ELECTRIC DISCHARGE. The amount of energy necessary to remove an electron from an atom is called the ionization energy. The principle of ionization of gases by various types of radiation is used in the detection and measurement of radiation (see IONIZATION CHAMBER; CLOUD CHAMBER) and in the separation and analysis of isotopes in the mass spectrograph (q.v.). The atmosphere always contains a certain number of ions produced by ultraviolet light and cosmic radiation; see IONOSPHERE.

IONIZATION CHAMBER, a term applied to a variety of instruments designed to detect and measure ionizing particles of radiation, such as alpha, beta, gamma, and cosmic rays. See IONIZATION; RADIATION. An ionization chamber consists essentially of a closed vessel containing a gas and equipped with two electrodes at different electrical potentials. The electrodes, depending on the type of instrument, may consist of parallel plates or coaxial cylinders, or the walls of the chamber may act as one electrode while a wire or rod inside the chamber acts as the other. When ionizing particles of radiation enter the chamber they ionize the gas between the electrodes. The ions which are thus produced migrate to the electrodes of opposite sign (negatively charged ions move toward the positive electrode and vice versa), creating a current which may be amplified and measured directly with an electrometer (see ELECTRIC METERS), or amplified and recorded by means of electronic circuits.

Ionization chambers adapted to detect individual ionizing particles of radiation are called counters. The *Geiger-Müller counter* is the most sensitive and widely used instrument of this type. It was developed by the German physicist Hans Geiger (1882-1946), from an instrument first devised by Geiger and the English physicist Ernest Rutherford, and was later improved by Wilhelm Müller. The counting tube is filled with a gas or a mixture of gases at low pressure, the electrodes being the thin metal wall of the tube and a fine wire, usually made of tungsten, stretched lengthwise along the axis of the tube. A strong electric field maintained between the electrodes accelerates the ions; these then collide with further atoms of the gas, detaching electrons and thus producing more ions. When the voltage is raised sufficiently, the rapidly increasing current produced by a single particle sets off a "discharge" throughout the counter. In order to prevent the current caused by one particle from continuing to flow indefinitely, the discharge is automatically "quenched" after a fraction of a second. The external circuits may be so arranged that the voltage drops as soon as the current passes, thereby extinguishing the discharge. The counter then gradually reverts to its former condition and is ready for the discharge caused by the next particle. In some cases the tube is filled with a mixture of gaseous organic chemicals which form a layer of vapor on the electrode surface as soon as the discharge passes and temporarily prevent the further emission of electrons. The pulse caused by each particle is amplified electronically and then actuates a loud speaker, or a mechanical or electronic counting device.

IONOSPHERE, name given to a layer or layers of ionized air in the earth's atmosphere extending from about 50 m. above the earth's surface to the limits of the atmosphere. At these altitudes the air is extremely thin, having about the density of the gas in a vacuum tube, and when the atmospheric particles are ionized by ultraviolet radiation from the sun or by other radiation they tend to remain ionized, since few collisions occur between ions.

The ionosphere exerts a great influence on the propagation of radio signals. Energy which is radiated from a transmitter upward toward the ionosphere is in part absorbed by the ionized air and in part refracted or bent downward again toward the surface of the earth. The bending effect makes possible the reception of radio signals at distances much greater than would be possible for waves which traveled along the surface of the earth. Such refracted waves, however, reach the earth only at certain definite distances from the transmitter; the distance depends on the angle of refraction and the altitude. Hence a radio signal may be receivable at a distance of 100 m. from the transmitter but inaudible at 500 m. This phenomenon is known as *skip*. In certain other areas the ground-wave signals and the refracted signals from the ionosphere may reach the receiver and interfere with each other, producing the phenomenon known as *fading*. The amount of refraction in the ionosphere decreases with the frequency and for very high frequencies is almost nonexistent, and so long-distance transmission of high-frequency radio waves such as those used for frequency modulation and television is impossible.

The ionosphere is usually divided into two main layers; a lower or *E layer* (sometimes called the Kennelly-Heaviside layer) which is between 50 and 70 m. above the earth's surface and which reflects radio waves of low frequency; and a higher *F layer* (sometimes called the Appleton layer) which is 130 m. or more above the earth and which reflects high-frequency radio waves. The F layer rises during the night and therefore changes its reflecting characteristics.

IOWA, an Indian tribe of the Siouan family (q.v.), first encountered by white men about the beginning of the 18th century in Minnesota. The precise name of the tribe (the members of which originally called themselves *Pahotcha* or *Pahucha,* "dusty noses") was long a matter of dispute, largely through confusions arising from a variety of more or less phonetic spellings of the same basic name in English and French. The tribe existed, however, as a definite entity throughout its history, and was well-known to French traders and later to American explorers and settlers. Under the pressure of white settlement the Iowa Indians wandered southward to the areas now included in the States of Missouri and Iowa as well as in Minnesota. In 1861 they ceded part of their land to the U.S., and were settled upon reservations in Kansas and Oklahoma, where they remain to the present day with a population of about 650. The primitive economy of the Iowa Indians conformed in the main to the typical patterns of the Plains Indians, being based almost entirely upon agriculture and buffalo-hunting. Their culture was similar, though in most respects somewhat inferior, to that of the Omahas (q.v.).

IOWA, one of the West North Central States of the United States, bounded on the N. by Minnesota, on the E. by the Mississippi R., which separates it from Wisconsin and Illinois, on the S. by Missouri, and on the W. by the Big Sioux and Missouri rivers, which separate it from South Dakota and Nebraska respectively. It ranks as the twenty-fourth State of the Union in area, the twenty-second (1950) in population, and the sixteenth in order of admission after the thirteen original States, having been admitted on Dec. 28, 1846. Des Moines (q.v.) is the State capital and largest city. In descending order of population (1950), other cities with over 25,000 inhabitants are Sioux City, Davenport, Cedar Rapids, Waterloo, Dubuque, Council Bluffs, Ottumwa, Burlington, Clinton, Mason City, Iowa City, and Fort Dodge (qq.v.). Iowa somewhat resembles a rectangle in shape. The distance between the northernmost and southernmost points in the State is about 210 m.; the distance between the easternmost and westernmost points is about 310 m. The area of the State is 56,280 sq.m., including 294 sq.m. of inland water surface; pop. (1950) 2,621,073.

Physiographically, Iowa falls within the province of the Interior Plain of North America. The terrain, extensively glaciated during the Pleistocene epoch, consists almost entirely of smooth, gently undulating or level prairie (q.v.). Diversification of relief is most pronounced in the N. central region, which contains numerous low hills, lakes, and ponds, and in the N.E. section, characterized by steep

Iowa Development Commission

Iowa State Capitol in Des Moines

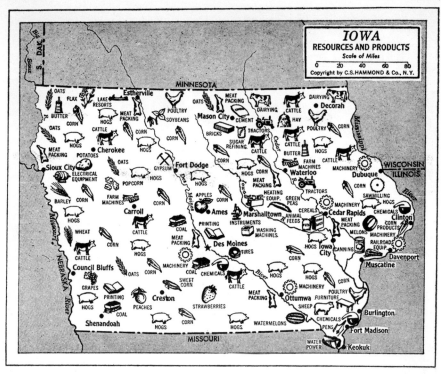

IOWA
RESOURCES AND PRODUCTS
Scale of Miles
0 20 40 60 80
Copyright by C.S. HAMMOND & Co., N.Y.

river gorges up to 400 ft. in height. Another hilly region is situated in the w., parallel to the Missouri R. Iowa has an average elevation of 1100 ft. above sea level. The highest point, in the N.E. portion of the State, is 1675 ft. above sea level; the lowest point, in the S.E., is 480 ft. above sea level. Approximately two thirds of the State is drained by direct affluents of the Mississippi R., which forms the entire E. boundary; the remainder is drained by the affluents of the Missouri R., part of the w. boundary of the State. The divide between the two drainage systems extends obliquely across the State from N.W. to S.E. The Mississippi affluents flow generally S.E. from the divide, and the Missouri affluents flow generally s.w. Among the principal affluents of the Mississippi are the Des Moines, largest stream within the State, Upper Iowa, Turkey, Wapsipinicon, Cedar, Iowa, and Skunk rivers. The principal affluents of the Missouri are the Big Sioux, Little Sioux, Nishnabotna, and Nodaway rivers. Among the principal lakes are Spirit Lake, East and West Okoboji Lakes, Clear Lake, and Storm Lake.

The climate of Iowa is characterized by wide seasonal variations in temperature.

Temperatures as high as 118°F. and as low as −47°F. have been recorded, but the annual absolute range of temperature averages about 118°F. Temperatures in July and January average about 74°F. and 18°F. respectively. The mean annual temperature is almost 47.5°F. In the vicinity of Des Moines the mean January temperature is about 21°F. and the mean July temperature is about 76°F. The maximum and minimum temperatures recorded in the Des Moines area are 110°F. and −30°F. Mean annual precipitation is nearly 32 inches. About four fifths of the total falls between the end of March and the first of November.

Iowa maintains eighty-eight State parks totaling 23,400 acres and ten State forests totaling 13,800 acres, and there are ten community forests totaling 14,100 acres. These parks and forests include many diversified types of scenery, including river gorges and bluffs, caves, mineral springs, streams, lakes, forests, and several small areas of desert. Noteworthy among the parks, many of which contain accommodations for vacationists and a variety of recreational facilities, are Lacey-Keosauqua State Park (2216 acres), near Keo-

Iowa Devel. Comm.; Des Moines C. of C.

CITIES IN IOWA

Above: Aerial view of the Loop district in Cedar Rapids, showing the civic center located on an island in the Cedar River.

Left: Walnut Street, popular shopping center in the city of Des Moines.

lakes, and the State game preserves are well stocked with ring-necked pheasants, ducks, and geese.

Iowa is one of the foremost agricultural and stock-raising States of the United States. About 95 percent of the area of the State is arable, and the soil is remarkably fertile. In a recent year farms numbered nearly 200,000. These farms included almost 34,715,000 acres and had a value in excess of $5,500,000,000, a total exceeded only in Texas. The average farm in Iowa includes about 174 acres. Only about 9 percent of the farms are less than 30 acres in size, and farms of over 1000 acres number less than 3 percent of the total. Iowa is the chief hog-raising and egg-producing State of the Union. Over 11,465,000 hogs were numbered among the livestock population in a recent year, and almost 4,800,000,-000 eggs were produced. The State is also a major source of beef cattle, which recently numbered over 4,500,000 head. Among other livestock were more than 890,000 dairy cattle and about 1,280,000 sheep. In a recent year the total cash income from marketed livestock amounted to more than $2,070,000,000, considerably exceeding the total for any other State.

The State ranks first in the Union in the

sauqua; Backbone State Park (1412 acres), near Strawberry Point; Lake Wapello State Park (1130 acres), near Drakesville; Ledges State Park (896 acres), near Boone; Geode State Park (884 acres), near Danville; Stone State Park (882 acres), near Sioux City; McGregor State Park (576 acres), near McGregor; Lake Ahquabi Recreation Preserve (770 acres), near Indianola; White Pine Hollow State Forest (650 acres), near Luxemburg; Heery Woods Recreation Preserve (380 acres), near Clarksville; and Preparation Canyon State Forest Preserve (186 acres), near Moorehead. Trout, carp, catfish, pike, and bass are plentiful in the streams and

production of corn and oats, with an average annual harvest of about 532,800,000 bushels and 205,200,000 bushels, respectively. Other leading crops, together with approximate, average, annual yield, are hay, 5,500,000 tons; soybeans, 33,535,000 bushels; wheat, 4,160,-000 bushels; popcorn, 56,800,000 pounds; potatoes, 2,880,000 bushels; and rye, 210,000 bushels. Cash receipts from the sale of crops in a recent year amounted to nearly $291,000,-000, and Federal government payments were about $11,700,000, making a total farm income of about $2,372,000,000. This total was exceeded only in California and Texas.

According to a recent survey Iowa contains about 3850 manufacturing and food-processing establishments employing about 167,000 production workers. The output of these establishments for the year had an approximate value of $2,700,000,000. Meat packing, poultry dressing and packing, the manufacture of dairy products, and the processing of other farm products are the principal manufacturing industries. Printing and publishing, cement making, and the production of bakery products, pearl buttons, washing machines, furnaces, agricultural implements and lawn mowers, railroad equipment, automobile accessories, fountain pens, cosmetics, and non-alcoholic beverages are other important industries of the State.

Right: Boat pushing a barge on the Mississippi River near Davenport, Iowa.
Below: Field of corn on typical Iowa farm.

Davenport C. of C.; Iowa Devel. Comm.

Iowa has a variety of productive mineral deposits, including coal, limestone, clay, gypsum, sand, gravel, and building stone. In a recent year the total value of the mineral production of the State was over $41,000,000.

The State is served by an extensive network of transportation facilities, including twelve trunk-line railroads, with an aggregate of about 8600 m. of main-track lines, and a number of inland-water carriers operating on the Mississippi R. Excluding roads within urban areas, the highway system consists of about 101,500 m. of roads; nearly 70,000 m. are surfaced, about 9730 m. are maintained by the State, and about 92,000 m. are locally maintained. The State has about 150 commercial and municipal airports, including 61 that are equipped for night flying.

Attendance at the public schools of Iowa is compulsory, during a minimum period of 120 school days annually, for all children between the ages of seven and sixteen. Public elementary and secondary schools, in a recent year, numbered over 9110, with 460,500 pupils instructed by nearly 22,000 teachers. The State has twenty-three universities and colleges, and thirty-three junior colleges. Among the outstanding institutions are the University of Iowa (see IOWA, UNIVERSITY OF), at Iowa City; the State College of Agriculture, at Ames; Grinnell College, at Grinnell; Cornell College, at Mount Vernon; Drake University, at Des Moines; Coe College, at Cedar Rapids; Morningside College, at Sioux City; and Iowa State Teachers College, at Cedar Falls. Iowa has consistently had one of the lowest illiteracy rates of all the States in the United States.

Iowa is governed according to the constitution of 1857. Executive authority is vested in a governor and lieutenant governor, elected for two-year terms, a secretary of state, a secretary of agriculture, a treasurer, an auditor, an attorney general, and certain other appointed officials. Legislative authority is vested in a general assembly consisting of a senate of 50 members, and a house of representatives of 108 members. Members of the senate are elected for four-year terms, and members of the house of representatives for two-year terms. Judicial authority is vested in a supreme court consisting of 9 members, a district court consisting of 70 members, and various minor courts. The State is divided into 99 counties. It is represented in the Congress of the United States by two senators and by eight representatives.

History. When visited (1673) by the French explorers Jacques Marquette and Louis Joliet, the first white men to reach the region included in present-day Iowa, it was inhabited by the Illinois and Iowa tribes of the Siouan linguistic stock. These tribes were later expelled from their ancestral domains by the Sacs and Foxes, Indians of the Algonquian stock. In 1680 the Iowa region was partly explored by the Flemish missionary Louis Hennepin. The French government formally claimed the region in 1682. More than 100 years elapsed before Iowa began to figure significantly in the colonial history of North America. However, in 1762 France ceded the region, together with other French possessions w. of the Mississippi R., to Spain.

In 1788 the French-Canadian pioneer Julien Dubuque (1762–1810) obtained from the Fox Indians the grant of a tract of land containing rich lead deposits and including the site of the city now bearing his name. He built a fort there, carried on the mining of lead, and traded with the Indians, but on his death the settlement was abandoned. Meanwhile, in 1803 the region had become a possession of the United States as a part of the Louisiana Purchase (q.v.). The Iowa region successively formed a part of the Territories of Louisiana (1805–12), Missouri (1812–21), Michigan (1834–36), and Wisconsin (1836–38); between 1821 and 1834 it was an unorganized area of the United States.

In 1808 the Federal government established Fort Madison, but the garrison was withdrawn in 1813 because of the hostility of the Indians. The Indians relinquished their title to an area of almost 9000 sq.m. in what is now Iowa following the defeat of the uprising (1832) led by the Sac chieftain Black Hawk, and thereafter increasing numbers of settlers arrived in the region. Dubuque was founded in 1833; other towns, including Davenport and Burlington, were founded during the next few years. Practically from the beginning the economy was based largely on livestock raising and the cultivation of corn.

All of the present-day State and parts of what are now Minnesota, North Dakota, and South Dakota were separated from Wisconsin Territory in 1838 and merged as Iowa Territory. By 1840 the Territorial population totaled more than 40,000. The Territory applied for admission to the Union in 1844, following the adoption of a constitution. After delays resulting from Congressional debates over the proposed State constitution and boundaries Iowa became (Dec. 28, 1846) the twenty-ninth State of the Union.

The influx of settlers continued, even after a massacre of Whites by Sioux Indians at Spirit Lake in March, 1857. In the same year the original constitution of 1846 was revised and Des Moines was made the capital of the State. Iowa, a strong antislave State, zealously supported the Union cause in the Civil War.

The development of the State was greatly accelerated by the building of railroads. With the rise of powerful railroad corporations there ensued a continuous conflict between the State legislature and the companies in regard to the taxation of railway property and the regulation of rates. In 1872 an act taxing railway property was passed, and in 1873 agitation stirred up by the Patrons of Husbandry (see GRANGE, NATIONAL) against the heavy rates imposed by the companies led to the creation of a board of railroad commissioners for the purpose of determining a maximum rate. The lowering of rates by the commissioners caused repeated appeals by the railroads to the courts. In general, however, the railroads maintained the advantage, although making various concessions. A Prohibition amendment adopted in 1882 was promptly declared unconstitutional by the courts. A new Prohibition law went into effect in 1884 and for some years proved fairly adequate. A very large part of the population, however, was opposed to sumptuary legislation, and in 1890, under the protection of the interstate commerce laws, a successful attempt was made to evade the antiliquor regulations by the importation of alcoholic products from other States. In 1894 the courts declared the Prohibition laws unconstitutional.

From 1846 to 1854 the majority of the voters in the State of Iowa voted Democratic in Presidential elections. From 1854 to 1916 the majority vote was for the Republican Party candidate. In 1920, 1924, and 1928 the vote was Republican; in 1932 and 1936, Democratic; and in 1940 and 1944, Republican. In 1948, 523,502 ballots were cast for the Democratic incumbent, President Harry S. Truman, and 488,933 ballots for the Republican candidate Thomas E. Dewey. The Republicans carried the State in 1952, their candidate General Dwight D. Eisenhower receiving 803,747 votes, as against 452,404 votes for the Democratic nominee Adlai E. Stevenson.

IOWA CITY, county seat of Johnson Co., Iowa, situated on the Iowa R., 120 miles E. of Des Moines. It is served by two railroads, and maintains a municipal airport. The city is the center of a productive farming and livestock-raising area, and is the site of the State University of Iowa (see IOWA, STATE UNIVERSITY OF). By virtue of the hospitals and medical-research departments associated with the university, Iowa City is the medical center of the State. A State music festival is held in the city annually. The site of Iowa City was chosen for the capital of the Territory of Iowa in 1839, and after the admission (1846) of Iowa to the Union the city became the State capital. In 1857 the capital was changed to Des Moines, a more central location. Pop. (1950) 27,212.

IOWA STATE COLLEGE OF AGRICULTURE AND MECHANICAL ARTS, a coeducational state institution of higher education, founded in 1858 and opened in 1868, at Ames, Iowa. The college offers courses in agriculture, science, engineering, home economics, and veterinary medicine, leading to bachelor's, master's and doctor's degrees. The college, in which tuition is free to Iowa residents, is partly supported by Federal funds. In a recent year the faculty numbered about 925, about 7200 students were enrolled, and the library contained 410,000 volumes.

IOWA STATE TEACHERS COLLEGE, a coeducational institution of higher learning, founded in 1876 as Iowa State Normal School, at Cedar Falls. The present name was adopted in 1909. The college, which is maintained by the State, offers instruction in industrial arts, the liberal arts, science, agriculture, home economics, and music, leading to bachelor's and master's degrees in education. In a recent year the faculty numbered about 195 and approximately 2350 students were enrolled.

IOWA, STATE UNIVERSITY OF, a coeducational State institution of higher learning, founded in 1847, and opened in 1855 at Iowa City. The university includes colleges of liberal arts, law, medicine, nursing, dentistry, pharmacy, engineering, education, and commerce, as well as a graduate college; schools of fine arts, social work, journalism, and religion; and a division of physical education. It grants bachelor's, master's, and doctor's degrees. In 1947 the university instituted a course in social science, called the "Great Issues" course, for the examination of vital problems of labor-management relations, higher education, and social security. In a recent year the faculty numbered about 565, and over 7300 students were enrolled.

IPATIEFF or **IPATIEV,** VLADIMIR NIKOLAEVICH (1867-1952), Russian-American chemist, born in Moscow, and educated at the University of St. Petersburg (now Leningrad). He was professor of chemistry at the University of St. Petersburg from 1906 to 1915. During World War I he was chairman of the Chemical Commission of Russia. He emigrated to the United States in 1931, and was professor of chemistry at Northwestern University from 1931 to 1935. Ipatieff's greatest contributions were in the field of high-pressure catalytic reactions. He discovered new catalytic agents important in the manufacture of fuels and dyes, and was the first to point out the action of promoters (agents which activate catalysts). Among his many industrial applications of the theory of catalysis were a polymerization process for making high-octane gasoline and a synthesis of isoprene, a compound used in making synthetic rubber. His writings include *Text Book of Organic Chemistry* (1903), *Aluminum Oxide as Catalyst* (1929), and *Catalytic Reactions at High Pressures and Temperatures* (1936).

IPECAC, common name of a tropical creeping plant, *Cephaëlis ipecacuanha,* which is a source of alkaloid drugs. Ipecac is a member of the Madder family, native to forests of Brazil and adjoining South American countries. It is a small, shrubby plant bearing flowers which are composed of a five-parted united calyx, a five-lobed corolla, five stamens, and a single pistil. The fruit is a small purple berry. The root of ipecac has a ringed surface, giving the appearance of small quoits strung on a central woody cord. The root yields two colorless crystalline alkaloids, *emetine,* $C_{29}H_{40}N_2O_4$, and *cephaëline,* $C_{28}H_{38}N_2O_4$. Emetine is a white, odorless, bitter powder, soluble in alcohol. It acts as a violent emetic in doses of 1/18th of a grain or even less, and is a powerful poison. It is a chemotherapeutic agent for treatment of amebic dysentery (q.v.). Minute doses are often included in barbiturate sleeping pills; when a dangerous dose of the latter is taken, sufficient emetine is introduced to force the stomach to empty.

Several unrelated emetic plants are called ipecac, including *Euphorbia ipecacuanha,* the wild ipecac, and a species of *Gillenia* (q.v.).

IPHIGENIA, in Greek legend, daughter of Agamemnon, King of Mycenæ, and Clytemnestra. Because Agamemnon had offended Artemis (q.v.), the goddess of wild life, the Greek fleet, commanded by Agamemnon and sailing to attack Troy (q.v.), was detained by calm and a plague at Aulis. When Calchas the seer declared that only the sacrifice of Iphigenia would appease Artemis, Agamemnon sent for his daughter on the pretense that she would be married to the warrior Achilles. Then, as Iphigenia was about to be slain, Artemis relented and, substituting a hind on the sacrificial altar, carried Iphigenia away in a cloud to Tauris. There Iphigenia became a priestess of Artemis, and was required, according to the local custom, to sacrifice all strangers. When her brother Orestes (q.v.) came to Tauris and was on the point of being sacrificed, Iphigenia saved him; together they fled, taking with them a sacred wooden statue of Artemis. The city-states of Sparta and Brauron later claimed to have the original statue. According to the Greek poet Hesiod (q.v.),

Iphigenia was transformed into the goddess Hecate (q.v.).

The story of Iphigenia has been the inspiration for a number of the world's greatest tragic dramas, from classical to modern times, including *Iphigenia among the Tauri* and *Iphigenia at Aulis,* by the Greek playwright Euripides; *Iphigenie* (1674) by the French dramatist Jean Baptiste Racine; and *Iphigenie auf Tauris* (1789) by the German writer Johann Wolfgang von Goethe. Iphigenia is also the subject of two operas by the German composer Christoph Gluck, *Iphigénie en Aulide* (1774) and *Iphigénie en Tauride* (1779).

IPPOLITOV-IVANOV, MIKHAIL MIKHAILOVICH (1859-1935), Russian composer, born in Gatchina, near St. Petersburg, and educated at the St. Petersburg conservatory. In 1882 he became director of the Tiflis Music School; in 1893 he was appointed professor and later director of the Moscow conservatory. The Soviet government honored him with the title of "People's Artist of the Republic" in 1923, and in 1925 he became the conductor of the Moscow Opera. Ippolitov-Ivanov wrote many works in all forms, much of which reflects his interest in Caucasian music; his most popular composition is the orchestral suite, *Caucasian Sketches* (1894). His literary works include *On the National Songs of Georgia* and his memoirs, *Fifty Years of Russian Music in My Memories* (1934).

IPSWICH, a commercial and mining town of Stanley County, Queensland, Australia, located on the Bremer R., 23½ m. by rail s.w. of Brisbane. The most important coal field in Queensland is located in and around Ipswich, and the surrounding area is a rich agricultural region. Among the manufacturing establishments of the town are sawmills, metal foundries, and woolen mills. Ipswich was founded in 1829 and incorporated in 1860. Pop. (1950) 34,030.

IPSWICH, a county borough and county seat of East Suffolk County, England, situated on the Gipping R., 69 m. by rail N.E. of London. The site contains the remains of a Roman villa and of a Saxon settlement. Ipswich was chartered in 1200 and incorporated in 1464. Several Tudor structures are still standing, notably Sparrowe's house, dating from 1567, and the Christchurch Park mansion, built in 1549. Other points of interest include Wolsey's Gateway, all that remains of a college founded by Thomas Cardinal Wolsey during the reign of Henry

VIII, and several churches built in the perpendicular style of early English architecture. Among the principal industrial establishments are railway shops, engineering works, paper mills, fertilizer plants, and clothing and furniture factories. Pop. (1951 prelim.) 104,788.

I.Q. See PSYCHOLOGICAL TESTING.

IQUIQUE, seaport and capital of Tarapacá Province, Chile, situated on the Pacific Ocean, 820 miles N. of Valparaíso. It originated as a fishing village, but after 1830 became active in the nitrate trade, and is now one of the principal ports of Chile, exporting chiefly nitrate of soda and iodine. Railway lines connect Iquique with various mining centers in the interior of the province and with other coastal cities. Iquique lies in a desert area, and water is piped from 50 m. inland. The port belonged to Peru until 1879, when it was captured by the Chileans during the War of the Pacific. It was formally ceded to Chile by treaty in 1883. Pop. (1949 est.) 35,985.

IQUITOS, a tribe of South American Indians living in Peru and Ecuador and inhabiting a number of settlements on the banks of the Marañón, Tigre, and Nanay rivers. They carry on an active trade, exchanging rubber and other native products for a variety of imports. Contact with white civilization and Christian missionaries has not greatly affected their primitive culture; the tribe is still pagan, following an animistic religion and worshiping images carved in the shapes of birds and other animals. They are known for their skillful preparation of a fermented liquor, *chicha,* made from cane sugar or corn, which they also mix with the roots of an unidentified plant to produce an opiate.

IQUITOS, capital and river port of Loreto province, Peru, on the Marañón R., near the point where the Marañón unites with the Ucayli R. to form the mainstream of the Amazon. Although situated 2330 m. from the Atlantic Ocean, the port is regularly visited by ocean-going vessels. Iquitos is also served by several air lines. The principal exports are tobacco, cotton, rubber, tagua nuts, vanilla, and sarsaparilla. Pop. (1950 est.) 42,018.

IRAN, a kingdom located in s.w. Asia. The country is bounded on the N. by the U.S.S.R. and the Caspian Sea, on the E. by Afghanistan and Baluchistan, on the s. by the Gulf of Oman and the Persian Gulf, and on the w. by Iraq and Turkey. The extreme length of the country is 450 m. from E. to w.,

and the maximum width is 365 m. The capital and the largest city of the country is Teheran (q.v.). Other leading cities are Abadan, Ardebil, Hamadan, Isfahan, Kazvin, Kerman, Kermanshah, Meshed, Resht, Shiraz, and Tabriz (qq.v.). Iran is composed of ten major political divisions. These are the ûstans, or provinces, of Azerbaijan, Fars, Isfahan, Kerman, Kermanshah, Kirman, Khurasan, Khuzistan, Laristan, and Luristan. Area, 628,060 sq.m.; pop. (1951 est.) 19,-139,563.

Iran is a great tableland from 4000 to 8000 ft. above sea level. A desert, 800 m. long and from 100 to 200 m. wide, stretches across the country from the Elburz Mts. in the N. to the Gulf of Oman in the s.E. The w. region is broken by small mountain ranges. In the N.w. is Lake Urmia, a large body of salt water, and beyond it, along the Turkish border, rise the Zagros Mts.; the highest peak in this range is Mt. Alijuk, about 14,000 ft. above sea level. The highest peak in Iran is Mt. Demavend in the Elburz Mts., 18,600 ft. above sea level.

The country is divided climatically into three main regions: the extremely hot coast along the Persian Gulf and the Gulf of Oman; the temperate but arid central highland; and the tableland of the intensely cold Elburz Range beyond which, on the s. shore of the Caspian Sea, lies a fertile narrow coastal plain. The annual average rainfall for the country is about ten inches, with the exception of the N. coastal plain, which receives about fifty inches a year.

The flora of the plateau is poor in variety; the predominant trees are the konar, cypress, dwarf oak, walnut, and mulberry. Such medicinal plants as gum tragacanth, gum arabic, asafoetida, and the opium poppy are found throughout Iran. The rose is the pre-eminent flower of the country. The fauna includes the rabbit, fox, wolf, hyena, jackal, leopard, deer, porcupine, ibex, bear, badger, weasel, and tiger. Pheasants and partridges are found inland; pelicans and flamingoes breed along the coast of the Persian Gulf.

Iran is principally an agrarian country. Most of the tillable land is divided into large, irrigated, privately owned estates. The chief crops are wheat, barley, and rice. Other agricultural products are tobacco, tea, dates, apricots, sugar beets, corn, cotton, and the opium poppy.

The country has a broad diversity of mineral deposits, but is especially noted for the production of petroleum. The principal

Iranian oil fields, located at the head of the Persian Gulf in the s.w. region, are considered the richest oil fields in existence. They were exploited by the Anglo-Iranian Oil Company (A.I.O.C.); the concession was granted in 1901 and abrogated in 1951. In a recent year these fields produced 31,750,147 long tons of crude petroleum. The mineral deposits of Iran include copper, lead, nickel, manganese, iron, marble, cobalt, borax, sodium, sulfate, sulfur, rock salt, and turquoise. Most of these deposits are relatively undeveloped; in 1939 Iran granted the Dutch company, Algemeen Exploratie Mattschappij, a concession to explore and develop the mineral resources in certain regions of the country.

The industries of Iran depend heavily upon its agricultural production and its natural resources. The fisheries of the Persian Gulf and the Caspian Sea, produce trout, carp, sturgeon, sheatfish, salmon, and herring. Persian carpets, silk, cotton, and wool textiles, chemicals, and wine are produced. Other important industries are the refining of oil, smelting of copper, and the processing of hides, tobacco, sugar beets, and rice.

Iran depends heavily on foreign sources for most manufactured necessities; the vast petroleum wealth enables it to maintain a favorable balance of trade. The leading imports, in a recent year, in order of their importance, were cotton piece goods, machinery and tools, sugar, tea, woolen textiles, automotive vehicles, rubber, paper, and drugs. The leading exports of the same year were oil (about 86%), fruits, wool, leather, and raw cotton. The value of Iranian imports in a recent year was about $230,000,000, and for the same year the value of the exports was about $352,000,000. Trade is chiefly with the United States, the United Kingdom, the Soviet Union, and Germany.

The Iranian railway system has over 1900 m. of track. The highway system of the country is government maintained, as are the telegraph facilities and radio stations. Commercial vessels navigate Lake Urmia and the Karun R. Iranian air services operate both domestic and foreign flights; foreign air services connect Teheran with other Asiatic cities and with a few large European cities. Regular service is maintained by numerous foreign and domestic steamship lines.

For a detailed account of the people of Iran, see IRANIAN. Sunnites (q.v.), orthodox Mohammedans, comprise the largest religious group. Other denominations are Christians of the Armenian Church, Jews, Nestorians (q.v.), and Parsis (see PARSEE). Over 500,-000 pupils are enrolled in the country's schools, which number more than 4400. Institutions of higher learning include universities at Teheran and Tabriz, and colleges at Isfahan, Meshed, and Shiraz.

The government of Iran is a constitutional monarchy, based on the constitution of December 30, 1906. The supreme executive authority is vested in the shah, or king; he is aided by a cabinet of fourteen members including a prime minister appointed by the shah. Legislative authority is vested in the parliament, a unicameral body consisting of 136 popularly elected members. The highest judicial authority is the supreme court located in Teheran. Eight courts of appeal decide upon the cases referred to them from the numerous minor courts throughout the country.

History. The cross-references in the following account of the history of Iran direct the reader to articles presenting the same or related material in greater detail. For the history of Iran prior to 1935, see PERSIA; see also PERSIAN ART; PERSIAN LITERATURE.

In 1935 Riza Shah Pahlevi (q.v.) officially

British Information Services

A typical farmer of southern Iran

British Information Services

Shrine of Shah Nametullah in the village of Mahun, near Kerman in central Iran

changed the name of his country from Persia to Iran and initiated a number of westernizing reforms. The first decree ordered the Sunnites to wear western hats instead of their traditional fezzes. Most of the population obeyed without protest; a minority, led by Mohammedan priests, rioted; several were killed. The government next abolished all feudal titles and began a long-range program for the economic modernization of the country. Early in 1936 the shah's wife and daughters appeared in public without veils, breaking an ancient tradition of the country; most Iranian women no longer wear veils. In 1936 Iran signed a treaty of friendship and nonagression with Iraq, Turkey, and Afghanistan. Early in World War II, Germany, Turkey, Great Britain, and the U.S.S.R. attempted unsuccessfully to form alliances with Iran. In 1941, however, both Great Britain and the U.S.S.R. occupied areas of Iran to protect the oil fields from possible German seizure. As a result of the Allied invasion all Axis nationals were expelled, all Axis consulates and legations were closed, the Allies assumed control of all Iranian communications facilities, and Riza Shah Pahlevi, who had been friendly to Axis interests, abdicated. The shah's son, Mohammed Riza Pahlevi (q.v.), succeeded his father; he adopted a pro-Allied policy, and granted the parliament's demand for liberal reforms. In January, 1942, Iran, Great Britain, and the U.S.S.R. signed a treaty guaranteeing Anglo-Soviet respect for Iranian territorial integrity and military aid to fulfill this pledge. The Allies also agreed to consult the Iranian government on all economic, political, and military measures affecting the domestic policy, to withdraw the occupation forces as soon as possible, and to provide economic assistance to Iran.

By 1943, the U.S.S.R. and Great Britain, with the assistance of U.S. military forces and Lend-Lease (q.v.), had made extensive improvements in Iran's transportation facilities in order to increase the country's value in the transfer of military supplies to the Russian fighting front. Iran complained, however, that the U.S.S.R. had completely isolated its occupation zone from outside contact. The Soviet government defended its action by explaining that it was protecting itself against possible Anglo-American expansion in Iran. This dispute was adjusted in November, 1944, by the Teheran Conference attended by Franklin D. Roosevelt, Winston Churchill, and Joseph Stalin. The Declaration on Iran, produced by this conference and issued on December 1, stated that the three governments were "at one with the government of Iran in their desire for the maintenance of the independence, sovereignty, and territorial integrity of Iran." In the

British Information Services

*Woman of Iran making cheese by shaking
milk in goatskin, supported on tripod*

following year, however, the U.S.S.R. demanded that the Iranian government grant it permission to exploit the oil resources in its occupation zone. The British and American governments also proposed that the Iranian government grant them oil rights in the s.e. portion of the country. The shah refused to commit himself on these plans and adopted a policy of delay.

By the early part of 1945 it became safe for Allied shipping to use the Bosporus and the Dardanelles to send war material to Russia, eliminating the overland route through Iran. In May the government of Iran requested the occupying countries to withdraw their troops. The United States agreed; however, neither the U.S.S.R. nor Great Britain would consent. After prolonged negotiations, Great Britain and Russia agreed to withdraw from Iran by March 2, 1946. However the Iranian government became increasingly concerned over the Soviet occupation. Iranian officials claimed that they were not permitted to enter the Soviet-occupied provinces of Azerbaijan and Kurdistan in order to quell anti-Iranian disturbances provoked by pro-Soviet forces. By mid-November, Azerbaijan was the site of an independence movement supported by Soviet authorities.

Iran signed the Charter of the United Nations at San Francisco on June 26, 1945,

becoming one of the original members of that organization. In the latter part of 1946, the U.S.S.R. began to press for immediate action on the part of Iran for the formation of a Russo-Iranian oil company. Iran, counting on United States aid, announced in October, 1947, the rejection of the Soviet oil plan and the establishment of a five-year oil program whereby Iran would develop its own oil resources. On July 29, 1948, the United States made a $26,000,000 loan to Iran for the purchase and repair of surplus American army equipment. The U.S.S.R. charged that the United States was arming Iran for aggressive warfare. The U.S. Secretary of State, Dean G. Acheson, denied these charges and stated that the only interest of the United States in Iran was the maintenance of that country's security.

In the realm of domestic politics outstanding developments during 1949 included the outlawing of the pro-Soviet Tudeh (Masses) Party, enactment of legislation making Parliament a bicameral body, and growth of popular antagonism over foreign oil concessions. In response to public sentiment on the oil question, the government obtained (July) from the British-owned Anglo-Iranian Oil Co. an agreement to double royalty payments on petroleum taken from Iranian fields. Parliament failed to ratify the agreement, which was characterized as unsatisfactory by various members.

Severe economic difficulties developed during the first half of 1950, causing several political crises. In June General Ali Razmara accepted the premiership. A vigorous executive, he succeeded in improving the economic situation. He strongly opposed nationalization of the oil industry, however, and on March 7, 1951, he was assassinated by a nationalist fanatic. Ali Razmara was succeeded by Hussein Ala (1882–   ) but the new government fell on April 27. Two days later Mohammed Mossadegh (1880–   ), leader of a coalition of nationalist groups (National Front) and vigorous supporter of oil nationalization, became premier. Legislation to nationalize the oil industry was approved by Parliament within a few weeks and became effective May 2. Attempts to settle the ensuing crisis in Anglo-Iranian relations through direct negotiation between the two countries ended in failure. The efforts (July) of the United States to mediate the dispute were to no avail. On Oct. 3 Great Britain, deciding against the use of force, acceded to an Iranian ultimatum and withdrew the A.I.O.C.

technical staff from the Abadan refinery. Later in the month, when Great Britain brought the dispute before the U.N. Security Council, Premier Mossadegh flew to New York to present the case for Iran. The Council agreed to postpone debate until the International Court decided on the Court's competence to deal with the dispute. On Dec. 26 Iran rejected a proposal made by the International Bank that the oil industry be administered by the Bank or by some other international authority pending final settlement. In May, 1952, Mossadegh appeared before the International Court, at the Hague, and argued that it had no jurisdiction in the case.

Parliamentary (lower-house) elections had been completed meanwhile, and early in July Mossadegh, having resigned in accordance with constitutional procedure, was requested by the shah to resume the premiership. Mossadegh's acceptance was based on various conditions, notably that he receive control of the army and the right to rule by decree for six months. The shah, constitutional head of the army, rejected the former condition, and on July 16 Mossadegh resigned. Former premier Ahmed Ghavam es Sultaneh (1875–) agreed the next day to form a new government. Mossadegh's supporters responded to this development with riotous demonstrations and a general strike (July 21), which forced Ghavam's resignation. On July 22 Mossadegh was designated premier; the same day the International Court ruled that it had no jurisdiction in the Anglo-Iranian dispute. The lower house subsequently granted the premier unlimited power for six months.

On Aug. 30 Iran turned down a joint Anglo-American proposal designed to break the oil deadlock. In the proposal Great Britain for the first time accepted the Iranian nationalization law as valid, but still insisted that compensation be based upon potential revenue losses as well as upon the physical assets of the A.I.O.C. Iran broke off diplomatic relations with Great Britain on Oct. 22.

Early in 1953 the Parliament extended Mossadegh's dictatorial powers for a year. The premier demanded (April) that the shah be stripped of all his powers. In May he appealed to the United States for emergency economic aid. The U.S. government refused (July) any special assistance; Iran was reminded it had received $47 million military and Point Four funds.

The dissension between pro- and anti-Mossadegh forces reached a climax during the summer of 1953. The premier dissolved the lower house on the basis of a plebiscite (Aug. 3–10) in which he suspended the secret ballot. The shah, who opposed many of Mossadegh's policies, including his uncompromising stand on the oil question, demanded (Aug. 16) the premier's resignation. Mossadegh refused to resign, his followers rioted against the royalists, and the shah fled to Rome. After three days of sanguinary disorders the royalists, supported by the army and police, won control of Teheran, and Mossadegh and several aides were placed under arrest. The shah returned in triumph on Aug. 22; the next day Maj. Gen. Fazlollah Zahedi (1897–), who had been designated premier by the shah on Aug. 16, formed a government. On Sept. 5 the U.S. government granted Iran an emergency loan of $45 million. Iran resumed diplomatic relations with Great Britain on Dec. 5.

Mossadegh was sentenced (Dec. 21) to three years' solitary confinement for leading a revolt against the shah. His appeal for a new trial by the Supreme Court was denied on Jan. 3, 1954.

IRANIAN, a name applied to a group of peoples, some of whom are almost or altogether extinct, generally speaking languages of the Iranian branch of the Indo-Iranian languages (q.v.). They now number some

British Information Services

Harvest time in southern Iran

15,000,000, and inhabit the plateau lying between Asia Minor and the Caspian Sea on the west and the Hindu Kush Mountains on the east, a region of which modern Iran forms the chief part. The chief Iranian peoples are the modern Persians (the descendants of the ancient Medes and Persians), the descendants of the ancient Bactrians, and the partly-civilized Kurds. Outlying groups include the Tates and Azerbaijanis, the Sart of Russian Turkestan, and members of the populations of such areas as Afghanistan and Baluchistan, who are physically of the Iranian type but now speak Turkish dialects.

The situation of the Iranian plateau between India and China on the one hand and Asia Minor and Arabia on the other has made the region an absorber and transmitter of cultures, a melting pot of racial strains, a great highway of commerce, and a theater of religious disputes. Neighboring peoples such as the Dravidians and Semites, and nomadic peoples and tribes such as the Uzbeks, have introduced varieties of culture levels and admixtures of foreign physical types which make a simple ethnological description of the Iranians impossible. Moreover, the spread of Iranian culture through commerce, particularly by the ancient Persians and Parsis, has made Iranian influence felt from the Red Sea on the west to India on the east and Siberia and China on the north. These commercial activities, along with the colonizations which accompanied them, has resulted in further intermixture of the Iranian stock with the stocks of nearly all the known peoples of Asia Minor and Central Asia.

In religion the history of the Iranians exhibits great variations of belief and influence. Originally, they shared many of the dogmas and myths of India, and may even at some prehistoric time have been identical with the Indians in culture and race. In time, however, the body of essentially Indian beliefs, which included Mithraic, Avestan, and Vedic elements, and was based upon fire and sun worship, gave way to a new and peculiarly Iranian creed, Zoroastrianism (q.v.). Zoroastrianism persisted until well into the Christian Era as the dominant religion of the region, and greatly influenced the theology of Judaism; in the 7th century A.D. Zoroastrianism in the Iranian region fell before the new Mohammedan faith, and the Iranians became and have remained fanatic Moslems. They have not, however, adopted any of the orthodox Mohammedan sects, but give their allegiance to Shiism (q.v.).

IRAQ, or IRAK, a kingdom of s.w. Asia, bounded on the N. by Turkey, on the w. by Syria, on the s.w. by Jordan, on the s. by Saudi Arabia, the State of Kuwait, and the Persian Gulf, and on the E. by Iran. Roughly triangular in shape, the country has an extreme length from N. to s. of about 600 m., an extreme width of about 400 m., and a total area of approximately 168,000 sq.m. Pop. (1950 est.) 5,100,000.

Iraq is divided into fourteen administrative units called *liwas*. The capital and largest city is Baghdad (q.v.). Other leading cities are Basra, Mosul, and Kirkuk (qq.v.).

Physical Features and Climate. The N. portion of Iraq, known as the Al Jazira, is mountainous. Elevations of nearly 7000 feet above sea level are reached near the Turkish border, and in the N.E. part of the country are heights of over 5000 feet. Further s. the country slopes downward to form a broad central alluvial plain, which is occupied by the valley between the Euphrates R. (q.v.) on the w., and the Tigris R. (q.v.) on the E. The extreme s.E. portion of Iraq is a low-lying, marshy area adjacent to the Persian Gulf, on which Iraq fronts for a distance of about 25 m. West of the Euphrates, the land rises gradually to meet the Syrian plateau, a desert region.

Present-day Iraq occupies the greater part of the ancient land of Mesopotamia (q.v.), the plain between the Tigris and Euphrates rivers. The two rivers flow through Iraq from N.W. to s.E. They meet about 120 miles N. of the Persian Gulf to form the Shatt al Arab, which drains into the Gulf. The chief tributary of the Euphrates is the Belik, which joins the river near the town of Rakka; the main affluents of the Tigris are the Greater and the Lesser Zab, and the Diyala rivers. Level terrain separates the Tigris and Euphrates rivers in the lower part of their course, and in ancient times the two rivers were joined by a network of canals and irrigation ditches, which directed the water of the higher lying and more westerly Euphrates across the valley into the Tigris.

Most of Iraq has a continental climate with extremes of heat and cold. However, the mountainous N. portion of the country has cool summers and cold winters, often accompanied by snow. In central Iraq the summers are long and hot and the winters short and cool. The mean January tempera-

British Information Services

PEOPLE IN IRAQ

Above: A Yezidi. Right: An Arab tribesman.

ture in Baghdad is 49° F; for the months of July and August it is 92°F, and temperatures as high as 123°F have been recorded. In the s. area around the Persian Gulf some of the highest atmospheric temperatures in the world have been recorded, and humidity is high. In the N.E. highlands rainfall is considerable during the months from October to May, but further s. on the central alluvial plain precipitation is slight, averaging about 6 inches annually. The area adjacent to the Syrian desert gets little or no rainfall.

Flora and Fauna. Throughout Iraq the vegetation is scanty. The s. and s.w. parts of the country are desert areas. There are few trees, except for the cultivated date palm and the poplar. Among the fauna are cheetahs, gazelles, antelopes, wild asses, lions, hyenas, wolves, jackals, wild pigs, hares, jerboas, and bats. There are a number of birds of prey, including vultures, buzzards, ravens, owls, and various species of hawk. In addition, there are ducks, geese, partridges, and sand grouse. Lizards are fairly common.

Economy. Iraq has an agrarian economy. Approximately 10% of the land is under cultivation, and it is believed that about 20% of the country is arable. The principal crops are wheat, barley, and dates; about 350 different varieties of date palm are cultivated.

Other important crops are rice, sorghum, corn, millet, citrus fruits, tobacco, and cotton. The raising of livestock is an important occupation for the nomadic and seminomadic tribes. It is estimated that in a recent year there were in Iraq approximately 822,000 cattle, 7,000,000 sheep, 1,850,000 goats, 413,000 donkeys, 130,000 water buffaloes, 291,000 camels, and 52,000 mules. The world-famed Arab horse is extensively bred; there were about 184,000 horses in a recent year.

Oil is the most important natural resource. The oil fields occur in three main regions: around the Persian Gulf, near Basra; in the N. central part of the country, near Mosul and Kirkuk; and in the E. central part of Iraq, near the town of Khaniqin. Small deposits of various minerals are found, principally ores of iron, gold, lead, copper, silver, platinum, and zinc. Sulfur, salt, and gypsum are fairly abundant, and there are seams of brown coal in commercially exploitable quantities at various sites.

The most valuable industry of the country is the production of oil for export and for domestic use. In 1939 Iraq ranked eighth among the nations of the world in the amount of oil produced. There are four major oil companies owning oil concessions in the country which are at present actively engaged in the production and refining of oil. Annual leases and royalties paid the Iraqi government by these companies, which are owned by foreign capital, furnish the great portion of the yearly national income. The most important oil company is the Iraq Petroleum Company (controlled by British, American, Dutch, and French interests), which owns oil concessions in the Kirkuk area and has constructed pipe lines to Haifa, Israel, and Tripoli, Lebanon, and Baniyas, Syria. A subsidiary of the Anglo-Iranian Oil Company produces and refines oil for distribution in Iraq. The annual production of oil recently totaled about 8,349,000 metric tons.

Other industries in Iraq include the manufacture of glass, cigarettes and other tobacco products, vegetable oils, soap, woolen textiles, and brick and tile.

Imports in a recent year totaled about $18,200,000, and consisted chiefly of cotton, silk, rayon, and wool textiles, and clothing, iron and steel, automotive vehicles, machinery, electrical equipment, paper products, chemicals, sugar, tea, soap, cement, lumber, coffee, chemicals, and pharmaceuticals. Recent annual exports, excluding oil exported by foreign-owned companies, were valued at $21,-270,000, and consisted chiefly of dates, barley, wool, wheat, cotton, livestock, millet, and rice. Iraq furnishes about 80% of the world's supply of dates, and in a recent year the country exported about 208,000 tons. Also, in a recent year, Iraq exported approximately 462,000 tons of barley. The bulk of Iraq's foreign trade is with Great Britain.

Communications. Iraq is connected with Syria, Turkey, Egypt, and Europe by means of a railroad line which links the town of Tel Kotchek, on the Syrian frontier, with the main Iraq railroad line running from Mosul in the N. to Baghdad, thence to the port of Basra, near the Persian Gulf. There are also branch lines from Baghdad to Kirkuk and to Khaniqin. Altogether, there are about 1000 m. of railway in Iraq. Approximately 4000 m. of roads exist, of which about 1750 m. are surfaced, the remainder consisting of dirt roads and tracks. Regular air-line service is maintained from Europe and the Far East to Iraq, and there are airports at Baghdad, Basra, and Habbaniya, and seaplane bases at Basra and Habbaniya. Basra, on the Shatt al Arab, is the only port for ocean-going vessels, but river steamers are able to navigate on the Tigris from Basra to Baghdad.

People, Religion, and Education. About 75% of the population of Iraq is Arab.

Kurds (q.v.), dwelling in the highlands of N. Iraq, comprise about 18% of the population. Some historians believe these people to be the descendants of the ancient Kassite (q.v.) invaders of Iraq. There are also Jews, Turks, and Iranians in Iraq. The Jews are descendants of the Old Testament Jews made captive by the armies of Nebuchadrezzar. In the rural areas of the country many of the people still live in tribes leading a nomadic or seminomadic existence, keeping herds of camels, horses, and sheep. The chief languages spoken in Iraq are Arabic and Kurdish.

The majority of the population is Mohammedan and belongs to one or the other of the two chief moslem sects, the Shiite and Sunnite Moslems. Several of the holy cities of the Shiite sect, notably Najaf and Karbala (q.v.), are situated in Iraq. There are a few Christian sects in Iraq, among them being the Nestorians (q.v.), the Jacobite Christians, and offshoots of these two churches, respectively known as "Chaldean" and "Syrian" Catholics. In addition, several smaller religious groups exist, such as the Yezidis (q.v.), who live in the hill country N. of Mosul, and a group known as the "Mandaean Baptists" (see MANDAEANS) living in Baghdad and Amara.

Educational facilities include a system of primary-school instruction, which is free and compulsory for children between the ages of six and twelve, and a system of free secondary schools for young people of the ages of thirteen and eighteen. Instruction is in Arabic. Higher instruction is furnished by six normal schools, with about 1500 students, and by colleges of engineering, medicine, pharmacy, and law, as well as a Higher Teachers' Training College and a military college.

Government. Iraq is a limited constitutional monarchy, with the chief executive authority vested in a prime minister and a cabinet. Legislative authority resides in a bicameral legislature, consisting of an upper house, the senate, composed of 20 members appointed by the king, and a lower house, composed of 115 elected deputies. The country is at present governed under an Organic Law, passed by a constituent assembly in 1924. Subsequent modifications in the Organic Law permit the king to dismiss his government. Suffrage is restricted to males over the age of twenty.

History. For the history of the land of Mesopotamia up to and including the period

British Information Services

Dhows on a river in Iraq

of Turkish conquest, the reader is referred to the separate articles ASSYRIA; BABYLONIA; MESOPOTAMIA; PERSIA; SUMER; TURKEY.

The history of modern Iraq properly begins with the last phase of Turkish rule, during the 19th century. For several centuries following the Turkish conquest of Mesopotamia, completed in 1534, Turkish rule in Mesopotamia had been exercised through local sovereigns, and many of the nomadic Arab tribes were never fully brought under Ottoman control. In 1831, however, Sultan Ali Riza Pasha deposed the last local Mesopotamia ruler, and the province of Iraq, then subdivided into the three vilayets of Mosul, Baghdad, and Basra, came directly under Turkish administration. The Arabs then began to feel the weight of the new and more efficient methods of Turkish administration, particularly with regard to tax collecting, and a spirit of Arab nationalism, outcome of their resentment of the centralized authority of the Empire, began to develop. In the latter part of the 19th century the British and the Germans became rivals in the commercial development of the Mesopotamian area. The British government first became interested in Iraq as a direct overland route to India, and in 1861 established a steamship company for the navigation of the Tigris to the port of Basra. Meanwhile, the German government was planning the construction of a railroad in the Middle East, to run "from Berlin to Baghdad", and was successful over British opposition in obtaining a concession to build a railroad to the Persian Gulf. Despite this defeat the British government managed to consolidate its position on the Persian Gulf by concluding treaties of protection with the Arab chieftains of the area. British financiers were also successful in obtaining, in 1901, a concession to exploit the oil fields of Iran; in 1909 the Anglo-Persian Oil Company (now Anglo-Iranian Oil Company) was formed to work the concession. Meanwhile, the Arab nationalist movement was becoming an organized political force, through the establishment, after 1908, of an Arab nationalist secret society, Al-Ahd ("The League").

Turkey entered World War I as an ally of the German Empire. British forces invaded southern Mesopotamia in November, 1914, and gradually pushed northward against heavy Turkish opposition. In March, 1917, the British occupied Baghdad. Mesopotamia was fully under British military control by October, 1918.

Early in the war, in order to ensure the interest of the Arabs in a military uprising against the Turks, the British government had promised a group of Arab leaders that their people would receive independence if a revolt proved successful. In June, 1916, an uprising occurred in the Hejaz, led by Faisal al-Husein (see FAISAL I), later to become the first king of Iraq. Under the leadership of General Edmund Henry Hynman Allenby (q.v.) and the tactical direction of Col. Thomas Edward Lawrence (q.v.), the Arab and British forces achieved dramatic successes against the Turkish army, and succeeded in liberating the Arabian territory. In 1918 an armistice was signed with Turkey and at that time the British and French governments issued a joint declaration of their intention to assist in the establishment of independent Arab nations in the Arab areas formerly controlled by Turkey. However, there was delay in implementing this policy, because a secret British-French-Russian agreement, the so-called Sykes-Picot Agreement, had stipulated that Britain and France would have spheres of influence and possibly territory in Arabia: France in Syria, and Great Britain in Mesopotamia. This informal understanding was reinforced in April, 1920, at the San Remo session of the Supreme Council of the Allied Powers, by the decision of the Council to award the mandates of Syria and Lebanon to France, and the mandates of Palestine and Mesopotamia to Great Britain.

In July, 1920, when the Mesopotamian Arabs learned of the decision of the Supreme Council they began an armed uprising against the British government, then still in occupation of Iraq. The British were forced to spend 40 million pounds in quelling the revolt, and the government of Great Britain concluded it would be expedient to terminate its mandate in Mesopotamia as speedily as possible. The British Civil Commissioner in Mesopotamia, Sir Percy Cox, thereupon drew up a plan for a provisional government of the new state of Iraq: Iraq was to be a kingdom, with a government directed by a council of Arab ministers and under the supervision of a British high commissioner. Emir Faisal al-Husein was invited to become the ruler of the new nation. In August, 1921, a plebiscite elected him king of Iraq by 96% of the votes cast.

The integrity of the new state was menaced from without by Arabia on the s. and Turkey on the N.; and from within by various groups with separatist aspirations, such as the Shiite Moslems of the Euphrates R. area, and the Kurdish tribes of the N., acting in conjunction with Turkish armed forces endeavoring to reclaim the lands in the Mosul area for Turkey. The British were thus forced to maintain an army in Iraq. The Turkish-inspired revolts were not suppressed until the fall of 1925, and in that same year a treaty was concluded with Arabia to determine the boundaries between Iraq and the Nejd territory in Arabia. Meanwhile, agitation against the British mandate continued in Iraq, and King Faisal formally requested that the mandate under which Great Britain held Iraq be transformed into a treaty of alliance between the two nations. The British government concurred, and in October, 1922, a 20-year treaty of alliance and protection between Great Britain and Iraq was signed. The treaty was subsequently revised to be binding for only four years after the cessation of hostilities between Turkey and Iraq, and in its revised form placed Iraq under an obligation to expand its army and to assume part of the debts of the former Turkish Empire. The revised treaty was approved by the League of Nations in September, 1924, and was ratified by Great Britain and Iraq in the same year. In 1924, the dispute between Turkey and Iraq as to the possession of the Mosul oil area was adjudicated in Iraq's favor by the Council of the League of Nations.

In spring, 1924, a constituent assembly was convened and passed an Organic Law establishing the permanent form of the government of Iraq. Elections for the first Iraqi parliament were held in March, 1925. In the same year a concession was granted to an internationally owned oil company, the Turkish Petroleum Company, to develop the oil reserves of the Baghdad and Mosul regions. According to the terms of the treaty negotiated with Turkey in 1924, Iraq was to pay the Turkish government 10% of the profits of the undertaking. In 1926 a second treaty signed by Iraq and Turkey provided a more definitive settlement of the Turkish-Iraqi boundary dispute over the Mosul area. In 1927 King Faisal requested the British to support Iraq's application for admission to the League of Nations; the British refused to take the step at that time, but negotiated another treaty of alliance with Iraq, in which they pledged themselves to support Iraq's application for admission to the League in 1932. This treaty was the first to recognize Iraq formally as an independent state. In return for this concession the treaty stipulated that Iraq was to permit the British to erect and maintain three air bases in Iraq,

British Information Services

*Above: Musicians playing at a Yezidi cere-
monial dance in northern Iraq. Right: Twin
cones of a Yezidi religious shrine.*

and to permit British supervision of the
training of the Iraqi army.

In June, 1930, a third treaty between Great
Britain and Iraq provided for a recommendation by Great Britain that Iraq be admitted to the League of Nations as a free
and independent state in 1932; the recommendation was made in that year, and the
mandate was formally terminated. In October, 1932, Iraq took its place in the League
of Nations as an independent sovereign state.
King Faisal I died in 1933, and was succeeded
by his son, King Ghazi I.

In 1931 the exploitation of the oil reserves
in Iraq was further advanced by an agreement signed by the Iraqi government and
the Iraq Petroleum Company, an internationally owned organization composed of companies of Royal-Dutch Shell, the Anglo-
Persian Oil Company, French oil companies,
and the Standard Oil Companies of New
York and New Jersey. The agreement
granted the Iraq Petroleum Co. the sole
right to develop the oil fields of the Mosul
region, in return for which the Company
guaranteed to pay the Iraq government annual royalties of 400,000 pounds. In 1934

the Company opened an oil pipe line from
Mosul to Tripoli, and a second to Haifa was
completed in 1936.

In 1936 the Iraq government, under King
Ghazi (ruled 1933-39), began to move in the
direction of a general alliance with the other
nations of the Arab world in forming the
so-called Pan-Arab movement. A treaty of
nonaggression, reaffirming a fundamental
Arab brotherhood, was signed with the king
of Saudi Arabia in the same year, and the
treaty invited other Arab nations to join in

the agreement. In October of the same year a leader of the Pan-Arab movement, General Bakr Sidqi, led a revolt which seized control of the government, dissolved the Iraqi parliament, and created a dictatorship. The newly established regime formed a party, the so-called "Society for National Reform", and began an ambitious program of internal development which featured the construction of railroads and highways, as well as the development of irrigation projects. In 1937 General Sidqi was assassinated by a Kurdish soldier and a new cabinet was formed which continued the policies of the preceding administration in favor of the Pan-Arab movement. In April, 1939, King Ghazi was killed in an automobile accident, leaving his three-year-old son Faisal the titular king under the regency of Crown Prince Emir Abdul-Ilah.

In accordance with its treaty of alliance with Great Britain, Iraq broke off diplomatic relations with Germany early in September, 1939, and during the first few months of World War II Iraq had a pro-British government under Premier General Nuri es-Said. In March, 1940, however, es-Said was replaced by Rashid Ali Al-Gailani, an extreme Arab nationalist, who at once embarked on a policy of non-co-operation with the British. Al-Gailani's policy was backed by the Grand Mufti of Palestine, whose extremely anti-British sentiments had placed him in exile in Baghdad; and it received considerable financial support from the German government, which had recently occupied Bulgaria, and was interested in acquiring control of Iraq's oil fields. British pressure for the implementation of the Anglo-Iraqi alliance precipitated a military revolt on April 4, 1941, in which Abdul-Ilah was forced to flee the country, and a new pro-Axis government under Premier Al-Gailani was formed. Alarmed at this development, the British at once landed troops at Basra. Declaring this action a violation of the treaty between Great Britain and Iraq, Al-Gailani mobilized the Iraqi army, and war between the two countries broke out on May 2. Germany and the other Axis-dominated nations of Europe at once recognized the new Iraqi government, and the Soviet Union began negotiations for the establishment of diplomatic relations with Iraq. However, more substantial aid from the Axis Powers was not forthcoming, and the British advance from Basra to Baghdad met with comparatively little resistance. On May 31, 1941, the government of Iraq conceded defeat. The armistice terms provided for the re-establishment of British control over Iraq's transport, a provision of the 1930 treaty of alliance. Shortly afterward a pro-British government was formed under Premier Jamil al-Midfai, later superseded by a government under General Nuri es-Said.

In 1942 Iraq became an important supply center for British and American forces operating in the Middle East, and for the transshipment of arms to the Soviet Union. Though several of the leaders of the 1941 pro-Axis coup, notably the Grand Mufti and Al-Gailani, had fled the country, other ringleaders were tried and several were sentenced to death. Nevertheless, anti-British propaganda by German agents continued in Iraq. Officially, the Iraqi government began to move in the direction of declaring war on the Axis and affiliating with the United Nations. Tentative negotiations for a Lend-Lease (q.v.) agreement were begun. On January 17, 1943, Iraq declared war on the Axis, the first independent Moslem state to do so. Meanwhile, Iraq's continuing assistance to the Allied war effort made possible a stronger stand by Arab leaders on behalf of a federation of Arab states. Premier Nuri es-Said continued to confer with the leaders of the Arab nations of Trans-Jordan, Lebanon, and Syria regarding the establishment of a federated Arab state, the so-called Greater Syria, and in August, 1944, submitted an eight-point program for such a state (to include Palestine, in addition to Syria, Trans-Jordan and Lebanon) to a preliminary Pan-Arab conference. However, the plan proved unpopular with the delegates of the conference, and the matter was dropped.

Throughout 1945 and 1946 the Kurdish tribes of northeastern Iraq were in a state of unrest, supported, it was believed, by the Soviet Union. The British, fearing Soviet encroachment on the Iraqi oil fields, moved troops into Iraq. In 1947 General Nuri es-Said began to advocate a new proposal for a federated Arab state: this time he suggested that Trans-Jordan and Iraq be united, and began negotiations with the king of Trans-Jordan regarding the effectuation of his proposal. In April, 1947, a treaty of brotherhood and alliance was signed by the two kingdoms, providing for mutual military and diplomatic aid.

In 1948 the British government negotiated another treaty of alliance and defense with the Iraqi government to replace the 1930 agreement. Among the provisions incorporated into the new treaty was maintenance of two air bases in Iraq by the British. Opposition to the new treaty was widespread in Iraq, particularly among nationalist student organizations, and severe riots led to the downfall of the cabinet sponsoring the agreement. The treaty was officially rejected by the Iraqi government in February, 1948.

Immediately following the declaration of independence by Israel (q.v.) in May, 1948, the armies of Iraq and Trans-Jordan invaded Palestine. Throughout the rest of the year Iraqi armed forces continued to fight in Palestine and the nation continued to work politically with the state of Trans-Jordan. In September it joined King Abdullah of Trans-Jordan in denouncing the establishment of an Arab government in Palestine as being "tantamount to recognizing the partition of Palestine", which Iraq had long consistently opposed. With the general defeat of the Arab forces attacking Israel, however, the government of Iraq prepared to negotiate an armistice, represented by Trans-Jordan. On March 11, 1949, a "cease-fire" agreement between Israel and Trans-Jordan was signed, but Iraqi units continued to fight the Jews in an Arab-occupied area in N. central Palestine. Trans-Jordanian troops replaced the Iraqi units in this area under the terms of the armistice agreement, signed on April 3, 1949. Late in October, 1949, the Israeli government charged Iraq with conducting a pogrom against the 150,000 Jewish citizens of the country. Hundreds of Jews had been arrested, tortured, and deprived of their property, according to the accusation. Iraq replied that forty Jews had been arrested for assaulting Bagdad's chief rabbi, a foe of Zionism.

In December, 1949, Iraq obtained an $8 million railroad-development loan from Great Britain. Further development of the national economy was assured during 1950 through additional loans, notably one from the International Bank for Reconstruction and Development. In May, 1950, the Iraqi government announced completion of arrangements for the transfer by air transports of over 50,000 Iraqi Jews to Israel. The mass migration, popularly known as Operation Ali Baba, began on May 20.

Royalties paid to the government of Iraq by the Iraq Petroleum Co. were substantially increased under an accord reached in August, 1950. In April, 1951, the company agreed to another increase in royalty rates. By the terms of an even more advantageous arrangement, concluded in February, 1952, Iraq obtained 50 percent of the profits. Seventy percent of the oil royalties was to be allocated to the National Development Board (established 1950), mainly for the financing of flood-control and irrigation projects along the Tigris and Euphrates rivers and of a $470-million, five-year plan to modernize Iraqi farming methods.

Meanwhile, in January, the U.S. government, taking note of the failure of Iraq to contribute to the defense of the non-Soviet world and to develop its own capacity for self-defense, had announced that the country would be denied American technical and economic aid. On Aug. 8 Iraq ratified the Arab League collective-security pact.

On Nov. 18 the Kirkuk-Baniyas 556-mile pipe line of the Iraq Petroleum Company was formally opened. The line made possible a vast increase (more than double, according to estimates) in the output of Iraqi oil. Rioting provoked by the government's failure to effect electoral reforms based on direct suffrage broke out on Nov. 23. Communists and nationalist extremists took advantage of the situation to attack British and American properties. A military junta immediately quelled the disturbances and imposed martial law. The junta dissolved all political parties and appointed a committee to prepare a new electoral law. In addition, import and export duties were reduced and taxes on land, fruit and vegetables were abolished in an effort to overcome inflationary pressures in the economy.

Parliamentary elections, the first based on direct suffrage, took place on Jan. 17, 1953. Constitutional government was re-established on Jan. 29. King Faisal II formally assumed the throne on May 2, 1953, his eighteenth birthday. By the end of the year Iraq, like the rest of the Arab world, was no nearer to signing a formal peace treaty with Israel.

IRAWADI. See IRRAWADDY.

IRELAND, in physical geography, the second-largest island (after Great Britain) of the British Isles, situated in the North Atlantic Ocean, and separated from Great Britain by St. George's Channel on the S.E., the Irish Sea on the E., and by North Channel on the N.E. In political geography, the island of Ireland is divided into Northern Ireland (q.v.), a constituent part of the United Kingdom, and the Republic of Ireland, formerly Eire. The island is divided into four historical districts, namely Connacht, Leinster, Munster, and Ulster provinces, and thirty-two administrative units, called counties. The republic consists of Connacht, Leinster, and Munster provinces, totaling twenty-three counties, and part (three counties) of Ulster Province. Northern Ireland consists of six counties, the remainder of Ulster province. The area of the island is 31,840 sq.m. (Republic of Ireland, 26,602 sq.m.; Northern Ireland 5238 sq.m.) ; pop., about 4,319,000, including Republic of Ireland (1951) 2,958,878.

In a N. and S. direction the maximum length of Ireland is 302 m.; its extreme width is 174 m. Malin Head, at lat. 55°27′ N., and Mizen Head, at lat. 51°27′ N., are respectively the northernmost and southernmost points on the island; the respective easternmost and westernmost points are demarcated by long. 5°25′ W. and long. 10°30′ W.

The E. coast of Ireland is comparatively regular and has few deep indentations; the W. coast is fringed by drowned valleys, steep cliffs, and hundreds of small islands torn from the mainland mass by the destructive influences of the Atlantic. Topographically, the surface may be described as basin-shaped. The chief physiographic features are a region of lowlands, occupying the central and E. central section, and a complex system of low mountain ranges, lying between the lowlands and the periphery of the island. Among the principal ranges are the Mourne Mts. in the N.E., rising about 2000 ft. above sea level; the Mountains of Donegal in the N., containing Mt. Errigal, 2466 ft.; the Sperrin Mts. in the N.W., containing Sawel Mt., 2240 ft.; the Maumturk Mts. in the W., containing Mt. Twelve Pins, 2336 ft.; the Caha Mts. in the S.W., containing Mt. Knockboy, 2323 ft.; the Boggeragh Mts. in the S., rising 2100 ft.; and the Wicklow Mts. in the E., rising over 2000 ft. Carrantual (3414 ft. above sea level), located in the S.E. section of the island, is the highest point in Ireland. The central plain has an extreme length of about 100 m. from E. to W. and a maximum width of about 50 m. from N. to S. Numerous bogs and lakes are contained in the plain. The principal rivers of Ireland are the Shannon and the Erne (qq.v.), which are in reality chains of lakes joined by stretches of river. The N. portion of the central plain is drained by the Erne R. The center of the plain is drained by the Shannon, which empties into the Atlantic Ocean through a wide, lengthy estuary. Nearly half of the Shannon, above the estuary, is made up of Allen, Ree, and Derg lakes. All the principal rivers of Ireland flow from the plain, and an interior canal system facilitates communications.

The climate of Ireland is typically insular. Due to the moderating influence of the prevailing warm, moist winds from the Atlantic Ocean, the mean winter temperature ranges from 40°F. to 45°F., about 20°F. to 30° F. higher than that of other places in the same latitude in the interior of Europe or on the E. coast of North America. The oceanic influence is also very pronounced in summer, the mean summer temperature of Ireland, 59°F. to 62°F., being from 5°F. to 10°F. lower than that of other places on the same parallels of latitude. The rainfall averages 40 inches a year.

The flora of Ireland consists largely of English migrants, which in turn came from the W. portions of the European continent. Sedges, rushes, ferns, and grass are the principal flora. The fauna differs in no marked degree from that of England or France. The great Irish deer and the great auk, or garefowl, were exterminated in prehistoric times; and, since civilization took root in Ireland, the island has lost its bears, wolves, wild cats, beavers, native cattle, and other species of animals. Remaining are the small rodents of the woods and fields and such small birds as belong to the fields, gardens, and shore. There are no serpents in Ireland, and the only reptile is the lizard.

History. To supplement the following account of the history of the island of Ireland, the reader is directed to the related articles entitled CELTIC CHURCH; CELTIC PEOPLES AND LANGUAGES; GAELIC LANGUAGE; IRELAND, CHURCH OF; IRISH LITERATURE. See also ENGLAND: *History;* GREAT BRITAIN: *History.*

According to native legends Ireland was inhabited first by various tribes, the most important of which were the Nemedians, Fomorians, Firbolgs, and Tuatha De Danann (q.v.). These tribes are said to have been eventually subdued by Milesians (Scots). Although Ireland is mentioned under the name of Ierne in a Greek poem, written in the 5th century B.C., and by the names of Hibernia (q.v.) and Juverna by various classical writers, little is known with certainty of its inhabitants before the 4th century A.D., when, called the Scoti, they harried the Roman province of Britain. These expeditions were continued, and extended to the coast of Gaul, until the time of Loigaire MacNeill, about 430 A.D., in whose reign St. Patrick (q.v.) attempted the conversion of the natives. Although Christianity had been previously introduced in some parts of Ireland, St. Patrick encountered great obstacles,

Assoc. Brit. & Irish Rys.

Travelers on Dunloe Gap Road, near Killarney in County Kerry, Ireland

and the new faith was not fully established in the island until a century after his death (about 461).

From early times each province of Ireland appears to have had its own king; according to legend these kings were subject to the *ard-ri,* or monarch, to whom the central district, called Meath, was allotted, and who usually resided at Tara (q.v.). Each clan was governed by a chief selected from its most important family. The laws were dispensed by professional jurists styled *brehons,* who received great consideration and were endowed with lands and important privileges.

In the 6th century extensive monasteries were founded in Ireland, in which religion and learning were zealously cultivated. From these establishments numerous missionaries went forth during the succeeding centuries, while many students of distinction from England and the Continent visited Ireland and received instruction. The progress of

Irish civilization was checked by the incursions of the Scandinavians, begun toward the close of the 8th century, and continued for more than two centuries. The Northmen established settlements on the E. coast of Ireland, and conducted raids in the interior until their signal overthrow at the battle of Clontarf, near Dublin, in 1014, by Brian Boru (q.v.).

The first step toward an Anglo-Norman conquest of Ireland was made by Henry II of England, who is said to have obtained in 1155 a bull from Pope Hadrian IV authorizing him to take possession of the island, on condition of paying to the papal treasury a stipulated annual revenue. This bull is thought to have been a forgery. At all events, nothing was done until Dermod Macmurrough, the deposed king of Leinster, sought refuge at King Henry's court and obtained permission to enlist the services of English subjects for a recovery of his kingdom.

Dermod, returning to Ireland in 1169, with the aid of his foreign mercenaries and numerous Irish allies, succeeded in recovering part of his former territories and in capturing Dublin and other towns on the E. coast. After his death the succession to the kingdom of Leinster was claimed by his son-in-law Richard, Earl of Pembroke, surnamed "Strongbow". In 1172 Henry, with a formidable army, visited Ireland, received homage from several minor Irish chiefs and from the principal Norman leaders, and granted to the latter charters authorizing them, as his subjects, to take possession of portions of the island. The chief Anglo-Norman adventurers, however, encountered formidable opposition before they succeeded in establishing themselves on the lands which they claimed. The government was intrusted to a viceroy, and the Norman legal system was introduced into such parts of the island as were reduced to obedience to England. The youthful Prince John was sent by Henry into Ireland in 1185, but the injudicious conduct of his council excited disturbances, and he was soon recalled to England. John made a second expedition to Ireland in 1210, to curb the refractory spirit of his barons, who had become formidable through alliances with the Irish.

During the 13th century various Anglo-Norman adventurers succeeded in firmly establishing themselves in Ireland by the assistance or suppression of native clans. The Fitzgeralds (q.v.) acquired power in Kildare and East Munster; the Le Botillers, or Butlers, in West Munster; and the De Burghs, or Burkes, in Connacht. After the battle of Bannockburn, in 1315, Edward Bruce, the younger brother of David Bruce, king of Scotland, invaded Ireland and attempted unsuccessfully to overthrow the English there. The pope, at the instigation of England, excommunicated Bruce and his Irish allies. Although Bruce's enterprise failed, the general result was a decline of English power in Ireland.

The descendants of the most powerful Anglo-Norman settlers in Ireland gradually became identified with the native Irish, whose language, habits, and laws they adopted to so great an extent that the Anglo-Irish Parliament passed, in 1366, the Statute of Kilkenny, decreeing excommunication and heavy penalties against all those who followed the custom of, or allied themselves with, the native Irish. This statute, however, remained inoperative; and although Richard II of England later in the 14th century made expeditions into Ireland with large forces, he failed to effect any practical result. The power and influence of the natives increased so much at the time of the War of the Roses that the authority of the English crown became limited to the area known as the English Pale, a small coastal district around Dublin (q.v.) and the port of Drogheda. In the War of the Roses, the struggle in England between the houses of York and Lancaster, Ireland supported the losing house of York.

The participation of the Anglo-Norman nobility of the Pale in the War of the Roses greatly impaired English strength in Ireland. When Henry VII came to the throne of England, he left Gerald, Earl of Kildare, as viceroy of Ireland, although Kildare belonged to the Yorkist party. However, the assistance rendered by Kildare to the Yorkist pretenders finally compelled the king, in 1494, to replace him with Edward Poynings, an English soldier and diplomat. Poynings represented the purely English interest, as distinct from the Anglo-Norman interest, which up to that time had prevailed in Ireland. He at once summoned the Parliament of Drogheda, which enacted legislation providing for the defense of the Pale and the reduction of the power of the Anglo-Irish lords. The nobility was forbidden to oppress the inferior baronage, to make exactions upon the tenantry, or to assemble their armed retainers; and the Statute of Kilkenny, which compelled the English and Irish to live apart and prohibited Irish law and customs in the Pale, was confirmed. All state offices, including the judgeships, were filled by the English king instead of by the viceroys, and the entire English law was declared to hold for the Pale. Most important of all was the so called Poynings Law, which made the Irish Parliament dependent upon the English king, by providing that all proposed legislation should first be announced to the king and meet with his approval, after which he would issue the license to hold Parliament.

Henry VII eventually re-established the Earl of Kildare, the most powerful of the Irish nobles, as viceroy, and under Kildare's rule the Pale grew and prospered. His family, the Geraldines, rebelled and was overthrown during the reign of Henry VIII (q.v.). Henry VIII in 1537 attempted to introduce the Reformation into Ireland, and the dissolution of the monasteries was begun. Somewhat later, relics and images were destroyed and the dissolution was completed. The native chieftains were conciliated by a share of the spoils and received English titles, their lands being regranted under English tenure. It was Henry's policy thus to conciliate the Irish and to leave them under their own laws. An English commission held courts throughout the island, but Irish right was respected, and the country remained peaceful. In the Parliament of 1541, attended for the first time by native chieftains as well as by the lords of the Pale, Henry's title of Lord of Ireland, which had been conferred by the pope, was changed to that of King of Ireland.

The religious changes under Edward VI and Mary Tudor (qq.v.) had little effect upon Ireland. Although Mary was herself a Catholic, she was the first to begin the colonization of Ireland by English settlers. The Irish people of King's and Queen's County were driven out and their lands given to English colonists. Queen Elizabeth at first followed her father's policy of conciliating the Irish chieftains, but the rebellion of Shayne O'Neill (q.v.), an Ulster chief, caused her policy to become more severe; an act was passed making all Ireland shireland, and the commissioners of justice were invested with military powers, which they used in arbitrary fashion. The religious wars of Elizabeth were attended by rebellions of the Irish Catholics. The Earl of Desmond, a member of the great house of Geraldine, which ruled over the larger part of Munster, was defeated after a long struggle. Hugh O'Neill, called by the English the Earl of Tyrone (q.v.), annihilated an English army on the Blackwater and also defeated the Earl of Essex (see DEVEREUX, ROBERT, 2nd EARL OF ESSEX), whom Elizabeth had sent against him. However, about 1603 Tyrone was compelled to submit to the English. During the war the greatest cruelty and treachery were practiced on both sides. In order to destroy Irish resistance, the English devastated villages, crops, and cattle, putting to death all the inhabitants within reach. The greater part of Munster and Ulster was laid desolate, and many more people died from hunger than from the war.

Under Elizabeth and James I the Anglican state church was extended over Ireland, not only obtaining all that belonged to the church of the Pale, but being invested with the establishment belonging to the Celtic church as well. An ancient feud existed between the two Irish churches, and they were intensely hostile to each other. The church of the Pale was affected by the Reformation, but the Celtic church had become increasingly Roman. Nearly the entire Celtic population of Ireland, and the majority of the inhabitants of the Pale, remained Catholic, and the Anglican church served as a political instrument for the English rulers in Dublin Castle.

During the reign of James I English law was pronounced the sole law of the land. Warfare between the earls of Tyrone and Tyrconnell, traditional rivals, gave pretext for the confiscation of the land in six counties of N. Ulster. The last vestiges of the independence of the Irish Parliament were destroyed by the creation of forty boroughs out of small hamlets, a political maneuver which secured a permanent majority to the English crown.

The stern but vigorous rule of the Earl of Strafford, the viceroy of Charles I, produced order and prosperity in Ireland. By balancing the number of Catholics and Protestants in Parliament and holding out to the former the promise of toleration, he succeeded in obtaining liberal funds for the Tudor king in his conflict with the English Parliament. The native Irish, who had been dispossessed in Ulster and elsewhere, made use of the English situation to regain their possessions. Under the leadership of Roger (Rory) O'More, a conspiracy was formed in 1641 to seize Dublin and expel the English. The Irish succeeded in driving the English settlers out of Ulster and committed many outrages. It has been estimated by English writers that at least 30,000 were put to death by the Irish, but this number is thought to be exaggerated; the Scots in Ulster were, as a rule, spared. The insurgents were soon joined by the Catholic lords of the Pale, and together they chose a supreme council to govern Ireland. Charles I sent the Earl of Glamorgan to treat with them, and the Earl went so far as to promise them the predominancy of the Catholic church in Ireland as the price of their assistance to Charles. In 1647 the alliance between the lords of the Pale, who desired nothing beyond toleration for their religion, and the native Irish, who hoped for the restoration of the ancient land system, came to an end. In 1648 the Earl of Ormond returned as the viceroy of Charles I and made an alliance with the Catholic lords, thereby securing Ireland to the Royalist party.

In 1649 Oliver Cromwell (q.v.) landed at

Dublin, which the Catholics had been unable to take. With his well-disciplined forces, 10,000 men of the New Model army, he stormed Drogheda and captured its garrison of 2000 men. At Wexford occurred another Cromwell victory. Cromwell's successors, Henry Ireton and Edmund Ludlow (qq.v.), successfully concluded the war, and a great part of the best land of Munster, Leinster, and Ulster was confiscated and divided among the soldiers of the Parliamentary army. The Catholics and Loyalist landowners were banished to Connacht. A portion of the land confiscated at this time was restored under Charles II, but at least two thirds of the land in Ireland remained in the hands of the Protestants. The viceroyalty of Ormond, while maintaining the Protestant ascendency, did much to restore order and promote industry. James II (q.v.), however, reversed the policy of Charles II. Under James' viceroy in Ireland, the Earl of Tyrconnell, Catholics were advanced to positions of state and placed in control of the militia, which Ormond had previously organized. Consequently the entire Catholic population sided with James II in the English revolution of 1688, and, in 1689, when James landed at Dublin with his French officers, Tyrconnell had an Irish army ready to assist him. The Protestant settlers were driven from their homes and found refuge in the towns of Enniskillen and Londonderry. James attempted to capture Londonderry, but was hampered by the lack of artillery, and the city was relieved by way of the sea. His Parliament of 1689 restored all the lands that had been confiscated since 1641 and passed an act of attainder against the partisans of William III (q.v.). In the following year William landed in Ireland and, in July, 1690, in the battle of the Boyne (q.v.), he defeated the Irish forces. He failed, however, to capture the town of Limerick, which was bravely defended. A brilliant tactic of the Irish patriot Patrick Sarsfield (q.v.) destroyed William's heavy artillery, and he was forced to retire. The next year his generals defeated the Irish army at the town of Aughrim, and Limerick was forced to capitulate. By the terms of the Treaty of Limerick, Catholics were permitted a certain amount of religious freedom, and the lands they had possessed under Charles II were to be restored.

The Parliament of England forced William to break the concession of the Treaty of Limerick regarding the restoration of the land, and the Parliament of Ireland violated the terms granting religious toleration by enacting the Penal Laws, directed mainly against the Roman Catholics. Irish commerce and industries were deliberately crushed by the English. By enactments in 1665 and 1680 the Irish export trade to England in cattle, milk, butter, and cheese was forbidden. The trade in woolens, which had grown up among the Irish Protestants, was likewise crushed by an enactment of 1699, which prohibited the export of woolen goods from Ireland to any country whatever. Small amends for these injuries were made by leaving the linen trade undisturbed. The result of all these measures was the gradual economic decline of Ireland. A large percentage of the population emigrated, the Catholics to Spain and France, and the Protestants to America.

The American Revolution awakened much sympathy in Ulster, especially among the Presbyterians, who, being disqualified from holding office, desired a general emancipation including that of the Catholics. In 1778 the Irish Parliament passed the Relief Act, removing some of the most oppressive disabilities. Meanwhile the Irish Protestants, under the pretext of defending the country from the French who had entered into an alliance with the Americans, had formed military associations of volunteers, with an 80,000 membership. Backed by this force they demanded legislative independence for Ireland, and on motion of Charles Fox (q.v.) the British Parliament repealed the Poynings Law and much of the anti-Catholic legislation. The Irish Parliament, however, was composed entirely of the Protestants of the established church, who were unwilling to extend the suffrage to Catholics.

The principles of the French Revolution found their most powerful expression in Ireland in the Society of United Irishmen, which organized the rebellion of 1798. The peasantry rose in Wexford and, although insufficiently armed, made a brave fight. At one time Dublin was in danger, but the insurgents were defeated by the regular forces at Vinegar Hill. A French force of 1100 landed in Killala Bay, but was too late to render effective assistance. William Pitt (q.v.) the Younger, the British prime minister, thought that legislative union of the two countries, together with Catholic emancipation, was the only remedy for Catholic rebellion and Protestant tyranny in Ireland. By a lavish use of money and

Can. Pac. Ry.; Assoc. Brit. & Irish Rys.

SCENES IN IRELAND

Above: Early castle bordering the harbor at Carrickfergus, County Antrim. Right: A fisherman casting in the Maigue River, in County Limerick, southwestern Ireland.

distribution of patronage, he induced the Irish Parliament to pass the Act of Union. On January 1, 1801, the Union was formally proclaimed.

The history of Ireland after the Union was principally concerned with the struggle for Irish civic and religious freedom and for separation from Great Britain. Hardly had the Union been carried out when dissatisfaction in Ireland gave rise to the armed outbreak of July 23, 1803, under Robert Emmet (q.v.). It was easily suppressed, and for some time there were no further armed revolts. In 1823 the Catholic Association was founded, which demanded complete Catholic emancipation. Catholic emancipation in Ireland was finally obtained: in 1828 Catholics were permitted to hold local office, and in 1829 they were allowed to sit in Parliament. The struggle then turned upon the tithes, which all Irish, Catholics included, were compelled to pay for the maintenance of the Anglican church in Ireland. Great cruelties were perpetrated on both sides during the so-called Tithe War, which was coupled with a renewed emphatic demand for the repeal

of the Act of Union. Various societies were formed to carry on the agitation, and there was considerable lawlessness, fostered by the so-called Ribbon Society. See O'CONNELL, DANIEL.

The reform of the Irish Parliament in 1832 increased the number of Irish members

Associated British & Irish Railways

Trinity College in the city of Dublin, Ireland

from 100 to 105 and, more important, it gave the middle class more power, weakening the pro-English aristocracy. In 1838 a bill was passed converting the tithes into rent charge, to be paid by the landlords; as a result, agitation in connection with the Anglican church ceased to be acute for a time. From 1845 to 1847 rent-racked Ireland suffered a disastrous famine resulting from the failure of the potato crop. Again large numbers of people emigrated, especially to America; it has been estimated that by the end of 1848, through emigration and deaths resulting from famine, the population of Ireland decreased by a half million.

In the third quarter of the 19th century many ecclesiastical and agrarian reforms were effected in the country. However, agitation for Home Rule (q.v.) assumed a leading place in Irish politics, the cause finding a champion of great ability in Charles Stewart Parnell (q.v.). At that time, also, many secret societies were working for the establishment of an Irish republic. In 1867 the more extreme members of these societies, calling themselves the Invincibles, started an abortive rebellion in counties Dublin and Kerry; in 1882 they were responsible for the murder of the British chief secretary for Ireland, Lord Frederick Charles Cavendish, and the undersecretary, Thomas Henry Burke, in protest against the Coercion Act

of 1881, which gave the lord lieutenant of Ireland power to arrest any person on mere suspicion of treason, intimidation, and the like. The Crimes Act, which was passed soon after the dual murder, made the provisions of the Coercion Act more stringent. Meanwhile, in England, Prime Minister William Ewart Gladstone (q.v.) attempted to resolve the Irish question by a Home Rule bill, which he formally introduced in 1886. The bill gave the Irish Parliament the right to appoint the executive of Ireland; however, the taxing power was still retained by the British Parliament. Parnell accepted the bill, but it was greatly opposed in Ulster and in England. Gladstone introduced another Home Rule bill in 1893, which, however, failed to pass the British House of Lords. During the last quarter of the 19th century and the first decade of the 20th century there developed in Irish life two new forces which to a large degree stood apart from political and religious struggles: the Irish Agricultural Organization Society, inaugurated in 1894, and the Gaelic League, founded in 1903. The former aimed to do in the economic field what the latter attempted to do in the intellectual, that is, to rehabilitate Ireland from within. In 1900 Arthur Griffith (q.v.) founded the Sinn Fein (q.v.), an organization to promote Irish economic welfare and to achieve the complete political independence of Ireland. The Sinn Fein became the most important political party in the country, and the leading factor in the eventual attainment of Irish independence.

For details leading to the formation of the Irish Free State in 1922, Eire in 1937, and the Republic of Ireland in 1949, see IRELAND, REPUBLIC OF; see also NORTHERN IRELAND.

IRELAND, CHURCH OF, in general usage, the Christian Church in Ireland; more specifically, the Protestant Episcopal Church which became the established church (see ESTABLISHMENTS, ECCLESIASTICAL) at the time of the Reformation (q.v.). The early Irish Church was a branch of the Celtic Church (q.v.) consolidated by Saint Patrick in the 5th century. At the time of the Reformation, most of its members resisted the efforts of the English to break their allegiance to Rome, and to impose the changes in doctrine and rite accompanying the religious revolt in England. After the establishment of the Protestant Episcopal Church in Ireland, Roman Catholics were placed under serious civil disabilities; they were not permitted to teach or to act as guardians, and a tithing tax was imposed on them for the support of the established church. When political union with England was effected in 1800-01, the established churches of the two countries were also united. Disabilities on the nonconforming Catholics were removed in 1829, and the tithing tax was remitted in 1838.

In 1871 the Church of Ireland was disestablished and was separated from the Church of England; thereafter it continued as an independent body, governed by a general synod. In a recent year its communicants in all of Ireland numbered about 490,000, almost 12 percent of the total population; 70 percent of all communicants are concentrated in Northern Ireland, where they constitute over 25 percent of the population.

IRELAND, NATIONAL UNIVERSITY OF, a coeducational institution of higher education, including three constituent colleges, at Cork, Galway, and Dublin respectively. Of these three bodies, those at Cork and Galway were founded as colleges of Queen's University in 1845 and, when that organization was dissolved in 1907 and the National University of Ireland was founded, were taken over as constituent colleges of the latter body; the Dublin branch was established

in 1909. The colleges include faculties of arts, Celtic, commerce, engineering and architecture, law, medicine, philosophy and sociology, and science. In a recent year the combined faculties numbered over 500 members, and over 7000 students were enrolled. The University, which is famous for its Celtic studies, has in its library the Zimmer collection of Celtic books.

IRELAND, NORTHERN. See NORTHERN IRELAND.

IRELAND, REPUBLIC OF, a republic comprising about five sixths of the island of Ireland (q.v.). Geographically, it consists of the provinces of Leinster, Munster, and Connacht (qq.v.), and part of the province of Ulster (q.v.). The remainder of Ulster, which occupies the N.E. portion of the island, constitutes Northern Ireland (q.v.), a constituent part of the United Kingdom (q.v.). Ireland has a total area, excluding that of the larger lakes and inland waterways, of 26,061 sq.m.

The capital and largest city is Dublin (q.v.). Cork (q.v.) is the chief port and second-largest city. Other important cities and towns include Dun Laoghaire, Limerick, Waterford, Galway, Mullingar (qq.v.), Cobh, Wexford, and Ennis. For administrative purposes, Ireland is divided into 26 counties, each described in a separate article, and 4 county boroughs, which are coextensive with the cities of Dublin, Cork, Limerick, and Waterford. The counties are Carlow, Dublin, Kildare, Kilkenny, Laoighis, Longford, Louth, Meath, Offaly, Westmeath, Wexford, and Wicklow, in Leinster Province; Clare, Cork, Kerry, Limerick, Tipperary, and Waterford, in Munster Province; Galway, Leitrim, Mayo, Roscommon, and Sligo, in Connacht Province; and Cavan, Donegal, and Monaghan, in Ulster Province. The population of the Republic of Ireland (1951 prelim.) is 2,958,878.

Physiography and Climate. See IRELAND.

Agriculture. Ireland is primarily an agrarian country, with more than two thirds of the total area occupied by agricultural enterprises. The chief of these, in terms of wealth produced, is stock raising. In a recent year, livestock included nearly 4,211,000 head of cattle, about 2,580,000 sheep, more than 426,000 pigs, and approximately 464,500 horses. Poultry production is also important. Annual wool production recently approximated 8000 tons, and butter production exceeded 30,000 tons. The principal field crops are hay, potatoes, and turnips, the respective annual yields of which recently totaled about

4,312,000, 3,000,000 and 2,555,000 tons. Among other leading crops are mangels, sugar beets, oats, wheat, barley, and cabbage.

Manufacturing and Other Industries. Ireland has a wide diversity of manufacturing enterprises, most of which were developed in the decades following 1930. The food-processing industries rank first in the value of commodities produced, the most important being brewing, grain milling, sugar refining, meat packing, and the manufacture of dairy products, margarine, confections, and jam. Other important manufactured articles include tobacco products, woolen and worsted goods, clothing, furniture, soap, candles, whiskey, building materials, boots and shoes, cotton and linen textiles, hosiery, paper, leather, and chemical products. Ireland also has a number of printing, bookbinding, and automobile-assembly plants.

The fishing industry contributes substantially to the national wealth. Fishing craft of all types number about 3500. These are manned by crews totaling more than 10,000 men and boys. The annual catch, consisting mainly of herring, plaice, mackerel, cod, whiting, and shellfish, is valued at nearly £700,000.

The mineral deposits consist chiefly of peat, coal, and gypsum. Of these, only peat is mined in commercially important quantities.

Commerce. The annual commodity exports and imports of Ireland were valued recently at about £75,500,000. The value of exports, consisting predominantly of livestock and foodstuffs, amounted to about £34,850,000. The United Kingdom was the principal market for these exports, receiving more than 99%, by value, of the total. The United Kingdom, Canada, the United States, Argentina, Brazil, the Netherlands West Indies, and Portuguese Guinea supplied the bulk of the imports, composed largely of coal, iron, steel, textiles, tobacco, oil and gasoline, wheat, corn, tea, and clothing. The net tonnage of the national merchant marine totals less than 45,000, and most of the foreign trade of Ireland is transported in foreign-flag carriers.

Communications. Ireland has approximately 2500 m. of mainline railway trackage linking all important points on the island, and an extensive network of motorbus carriers. Navigable inland waterways, totaling 650 m. in length, supplement the railway lines. Several international air-transport systems provide

Pan American World Airways

A busy intersection in Dublin, capital and largest city of the Republic of Ireland

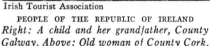

Irish Tourist Association

PEOPLE OF THE REPUBLIC OF IRELAND
Right: A child and her grandfather, County Galway. Above: Old woman of County Cork.

regular service between Ireland and major world points. Passenger travel between Ireland and all parts of the world is also facilitated by numerous steamship lines.

People, Languages, and Religion. The population of Ireland is composed overwhelmingly of people of Celtic origin. Most of the inhabitants are English-speaking; the remainder employ Gaelic, also known as the Irish language, the traditional tongue of Ireland. The study of this language is compulsory in all schools maintained by the state. Approximately 94% of the population are communicants of the Roman Catholic Church, which has a privileged status in the republic. Among the more important of the other religious denominations are the Protestant Episcopal, Presbyterian, and Methodist. Freedom of worship is guaranteed to all citizens by the terms of the constitution of Eire. See CELTIC PEOPLES AND LANGUAGES; IRISH LITERATURE.

Education. Ireland has a free public-school system, with attendance at elementary schools compulsory for all children under fourteen years of age. Enrollment in elementary schools, of which there are about 5000, approximates about 455,000 pupils. Secondary schools, controlled chiefly by religious orders and subsidized to a certain extent by the state, total about 385, with an enrollment of about 42,000. The principal schools of higher learning are the University of Dublin (see DUBLIN,

UNIVERSITY OF) and the National University of Ireland. Attendance at the latter institution, which was founded in 1909 and has constituent colleges at Dublin, Cork, and Galway, recently totaled about 5000 students. Ireland also has several state-subsidized training colleges, various technical schools situated in the larger communities, and a network of so-called winter classes which provide agricultural instruction for residents of the rural regions.

Government. The government of Ireland is based on the constitution of 1937, as amended. By the terms of this document, which proclaims Ireland a sovereign, independent, democratic state, executive power is vested in the government (cabinet), consisting of not more than fifteen members, nor less than seven. The government, responsible to the lower house of the national legislature, is headed by the Taoiseach, or prime minister. This official is nominated by the lower house and appointed by the president of Ireland. The members of the government head the various administrative departments, or ministries. They are nominated by the prime minister and, subject to the approval of the lower house, appointed by the president. The president of Ireland is elected by direct popular vote for a seven-year term. Besides those already indicated, his duties include supreme command of the armed forces of the nation, the right to refer legislation of questionable constitutionality to the supreme court, and the power, under certain circumstances, to submit legislation to a referendum of the voters. Legislative authority in Ireland is vested in a bicameral legislature known as the Oireachtas. This is composed of the lower house, or Dail Eireann (q.v.), and the senate, or Seanad Eireann. The members of the Dail are elected for five-year terms by proportional representation. Eleven members of the senate, which may not veto legislation enacted by the Dail and is otherwise restricted in authority, are selected by the prime minister, and six members are elected by the universities. The Dail and the county councils elect the remainder by proportional representation from five panels of candidates. These are representative of national culture, labor, agriculture and the fisheries, public administration and social services, and commerce and industry. Judicial authority is vested in a supreme court, a high court, a court of criminal appeal, a central criminal court, a circuit court, and a district court. All of the judges and justices of these courts are appointed by the president of Ireland. The supreme court, which is the court of final appeal, consists of four judges and a chief justice, who is also an ex-officio member of the high court. The latter court, consisting of five judges and a president, who is an ex-officio member of the Supreme Court, determines all questions of law and fact arising from both criminal and civil cases, and also has original jurisdiction in appeals involving constitutionality of laws. The court of criminal appeal, composed of a judge of the supreme court and two judges of the high court, handles appeals from the lower courts. Decisions of this court are final except in cases involving points of law sufficiently important to warrant review by the supreme court. The central criminal court, presided over by a judge of the high court, has jurisdiction in all cases involving a major felony, including murder and high treason. Lesser crimes and most civil cases are tried before the circuit court. The district court hears cases involving misdemeanors and minor civil claims.

History. Irish liberation from British rule was achieved as the result of a struggle extending over several centuries and marked by numerous rebellions. An account of these events will be found in the article IRELAND. Following the Easter Rebellion (q.v.), an uprising of Irish nationalists on Easter Monday, April 24, 1916, the Sinn Fein (q.v.) became the most influential political party in

Ireland. This party, founded in 1900 by Arthur Griffith (q.v.), a journalist of Dublin, campaigned in the Parliamentary election of 1918 on a program that called for the severance of all ties with Great Britain, an end to the separatist movement in northern Ireland, and the establishment of an Irish republic. Candidates of the Sinn Fein won 73 of the 106 seats allotted to Ireland in the British Parliament.

In January, 1919, the Sinn Fein caucus assembled in Dublin as the Dail Eireann or national assembly. Proclaiming the independence of Ireland, the Dail forthwith formed a government, with Eamon de Valera (see DE VALERA) as president. British refusal to recognize this government precipitated armed hostilities. These consisted chiefly of guerrilla attacks by Irish insurgents, later called the Irish Republican Army, on British forces, particularly the Royal Constabulary (see BLACK AND TANS); and vigorous reprisals by the British. In the course of the war, the British Parliament enacted, in December, 1920, a Home Rule Bill, providing separate parliaments for part (six counties) of Ulster Province and for the remainder of Ireland. By the terms of the Bill, Great Britain retained effective control of Irish affairs. The people of Northern Ireland, as the six counties in Ulster Province were known, ratified the legislation in May of the following year and elected a parliament. Although the rest of Ireland also elected a parliament in May, 1921, under the legislation, the Sinn Feiners, comprising the overwhelming majority, refused to recognize the other provisions of the Home Rule Bill. The warfare against the British continued until July 10, 1921, when a truce was arranged. Subsequent negotiations led to the signing, in December, 1921, of a peace treaty by representatives of the second Dail Eireann and the British government. By the terms of the treaty, all of Ireland except the six counties comprising Northern Ireland was to receive Dominion status identical with that of Canada. After considerable debate, in which the opposition, led by de Valera, objected strenuously to a provision that virtually guaranteed a separate government in Northern Ireland and to an article that required members of the Dail to swear allegiance to the British sovereign, the Dail ratified the treaty (January 15, 1922) by a vote of 64 to 57. Ratification brought into being the Irish Free State, with Arthur Griffith as president and Michael Collins (q.v.), another prominent member of the Sinn Fein party,

Pan American World Airways

A house on the shore of Lake Leane, County Kerry, Republic of Ireland

as premier of the provisional government.

Under the leadership of De Valera, the dissident Sinn Fein grouping, termed the Republicans, later known as the Fianna Fail ("men of destiny"), called for a resumption of the struggle against Great Britain and instituted a campaign, including insurrectionary acts, against the provisional government. With the question of the treaty the chief issue, an election for a provisional Dail was held in June, 1922. Candidates supporting the treaty won a majority of the seats. The Republicans, refusing to recognize the authority of the new Dail, proclaimed a rival government and intensified their attacks on the Free State. In the course of the ensuing struggle, thousands were killed on both sides and scores of Republicans were executed. Meanwhile, the provisional Dail, headed now by William Thomas Cosgrave (q.v.), drafted a constitution. This was adopted on October 11, 1922. Following approval by the British Parliament, it became operative on December 6. The official government of the Irish Free State was instituted at once, with Cosgrave assuming office as president of the executive council. In April, 1923, the Republicans declared a truce in hostilities in order to participate in the forthcoming national elections, and public order was gradually restored. Neither the Sinn Fein Party nor the Republican Party secured a majority in the elections held late in August, 1923. However, the Republicans boycotted the Dail, and Cosgrave, supported by a coalition of parties, retained power. The boundary between the Free State and Northern Ireland was established in December, 1925. During the next few years, agreement was reached with the British government on various mutual

problems, and the national economy was substantially strengthened by a series of measures, notably the initiation of a hydroelectric project on the Shannon R.

Although the Republicans gradually increased their representation in the Dail during this period, they continued their boycott until August, 1927. They then assumed their seats, a total of 57, in the newly elected Dail. Partly as a result of the failure of the government to cope with domestic difficulties brought on by the world economic crisis of the early thirties, Cosgrave's party lost several seats to the Republicans in the elections of February, 1932. De Valera thereupon became head of the government. Legislation which he sponsored in the following April included provisions for the abrogation of the oath of allegiance to the British crown. This bill, which also would have virtually ended the political ties between Great Britain and the Free State, received the approval of the Dail, but was rejected, in effect, by the senate. In his next move against the British, De Valera withheld payment of annuities owed by Irish citizens to investors in Great Britain. By previous land-purchase acts, the English investors, through the British government, had loaned money to the Irish for the purchase of farm land. The withholding of the payment of annuities led to a protracted tariff war between the two countries, with serious damage resulting to the economy of the Free State. In another significant move, De Valera secured repeal of a law restricting the activities of the Irish Republican Army. The electorate registered approval of his program in elections held in January, 1932, in which a majority of Republicans were returned to the Dail.

With this mandate from the people, De Valera systematically developed his program for the gradual elimination of British influence in Irish affairs, obtaining abrogation of the oath of allegiance, limitations on the powers of the British governor general, and other anti-British measures. Simultaneously, the government initiated measures designed to give the country a self-sufficient economy. Steps taken included high income taxes on the rich, high tariffs on luxury goods, and control of foreign capital invested in Irish industry. During 1934, De Valera's government successfully met the challenge to Irish democracy of a fascist movement led by Owen O'Duffy. The Republican Party won a decisive victory in the elections held that year. In June, 1935, De Valera severed his political ties with the Irish Republican Army, which was extremely critical of many of his policies, and imprisoned a number of its leaders. It became general knowledge, meanwhile, that the draft of a new constitution was in progress. In 1936, the Republicans, in coalition with other groups in the Dail, finally secured passage of legislation abolishing the senate, long inimical to De Valera's policies. The Dail functioned as a unicameral legislature for the remainder of its term. In connection with the events surrounding the abdication of the British sovereign Edward VIII, the Dail enacted in 1936 a bill that deleted all references to the king from the constitution of the Free State, and abolished the office of governor general. Parallel legislation, known as the External Relations Act of 1936, restricted the association of the Free State with the British Commonwealth of Nations to joint action on certain questions involving external policy, specifically the approval of the trade treaties of the Free State and the appointment of its foreign envoys in the name of the British Crown.

The five-year term of office of the Dail expired in June, 1937. In the subsequent election the Republican Party won a plurality of the seats in the Dail. The new constitution, which abolished the Irish Free State and established Eire as a "sovereign independent democratic state", was approved by the voters in a plebiscite conducted simultaneously with the election. In addition to fundamental changes in governmental organs and procedures, this document promulgated various innovations in constitutional law. It prohibited divorce, empowered the state to censor the press, and projected the elimination of the employment of women in industry. Although the constitution specifically applied to all of Ireland, it provided that the laws of Eire should be executed, pending unification with Northern Ireland, only within the territory of the republic. The constitution contained no references to the British sovereign or to the Commonwealth of Nations. However, a subsequent statement by De Valera indicated that Eire's relations with the United Kingdom would be governed by the External Relations Act of 1936. In 1938 Douglas Hyde (q.v.) became the first president of Eire, and De Valera received the premiership.

Major differences between Eire and Great Britain were reconciled in a treaty adopted in April, 1938. The British government agreed to withdraw its forces from naval bases in Eire. On its part, the government of Eire accepted a British proposal for the settlement of the annuities debt to Great Britain. A mutually satisfactory conclusion of the tariff war between the two nations was drafted. In the ensuing period, the Irish Republican Army launched a campaign of terror and violence against Northern Ireland, Great Britain, and the government of Eire.

Shortly after the outbreak of World War II, the government of Eire proclaimed Irish neutrality in the conflict. Although many citizens of Eire volunteered for service with the armed forces of the United Kingdom, and despite a number of German bombings of Irish territory, including Dublin, Eire maintained neutrality throughout the war. Its commercial relations with Great Britain during the war period were prosperous. In the postwar period, economic dislocations in Great Britain and Europe subjected the economy of Eire to various strains, with a severe coal shortage and inflationary prices figuring prominently among national problems. Sean Thomas O'Kelly (q.v.), a leading member of Fianna Fail, was elected president of Eire in June, 1945, succeeding Douglas Hyde. Shortly after election, Premier De Valera disclosed that Sean McAteer, a leader of the outlawed Irish Republican Army, had been seized and interned. McAteer was accused of conspiring against the government. Arrests of other I.R.A. leaders followed.

In the elections of February, 1948, Fianna Fail lost its absolute majority in the Dail, obtaining only 68 of the 147 seats. De Valera was subsequently defeated in the Dail for the premiership by John A. Costello, candidate of a six-party coalition opposed to Fiann Fail. Costello, a veteran of the Easter Rebellion and the first attorney general of Eire, stated that the program of his cabinet called for lower prices and taxes, additional housing, expanded industrial production, and closer commercial relations with the United Kingdom. Soon after assuming office, Costello announced the release of all political prisoners in Eire.

The few remaining ties between Eire and the United Kingdom were severed by the terms of the Republic of Ireland Bill of 1948, approved by the Dail, in its second and decisive reading, on Nov. 26, 1948. Under the provisions of this law, effectuated on Easter Monday, April 18, 1949, Eire became a republic (officially styled Republic of Ireland), formally free of allegiance to the British crown and of association with the Commonwealth. Early in 1949 the British Parliament began consideration of legislation continuing the constitutional status of Northern Ireland as a part of the United Kingdom and defining the status of Irish citizens in Great Britain and the colonies. The Republic conducted an intensive campaign against the section dealing with Northern Ireland, but the bill was adopted on May 11. Under the law citizens of the Republic obtained all the privileges of British citizenship. De Valera was elected premier in June, 1951, after defections among the government coalition.

IRENÆUS (Gr., "Peacemaker"), SAINT (fl. 170-90), Christian prelate and a Father of the Greek Church, born in Asia Minor. There, as a child, he heard St. Polycarp, the disciple of St. John, preach. In 177 Irenæus was appointed bishop of Lyons; as bishop he made many converts among the Gauls and was an active opponent of the heresy of Gnosticism (q.v.). About 180 he wrote *Refutation and Overthrow of Gnosis, falsely so called,* a work which is now usually referred to as *Against the Heresies.* The 6th-century chronicler St. Gregory of Tours described the martyrdom of St. Irenæus, reputedly under the Roman emperor Septimius Severus in about 202, but no earlier description of this occurrence exists. His feast is celebrated on June 28th.

IRENE (752–803), Empress of the Eastern Roman Empire, born of humble family in Athens. In 769 she married Emperor Leo IV, and by the time he died, eleven years later, she had established her power over the empire, which she continued to rule as regent during the minority of her son Constantine VI. She restored the practice of image worship, and in 787 summoned the second Council of Nicæa (See NICÆA), which supported her view of the veneration due to sacred images, and reunited the Eastern Church with that of Rome. Irene's reign was troubled by a struggle for power with her son Constantine, whom she finally had imprisoned and blinded in 797. Subsequently her rule was uncontested until, in 802, the patricians revolted and deposed and exiled her. Irene spent the last year of her life on the island of Lesbos.

IRETON, HENRY (1611-51), English soldier and regicide, born in Attenborough, Nottinghamshire, and educated at Trinity College, Oxford University. He joined the army which supported Parliament in its struggle against the crown at the outbreak of the Great Rebellion (q.v.) in 1642 and fought throughout the early campaigns. At the battle of Naseby in 1645, he was wounded and captured by the royalists, but made his escape. Ireton was elected to Parliament in October, 1645. He attempted at first to promote moderate means of governmental reform, but later became convinced that it was useless to deal with King Charles I, helped to bring about his trial, and was one of the signers of the royal death warrant in 1648. Ireton went to Ireland as Oliver Cromwell's second-in-command in 1649 and commanded the troops which captured Carlow, Waterford, and Duncannon in 1650 and Limerick in 1651. He died of a fever shortly afterward. Ireton's stern character and military and political talents were greatly admired by Cromwell, whose daughter Bridget he married in 1646.

IRIDACEAE, or IRIS FAMILY, family of monocotyledonous plants, most of which are herbaceous perennials, belonging to the Lily order. The family comprises about sixty genera and eight hundred species native to temperate and tropical countries all over the world. Plants of the family have two-ranked, lance-shaped leaves which arise from underground tubers or rhizomes. The flowers have a six-parted perianth, three large stamens, and a single pistil composed of three carpels. The fruit is a many-seeded, three-celled capsule. The family includes many familiar genera of garden plants, including *Iris, Crocus,* and *Gladiolus* (qq.v.).

IRIDIUM, a metallic element of the platinum group, symbol Ir, atomic number 77, atomic weight 193.1. It was discovered by the English chemist Smithson Tennant (1761-1815) in 1804, and received its name from the iridescent nature of some of its compounds. It is an extremely rare metal, ranking sixty-first in order of abundance of the ele-

Peter Henderson & Co.

Left: Dutch iris, a bulbous type. Right: A variety of bearded iris.

ments in the earth's crust, and is found in alluvial deposits alloyed with platinum as platiniridium, or with osmium as osmiridium.

Iridium is a white, brittle, extremely hard metal, with m.p. 2350°C. (4262°F.). Its specific gravity of 22.4 is exceeded only by osmium, which is a fraction of one percent denser. It is extremely inert chemically, resisting even the action of aqua regia. In its chemical compounds it forms divalent and trivalent salts. It is used chiefly as an alloying material for platinum (q.v.); the alloy, which contains about ten percent iridium, is far harder than pure platinum. Platinum-iridium alloys containing larger percentages of iridium are used in making precision instruments, surgical tools, pen points, and standard weights and lengths.

IRIGOYEN, HIPÓLITO (1850–1933), Argentine statesman, born in Buenos Aires, and educated at the law school of the Colegio of San José. After holding several minor civil and political posts, Irigoyen took an active part in the revolution of 1890, and was subsequently the leader of the Radical Party. In 1916 he was elected president of Argentina, and during his administration he instituted social reforms benefiting labor, public health, and education. When, in 1917, during World War I, President Woodrow Wilson of the United States appealed to the Latin American countries to support the United States against Germany, Irigoyen opposed Argentina's entry into the war. At the end of his term in 1922, he retired as required by the Argentine constitution; he was re-elected for the term of 1928 to 1934. He lived simply, refusing to occupy the presidential palace and giving his salary to charity; he was immensely popular. In September, 1930, he was forced out of office by an uprising of the military, and was replaced by General José Francisco Uriburu.

IRIS, in anatomy. See EYE.

IRIS, genus of herbaceous plants belonging to the family Iridaceae. The genus contains about two hundred species native to temperate regions of the Northern Hemisphere. The plants have sword-shaped leaves arising from rhizomes or bulbs. The flowers, which are borne on long stalks, have three petal-like sepals, three petals, three stamens, and a single pistil. The fruit is a leathery loculicidal capsule. The common blue flag, *I. versicolor,* has violet-blue flowers spotted with green, yellow, and white. It is native to wet areas of E. United States. The blue flag is the State flower of Tennessee. Flagon or yellow flag, *I. pseudacorus,* the common bright yellow iris of European marshes, is naturalized in wet areas of New England, New Jersey, and New York. The fleur-de-lis or flower-de-luce, *I. germanica,* has bright-purple flowers with bright-yellow, beardlike tufts on the upper surfaces of the sepals. It is native to Europe and naturalized in E. United States. The Florentine iris or orris, *I. florentina,* is a native of S. Europe which has white, pale blue, or blue-gray flowers. Powdered rootstock of fleur-de-lis and Florentine iris, called *orrisroot,* is used in the manufacture of perfumes and toothpowders, and was formerly used in medicine for its emetic, cathartic, and diuretic properties.

Cultivated Varieties. Most of the common wild species of iris have long been cultivated in gardens. Since the latter part of the 19th century, however, many new hybrids have been developed, and exotic Asiatic irises have been brought under cultivation. Cultivated irises are divided into three general categories: (1) bearded irises, with beards like those of the fleur-de-lis; (2) beardless irises; and (3) bulbous irises. The first two of these categories include irises which grow from rootstocks called rhizomes, and the third contains those which grow from bulbs.

Bearded irises include dwarf varieties, such as the early-blooming crested dwarf iris, *I. cristata,* many varieties of intermediate size, and a large number of tall varieties. Bearded irises grow well in almost any soil which is well-drained and exposed to the sun. The rhizomes overgrow and crowd each other, and are dug up and divided every three to five years.

Beardless irises require heavy soils and moist conditions. Some of the beardless varieties are descended from such swamp species as the blue flag, but most cultivated varieties belong to a group commonly called Siberian irises, which includes several Asiatic species such as *I. chrysographes* and *I. forresti.*

The bulbous irises include the Spanish, English, and Dutch varieties. English irises actually originated in Spain, and Dutch irises are hybrids between cultivated Spanish varieties and a large Algerian species, *I. tingitana.* The bulbous irises range in color from white through yellow, blue, and bronze. Spanish and Dutch irises require light, well-drained soil; English irises grow best in heavy, moist soil.

IRIS, in Greek mythology, the goddess of the rainbow. According to the poet Hesiod (q.v.), she was the daughter of the ocean nymph Electra and of Thaumas, son of Pontus, the sea. In the *Iliad* by the epic poet Homer, Iris was also the messenger of the gods, particularly of Zeus, father of the gods, and his wife Hera. In art she is frequently represented as a young winged maiden holding a herald's staff.

IRISH CHURCH. See IRELAND, CHURCH OF.

IRISH FREE STATE. See IRELAND, REPUBLIC OF.

IRISH LANGUAGE. See GAELIC LANGUAGE.

IRISH LITERATURE, the literature written either in the Gaelic language (q.v.) or in English by writers of Irish birth. For Irish authors or literary movements connected with English life, see ENGLISH LITERATURE.

IRISH LITERATURE IN GAELIC. The history of the Irish literature written in Gaelic may be divided into three periods: Old Irish, dating from about the 5th century A.D. to the 11th century; Middle Irish, from the 11th to the middle of the 17th century; and Modern Irish, from the middle of the 17th century to the present time.

Old Irish Period. The earliest examples of Irish literature written in Gaelic are the ancient ogam inscriptions, which consist mainly of proper names inscribed on tombstones in a primitive form of the Gaelic language; the ogam inscriptions date from the 5th and 6th centuries. The few extant manuscripts of the Old Irish Period date from the 7th to the 10th century. They include a sermon written partly in Latin and partly in Gaelic; a short sketch of the life of Ireland's patron saint, St. Patrick; and a few poems and incantations. The scarcity of literary works of this period is the result of the invasions of Ireland by the Norsemen, who settled on the coasts of Ireland and from these points ravaged the interior, sacking and burning the monasteries, which were the centers of learning and contained libraries of manuscripts. The manuscripts of the time still extant are those which were carried off and preserved on the European continent by Irish scholars fleeing the invaders. Many of the tales composed in the Old Irish period survived and were written down in collections compiled during the following period.

Middle Irish Period. The great victory of the Irish over the Norsemen at the battle of Clontarf (see IRELAND: *History*), in 1014, freed Ireland from Norse domination and was indirectly a great stimulus to literature. A great number of manuscripts, dating chiefly from the period 1100 to about 1500, are extant. Among the more important manuscripts are the *Liber Hymnorum,* a compilation of hymns which date from the 7th to the 11th century; and a number of collections, compiled from the 12th to the 16th century, of romances, and of ecclesiastical and religious material, both dating from the 9th and 10th centuries. Among the books of romances are *Lebor na h-uidre,* the *Book of Leinster, The Yellow Book of Lecan,* and *The Great Book of Lecan;* the *Leabhar Breac* ("Speckled Book") is a religious work.

The chief literary works of the Middle Irish Period are the heroic sagas or tales of heroes, written partly in verse and partly in prose. These sagas fall into three principal divisions: a mythological cycle; the Ulster or Red Branch cycle; and the Fenian or Ossianic cycle. The mythological cycle consists of sagas dealing with events in Ireland from earliest pagan times to the beginning of the Christian era; they narrate stories of the earliest conquest of Ireland and of the old Irish heroes, who were believed to be descended from the Celtic gods and who fought one another for supremacy in Ireland. Two of the best-known of these sagas are the *Death of the Children of Tuireann* and *The Tragedy of the Children of Lir.*

The Ulster of Red Branch cycle contains nearly one hundred tales of the heroes of the kingdom of Ulster, one of the three kingdoms into which Ireland was divided at the beginning of the Christian era. The two principal heroes are King Chonchobor of Ulster and the brave warrior Cuchulainn. Among the more important of the sagas of the Ulster cycle are *Táin Bó Cualnge,* or *The Raid of the Cattle of Cooley; Deirdre and the Sons of Uisneach;* and *The Death of Cuchulainn.* The adventurous tales of this cycle are generally considered the most important contribution Ireland has ever made to world literature. They are not only vividly and dramatically written, but furnish the best existing record of the ways of life of the Celtic (see CELTIC PEOPLES AND LANGUAGES) or Irish people in early Christian times.

The sagas of the Fenian or Ossianic cycle deal chiefly with the life and adventures of Finn Mac Cool, a legendary Irish chieftain and bard of the 2nd and 3rd centuries A.D., and his followers, known as the Fianna. Ossian (q.v.) was either his son or his associate; he was also a warrior and a bard. Many of the poems of the cycle are ascribed either to Finn or to Ossian. Among the better-known stories of this cycle are *Agallamh na Seanórach* or *Dialogue of the Ancients; Os-sian and Evir-Alin;* and *Pursuit of Diarmid and Grainne.*

In addition to the tales in the three above-mentioned cycles, many other tales or groups of tales came into existence during the Middle Irish period. Among them are the *Immrama,* containing stories of marvelous voyages, including the *Voyage of Bran;* the satiric *Vision of MacConglinne;* and the story *Sons of Eochaid Muigmedoin.*

During both the Old Irish and Middle Irish periods, the poets, represented until the 13th century by a class of literary men noted for storytelling and known as *filid* (plural of *fili*), and from the 13th to the 16th century by the class known as bards, occupied a special position in the social order of Ireland. Poets were admired and honored throughout the land, permitted to reside at the courts of kings and nobles, and were generally regarded as the custodians of Irish culture; they took the place, after the coming of Christianity, of the druids of the pagan religion (see DRUIDISM) of ancient Ireland. Few of the filid and bards who flourished previous to the 13th century are known by name; the outstanding bards of the 13th to 15th century were the patriotic poet Gilbride Albanach McNamee (13th century), the religious poet Donough Mor O'Daly (13th century), and Teig Og O'Higgins (15th century). The most famous poet of the late Middle Irish Period was Teig Dall O'Higgins (d. about 1617), whose works were not published until 1922 and 1926. In prose the latter part of the Middle Irish period was distinguished by the historical and religious works of Geoffrey Keating (1570-about 1650), author of *History of Ireland.*

Modern Irish Period. The middle of the 17th century was marked historically by the conquest of Ireland by the English under Oliver Cromwell and later other generals (see IRELAND: *History*). The most fertile areas of the country were appropriated by the Presbyterian conquerors, and the native owners, who adhered to the Roman Catholic faith, were driven out and forced to settle on comparatively unproductive lands. The Gaelic-Irish literature of this period of English ascendancy consisted chiefly of religious books which, printed abroad and smuggled into Ireland and circulated secretly, served to keep alive the Catholic faith; and of poems, in which the glories of ancient and free Ireland were sung and laments were made on the course of contemporary events. Among the best-known poets of the 17th and 18th centuries were Pierce Ferriter (d. 1653), David O'Bruadar (d. about 1697), John O'Neaghtan (d. about 1720), Egan O'Rahilly (flourished between 1700 and 1726), Turlough O'Carolan (1670-1738), Owen Roe O'Sullivan (d. 1784), Teig Gaolach O'Sullivan (d. about 1795), and Brian Mac Gidla Meidhre (d. 1808), famous for his poem of nearly 1000 lines entitled *Midnight Court,* considered to be the best long-sustained Gaelic poem in Irish literature. The best-known poet of the 19th century is Anthony Raftery (1784-1835).

Throughout the 19th century, principally because of depopulation, caused by the potato famine of 1847, among the Gaelic-speaking people, the Gaelic language, both written and spoken, fell into disuse. Toward the end of the century efforts were made not only to restore Gaelic as a spoken language, but also to stimulate the writing of literary works in Gaelic. A revival of interest in the language was accomplished by the work of various societies, particularly the Gaelic League (q.v.) founded in 1893, and by the works of such scholars and writers as Douglas Hyde (q.v.), Canon Peter O'Leary (d. 1920), Patrick O'Conner (d. 1928), and Padhraic Pearse (q.v.). This so-called Gaelic revival resulted, in the last decade of the 19th and in the first half of the 20th century, in the publication of many collections of Irish folk tales, and in the writing of a considerable number of works of fiction and plays in Gaelic.

IRISH LITERATURE IN ENGLISH. Simultaneously with the decline of the popularity of Gaelic, which began about the end of the 18th century, occurred the beginnings of Irish literature in the English language. The earliest Irish-English literature was of two types: the pastoral, patriotic, convivial, and humorous verse written by anonymous poets of the people, and which included such well-known examples as *The Wearin' of the Green, The Boyne Water,* and *Irish Molly O;* and sophisticated verse written by known poets. The principal writers of the second type were Thomas Moore (q.v.), author of *Irish Melodies* (1807) and *National Airs* (1815); Gerald Griffin, the author of the poem *Eileen Aroon,* and many other poems; and Francis Mahony, better known as "Father Prout", the author of the famous poem *The Bells of Shandon.* Charles Lever and Samuel Lover (q.v.), both better known as novelists (see below), were the authors of the words of two of the best-known of Irish comic songs, respectively

The Widow Malone and *The Widow Machree.*

From about the middle to the end of the 19th century two classes of poets dominated Irish poetry written in English: patriotic and lyric. To the first class, the need to arouse the Irish people to a sense of nationalism was stronger than their impulse to write poetry distinguished for its formal or esthetic perfection; their work was characterized by flamboyant diction and fiery emotion and was important for its political effect. Among these poets, who contributed much of their work to the *Nation* (founded 1842), a journal devoted to the promotion of the cause of Irish nationalism, were Thomas Osborne Davis (*Lament of Owen Roe O'Neill*); Joseph Sheridan LeFanu, also a novelist; Denis Florence McCarthy (*The Bell-founder,* 1857); Jane Francesca Elgee, Lady Wilde (about 1820-96), who wrote under the name of "Speranza"; and Thomas D'Arcy McGee. The most outstanding of the lyrical poets were James Clarence Mangan (*Dark Rosaleen*); Jeremiah Joseph Callanan (1795-1829); Edward Walsh (1805-50); Sir Samuel Ferguson (*Lays of the Western Gael,* 1867); Aubrey Thomas de Vere (*The Foray of Queen Maeve and Other Legends of Ireland's Heroic Age,* 1882); and William Allingham (*Irish Songs and Poems,* 1887).

Much distinguished work in fiction was done in the 19th century by Irish authors writing in English. The writers of tales and novels of the century fall into two principal categories: one consisted of those who were Protestants and who treated Irish life from the point of view of the Anglo-Irish upper classes or gentry; the other comprised Catholic writers of Celtic stock, whose works dealt principally with the lives of the Irish Catholic peasantry. Among the important writers of the first group were Maria Edgeworth (*Castle Rackrent,* 1800, and *Ormond,* 1817); Lady Sydney Morgan (*The Wild Irish Girl,* 1806); William Hamilton Maxwell, writer of tales of military life, including *Stories of Waterloo* (1829); Samuel Lover (*Rory O'Moore,* 1837, and *Handy Andy,* 1842, both stories of the Irish peasantry, treated in general as consisting of good-natured and comic figures); and Charles Lever (*Harry Lorrequer,* 1839, and *Jack Hinton,* 1843). Among the Catholic writers of fiction were the Banim brothers, John and Michael, noted for their stories of the life of the poverty-stricken Irish peasant (*Tales of the O'Hara Family,* 6 vols., 1825-

James Joyce (from a drawing)

26); Gerald Griffin (*The Collegians,* 1829, a tale of middle-class Irish life); and William Carleton (*Fardorougha the Miser,* 1839). Other eminent Irish novelists of the 19th century were Joseph Sheridan LeFanu (*Uncle Silas,* 1864), Charles J. Kickham (*Sally Cavanagh,* 1869), and Emily Lawless (*Hurrish,* 1886). For discussion of the work of Irish writers in English who are closely identified with English life and literature, such as Jonathan Swift, Oliver Goldsmith, Richard Brinsley Sheridan, Oscar Wilde, George Bernard Shaw, James Joyce, and Liam O'Flaherty, see DRAMA: *British Drama;* ENGLISH LITERATURE; and the articles under the names of the writers.

The last decade of the 19th century witnessed a remarkable revival in Irish literature written either in Gaelic (see *Modern Irish Period,* above) or in English. The principal Irish writers in English who are identified with this movement are the poets William Butler Yeats and George W. Russell ("A.E."); the playwrights John Millington Synge and Sean O'Casey; the novelist and playwright George Moore; and the poet and fiction writer James Stephens. For a discussion of their work see the individual articles under their names; and also ENGLISH LITERATURE: *The Irish Renaissance and Other Twentieth-Century Irish Literature;* and AB-

BEY THEATRE. In addition to the above-mentioned, other Irish writers in English prominent in the Irish Renaissance were the poets William Larminie (*Fand and Other Poems,* 1892); Agnes Skrine, who wrote under the pen name "Moira O'Neill", and among whose works is *Songs from the Glens of Antrim* (1900); Jane Barlow (*Ghostbereft,* 1902); John Todhunter (*Sounds and Sweet Airs,* 1905); Nora Hopper (*Father Felix's Chronicles,* 1907); the religious poet Katharine Tynan (*Herb o' Grace,* 1918); and Alfrde Perceval Graves (*Book of Irish Poetry,* 1925). Most of these poets used the personages and events of the Irish sagas as material for their work. Notable translations into English were made of the Gaelic romances by Lady Augusta Gregory (*Cuchulain,* 1902, and *Gods and Fighting Men,* 1904); Thomas William Rolleston (*Myths and Legends of the Celtic Race,* 1911); and Douglas Hyde (*Legends of Saints and Sinners from the Irish,* 1915). Among representative fiction writers of the period of the Irish Renaissance were Standish James O'Grady, author of many Irish historical romances (*The Coming of Cuchulain,* and *The Chain of Gold*); Jane Barlow (*Flaws,* 1911); and James Owen Hannay ("George A. Birmingham") among whose writings are the novels *The Seething Pot* (1905), *Wild*

William Butler Yeats

Justice (1930), and *The Search for Susie* (1941).

IRISH SEA, part of the Atlantic Ocean, located between N. Ireland on the W. and N. England and s.w. Scotland on the E. It is connected with the Atlantic on the N.W. by the North Channel and on the s. by St. George's Channel.

IRISH SETTER, a type of hunting dog (see FIELD DOG OR BIRD DOG) which reputedly originated in Ireland several hundred years ago. It is not definitely known from what other breeds this dog developed, but the type is believed to have sprung from a cross between the Irish water spaniel and the Irish terrier, or to have developed from a combination of English setter, Gordon setter, spaniel, and pointer. The Irish setter was first brought to the United States toward the end of the 19th century. The dog has a long body and deep, narrow chest; a long, lean head, with moderate-sized ears that hang close to the head; and hazel or rich-brown eyes. Its forelegs are strong and sinewy; the upper part of the hindlegs is long and muscular, the lower part short and strong. The tail is moderately long, tapers to a fine point, and has a fringe of fairly long hair. The coat of the Irish setter, which is characteristically mahogany red or golden chestnut in color, is of moderate length and lies flat. Because of its speed and endurance, the dog is a valuable aid in bird hunting, but it is frequently used only as a pet or for show purposes. The Irish setter is vigorous, hardy, and long lived.

IRISH TERRIER, a small variety of terrier (q.v.) which originated in Ireland reputedly several centuries ago. The dog is useful for hunting woodchucks, rabbits, rats, and larger game, and has been trained to act as a

Irish water spaniel

retriever on land and in water; it has also been employed in war as runner or messenger. Its companionability and loyalty to its master make it an admirable pet and watchdog. The Irish terrier has a long head with a flat skull; dark-hazel eyes; small, v-shaped ears; and long, sloping shoulders. Its coat is dense and wiry, lying close to the body, and is a bright or a golden red in color. The Irish terrier is about 18 inches high at the shoulder; the dog weighs about 27 pounds; the bitch, about 25.

IRISH WATER SPANIEL, a sporting or hunting dog, a variety of the spaniel (q.v.). The dog originated in Ireland from a number of cross breeds, including the poodle. Before 1859 two types of Irish water spaniel existed, the "South country" and the "North country"; the modern breed is largely derived from the "South country" variety. The Irish water spaniel is particularly useful as a retriever of game from water; because its curly coat may catch on branches of trees and bushes, the dog is less often used for retrieving on land. The animal has a large skull, a square muzzle, and a large, liver-colored nose; a topknot of long curls; hazel-colored, medium-sized eyes; long ears; and a short tail, thick at the root and tapering to a fine point. The coat consists of a dense covering of tight ringlets; the color is a solid liver. The male stands from 22 to 24 inches high at the shoulder; the bitch, 21 to 23. The male weighs 55 to 65 pounds; the bitch, 45 to 58.

IRISH WOLFHOUND, a hunting dog of the hound variety, the tallest dog known. The Irish wolfhound originated in Ireland in remote antiquity. It was known in Rome

Irish setter

in the 4th century A.D., and early Celtic literature contains many stories concerning Celtic heroes and their wolfhounds, which were used principally to hunt the wolf and elk. The breed became almost extinct in Ireland and Europe in the middle of the 19th century, but was rehabilitatd by the Scottish dog breeder Captain G. A. Graham. Today the Irish wolfhound is occasionally used for hunting large animals, such as the timber wolf, but is more often kept as a pet because of its loyalty, intelligence, and fearlessness as a watchdog. The Irish wolfhound is from 31 to 34 inches high at the shoulder and weighs up to 135 pounds; the bitch is about 28 inches high and weighs about 90 pounds. The dog has a long head and a long muzzle; small ears; dark eyes; a very deep chest; muscular shoulders; a rough, hard coat which is especially wiry over the eyes and the underjaw; and a long, slightly curved tail. The color of the Irish wolfhound may be gray, brindle, fawn, pure white, black, or red.

IRKUTSK, city and capital of Irkutsk Region, Russian Soviet Federated Socialist Republic, situated at the junction of the Irkut and Angara rivers, several m. below the exit of the Angara from Lake Baikal. It was founded by the Cossack chief Ivan Pokhabov in 1652 as a station for the collection of the fur tax from the Buriat inhabitants of the region. Later it became a trade center for furs from Siberia and China and for gold from the Siberian mines. For many years Irkutsk has been the cultural center of the surrounding region. It contains historical and art museums, theaters, libraries, and several institutions of higher learning. Between 1918 and 1921 considerable revolutionary activity took place in the city; the anti-Bolshevik leader Aleksandr Vasielievich Kolchak (q.v.) was executed there in 1920. The modern city is served by an air line and by a railway. Industrial establishments include breweries, lumber mills, machine shops, airplane factories, and glass, chemical, aluminum, and leather works. Iron, coal, manganese, gold, mica, asbestos, bauxite, and salt are mined in the vicinity. Pop., about 243,000.

IRON, a metallic element, atomic number 26, atomic weight 55.85, symbol Fe. Iron metal was known and used for ornamental purposes and weapons in prehistoric ages; the earliest specimen still extant, a group of oxidized iron beads found in Egypt, dates from about 4000 B.C. The archeological term Iron Age (q.v.) properly applies only to the period when iron was used extensively for utilitarian purposes, as in tools, as well as for ornamentation. The beginnings of modern processing of iron can be traced back to Germany in the middle of the 14th century.

Metallic iron occurs in the free state in only a few localities, notably w. Greenland. It is found in meteors, usually alloyed with nickel. In chemical compounds the metal is widely distributed over the world and ranks fourth in abundance among all the elements in the earth's crust; next to aluminum it is the most abundant of all metals. The principal ore of iron is hematite. Other important ores are goethite, magnetite, siderite (qq.v.), and bog iron or limonite. Pyrite (q.v.), the sulfide ore of iron, is not processed as an iron ore, because it is too difficult to remove the sulfur. For processing of iron ore see IRON, METALLURGY OF. Small amounts of iron occur in combination in natural waters, in plants, and as a constituent of blood.

By far the greatest amount of iron is used in processed forms, such as wrought iron, cast iron, and steel. Commercially pure iron is used for the production of galvanized sheet and of electromagnets. Iron is employed for medicinal purposes in the treatment of anemia when the amount of hemoglobin (q.v.) or the number of red blood corpuscles in the blood is lowered. It is also used in tonics.

Pure iron is a bright, silvery-white metal, with melting point 1535° C. (2795° F.), boiling point about 3000° C. (5432° F.), specific gravity 7.86, and hardness ranging from 4 to 5. It is soft, malleable, and ductile. Iron is easily magnetized at ordinary temperatures; it is difficult to magnetize when heated, and at 790° C. (1454° F.) the magnetic property disappears.

The metal exists in three allotropic forms, ordinary or α-iron, γ-iron, and δ-iron. The internal arrangement of the atoms in the crystal lattice changes in the transition from one form to another. The transition from α-iron to γ-iron occurs at 912° C. (1673° F.) and the transition from γ-iron to δ-iron occurs at 1400° C. (2552° F.). The different physical properties of the allotropic forms and the difference in the amount of carbon taken up by each of the forms play an important part in the formation, hardening, and tempering of steel.

Pure iron, prepared by the electrolysis of ferrous sulfate solution, has limited use. Commercial iron invariably contains small amounts of carbon and other impurities which alter its physical properties, and the mechanical properties of iron are considerably improved by the further addition of carbon and other alloying elements; see IRON, METALLURGY OF.

Chemically, iron is an active metal. It combines with the halogens, sulfur, phosphorus, carbon, and silicon. It displaces hydrogen from most dilute acids. It burns in oxygen to form ferrous ferric oxide, Fe_3O_4. When exposed to moist air, iron becomes corroded, forming a reddish-brown, flaky, hydrated ferric oxide, commonly known as rust. The formation of rust is an electrochemical phenomenon, in which the impurities present in iron form an electrical "couple" with the iron metal. A small current is set up, water from the atmosphere providing an electrolytic solution; see ELECTROCHEMISTRY. Water and soluble electrolytes such as salt accelerate the reaction. In this process the iron metal is decomposed and reacts with oxygen from the air to form the rust. The reaction proceeds faster in those places where rust accumulates, and the surface of the metal becomes pitted. See CORROSION.

When iron is dipped into concentrated nitric acid it forms a layer of oxide which renders it passive, i.e., it does not react chemically with acids or other substances. The protective oxide layer is easily broken by striking or jarring the metal, which then becomes active again.

Compounds of Iron. Iron forms ferrous compounds in which it has a valence of two, and ferric compounds in which it has a valence of three. Ferrous compounds are easily oxidized to ferric compounds. The most important ferrous compound is ferrous sulfate, $FeSO_4$, usually occurring as pale green crystals containing seven molecules of water of hydration, and called green vitriol or copperas. It is obtained in large quantities as a by-product in pickling iron and is used as a mordant in dyeing, as a tonic medicine, and in the manufacture of ink (q.v.) and pigments.

Ferric oxide, an amorphous red powder, is obtained by treating ferric salts with a base or by oxidizing pyrite (q.v.). It is used both as a pigment, called iron red or Venetian red, and as a polishing abrasive, called rouge (q.v.).

Ferric chloride, obtained as dark green, lustrous crystals by heating iron in chlorine, is used in medicine as an alcoholic solution, called tincture of iron.

The ferrous and ferric ions combine with cyanides to form complex cyanide compounds.

Ferric ferrocyanide, $Fe_4[Fe(CN)_6]_3$, a dark blue, amorphous solid, formed by the reaction of potassium ferrocyanide with a ferric salt, is called Prussian blue. It is used as a pigment in paints, and in laundry bluing to correct the yellowish tint left by the ferrous salts in water. Potassium ferricyanide $K_3Fe(CN)_6$, called red prussiate of potash, obtained from ferrous ferricyanide $Fe_3[Fe(CN)_6]_2$ or Turnbull's blue, is used in processing blueprint paper.

Iron undergoes physicochemical reactions with carbon, which are essential to the formation of steel. See FERRITE; PEARLITE.

IRON AGE, archeological term denoting the period of time during which a civilization has used iron for weapons and tools. In advanced civilizations the Iron Age succeeded the Bronze Age (q.v.); in certain primitive civilizations, such as those of the North American Indians, it immediately followed the Stone Age (q.v.), having been introduced by conquerors whose conquests were due, in large part, to iron weapons, or by tradesmen from more civilized areas.

The Iron Age seems to have begun in Egypt and Asia Minor at about the 14th century B.C., and to have remained confined within this region for about 300 years. The first appearances of iron-using cultures in Europe were in the upper Danube region, in Italy (see HALLSTATT CULTURE; VILLANOVA CULTURE), and in Greece and the Grecian Islands, about 1000 B.C. These cultures continued to use bronze for ornament but developed iron weapons. The Hallstatt culture spread southward and westward over Europe, reaching Britain about 500 B.C., in the middle of the so-called prehistoric, Central European Iron-Age culture.

La Tène culture, so called because abundant remains of it were found in the La Tène region of Lake Neuchâtel, Switzerland, was predominant among the Celts of Germany, France, and Switzerland between 500 B.C. and about 100 A.D., and was spread to Ireland about 350 B.C. Hallstatt and La Tène cultures differ chiefly in pottery styles and burial fashions rather than in iron implements. See ARCHEOLOGY.

Though European cultures are still considered by anthropologists to be in the Iron Age, the displacement of iron by steel and by lighter construction materials, such as aluminum and plastics, is a predominant feature of our times. Moreover, the construction of machinery and the fission of atomic nuclei have had greater recent impact on the forms

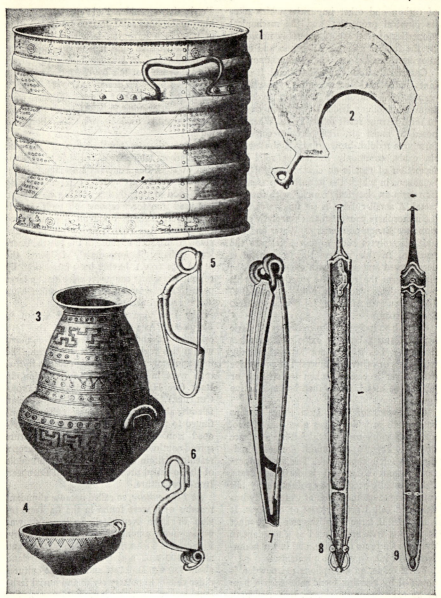

IMPLEMENTS OF THE IRON AGE. *1, a Hallstatt bucket; 2, razor from northern Italy's earliest Iron-Age culture; 3, and 4, vessels of the Villanova type; 5, 6, and 7, clasps, called fibulae, of the La Tène culture; 8, and 9, swords of the La Tène culture.*

of society than have changes in materials of construction.

IRONBARK TREE. See EUCALYPTUS.

IRON CHANCELLOR, THE. See BISMARCK-SCHÖNHAUSEN, OTTO VON.

IRON CURTAIN, THE, a metaphorical expression describing the system of controls established by the governments of the Soviet Union and of the countries under its influence to prevent the free flow of information and the normal transit of persons in either direction across the borders of those countries. The expression was first used, in the sense of an opaque and almost impenetrable wall surrounding the Soviet Union and its satellite states, by the English statesman Winston Churchill in a speech delivered at Fulton, Mo., on March 6, 1946; it immediately became popular in the United States and other countries outside the Iron Curtain.

IRON DUKE, THE. See WELLINGTON, ARTHUR WELLESLEY.

IRON LUNG, common name for an apparatus for producing artificial respiration (see RESPIRATION, ARTIFICIAL) by rhythmically altering air pressure applied against the outside chest walls of a person who cannot breathe normally. The iron lung is most valuable in treating victims of infantile paralysis who have complete peripheral paralysis from the neck down. Early forms of the iron lung consisted of an airtight chamber into which the entire body of the patient, except for the head, was inserted; recently, improved respirators utilizing the same principle have been developed which enclose merely the chest. As part of the treatment, the patient is frequently permitted normal breathing outside the iron lung for periods ranging from minutes to hours; with the aid of the iron lung the respiratory muscles of the patient are gradually brought into use and may completely recover.

IRON MASK, THE MAN IN THE, a mysterious prisoner in the Bastille, Paris, during the late 17th century. The complete secrecy which concealed his identity has aroused many romantic conjectures, the most famous of which is the theory, utilized by the novelist Alexandre Dumas, père, that the prisoner was a secret brother of King Louis XIV of France. Other legends claim that he was an intriguing Italian minister of state, Count Mattioli, or an English agent inimical to French interests. Serious consideration of the records shows that, though the prisoner was carefully sequestered and even masked, his features were concealed by no more severe a material than velvet. Although many scholars have scrutinized contemporary records, no sure trace of the true identity of the Man in the Iron Mask has as yet been discovered, and the only reliable information available is that he was brought to the Bastille in 1698 by the new governor of the prison, Bénigne d'Auvergne de Saint-Mars, and that his death was recorded in 1703 under the name of "Marchioly", at which time he was described as being "aged about forty-five".

IRON, METALLURGY OF, the science and technology of iron and its alloys, particularly those containing a small percentage of carbon. The differentiation between different kinds of iron and steel is sometimes confusing because of the nomenclature used. Steel in general is regarded as an alloy of iron

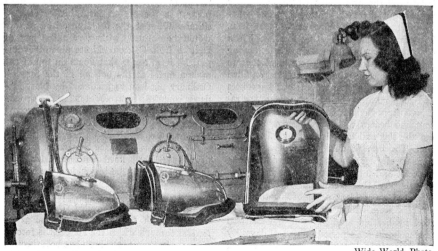

Wide World Photo

Three lightweight chest respirators are shown next to an old-type iron lung. The newer, plastic device is about 400 times lighter than the metal machine in the background.

and carbon, often with an admixture of other elements. However some alloys which are commercially called irons contain more carbon than commercial steels. *Open-hearth iron* and *wrought iron* contain only a few hundredths of 1 percent of carbon. Steels of various types contain from 1/25 percent to 2¼ percent of carbon. *Cast iron, malleable cast iron,* and *pig iron* contain amounts of carbon varying from 2 to 4 percent. A special form of malleable iron, not produced in the U.S. and containing virtually no carbon, is known as *white-heat malleable iron.* These are the chief types of iron and steel, but other special types are mentioned below. A special group of alloys, known as *ferroalloys,* is used in iron and steel manufacture. These ferroalloys typically contain about four parts of an alloying element, such as manganese, silicon, or chromium, to one of iron. Alloys of iron with other metals, such as stainless steel and Duriron, are called "iron" or "steel" arbitrarily, without regard to their carbon content.

History. The exact date at which mankind discovered the technique of smelting iron ore to produce usable metal is not known. The earliest iron implements discovered by archeologists in Egypt date from about 3000 B.C., and iron ornaments were used even earlier; the comparatively advanced technique of hardening iron weapons by heat treatment was known to the Greeks about 1000 B.C. The alloys produced by early iron workers, and, indeed, all the iron alloys which were made until about the 14th century A.D., are what would today be classified as wrought iron. They were made by heating a mass of iron ore and charcoal in a forge or furnace having a forced draft. Under this treatment the ore was reduced to a sponge of metallic iron filled with a slag composed of metallic impurities and charcoal ash. This sponge of iron was removed from the furnace while still incandescent and beaten with heavy sledges to drive out the slag and to weld and consolidate the iron. The iron produced under these conditions usually contained about 3 percent of slag particles and 0.1 percent of other impurities. Occasionally this technique of ironmaking produced, by accident, a true steel rather than wrought iron. Iron workers learned to make steel by heating wrought iron and charcoal in clay boxes for a period of several days. By this process the iron absorbed enough carbon to become a true steel.

After the 14th century, the furnaces used in smelting were increased in size, and increased draft was used to force the combustion gases through the "charge", the mixture of raw materials. In these larger furnaces, the iron ore in the upper part of the furnace was first reduced to metallic iron and then took on more carbon as a result of the gases forced through it by the blast. The product of these furnaces was pig iron, an alloy which melts at a lower temperature than steel or wrought iron. Pig iron (so called because it was usually cast in stubby, round ingots known as "pigs") was further refined to make steel.

Modern steelmaking employs blast furnaces which are merely refinements of the furnaces used by the old ironworkers. The conversion of pig iron to steel is carried out in three kinds of furnace: the *Bessemer furnace* or *converter* introduced in 1855 by Sir Henry Bessemer (q.v.) ; the *open-hearth furnace* introduced about ten years later in England; and the *electric furnace.* More than 90 percent of the steel manufactured in the U.S. is made in open-hearth furnaces.

Pig-Iron Production. The basic materials used for the manufacture of pig iron are iron ore, coke, and limestone. The coke is burned as a fuel to heat the furnace and in so doing gives off carbon monoxide which combines with the iron oxides in the ore, reducing them to metallic iron. This is the basic chemical reaction in the blast furnace and has the equation: $Fe_2O_3 + 3CO = 3CO_2 + 2Fe$. The limestone in the furnace charge is used as an additional source of carbon monoxide and as a "flux" to combine with the infusible silica present in the ore to form fusible calcium silicate. Without the limestone, iron silicate would be formed, with a resulting loss of metallic iron. Calcium silicate plus other impurities form a *slag* that floats on top of the molten metal at the bottom of the furnace. Ordinary pig iron as produced by blast furnaces contains: iron, about 92 percent; carbon, 3 or 4 percent; silicon, ½ to 3 percent; manganese, ¼ to 2½ percent; phosphorus, 1/25 to 2 percent; and a trace of sulfur.

A typical blast furnace consists of a cylindrical steel shell lined with firebrick. The shell is tapered at the top and at the bottom and is widest at a point about one third of the distance from the bottom. The lower portion of the furnace, called the *bosh,* is equipped with several tubular openings or *tuyères* through which the air blast is forced. Near the bottom of the bosh is a hole through which the molten pig iron flows when the furnace is tapped, and above this hole, but below the tuyères, is another hole for drain-

Chicago Association of Commerce; Standard Oil Co. (N.J.)

METALLURGY OF IRON. *Left: Ramp through which skip cars carry iron ore, coke, and limestone to the blast furnace, in the manufacture of pig iron. Right: Worker in a pig-iron pile.*

ing the slag. The top of the furnace, which is about 90 ft. in height, contains vents for the escaping gases and a pair of round hoppers closed with bell-shaped valves through which the charge is introduced into the furnace. The materials are brought up to the hoppers in small dump cars or *skips* which are hauled up an inclined external *skip hoist.*

Blast furnaces operate continuously. The raw material to be fed into the furnace is divided into a number of small charges which are introduced into the furnace at ten- to fifteen-minute intervals. Slag is drawn off from the top of the melt about once every two hours, and the iron itself is drawn off or *tapped* about five times a day. The process of tapping consists of knocking out a clay plug from the iron hole near the bottom of the bosh and allowing the molten metal to flow into a brick-lined gutter and thence into a large, brick-lined metal bucket which holds as much as one hundred tons of metal. Any slag that may flow from the furnace with the metal is skimmed off before it reaches the bucket. When the bucket is full it is lifted by a crane and carried to the pig-casting machine. There the metal is poured from the bucket and is directed into a series of molds which are carried into and out of the machine by an endless-chain conveyor. As the molds leave the machine they pass through water

sprays which cool the metal sufficiently so that the pigs may be dropped from the molds and be further cooled by water.

In many cases blast furnaces are operated in conjunction with Bessemer converters or open-hearth furnaces as part of a single steel-producing plant. In such cases the molten pig iron is not made into pigs but is used, while still molten, to charge the steel furnaces. Usually the molten metal from several blast furnaces is mixed in a large ladle before it is converted to steel, to minimize any irregularities in the composition of the individual melts.

The air used to supply the blast in a blast furnace is preheated to temperatures between 1000° and 1600° F. (538° to 871° C.). The heating is performed in *stoves,* cylinders containing networks of firebrick. The bricks in the stoves are heated for several hours by burning blast-furnace gas, the waste gases from the top of the furnace. Then the flame is turned off and the air for the blast is blown through the stove. The weight of air used in the operation of a blast furnace exceeds the total weight of the other raw materials employed. A furnace producing 1150 tons of pig iron per day requires about 850 tons of coke, 400 tons of limestone, 2000 tons of ore, and 4000 tons of air.

An important development in blast furnace

technology was introduced after World War II in the pressurizing of furnaces. By "throttling" the flow of gas from the furnace vents it is possible to build up the pressure within the furnace to 10 pounds per square inch or more, thus increasing the flow of air through the furnace without increasing the "wind" which normally blows an appreciable portion of iron-ore dust out of the furnace. The pressurizing technique makes possible better combustion of the coke and higher output of pig iron. The output of many blast furnaces can be increased 25 percent by pressurizing. Experimental installations have also shown that the output of blast furnaces can be increased by enriching the air blast with oxygen.

Other Methods of Iron Refining. Although almost all the iron and steel produced in the world is made by the blast-furnace process, other methods of iron refining are possible and have been practiced to a limited extent. One such method is the so-called *direct* method of making iron and steel from ore, with making pig iron. In this process iron ore and coke are mixed in a revolving kiln and heated to a temperature of about 1740° F. (949° C.). Carbon monoxide is given off from the heated coke just as in the blast furnace and reduces the oxides of the ore to metallic iron. The secondary reactions which occur in a blast furnace, however, do not occur, and the kiln produces so-called *spongy iron* of great purity. Virtually pure iron is also produced by means of electrolysis (q.v.), by passing an electric current through a solution of ferrous chloride. Neither the direct nor the electrolytic processes has any great commercial significance.

Bessemer Process. Although the Bessemer process is less important than the open-hearth process from the standpoint of modern tonnage steel production, it has great historical importance as the first practical process for making steel in large quantities. Essentially the production of steel from pig iron by any process consists of burning out the excess carbon present in the iron. The Bessemer process has been little changed since it was first introduced. From 10 to 20 tons of molten pig iron are poured into a pear-shaped vessel 15 to 20 feet high, called a *converter.* Cold air is blown into the molten iron from the bottom of the converter for a period of about 20 minutes. This air blast causes impurities in the iron to burn, and the combustion maintains the iron in a molten state. Just before the end of the "blow" a small quantity of an alloy called *spiegeleisen* is added to the mol-

ten metal in the converter. This alloy contains iron with an admixture of about 15 percent of manganese and 5 percent of carbon. The manganese serves to remove oxygen from the melt and carbon alloys with the iron to form a steel. At the end of the blow the entire converter is tilted and the molten metal is poured from its open top into ladles. From the ladle the steel is poured into cast-iron molds which form ingots, usually about 5 ft. long and 19 in. square. These ingots, which are the raw material for all forms of fabricated steel, weigh about 2½ tons in this size.

In the original Bessemer process, the converter was lined with silica bricks, and heat was obtained in part by the combustion of silicon impurity in the iron. This process is sometimes called the *acid Bessemer process* because of the acidic reaction of silica. A variation is the *basic Bessemer process* in which the converter is lined with basic dolomite bricks and in which most of the heat is obtained from the burning of phosphorus. The acid process is adapted to iron obtained from ores which are nearly free of phosphorus, and is the one usually used in the U.S. In Europe, where iron ores often contain large quantities of phosphorus, the basic process is extensively employed.

Open-Hearth Process. One of the difficulties in the manufacture of steel is its high melting point—approximately 2500° F. (1371° C.)—which prevents the use of ordinary fuels and furnaces. To overcome this difficulty the open-hearth furnace was developed; this furnace can be operated at a high temperature by regenerative preheating of the fuel gas and air used for combustion in the furnace. In regenerative preheating the exhaust gases from the furnace are drawn through one of a series of chambers containing a mass of brickwork and give up most of their heat to the bricks. Then the flow through the furnace is reversed and the fuel and air pass through the heated chambers and are warmed by the bricks. By this means open-hearth furnaces can reach temperatures as high as 3000° F. (1649° C.).

The furnace itself consists typically of a flat, rectangular brick hearth about 20 feet by 35 feet, which is roofed over at a height of about 8 feet. In the front of the hearth is a series of doors opening out onto a working floor in front of the hearth. The entire hearth and working floor are one story above ground level and the space under the hearth is taken up by the heat-regenerating chambers of the furnace. A furnace of this size has a capacity

Chi. Assoc. of Comm.; Wheeling Steel
Corp.; Otis Steel Co.

METALLURGY OF IRON

*Above: Slag pouring from brick-
lined bucket just filled with
molten steel from open hearth.
Right: Rolling mill where red-
hot ingots of steel are shaped.
Below: Delivery end of hot mill
where metal sheets are cooled.*

of about 100 tons of steel every 11 hours.

The furnace is charged with a mixture of pig iron (either molten or cold), scrap steel and iron ore which provide additional oxygen, with a small admixture of limestone for flux and fluorspar to make the slag more fluid. The proportions of the charge vary within wide limits, but a typical charge might consist of 125,000 lbs. of scrap steel, 25,000 lbs. of cold pig iron, 100,000 lbs. of molten pig iron, 26,000 lbs. of limestone, 2000 lbs. of iron ore, and 500 lbs. of fluorspar. After charging, the furnace is lighted and the flames play back and forth over the hearth as their direction is reversed by the operator to provide heat regeneration.

Chemically the action of the open-hearth furnace consists in lowering the carbon content of the charge by oxidization and of removing such impurities as silicon, phosphorus, manganese, and sulfur, which combine with the limestone to form slag. These reactions take place while the metal in the furnace is at melting heat, and the furnace is held at between 1540° and 1650° C. (2800° and 3000° F.) for many hours until the molten metal has the desired carbon content. Experienced open-hearth operators can often judge the carbon content of the metal by its appearance, but the melt is usually tested by withdrawing a small amount of metal from the furnace, cooling it, and subjecting it to physical examination or chemical analysis. When the carbon content of the melt is that desired, the furnace is tapped through a hole at the rear. The molten steel then flows through a short trough to a large ladle set below the furnace at ground level. From the ladle the steel is poured into cast-iron molds which form ingots like those produced in the Bessemer process.

Finishing Processes. Steel is marketed in a wide variety of sizes and shapes, such as rods, pipes, railroad rails, tees, channels and I-beams. These shapes are produced at the steel mill by rolling and otherwise forming heated ingots until they reach the required shape. The working of steel fresh from the furnace also improves the quality of the steel by refining its crystalline structure and making the metal tougher.

The basic process of working steel is known as hot-rolling. In hot-rolling, the cast ingot is first heated to bright-red heat in a furnace called a *soaking pit*, and is then passed between a series of pairs of metal rollers which squeeze it to the desired size and shape. The distance between the rollers diminishes for each successive pair as the steel is elongated and reduced in thickness.

The first pair of rollers through which the ingot passes is commonly called the *blooming mill* and the square billets of steel which it produces are known as *blooms*. From the blooming mill, the steel is passed on to *roughing mills* and finally to *finishing mills* which reduce it to the correct cross section. The rollers of mills used to produce railroad rails and such structural shapes as I-beams, H-beams, and angles are grooved to give the required shape.

Modern manufacturing requires a large amount of comparatively thin sheet steel, and special *continuous mills* have been developed for rolling such strips and sheets in widths as great as 8 feet. These continuous mills have the added advantage of processing the thin sheet so rapidly that it does not have time to cool and become unworkable. In a typical continuous mill a slab of steel is fed through a series of ten rollers all located in a straight line, being carried from one roller to the next on a moving conveyor. The original slab is 35 inches wide, 13 feet long, and about 4½ inches thick. After passing through the mill the steel is reduced to a strip .05 inches thick, 35 inches wide, and nearly 1200 ft. long. The successive pairs of rollers in the continuous mill are arranged to revolve with increasing speed to compensate for the elongation of the sheet. As it leaves the final pair of rollers, in the example given, the sheet is traveling at a rate of about 15 miles per hour. Continuous mills are equipped with a number of accessory devices including edging rollers, descaling devices, and devices for coiling the sheet automatically when it reaches the end of the mill. The edging rollers are sets of vertical rolls set opposite each other at either side of the sheet to insure that the width of the sheet is maintained. Descaling apparatus removes the scale that forms on the surface of the sheet by knocking it off mechanically or loosening it by means of an air blast or by bending the sheet sharply at some point in its travel. The completed coils of sheet are dropped on a conveyor and carried away to be annealed and cut into individual sheets.

Steel pipe is made by two methods. Cheaper grades of pipe are shaped by bending a flat strip or *skelp* of hot steel into cylindrical form and welding the edges to complete the pipe. For the smaller sizes of pipe, the edges of the skelp are usually overlapped and passed between a pair of rollers curved to correspond with the outside diameter of the pipe. The pressure on the rollers is great enough to weld the edges together. Seamless pipe or tubing is made from solid rods by passing them between a pair of inclined rollers which have a pointed mandrel set between them in such a way that it pierces the rods and forms the inside diameter of the pipe at the same time that the rollers are forming the outside diameter.

Other processes of steel fabrication, sometimes employed in steel mills, include forging, founding (qq.v.), and drawing the steel through dies (q.v.).

Wrought Iron. The process of making the tough, malleable alloy known as wrought iron differs markedly from other forms of steel making. Until comparatively recent years this process, known as *puddling,* required a great deal of hand labor, and it was impossible to produce wrought iron in tonnage quantities. The development of new processes involving the use of Bessemer converters and open-hearth furnaces has made possible the production of large quantities of wrought iron.

The puddling furnace has a low, arched roof and a depressed hearth on which the crude metal lies, separated by a wall from the combustion chamber in which bituminous coal is burned. The flame in the combustion chamber surmounts the wall, strikes the arched roof, and "reverberates" upon the contents of the hearth. After the furnace is lit and has become moderately heated, the puddler, or furnace operator, "fettles" it by plastering the hearth and walls with a paste of iron oxide, usually hematite ore. The furnace is then charged with about 600 pounds of pig iron and the door is closed. After about 30 minutes the iron is melted and the puddler adds more iron oxide or mill scale to the charge, working the oxide into the iron with a bent iron bar called a *raddle.* The silicon and most of the manganese in the iron are oxidized and some sulfur and phosphorus are eliminated. The temperature of the furnace is then raised slightly, resulting in the formation of carbon monoxide gas. As the gas is evolved the slag puffs up and the level of the charge rises. As the carbon is burned away the charge becomes more and more pasty, and finally the bath drops to its former level. About this time grains of nearly pure iron begin to form, and the puddler stirs the charge with the raddle to insure uniform composition and proper cohesion of the particles. When the action is completed, the resulting pasty, spongelike mass is separated into lumps, called balls, of about 180 to 200 pounds each. The balls are withdrawn from the furnace by means of tongs and are placed directly in a squeezer, a machine in which the greater part of the intermingled siliceous slag is expelled from the ball and the grains of pure iron are thoroughly welded together. After squeezing, the iron is cut into a number of flat pieces which are piled on each other, heated to welding temperature, and then rolled into a single piece. This rolling process is sometimes repeated to improve the quality of the product.

The modern technique of making wrought iron utilizes molten iron from a Bessemer converter and molten slag, which is usually prepared by melting iron ore, mill scale, and sand in an open-hearth furnace. The slag is maintained at a temperature several hundred degrees above its melting point and several hundred degrees below the melting point of the pig iron. When the molten iron, which carries large amount of gas in solution, is poured into a ladle containing molten slag, the metal solidifies almost instantly, releasing the dissolved gas. The force exerted by the gas shatters the metal into minute particles, which are heavier than the slag and accumulate in the bottom of the ladle, agglomerating into a spongy mass similar to the balls produced in a puddling furnace. After the slag has been poured off the top of the ladle, the ball of iron is removed and pressed, reheated, and rerolled.

Electric-Furnace Steel. The composition of the alloy steels used for cutlery, machine tools, and other specialized purposes must be rigidly controlled, for slight variation in the percentage of alloying elements may greatly alter the properties of the resulting alloy. Because of the complex chemical reactions of the open-hearth furnace, the composition of steel made by this process cannot precisely be governed. For this reason tools steels and other special steels are usually manufactured by electric furnaces; see ELECTRIC FURNACE. Formerly arc furnaces were generally used for steelmaking, but the induction furnace has been increasingly employed since the early 1930's. The electric furnace has several advantages for the controlled production of steel alloys, the most important of which is the absence of combustion gases which produce impurities in the steel. Steels refined in the electric furnace have an extremely low oxygen and sulfur content and their composition is governed almost entirely by the materials used. Prior to the introduction of the electric furnace, quality alloy steels were usually furnace-melted in graphite or clay crucibles. Steel scrap is generally used as the basic raw material for making alloy steels, but the electric furnace can also be used for the production of steel from pig iron. The other elements required in the alloys are supplied by the addition of such ferroalloys as ferromanganese and ferrochromium.

Types of Steel. Steel technologists and engineers have developed thousands of types of steel of different compositions suitable for specific uses. In general, steels with a low carbon content are used when ductility is desired, and steels with high carbon content when hardness is desired. Steels having between .04 and .12 percent of carbon are employed for drawing and stamping and for the manufacture of nails and rivets; steels having between .08 and .25 percent of carbon are used for general structural purposes and for machine parts; steels having between .25 and .50 percent of carbon are used for steel castings and for machine parts requiring hardening; steels with .45 to .75 percent of carbon for railroad rails and wheels and spring wire; steels with .75 to 1.25 percent of carbon for drills, cutting tools, and ball bearings; and steels with 1.25 to 2.25 percent of carbon for files, drawing dies, and tools subject to excessive abrasion.

A large group of special steels is described as *tool steels.* These alloys vary widely in composition and properties, but all possess the property of being hardened, by suitable heat treatment, for use in cutting operations. One of the most important types of tool steel is described generically as *high-speed steel.* Alloys which fall into this category retain their hardness even when subjected to high temperatures. The name "high-speed steel" refers to the ability to cut efficiently when used in lathes and other machine tools operating at high speeds. Most high-speed steels contain a large percentage of tungsten—sometimes as much as 18 percent—together with chromium, vanadium, and molybdenum.

Stainless steels are alloys which have a strong resistance to rusting and corrosion. The simplest stainless steels are alloys containing about 12 percent of chromium. By increasing the amount of chromium and adding nickel to the alloy, it is possible to make steel which also resists corrosion and scaling at high temperatures. An extremely thin layer of stable oxide which covers such steels gives them their corrosion resistance.

For properties of alloy steels see articles on the various alloying elements, including chromium, cobalt, manganese, molybdenum, nickel, silicon, tungsten, and vanadium.

Structure of Steel. The physical qualities of various types of steel and of any given steel alloy at varying temperatures depend entirely upon the crystalline structure of the metal. Prior to heat treatment all steels are a mixture of three substances: ferrite, pearlite (qq.v.), and cementite. Ferrite is iron containing small amounts of carbon and other elements in solution and is soft and ductile. Cementite, a compound of iron and a greater amount of carbon, is extremely brittle and hard. Pearlite is an intimate mixture of ferrite and cementite having a specific composition and characteristic structure, minimum melting point, and physical characteristics intermediate between its two constituents. The toughness and hardness of a given steel depend upon the varying percentages of these three ingredients. As the carbon content of a steel increases, the amount of ferrite present decreases and the amount of pearlite increases until, when the steel has .8 percent of carbon, it is entirely composed of pearlite. Steel with still more carbon is a mixture of pearlite and cementite, but very high-carbon steels before hardening are largely composed of ferrite in which particles of cementite are embedded. Raising the temperature of steel changes ferrite and pearlite to an allotropic form of iron-carbon alloy known as austenite, which has the property of dissolving all the free carbon present in the metal. If the steel is cooled slowly the austenite reverts to ferrite and pearlite, but if cooling is sudden, the austenite is "frozen" or changes to martensite, an extremely hard allotrope which resembles ferrite but which contains carbon in solid solution.

Heat Treatment of Steel. The basic process of hardening steel by heat treatment consists of heating the metal to a temperature at which austenite is formed — usually in the neighborhood of 1400° F. (760° C.) — and then cooling or *quenching* it rapidly in a water or oil bath. Such hardening treatments set up large internal strains in the metal and these are relieved by *tempering* or *annealing*, which consists of reheating the steel to a lower temperature and allowing it to cool gradually, usually in air.

Many variations of this basic process are practiced. Metallurgists have discovered that the change from austenitic to martensitic structure takes place during the latter part of the cooling period and that this change is accompanied by a change in volume which may crack the metal if the cooling is too swift. Three comparatively new processes have been developed to avoid such cracks. In *time-quenching* the steel is withdrawn from the quenching bath when it has reached the temperature at which the martensite begins to form, and is then cooled slowly in air. In *martempering* the steel is also withdrawn from the quench at the same point, and is then placed in a constant temperature bath until the transformation to martensite is complete before it is further cooled to room temperature. In *austempering* the steel is quenched in a bath of metal or salt held at a constant temperature equal to the temperature at which the structural change takes place and is held in this bath until the change is complete before being subjected to the final cooling.

Another method of heat treating steel to harden it is known as *casehardening*. In this process a finished piece of steel is given an extremely hard surface by heating it with carbon or nitrogen compounds; these compounds react with the steel, either raising the carbon content or forming nitrides in the surface layer of the steel. For *carburizing*, the piece is usually packed in charcoal or coke. *Cyaniding* consists of hardening in a bath of molten cyanide salt to form nitrides, and *nitriding* accomplishes the same result by heating the steel in an atmosphere of ammonia gas.

IRONWEED, common name of perennial herbs of the genus *Vernonia,* belonging to the Thistle family. The genus is native to N. North America and contains about ten species. Flowers of the genus, which are borne in cymes, produce disk-shaped heads surrounded by purple or white ray flowers. The fruit is a cylindrical, ribbed achene. The New York ironweed, *V. noveboracensis,* has purple or nearly purple heads. It grows on low ground on the coasts of E. United States and on the shore of Lake Erie. Illinois ironweed *V. illinoensis,* has reddish-purple flowers, and grows on the prairies of N.E. and central United States.

IRONWOOD, common name applied to a wide variety of trees or shrubs which have exceptionally hard or heavy wood, and to the wood itself. The name is applied generally to ebony, *Millettia,* and *Sideroxylon* (qq.v.), but is applied to scores of other trees in local usage. In Australia, for example, the name "ironwood" is applied primarily to members of the genus *Casuarina.* Important North American trees and bushes commonly called ironwood include buckwheat tree, hornbeam, leatherwood, mesquite, ocean spray

(qq.v.), and guaiacum. The black ironwood, *Krugiodendron ferreum,* a tree of the Buckthorn family which grows in Florida and the West Indies, is one of the few trees which produces wood that will not float in water.

IRONY (Gr. *eiron,* "a dissembler in speech"), in its original meaning in ancient Greece, a form of speech in which words are used to dissemble the true meaning of the speaker. One ancient form of irony, called Socratic irony, was used by the philosopher Socrates in his disputations with the Sophists; Socrates pretended ignorance in order, by skillful questioning, to make conspicuous the errors in reasoning of his opponents. Another ancient form, called dramatic irony, was a favorite device of the Greek dramatists, who put into the mouths of their characters words which had only a trifling import within the play but conveyed to the audience significant hints of the approaching tragic culmination of the drama. Subsequently, writers of all ages, including Shakespeare, have made use of both ancient forms of irony.

Through a later extension of its original meanings, irony, in speech and literature, has come to signify an expression in which words are employed to convey a meaning contrary to their literal sense, and by this means to express humor or ridicule. Shakespeare has made frequent use also of this form of irony. A notable example occurs in his play *Julius Cæsar*: Mark Antony, speaking of Cæsar who had been slain by Brutus and his fellow-conspirators, refers repeatedly to Cæsar's assassins as "honorable men", in such a way as to arouse his hearers' wrath against them. In another sense, as in the expression "the irony of fate", irony signifies an outcome of affairs or events contrary to, and as if in mockery of, the logical or anticipated outcome.

IROQUOIAN FAMILY, one of the most important linguistic families of the North American Indians, deriving its family name from that of the Iroquois (q.v.), and usually subdivided into two groups of tribes. The northern tribes, of which the Iroquois proper were the most important, ranged from the St. Lawrence R. and the shores of lakes Erie, Ontario, and Huron in the north, through eastern Pennsylvania as far south as Maryland. The southern tribes, of which the Cherokees (see CHEROKEE INDIANS) were the most important, lived in part of Virginia and in the Carolinas, Georgia, Tennessee, and Kentucky. The Tuscaroras (q.v.), originally a southeastern subdivision, moved north in the 18th century to join the Iroquois. Other important Iroquoian tribes scattered throughout this vast region were the Conestoga, Erie, and Huron (qq.v.).

The entire body of Iroquoian tribes, though displaying considerable diversity, shared certain cultural as well as linguistic characteristics. All were agricultural, with corn as their chief crop, and more or less sedentary. They lived in sizable towns, around which they erected log palisades, and which contained large communal houses. Tribal organization was totemic and matrilineal, with interlocking political and religious organizations of clans within tribes and tribes within large confederacies or leagues, of which that of the Iroquois was the most notable. All the Iroquoian tribes were skilled in war, and warfare was common and was carried on with great ferocity. A completely defeated tribe was never permitted to retain its autonomy, though in some cases defeated enemies were adopted by and incorporated into a conquering Iroquoian tribe.

IROQUOIS, an important confederacy of North American Indians of the Iroquoian Family (q.v.), founded in the 16th century in the region now included in central New York State. The original confederacy consisted of five tribes, the Mohawks, Onondagas, Cayugas, Oneidas, and Senecas (qq.v.), and was known as the Five Nations or the League of Five Nations. Sometime during the years between 1715 and 1722, however, the Tuscaroras (q.v.), an Iroquoian tribe originally of North Carolina, which had emigrated to New York, was formally admitted to the confederacy, and the name of the league was correspondingly changed to the Six Nations or the League of Six Nations. As representative members of the Iroquoian family, and the ones first encountered and later most intensively studied by white men, the Iroquois gave their name to the family of which they are a part.

The Iroquois followed an agricultural economy, based in the main upon corn, with supplementary crops of pumpkins and tobacco and later of orchard fruits such as apples and peaches. They made fine pottery, splint baskets, and mats of corn husk, and used wampum as a medium of exchange. Public records were woven into the designs of larger wampum belts. Each town contained several long, bark-covered communal houses, which had both tribal and political significance; along the inner sides of these houses the various families of a clan lived in semi-private compartments, and the central areas were used as social and political meeting places. The common council of the entire confederacy met in such a meeting place in a constituent town for their deliberations and ceremonies. These councils were fairly democratic in composition; delegates were elected by members of various lineages, and each delegate represented both a tribe and one of the matrilineal clans within a tribe. The office of delegate was restricted to chiefs, and every delegate had to meet the approval of both tribal and league councils. The league as a whole had no single head, and deliberative decisions were usually made by a unanimous vote of the league council.

The complexity and stability of this political organization, together with a carefully nurtured skill in warfare and the early acquirement of firearms, enabled the Iroquois to achieve and maintain a position of great power during the colonial period of American history. During their formative period in the 17th century they broke up the tribal confederacies to their west, notably that of the Hurons (q.v.), and continued the expansion of the territory under their dominion until by 1720 they had subdued all the tribes in a vast region extending from the Atlantic Ocean to the Mississippi R. and from the St. Lawrence R. to the Tennessee R.

In their relations with white men, the Iroquois from the start played the role of an independent power. During the colonial period they held the balance of power between the French and English, particularly in the area around the Canadian border. With few exceptions, chiefly those of the Mohawks and Cayugas, who came under the influence of French Jesuit missionaries, the Iroquois allied themselves with English interests. They bitterly opposed the extension of French settlement southward from Canada, and they were responsible for preventing the English colonies from being flanked on the west by the French.

At the outbreak of the American Revolution, the league council declared for neutrality, but allowed each of the six component tribes to take sides as it saw fit. Most of them, with the exception of the Oneidas and a part of the Tuscaroras, joined the British. After the Revolution the Mohawks, under their leader Joseph Brant (q.v.), crossed into Canada; they were followed in this emigration by the Cayugas, and both tribes were eventually settled on two reservations to the north of lakes Erie and Ontario. The Tuscaroras are scattered, though some hundreds have found a home among the Mohawks; most of the Oneidas are settled at Green Bay, Wis. and most of the Senecas in w. New York; Onondagas still hold their valley near Syracuse, N.Y. Despite their political importance, the Iroquois probably never exceeded 25,000 in number; at the present time they number about 6000.

IRRATIONAL NUMBERS. See RATIONAL NUMBERS.

IRRAWADDY, the principal river of Burma, formed N. of Myitkyina, Upper Burma, by the confluence of the Mali and Nmai rivers. From Myitkyina the river flows generally s. for about 1350 m.; it branches into several mouths near Henzada, forming an extensive delta, and empties into the Bay of Bengal. The largest tributary of the Irrawaddy is the Chindwin R.; other tributaries include the Mu and Myitnge. In Upper Burma the Irrawaddy traverses three narrow gorges, but s. of Mandalay, the chief city on its banks, the river ranges from 1 to 4 m. in width; it is navigable by shallow-draft steamers all the year round to Bhamo, a distance of almost 1000 m., providing the main means of communication between important points in the interior and the s. port cities, especially Rangoon. In addition to Mandalay, Bhamo, and Henzada, Irrawaddy ports include Katha, Myingyan, and Prome.

IRREDENTISM (It. *Italia irredenta,* "unredeemed Italy"), a term originally applied to a policy advocated in Italy in the 19th century, for the acquisition of foreign territories claimed as Italian because of previous Italian sovereignty over them or of ethnic affinity between the Italian people and the population of those regions. The territories so claimed included the city of Nice in France, the Mediterranean islands of Corsica and Malta, and the regions of Austria-Hungary and Switzerland with large Italian-speaking populations. The Italian irredentist movement originated about 1878, and was essentially a manifestation of the intensely nationalist movement which had succeeded in 1871, after decades of struggle, in creating a united Italian nation; see ITALY: *History.*

By extension, especially after World War I, the designation "irredentist" was applied to movements in other countries, for the inclusion within their national boundaries of areas of which those countries had been previously deprived. A number of the provisions of the Treaty of Versailles (1919), which redefined the boundaries of several European states, thereby laid the basis for irredentist claims.

A notable example of such claims was the movement in Hungary for the recovery of the province of Transylvania from Romania. Later examples include the Greek claims to southern Albania after World War II, and Yugoslav claims to Trieste, formerly belonging to Italy, and to Carinthia, formerly part of Austria. See sections on history in articles on these countries. See also IMPERIALISM.

IRRIGATION, the application of water to farmlands by artificial means. Irrigation is practiced in all parts of the world where the natural rainfall is insufficient to provide the water needed for plant growth. In certain areas, such as the southwestern U.S., not enough rain falls during the year to permit crop raising; in other areas the rainfall is inadequate during the growing season; and in certain cases growers of high-priced crops use irrigation as insurance against periods of drought. The custom of irrigating land is of very ancient origin. According to historical records irrigation was practiced by the Egyptians at least as early as 2000 B.C., and it is probable that the practice is even older. Many of the more primitive forms of irrigation, such as the bucket and the water wheel described below, are still in use.

In general irrigation can be divided into two types: irrigation using ordinary surface water such as the water of streams, rivers, and lakes; and irrigation employing subsurface water from wells. The general conditions of terrain and climate and the availability of water govern the type of irrigation used in a given locality.

Undoubtedly the earliest method of irrigation was manual: the farmer dipped a bucket into a stream and poured the water into small furrows or channels which he had dug through his fields. This laborious technique was soon supplanted by various mechanical devices which enabled the farmer to irrigate his fields with the expenditure of less energy. The simplest of such devices consists of a bucket set on one end of a counterweighted pole. By the use of this pole-and-bucket arrangement, which in Egypt is called a *shadoof,* the agriculturist is able to move a much greater volume of water than he can by his own unaided efforts. In many parts of the world water wheels are used for the same purpose. These consist of an endless chain of buckets or scoops arranged to run over pulleys. The buckets at the lower end of the chain dip into the stream and are raised up and tilt as they go around the upper pulley, discharging their contents into the system of irrigation canals or into a reservoir which feeds the canals. In some cases water wheels are driven by a man walking on a set of treadles and in others by draft animals turning a simple windlass.

Occasionally primitive farmers utilized the principle of Archimedes' screw to lift water from the stream to their fields. In most cases the device used consists of an inclined cylinder containing a helical partition or diaphragm running through its length. The lower portion of the cylinder is placed in the water and the upper portion is set over the reservoir of the irrigation system. When the cylinder is rotated, water is forced up through it along the screw and empties into the reservoir. Devices of this kind are commonly turned by animals. These primitive water-lifting devices have been supplanted by pumps, especially in technically advanced countries. They are, however, still found in many countries such as Egypt, India, and China.

All such devices as those described above are inefficient and labor-consuming, and since very early times men have endeavored to lighten the labor of irrigation by bringing the water to their fields by utilization of the force of gravity. Such irrigation is accomplished by building permanent works which either divert the flow of a stream or river, or raise its level to a point at which it is higher than the surrounding fields. The most important methods of accomplishing these ends are the use of canals and dams. If a canal is dug from a point some distance upstream from the field to be watered, it is possible to arrange the gradient so that the flow of water in the canal will be delivered to the field. The water level of streams is more often raised artificially by building dams or weirs behind which water rises to the desired height. Such dams also can act as reservoirs, impounding water in dry seasons, so that the farmers served by the dam can always be insured of an adequate supply. The dams used for irrigation range from simple earthen structures to enormous masonry dams such as Grand Coulee Dam in the State of Washington. See RECLAMATION.

In the distribution of irrigation water, two techniques are available. The water may be distributed over the entire cultivated area, allowed to stand until the ground is thoroughly impregnated, and then drained away; or the water may be led through the fields through small parallel channels or furrows from which it can percolate into the soil. The former system is particularly adapted to the use of flood waters which ordinarily occur only once a year, but the system using channels is far more flexible and far more common.

The use of wells for irrigation almost invariably requires the construction of a channel system similar to that outlined above. In some instances, however, two other forms of water distribution are employed: overhead irrigation, and subterranean irrigation. In overhead irrigation the water is carried in a system of sprinkler pipes which rise over the crops and which are arranged to spray the area on one or both sides of the pipes. Frequently in such systems, the sprinkler pipes are portable and can be moved from one part of the field to another. Portable systems of this kind require more work on the part of the farmer but are far cheaper than permanent installations to cover the entire irrigated area. Underground irrigation systems are made up of networks of perforated pipes which are buried below the surface of the fields at such a depth that the roots of the crops will not reach them. When water flows through the pipes it percolates into the soil and soaks upward into the root area. Underground irrigation systems are effective for some types of annual crops but are never used for the irrigation of fruit orchards or for any crops the roots of which might grow deep enough to enter the pipes and clog them.

In any irrigation system drainage (q.v.) is of the first importance. All natural surface fresh water contains a certain amount of dissolved salts which become injurious to plant life if they are concentrated. If no provision were made for the drainage of irrigated fields, the soil would soon become saturated with salts and be worthless for agriculture. Except in the case of loose or sandy soils which provide natural drainage, good irrigation practice demands the construction of suitable drain channels which are usually set parallel to the irrigation channels and between them.

Amount of Water. The calculation of the amount of water needed for adequate irrigation is of vital importance not only to individual farmers who are irrigating their land but also to governmental and other agencies which are planning irrigation projects, dams, and similar public works. Approximately 300 to 500 lb. of water are needed annually to produce 1 lb. of dry crop. Besides this minimal requirement, allowance must be made for evaporation from the soil, for runoff of water on the surface, and for the percolation of water in the ground to depths below the growing zone of the crops. The entire amount

Stockton Chamber of Commerce; State Crop Growers' Association

MODERN IRRIGATION. *Top: A concrete-lined irrigation canal in San Joaquin County, California. Bottom, left: Field of sugar beets irrigated by general flooding of the area. Bottom, right: Irrigated field with canals between each furrow.*

of water required (that needed by the plants and that needed to offset the losses inherent in the nature of the soil, the type of terrain, and the irrigation system itself) is known as the *duty of water*. The duty of water is usually expressed in terms of the number of acres which can be irrigated by a "second-foot", that is, a flow of 1 cubic foot of water per second. A second-foot of water is sufficient to cover an area of 100 acres 21.6 in. deep in the course of 90 days, which is about the length of the average crop-growing season. The duty of water varies within quite wide limits, but the figure of 100 acres per second-foot is often taken as an average in the irrigated areas of western U.S. In deciding the values of farm land in districts where irrigation is necessary the duty of water and the water supply available are the most important factors. Among the principal irrigated farm products are forage crops, potatoes, cotton, rice, sugar cane, fruits, berries, and grains. Irrigated farms produce nearly twice the average farm yield. When combined with other methods of soil management, irrigation may yield as much as three times the average farm production. See SOILS and SOIL MANAGEMENT.

IRRITABILITY, property of responding to environmental changes, possessed by all living cells, tissues, and organisms. Irritability is one of the primary characteristics of living things; see LIFE. The protoplasm which comprises living matter responds to the stimuli of environmental change in various ways, such as change in shape, initiation of movement, cessation of movement, or change in rate of growth. Irritability may be temporarily lost; during such a period the protoplasm is said to be in a state of *rigor*. Loss of irritability can be caused by fatigue, which is the result of prolonged or repeated stimulation, or by unfavorable conditions, such as insufficient moisture, abnormally low or high temperature, or lack of oxygen. Anesthesia (q.v.), used in medical and surgical treatment, is essentially a partial or complete temporary loss of irritability of all or part of the nervous system. All healthy protoplasm is capable of temporary loss of irritability and subsequent recovery; when irritability is permanently lost, however, the protoplasm is dead.

A given stimulus does not produce an equal reaction in all cells, tissues, or organisms. Stimuli applied to plants, which do not have nervous systems, generally evoke a reaction only after the lapse of a long period of time. However, in plants of the genus *Mimosa,* called sensitive plants (q.v.), the reaction to

such stimuli as touch or the approach of heat may be completed in a few seconds. In higher animals, all of which possess nervous systems, the irritability of all but very localized areas of living tissue is controlled by the nervous system. Irritability reactions are much more noticeable in animals than plants because nerve cells of animals possess the unique property of producing the same reaction regardless of the intensity of the stimulus, whereas plant cells react in proportion to the stimulus. Irritability reactions controlled by the portion of the nervous system called the *autonomic nervous system* (q.v.), may be confined to local areas of the body; reactions of the *central nervous system,* however, affect parts of the body other than that to which the stimulus is applied; see NERVOUS SYSTEM.

All activity of any living thing results from response to stimuli, but such irritability is usually the result of highly involved complexes of stimuli which are exceedingly difficult to analyze. Most plants, for example, respond to gravity by producing roots which grow in the direction of gravitational pull and stems which grow in the direction away from gravitational pull; stems of some slender, herbaceous plants, however, respond to gravity only in the presence of light, and lie prostrate in the dark; see TROPISM.

IRULAS (Tamil, *irul,* "darkness"), a dark-skinned tribe living in the forests of s. India among the Nilgiri Hills (q.v.) and speaking a corrupt form of the Tamil language (see INDIAN LANGUAGES). The tribe contains about 85,000 members, all in a primitive state of culture. The Irulas worship Vishnu, though their religious thought and ceremonies are of the simplest kind; marriage rites, for example, have little religious significance, consisting almost entirely of a feast. Other Indian peoples, however, ascribe certain supernatural powers to the Irulas despite their backwardness and poverty, and they are popular as fortunetellers.

IRVING, SIR HENRY, assumed name of JOHN HENRY BRODRIBB (1838–1905), English actor and theatrical manager, born in Keinton-Mandeville, Somerset, and educated in London. He made his first appearance on the stage at Sunderland in 1856, playing the part of Gaston, Duke of Orleans, in *Richelieu,* by Sir Edward Bulwer-Lytton. At that time he began to use the name of Henry Irving, and later adopted it by royal license. After touring the provinces of England for ten years, Irving began to appear in plays in London in 1866; in 1870 he gave his first notably popular performance as Digby Grant in *The Two Roses,* by James Albery. Later, Irving was engaged by the Lyceum Theatre, with which he continued to be associated as an actor for thirty years, and as manager from 1878 to 1899. Irving's regime as manager at the Lyceum was notable for the artistry of his productions, particularly of Shakespeare's plays, and the distinction of his acting company, the leading lady of which for twenty-two years was Ellen Terry (q.v.). The originality of his interpretation as an actor of the tragic Shakespearean roles of Shylock, Richard III, Hamlet, Macbeth, Othello, Iago, and King Lear aroused both criticism and great admiration. Some critics contended that his pronounced idiosyncrasies of voice and manner detracted from the value of his interpretations; others pointed out that his success in creating vivid characters more than made up for any mannerisms. Irving also met with great success in the title role of *Becket* (1893), by Alfred, Lord Tennyson. He was knighted in 1895. Irving made eight acting tours in the United States between 1883 and 1904. He died on tour at Bradford, England, and was buried in Westminster Abbey. He wrote and delivered many lectures on his profession, a number of which were collected and published in book form in *The Stage* (1878), *English Actors* (1886), and *The Drama* (1893).

IRVING, WASHINGTON (1783–1859), American author, born in New York City. He studied law at private schools and, after serving in several law offices and traveling in Europe for his health from 1804 to 1806, was eventually admitted to the bar in the latter year; but his interest in the law was neither deep nor long-lived, and he began to contribute satirical essays and sketches to New York newspapers as early as 1802. A group of these pieces, written from 1802 to 1803 and collected under the title *Letters of Jonathan Oldstyle, Gent.,* won for Irving his earliest literary recognition. From 1807 to 1808 he was the leading figure in a social group including his brothers William and Peter and his brother-in-law J.K. Paulding; together, they wrote *Salmagundi, or, the Whim-Whams and Opinions of Launcelot Langstaff, Esq., and Others,* a series of satirical essays and poems on New York society. Irving's contributions to this miscellany established his reputation as an essayist and wit, and this reputation was enhanced by his next work, *A History of New York* (1809), ostensibly written by Irving's famous comic creation, the Dutch-Amer-

Sir Henry Irving

ican scholar Diedrich Knickerbocker. The *History* professes to be an account of New York during the period of Dutch occupation; actually, it is a whimsical satire on the pedantry of antiquarians and a conservative Federalist critique of Jeffersonian democracy. Generally considered to be the first important contribution to American comic literature, and a great popular success from the start, it brought Irving considerable fame and financial reward.

In 1815 he went to Liverpool, England, as a silent partner in his brothers' commercial firm. When, after a series of losses, the business went into bankruptcy in 1818, Irving turned to writing for a living. In England he became the intimate friend of several leading men of letters, including Thomas Campbell, Sir Walter Scott, and Thomas Moore. Under the pseudonym of Geoffrey Crayon he wrote the essays and short stories collected in the *Sketch Book* (1820), his most popular work, which was widely acclaimed for its geniality, grace, and humor both in England and the United States. Two of the stories, *Rip Van Winkle* and *The Legend of Sleepy Hollow,* are classics in American literature (q.v.).

From 1826 until 1829 he was a member of the staff of the U.S. legation in Madrid, Spain. During this period and after his return to England he wrote several historical works, the most popular of which was the *History of Christopher Columbus* (1828). Another well-known work of this period was *The Alhambra* (1832), a series of sketches and stories based upon Irving's residence in 1829 in an ancient

Washington Irving

Moorish palace at Granada, Spain. In 1832, after an absence which had lasted seventeen years, he returned to America, where he was welcomed as a national figure.

In 1842 he was appointed U.S. minister to Madrid, where he lived until 1846, continuing his historical researches and writing. He returned to the United States again in 1846, settling at *Sunnyside,* his country home near Tarrytown, N. Y.; there he spent his remaining years, the acknowledged leader of American literature.

To his contemporaries, Irving was of particular importance as the first American writer to obtain real recognition in England. His popular but elegant style, based upon that of Joseph Addison and Oliver Goldsmith (qq.v.), and the ease and picturesque fancy of his best work commanded an international audience. To a certain extent his romantic attachment to Europe resulted in thinness and overrefinement of material; much of his work deals directly with English life and customs, and he never attempted to come to terms with the democratic American life of his time. On the other hand, American writers were encouraged by Irving's example to look beyond America for subject matter. He was also the discoverer, for Americans at least, of the effectiveness of the short story as a form of art.

Among his other works are *Bracebridge Hall* (1822), *Tales of a Traveller* (1824), *A Chronicle of the Conquest of Granada* (1829),

The Crayon Miscellany (1835), *Oliver Goldsmith* (1849), and *Life of Washington* (5 vols., 1855–59).

IRVINGTON, town of Essex Co., N.J., adjoining Newark on the s.w. It is a residential and manufacturing center, with diversified industries. Among the principal manufactures are chemicals, hardware, machine tools, jewelry, optical goods, plastics, paints and varnishes, writing materials, sporting goods, and toys. Founded in 1692, the town was known as Camptown for 160 years. It was renamed (1852) in honor of the American author Washington Irving. Irvington was incorporated in 1898. Pop. (1950) 59,201.

ISAAC (Heb., "laughter"), in the Old Testament, one of the Hebrew patriarchs, son of Abraham and Sarah when they were 100 and 90 years old, respectively. In the Book of Genesis, the Biblical account relates that Abraham prefers Isaac to his half-brother Ishmael (q.v.), son of Abraham and Hagar, because Isaac is the child of Abraham's "true" wife, Sarah. Abraham yields to Sarah's request that Ishmael and Hagar be driven into the wilderness. While he is still young, Isaac is taken by Abraham in obedience to divine prompting, to be sacrificed on Mount Moriah, but God intervenes and provides a ram as a substitute, telling Abraham to spare Isaac, and promising to make the boy the father of a great nation. Later, Isaac has two sons, Esau and Jacob, and prefers the former to the latter, but, when blind, is tricked by Jacob into giving the latter his blessing. Isaac lived to an age of 180 years.

Archeologists and Bible scholars have drawn several parallels between the Biblical narrative and the history of the Semitic tribes. Abraham is thought to represent the original nomadic stock out of which the Hebrew and Edomite tribes separated; see JEWS: *History.* Isaac is believed to represent the tribes that joined to form the Hebrew confederacy and to give allegiance to the God, Yahweh, or Jehovah, originally a tribal deity; and Ishmael is believed to represent the tribes of Edom. Isaac was a relatively minor figure compared to the other two great Biblical patriarchs, Abraham, his father, and Jacob (qq.v.), his son; but a number of the details of the Biblical account are believed by scholars to have major symbolic importance. The story of his birth is believed to be a deliberate attempt by early Hebrew writers to alter the traditions of the Semitic tribes in order to strengthen adherence to the Hebrew confederacy, a military and political alliance, by suggesting that it had divine inspiration. In making Isaac the legitimate son, and Ishmael the illegitimate son, of their common ancestor, the Hebrews claimed superiority over the independent Edomite tribes. Finally, the rivalry between Isaac's two sons is thought to reflect again the rivalry between Edom and the Hebrews.

ISABELLA I (1451–1504), Queen of Castile, known as the Catholic. She was the daughter of John II, King of Castile and León, by his second wife, the Infanta Isabella of Portugal. In 1469 the Princess married Ferdinand of Aragon (see FERDINAND, known as *the Catholic*), and on the death of her brother Henry IV, in 1474, Isabella and Ferdinand, jointly, succeeded to the throne of Castile and León. A war with Portugal was terminated in Isabella's favor in 1479, and the same year Ferdinand succeeded to the throne of Aragon as Ferdinand V. This union of the two chief Spanish kingdoms laid the foundation of Spain's future greatness. Toward the end of the campaign against the Moors of Granada, in 1492, the Queen of Castile earned her greatest title to fame by her acquiescence in the plans of Columbus, who was then a suppliant at court.

ISABELLA II (1830–1904), Queen of Spain from 1833 to 1868, daughter of Ferdinand VII by his fourth wife, born in Madrid. By a decree which set aside the Salic Law in Spain, the Infanta Isabella ascended the throne on the death of her father in September, 1833, her mother being appointed Queen Regent. An insurrection in favor of her uncle, Don Carlos, raged with great violence until 1840, when the cause of the court triumphed. In 1846 the Queen married her cousin, Don Francisco d'Assisi, elder son of Ferdinand VII's youngest brother. In September, 1868, a revolution broke out, headed by Francisco Serrano, Juan Prim y Prats, and Juan Topete y Carballo, ending in the formation of a Republican provisional government and the flight of Isabella to France. In 1870 she abdicated in favor of her son, Alfonso XII, who succeeded to the throne in 1875. See SPAIN.

ISABEY, EUGÈNE LOUIS GABRIEL (1804–86), French landscape and marine painter, born in Paris, the son and the pupil of the French miniaturist Jean Baptiste Isabey. In 1830 he accompanied the French expedition to Algiers as royal marine painter. Later he settled in Paris, distinguishing himself in painting by his bold, dramatic treatment of seascapes with shipwrecks and stormy skies. Typical examples are "Hurricane at Dieppe" and "The Old Barks" at the Versailles Museum, "Burning of the Steamer Austria" at the Bordeaux Museum, and his best-known work "Embarkation of De Ruyter and De Witt" at the Luxembourg, Paris.

ISAIAH, ISAIAS, or **ESAIAS,** one of the Books of the Bible, in the Old Testament. The Book recounts events in the life and the teachings of the prophet Isaiah. It is one of the longest and greatest of the prophetic Books, believed by most modern scholars to be a composite work written by perhaps six, or more, authors. The greater part of the Book was probably written after the Babylonian Exile; see JEWS: *History*. It has two main parts, Chapters 1 to 39 and Chapters 40 to 66, each divided into sections. The first part has four principal sections. Chapters 1 to 12 tell of the alliance of Israel, the northern Hebrew kingdom, with Syria against Judah, the southern Hebrew kingdom; and how Isaiah warned that Israel, as well as Judah, was endangered by Syria. They also contain a description by Isaiah of the Messiah (q.v.) as the perfect ruler, and a lyric in praise of Yahweh or Jehovah. Chapters 13 to 23 are a collection of ten prophecies about the nations bordering Israel and Judah, predicting the fall of those nations. Chapters 24 to 35 contain prophecies by Isaiah of the judgment to be passed on the whole world, except the Hebrews, and include a description of the Messianic age. Chapters 36 to 39 contain commentary on the events related in the discourses of Isaiah. The second part of the Book of Isaiah has three principal sections. Chapters 40 to 48 set forth the hope of the Hebrew exiles after the fall of Babylon. Chapters 49 to 55 indicate the difficulties encountered in the reorganization of the kingdom of Judah, and relate how Isaiah exhorted the Babylonian Jews to return to their homeland. Finally, in chapters 56 to 66 Isaiah asserts that the difficulties of the Jews are no longer owing to outside oppressors, but to the wickedness of the people; and describes his attempt to rekindle religious fervor through promises of salvation.

It is the opinion of most modern scholars that only a small proportion of the discourses in the Book of Isaiah emanated from the prophet Isaiah, who was born into an aristocratic family of Jerusalem about 760 B.C. and died about 700 or 690 B.C. They also believe that none of the discourses attributed to him were preserved in their original form. Never--

theless, the spirit of the discourses is ascribable to him, and is probably also typical of a number of lesser prophets who followed him. The great importance of Isaiah to subsequent Jewish and Christian thought is twofold. He dispelled the confusion and abated the desperation of the Hebrew people at a time when they were beset by powerful enemies, with the first consistent references to the coming of the Messiah, thus preparing the way for the later acceptance of Jesus as the Saviour. He also countered the prevalent warlike spirit of his time with the first moving assertion of a God of love and mercy, as opposed to a God of vengeance, thus laying the basis for the development of a theology which emphasizes personal responsibility for moral action, rather than sacrifice to and appeasement of God.

The grandeur of Isaiah's conceptions, his uncompromising emphasis on ethical principles, the vigor of his style, and his command of invective, sarcasm, and irony, mark him as one of the most powerful and gifted of Hebrew prophets. His admonition that only through righteous conduct can a people be saved made less impression on his own generation than on those of the exilic and postexilic periods; but his fervor and inspiration were largely responsible for the preservation of the Hebrew faith during the Babylonian Exile, and later, during the long dispersion in the Christian era.

ISÈRE, department of France, situated in the S.E. section of the country and comprising part of the former province of Dauphiné. Several spurs of the Alps occupy the S. portion of Isère; the terrain in the N. is generally flat. The department is watered by the Rhone R., which partially bounds it in the W. and N., and by the Isère, the Drac, and Romanche rivers. Agriculture is the principal occupation, and grains, grapes, mulberries, chestnuts, and tobacco are raised. The mining of coal and iron, and the manufacture of cement, gloves, paper, silk goods, and metalware are other industries. Grenoble, the capital, and Vienne (qq.v.) are the chief towns. Area, 3178 sq.m.; pop. (1952 est.) 596,000.

ISEULT. See TRISTRAM.

ISFAHAN, formerly ISPAHAN (anc. *Aspadana*), city and capital of the province of the same name, Iran, situated on the N. bank of the Zayinda Rud, at the junction of roads extending to Teheran, Yezd, and Shiraz. The city is a trading and industrial center, with extensive bazaars and with factories producing leather goods, textiles, ceramics, lacquer ware, silver filigree, and other metal work. Local manufactures and agricultural products comprise the city's principal articles of trade.

Isfahan was renowned in former times for its architectural grandeur and for the beauty of its public gardens. Most of the gardens and many of the edifices, which included nearly 2000 caravanseries, almost 300 public baths, over 160 mosques, and several palaces, are now in ruins, but a number of imposing structures have been preserved or restored. In the central part of the city is the Masjid-i-Shah, a royal mosque completed in 1611. Faced with colored, enameled tile, it is authoritatively regarded as one of the world's most magnificent edifices. Maidan-i-Shah, a rectangular garden 3360 ft. long and 1044 ft. wide, adjoins the royal mosque. Nearby is another mosque (built in 1621), famous for the beauty of its interior mosaics and painted tiles. The central plaza affords access also to Hasht Behesht ("Eight Paradises"), the former royal palace of Persia (now Iran). The throneroom, Chihil Si-Tun ("Hall of Forty Columns"), is one of the features of this structure. Additional points of interest in Isfahan include the Cathedral mosque, or Masjid-i-Jami, notable for its dome chambers, especially one dating from 1088; the Madrassa Mader-i-Shah Sultan Hussein, a magnificent building constructed (1710) as a school for dervishes and mullahs; several bridges spanning the Zayinda Rud, including a 17th-century structure with galleries and arcades; and remnants of the walls that formerly surrounded the city.

The origins of Isfahan are obscure. In legendary accounts it is variously described as having been founded by the eponymous hero of the Persian people and by some of the Jews who were led into captivity by the Chaldean king Nebuchadrezzar. As *Aspadana*, the city formed part of ancient Media (q.v.). Occupied by invading Arabs about the middle of the 7th century, it became one of the most prosperous commercial centers of Islam. The Mongol conqueror Tamerlane captured the city in 1387, during his invasion of Persia, and reputedly massacred 70,000 of the inhabitants.

During the reign of the Persian shah Abbas I (1557?–1628) Isfahan was made the national capital. Under his patronage the city attained the peak of its growth, commercial prosperity, and architectural splendor. According to an unofficial estimate the population then numbered at least 600,000. Invading Afghans captured Isfahan in 1722, and the seat of the Persian government was removed to Shiraz. The Afghans were expelled in 1729, but the city never fully recovered from the dislocations consequent on their occupation.

Isfahan Province, situated in the central part of Iran, is generally mountainous. Farming is the chief occupation; the principal crops are cereals, cotton, the opium poppy, and tobacco. Area of province, 100,000 sq.m.; pop., about 1,400,000. Pop. of city (1949 est.) 192,000.

ISHBOSHETII. See SAUL.

ISHMAEL, in Biblical history, the elder son of Abraham and the reputed ancestor of a group of Arabian tribes. His story is related in Genesis 16, 21, and 25 as follows. Ishmael's mother was Hagar, Egyptian handmaid to Abraham's wife Sarah, who was barren. About thirteen years later, in answer to her prayers, Sarah conceived and was delivered of a son, Isaac. Having satisfied Abraham with issue, Sarah demanded that Hagar and Ishmael be put out of the house. Hagar and her son thereupon fled to the s. Ishmael settled in the wilderness, married an Egyptian woman, and became the progenitor of twelve tribes of desert nomads. The region occupied by these *Ishmaelites* included most of central and N. Arabia. The Mohammedans regard themselves as the descendants of Ishmael, but maintain that Hagar was the true wife of Abraham, and Ishmael his favored son. They further contend that Ishmael, not Isaac, was offered to be sacrificed by Abraham, and transfer the scene of the intended sacrifice from Moriah, in Palestine, to Mt. Ararat, near Mecca.

ISHTAR, the chief goddess of the Babylonians and the Assyrians, and the counterpart of Astarte (q.v.), a Phenician goddess. The name appeared in different forms in every part of the ancient Semitic world; thus it was Athtar in Arabia, Astar in Abyssinia, and Ashtart in Canaan and Israel. The sex of the divinity also varied, since Athtar and Astar were male deities. Ishtar of Erech (in Babylonia) was a goddess worshiped in connection with the evening star, but Ishtar of Akkad was a god identified with the morning star. As a goddess, Ishtar was the Great Mother, the goddess of fertility and the queen or mistress of heaven. On the other hand, her character had destructive attributes; she was considered, especially by the Assyrians, a goddess of hunting and war, and was depicted with sword, bow, and quiver of arrows. Among the Babylonians, Ishtar was distinctly the mother goddess and was portrayed either naked and with prominent breasts, or as a mother with a child at her breast. As goddess of love she brought destruction to many of her lovers, of whom the most notable was her consort Tammuz (q.v.), the Babylonian counterpart of Adonis (q.v.).

ISIDORE OF SEVILLE, SAINT, or ISIDORUS HISPALENSIS (560?–636), Spanish ecclesiastic and scholar, born probably in Cartagena. He became archbishop of Seville in 600, and was an influential member of the ecclesiastical councils held at Toledo (610 and 633) and Seville (619), which reorganized the Christian Church in Spain. He was known as the most learned scholar of his day; his greatest work was the *Originum seu Etymologiarum Libri XX* (622–33), an encyclopedic work in twenty volumes, which contains evidence of his extensive reading in many fields of knowledge.

ISIS, in ancient Egyptian religious mythology, the goddess of fertility and motherhood. According to the Egyptian belief (see EGYPTIAN RELIGION), she was the daughter of Keb and Nut ("Earth" and "Sky"), the sister-wife of Osiris, judge of the dead, and the mother of Horus, god of day. After the end of the New Kingdom in the 4th century B.C. (see EGYPT: *History*), the center of Isis-worship, which was then reaching its greatest peak, was on Philæ, an island in the Nile River, where a great temple was built to her during the XXXth Dynasty. Ancient myths described Isis as having great magical skill; and she was represented as human in form though she was frequently described as wearing the horns of a cow. Her personality was believed to resemble that of Athor, the goddess of love and gaiety.

The cult of Isis spread from Alexandria throughout the Hellenic world after the 4th century B.C. It appeared in Greece in combination with the cults of Horus, her son, and Serapis (q.v.), the Greek name for Osiris. The Greek historian Herodotus identified Isis with Demeter (q.v.), the Greek goddess of earth, agriculture, and fertility. The tripartite cult of Isis, Horus, and Serapis was later introduced into Rome by the consul Lucius Cornelius Sulla (q.v.) in 86 B.C., and became one of the most popular branches of Roman religious mythology. It later received a bad reputation through the licentiousness of some of its priestly rites, and subsequent consuls made efforts to suppress or limit Isis worship. The cult died out in Rome after the institution of Christianity, and the last remaining Egyptian temples to Isis were closed in the middle of the 6th century A.D.

ISLÂM, or (Ar.) Eslam, the proper name of the Mohammedan religion, designating complete and entire submission of body and soul to God, His will and His service, as well as to all those articles of faith, commands, and ordinances revealed to and ordained by Mohammed the prophet. See Mohammedanism.

ISLAND, any comparatively small body of land completely surrounded by water. From the geographical point of view the only difference between an island and a continent is in size. The smallest continent is Australia with an area of about 2,974,000 square miles, and the largest island is Greenland, with an area of 827,300 square miles. From the biological point of view islands differ from continents in that their isolation controls the number and variety of animal and plant species found on islands, and frequently two islands comparatively near each other have very different flora and fauna; see Geographical Distribution.

Islands are formed in a number of ways. Islands close to the shores of continents may be created when the continental coastline subsides, leaving islands which were formerly the peaks of coastal mountains. Such islands are found off the coasts of Maine, Norway, and Scotland. Subsidence may also cut off comparatively large land masses such as those of the British Isles, Sicily, and Japan. Islands are also sometimes formed at the mouths of large rivers as a part of the formation of deltas; see Delta. Islands in the deeper part of the ocean may be formed by the emergence of the peaks of subterranean mountain ranges, and such islands are frequently enlarged by the deposition of coral reefs; see Coral Reefs. In some cases the original island has submerged far below the surface, and the entire visible structure is composed of coral. A number of oceanic islands are of volcanic origin, such as the Azores and the Hawaiian Islands.

The ten largest islands in the world are: Greenland, 827,300 sq.m.; New Guinea, 316,-861 sq.m.; Borneo, 290,012 sq.m.; Madagascar, 228,642 sq.m.; Baffin Island, 211,000 sq.m.; Sumatra, 167,620 sq.m.; Honshu (Japan), 89,009 sq.m.; Great Britain, 84,186 sq.m.; Victoria (Canada), 80,340 sq.m.; and Ellesmere Island, 77,392 sq.m.

ISLAND NUMBER TEN, BATTLE OF, a military engagement of the American Civil War, fought during the late winter and early spring of 1862 in and around Island Number Ten, situated in the Mississippi R., N.W. Ten-

nessee. The battle was joined when a task force of Union gunboats, operating upstream of the island, opened a bombardment of the island's Confederate garrison, about 7000 men belonging to the army of Gen. Pierre Beauregard. Confederate fortifications on the w. bank of the river opposite the island were reduced early in the action by Union troops under the command of Gen. John Pope, who then succeeded in crossing the river. Meanwhile, Union warships ran the gauntlet of Confederate batteries on the island, cutting off the sole avenue of retreat of the Confederate forces. On April 8 the Confederate garrison on Island Number Ten was surrendered by Gen. W. W. Mackall, its commandant. Island Number Ten disappeared, in the course of time, as the result of the eroding action of the Mississippi R.

ISLANDS OF LANGERHANS. See Pancreas.

ISLAY. See Plum.

ISLE OF MAN. See Man, Isle of.

ISLE OF THANET. See Thanet, Isle of.

ISLE ROYALE NATIONAL PARK, a national park in Keweenaw Co., Mich., established in 1940. It contains Isle Royale, largest island in Lake Superior. The island is about 45 m. in length, has a maximum width of 9 m., and is noted for its extensive forests containing varieties of wildlife no longer common to the mainland. Moose, beaver, minks, lynxes, and coyotes are among the animals found within the park, in addition to numerous species of birds. Fish, especially brook trout, perch, and pickerel, are abundant. The park also contains prehistoric copper mines of unknown origin, and many artifacts of the Stone Age. Semiprecious stones, including Thompsonite and other zeolites, and agate, are found at Thompsonite Beach. The park area covers about 133,700 acres.

ISLETA, a Pueblo Indian tribe of Tanoan (q.v.) stock, living on the west bank of the Rio Grande River about 10 miles s. of Albuquerque, N.M. The pueblo which it inhabits contains one of the three largest settlements of Pueblo Indians, ranking after Zuñi and Laguna (qq.v.), and containing a total population of about 1350. The Isleta Indians are peaceable and industrious, and even under U.S. authority (their pueblo has been secured to them as the Isleta Indian Reservation) have been entirely self-supporting. A branch of the tribe has been established under mission auspices at Isleta del Sur, a small pueblo on the north bank of the Rio Grande, located about 14 m. below El Paso, Tex.

ISLEWORTH. See HESTON AND ISLEWORTH.

ISLIP, a township of Suffolk Co., N.Y., situated on the s. shore of Long Island. It comprises various villages, including Sayville, Bayport, Oakdale, East Islip, Central Islip, Brentwood, and West Islip, and covers an area of about 16 m. in length and 8 m. in width. Also included in the township is Fire Island (q.v.). Islip is a noted summer-resort center, and contains many large estates, excellent bathing beaches, and facilities for yachting, golfing, and other sports. The principal industries are dairying, oystering, clamming, and fishing. The township of Islip was incorporated in 1710, and is the site of several private preparatory schools, and two State hospitals for the insane. Pop. (1950) 71,-465.

ISMAILIA, town of the Canal administrative division, Egypt, located on the N.W. shore of Lake Timsah, 93 m. by rail N.E. of Cairo and about 50 m. from the Mediterranean Sea. It was laid out in 1863 under the supervision of Ferdinand de Lesseps, French promoter of the Suez Canal, as part of the Canal project. The town was named for Ismail Pasha, Khedive of Egypt (1863–79). Pop. (1947) 53,594.

ISMAIL PASHA or **ISMAIL I** (1830–95), viceroy and khedive of Egypt, second son of the military leader Ibrahim Pasha (q.v.), born in Cairo, and educated in Paris. He succeeded his uncle, the viceroy Said Pasha, in 1863. Four years later the sultan of Turkey granted him the title of khedive, with the right to pass the title to his son. Ismail thereupon embarked on a large program of public works and administrative reforms. As a result the government debt rose from £3,000,000 in 1863 to £100,000,000 in 1874. As the financial situation of the government became worse, France and Great Britain assumed control of Egyptian finances. Ismail was compelled to abdicate in favor of his son Tewfik Pasha in 1879, and subsequently lived in retirement in Naples and in his palace near Constantinople (now Istanbul).

ISOCRATES (436–338 B.C.), an Athenian orator and rhetorician. He was a pupil and follower of the philosophers Socrates and Plato (qq.v.); in his dialogue *Phædrus*, the latter characterized Isocrates as a youth of great promise. During the reign of the Thirty Tyrants in Athens (see GREECE: *Ancient History*), Isocrates absented himself from the city and established a school of rhetoric on the Ionian island of Chios. He returned about 403 B.C. and worked for a decade writing legal speeches for clients. After 392 he founded a school near the Lyceum (q.v.), in which he taught young men from all parts of the Greek-speaking world the arts of writing essays and of oratory. The subject matter was derived from the political issues of the day, and the instruction was characterized by a breadth and an elevation of moral tone which set it apart from the mere ingenuity and specious effectiveness of the Sophists (q.v.), his rivals among teachers of rhetoric and disputation. Isocrates' illustrious pupils included the orators Hyperides, Isæus, and Lycurgus (q.v.). Isocrates persistently advocated the unification of the Greek city-states in a strong alliance against the threat of a Persian invasion. He advanced the hope of a union between Athens and Sparta in his famous speech *Panegyricus* (380 B.C.). When he failed to influence the city-states to unite, Isocrates urged various eminent military men to assume the leadership of the Greeks in a war against Persia. The *Philippus* (346 B.C.) is such an appeal to Philip of Macedon. The *Aeropagiticus* and *On the Peace* (both 355 B.C.) deal with Athenian politics and the waning of Greek democracy.

Including those already mentioned, the extant works of Isocrates number twenty-one speeches and nine letters. The letters deal with such varied topics as education, the art of speaking, the power of beauty, counsel to despots, and appeals to leaders, and include *Against the Sophists* (391–390 B.C.), *Encomium on Helen* (370), *Archidamus* (366), *Antidosis* (353), and *Panathenaicus* (339). Isocrates, pre-eminent as a rhetorician, also occupies a distinguished place in the history of Attic prose. His style is marked by flowing cadence, complex sentence structure, and frequent use of antithesis. The standards set by Isocrates were followed by the Greek orator Demosthenes, and the Roman orator Cicero (qq.v.), through whom the influence of Isocrates was transmitted to the literature of modern Europe.

ISOETACEAE. See QUILLWORT.

ISOGAMY. See GAMETE.

ISOMETRIC PERSPECTIVE. See DRAFTING.

ISOMORPHISM. See CRYSTAL.

ISOPODA, an order of crustaceans in the subclass Malacostraca, containing many small aquatic and some terrestrial species, the best known of which are the wood louse and gribble (qq.v.). Isopods are small, flat, oval animals which, unlike other crustaceans such as crabs and lobsters, have no carapace (horny shield covering the body). The body is made up of seven free thoracic segments, each of which is equipped with a pair of legs. Many species are parasitic on fish or on other crustaceans.

ISOPTERA. See TERMITE.

ISOSPONDYLI. See FISH: *Classification.*

ISOSTASY. See GEOLOGY: *Formation of Mountains.*

ISOTOPES, forms of an element having the same atomic number but different atomic weights. Isotopes of the same element differ from each other only in the number of neutrons in the nucleus. The configuration of electrons around the nucleus is the same for all isotopes of a single element; hence their chemical properties are identical. See ATOM AND ATOMIC THEORY.

Experiments with radioactive materials early in the 20th century indicated that radioactive substances which were chemically inseparable might differ from each other only in the structure of their nuclei. The existence of stable isotopes was first demonstrated in 1912 by the English physicist Sir Joseph John Thomson who showed, by passing neon through a discharge tube and deflecting the neon ions by means of magnetic and electric fields, that the stable (nonradioactive) element neon exists in more than one form. Thomson found two isotopes of neon, one of atomic mass 20 and another of mass 22. Later experiments showed that naturally occurring neon contains 90% of Ne-20 (the isotope with mass 20), 9.73% Ne-22, and 0.27% Ne-21. The work on isotopes was continued by many scientists, chief among whom was Francis William Aston (q.v.); their work in detecting and studying isotopes was accelerated by the development of the mass spectrograph (q.v.).

It is now known that most elements in the natural state consist of a mixture of two or more isotopes. Among the exceptions are beryllium, aluminum, phosphorus, and sodium. The chemical atomic weight of an element is the weighted average of the individual atomic weights, or atomic masses, of the isotopes. For example chlorine, atomic weight 35.457, is composed of Cl-35 and Cl-37, occurring with an abundance of 76% and 24% respectively. All the isotopes of elements with atomic numbers higher than eighty-three (above bismuth in the periodic table) are radioactive, and a few of the lighter isotopes, such as potassium-40, are radioactive. About 274 naurally occurring stable isotopes (radio-isotopes) are known.

Artificially produced isotopes are made by bombarding naturally occurring atoms with neutrons from an atomic pile or with protons, electrons, or other particles from such instruments as the cyclotron and betatron. Over 400 such isotopes have been produced, all of which are radioactive. See ATOMIC ENERGY AND ATOMIC BOMB; RADIOACTIVITY; RADIOCHEMISTRY.

The separation of isotopes of the same element from each other presents enormous difficulties. Chemical separation is impossible, because isotopes of the same elements have the same chemical properties; physical methods are generally based on the extremely small difference in physical properties caused by the differences in mass of the isotopes. The isotopes of hydrogen, deuterium or H-2 and ordinary hydrogen or H-1, were the first to be separated in appreciable quantities. This separation was accomplished about 1934 (see DEUTERIUM) by taking advantage of the fact that heavy water (water containing deuterium) breaks down much less rapidly than ordinary water when using nickel electrodes in the electrolysis. See HYDROGEN BOMB.

Before 1940 many methods were used for the separation of small amounts of isotopes for research purposes. Of the many methods used, some of the most successful were the centrifuge method, fractional distillation, thermal diffusion, ion exchange, gaseous diffusion, and electromagnetic separation. Each of these methods depends on the small difference in weight of the isotopes to be separated, and is most effective with the hydrogen isotopes, where the difference in mass between the two substances amounts to 100%; by contrast, the difference in mass between the carbon isotopes C-12 and C-13 or between the neon isotopes Ne-20 and Ne-22 amounts to only about 10%, and between the uranium isotopes U-235 and U-238 to only a little over 1%. This factor of 10 to 1 or 100 to 1 makes the separation far more than 10 or 100 times as difficult.

The net result of any single process of isotope separation is the separation of the original material into two "fractions", one of which contains a slightly higher percentage of the heavy isotope than the original mixture, while the other contains slightly more of the light isotope. To obtain an appreciable "enrichment" in the desired isotope, it is necessary to separate further the enriched fraction. This process is usually carried out by means of a "cascade", comprising a large number of stages. The enriched fraction from any stage becomes the raw material for the next stage, while the depleted fraction, which still contains a considerable percentage of the desired isotope, is mixed with the raw material for the preceding stage. Even the depleted material from the original stage is "stripped" in additional stages when the raw material (e.g., uranium) is scarce. Suitable apparatus is designed to make the flow from stage to stage automatic and continuous. Such a cascade is extremely flexible, and units can be shifted from one stage of the separation to another as desired. For example, in the separation of uranium, a large amount of material must be handled at the beginning, where the desired U-235 is mixed with about 140 times as much U-238; at the end of the process the U-235 is almost pure, and the volume of material (and hence the number of units required) is much smaller. Furthermore, by merely changing the piping, it is possible to shift stages to compensate for addition at an intermediate stage of material which results from preliminary enrichment by a different process.

In the centrifuge method the apparatus is so arranged that there is a downward flow of vapor in the outer part of the rotating cylinder and an upward flow in the central region of the cylinder. The centrifugal force acts more strongly on the heavy molecules than on the light ones, increasing the concentration of the heavy isotopes in the outer region; see BEAMS, JESSE W. In separation by fractional distillation a mixture containing various isotopes is distilled. The molecules of the fraction having the lower boiling point (the lighter isotopes) tend to concentrate in the vapor stream and are collected. See DISTILLATION.

Separation of isotopes by thermal diffusion depends on the tendency for one type of molecule to concentrate in a cold region and for another type to concentrate in a warm region. This tendency varies not only with molecular weights but with the forces between molecules; in the case of some gases the heavier isotopes collect in the warm region and in other cases the heavier isotopes concentrate in the cold region. A simple form of thermal-diffusion apparatus consists of a tall, vertical tube containing a heated wire stretched along the axis of the tube, producing a temperature difference between the periphery and the center of the tube. A thermal-diffusion plant was constructed at Oak Ridge, Tenn., in 1944 to effect a preliminary separation of uranium isotopes.

The gaseous-diffusion and electromagnetic methods of separating isotopes of uranium afforded the first large-scale separation ever achieved. The problem of separating U-235 from U-238 arose in 1940 after the demonstration of the susceptibility of the 235 isotope to fission by neutrons. U-235 exists in naturally occurring uranium to the extent of seven parts to a thousand of U-238. By the end of 1941, using the best techniques available, the American physicist Ernest O. Lawrence was able to produce a millionth of a gram of the fissile isotope in an hour by the electromagnetic method. Under the auspices of the atomic-bomb project, the various methods for separating isotopes were considered and the gaseous-diffusion and electromagnetic methods were put into large-scale operation for the production of about one kilogram (2.2 lbs.) per day of U-235 to be used in atomic bombs; see ATOMIC ENERGY AND ATOMIC BOMB.

The gaseous-diffusion method exploits the different rate of diffusion (q.v.) of gases of different molecular weight. The rate of diffusion of a gas is inversely proportional to the square root of the mass; light atoms diffuse through a porous barrier faster than heavier atoms. In the separation of uranium isotopes, the only gaseous compound of uranium, the fluoride of uranium, UF_6, is used. The uranium hexafluoride is pumped continuously through porous barriers. The difference in weight between U-235 and U-238 is slightly greater than 1%, but the difference in weight between the fluorides is slightly less than 1%. The enrichment factor, which depends on the square root of the above difference, is theoretically 0.43% for an instantaneous process or 0.30% for a continuous process, but in actual practice an enrichment factor of only about 0.14% per stage has been achieved. To produce 90% U-235 from 0.7% U-235, 4000 such stages are required. The process requires thousands of miles of pipe, thousands of pumps and motors, and intricate control mechanisms. The principal gaseous diffusion plant, constructed at Oak Ridge, Tenn., in 1943–44, is the largest continuous process plant in the world. The building is approximately one mile long, a twelfth of a mile wide, four stories high, and built in the shape of a U. The porous barriers through which the uranium gas is diffused contain billions of holes per square inch, each hole a few ten millionths of an inch in diameter. The barriers are very thin, but are strong enough to withstand considerable pressure. The total area of barrier material used in the plant is measured in square miles.

Although the gaseous-diffusion method of isotope separation yielded the large amounts of U-235 required by the atomic-bomb project, the first comparatively large amounts of the isotope were produced by electromagnetic means at Oak Ridge, Tenn. A series of separator units was built in which an ionic beam obtained from a uranium compound was passed through a magnetic field. Since the radius of the curvature of the path of the ions deflected by the beam depends on the mass of the ion, ions of different mass complete their path at different positions and the uranium isotopes are appreciably separated.

The electromagnetic method was operated in stages similar to the cascades except that they were not continuous. Material processed in one unit was sent on to the next stage for further enrichment. The chief advantage of the electromagnetic separation is the large separation affected in one operation. The chief disadvantage is the small amount of material that can be treated in one operation. At the end of the war the electromagnetic plant was closed down in favor of the gaseous-diffusion plant.

For the application of isotopes to biological, medical, chemical, and physical research, see RADIOCHEMISTRY; TRACERS.

ISOTOPE TRACERS. See TRACERS.

ISRAEL, a republic in the Middle East embracing part of the territory of what was formerly Palestine, proclaimed on May 14, 1948, and constituting the first Jewish national state since 70 A.D., when Jerusalem was destroyed by Roman soldiers and Judea (see JEWS) became a Roman province. Israel was created following a resolution of the United Nations General Assembly on Nov. 29, 1947, setting a date for the termination of the British mandate for Palestine, which had been established by the League of Nations in 1922, and recommending partition of the country into separate Arab and Jewish states. By the terms of the U.N. resolution, the Jewish state consisted of three major areas: extreme N.E. Palestine, bounded on the E. by the Jordan R. and extending about 20 m. at its greatest distance w., and bounded on the N. by Lebanon, from which it extends s. about 60 m.; a coastal strip along the Mediterranean Sea, about 80 m. long from Acre in the N. to Isdud in the s., and ranging from about 5 to 25 m. in width; and an area in the s., including most of the Negeb (q.v.) desert region and all s.E. Palestine, but excluding a coastal strip,

about 5 m. wide, extending from Isdud to the frontier of Egypt. The seaport of Jaffa (q.v.), in the Jewish coastal region, was awarded to the Arabs as a Mediterranean port, but was captured by the Israelis and incorporated into the state of Israel in 1948. The main cities awarded to the Jewish state under this plan were Haifa, the chief port of Palestine, Tel Aviv, the largest city and leading industrial center of Palestine, Safed, and Tiberias (qq.v.). After the proclamation of the state of Israel, Sarona (q.v.), formerly a N.E. suburb of Tel Aviv, was made its capital. In 1950 the seat of government of Israel was removed to the New City of Jerusalem. The total area of the Jewish state is 8048 sq.m. The population (1952 est.) is 1,607,000, including about 1,430,000 Jews, 125,000 Mohammedans, 37,000 Christians, and 15,000 Druses.

For physical features, climate, flora and fauna, and for the detailed history of the region before 1947, see PALESTINE.

Production and Industry. Israel is primarily an agricultural country, the most important crop being citrus fruits. In a recent year about 135,000 dunams (29,700 acres; 1 dunam equals .22 acre) were devoted to citrus cultivation by Jewish farmers. (This figure decreased from a high of 139,000 dunams in 1939 as a result of the ruinous effects of Arab-Jewish fighting.) Other principal crops are olives, barley, wheat, tomatoes, millet, potatoes, figs, corn, and durra. The greatest farming regions in Israel are Esdrælon (q.v.), or the Plain of Jezreel, in the N.E., and Sharon, the plain along the Mediterranean coast. Irrigation projects are planned to reclaim part of the Negeb desert as a third great agricultural region.

The development of Jewish farming in Palestine occurred almost entirely after the beginning of the 20th century, prior to which there were only a few scattered Jewish settlements. Various Zionist organizations, notably the Jewish National Fund (*Keren Kayemeth*), the Palestine Foundation Fund (*Keren Hayesod*), the Palestine Jewish Colonial Association (P.I.C.A.), and the Jewish Colonial Association (I.C.A.), created Jewish farming settlements on land purchased from the British mandatory government of Palestine or from Arab landowners (see ZIONISM). Jewish settlements are organized into three principal types, colonized by Jewish immigrants, most of whom were not originally farmers. The most distinctive type of farm colony is the communal or co-operative settlement, in which the workers live in communal dwellings and share the work and profits equally. In a second type, the workers' smallholders' settlements, individual farms are worked separately, but the produce is pooled and marketed by the settlement unit. Both these types of settlement are established on land owned by one of the various colonial organizations, principally the Jewish National Fund, but leased to the settlers. In a third type, the smallholders' settlements, individual farms are worked as private enterprises. In addition to the above, several other types of agricultural settlements, intermediate between the collective and free-enterprise communities, have evolved in recent years.

Industrial enterprise in Israel began even later than agricultural settlement. The major impetus to Jewish industry occurred in the 1930's, with the arrival of great numbers of technicians as refugees from Nazi Germany and German satellite countries. Factories are primarily concentrated in Haifa and Tel Aviv, where most of Israel's industry is situated. The principal industrial products are glass, made with potash from mines and processing plants near the Dead Sea (q.v.), false teeth, bricks, pharmaceutical products, soap, cosmetics, olive oil, wine, textiles, and extracts and other by-products of citrus fruitgrowing. A large diamond cutting and polishing industry was established after the beginning of World War II, when Jewish diamond workers fled from the German occupation of Belgium and Holland. In addition, the city of Haifa is the terminus of one of the largest oil pipe lines in the Middle East, and is the site of oil refining and shipping installations. In a recent year, exports, including citrus fruits, were valued at $46,800,000. The principal imports are machinery, grain and flour, vehicles, iron and steel products, and fuel. The principal exports are citrus fruits, wines and liquors, polished diamonds, chemicals, textiles, and other manufactured goods. Imports in a recent year were valued at about $343,000,000.

People. About 25,000 Jews lived in Palestine in 1882, before the first great Jewish immigration to that country. The present size of the Jewish population is almost entirely a result of immigration which occurred in a series of great waves, called *aliyoth* (Heb., "ascents"): about 1884, following the beginning of a Jewish nationalist movement in central and E. Europe; from about 1905 to 1925, mainly composed of European youth and socialists who founded many of the communal

settlements; from about 1932 to 1939, chiefly refugees from Nazi persecution, and European businessmen with capital to invest in Jewish industry; and following World War II, principally displaced persons from Europe. Also, a steady influx of Yemenite (see YEMEN) and other Middle Eastern Jews began with the establishment of the British mandate. In a single decade (1935–45), the *Yishuv* (Jewish community in Palestine) grew from a population of about 335,000 to more than 554,000. About 135,700 of the 1935–45 immigrants came from Europe, mainly from Poland (55,313) and from Germany, including Austria (29,931). Altogether, over 726,000 immigrants were admitted to the new state from the time of the proclamation of Israel in 1948 through 1952, more than doubling the Jewish population of the country. The greatest number to arrive in one year, 250,000, were admitted in 1949. In a recent year, the principal occupational groups were: 23% in industry, 17% in commerce, 14% in agriculture, 10% in building, and 8% in the various professions.

Communications. The only Israeli port with modern harbor facilities, where vessels of any size can be docked and serviced, is Haifa, of great strategic importance, with the best natural harbor on the eastern Mediterranean. All ships arriving at Tel Aviv or Jaffa, now controlled by Israel, must be serviced by lighters. Internal communication facilities include about 330 miles of railroad, both wide and narrow gauge, concentrated almost entirely along the Mediterranean coast and in the N. Haifa is connected with Istanbul, Turkey, by a direct rail line. About 1590 miles of paved road connect all parts of Israel. Several international air lines service the country through the Lydda airport, near Tel Aviv.

Government. The basis for the government of the Jewish state was outlined in the U.N. resolution of Nov. 29, 1947, which prescribed a democratic, parliamentary form of government. The resolution further specified that the Jewish legislature should be elected on the basis of proportional representation (q.v.) and that the franchise for the election of a constituent assembly should be given to all citizens over eighteen years of age. Personal rights and rights of religious minorities were to be protected, and Moslems and Christians were to be allowed freedom of transit to visit their holy places. Immediately after the proclamation of the state of Israel on May 14, 1948, a provisional government organized the administration of the new republic. In Octo-

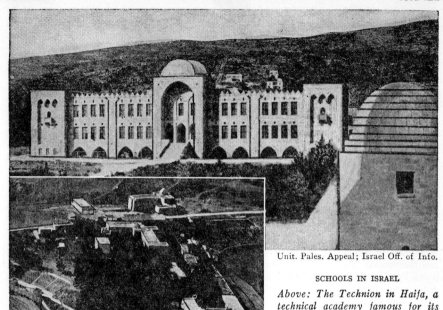

Unit. Pales. Appeal; Israel Off. of Info.

SCHOOLS IN ISRAEL

Above: The Technion in Haifa, a technical academy famous for its agricultural training facilities.
Left: Aerial view of the Hebrew University, near Jerusalem.

ber, 1948, the provisional government appointed a commission to draft a constitution embodying the specifications of the U.N. resolution. Elections to choose a 120-member *Knesset* (constituent assembly) were held on Jan. 25, 1949. Dr. Chaim Weizmann (q.v.) was elected president by the *Knesset,* and David Ben-Gurion (q.v.) became prime minister of the provisional government. Though the Jewish religion is separate from the government, Israel observes the traditional Jewish Sabbath from sundown Friday to sundown Saturday; and the Jewish holy days, such as Passover, Rosh Hashonah, and Yom Kippur, are celebrated as national holidays.

Education. In a recent year about 900 Jewish primary and secondary schools were in existence in Israel, divided into three main categories: general schools, called General Trend; schools established and operated by various labor political parties; and schools owned or operated by Jewish religious groups. There is also a fourth and smaller group of nonaffiliated schools. About 197,000 students, between the ages of six and seventeen were enrolled in these schools. Separate schools were maintained for Arab children. Israeli Jewish schools teach in Hebrew, but Arabic is a secondary language in secondary

schools. A technical academy, the Technion, was established in Haifa. Hebrew University, one of the foremost universities in the Middle East, is situated in Jerusalem. Law schools were established at Tel Aviv and in the Jewish portion of Jerusalem. In a recent year the government budget included £I 8,280,000 for education.

History. The movement for an independent Jewish state in Palestine had its roots in the beginning of organized Jewish settlement during the 19th century. The first modern Jewish agricultural colony, Petah Tiqva, was founded about 1870, and a number of others followed soon thereafter. In the last decade of the century, Theodor Herzl (q.v.), an Austrian writer, brought about the formation of a world Zionist organization, and initiated the development of Zionism into an effective political force. The movement rapidly gained adherents during the first decade of the 20th century, as anti-Semitism and pogroms (q.v.) in eastern Europe stimulated Jewish nationalism and caused growing numbers of Jews to see in Zionism a solution to their problem. Meanwhile, the earliest settlements in Palestine, attacked occasionally by marauding Arabs, organized a loose defensive group known as *Hashomer* (Heb., "Watchmen").

This group was the antecedent of the Israeli army, and it came into being in response to the Jews' first confrontation with Arab opposition, one of the two major obstacles to the achievement of their own state. The other important obstacle, opposition from the country which controlled Palestine, appeared to be eliminated after British troops, supported by specially recruited Jewish forces under Vladimir Jabotinsky (q.v.), ousted the Turks from Palestine during World War I, in 1918. The year before, Arthur James Balfour (q.v.), then foreign secretary of Great Britain, had stated that Britain pledged itself to support the establishment of a Jewish "National Home" in Palestine; see BALFOUR DECLARATION.

This pledge was incorporated into the League of Nations mandate for Palestine in 1922, under which Britain was instructed to

Below: Young men and women of Israel eating breakfast before beginning their day's work in the fields of a new co-operative settlement. Right: Modern buildings and ploughed fields of the Massada-Ain Hakoreh colony in the Beisan region of Palestine. Before the Israelis settled here it was a barren plain.

Keystone; United Palestine Appeal

"facilitate" Jewish immigration and settlement upon the land; and its intention was supported by Faisal, king of the newly created Arab state of Iraq (q.v.), in an exchange of letters with Dr. Chaim Weizmann (q.v.). However, the post-war influx of Jewish immigrants was met by two setbacks. The mandatory government detached Trans-Jordan, a part of Palestine under the mandate, from the rest of Palestine, and forbade the

entry or settlement of Jews; and Palestinian Arabs began to organize political opposition to Zionism. During the following decade, Jews increasingly charged that British officers of the Palestine government were encouraging overt Arab acts of opposition in order to furnish a basis for the restriction of Jewish immigration; and British authorities declared in answer that Jewish and Arab counterclaims were such that neither side could expect full satisfaction. After the advent of the Nazi regime in Germany, in 1933, Jews faced with persecution left Europe in increasing numbers; and the Jewish population of Palestine began to swell. In 1936, fierce Arab rioting broke out in protest against further Jewish immigration, and deaths occurred daily for the next three years. In response to this rioting, two Jewish armed forces were organized. In 1936, the *Hashomer* was abandoned, and the *Haganah* ("Defense") was created as an underground army, enlisting large numbers of able-bodied Jewish men and women. The *Haganah* operated on a principle of "self-restraint", and dedicated itself solely to defending Jewish lives and property. In 1937, the smaller *Irgun Zvai Leumi* ("National Military Organization") was founded. Following the political leadership of Vladimir Jabotinsky, then head of the militant New Zionist Organization, the *Irgun* sought out and conducted retaliatory attacks against Arabs, on the theory that Arab rioting was encouraged by the British and could not be halted merely by defensive tactics.

In 1939, on grounds of being obliged to find some means of restoring order in Palestine, the British government issued a White Paper. This document asserted that "a" Jewish national home had already been established in Palestine, with the existence there of a large and flourishing community. By thus implying that the term "national home" did not mean a state, but simply a functioning community, the British claimed that this part of the mandatory obligation already had been satisfactorily discharged. Then, on the ground that Britain was obliged to respect the wishes of the "local inhabitants", the White Paper assured the Arabs of a continuing majority in Palestine by restricting further Jewish immigration to 75,000, to be apportioned over the ensuing five years. It also severely limited Jewish purchase of Palestinian land. The result was a virtual cessation of Arab violence, and the first beginnings of anti-British violence by Jews, conducted by the Irgun.

Following the outbreak of World War II,

both the *Haganah* and the *Irgun* placed themselves at the disposal of the anti-Hitler war effort. About 30,000 Palestinian Jews enlisted in the British Middle Eastern forces, and distinguished themselves, notably, in the North African and Italian campaigns. However, the *Irgun,* whose commander was killed while on a British mission, was split in 1940 by a small faction, the Fighters for the Freedom of Israel, or "Stern Group." Its leader, Abraham Stern, killed in 1942 by British police who claimed that he attempted to escape after being apprehended by them, believed that the rescue of Jews from Europe, almost halted by the Palestine government, was of primary importance; and his group attempted to force elimination of immigration restrictions through assassination of important British officials throughout the war. The collapse of Germany, and the subsequent disclosures about the fate of European Jewry, produced an immediate clamor among Palestinian Jews for admission of the concentration-camp survivors. When the election of a Labor government in Britain, in August, 1945, failed to produce a change in immigration policy, anti-British fighting flared again. The Stern Group and the larger and stronger *Irgun* claimed that the British administration had become an unlawful occupation regime by violating the immigration and land settlement provisions of the mandate. Both of these underground forces, and, occasionally, the *Haganah,* attacked British police stations, arsenals, communications, and coastal lookouts. The latter were attacked specifically because they were used in intercepting the "illegal" immigrant ships, by which the powerful *Haganah* was attempting to smuggle refugees into Palestine.

A two-year crisis of continuously mounting intensity began. While Arabs, impressed by Jewish strength, looked on passively, the British government and the Jewish groups jockeyed for position. Under David Ben-Gurion, the Jewish Agency, the official Zionist and semigovernmental organization of Jewish Palestine, denounced what it called the "terrorism" of the *Irgun* and the Stern Group; but its hand was strengthened by their activities, which it told the government it could not prevent unless concessions were granted. Meanwhile, Jews and other sympathizers in America, aroused by the reports of fighting and of captured immigration ships, contributed increasing amounts of money for support of these activities, and put pressure on the Government of the United States to urge a change in British policy. The British refused to increase the immigration quota, and began to intern captured would-be immigrants on the island of Cyprus. Early in 1947, the imminent execution of the captured *Irgun* member, Dov Gruner, when he refused to recognize the jurisdiction of a British military tribunal by declining appeal of his case to a higher court, brought the tension to fever pitch. In March, the British army imposed martial law on Tel Aviv and the Jewish sections of Jerusalem; and Gruner was hung in April. Three other Irgunists were hung shortly thereafter. Having warned that it would retaliate if its members were executed, the *Irgun* captured two British soldiers and hung them in a forest near Natanya.

The economic dislocations caused by martial law had failed to force the Jewish Agency to use the *Haganah* to combat the *Irgun* and the Stern Group, and the hanging of the British soldiers produced a clamor in the British press for a change in Palestine policy. The Palestine government had succeeded only in strengthening and uniting its opposition; and greater repressive measures were likely to produce an explosion in which the Jewish Agency would be forced to permit the *Haganah* to form an outright alliance with the more militant underground groups. On the other hand, to allow Jewish immigration would antagonize the nations of the Arab League (q.v.), whose anti-Zionism Britain had never discouraged. Accordingly, the British government decided to submit the Palestine problem to the United Nations, which would either take responsibility out of British hands, or give official approval to British policy.

Fighting in Palestine ceased when a special meeting of the U.N. General Assembly resulted in the appointment of an eleven-nation investigation commission, the United Nations Special Committee on Palestine (U.N.S.C.O.P.). The Jews waited to see what the commission would produce; and the British allowed the Arabs to speak for themselves in the U.N. and bear the burden of opposition to Zionism. The U.N.S.C.O.P. proceeded to Palestine in the summer of 1947, and, on Aug. 31, submitted a majority report recommending the partition of the country into separate Arab and Jewish states, and the creation of an international zone including Jerusalem and its environs. Both states were to have democratic governments, and were to co-operate with each other economically. A detailed plan of partition procedure was passed by the General Assembly on Nov. 29. However, representatives of the Arab nations belonging to the U.N. walked

Wide World Photo

Steer being unloaded from a ship, in Haifa

out of the meeting after the vote, declaring their refusal to accept the plan.

Fighting broke out in Palestine immediately after the vote of the General Assembly. Bands of Arabs attacked Jewish farms and settlements, and Jews retaliated with attacks on Arabs. The five-nation commission (Bolivia, Czechoslovakia, Denmark, Panama, the Philippines), appointed to supervise the partition, was hampered by lack of military forces to assist its implementation, and by the fact that, being only in the form of a recommendation, the U.N. resolution was not binding upon the British, who refused to let the commission enter Palestine until the following spring. As the communal fighting increased, the British failed to evacuate a port on Feb. 1, for Jewish use in bringing refugees and supplies, as specified in the U.N. timetable. Meanwhile, Palestine Arabs were being reinforced by detachments of irregulars, trained and armed in the surrounding Arab countries. The British abandoned more and more of the administration of the country, which was taken up haphazardly by local Jewish and Arab authorities, and announced that they would depart completely on May 15. The failure to provide for

Jerry Cooke; Keystone

Above: Truckloads of oranges at a co-opera-
tive canning plant at which they will be
processed to make juice for export, in Israel.
Left: Teen-age girls helping to plant the
crops on an Israeli farm settlement.

an orderly transfer of governmental facilities
and authority produced widespread confusion,
greatly hampering the work of implementing
the U.N. recommendations, and encouraging
the communal warfare. In February, the Palestine Commission requested an international
military force to quell the fighting and implement partition; but neither the U.S. nor
the U.S.S.R., the dominant powers in the U.N.,
approved of this proposal.

On May 13, the Arab League declared that
the forces of its member nations would enter
Palestine immediately after the British departure to "administer" it until an Arab state
could be established throughout the country.
On May 14, the British High Commissioner
for Palestine and the last of the British troops
sailed from Haifa harbor. That night, the
state of Israel was proclaimed by Jewish leaders, and a provisional government was established. Almost simultaneously, the regular armies of Syria, Lebanon, Egypt, Iraq, and
Trans-Jordan crossed the Palestine frontier

and attacked Jewish settlements. The state of Israel began its official existence at midnight. Eleven minutes later, it was accorded *de facto* (in fact) recognition by the U.S.; and two days later, it was recognized *de jure* (in law) by the U.S.S.R. The Israeli provisional government was headed by David Ben-Gurion, prime minister and defense minister, and Moshe Shertok (now Sharett), foreign minister. Other ministries were: interior, agriculture, communications, finance, supply, social welfare, labor and social insurance, justice, immigration, religious affairs, health, education, and police. On May 16, Dr. Chaim Weizmann was elected president of the council of the provisional government.

The Israelis were at first hard pressed. Lacking sufficient arms, they had only their manpower to throw against the advancing Arab armies, and suffered heavy initial casualties. In addition, the Israeli army, formed from the *Haganah*, did not yet embrace the *Irgun* and the "Stern Group". These kept most of their effectives in Jerusalem, since Israel did not yet claim that city, and they wanted to effect its inclusion in the new state. Jewish forces had cleared Haifa and seized Jaffa before the state was established, and their main danger was no longer internal. Lebanese troops, and Lebanon-supported irregulars, occupied western Galilee; and Syrian army units attacked Israeli settlements in eastern Galilee. Iraqi troops occupied the strategic Tulkarm-Jenin-Nablus "triangle" in the northern Judean hills; and Trans-Jordan forces, British armed and led, constituting the strongest Arab army, attacked Jerusalem and destroyed Israeli settlements south of Bethlehem. Egyptian troops moved up the Mediterranean shore from the south, taking Gaza, and struck inland to occupy Beersheba and Hebron. This over-all situation represented the high-water mark of the Arab advance.

The U.N. proposed a truce and appointed Count Folke Bernadotte, head of the Swedish Red Cross, as U.N. mediator to conciliate the adversaries. The Arabs at first rejected the truce proposal; but, when their attack bogged down, they announced their acceptance of the cease-fire proposal. A four-week truce went into effect on June 11, 1948. During the breathing space thus provided, the Israelis managed to strengthen their forces, and, when the truce ended on July 9, they launched offensives in the northern and central sectors, capturing western Galilee, thus gaining all of northern Palestine, and capturing Lydda, important for its airport and its location near the strategic Tel Aviv-Jerusalem highway. Under the circumstances, the Arabs readily agreed to another truce, which went into effect on July 17.

While trying to bring about a permanent armistice, Bernadotte was killed by unidentified assassins on Sept. 17, in the Israeli-held part of Jerusalem. Three days later, the Israeli government required the disbanding of non-governmental military forces; and the *Irgun,* most of whose members had already been transferred to the Israeli army, and the "Stern Group" disbanded as military units, and became political parties. The Bernadotte plan for conciliation, which the Count had completed shortly before his death, was presented to the U.N. by Dr. Ralph Bunche, Bernadotte's American assistant, who became acting mediator. Recognizing Israel as an established fact, the plan called for its admission into the U.N. and a final arrangement of boundaries, giving w. Galilee to Israel and the Negeb region to the Arabs, and placing Jerusalem under U.N. administration. Jews and Arabs both objected: the Arabs continued to oppose the existence of any Jewish state, and Israel maintained that surrender of the Negeb would reduce the state by two-thirds of its territory. The plan, though supported by Britain, failed to receive U.N. approval, and was abandoned.

Charging Egyptian truce violations, in October, 1948, Israel launched an attack which cleared most of the Negeb desert region. The fighting was stopped and the new front stabilized through the mediation of Dr. Bunche, and armistice talks between Israel and Egypt were begun on the island of Rhodes (q.v.) under U.N. sponsorship. After the talks had continued for some weeks without apparent success, Israeli again attacked in the Negeb, with one of its detachments striking more than 40 miles into the Sinai Peninsula, in Egypt, before withdrawing to Israeli territory. This fighting between Israel and Egypt was also halted by the intervention of Dr. Bunche, and an agreement was signed on February 24, 1949. Under its terms, Israel retained the entire Negeb except for a small coastal strip, including Gaza, which remained in Egyptian hands. During the second period of Negeb fighting, Israeli forces shot down five British planes which flew over the battle area. A tense situation developed, in which British troops were moved into the Trans-Jordan port of Aqaba, within sight of Israeli territory on the Red Sea, and the British government was attacked in London newspapers for having allowed its personnel to become involved in the Palestine fighting. Israeli soldiers raced to occupy their Red Sea territory near Aqaba, but, after strong pressure from the U.S., they met with no British interference, and the tension diminished. On March 11, Trans-Jordan signed an armistice agreement with Israel, under which the New City of Jerusalem remained in Israeli possession, and the Old City remained under Arab control. The agreement also provided for the withdrawal of Trans-Jordan forces along some portions of the front in order to adjust Israel's borders. On March 23, Lebanon signed an armistice, and, with the withdrawal of Iraqui troops from all of Palestine, and an Israeli-Syrian armistice in process of negotiation, fighting ceased on all fronts.

Meanwhile, on January 25, the new republic held its first elections. More than 350,000 persons voted, including Arabs, who are permitted to elect their own delegates to the *Knesset*. The largest vote was given to the *Mapai* (Palestine Labor Party), headed by Prime Minister Ben-Gurion, which received about 35 percent of the total, and advocated an internal program of moderate socialization. The Russian-oriented *Mapam* (United Labor Party) received about 14 percent of the total with advocacy of a program of intensive socialization. A bloc of religious parties, advocating strict observance of Jewish religious strictures, received about 13 percent of the vote. The controversial *Tnuat Hacherut* ("Freedom Movement"), the political outgrowth of the *Irgun,* led by Menachem Begin, sponsored a program reminiscent of the American "New Deal" and a foreign policy designed to secure the inclusion in Israel of all of Palestine, including Trans-Jordan, and received about 12 percent of the vote. A number of smaller parties received total votes ranging from 8 percent to less than 1 percent. Ben-Gurion became prime minister of the government, with the support of the religious bloc and some of the smaller parties. On February 17, Chaim Weizmann was elected the first president of Israel by the new *Knesset*.

Despite a $100,000,000 loan granted by the U.S. Export-Import Bank and large-scale financial assistance from Jewish communities elsewhere in the world, the new state faced great economic difficulties from the beginning of its existence. The fighting had drained Israeli resources, and there was the additional problem of sheltering and absorbing the hundreds of thousands of new immigrants who,

often penniless, poured into the country. Accordingly, a drastic austerity program was inaugurated, modeled after the one in Britain. It included price and production controls, rationing of essential items, including housing, and construction projects. The principal domestic bulwark of the political and economic program of Prime Minister Ben-Gurion was the *Histadrut* ("Organization"), the General Federation of Jewish Labor, organized by Ben-Gurion and other socialists during the 1920's. Not simply a federation of trade unions, the *Histadrut* was an unusual combination of political and economic power, providing the basis for strength of both the *Mapai* and *Mapam* parties, and constituting the most powerful single employer and owner of capital in Israel. It monopolized Israeli transportation, one of its holding companies dominated the construction industries, and it had important and often controlling interests in the food-processing, leather, publishing, textile, chemical, metal, fabricating, wood-manufacturing, and other industries; and an estimated two-thirds of the Israeli population were directly or indirectly dependent upon the *Histadrut* for their livelihood.

Israel's application for membership in the U.N. was approved by the Security Council on March 4, 1949, and by the General Assembly on May 11. On December 9 the General Assembly affirmed (38 to 14, with 7 abstentions) its previous (1947) decision to internationalize Jerusalem and environs. Both Israel and Trans-Jordan vigorously opposed the Assembly action. The Israeli foreign minister, characterizing the U.N. majority as victims of "incredible light-mindedness", notified the Assembly that his country intended to keep the New City. Later in December Prime Minister Ben-Gurion announced that Jerusalem would soon replace Tel Aviv as capital of Israel. The change was officially proclaimed on January 23, 1950.

More than 243,500 immigrants reached Israel during 1949. Absorption of the newcomers, many of whom were penniless and unskilled workers, was attended by serious difficulties. In mid-November persons in immigration camps totaled 104,000. The rate of immigration lessened appreciably during the final months of the year, and by January 1, 1950, the number of immigrant-camp residents had been reduced to 78,600. Israel planned to receive 150,000 immigrants, including 65,000 European invalids, during 1950, according to official estimates. On May 20 Israel began (by air transports) the mass evacuation, popularly known as "Operation Ali Baba", of over 50,000 Iraqi Jews. The nation's economic plight, seriously aggravated by the failure of industrial development to keep pace with population growth, worsened during 1950. To offset the effects of the resultant adverse balance of trade, the government instituted various austerity measures. Popular opposition contributed to the nation's first cabinet crisis. On October 15 Prime Minister Ben-Gurion resigned after losing a vote of confidence in the Knesset. He agreed, however, to remain in office on a temporary basis. A congress of U.S. Jewish organizations voted on October 26 to raise $1 billion to help finance a three-year development program for Israel. Announcement of this plan eased domestic political tensions. On October 30 the Knesset approved a new cabinet, with Ben-Gurion as prime minister. Late in December the U.S. Export-Import Bank approved a $35-million loan to Israel. Legislation approving a $500-million bond issue in the U.S. was adopted by the Knesset on February 27, 1951.

Israel's relations with the neighboring Arab states during 1950 were marked by mutual antagonisms. As a consequence U.N. attempts to arrange a final Israeli-Jordani peace settlement were unsuccessful. During the spring of 1951 Israeli and Syrian troops clashed frequently in the Huleh swamp region, a demilitarized zone near the Syrian border. Occasioned by Syrian opposition to an Israeli reclamation project in the area, the fighting ended early in May, when both sides agreed to obey a U.N. cease-fire order. The U.N. later granted Israel authority to resume activities in certain uncontested areas, pending settlement of the dispute. On July 12 Israel demanded that the U.N. Security Council compel Egypt to end its three-year blockade of shipping en route to Israel via the Suez Canal. The Council approved such a resolution on Sept. 1. Egypt immediately rejected it because of Israel's failure to abide by previous U.N. resolutions on partition, repatriation of Arab refugees, and the internationalization of Jerusalem. The next day the Arab League tightened its economic blockade of Israel.

Meanwhile, on Feb. 14, Prime Minister Ben-Gurion resigned, chiefly because of disagreement within the coalition on the question of whether education in the immigrant camps should be religious or secular. After negotiations to form a new government ended in failure, the prime minister agreed to remain in office pending general elections. The latter were held on July 30. *Mapai,* the government party, failed to increase its strength in the

Knesset; the conservative General Zionist party increased its seats to 20, a gain of 7. Long weeks of discussion with the General Zionists on the possibility of a coalition proved fruitless. Finally, on Oct. 7 Ben-Gurion formed a cabinet with the aid of the *Mizrachi* (religious) parties, which had previously opposed him on the education question. Israel signed a treaty of friendship, commerce, and navigation with the United States on Aug. 23.

Although Israel made some progress toward solving its economic problems during 1952, drastic measures were still necessary. On Feb. 13 the government devaluated the Israeli pound in order to attract foreign investment and the tourist trade. In an attempt to control inflation, a compulsory tax was levied (June 8) on individual bank deposits above 50 Israeli pounds. Meanwhile financial assistance was secured (Feb. 27) from the U.S. government in the form of a $50 million grant-in-aid for the relief and resettlement of refugees in Israel. Economic pressures were lessened during the year by a marked decrease in immigration. Only 23,370 immigrants entered the country, as contrasted with 173,901 during 1951. West Germany signed an agreement on Sept. 10 with the government providing for the payment to Israel over a twelve-year period of $715 million in the form of capital goods as reparations for the destruction of Jewish life and property under the Nazi regime.

President Chaim Weizmann died on Nov. 9 and Yitzhak Ben-Zvi (1884–   ), *Mapai* leader and close associate of Ben-Gurion, was installed as Israel's second president on Dec. 10. The coalition cabinet resigned (Dec. 19). Ben-Gurion formed (Dec. 22) a new cabinet composed of *Mapai* and General Zionist members.

Anticommunist extremists bombed the Soviet legation in Tel Aviv on Feb. 9, 1953. The Israeli government, which had long protested against alleged anti-Semitic and anti-Zionist activities in the Soviet bloc of states, denounced the bombing. On Feb. 12 the U.S.S.R. severed diplomatic relations with Israel. Tensions between the two countries lessened following the death (March) of Soviet premier Joseph Stalin. Israel and the U.S.S.R. renewed diplomatic relations on Aug. 5.

Violations of the truce agreements by both sides continued to embitter Israeli-Arab relations throughout 1952 and 1953. On Oct. 15, 1953, an Israeli raid on the Jordan village of Kibya resulted, according to various reports, in the loss of from 32 to 66 lives. The

Israeli Office of Information

President Chaim Weizmann (center) and David Ben-Gurion (right) meeting in Israel with American ambassador James McDonald after American recognition of the new state

Israeli government disclaimed official responsibility for the raid and charged that 150 Israelis were killed in border clashes during 1953 alone. On Oct. 27 the chief of the Palestine Truce Supervisory Organization, testifying before the U.N. Security Council, stated that the failure to replace the long-standing armistice agreements with formal peace treaties had increased Israeli-Arab tensions to the breaking point. Israel announced (Nov. 23) its intention of invoking the Jordan armistice-agreement clause providing for direct talks on border disputes. On Nov. 24 the Security Council strongly censured Israel for the Kibya raid. See also UNITED NATIONS: *The Palestine Problem.*

Meanwhile Syria and Jordan had registered strong protests against Israeli construction of a canal for a hydroelectric project on the Jordan River. The two countries lodged (Sept. 22) a complaint with the U.N. Security Council that the project would deprive them of water for irrigation. When Israel failed to halt work on the canal pending U.N. investigation, the U.S. government announced (Oct. 20) that financial assistance to Israel would be suspended. Israel halted construction on Oct. 28 and U.S. economic aid was resumed.

On the domestic political scene, Prime Minister Ben-Gurion resigned (Dec. 6) for health reasons; he was succeeded by Foreign Minister Moshe Sharett.

Jordan informed the U.N. on Jan. 4, 1954, that it would not comply with the Israeli request for direct talks and would negotiate only through the Mixed Armistice Commission. The U.S.S.R. vetoed (Jan. 22) a Security Council resolution to allow Israel to continue construction of the Jordan River project providing that the chief of the Palestine Truce Organization ruled that it was not detrimental to Syria or in violation of the Israeli-Syrian armistice.

ISRAEL. See JACOB.

ISRAEL, KINGDOM OF, the northern Hebrew kingdom in ancient Palestine (q.v.) ; see also JEWS.

ISSACHAR, name of the ninth son of Jacob (q.v.), and traditional founder of the tribe of Israel that bore his name. According to the Jewish historian Josephus, the land of Issachar "extended in length from Carmel to the Jordan, in breadth to Mount Tabor." The territory was among the most fertile lands in Israel during Biblical times.

ISSUS, town of ancient Asia Minor, located near the site of present-day Alexandretta, Syria. It was a seaport, built on a narrow strip of coast between high mountains and the Gulf of Issus (now Alexandretta). Issus is celebrated as the site of three battles. In the first occurred the defeat of the Persian king Darius III by Alexander the Great in 333 B.C. In a second battle, in 194 A.D., Lucius Septimius Severus (q.v.) defeated Pescennius Niger, a rival claimant to the Roman throne. Emperor Heraclius of the Eastern Roman Empire, in the third battle at Issus, in

622 A.D., was victorious against the Persians during a war to regain territory formerly lost to the Persians.

ISSY-LES-MOULINEAUX or **ISSY,** a town in the department of Seine, N. central France, located near the Seine R., about 2 miles s.w. of Paris, of which it is a suburb. Manufactured products include paint, cement, chemicals, vegetable oil, silk, and shoes. Pop. (1947) 42,449.

ISTANBUL, formerly CONSTANTINOPLE, the largest city of Turkey and capital of the il of the same name. The city proper is situated on the European mainland, at the s. extremity of the strait of Bosporus (q.v.); a part of the present-day metropolis, however is Üsküdar (Scutari) on the E. bank of the Bosporus, on the Asiatic shore. Istanbul proper is bounded on the N. by an inlet of the harbor known as the Golden Horn, on the E. by the Bosporus, and on the s. by the Sea of Marmara. Among its chief sections are Galata, the mercantile quarter, and Pera, the foreign quarter. Istanbul proper, which is commonly called Stambul, was founded as Constantinople in 328 A.D. by the Roman emperor Constantine the Great by enlarging the ancient town of Byzantium (q.v.). Constantinople was built, like Rome, on seven gently sloping hills, and in medieval times was a walled city. The walls, the most famous of which are those erected by Theodosius II in 447, are today largely in ruins.

Istanbul is historically important, first as the capital of the Byzantine, or Eastern Roman, Empire (330–1453), and later as the capital of the Turkish, or Ottoman, Empire, which succeeded the Byzantine. The contributions to civilization emanating from the city during the period of Byzantine rule are considered by many to be equal to those from Athens, Jerusalem, Rome, and Paris, vitally affecting the development of Roman law, Greek philosophy and art, and the course of Christian theology and church history (see BYZANTINE EMPIRE). After the founding of the city by Constantine the Great it became the major center of Hellenistic culture. As a result of the Turkish conquest in 1453, the Greek scholars of Constantinople fled to western Europe, where their teachings played a vital role in the Renaissance. The Turkish conquest also closed to the nations of western Europe the direct trade route to the East, thereby forcing the navigators of Spain, Portugal, and Italy to search for a new way to the East; their search eventually led to the discovery of the Americas. (See COMMERCE.)

Istanbul is famous as one of the most often besieged cities in the world. Prior to the Turkish conquest it was assailed by the Arabs from 673 to 677, and in 718; by the Bulgarians in 813 and 913; and by the armies of the Fourth Crusade (see CRUSADES), which twice succeeded in taking the city, in 1203 and 1204.

Philip Gendreau, N.Y.

Aerial view of the city of Istanbul. Spanning the Golden Horn is the Galata Bridge.

In 1453 Constantinople fell to the Turks, and became the capital of the Ottoman, or Turkish, Empire; it was the capital of present-day Turkey until 1923, when the newly founded Turkish Republic declared Angora (now Ankara) the capital. During World War I the city was the objective of the Allies' disastrous Gallipoli Campaign (q.v.), and Allied airmen raided the city in 1916 and 1917. It was occupied by Great Britain, France, and Italy from 1918 to 1923.

Istanbul is noted for the picturesqueness of its location and its excellent harbor. The city contains numerous imposing buildings, the most famous of which is the mosque, Hagia Sofia, built about 538 in classic Byzantine architectural style by the emperor Justinian as the Christian church of Santa Sophia (see SAINT SOPHIA), and converted into a mosque by Mohammed II in 1453. It is now the second most important mosque in the Moslem world, the first being that in Mecca. Other mosques in Istanbul are those of Achmet, Suleiman the Magnificent, and Bajazet. The city contains numerous bazaars and palaces. The so-called Great Bazaar, with its long avenues lined with counters and stalls, is the center of the commercial life of the city. Among the palaces, the Old Seraglio is famous as the residence of the Byzantine emperors and Turkish sultans; but the Dolma Bagtcheh, on the Bosporus, is of greater architectural beauty. Istanbul is a city of striking contrasts, with handsome modern buildings, such as the Admiralty and the villas of the well-to-do residential districts, set against the squalor in which the majority of the inhabitants live. It is one of the most cosmopolitan cities in the world, with large minorities of Greeks, Albanians, Bulgarians, and other European nationalities, as well as groups from neighboring Near Eastern countries and Africa. Educational institutions include the University of Istanbul and, near Scutari, a medical school. The Greek and Armenian communities maintain private schools. Robert College, an American institution, dates from 1863.

The principal products of Istanbul are cigarettes, sweetmeats, embroideries, and handmade articles of iron, brass, and wood. Because of the development of modern railway facilities throughout the Near and Middle East, the port of Istanbul no longer enjoys its position as the chief trading center of the region, although there is still considerable exporting of cereal grains, wool, silk, carpets, and hides, and other products of the province

and the Turkish interior. Pop. of city (1950) 1,000,022. Area of province, 2116 sq.m.; pop. (1950) 1,179,666.

ISTHMIAN GAMES, one of the four national festivals of ancient Greece (see GAMES, ANCIENT), so called because the celebrations took place on the Isthmus of Corinth. The games were held in honor of Poseidon, god of the sea; according to tradition, they had been founded either by him or by the legendary Attic hero Theseus. Available records indicate that the first Isthmian Games were held in 582 B.C.; thereafter they were held biannually in the spring. Athletic, equestrian, and musical competitions were featured. The victors were originally awarded wreaths of parsley or wild celery; later, the wreaths were of fir or pine needles. The games are believed to have continued until about the 4th century A.D., when the acceptance of Christianity as the religion of the Roman empire, which then included Greece, brought an end to the practice of many pagan customs.

ISTRIA, mountainous peninsula of Yugoslavia, projecting into the Adriatic Sea, between the gulfs of Trieste and Quarnero. Ancient Istria, or Histria, was the home of Illyrian pirates. It was conquered by the Romans in 177 B.C., by the Franks in 789, and by the dukes of Carinthia in the 10th century. During the Middle Ages it was held by various nobles and in the 18th century it became a crownland of Austria. By the terms of the Treaty of Rapallo (1920), following World War I, Istria was awarded to Italy. The peninsula then became known as the province of Pola, in the region of Venezia Giula. After World War II the Free Territory of Trieste was partitioned from Pola. The remainder of the peninsula was ceded to Yugoslavia. Monte Maggiore (4753 ft.) is the highest peak of Istria. Olives, grains, melons, figs, and wine grapes are the chief agricultural products; fishing, shipbuilding, and the manufacture of wine and lumber are important industries. Area, 1435 sq.m.; population, about 294,000.

ITALIAN ART AND ARCHITECTURE, a term which in its broadest sense includes a number of styles in art and architecture which appeared in Italy after Roman times. The Early Christian, Byzantine, Romanesque, Gothic, and Renaissance periods succeeded one another in the thousand years from the 5th to the 15th century. Only the Renaissance period, however, had a uniquely Italian character, inasmuch as the others were in-

Interior of the Church of Jesus, built by Giacomo da Vignola, in Rome

ternational in scope or had their greatest development in other countries. Men of the Renaissance found models for painting, sculpture, architecture, and writing in classical remains that were being unearthed at the time. Italy of the Renaissance was the cultural capital of the entire Western world, and took the lead in all the arts from the 15th to the 17th century. In the Renaissance for the first time after the Roman Empire the names of artists became generally known and the creative work of painting and building was no longer cloaked in the group anonymity common to the work of medieval guilds and bands of artisans. Artists and architects became famous as individuals and sought to develop their personal styles; the pattern they established has continued in use to the present day.

Further information on individual architects, painters, and sculptors will be found in separate articles on many of the persons mentioned below.

ARCHITECTURE. Renaissance architecture is divided into three periods: (1) Early Renaissance, from about 1420 to 1500; (2) High Renaissance, from about 1500 to 1580; and (3) Baroque, from 1580 to 1780. In general, Renaissance architecture differs from Gothic, the preceding style, in emphasizing horizontal rather than vertical lines, round rather than pointed arches, and the carrying of roof structures on continuous walls rather than on isolated thrust-absorbing members.

Early Renaissance. Architectural experiments of this period took the form of decorative use of classical motifs taken from Roman coins, candelabra, and busts, applied in terracotta to façades of buildings that remained Gothic in mass and plan. The finely chiseled and highly detailed ornamentation is close in feeling to contemporary goldsmith work. The best examples occur in the north in Lombardy, for instance, on the façade of the Certosa at Pavia. This style was carried by the Lombards to Venice, where it gave rise to the most richly decorative of all the local Renaissance schools of building, through the free use of multicolored marble incrustations and surface carving. More important to the full revival of classic types of building mass and plan was the work at Florence of Filippo Brunelleschi, the greatest designer of the Early Renaissance. In the Pazzi Chapel (1425) and the two great basilican churches of Santo Spirito and San Lorenzo he used Roman moldings and details to emphasize the structural lines of the buildings. The Riccardi Palace, built by Michelozzo for the Medici family during this first period of the Renaissance, also shows Roman inspiration in scale and minor details, although it is fundamentally a contemporary Florentine palace type. Leon Battista Alberti was the first to attempt strictly classical exterior design in both religious and secular architecture by an integrated use of superposed orders, pilasters, entablatures, and Roman arches. Florentine architects of later date, such as Bernardo Rosselino and Francesco di Giorgio, carried the new style to Pienza, Siena, and Cortona; others such as Benedetto and Giuliano da Maiano, Luciano da Laurana, and Giuliano da Sangallo, brought it to Naples, Urbino, and Rome. Laurana's ducal palace at Urbino was regarded by contemporaries as the ideal princely residence.

High Renaissance. Bramante, a native of Lombardy, outgrew the goldsmith and decorator limitations of most of his compatriots and predecessors. He was a master builder, and the first to synthesize structure, space, and detail in the classic manner. Severe and grandiose, given to plain surfaces and colossal details, the new style was embodied in the small, domed structure called the Tempietto and in the designs for the Vatican and St. Peter's, in Rome (1503–06). The center of the new movement had shifted from Florence to Rome, where ancient remains could be seen in every street and where powerful popes gave the impetus to ambitious building projects, both religious and secular. The study of the Roman architect Vitruvius (see VITRUVIUS POLIO, MARCUS) and the measuring and drawing of Roman ruins became a standard part of every architect's training. After Bramante, the younger architects Raphael, Baldassare Peruzzi, and Antonio da Sangallo took the lead, and their formal, symmetrical use of tiers of

Roman orders and pedimented windows may be seen in the Farnesina, Massimi, and Farnese palaces. Michelangelo, a giant figure in architecture as well as in painting and sculpture, ushered in a new phase of personal adaptation of classic elements. Earlier lessons learned from Vitruvius and Roman ruins had been thoroughly assimilated, and now a freer play of personal stylistic elements became dominant. The dome, either single or grouped, and the tunnel and cross vaults, often coffered, continued the orthodox forms of roofing, but internal piers became heavier, columns frequently took the place of pilasters on the exterior, and the single, colossal order (see ORDER), replacing tiers of superposed orders, reigned supreme. St. Peter's at Rome, remodeled by Michelangelo, became the archetype for Renaissance churches. His Capitoline group of buildings in Rome established the free use of balustrades and sculptured figures as architectural adjuncts to the façade itself. Certain elements of the Capitoline group as well as details of the interior of the Laurentian Library in Florence foreshadow Baroque architectural freedom. The more sedate work of Giacomo da Vignola set the style for villa architecture centering in Rome. He built the Villa Caprarola and the Villa de' Papa Giulio.

The continuing domination of classic formulas is seen both in the writings and work, especially at Vicenza, of Andrea Palladio. This phase is known as the Classisima, although the term Palladian has also been used for the scientific-theoretical style which was exemplified also by Vignola, Sebastiano Serlio (1475–1554), and Vincenzo Scamozzi (1552–1616), all of whom published books on architecture in addition to practicing as architects. Palladio's sober, carefully studied interrelation of classic elements was first embodied in the arcade around the basilica at Vicenza, which was followed by examples such as the Chieregati and Barbarano palaces, and the Teatro Olimpico. He also built in Venice the churches of Santa Maria Maggiore and the Redentore.

Baroque. Opposed to Classisima or Palladian severity, the Baroque style was characterized by defiance of tradition, broken lines and curves, unexpected theatrical perspectives, and unusual placement of figures and objects. Associated with the Counter Reformation demand for lavish and appealing effects in the churches aimed at holding and attracting worshipers, the style made use of richly colored marbles and decorative cupids, scroll-.

ITALIAN ARCHITECTURE
Above: St. Peter's Cathedral in Rome, outstanding example of High Renaissance style in Italian architecture. Right: Building at Vicenza built in classical style of Palladio.

work, and animated figures, and often imitated drapery in metal and stone. Domenico Fontana, Carlo Maderna, Giovanni Lorenzo Bernini, and Francesco Borromini were its greatest representatives. One of the most grandiose works of the style is Bernini's colonnade and approach to St. Peter's, Rome. See also the article BAROQUE.

Following the Baroque period, Italian styles no longer dominated the European scene. In the 18th century, France set the architectural styles, and French Rococo and the later archeological Neoclassic were imitated all over Europe, including Italy. The huge palace grounds of Caserta, near Naples, reminiscent of Versailles, is one of the few ambitious architectural projects carried out in Italy after the Renaissance and before recent times. Italian 19th-century building showed the eclectic stylistic trends common to the western world. The 20th century brought the collective efforts sponsored by the Fascist government under Benito Mussolini. Many modern ferroconcrete and glass railroad stations, factories, public buildings, and housing settlements were constructed with state backing. Notable examples are the modern piazza at Brescia, the railroad station at Florence, and the new town of Sabaudia in the Pontine marshes.

SCULPTURE. The 13th-century sculptor Niccolo Pisano employed both medieval and classical forms in his work. His son Giovanni

ITALIAN ART

Above: Detail from "Marriage of the Virgin," by Raphael. Left: Drawing by Leonardo da Vinci in which the character of the subject is shown, despite his fanciful armor.

Pisano was the dominant influence on Italian sculpture of the 14th century because his large, expressive forms gave new life to the Gothic formula. A greater realism and renewed interest in classic forms took place in the 15th century; the nude human figure as a subject for grand concepts made its reappearance in sculpture. Lorenzo Ghiberti produced a pair of bronze doors for the baptistery of the church of San Giovanni in Florence, a delicate masterpiece of relief sculpture which became known as "the Gates of Paradise" and influenced all similar projects after that time. Jacopo della Quercia combined in his relief of "Adam and Eve", at Bologna, the robust quality of the antique with the dramatic spirit of the Renaissance. Donatello, the outstanding sculptor of the 15th century, acquired a complete knowledge of human anatomy, and gave humanness of expression to his grand classic forms. His work represented a vigorous pageant of life as contrasted to a medieval religious symbolism. His dramatic figure "Lo Zuconne" in the Campanile, Florence, is the embodiment of the Early Renaissance spirit. Antonio Pollaiuolo and Andrea del Verrocchio were representative of the scientific realism in Florentine sculpture of the late 15th century. Verrocchio's equestrian statue of "Colleoni" in Venice utilized a forceful realism and a monumental scaling to achieve a new power.

The dominant personality in High Renaissance sculpture was Michelangelo. His work represented a vigor, drama, and exaltation unique within the realm of Western sculpture. The climax of his style was reached in the Medici Tombs, for which he designed both the architecture and sculpture; in the nude figures "Night" and "Day" he used the human form as universal symbols. Benvenuto Cellini utilized the Michelangelesque forms for decorative purposes; his rendering of graceful detail and his remarkable work as a goldsmith made him extraordinarily popular. The Baroque style, with its insistence on exaggerated emotional effects and sharply illustrative technique, was summed up in the work of Giovanni Lorenzo Bernini. "The Fountain of the Four Rivers" at Rome, executed by assistants of Bernini after the master's design, displayed the lavishly ornamental character of the Baroque.

PAINTING. From the 13th century through the 16th the development of Italian art centered in Siena, Florence, and Venice. Siena was the most isolated center, and the character of Sienese art remained close to the Ro-

Frick Collection

"Man in a Red Cap," painting by Titian

manesque-Byzantine tradition. To this tradition the Sienese school added a touch of naturalism and delicate sentiment in order to illustrate Biblical tales more clearly. Duccio di Buoninsegna, the greatest master of the Sienese school, introduced a more rhythmic and complex style of composition into painting. He also added a gracious characterization to the figures in his paintings of early Christian legends. Among other notable painters of Siena were the brothers Ambrogio and Pietro Lorenzetti, Simone Martini, and Stefano di Giovanni, known as "Sassetta". They added refinement of color and subtlety of composition to the native tradition. Elements of pathos, narration, and rich decoration were revealed by a rare purity of style within the framework of small panels and altarpieces.

At the close of the 13th century, Giotto, one of the supreme artists of medieval Italy, transformed the role of painting into one of grandeur, naturalism, and depth of human feeling by his series of murals at Padua and Assisi. The monumental scale of his designs established Florence as the fountainhead of European art, and the bold innovations in his work paved the way for the work of the Renaissance. At the beginning of the 15th century Masaccio introduced a new ease and freedom of gesture in the figures of murals.

"The Blood of the Redeemer," painting by Giovanni Bellini

Aerial perspective, that is, the effect of atmosphere suffusing distant objects, and the constructing of figures by strong areas of light and shade were Masaccio's special contributions. His mural "The Tribute Money" in the Branacci Chapel, Florence, exemplified his art at its peak. Andrea del Castagno combined an austerity with a sculptural solidity that foreshadowed the grand art of Michelangelo. Castagno's "Last Supper" welded a vigorous realism to bold, complex space composition. Other 15th-century masters were Paolo Uccello, Andrea Mantegna, and Piero della Francesca. Francesca, in his set of frescoes at Arezzo, representing the "Story of the True Cross", revealed a world of arrested action and a mood of withdrawal from the ordinary aspects of life in his classically articulated designs and monumental figure groupings. In his works, the union of the physical and the spiritual was lifted to the level of sublime detachment. In contrast to Piero della Francesca, Domenico di Tommaso Ghirlandajo and Benozzi Gozzoli were popular illustrators of the Bible in terms of everyday life; their work was full of picturesque sentiment and tapestrylike detail. The gentle and spiritual art of Giovanni da Fiesole, known as Fra Angelico, was suffused with a lyrical religious sentiment, and stood apart from the main currents of the time, being more closely related to the early Sienese masters. His devout life as a Dominican monk was undoubtedly a chief factor in lending his art its rare grace and fervor.

The exploration of the external world, based upon the rational interpretation of experience as opposed to medieval mysticism, was the fundamental principle of the early Renaissance. The mastery of the physical world in terms of realistic images was a long and involved process. Uccello experimented with new principles of perspective (lines converging into space) in his famous battle pictures, such as "Battle of San Romano", now in the Uffizi Gallery, Florence. Piero della Francesca had written books on scientific perspective. Antonio Pollaiuolo made exhaustive studies of the nude in contorted postures and contributed to the study of anatomy during this period. Luca Signorelli, through analysis of the structure of the skeleton and dissection of cadavers, acquired a remarkable skill in rendering physical movement. In his mural "Torments of the Damned" (Cathedral, Orvieto), the writhing of men in agony is vividly portrayed. Sandro Botticelli illustrated myths from antiquity in elaborately decorative

National Gallery of Art, Mellon Collection

ITALIAN SCULPTURE

*Above: A portrait bust of Giovanni Lorenzo
Bernini, the 17th-century Italian sculptor.
Right: "Madonna and Child," by Donatello.*

paintings, full of nostalgic charm and sensu-
ousness. He added to Italian art one of the
most intricately graceful uses of line ever created by a Western artist. Moreover, his art
represented the beginning of a secular art that
eventually superseded religious painting in the
course of the 16th century. "The Birth of
Venus" (Uffizi) is Botticelli's supreme example in this field.

Leonardo da Vinci, working at the end of
the 15th and the beginning of the 16th century, summed up for the Renaissance both
the passion for scientific inquiry and the spirit
of humanism in art. He examined thoroughly
formalistic problems of space, anatomical and
psychological aspects of character, and chi-
aroscuro (q.v.) effects to lend mystery and
drama to his work. His mural "The Last
Supper" (in the monastery of Santa Maria
delle Grazia, Milan) and the "Mona Lisa"
(Louvre, Paris) are his most famous examples. He exerted a great influence on the
work of 16th-century painters, particularly
that of Raphael and Michelangelo. Michelangelo, one of the giant figures of the 16th

century, was a sculptor, architect, painter,
and poet. He created a grand concept of the
human form, more expressive and monumental than it had ever been before. His decorations for the ceiling of the Sistine Chapel in
the Vatican recorded the epic of mankind
from the Creation to the Last Judgment.
Michelangelo's figures create a sense of superhuman conflict with the universe. Raphael
combined some of the lyric qualities of Leonardo da Vinci with the dramatic power of
Michelangelo, adding a gracious harmony and
sentiment of his own. He painted many fine

"Moses," sculpture by Michelangelo at the Church of S. Pietro in Vincoli, Rome

portraits and popular versions of the Madonna, and created one of the finest series of frescoes of his period, "The School of Athens" in the Vatican at Rome. In representing groups of scholars and philosophers surrounded by spacious architectural vaults, he summed up, pictorially, the homage of Renaissance man to ancient Greece.

Venetian painting represented both a more luxurious and a more worldly attitude toward life than did either the Sienese or Florentine schools. The founder of the great age of painting in Venice, during the 15th century, was Giovanni Bellini, whose work covered all phases of religious humanism, and in several late paintings created the beginning of secular and Romantic art. His favorite subject was the Madonna and Child, many versions of which express a human warmth, grace, and serenity unequaled in Italian painting. Among his late works is a splendid bacchanale, "The Feast of the Gods" (National Gallery, Washington, D.C.), which combines a paganism with a lofty classical spirit. This picture represented the dawn of Romanticism in Renaissance art, and its mood and spirit was both sustained and deepened in the work of Bellini's pupil Il Giorgione. The Romantic motifs of this painter, such as the "Sleeping Venus" (Dresden) and the "Pastoral Symphony" (Louvre, Paris), together with his use of sensual forms, richness of color, and an Arcadian landscape world, broke through the boundaries of religious painting and created a poetical sphere in art which proclaimed the glory of the physical life. With Titian, pupil of Bellini and Giorgione, art flowered into a full-bodied, vigorously sensual experience, a frank expression of the dominance of man's individuality. Portraiture assumed a major role in the history of painting, representing the glory and beauty of Venetian society as exemplified by wealthy princes, merchants, and their families. Titian recorded the fullest splendor of the High Renaissance. The herculean compositions of Il Tintoretto and the sumptuous festival scenes of Paolo Veronese were rooted in the tradition of Titian and complete the history of Renaissance painting.

In the 17th century Italian painting became both academic and eclectic. The painters attempted to create a lofty style by a cold imitation of the great previous masters. Lodovico and Annibale Carracci of Bologna were the leading exponents of the new manner. Their elaborate works are characterized by bombast and theatricality. A realistic movement was led by Michelangelo da Caravaggio, who painted scenes of everyday life with striking light effects and careful representation of nature. His work was immensely popular and exerted a wide influence on painters. With Caravaggio, a new, more obviously illustrative current entered the mainstreams of art.

The 18th century was dominated by Giovanni Battista Tiepolo (1696–1770), whose large fresco decorations emulated the work of Veronese, but were more light and airy in tone. His style was both highly skillful and theatrical in character. In Venice, too, a group of painters developed a school of architectural and landscape art, depicting canal scenes surrounded by buildings and bridges. It was an intimate, localized school of painting, and its best-known masters were Antonio Canaletto, his pupil Bernardo Bellotto (1724–80), and Francesco Guardi. Pietro Longhi painted the everyday life, manners, and frivolities of well-to-do Venetians. Giambattista Piranesi made great contributions as engraver and architect. His fantastic prints of prisons and grand architectural interiors were daring in conception. Antonio Canova (1757–1822) was the leader of the Classic Revival in Italy, spurred by a renewed interest in Greek sculpture of the highly graceful Hellenic period.

Though Italy still remained an art center during the 19th century, the mainstream of art was developed in Spain and France. In modern times, Italy's chief contributions to painting were the movement of Futurism (q.v.) initiated by Gino Severini and Umberto Boccioni (1882–1916), and a metaphysical, surrealist school of painting founded by Giorgio di Chirico and Carlo Carra (1881–). See also BYZANTINE ART; FLORENTINE SCHOOL; FRESCO; RENAISSANCE; SIENESE SCHOOL; VENETIAN SCHOOL.

ITALIAN EAST AFRICA, former Italian colonial State in E. Africa, comprising Eritrea, Ethiopia, and Italian Somaliland (qq.v.), and established under the terms of legislation adopted on June 1, 1936. Ethiopia was incorporated with Italian Somaliland in the new colony of Italian East Africa. Addis Ababa, the capital of Ethiopia, was the capital of the new colonial state. Italian East Africa was divided into five administrative regions.

Between January and December, 1941, during World War II, British, Ethiopian, and other Allied military contingents conducted a successful offensive against the armed forces of Italy in Italian East Africa. Eritrea and Italian Somaliland were placed under British occupation, and Ethiopia was re-established

The Italian greyhound

(January, 1942) as a sovereign state.

By the terms of the peace treaty imposed (1947) on Italy after the war, the Italian government abjured all claims to its former African possessions; disposition of the former possessions was made the responsibility of the "Big Four" Powers (the United States, the United Kingdom, the Soviet Union, and France). In 1948 the "Big Four", having failed to reach agreement on disposition, referred the problem to the General Assembly of the United Nations. The General Assembly approved (November, 1949) a plan granting independence to Italian Somaliland after ten years as a U.N. Trust Territory under Italian administration and postponing disposition of Eritrea pending preparation of recommendations by a special U.N. commission. Italy assumed the trusteeship over Italian Somaliland on April 1, 1950. On Dec. 2, 1950, the General Assembly adopted a plan providing for the creation of an Ethiopian-Eritrean federation, under the Ethiopian crown. The federation was established on Sept. 15, 1952.

ITALIAN GREYHOUND, a dog of the toy class; a miniature type of greyhound (q.v.). The Italian greyhound is believed to have originated in Asia Minor over two thousand years ago by the interbreeding of small specimens of the full-sized greyhound. From Asia Minor the breed spread into southern Europe and then into England, where it became a favorite of queens and ladies of the nobility. The Italian greyhound was introduced into the United States in the late 19th century. The dog has a long and narrow head; large, bright eyes; soft and delicate ears; a deep, narrow chest; a back that curves and droops at the hind quarters; and a rather long tail which is held low. The dog is of various colors, in-

cluding white, fawn, red, blue, and black, and weighs about eight pounds. Although it originated in warm regions, the Italian greyhound thrives equally well in northern climates. Its slender form, graceful movements, and intelligence make it a great favorite as a pet.

ITALIAN LANGUAGE, a term used generically to denote those modern types of Latin speech spoken in the Italian peninsula, in Sicily, Corsica, and Malta, along the N.E. shore of the Adriatic Sea, and on the southern watershed of the Alps as a whole. Considered as a single language with numerous dialects, Italian is one of the group of Neo-Latin or Romance languages (q.v.) which are the direct offspring of the Latin tongue as spoken by the Romans and imposed by them upon the nations under their dominion. The chief subdivisions of the Romance group are French, Spanish, Portuguese, Provençal, Romanian, and Italian, though certain Italian dialects are so peculiar that they are classified as a separate branch of Romance or in another language system altogether. Of all the Romance languages, Italian retains the closest resemblance to Latin. The struggle between the written but dead language and the various forms of the living speech, most of which were derived from Vulgar Latin (see LATIN), was nowhere so intense or so protracted as in Italy.

During the long period of evolution many dialects sprang up. In the north and northwest the *Gallo-Italian* dialects predominate; they were Piedmontese, Lombard, Ligurian, and Emilian or Bolognese, all of which display a close affinity to French in their pronunciation and truncated terminations. The *Venetian* dialect is spoken in the Italian Tirol and parts of what used to be Dalmatia and Istria, in addition to the Venetian area itself. South of these districts the centro-southern *Italian* dialects are found; these are Tuscan, Corsican, north Sardinian, Roman (with which are included the closely related dialects of Umbria and The Marches), Campanian (with which are included Abruzzese and Apulian), Sicilian, and Calabrian. South and central Sardinian dialects are so distinct from this entire group of dialects that they constitute a separate branch of the Romance languages, while an Italian dialect of the eastern Alps, Friulian, which is spoken in N.E. Venetia, is considered by most philologists to be a member of the Rheto-Romansch languages.

The multiplicity of these dialects, and their individual claims upon their native speakers as a "pure" Italian speech, presented a peculiar difficulty in the evolution of an accepted form of Italian which would reflect the cultural unity of the entire peninsula. Even the earliest popular Italian documents, produced in the 10th century, are dialectal in language, and during the following three centuries Italian writers wrote in their native dialects, producing a number of competing regional schools of literature between which communication in the vulgar tongue was almost impossible. In the 14th century the Tuscan dialect began to predominate, because of Tuscany's central position in Italy, and because of the aggressive commerce of its most important city, Florence. Moreover, of all the Italian dialects, Tuscan departs least in morphology and phonology from classic Latin, and therefore harmonizes best with the Italian traditions of Latin culture. Finally Florentine culture produced the three literary artists who best summarized Italian thought and feeling of the early Renaissance and late Middle Ages: Dante Alighieri, Francesco Petrarch, and Giovanni Boccaccio (see ITALIAN LITERATURE). Grammarians in the 15th and 16th centuries attempted to confer upon the pronunciation, syntax, and vocabulary of 14th-century Tuscan the status of a central and classic Italian speech. Eventually this classicism, which might have made Italian another "dead" language, was widened to include the organic changes inevitable in a living tongue. In the dictionaries and publications of the Accademia della Crusca, founded in 1583, which have been accepted by Italians as authoritative in Italian linguistic matters, compromises between classic purism and living Tuscan usage have been successfully effected.

In modern Italian the Latin qualities of the Florentine dialect are preserved, but the vocabulary of Latin has been made to meet the changing conditions of Italian life. The simplicity of the phonetic and morphological changes from Latin, along with a nearly perfectly phonetic orthography, makes the acquisition of Italian easy for a person who knows Latin or any of its modern Romance forms.

ITALIAN LITERATURE, the literature written in the Italian language and dating from about the 13th century to the present. Previous to the 13th century, the literary language of Italy was Latin, which served for the writing of chronicles, historical poems, heroic legends, lives of the saints, religious poems, and didactic and scientific works. In the latter part of the 12th century and the early part of the 13th, a school of Italian poets arose who wrote, in the Provençal language (q.v.) and also in an Italianized form of French, poems in imitation of those of the Provençal troubadours (see TROUBADOUR). Subsequently, at the court of Frederick II in Sicily, a group of poets known as the Sicilian school, headed by the king himself, devoted themselves to writing similar poetry in the Italian language. In addition to those of the Sicilian school, poets in various other parts of Italy, including Tuscany, Milan, Verona, and Venice, also began to imitate and build upon the forms of Provençal poetry.

The first important native Italian poetry was that of the Franciscan monks, who wrote narrative poems based on the Gospels in simple and original forms that had great popular appeal; among this group of monks was Jacopone da Todi (1230?–1306), author of *Crucifixion* and *My Lady Poverty*. In the latter part of the 13th century, secular Italian poets began definitely to break away from the Provençal tradition. Among the poets who set up a new Italian style, which was known as the *dolce stil nuovo,* were the Bolognese poet Guido Guinizelli (1240?–74), whom Dante (see below) considered the father of Italian love poetry; and the Florentine poet Guido Cavalcanti. In the 14th century, with the work of Dante Alighieri, Francesco Petrarch, and Giovanni Boccaccio, Italian literature reached one of the highest peaks of its development. All three of these masters wrote in the Tuscan, or Florentine, dialect of the Italian language (q.v.); its use by them made Tuscan the cultural language of all Italy and the basis for modern Italian. Dante is famous for his *Divine Comedy* (q.v.), a long, philosophical poem considered one of the masterpieces of world literature. Petrarch is best known for his *Canzoniere* or *Rime,* sonnets and odes to his lady Laura; and for his study of the Greek and Latin classics and his achievement in reviving in Italy an interest in ancient literature and culture. Boccaccio is world famous for his prose work the *Decameron* (q.v.), published in 1353, a collection of one hundred tales in which every aspect of contemporary Italian life is vividly depicted.

The Italian literature of the 15th century was dominated by the literature of ancient Greece and Rome, knowledge of which was by this time widespread throughout Italy (see HUMANISM; RENAISSANCE). Considerable work in translation from classic writers

Left: Francesco Petrarch. Right: Dante Alighieri.

and in imitation of them was done in this century, but works of originality and of outstanding merit are lacking. The principal center of literary and scholarly activity in Italy during this time was Florence; other important centers of learning were Naples, Ferrara, Rome, Mantua, Venice, Bologna, and Milan. Among the important writers of the time were Luigi Pulci (1432–84), noted for his epic of chivalry *Il Morgante Maggiore* (28 cantos, 1483); Matteo Maria Boiardo, whose principal work is the unfinished historical epic *Orlando Innamorato* (1487); Domenico Burchiello, known for his coarse poetry written in a spirit of burlesque and very popular at the time; Antonio Cammelli (1440–1502), also a writer of burlesque poetry; Giovanni Mainardi (1396–1483), writer of prose tales, including *Le Facezie dell' Arlotto;* the great humanist Lorenzo Valla, among whose works are translations into Latin from Homer, Thucydides, and Herodotus, and the original work *De Elegentia Latinæ Linguæ* (6 vols., 1471); and Jacopo Sannazaro, author principally of *Arcadia* (1504), one of the earliest of modern pastorals in prose, and the model for much subsequent work of this type in Italy and elsewhere.

Italian literature in the 16th century remained characterized by imitation of the literature of ancient Greece and Rome, but was also influenced by the writings of Dante, Petrarch, and Boccaccio. In spite of the tendency to imitate, a considerable body of original literature was written, principally by three writers. One was Lodovico Ariosto, whose chivalric epic poem *Orlando Furioso* (1516), a sequel to the *Orlando Innamorato* of Boiardo, is famous for its analysis of love in many aspects. Torquato Tasso, considered the greatest literary genius of the time, is noted for creating a new type of epic, the Christian or crusading epic, and wrote the best example of this type, *Gerusalemme Liberata* (1575), which deals with the events of the First Crusade. The third of the outstanding writers of the century was Niccolò Machiavelli, who in his works stressed the part that materialistic forces play in human events; he is world famous for his treatise on politics *Il Principe* ("The Prince", 1513). The lyric poets of the 16th century derived their inspiration largely from Petrarch. Important among them were the Venetian ecclesiastic, scholar, and poet Pietro Bembo, author of numerous *Rime* and a prose work (*Prose della Volgar Lingua,* 1525) urging writers to imitate classic literature and that of Dante, Petrarch, and Boccaccio; Angelo di Constanzo (1507–91); and Bernardino Rota (1509–75). The Petrarchian idealization of love, which was the chief characteristic of the work of the above-mentioned and numerous other lyric poets, had great influence on the work of the group of contemporary French poets known as the *Pléiade* (q.v.) and on that of the two English poets Sir Thomas Wyatt and Sir Philip Sidney. Satiric poetry also flourished in Italy in the 16th century, notably in the works of Francesco Berni (1497–1536), author of a satiric type of sonnet from which is derived the term "bernesque", signifying jocose poetry; and Antonio Francesco Grazzini (1503–84), whose work is largely imitative of Berni's. In Italian drama, the most important development of the time was the creation of the type of improvised drama known as the *commedia dell' arte* (q.v.). During this period was written the earliest tragedy in Italian literature and also one of the earliest in world literature, *Sofonisba* (1515) by Giovanni Giorgio Trissino. The period was distinguished also by the dialogues, such as *Eroici Furori* (1585), by the great Italian philosopher Giordano Bruno; the noted biographical work *Vite de' Più Eccelenti Pittori, Scultori, ed Architetti Italiani* (1550) by Giorgio Vasari; the *Autobiography* (after 1558) of Benvenuto Cellini; and *Il Cortegiano* (1528) by Count Baldassare Castiglione, a dialogue in which he describes an ideal court life.

In the 17th century the intellectual life of Italy took its tone largely from the religious movement known as the Counter Reformation. Just as under this movement the individual was prohibited from seeking religious experience for himself and was bound by the rituals and forms of the Church, scholars and writers were restricted by traditions and rules, and for the most part devoted themselves rather to recombining into new works types of literature already in existence than to creating original works. Nevertheless some significant literature was written during this time. Among the writers of such work were Gabriello Chiabrera, author of epics, lyrics, pastorals, odes, and satires; Giambattista Marini, the chief exponent of the use in poetry of artificial and affected conceptions or conceits, a form of writing known as concettism (*Adone,* 1623); the satirist Traiano Boccalini (*Dispatches from Parnassus,* 1612); Alessandro Tassoni, known principally for his mock epic *La Secchia Rapita* (12 cantos, 1622); the scientist and historian Fra Paolo Sarpi, author of *History of the Council of Trent* (1619); and Tommaso Campanella, noted for his description of a utopian state in *City of the Sun* (1623).

The 18th century, in reaction against the principles that characterized the previous century, was a time of freedom of thought and a breaking away from outmoded traditions in

Left: Giovanni Boccaccio. Right: Lodovico Ariosto.

literature. The greatest literary development of the period took place in the drama (see DRAMA: *Italian Drama*). The outstanding dramatists of the century were Carlo Goldoni, author of approximately one hundred and fifty comedies, in which he turned the *commedia dell' arte* into a serious art form; and Count Vittorio Alfieri, author of nineteen tragedies in which he displayed a hatred of political tyranny and urged the revival of a national spirit in Italy. In the front rank of the Italian writers of this century was also the poet Giuseppe Parini, noted for his satiric epic *Il Giorno* (written after 1760), a vigorous criticism of the social injustices and the vices of the period. Other important writers of the century include Apostolo Zeno, the co-founder (1710) of the earliest Italian journal of literary criticism, the *Giornale dei Letterati d' Italia*, and the writer of a number of melodramatic librettos for operas; and Metastasio, who wrote opera librettos for the most important composers of the time, including Wolfgang Amadeus Mozart. Two famous autobiographies by Italians also appeared in the 18th century, that of Giovanni Jacopo Casanova, written between 1785 and 1798 and published in French as *Mémoires Écrits par Lui-Même* (12 vols., 1826–38); and the *Memorie Inutili* (3 vols., 1797) by the playwright Count Carlo Gozzi. A contemporary work which was of importance because it foreshadowed later Italian Romantic literature was the translation (1763) by Melchiorre Cesarotti of *The Poems of Ossian* by the Scottish author James Macpherson.

The influence which formed the literature of Italy from the beginning of the 19th century to 1861, when the Kingdom of Italy was established (see ITALY: *History*), was primarily the strong national consciousness which was at the time urging all of Italy into rebellion against the forces keeping its various sections from forming one nation. Other influences were devotion to the Catholic Church, and a romanticism which imitated the contemporary Romantic movements in the literature of France and Germany and also sought to promote political unification and Catholic ideals. The dominant tendencies of the period were best expressed by the novelists Ugo Foscolo and Alessandro Manzoni and the poet Count Giacomo Leopardi. Italian patriotism found a notable exemplar in Foscolo, and both patriotism and romanticism, the latter derived from the German master Goethe, permeate Foscolo's novel *Ultime Lettere di Jacopo Ortis* (1802). Devotion to the Church

as well as patriotism were the paramount characteristics of the work of Manzoni, the leader of the Italian Romantic school. He is famous for his novel *I Promessi Sposi* ("The Betrothed", 1825–26), a historical study of life in 17th-century Italy; the work is notable for its vivid description of a plague that devastated Milan, for its excellent characterizations, and for the beauty of its language. The third outstanding writer of the first half of the 19th century was the Romantic poet Leopardi, whose works are pessimistic in character; among them are *Canzoni* (1824), *Canti* (1836), and the satire in verse *I Paralipomeni della Batracomionmachia* (1842). Among other writers of historical novels in the first half of the 19th century were Marchese Massimo d'Azeglio (*Ettore Fieramosca*, 1833), Cesare Cantù (*Margherita Pusterla*, 1837), and Francesco Domenico Guerrazzi (*Beatrice Cenci*, 1854).

For the first two decades after the unification of Italy in 1861, Italian literature, largely influenced by the same spirit of scientific materialism that prevailed in the literature of other important European countries at the time, imitated the naturalism (q.v.) which was the leading literary school of France and Germany. The variety of naturalism that developed in Italy is known as *verismo* ("verism"). The veristic movement in Italy was succeeded by an esthetic one, led by Gabriele D'Annunzio, which stressed elaborate beauty of language, egotism, and violent emotion, and frequently took for subject matter corrupt forms of sophisticated life. In reaction against both naturalism and the estheticism of D'Annunzio, the Italian writers of the early part of the 20th century interested themselves in social problems. Between 1905 and 1914 Italian literature was also influenced by the artistic movement known as Futurism (q.v.); the literary phase of Futurism originated in Italy under the leadership of Emilio Filippo Tommaso Marinetti. After World War I, Italian literature, like all other forms of Italian culture, was dominated by the Fascist political movement (see FASCISM). Although the Fascist regime endeavored to encourage the development of literature by the granting of prizes, subsidies, and pensions to writers, no significant literary work was done in Italy during the period (1922–44) of Fascist control. A number of leading Italian writers left Italy to avoid the tyranny of the Fascist government; among them were Giuseppe Antonio Borgese (1882–1952), who settled in the United States; and Ignazio Silone, who between 1931 and 1944 lived at first in Germany and then in Switzerland.

Below in alphabetical order are grouped representative Italian writers of the period from 1861 to the present, together with characteristic works. For further evaluation of their work and their place in Italian literature, see separate articles under the names of authors listed without birth and death dates.

Novelists and Writers of Short Stories: Sibilla Aleramo (1879–), noted particularly for her novel *Una Donna* (1906); Antonio Beltramelli (1879–1930), among whose works are *Il Cavalier Mostardo* (1921) and *L'Uomo Nuovo* (1923); Massimo Bontempelli (1884–), author of *La Vita Operosa* (1920) and *Il Figlio di Due Madri* (1933); Giuseppe Antonio Borgese (1882–1952), author of *Il Pellegrino Appasionato* (short stories, 1933); Carlo Collodi (pseudonym of Carlo Lorenzini, 1826–90), famous for his story for children *Le Avventure di Pinocchio* (1882); Luigi Capuana (1839–1915), among whose works is the novel *Il Marchese di Roccaverdina* (1901); D'Annunzio (*Il Piacere,* 1889, and *Notturno,* 1921); Grazia Deledda, writer of stories of Sardinian peasant life, who won the Nobel Prize for literature in 1926 (*Racconti Sardi,* 1893, and *Annalena Bilsini,* 1928); Antonio Fogazzaro (*Il Santo,* 1905, and *Leila,* 1910); Alfredo Panzini (1863–1939), who wrote the novels *Io Cerco Moglie* (1920) and *Il Bacio di Lesbia* (1937); Matilda Serao, author of psychological novels, including *Storia di Due Anime* (1904) and *Mors Tua* (1926); Ignazio Silone (*Pane e Vino,* 1937, and *The Seed Beneath the Snow,* published in English only, 1942); Federigo Tozzi (*Tre Croci,* 1920, and *Il Podere,* 1921); and Giovanni Verga (*Cavalleria Rusticana,* 1880).

Poets: Giosuè Carducci, winner of the Nobel Prize for literature in 1906, and among whose works in verse are *Satana e Polemiche Sataniche* (1879) and *Odi Barbare* (1887); D'Annunzio (*Laudi del Cielo, del Mare, della Terra, e degli Eroi,* 1903); Giuseppe Chiarini (1833–1908), noted for his translation (1880) of *Atta Troll* by the German poet Heinrich Heine; and Giovanni Pascoli (*Myricae,* 3 vols., 1892, 1895, and 1897).

Critics, Philosophers, Historians, and Essayists: Benedetto Croce, the philosopher, literary critic, and historian, among whose works are *Filosofia Come Scienza dello Spirito, Saggio Sull'Hegel* (1906), *La Letteratura della Nuova Italia* (4 vols., 1914–15), and *Storia d'Europa nel Seculo Decimonono* (1932); Edmondo de Amicis (1846–1908), known for

Harper Bros.

Ignazio Silone

his *El Cuore* (1886), the journal of an Italian schoolboy; Francesco De Sanctis (1817–83), the founder of modern Italian literary criticism, among whose works is *La Letteratura Italiana nel Secolo XIX* (1897); the historian Guglielmo Ferrero, among whose works are *Grandezza e Decadenza di Roma* (1902–07) and *The Principles of Power: The Great Political Crises of History* (published in English only, 1942); the philosopher Giovanni Gentile (1875–1944), among whose works are *Origini e Dottrina del Fascismo* (1929) and *La Filosofia dell'Arte* (1931); and Giovanni Papini, world famous for his *Storia de Cristo* (1921; Eng. trans. *Life of Christ,* 1923).

ITALIAN REPUBLIC. See Cisalpine Republic.

ITALIAN SOMALILAND or **SOMALIA,** former colony of Italy in E. Africa, now constituting a United Nations Trust Territory administered by the Italian government, and bounded on the N. by the Gulf of Aden, on the E. by the Indian Ocean, on the S. and S.W. by the British crown colony of Kenya, and on the W. by Ethiopia and the British Somaliland Protectorate. Mogadiscio (pop., about 70,000) is the administrative center and chief seaport. Other important towns are Chisimaio (pop., about 10,000) and Brava (pop., about 4000). Area of Trust Territory, about 194,000 sq.m.; pop. (1950 est.) 1,000,000, including about 4500 Italians.

The coast line, approximately 1450 m. in length, is closely bordered by low, rocky hills; there are few natural harbors. Much of the interior consists of an arid plateau, which has an average elevation of about 3000 ft. and slopes gradually upward from the coast ranges. Only two rivers of consequence traverse the Territory, namely the Juba in the s. and the Webbe Shibeli in the s. central region. The valleys of these streams, especially the Juba, contain large tracts of fertile land, but the rest of the Territory is largely desert.

Farming and the raising of cattle, goats, sheep, and camels are the chief occupations. The leading crops are cotton, rice, corn, bananas, and sugar cane, grown principally in the fertile Juba Valley. Exports include cattle, hides, aromatic gums, essential oils, resin, cotton, kapok, bananas, and ivory; imports are iron and steel products, machinery, timber, and foodstuffs. Highways and secondary roads have an aggregate length of about 5300 m. A 70-mile railway links Mogadiscio with the towns of Adalei, Afgoi, and Villagio Duca degli Abruzzi.

Somalis comprise an overwhelming majority of the Population (see SOMALI). The predominant religious grouping is the Sunni sect of Mohammedanism.

Toward the close of the 19th century, through treaties negotiated with native Somali sultans and conventions with Great Britain, Ethiopia, and Zanzibar, Italy acquired a foothold along the coast of Somaliland. By the provisions of the Treaty of London (1915), which brought Italy into World War I on the side of the Allies, and in consequence of various agreements concluded after the war, Italian holdings in Somaliland were extended by additional territory, including the town of Chisimaio and the right bank of the Juba R. In 1936 Italy merged Italian Somaliland, Eritrea (q.v.), and newly conquered Ethiopia (q.v.), forming the colonial State of Italian East Africa (q.v.). In 1941 during World War II, British Imperial and Ethiopian forces defeated the Italian armies in East Africa and liberated Ethiopia. Italian Somaliland and Eritrea were placed under British occupation pending disposition of Italy's colonies.

By the terms of the Italian peace treaty adopted (1947) after World War II, Italy was forced to renounce title to its possessions in Africa, and responsibility for their disposition was allocated to the "Big Four" Powers (the United States, the United Kingdom, France,

and the Soviet Union). In 1948, the "Big Four", having failed to reach an agreement on disposition, referred the matter to the General Assembly of the United Nations. A plan granting independence to Italian Somaliland after ten years as a U.N. Trust Territory under Italian administration was approved by the General Assembly in November, 1949. The U.N. decision met vigorous opposition among Somali nationalists, particularly members of the Somali Youth League; protest demonstrations took place in many parts of the former colony. On April 1, 1950, after Italy had accepted the terms of a trusteeship agreement drafted by the U.N. Trusteeship Council, the British military government was replaced by a provisional Italian administration. Italian authority became final when, on December 2, the General Assembly approved the trusteeship agreement.

ITALIC LANGUAGES, an important subfamily of the western or "centum" Indo-European languages (q.v.), spoken chiefly in Italy and also, particularly in its comparatively recent Romance developments, in France, Spain, Portugal, Switzerland, and Romania. The entire subfamily is generally divided into three branches: *Sabellian,* a group of obscure dead languages formerly spoken in Italy; *Osco-Umbrian,* a smaller group of dead Italian languages containing only two members, Oscan and Umbrian; and *Latinian,* the major branch, which contains Latin, the most important dead language of Europe, and the entire group of languages (usually called in whole or part the Romance languages, q.v.) which represent the survival of Latin in territories once part of the Roman Empire.

The predominance of Latin during the period of the Roman Empire was in large measure the result of more or less deliberate political pressure; in prehistoric Italy, however, and even well into classical times, competitive Italic and non-Italic tongues claimed numbers of speakers who at times amounted to an actual majority of the population of the Italian peninsula. Etruscan, for example, which is not even an Indo-European language, was at one time the dominant language of western Italy north of the Tiber R.; and in southern Italy and Sicily, Greek, a Hellenic language, was spoken in numerous Greek colonies and maintained a close relationship with the Italic languages (see GREEK LANGUAGE). Of the Italic tongues themselves, Umbrian and Oscan are second in importance only to Latin, and became the repositories of extensive literatures; they were suppressed before the begin-

Above: Trajan's Triumphal Arch in Benevento, southern Italy. Right: The cathedral of St. Peter (bottom) and the piazza of St. Peter in the city of Rome.

ning of the Christian Era through the political influence of Rome. Oscan was the language of the Samnites (q.v.), and was spoken in most of the southern half of Italy except for the southernmost peninsulas. Umbrian, spoken in a well-defined area N.E. of Latium, is of importance chiefly because of its literature, which is of far greater extent than that of any other Italic language except Latin. Most of the texts in this tongue are contained in the so-called Eugubine tablets.

ITALY, a republic of S. Europe, formerly a kingdom. It comprises, in addition to the Italian mainland, the Mediterranean islands of Elba, Sardinia, and Sicily (qq.v.), and approximately 70 lesser islands. (For the territorial extent of Italy and its colonial possessions prior to World War II, see the *History* section of this article.) Italy is bounded on the N. by Switzerland and Austria; on the E. by Yugoslavia, the Adriatic Sea, and the Ionian Sea; on the S. by the Strait of Messina, which separates it from Sicily; and on the W. by the Tyrrhenian Sea, the Ligurian Sea, and France. The capital and largest city is Rome (q.v.); other cities with populations in excess of 100,000 are Milan, Naples, Turin, Genoa, Palermo, Florence, Bologna, Venice, Catania, Bari, Messina, Verona, Taranto, Padua, Brescia, Reggio di Calabria, Leghorn, Ca-

gliari, Parma, Spezia, Modena, Reggio nell' Emilia, Ferrara, and Bergamo (qq.v.). The area of Italy, including the islands and Vatican City (q.v.), an independent papal state, within Rome, is 116,235 sq.m.; pop. (1951) 47,138,235.

Physical Features. In physical geography, more than one half of Italy consists of the Italian peninsula, a long projection of the continental mainland. Remarkably similar in shape to a boot, the Italian peninsula extends generally southeastward into the Mediterranean Sea, of which the seas along its lateral coasts are arms. In a straight line from N.W. to S.E., the country is nearly 710 m. in length; with the addition of the S. peninsular extremity, which extends in a N. and S. direction, the length is about 846 m. The maximum width of the mainland portion of Italy is approximately 250 m. in an E. and W. direction; the maximum width of the peninsula is 150 m. The northern frontiers are occupied by the ranges of the Alps (q.v.), which extend in a wide arc from Ventimiglia on the W. to Gorizia on the E. Between the Alps and the Apennines (q.v.), the range which forms the backbone of the Italian peninsula, spreads the broad plain of Lombardy, comprising the valley of the Po R. (q.v.). The northern Apennines project from the Maritime Alps along the Gulf of Genoa to the sources of the Tiber R. Monte Cimone (7100 ft.) is the highest summit of the northern Apennines. The central Apennines, beginning at the sources of the Tiber, consist of several chains. In the E. portion of this rugged mountain district is Monte Corno (9560 ft.) (also known as the Gran Sasso d'Italia), the highest peak of the Apennines system. The s. Apennines stretch in a southeasterly direction from the valley of the Sangro R. to the coast of the Gulf of Taranto, where they assume a more southerly direction. Maximum elevations of the Apennines ranges of the Calabrian peninsula, as the s. extremity of the Italian peninsula is known, are Botte Donato (6330 ft.) and Aspromonte (6420 ft.). The Apennines form the watershed of the Italian peninsula. The main uplifts are bordered, particularly on the w., by less elevated districts, known collectively as the sub-Apennine region.

Only about one third of the total land surface of Italy is made up of plains, of which the greatest single tract is the plain of Lombardy. In this region are concentrated the richest and most extensive farming areas and the largest industrial establishments of Italy. The Lombard plain is also the most populous area of Italy. Among the small plains of the peninsula are those of Tuscany and Apulia; the fertile tract, to the N. of Naples, known as Campania in ancient times; that bordering on the Gulf of Manfredonia in the S.E.; and the Roman Campagna. The N. coast of Italy along the Adriatic Sea is low and sandy, bordered by shallow waters, and, except at Venice, not readily accessible to ocean-going vessels. From a point near Rimini southward, the E. coast of the peninsula is fringed by spurs from the Apennines. Along the middle of the w. coast, however, are three stretches of low and marshy land, known as the Maremma, the Campagna, and the Pontine Marshes.

The w. coast is broken up by bays, gulfs, and other indentations, which provide a number of natural anchorages. In the N.W. is the Gulf of Genoa, the harbor of the important commercial city of Genoa. Naples, another leading west-coast port, is situated on the beautiful Bay of Naples, dominated by volcanic Vesuvius (q.v.). A little farther s. is the Gulf of Salerno, at the head of which stands the port of Salerno. The S.E. end of the peninsula is deeply indented by the Gulf of Taranto, which divides the so-called heel of Italy

(ancient Calabria) from the toe (modern Calabria). The range of the Apennines continues beneath the narrow Strait of Messina and traverses the island of Sicily, on which the volcanic Mount Etna (q.v.), 10,741 ft. high, is located. Another active volcano rises on Stromboli, one of the Lipari Islands (q.v.), N. of the Strait of Messina.

Italy possesses many rivers, of which the Po and the Adige (qq.v.) are the most important. The Po, 418 m. long, is fed on its N. side by the snows of the Alps, and on its s. side by the heavy rains of the Apennines, and drains an area of approximately 30,000 sq. m. It is navigable from Turin to its outlet on the Adriatic Sea, and with its tributaries affords about 600 m. of inland waterways. The Adige, some 220 m. long, enters Italy from the Austrian province of Tirol, flows eastward, and, like the Po, empties into the Adriatic. The beds of these rivers are slowly being elevated by alluvial deposits from the mountains.

The rivers of the Italian peninsula are shallow, often dry during the summer season, and consequently of little importance for navigation or industry. The chief peninsular rivers are the Arno and the Tiber (qq.v.). From its sources in the Apennines, the Arno flows w. through a well-cultivated valley and the cities of Florence and Pisa. It has a short course of only 150 m. The Tiber rises not far from the sources of the Arno, and runs through the city of Rome. The two rivers are connected by a canal and the tributary called the Chiana (q.v.). Both the mainland and peninsular regions of Italy have numerous lakes. The principal lakes of N. Italy, in the order of size, are Garda, Maggiore, Como, and Lugano (qq.v.); the peninsular lakes, which are considerably smaller, include Trasimeno (q.v.), Bolsena, Bracciano, and Vico.

Climate. The climate of Italy is highly diversified, with extremes ranging from frigid, in the higher elevations of the Alps and Apennines, to semitropical along the coast of the Ligurian Sea and the w. coast of the lower peninsula. Climatic conditions on the peninsula are characterized by regional variations, resulting chiefly from the configurations of the Apennines, and are influenced by tempering winds from the adjacent seas. In the lowland regions and lower slopes of the Apennines bordering the w. coast from N. Tuscany to the vicinity of Rome, winters are mild and sunny and extreme summer temperatures are modified by cooling oceanic air currents. Temperatures in the same latitudes on the E. of the peninsula are much lower, chiefly because of the prevailing northeast winds. Along the upper E. slopes of the Apennines climatic conditions are particularly bleak and severe. The climate of the peninsular lowlands below the latitude of Rome closely resembles that of s. Spain. In contrast to the semitropical conditions prevalent in s. Italy and along the Gulf of Genoa, the climate of the Lombardy plain is continental in character. Warm summers and severe winters, with temperatures as low as 5° F., prevail in this region, which is shielded from oceanic breezes by the ranges of the Apennines. Heaviest precipitation occurs in Italy during the fall and winter months, when westerly winds prevail. The lowest mean annual rainfall, 18 in., occurs in the Apulian province of Foggia in the south; the highest, 60 in., occurs in the Venetian province of Udine in the northeast.

Flora and Fauna. The flora of the central and s. lowlands of Italy is typically Mediterranean. Among the characteristic vegetation of these regions are such trees as the olive, orange, lemon, palm, and citron. Other common forms of plant life, especially in the extreme s., are the fig, date, pomegranate, and almond trees, and the sugar-cane and cotton plant. The vegetation of the Apennines closely resembles that of central Europe. Dense growths of chestnut and oak trees occupy the lower slopes, and at higher elevations are extensive stands of pine and fir. The forests of Italy cover nearly 20% of the total land area.

Italy is low in the scale of European countries in regard to its fauna. The marmot (a stocky, short-legged rodent), chamois (a diminutive, goatlike antelope), and ibex (a wild goat with long curved horns) are found exclusively in the Alps. The bear, numerous in ancient times, is now virtually extinct, but the wolf and wild boar still flourish in the mountain regions. Another fairly common quadruped is the fox. Among the predatory species of bird life are the eagle, hawk, vulture, buzzard, falcon, and kite, confined for the most part to the mountains. The quail, woodcock, and partridge, and various migratory species of birds abound in many parts of Italy. Reptiles comprise several species of lizards and snakes, including three species of the poisonous viper family. The coastal waters of Italy teem with fish, of which the sardine, tunny, and anchovy have the greatest commercial importance. Fresh-water fish include eels and trout. Noteworthy insects are the scorpion and the tarantula.

Natural Resources. Italy is seriously deficient in such basic natural resources as oil, coal, and iron ore, and is consequently obliged to import these minerals in large quantity. Coal production in a recent year totaled about 1,166,000 tons, far less than the nation's requirement. The country normally leads the world in the output of mercury, however, and ranks prominently as a producer of sulfur. Production figures for mercury and sulfur in a recent year were about 1860 metric tons and about 1,856,000 metric tons respectively. Other mineral deposits are lead, manganese, zinc, and bauxite. Italy is also rich in various types of building stone, notably marble. Italian water power resources have been extensively utilized, and more than 1000 hydroelectric plants are in operation throughout the country. Italy also has more than 200 thermoelectric plants, which generate power from deposits of superheated steam in the volcanic regions.

Agriculture and Industry. The greater part of Italy's land area is devoted to agriculture, which engages approximately 15% of the population. Variations of climate, soil, and altitude favor the cultivation of all European crops. Italy is the first country after France in the production of the wine grape. The volume of wine produced in a recent year was about 1,004,000,000 gallons. See WINE: *Italian Wines.* Considerable quantities of the common Italian red wine are exported to France for dilution with French wines. The average national output of olive oil ranks second only to that of Spain. In a recent year over 350,000 metric tons of olive oil were produced in Italy. The chief field crops, with recent annual yields in metric tons, are wheat, 6,904,000; potatoes, 2,840,000; oats, 496,000; sugar beets, 5,957,000; corn, 2,750,000; rice, 690,000. Other important field crops are barley, rye, tomatoes, beans, tobacco, and hemp. Orchard crops, a prominent feature of the Italian economy, include olives, apples, oranges, figs, dates, pomegranates, and nuts. Dairy farming is a major Italian industry. Some fifty kinds of cheese are produced, the most notable being gorgonzola, bel paese, pecorino (made from ewe's milk), and parmesan. Livestock, in a recent annual estimate, numbered 12,875,000 sheep and goats; 8,325,000 cattle; 4,052,000 hogs; 800,000 horses; 773,000 donkeys; and 390,000 mules. Silk production is carried on in N. Italy and on the E. coast. The production of artificial silk in a recent year exceeded 135,000 tons.

Before World War II, Italy had approximately 730,000 industrial plants, which furnished employment to about 3,825,000 workers. The textile industry, largest and most important of Italy's manufacturing industries, normally satisfied domestic requirements, leaving a considerable surplus for export. Rapid recovery was made in this field following World War II. In a recent year textile production included 41,000 metric tons of wool yarn, 195,200 metric tons of cotton yarn, and 65,100 metric tons of rayon yarn. Textile manufactures recently constituted more than one third of Italy's exports. The chemical industry also figures prominently in the national economy. The chief chemicals, with recent annual production figures in metric tons, are superphosphate, 1,506,600; sulfuric acid, 2,291,600; and copper sulfate, 65,000. Steel and pig-iron output in a recent year totaled 3,050,000 metric tons and 1,048,000 tons respectively. Among other important Italian industries are the manufacture of automobiles, heavy machinery, electrical ware, foodstuffs, particularly macaroni, shipbuilding, the processing of hemp and tobacco, and sugar refining.

Commerce. Italy's dependence upon foreign markets for coal, petroleum, and other essential raw materials is reflected in an unfavorable balance of trade. To a certain degree, the consequent unfavorable fiscal balance is equalized by protective tariffs, remittances from Italian nationals in foreign lands, and the expenditures of tourists. Exports, valued in a recent year at about 1,027,400,000 Italian lire, include wines, raw silk, rayon textiles, cotton manufactures, wool manufactures, vegetables and fruits, motor cars, and heavy machinery; imports, which recently had an annual value of over 1,353,600,000 lire, are chiefly coal, petroleum, wool, cotton, and wheat. The bulk of Italy's export trade is with Switzerland, the United Kingdom, Argentina, Sweden, the United States, Germany, and France. Almost 25% of Italian imports are furnished by the United States. In the order of importance, other leading sources of Italian imports were Germany, the United Kingdom, Argentina, and France. Italian participation in the European Recovery Program (q.v.), initiated by the United States in 1947, to render financial assistance to the war-torn countries of w. Europe, substantially furthered the rehabilitation of the national economy.

Communications. The gross tonnage of the Italian merchant marine recently totaled approximately 3,271,000, about 629,000 gross tons less than in the period immediately preceding World War II. The Italian railway system had about 13,400 m. of lines in operation in a recent year. Approximately 75% of these lines, which included more than 3500 m. under electrification, are owned and operated by the state. Highways in a recent year totaled almost 106,000 m., including about 13,500 m. of state roads.

People, Language, and Religion. The Italian population, which consists almost entirely of native-born persons, belongs to the ethnic grouping known as the Caucasian Race (q.v.). The language spoken by the overwhelming majority of the people is Italian, one of the Indo-European family of languages (see ITALIAN LANGUAGE). As affirmed by the Lateran Treaty (q.v.) of 1929 between the Holy See (q.v.) and the Italian government, the official religion of Italy is that of the Roman Catholic Church, to which about 99% of the people belong. Communicants of the Protestant, Greek Orthodox, and Jewish faiths comprise most of the remainder. The Italian constitution guarantees complete freedom of worship to the religious minorities. Roman Catholic religious instruction is part of the curriculum of all primary and secondary schools.

Education. Italy compares unfavorably with the other countries of w. Europe in respect to the general diffusion of education. Primary education is free and compulsory for all children between the ages of 6 and 14. Graded instruction is furnished in three types of elementary schools, namely, *asili,* or maternal schools (3 years), which are maintained by the individual municipalities; lower schools (3 years); and higher schools (2 years). In a recent year, approximately 39,000 elementary schools employing about 168,000 teachers provided instruction for more than 4,800,000 pupils. Secondary education is available in classical and technical institutions. The former category is composed of *ginnasi, licei,* and teacher training schools; the latter consist of technical, industrial, commercial, agricultural, and nautical institutes. Classical schools, according to a recent tabulation, numbered about 580, and had a combined enrollment of approximately 163,200; technical schools within the same period numbered about 2200, and had a total of more than 440,000 students. In addition there are art institutes and academies of music. Unusual attention is given to higher education in Italy. During the last quarter of the 19th century, the gain in Italian university graduates was about seven times the corresponding rate of increase of the Italian population. Of Italy's 27 universities, six were founded in the 13th century and five were founded in the 14th century. The

Pan American World Airways

Gondola on a canal in Venice, Italy

oldest is the University of Bologna, dating from 1200. Other notable institutions are those of Padua, Pisa, Siena, Perugia, and Rome. Matriculation for all Italian universities in a recent year was almost 145,000.

Government. The government of Italy, as characterized in the constitution adopted in 1947, which became effective in January, 1948, is "a democratic republic founded on work". By the terms of the new constitution, the re-establishment of the Fascist Party (see FASCISM) is specifically prohibited; members and heirs of the House of Savoy (q.v.) are ineligible to vote or hold any public office and are, in fact, banished from Italian soil; and official recognition is no longer accorded to titles of nobility, although titles in existence prior to October 28, 1922, may be employed as part of the bearer's name. The Italian parliament consists of a senate and chamber of deputies elected by popular suffrage for terms of six and five years respectively. The senate has 344 members, of whom 237 are elected on a regional basis and 107 are appointed; the appointed senators include for-

mer deputies who were incarcerated by the Fascist regime and former premiers who, by the terms of the Italian constitution, are permitted to hold their seats for life. The chamber of deputies is composed of 574 members, each of whom must be at least 25 years of age. The president of the Republic is elected for a 7-year term in a joint session of the parliament augmented by three delegates from each of the 19 regional councils except the Valle d'Aosta, which sends one. Election of the president, who must be at least 50 years old, is ordinarily by a two thirds majority. The president has the right to dissolve the senate and chamber of deputies at any time during his tenure of office, the last six months excepted. Administratively, Italy is divided into 19 Regions, namely Piedmont, Liguria, Lombardy, Trentino-Alto Adige, Veneto, Friuli-Venezia Giulia, Emilia-Romagna, Tuscany, Marches, Umbria, Latium (including Vatican City), Abruzzi and Molise, Valle d'Aosta, Campania, Apulia, Basilicata, Calabria, Sicily, and Sardinia. Each region is in turn subdivided into provinces and communes. A constitutional court, analogous in function to the United States Supreme Court, is composed of fifteen judges, five of whom are appointed by the president of the republic, five by the senate and chamber of deputies jointly, and five by the supreme law court. The constitutional court is empowered to determine the legality of laws and decrees, to delineate the respective rights of the state and the regions, and to adjudicate disputes between the state and the regions and among the regions themselves.

History. The many cross-references interspersed throughout the following account of Italian history direct the reader's attention to more detailed articles on the same or related subjects. For information on important aspects of Italian culture, the reader's attention is directed to ITALIAN ART AND ARCHITECTURE and ITALIAN LITERATURE. For the history of Italy down to the 5th century A.D., see ROME: *History.* Additional data relative to the development of modern Italy are contained in the following articles: ETRURIA; FLORENCE; GENOA; LOMBARDY; MILAN; NAPLES; PAPAL STATES; SAVOY; SICILY; TUSCANY; VENICE.

In 476 A.D. the last independent Roman emperor of the West, Romulus Augustulus (q.v.), was dethroned by the invading Germanic chieftain Odoacer, who thereupon succeeded to the throne. In 488 Theodoric the Great, king of the Ostrogoths, invaded Italy, and, in the following year, slew Odoacer. Theodoric ruled until his death in 526. At that time Justinian I (q.v.), Emperor of the Eastern Roman Empire (see BYZANTINE EMPIRE), dispatched his two great generals Belisarius (q.v.) and Narses to expel the Germanic invaders from Italy. A fierce war ensued, ending in 552 with the death of Teias, the last of the Gothic kings. The Byzantine sway was of short duration, however, for in 568 Italy was invaded by the Lombards, another Germanic tribe. Alboin (q.v.), king of the Lombards, made Pavia the capital of his realm, and from that city launched a series of campaigns which presently deprived the Byzantine power in Italy of everything except the s. portion of the province and the Exarchate, or Greek Orthodox bishopric, of Ravenna in the north. After the death of Alboin in 573, the Lombards for a time had no king. Separate bands thereupon united under regional leaders known as *duces.* The Lombards, like the Goths before them, espoused the heretical creed called Arianism (see ARIUS), with the result that they were in perpetual religious conflict with the native Italians, who were overwhelmingly supporters of orthodox Christianity. This conflict was intensified as the temporal power of the popes increased. At length, Agiluf, a new Lombard king, became a convert to orthodox Christianity, and for some time comparative harmony prevailed. However, in order to consolidate their political power, the Lombards began to encroach on papal territory, even threatening the city of Rome, the very center of church authority. In 754 Pope Stephen II summoned help from the Franks (q.v.), who had accepted the spiritual authority of the Church a century earlier. Under the vigorous leadership of Pepin the Short (q.v.), and his son Charlemagne (q.v.), the Franks conquered the Lombards, deposing the last Lombard king in 774. On Christmas Day, 800, Charlemagne was crowned Carolus Augustus, Emperor of the Romans, by Pope Leo III.

When, in the 9th century, the Saracens (q.v.) subdued Sicily and threatened Rome, Pope Leo IV called to his aid Louis II, Charlemagne's great-grandson, who checked the progress of the invaders. The Moslems overran s. Italy after the death of Louis, and compelled the popes to pay tribute. For many years thereafter, the history of Italy is the record of the rise and fall of successive petty kings. Chief among these rulers were Guido of Spoleto, Berengar of Friuli, and Hugo of Provence. The period of anarchy ended in 962, when the Germanic leader, Otto I, after obtaining possession of N. Italy and the Lombard crown, was crowned emperor by Pope John XII. This event marked the establishment of both the Holy Roman Empire (q.v.) and the German nation (see GERMANY: *History*).

Until the close of the Middle Ages the Holy Roman Emperors claimed and, in varying degrees, exercised sovereignty over Italy, but for practical purposes Imperial authority became completely nominal by the beginning of the 14th century. Meanwhile, the south of Italy had remained under Byzantine and Lombard sway. In the 11th century, however, the Normans broke the Byzantine power and expelled the Lombards. The Normans united their territorial conquests in Italy, in 1127, with Sicily, which they had wrested from the Saracens. These developments coincided with a resurgence of papal power, long secondary to that of the emperors. Imperial and papal friction reached a peak in the great Investiture struggle. By the Concordat of Worms (q.v.), negotiated in 1122, the emperor sur-

Above: Boats in the harbor of Pirano, seaport town on the Gulf of Trieste, northern Italy. Right: Picturesque street on a hill in Castel di Sangro, town in central Italy.

rendered to the college of cardinals the right to elect the pope. Simultaneously with the increasing influence of the papacy, strong opposition to the continued rule of the Holy Roman Emperors appeared in the form of the rising Italian city-states. In Italy the feudal system (see FEUDALISM) had never attained the high degree of development which was characteristic of France and Germany. The relative weakness of Italian feudalism was due in great part to the survival of Roman traditions and to the large number of cities in Italy, for feudalism was a rural rather than an urban phenomenon. The northern cities in particular defied the power of Emperor Frederick I (q.v.) Barbarossa, who fought fierce but inconclusive wars with them. At length the Lombard League (q.v.), an alliance of Italian cities, was formed in 1167, Frederick was vanquished at Legnano in 1176, and in 1183, with the signing of the Peace of Constance, the cities of northern Italy secured virtual autonomy. A final and unsuccessful attempt to crush both the papacy and its allies was made by Frederick II, the last great ruler of the royal house of Hohenstaufen.

Italy itself was divided by the struggles between Imperial partisans and their opponents. These factions were known respectively as Guelphs and Ghibellines (q.v.), names which continued to be the designations of fiercely contending parties long after the Holy Roman Emperors had lost their hold upon the country.

In the second half of the 13th century a

new foreign power began to play an important role in Italian affairs. Charles of Anjou, the brother of Louis IX of France, answering an appeal by the pope to aid him against the Hohenstaufens, conquered the Kingdom of Sicily and Naples (see Two Sicilies), and overthrew Manfred, son of Frederick II, in 1266. Conradin of Swabia, the last of the male Hohenstaufens, was defeated in an attempt to recover the kingdom in 1267 and put to death. In 1282, however, Siciliy threw off the French yoke and placed itself under the power of Aragon (see Sicilian Vespers). Through commerce, some of the n. Italian cities had meanwhile grown wealthy and had established oligarchical governments which were tending to become democratic. The prosperous merchants of these cities, having secured their independence from the authority of the Holy Roman Emperors, soon began to contest the authority of their powerful nobles. Gradually these nobles were divested of their power and compelled to abandon their extensive land holdings. Venice, by its participation in the Fourth Crusade (see Crusades), had secured extensive possessions in the East. Pisa, Genoa, Milan, and Florence had likewise become powerful. A bitter struggle for ascendancy shortly developed between Genoa and Venice. The conflict ended with a Venetian victory toward the close of the 14th century.

In every city of n. and central Italy the population had long been divided into Guelphs and Ghibellines. The former party was substantially progressive in character, the latter, conservative. Civil strife was almost incessant, and the triumph of one party frequently resulted in the banishment of members of the other. On occasion, the banished party sought to regain power with the aid of other cities, so that city often warred against city, producing throughout the late Middle Ages a shifting succession of alliances, conquests, and temporary truces. This turbulent state of affairs was highly disadvantageous to commerce and industry, the chief interests of the northern cities. In consequence, the office of *podestà,* or chief magistrate, was established as an arbitrative agency to mediate the differences of the contending parties. It proved ineffective, however, and the *podestà* came in time to be primarily a judicial officer. His place as head of the city was taken by "a captain of the people", representing the dominant party. As military accomplishment was an essential requisite in this position, it was usually held by a noble. The people, desirous

of peace, acquiesced in the establishment of centralized authority. Hence, almost every city came to have its "despot", or absolute ruler, the office which in many cases became hereditary in some noble family, such as the Scalas at Verona, the Estes at Ferrara, the Malatestas at Rimini, and the Visconti and later the Sforzas at Milan. Under the rule of the despots wealth increased, life became more luxurious, and literature and the arts flourished. Gradually the smaller cities passed under the influence of the larger and stronger ones.

By the middle of the 15th century Italy had achieved a state of great prosperity and comparative tranquility. The country stood in the forefront of European nations in all that pertained to culture, having pioneered the way in the great revival of learning and the arts (see Renaissance). Pre-eminent in this revival was Tuscany, which had produced the great religious poet Dante Alighieri (q.v.) and the painter, artist, and sculptor Giotto di Bondone (q.v.). Toward the close of the century Italy became the object of a succession of aggressive wars, waged by France, Spain, and Austria, which culminated in the ascendancy of the Spanish and Austrian Hapsburgs (see Hapsburg). In 1494 Charles VIII of France undertook to conquer the Kingdom of Naples, then under the rule of the house of Aragon. Charles was induced to conduct this campaign by the Milanese regent Ludovico Sforza, and by the citizens of Florence, who were restive under the tyranny of the Medici (q.v.). He invaded Italy, occupied Naples, and concluded a treaty with Florence, by the terms of which the Medici were expelled and the pope was brought to submission. In consequence, however, of a league formed against him by Spain, the pope, the Holy Roman Emperor Maximilian I, and the Italian cities of Venice and Milan, Charles was forced to retire from Naples and fight his way out of Italy. This French invasion, although it produced no great political results, was highly important as one of the means by which Italian culture was disseminated throughout Europe.

In 1499 Louis XII, the successor of Charles VIII, subjugated Milan, and two years later Ferdinand V of Castile, called the Catholic, reunited the Two Sicilies under one crown. In 1508 France again entered the Italian scene, forming with Spain, the Pope, and Emperor Maximilian, the League of Cambrai against Venice. Three years later, Venice was joined by its former enemies, Spain and the Pope, in the Holy League, a new alliance directed against France. The French forces were driven out of Italy in 1513. The rivalry between the Holy Roman Emperor Charles V (Charles I of Spain) and Francis I of France produced further armed conflict. Another French invasion of Italy, with the Florentines, Genoese, and Venetians as allies, was at first attended with success, but resulted finally in defeat. In the Peace of Cambrai of 1529 Francis renounced all claims to territory in Italy. He later renewed the conflict with Charles V, but the Hapsburg domination over Italy could not be broken. On the extinction of the Sforza dynasty, in 1535, Charles V took possession of Milan, which became part of the Spanish realm. Naples remained for over 200 years in the possession of the Spanish Hapsburgs. Of all the free cities of Italy only four survived, and of these four Genoa and the Republic of Venice alone are worthy of mention. Venice, in its last notable achievement as an independent city, conquered the Peloponnesus in 1684, but lost it in 1715. Thereafter, and until as late as the 19th century, Italy was at the mercy of foreign powers, and partitioned as suited their policy.

Following the French Revolution (q.v.) the French general Napoleon Bonaparte (see NAPOLEON I) invaded Italy. His victories over the Imperial armies led, in 1797, to the Treaty of Campo Formio (see CAMPO FORMIO, TREATY OF), under which the Cisalpine Republic and the Ligurian Republic (qq.v.) were established, with their respective capitals at Milan and Genoa. Venice and the bulk of its territory were given to Austria. Napoleon, who made himself emperor in 1804, was crowned King of Italy at Milan in the next year. The following year he took possession of the Kingdom of Naples, which was given first to his brother Joseph Bonaparte, and, after the latter acceded to the Spanish throne, to the French general Joachim Murat. In 1808 Rome became part of the French Empire.

Napoleon's hold on Italy began to weaken following his defeat at Leipzig in 1813. The Austrians invaded N. Italy, and a British force occupied Genoa. The Congress of Vienna (see VIENNA, CONGRESS OF) led to a restoration, with only slight modifications, of the *status quo* prevailing in Italy before the Napoleonic Wars. The period succeeding the Napoleonic rule and extending to the final unification of Italy in 1870 was characterized by a growing movement for national unity and independence, which has been termed the *risorgimento*. French rule had introduced var-

ious progressive ideas which made a deep impression upon the Italian people. The advance of liberalism was obstructed, however, by autocratic Italian princes strong in their support of the Austrian tyranny. Despite the suppressive measures of their despotic rulers, the Italian people maintained a network of secret societies, notably the Carbonari (q.v.), which agitated ceaselessly for the establishment of constitutional government. Risings occurred in Naples and Piedmont, but were ruthlessly suppressed.

The French Revolution of 1830, which drove the Bourbons (see BOURBON) from the throne of France, had strong repercussions in Italy. In 1831 insurrections took place in Modena and in the Papal States. A congress of representatives from the insurgent Papal States (except Rome and a few cities in the March of Ancona) met in Bologna and adopted a constitution establishing a republican form of government. Austria quickly intervened, suppressed the revolutionary movement in the papal dominions, and placed Bologna under stringent military surveillance.

Upon the death of Charles Felix in 1831, the crown of the Kingdom of Sardinia passed to Charles Albert, Prince of Carignan and the scion of the younger line of Savoy. At this time the Italian patriot and scholar Giuseppe Mazzini (q.v.) issued an exhortation to the new king, who was known to hold more liberal views than others of his house, to become the leader and liberator of Italy. As the movement toward Italian unification gathered impetus, more and more of its supporters looked to the Sardinian monarchy for the realization of their objective, for it was abundantly clear that Austria, unrelenting in its reactionary policy, would have to be driven from the Italian peninsula by a power strong enough to assume the leadership in Italy. On the domestic front, Mazzini founded the secret political society known as Young Italy to support the principles of the Carbonari.

The movement toward a national uprising was quickened by Pope Pius IX, the first pope to be elected without the influence of Austria since the establishment of the Austrian hegemony over Italy. Immediately after his election, in 1846, he entered upon an extensive program of reforms in the Papal States. An amnesty was proclaimed for political offenders, political exiles were permitted to return, freedom of the press was introduced, the highest government offices were opened to laymen, and a council of notables was established to initiate new reforms. The pope's example was followed by a number of Italian princes. Broad reforms were introduced in Lucca, Tuscany, and notably, in Piedmont, where a great advance was made toward constitutional government. Instead of allaying the revolutionary movement, however, these reforms served only to intensify it. In January, 1848, the people of Palermo rose and drove out the forces of Ferdinand II of Spain, who thereupon granted his Italian subjects a constitution and summoned a separate parliament for Sicily. At the same time Leopold II issued a constitution for Tuscany, and Pope Pius IX consented to a constitution for the Papal States (March, 1848), albeit unwillingly, since he had begun to regard the course of events with apprehension.

The revolutionary outbreak in Vienna, which drove the statesman Prince Klemens von Metternich (q.v.) from power (see AUSTRIA: *History*), served as the signal for a rising in Milan on March 18. The Austrian troops were driven from the city after a five-day battle with the populace. On March 22 the Austrians were expelled from Venice, and on the following day a Venetian republic was proclaimed. The autocratic rulers of Parma and Modena were likewise put to flight. In Piedmont sentiment ran high for a war to drive the Austrians completely from Italian soil. Charles Albert, after considerable hesitation, finally mobilized his army and marched to the assistance of Lombardy, which he entered on March 25, acclaimed as the liberator of Italy.

Italian nationalist hopes received a check when, on July 25, the Piedmontese suffered an overwhelming defeat at the hands of the Austrians, who re-entered Milan on August 6. An armistice was concluded on August 9, by the terms of which Charles Albert was to evacuate Lombardy, Venetia, and the duchies of Parma and Modena. In spite of these reverses, the Sardinian king considered it his duty not to retire without making another attempt to free the Lombards from Austrian domination. Accordingly, in March, 1849, the armistice was suspended. Charles Albert met the Austrians in battle at Novara on March 23, was badly defeated, and on the following night abdicated the Sardinian throne in favor of his son, Victor Emmanuel II. Meanwhile, Pope Pius IX, who perceived that the revolutionary movement had exceeded his expectations in both scope and intensity, gave evidence of his intention to rescind the benefits he had conferred upon the Papal States.

Before he could act, an insurrection led by Mazzini drove him from Rome. The temporal power of the pontiff was abolished and Rome was proclaimed a republic. In April a French army was dispatched to suppress the Roman republic. Despite gallant Italian resistance led by the patriot Giuseppe Garibaldi (q.v.), the French occupied Rome in July, and the papal authority was re-established.

Victor Emmanuel II remained true to the cause of Italian independence. He adhered faithfully to the liberal constitution promulgated by his father, retained the tricolor flag, symbolic of free Italy, perpetuated the freedom of the press, and encouraged political refugees from the Italian mainland to make Sardinia their asylum. In 1852 Conte Camillo Cavour (q.v.) became the Sardinian prime minister. He negotiated an alliance with Great Britain, Turkey, and France in 1854, and after Sardinia had rendered these countries effective assistance in the Crimean War (q.v.), he urged, at the subsequent peace conference (1856) the immediate consideration of Italy as a problem of international concern. In 1858 Cavour arranged an agreement with the French Emperor Napoleon III providing for a joint declaration of war against Austria. The Franco-Italian coalition won (1859) the battles of Magenta and Solferino, but on the eve of complete victory Napoleon, through the influence of the Empress Eugénie and the clerical party in France, deserted the Italians and concluded the preliminary treaty of Villafranca (q.v.), in July, 1859, with the Austrians. In November, France, Austria, and Sardinia signed the Treaty of Zurich, by the terms of which Austria ceded all of Lombardy to France, which then transferred the Lombard cities of Mantua and Peschiera to Sardinia. In a plebiscite held in March, 1860 the people of Romagna and the duchies of Parma and Modena declared for union with Sardinia. As the price of French assistance in the war against Austria, Napoleon exacted from Sardinia the regions of Savoy and Nice, which became part of France.

Palermo rose, in April, 1860, against Francis II, successor of Ferdinand II on the throne of the Two Sicilies. In May, Garibaldi headed an expedition from Genoa against Sicily. Sicily was taken after nearly three months of fighting, and then Garibaldi crossed to the Italian mainland in a move against Naples. Meeting with negligible resistance, he entered Naples on September 7. Francis II fled after making a vain attempt to save his throne by the grant of a constitution and the promise of sweeping reforms. The Sardinian government, while openly in sympathy with Garibaldi's mission, had carefully abstained from affording any pretext for the intervention of the European powers. This diplomatic neutrality was threatened, however, when Garibaldi, not content with the conquest of the Two Sicilies, prepared to invade the Papal States. Meanwhile, the Sicilies, Umbria, and the Marches declared by plebiscite for union with Sardinia.

In February, 1861, the first Italian parliament was convened in Turin by Victor Emmanuel, on whom the title of King of Italy was formally conferred. The death of Cavour in June was a grave loss to the new Italian government. Soon thereafter Garibaldi went to Sicily with the object of organizing an expedition against Rome. In fear of French intervention, Victor Emmanuel issued a proclamation denouncing Garibaldi's action as rebellious. Undeterred, the Sicilians enthusiastically rallied to the cause of Roman liberation. In August, 1862, the royal government dispatched a Sardinian force against Garibaldi's volunteers, who had landed in Calabria. The insurgents were met by Victor Emmanuel's troops and compelled, after a brief engagement, to surrender. In 1866 Italy became the ally of Prussia in the Seven Weeks' War (q.v.) against Austria, by which the Italian kingdom acquired the territory of Venice. The following year Garibaldi headed a new expedition against the Papal States, but was defeated by a French force at Mentana. At length, in 1870, French reverses suffered in the Franco-German War (q.v.) obliged Napoleon III to withdraw his troops from the papal dominions, and on September 20 Italian forces made their triumphant entry into Rome. In October the Roman people declared overwhelmingly for union with the Italian kingdom. Rome became the capital of a united Italy on July 2, 1871.

In January, 1878, Victor Emmanuel died, and his eldest son, Humbert I, succeeded to the Italian throne. Mounting labor disturbances, for the most part in the industrial cities of N. Italy, culminated on July 29, 1900 in the assassination of Humbert by Angelo Breschi, an Italian anarchist. Humbert's son, the Prince of Naples, thereupon ascended the throne as Victor Emmanuel III. Meanwhile, prompted by the example of France and Great Britain, Italy launched upon the establishment of its colonial empire. Early in 1885 an Italian expedition occupied a portion of E. Africa, and five years later Italy's African

possessions were consolidated into the colony of Eritrea (q.v.). Encouraged by this success, the Italian premier Francesco Crispi (q.v.) laid ambitious plans for a vast colonial empire in Africa. In February, 1890, an Italian protectorate was established over the Somali coast s. of British Somaliland. After unsuccessful attempts by two private companies to administer the territory, the Italian government assumed complete control in 1905. A convention was signed (1906) by Italy, France, and Great Britain demarcating their respective spheres of influence in Africa. With the consent of France and Great Britain, Italy undertook, in 1911, the annexation of Tripoli (q.v.). On September 27, following Turkey's rejection of an Italian ultimatum, Italian troops occupied and blockaded the Libyan coast. By the Treaty of Lausanne, which concluded (October, 1912) the ensuing Italo-Turkish war, Italy's possession of the Libyan coast was confirmed.

Although Italy had been formally allied with both Germany and the Austro-Hungarian Empire since 1882, the Italian government declared its neutrality on the outbreak of World War I (q.v.) in August, 1914. In the spring of 1915, however, after signing the secret Treaty of London with the Allied powers, Italy declared war on Austria and Germany. The Italian role in World War I commenced with the occupation of the seaport town of Valona in s.w. Albania. Italy then dispatched a large force into the Trentino region, in the s. Tirol. In 1916 the Austrians launched a series of attacks N.E. of Trent and along the E. bank of the Adige R., capturing the towns of Asiago and Asiero. Most of the lost territory was later regained by the Italian commander in chief Luigi Cadorna (q.v.). Cadorna then mounted an offensive along the Isonzo R. in Venezia Giulia, capturing Gorizia on August 9. The Italian armies made little progress thereafter. On October 24, 1917, a combined Austrian and German force attacked between the Plezzo R. and the Avscek Valley, winning a speedy victory at Caporetto in Venezia Giulia. The Italian commander in chief withdrew from Gorizia and the Carso plateau, and by October 20, Austria threatened the Italian line from the Julian Alps to the Adriatic Sea. General Armando Diaz (q.v.) replaced Cadorna as Italian commander in chief, and Allied divisions were dispatched to the Italian front. The Austrians began a general offensive along the Piave R. on June 15, 1918, and succeeded in crossing to the opposite side, but were there repulsed. In July the Italians drove the Austrians from the Piave delta. American aviators serving with the Italian army were presently joined by the 332nd United States Infantry regiment. The third battle of the Piave opened on October 24, leading rapidly to the collapse of Austrian resistance and the suspension of hostilities on November 4. Italian casualties during World War I totaled 462,000. Following the general armistice concluded between the Allies and the Central Powers on November 11, 1918, Italy and Yugoslavia reached an agreement signalized by the signing of the Treaty of Rapallo (see RAPALLO, TREATY OF). A provision of this treaty established Fiume as a free state, connected with Italy by a territorial corridor along the Adriatic Sea (see FIUME; ANNUNZIO, GABRIELE D'). In August, 1920, Italy signed with Turkey the subsequently discredited Treaty of Sèvres, which granted the Italian government substantial concessions in Anatolia. Italy became one of the charter members of the League of Nations (q.v.) in January of the same year.

Throughout most of 1920, 1921, and 1922 Italy was torn by bitter political strife. Armed bands, with a strongly nationalistic program, and known as Fascisti (see FASCISM) clashed repeatedly with the Communists (see COMMUNISM) in Rome, Bologna, Genoa, Trieste, Alessandria, and Parma. On October 24, 1922, Benito Mussolini, leader of the Fascist movement, demanded that the Italian government be turned over to the Fascist Party, threatening to seize power by force if his demands were refused. Three days later, as the blackshirted Fascisti mobilized for a march on Rome, the Italian premier Luigi Facta resigned. Mussolini was thereupon summoned to the capital by King Victor Emmanuel and given a free hand in the formation of a new government. In the ensuing years, the history of Italy was, to a large extent, identified with the career of Mussolini. Many reforms were instituted and the administration was strongly centralized. Following clashes with Greece and Yugoslavia (qq.v.), the Italian government negotiated a treaty with the latter country by which Fiume was ceded to Italy.

The public indignation attending the murder of the influential Socialist deputy Giacomo Matteotti (q.v.), allegedly by Fascist gangsters, and the widespread charges that the crime had been perpetrated with the complicity of the Fascist government, provided Mussolini with a convenient pretext for suspending constitutional guarantees, ostensibly in the interests of law and order. The premier proceeded to consolidate his dictatorial power by forbidding the Italian parliament to initiate legislation; by making himself responsible to the king alone; by ordering parliament to authorize him to issue decrees having the force of law; by establishing absolute censorship of the press; by abolishing secret societies; and (in 1926) by suppressing all opposition parties. By the terms of an industrial law promulgated in 1926, thirteen syndicates or associations were recognized as having legal status. These syndicates were grouped into corporations, which included the employers and workers of the various industries. The same law prohibited strikes and lockouts, and established a labor court for the arbitration of disputes. A "Fascist Charter of Labor" was issued in 1927. Under a law established in the following year Italy's transformation into a corporative state was completed by the creation of a legislative body based directly upon economic representation. Another law of 1928 vested supreme power in the Fascist Grand Council. In 1929 Mussolini scored one of the greatest diplomatic triumphs of his career when he concluded the Lateran Treaty (q.v.) of reconciliation between the Italian state and the Holy See. This concordat, signed on February 11, settled the 60-year-old controversy concerning the temporal power of the Pope by the creation, at Rome, of Vatican City, a state in which the Holy See is the sole authority. Under the terms of the treaty the Vatican received 750,000,000 lire in cash and 1,000,000,000 lire in Italian state bonds (interest-bearing at 5%) as indemnity for the Pope's loss of temporal power at the time of Italian unification.

In 1932 Italy observed the 10th anniversary of the establishment of the Fascist regime. The celebration reached a climax on October 28, the day of the march on Rome. The festivities emphasized the material progress of the Italian nation in the preceding decade, notably the extensive reclamation of wasteland; modernization of agricultural procedures; construction of highways, railways, and hydroelectric projects; modernization of cities, ports and harbors; and excavation and restoration of the remains of ancient Roman civilization. Early in December, the Fascist government launched a comprehensive public works program designed to provide winter employment for some 300,000 men. In the sphere of international relations, Fascist foreign minister Dino Grandi vigorously advanced Italy's claim to colonial outlets in

Africa for the rapidly expanding Italian population. Despite Mussolini's avowed support of the arms reduction proposal set forth by United States President Herbert Hoover (q.v.), the Italian dictator revealed the real objectives of Fascist foreign policy in an article on Fascism, written for the *Encyclopedia Italiana*. In that article Mussolini asserted that "only war raises all human energies to the maximum and sets a seal of nobility on the peoples which have the virtues to undertake it". Although officially anti-Communist, Italy negotiated, for economic reasons, a treaty of neutrality, nonaggression, and friendship with the Union of Soviet Socialist Republics.

During the world economic depression, which began in 1929, the Fascist government was forced increasingly to intervene to prevent the collapse of normally sound industries. The construction of new factories or the expansion of old ones without governmental consent was prohibited. Toward the close of 1933, Mussolini announced that the Italian Chamber of Deputies would be called upon to legislate itself out of existence and to transfer its functions to the National Council of Corporations. The Chamber of Deputies was replaced in time by a Chamber of Fasci and Corporations, composed of some 800 appointive members of the National Council of Corporations. In their respective industries the corporations were later entrusted with regulating prices and wages, planning economic policies, and discharging other economic functions.

On the international scene, the appointment of Adolf Hitler (q.v.) as Chancellor of the Third Reich was greeted with enthusiasm by the controlled Italian press. Hitler in turn responded with expressions of sympathy and friendship for Italian Fascism. Meanwhile, in return for Italian support of a disarmament plan submitted by James Ramsay Macdonald, prime minister of Great Britain, Mussolini obtained British endorsement of a four-power pact, which projected a multilateral agreement among France, Great Britain, Germany, and Italy designed to safeguard the peace of Europe for ten years. After extensive alterations, designed to placate certain of the small European nations, the four-power pact was signed in Rome on June 7, 1933.

Intensification of Hitler's propaganda in Austria for an Austrian union with Germany led to the first test of the four-power pact. Italy, France, and Great Britain registered their opposition to the German policy, but without avail. Mussolini thereupon isolated Germany through the establishment of a Danubian economic confederation, and consolidated Italo-Austrian commercial *rapprochement* by a trade pact signed on August 31. The rift between Italy and Germany was widened by adverse Italian reaction to various features of the Nazi economic program. Imposition by the Nazi government of high tariffs on agricultural imports provoked charges in Italy of German discrimination against Italian products. In addition the Italians bitterly resented the new Nazi ban on foreign workmen, which resulted in the expulsion from Germany of thousands of Italian laborers. Italian newspapers displayed marked coolness toward Hitler's victory in the German election of November 12, 1933.

A temporary improvement in Franco-Italian relations resulted from Nazi attempts to force the incorporation of Austria into the Third Reich in 1934. In addition, Mussolini rushed 75,000 Italian troops to the Italo-Austrian frontier, announcing that he would intervene should Germany take overt action. In line with the Italian dictator's anti-German orientation was his conciliatory attitude toward Austria and Hungary, which led to the signing of the so-called Rome protocols on March 17. Designed as an economic bulwark against Germany, the protocols provided for reciprocal trade agreements among the signatory powers, pledged Italy to give priority to Austrian manufactures, and committed the three nations to a uniform foreign policy. Concerned over these developments, Hitler sought to restore Italo-German amity in a visit to Mussolini at Venice in June, 1934. The meeting brought agreement on a number of matters, including maintenance of Austrian independence, but the abortive Nazi putsch in Austria on the following July 25 nullified the general atmosphere of cordiality. Following the attempted putsch, Mussolini concentrated 48,000 additional troops along the Austrian border. Italy drew even closer to her allies of World War I when, in April, 1935, the Italian government, with France and Great Britain, formed the *Stresa Front* (see STRESA), a bloc organized in protest against Germany's repeated violations of the Versailles Treaty (see VERSAILLES, TREATY OF).

The event which upset European alignments and brought the Fascist and Nazi dictatorships into close accord was Italy's invasion of Ethiopia (q.v.), on October 3, 1935. Ethiopia, generally regarded as within the

Italian sphere of influence, was bound to the Fascist state by many commercial and diplomatic pacts. But Italy, bent on finding an outlet for its excess population and on acquiring vital natural resources, sought every opportunity to make Ethiopia an integral part of the Italian colonial empire. The Italo-Ethiopian war was preceded by a Franco-Italian accord concluded in January, 1935, in which Italy agreed to support French opposition to German rearmament in exchange for French territorial concessions in French colonial Africa and a share in the ownership and management of the Djibouti-Addis Ababa railway. In addition to the foregoing provisions, the agreement between the two countries contained a secret clause which subsequently gave rise to conflicting interpretations in Rome and Paris. Mussolini contended that Pierre Laval (q.v.), the French foreign minister, had given him a free hand to carry out his conquest of Ethiopia. Laval formally denied having made such a promise, although the reluctance with which he supported the League of Nations in its efforts to stop Italy seemed to belie his words. Great Britain, regarding Italy's aggressive expansion as a menace to British interests in Africa, vigorously opposed Mussolini's plan of outright seizure of Ethiopia.

On October 4, the day following the commencement of the Italian invasion of Ethiopia, the Council of the League of Nations declared Italy guilty of violating its obligations under the League Covenant, and the decision was made to impose economic sanctions against the aggressor. Throughout the months of the Ethiopian crisis relations between Italy and Great Britain were strained to the breaking point. A final attempt was made by Britain and France to come to terms with Italy through a proposal submitted by British foreign secretary Sir Samuel John Gurney Hoare and Laval. The proposal provided for an "exchange of territories" by which Ethiopia was to cede outright to Italy 60,000 sq.m. in Tigre and Ogaden provinces in return for a corridor of 3000 sq.m. extending through the Italian colony of Eritrea to the Red Sea and including the port of Assab. In addition, a zone of 160,000 sq.m. for Italian settlement and economic expansion was to be established in s. Ethiopia. The zone was to be controlled by League administrative bodies in which Italy was to be assigned "a preponderant but not exclusive role". Despite the liberality of the offer, Mussolini delayed acceptance until international protests consequent on publication of the Hoare-Laval formula forced its speedy repudiation by both the British government and the League of Nations. Public indignation and criticism aroused by the disclosure of the plan resulted in the dismissal of Sir Samuel Hoare from his post as foreign secretary and the downfall of the French government. Meanwhile, the League's failure to enforce sanctions against Italy, particularly its refusal to impose an embargo on oil shipments to the Fascist state, contributed in large measure to an Italian victory. On May 9, 1936, Mussolini formally annexed Ethiopia and proclaimed King Victor Emmanuel emperor.

The Fascist dictator's successful defiance of the League of Nations, and especially of Great Britain and France, gained for him and his party further popular favor within Italy and greatly enhanced Italian prestige in the sphere of European politics. Great Britain and France took the lead in terminating League sanctions against Italy, but for a time many countries refused to recognize Italy's conquest. On June 1, an Italian decree incorporated Ethiopia with Eritrea and Italian Somaliland (q.v.) into a single colony, Italian East Africa (q.v.). By way of showing his gratitude for German assistance rendered during the Ethiopian campaign, Mussolini completely reversed his former stand and used his influence to bring about an Austro-German agreement by which the Nazis in Austria received substantial political advantages. In October, after Germany had recognized the Italian conquest of Ethiopia in July, 1936, Hitler and Mussolini concluded an agreement providing for joint action in support of their common goals.

With the outbreak of civil war in Spain (see SPAIN: *History*) new stresses were imposed upon the Italian economy in consequence of Mussolini's active espousal of the Fascist insurgent cause of General Francisco Franco (q.v.). The Italian dictator pursued this policy in the hope of securing an economic and strategic foothold in the w. Mediterranean and also of checkmating France and the Soviet Union, which had, to some degree, rendered assistance to the Spanish loyalist, or pro-republican, forces. Italian troops played an important role at the battles of Malaga and Santander, the Italian air force participated in a number of Spanish engagements, and Italian submarines allegedly sank many neutral ships bound for loyalist ports with oil, food, and other supplies to the repub-

The Matterhorn, 14,780 feet high, towering over the village of Breuil, northern Italy

lican armies. On the Guadalajara front, however, Italian forces were routed by the Spanish loyalists in March, 1937. An official report placed Italian casualties at about 4000 killed and 15,000 wounded.

By 1937, the Berlin-Rome Axis had begun to produce results. Although Italian influence throughout the Danubian and Balkan regions was being progressively supplanted by that of Germany, Mussolini was compensated by German support of his expansionist policy in the Mediterranean area. Following Mussolini's visit to Germany in September, Italy announced its adherence to the Anti-Comintern Pact between Germany and Japan, and soon thereafter withdrew from the

League of Nations. The first major result of Italian policy toward Germany was Mussolini's refusal to render diplomatic or military assistance to Austria when that republic was absorbed by Germany in March, 1938. To allay Italian fears respecting German intentions toward the Tirolean territory acquired by Italy after World War I, Hitler, during a visit to Italy in May, reiterated his pledge that the Italo-German frontier would remain unchanged. An Italo-German accord was reached for the transfer of German-speaking Tirolese to the Third Reich. Meanwhile, the increasing influence of Nazi racist doctrine upon Fascist Italy found expression in a series of measures designed to curb the economic, political, and cultural activities of Italian Jews. These measures were presently supplemented by additional racist legislation, including a law that excluded all Jews from the civil and military administrations of the state and the Fascist Party. During the negotiations which led to the conclusion (September, 1938) of the Munich Pact (q.v.) and to the subsequent dismemberment of Czechoslovakia, Mussolini gave firm support to Hitler's provocative demands. The Rome-Berlin Axis was converted into a military assistance pact in May, 1939. This move followed the German seizure of Bohemia and Moravia (qq.v.), and the Italian annexation of Albania (q.v.).

At the outbreak of World War II (q.v.) in September, 1939, the Italian government took the position that it was under no obligation to render military assistance to Germany since Hitler had rebuffed an Italian proposal for the arbitration of German-Polish differences. The Fascist government followed its declaration of nonbelligerency by removing a number of strongly pro-German ministers and high-ranking military officials from office. At the same time Italy attempted to regain its former trade connections with the Balkan countries, thus entering into a certain amount of competition with Germany. German successes during the first year of the war provided Mussolini with substantial grounds for a reversal of his policy of nonbelligerency. On June 10, 1940, when France lay prostrate in defeat and Great Britain alone faced the powerful Nazi armies, Italy entered the war. The Italian government granted France an armistice on June 25. At the end of July Italian air and ground units took up positions in N. France for a projected joint assault with the Germans upon Great Britain. Fascist planes, however, were severely battered by craft of the Royal Air Force during the first Italian raid on Britain, and there were no further reports of Italian participation in the German air offensive.

As soon as the determination of Great Britain to fight on became clear, the Fascist press began to prepare the Italian people for a long and arduous war. In August, 1940, Italian forces in East Africa scored an important victory with the conquest of British Somaliland (q.v.), and the following month Fascist armies in Libya and Italian East Africa began a gigantic pincers movement designed to overwhelm the British defenses in Egypt. The Italian drive into Egypt shortly became stalled at Sidi Barrani. On October 28, 1940, Fascist forces in Albania invaded Greece.

The offensive was apparently designed to divert British naval and military forces from Egypt and to secure Italian air and sea bases on the Greek peninsula. Undertaken without adequate preparation, the invasion was completely frustrated by the valiant Greeks, who drove the Italians from Greece and Albania. This debacle, followed by British naval and military victories in the Mediterranean area and in Egypt, rocked the Fascist regime in Italy to its foundations. Italian prestige was shattered throughout the world, and two decades of Fascist diplomacy in the Balkans, the Near East, and Africa were undone. To stave off total military collapse, Mussolini was obliged to ask Hitler for aid. Thereafter, Italy was a distinctly subordinate member of the Axis coalition, and the direction of Italian policy in all fields fell increasingly under German control. Sweeping changes in the Fascist military hierarchy were instituted by Mussolini in an effort to restore morale and retrieve his government's damaged prestige. These replacements, following upon a succession of military reverses, served only to undermine confidence in both Mussolini and his regime. Rising political discontent among the Italian masses was spurred by a steady decline of living standards and by a general increase of economic difficulties caused, among other factors, by the Allied blockade and a poor wheat crop.

Meanwhile, relations between Italy and the United States, characterized for some time by a growing coolness, had reached a critical juncture in the period following the Italian entry into World War II. Franklin Delano Roosevelt, President of the United States, had publicly denounced Italy's entry into the war as a stab in the back of France. This statement was bitterly resented by the Fascist press, which retaliated by intensifying its attacks upon U.S. foreign policy and threatening America with early involvement in the war if the program of aid to Great Britain was extended (see LEND–LEASE).

For Italy the year 1941 was one of successive military and naval disasters and growing economic privation. In January and February Fascist Marshal Rodolfo Graziani suffered a crushing defeat in Libya. The Duke of Aosta surrendered the main Italian army in Ethiopia on May 19, and by the end of November the Italian colonial empire in East Africa was completely liquidated. Anti-Fascist sentiment spread among all sections of the Italian population, including the professional army officers, who held Mussolini and his associates responsible for Italy's military setbacks. However, the successful termination of the Balkan campaign, as a result of German intervention, tended in some measure to offset the Fascist reverses. Italy acquired portions of the Dalmatian coast, almost all the islands off the Dalmatian Peninsula, the Kossovo district of E. Yugoslavia, six of the Cyclades Islands in the Ægean Sea, the Mediterranean island of Corfu, and the Ciamura district on the Greek mainland, adjoining the Albanian frontier. By arrangement with Germany, almost all of Greece, including Athens, was occupied by Italian troops. Many Italians soon realized that their territorial gains in the Balkans were largely illusory, since actual control in these areas was exercised by the Germans. In addition, Italy was forced to pay an increasingly high price for Hitler's military assistance. Italian stocks of foodstuffs, raw materials, and other commodities began to run low, due in large part to heavy shipment to the Third Reich in return for German coal and oil. Italy declared war on the U.S.S.R. on June 22, 1941, on the day following the German invasion, and five weeks later the first Italian division was sent to the Russian front. As difficulties developed in the German offensive against the Soviet Union, Hitler became more pressing in his demands upon Mussolini for further aid.

At the same time Italo-American relations were rapidly approaching a showdown. In March the U.S. governmment had seized 28 Italian merchant ships in American ports and arrested officers and seamen who sabotaged the machinery of the vessels on orders from the Italian naval attaché in Washington, D.C. The immediate recall of the attaché was demanded, whereupon Italy forced the recall of the U.S. military attaché in Rome. When Italian assets in the United States were impounded in June, the Fascist government promptly took similar measures against American assets in Italy. Later in the same month all consular offices were ordered closed in both countries. The process of alienation was climaxed on December 11, four days after Japan's surprise air attack upon Pearl Harbor, Hawaii, when Mussolini announced Italy's declaration of war against the United States.

The military and political outlook for Fascist Italy in 1942 was one of unmitigated gloom. In North Africa, temporary Italo-German gains were liquidated by a vigorous British offensive which lifted the Axis siege of Tobruk in Libya and recaptured Bengasi.

Axis forces, including several Italian divisions, suffered serious reverses in the Soviet Union. Some 500,000 Italian troops occupying conquered Albania, Yugoslavia, and Greece suffered heavy losses by the action of organized guerrilla bands. At home the Italian people endured a bitter winter with very short rations of food and fuel. Manufactured goods were scarce and of poor quality. War industries were handicapped by acute shortages of materials and manpower. Increasing German control of all phases of Italian life, corruption and inefficiency among Fascist officials, and evasion of the rationing laws by the wealthy and influential contributed to the demoralization and unrest of the Italian people. In October the British Royal Air Force launched a series of bombing raids on the industrial cities of N. Italy, destroying or damaging a considerable portion of Italian war industry and causing heavy civilian casualties. Simultaneously, advancing British and American forces in North Africa established bomber bases in Algeria and Cyrenaica from which the cities and military installations of S. Italy were brought under attack. In the political sphere the prestige of Mussolini and his regime continued to decline. United States newspaper correspondents repatriated from Italy reported that the Fascist government had virtually no popular support and that only the presence of German troops enabled it to remain in power. The Italian dictator sought vainly through shake-ups in the Fascist Party and through the imposition of more stringent controls to stem the rising tide of defeatist and antiwar sentiment.

Early in February, 1943, Mussolini dismissed twelve of the most important members of his government and announced that he personally was assuming full responsibility for the management of political affairs and the conduct of military operations. With the collapse of Axis forces in Tunisia (q.v.) in May, Mussolini hastily increased the strength of the Fascist militia and ordered the establishment of a council of defense to prepare for an expected Allied invasion of the Italian mainland. All efforts to reinvigorate the Fascist Party, bolster military defenses, and restore the national morale were nullified, however, by the inexorable Allied air offensive. Following the capitulation of the strategic Italian island of Pantelleria in the Mediterranean, an emergency meeting of the Fascist directorate was convoked at which Mussolini's disastrous conduct of the war was bluntly assailed. Then, on July 10, Allied forces invaded

Sicily. Six days later, President Roosevelt and British Prime Minister Churchill addressed a joint radio message to the people of Italy urging their surrender to avoid greater devastation and warning that their continued toleration of the Nazi-controlled Fascist regime would have disastrous consequences. This admonition, though underscored by heavy Allied air raids on Naples, was scornfully rejected by the Fascists in a radio broadcast to the Italian nation on July 18. The next day Allied planes dropped leaflets over Rome advising of a possible raid on military installations in the vicinity of the Italian capital but giving assurance that the utmost care would be exercised to avoid destruction of residential buildings and cultural monuments. Some 500 Allied bombers, mostly American, then made a devastating attack upon the San Lorenzo and Littorio railway freight yards, on war factories, and on the Ciampino airfield.

The bombing of Rome precipitated a large-scale exodus of the Roman population and brought the political crisis in Italy to a climax. Peace demonstrations were touched off in many cities and strikes and sabotage in war industries were intensified. During the raid on Rome Mussolini was at Verona conferring with Hitler on measures to meet the next phase of the Allied invasion of Italy. The Italian dictator acceded to a German plan for a gradual withdrawal from Sicily and from s. and central Italy to a defense line extending through the s. limits of Tuscany. Rome was to be abandoned. In addition, the plan called for stripping the evacuated regions of all food stores and rolling stock in order to force the invading Allies to feed and sustain the population. Upon Mussolini's return to Rome he was confronted with a demand for the convening of the Fascist Grand Council to consider the Italian military crisis. The session was marked by stormy debate and concluded with a no-confidence vote of 19 to 5 against Mussolini. It was thereupon decided to submit the German defense plan to the king. Victor Emmanuel flatly rejected the plan. He then ordered the resignation of Mussolini and his government and summoned Marshal Pietro Badoglio (q.v.) to form a new ministry. The ousted dictator and a number of his chief aides were placed under arrest. On July 28 the Badoglio cabinet decreed the dissolution of the Fascist Party, the Fascist Grand Council, and the special Fascist tribunals for the defense of the state. The liquidation of all other Fascist organizations and institutions followed.

Despite the new government's announcement that the war would go on, the fall of Mussolini precipitated clamorous peace demonstrations throughout Italy. At the same time popular demands were made for the termination of martial law, the restoration of constitutional government, and the punishment of Fascist leaders. Meanwhile the Allies continued their advance in Sicily. On July 27 Prime Minister Churchill offered Italy the choice of breaking off its alliance with Germany or being visited with terrible destruction; two days later General Dwight Eisenhower (q.v.), Allied commander in chief, promised the Italian people an honorable peace and a beneficent occupation if they ended their assistance to the German war effort. The Badoglio government made two unsuccessful secret peace overtures to British officials early in August. Then, on August 15, a fully authorized representative of Premier Badoglio arrived in Lisbon, Portugal, with an offer to join the Allies against Germany when the Allied invasion of the Italian mainland began. At the direction of President Roosevelt and Prime Minister Churchill, General Eisenhower dispatched American and British staff officers to carry out negotiations with the Italian representative on the basis of Italy's unconditional surrender. The armistice was signed on September 3, the same day the British Eighth Army began the invasion of s. Italy. The Italian capitulation was kept secret at General Eisenhower's insistence, and did not become effective until the Allied commander in chief personally broadcast the announcement on September 8. The armistice was then confirmed by Premier Badoglio over the Rome radio. Among other things, the terms provided for (1) immediate cessation of hostilities between Italian and Allied forces, (2) Italian denial to the Germans, as far as possible, of facilities that might be employed against the Allies, (3) immediate surrender of all Allied prisoners or internees, (4) transfer of the Italian fleet and aircraft to points designated by the Allied High Command, (5) Allied requisitioning of Italian merchant shipping, (6) immediate surrender to the Allies of Corsica and all Italian territory, and (7) immediate and free Allied use of all airfields and naval ports in Italian territory.

General Eisenhower's announcement of the armistice set off a furious race between the Allies and the Germans for possession of the territories, bases, arms and supplies, communications, and other war facilities formerly

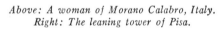

Above: A woman of Morano Calabro, Italy.
Right: The leaning tower of Pisa.

under Italian control. A large Anglo-American amphibious force landed on the beaches of Salerno just s. of Naples, hoping to drive inland and trap the German units facing the British Eighth Army farther south. British forces began a drive up the E. coast of the peninsula in co-ordination with other British units advancing from Calabria up the w. coast. The Germans were prepared for the emergency and acted swiftly. They attacked and held the invasion force at Salerno until German units in s. Italy could retire. They also seized outright the cities and strategic centers of N. and central Italy, disarmed all Italian troops except those under pro-Nazi commanders, and rounded up thousands of suspected enemies among Italian officials and civilians. On September 10 the Germans occupied Rome, from which King Victor Emmanuel and Premier Badoglio had fled two days previously to Allied-held territory in the s. of Italy. Complete Nazi domination was

likewise rapidly extended over Greece, Yugoslavia, and the Italian Ægean islands. The Allies were more successful in the race for control of the still powerful Italian fleet. In response to a message broadcast by Sir Andrew Browne Cunningham, Allied naval commander in the Mediterranean war theater, virtually all seaworthy Italian warships left their bases at La Spezia and other Italian-held ports to surrender to the Allies in accordance with the armistice terms.

In the political sphere the Germans sought to retain the support of pro-Fascist and anti-Allied Italians by announcing on September 9 that a "Fascist National Government" had been established in Italy in opposition to the Badoglio government, and was functioning in the name of Mussolini. The former Italian dictator had been rescued from prison in Arruzzi by a surprise raid of German parachute troops, thus balking Badoglio's promise to deliver the deposed dictator to the Allies. On September 23 the German radio announced the formation by Mussolini of an all-Fascist cabinet of the new Fascist regime, the name of which was changed to the Republican Fascist Government. In line with pledges made to the Allies and to the Italian people, Premier Badoglio declared war on Germany (October 13) and undertook to reorganize his government on a broader and more democratic basis. During the latter part of October he sought to induce leaders of various anti-German political groups to enter his cabinet. He conferred with Count Carlo Sforza (q.v.), former Italian foreign minister, who had just returned to Italy after a voluntary exile of almost fifteen years, and with leaders of six political parties, disbanded by Mussolini, which had united to form a National Liberation Front. These liberal elements served notice that they would consent to form a representative government only on condition that Victor Emmanuel abdicated. The king flatly refused to comply with this condition, and Badoglio declined any part in the move to oust him. As a temporary solution, the premier in the following month organized a "technical" government of nonparty experts to carry on the administrative functions. Allied policy had been based upon the subordination of political questions until the Germans were expelled from all of Italy and until the whole Italian people could determine their form of government by democratic process, but the violence of the controversy between opponents and supporters of the king made the implementation of such a policy increasingly difficult. On November 29 the Committee of National Liberation voted nonconfidence in the Badoglio government, called upon Victor Emmanuel to abdicate, and demanded that Crown Prince Humbert renounce his rights to the Italian throne. On February 11, 1944, the Allied Advisory Council for Italy turned over control of Sardinia, Sicily, Salerno, Potenza, Bari to the Italian royal government. Badoglio thereupon asked that Italy be received as an ally with full diplomatic relations. He also indicated that his administration would be democratically broadened after the liberation of Rome but that the king would not abdicate. Count Sforza denounced Prime Minister Churchill for supporting Victor Emmanuel and pointed out that the aged monarch had altogether discredited himself by his long support of the Axis.

At this juncture the U.S.S.R. assumed an active role in the Italian situation. Badoglio announced that he and Premier Joseph Stalin

(q.v.) had agreed upon an exchange of ambassadors between Italy and the Soviet Union. The Kremlin's action was widely interpreted abroad as a grant of diplomatic recognition to the royal regime and as Soviet endorsement of the House of Savoy. In other quarters, the Soviet move was seen as an attempt to strengthen the U.S.S.R.'s bargaining power in Italy vis-à-vis Great Britain and the United States. This view seemed to be borne out when, on March 28, the Communist leader Palmiro Togliatti (q.v.) returned to Italy from long exile in the Soviet Union to assume leadership of the Italian Communist Party. Four days later Togliatti called for a united front of all anti-Fascist forces and for a new provisional government capable of waging war against the Nazis. The king issued a formal statement, on April 12, announcing his decision to withdraw from public affairs and to appoint his son Humbert Lieutenant General of Italy, the appointment to become effective upon the entry of Allied troops into Rome. These developments cleared the way for a government representing the National Committee of Liberation. On April 17 Badoglio resigned and was at once asked by the king to form a new cabinet, representative of all parties. The formation of the cabinet was announced on April 21, the premiership being retained by Badoglio. This advance toward national unity and democracy was followed by the liberation of Rome by Allied armies on June 4. Victor Emmanuel then carried out his promise to transfer all royal authority to Humbert as Lieutenant General of the Realm (regent). Badoglio once more discharged the formality of submitting his resignation, whereupon Humbert requested him to form another cabinet. The party leaders of the Committee of National Liberation unanimously refused to serve under Badoglio. On June 9 the premiership was given to the 71-year-old statesman and ex-Socialist Ivanoe Bonomi, who succeeded in forming a coalition government. Count Sforza received one of the ministries without portfolio.

Because the new government was under Allied jurisdiction and control, its plans for the institution of broad domestic reforms and for vigorous participation in the war effort were largely nullified. American and British officials, fearful of internal developments that might impede the Allied war effort, vetoed or deferred all proposals for social and economic change. Allied authorities also looked with disfavor upon the Italian anti-Fascist volunteers and resistance fighters, most of whom were extreme radicals. Within the new cabinet, a large measure of agreement existed on basic political issues. Middle-class liberals and proletarian radicals were united in the belief that the armistice terms should be modified and that Italy should be allowed to reshape itself into a self-governing democracy. Communists and Socialists, elsewhere bitter adversaries, were unanimous in advocating economic reform. Even Communists and Catholics found areas of agreement, a small group of enthusiastic fusionists going so far as to call themselves Catholic Communists.

The winter of 1944–45 was a period of intense suffering in Italy, particularly in the ravaged areas left in the wake of the retreating Germans. Throughout the central provinces were burned villages, idle or flooded fields, and ruined factories, railroads, power plants, and bridges. Two million acres of arable land were out of cultivation. Prices of necessities rose prohibitively in an inflation made worse by the Allied issue of invasion currency. As a result of the widespread misery among the Italian people, the Action and Socialist parties subjected Premier Bonomi's leadership to sharp criticism. Bonomi resigned on November 26. During the ensuing political crisis, it became known that the British government had taken steps to prevent the appointment of Count Sforza as foreign secretary of the Italian cabinet. The United States government publicly rebuked Great Britain for its unilateral intervention in Italian affairs, but Sforza was excluded from Bonomi's new cabinet, which received the approval of the Allied Control Commission on December 9. In this situation, with the Action and Socialist parties excluded from the governing coalition and popular discontent with the monarchy increasing, the Italian Communist Party gave full support to Bonomi.

Meanwhile all of Italy N. of the Apennines remained under the tyranny of Mussolini's Republican Fascist regime, supported by the Nazis. Early in January Count Galeazzo Ciano (q.v.), Fascist foreign minister from 1936 to 1943, was placed on trial at Verona before a jury of Fascist party members for plotting Mussolini's overthrow. Ciano was condemned to death on January 10, along with seventeen other members of the defunct Fascist Grand Council. According to a news broadcast on the German radio, sentence was executed on January 11. Following the German withdrawal from Rome, investigation of secret files of the Fascist Party had produced a series of startling revelations respecting the early crimes of the Mussolini regime. Documents taken from these files established, after twenty years of Fascist denial and evasion, that Mussolini had been personally responsible for the murder of Socialist deputy Giacomo Matteoti. Early in November, the Commission for the Punishment of Fascist Crimes, headed by Count Sforza, disclosed that Count Ciano had instigated, in 1934, the murder of King Alexander of Yugoslavia and Foreign Minister Louis Barthou of France, and had drawn into a revolutionary conspiracy against the French Republic a number of prominent French public figures, including Admiral Jean Louis Darlan and Marshal Henri Philippe Pétain (qq.v.).

On February 25, 1945, the Allied Control Commission transferred to the Italian government most of its authority throughout the liberated regions of Italy (except military zones near the fighting front), thereby enabling the Italian cabinet to conduct foreign relations, make diplomatic appointments, and enact legislation without the ratification of the Control Commission. Industrial stagnation, mass unemployment, and skyrocketing inflation continued to frustrate the government's efforts to rehabilitate the national economy.

The final Allied offensive in Italy began on April 9, 1945, and by the end of the month the German armies on Italian soil had been completely smashed. On April 26 Mussolini, his mistress, and a number of his high-ranking colleagues were captured by Italian partisans at Nesso, near Lake Como. The entire group was summarily tried and, on April 28, executed. Italian partisans inflicted sanguinary vengeance on Mussolini's followers throughout N. Italy after the German surrender, which became effective on May 2. More than a thousand Fascists were shot in Milan alone.

In accordance with a previously made pledge to dissolve his government after the liberation of N. Italy, Premier Bonomi resigned on June 12. The period immediately preceding his resignation was marked by a bitter dispute with Yugoslavia regarding Venezia Giulia, which had been occupied by Yugoslav troops. By the terms of an Anglo-American accord with the Yugoslav government, Yugoslav forces evacuated Trieste and a strip of adjacent territory during the second week of June. This region was placed under the authority of the Allied military command pending final determination of its status. The remainder of Venezia Giulia remained under Yugoslav control.

A coalition government, representative of the entire Committee of National Liberation, succeeded the Bonomi cabinet on June 21. The new government, which was headed by Ferruccio Parri, a prominent anti-Fascist and leader of the Action Party, inherited, in addition to all of the economic problems of its predecessor, mounting popular demands for a Constituent Assembly and a referendum on the future of the monarchy. In the absence of a peace settlement of such matters as frontiers, reparations, and the status of the Italian colonies, the Parri government was little more than a stopgap regime, unable to grapple effectively with the economic, political, and social problems confronting Italy. The Italian people grew restive under these conditions, particularly after repeated failures of the "Big-Four" (France, Great Britain, the U.S., and the U.S.S.R.) Council of Foreign Ministers to reach agreement on a draft of the Italian peace terms. In October spokesmen for Italian monarchism and leaders of the Liberal Party accused Premier Parri of violating the truce on the question of the monarchy. Warning Italy to beware of resurgent Fascism and of possible civil war, Parri resigned on November 24. The ensuing crisis was accompanied by riotous demonstrations in s. Italy against the high cost of living. On November 30, after unsuccessful attempts by Vittorio Orlando, a conservative and Francisco Nitti, a leader of the Liberal Party, to form a government, the Committee of National Liberation offered the premiership to Alcide de Gasperi, a Christian Democrat and the foreign secretary of the Parri cabinet. In one of his initial moves, De Gasperi, who took office on December 9, proclaimed April 30, 1946, as the date for the election of a Constituent Assembly.

The first half of 1946 was a decisive period in Italian political history. The period was also one of unparalleled hardship for the great majority of the Italian people. By the beginning of March, the average daily ration of food had been reduced, as a result of general shortages, to 650 calories daily. The desperation caused by starvation and other privations found occasional expression in riotous demonstrations, but the general mood of the populace was apathetic. In consequence, the campaign leading up to the national referendum and elections, which were postponed until June, was attended by a minimum of violence. That a key sector of the Italian people opposed the monarchy was indicated when, on April 27, the convention of the Christian Democratic Party, composed largely of liberal Roman Catholics, voted three to one in favor of a republic. King Victor Emmanuel III abdicated on May 9, whereupon the Lieutenant General of the Realm ascended the throne as Humbert II.

Nearly 25,000,000 voters, approximately 89% of the eligible electorate, which included women for the first time in Italian history, cast ballots in the general elections of June 2 and 3. Of these voters, almost 12,718,000 (54.3%) voted for a republic. The vote for retention of the monarchy was approximately 10,719,000. On June 10, 1946, when the mandate of the people was officially proclaimed, Italy became a *de facto* republic. The cabinet transferred all royal powers to the premier shortly thereafter, and on June 13 King Humbert abdicated and left the country.

As a result of the balloting for the Constituent Assembly, the Christian Democrats, with nearly 6,000,000 votes and 207 seats, emerged as the first party of Italy. The Socialist and Communist parties won 115 and 104 seats respectively. Four minor parties shared the remaining 117 seats. The Liberal, Labor Democratic, and Action parties, components of the erstwhile Committee of National Liberation, practically disappeared as important factors in Italian politics. On June 28, Enrico de Nicola, a leading member of the Liberal Party and a compromise candidate of the Marxist and Christian Democratic parties, was elected provisional president of the republic by the Constituent Assembly. De Gasperi, who retained the premiership, reorganized the cabinet on July 12. The new government was a coalition of the three leading parties and the Republican Party.

In the deliberations preceding approval of the first Italian republican government by the Constituent Assembly, sharp verbal exchanges between the Communists and Christian Democrats indicated that the coalition would be an uneasy alliance. Communist charges of undue papal influence in the formulation of Christian Democratic policy was countered by Christian Democratic accusations that the Communist Party was an instrument of Soviet policy. The Communists were also accused of fomenting industrial strife, then rapidly attaining serious proportions in Italy. During the following months De Gasperi was subjected to increasingly violent attacks from the left. The friction between the two camps was intensified by a variety of factors, including the persistence of semifamine conditions and the chaotic state of Italian economy in general. In October the radical wing of the Christian Democratic Party attacked De Gasperi's policies. As the prestige of the De Gasperi government decreased, the Socialist and Communist parties drew more closely together, with the stated objective of taking power. The municipal elections of November, 1946, resulted in substantial Christian Democratic losses and corresponding gains by the Communist, Socialist, and rightist parties. On November 23 the Socialist leader Pietro Nenni warned that the alternative to early leftist assumption of power in Italy would be civil war. The mood of despair prevalent among the Italian people had been aggravated meanwhile by the preliminary decisions of the "Big-Four" Council of Foreign Ministers with respect to the Italian peace treaty. As revealed at the Paris Peace Conference, which opened on July 29, these decisions contemplated the internationalization of Trieste (see TRIESTE, FREE TERRITORY OF), the cession of most of the remainder of Venezia Giulia and several Adriatic islands to Yugoslavia, the cession of the Dodecanese Islands and certain small border areas to France, and the award of $100,000,000 in reparations to the U.S.S.R. The proposed treaty contained other stringent provisions, including the imposition of additional reparations on behalf of other nations victimized by Fascism, of severe restrictions on the Italian military establishment, and of British administration over Italian East Africa pending agreement among the "Big-Four" on the final disposition of the colonies.

On August 10 De Gasperi delivered an eloquent appeal for more lenient terms before the peace delegates, but the Conference adjourned, on October 15, without materially altering the original draft. The Italian treaty, identical in all important respects to the document prepared at Paris, was confirmed, along with the treaties for the other Axis satellite nations, at the next session of the Council of Foreign Ministers, which met in New York City from November 4 to December 6, 1946. Despite official Italian protests and popular manifestations in various parts of Italy, the treaty was signed by the Allied powers at Paris on February 10, 1947. Ratified (266–68) on February 10, 1947, by the Italian Constituent Assembly, with the Communist and Socialist delegates abstaining, the treaty became effective on September 15. Allied occupation forces withdrew from Italy during the next three months.

Although there was strong sentiment among the Italian people against the peace agreement concluded by the "Big Four" at New York, many were mollified and encouraged by the attitude of the United States government, which had not only helped to frustrate Soviet demands for harsher terms but had also, in January, 1947, concretely demonstrated its friendly intentions toward Italy. On a mission to Washington, D.C., early in the new year, De Gasperi had obtained $50,000,000 in payment of purchases by U.S. forces in Italy, a credit for $100,000,000 from the Export-Import Bank, immediate shipments of basic foodstuffs, and pledges of additional aid.

Significant events developed on the Italian political scene during De Gasperi's visit abroad. The Italian Socialist Party, reflecting the process of differentiation along ideological lines then gaining headway in Europe, split into two groupings on the issue of collaboration with the Communists. Pietro Nenni, foreign minister in De Gasperi's cabinet and a leader of the pro-Communist faction of the Socialist Party, resigned his government post on January 15, shortly after De Gasperi's return from America. Nenni's resignation was followed by that of the entire cabinet, but De Gasperi formed another coalition ministry on February 2. Both the Communist and Socialist parties were represented in the new government, but Count Sforza replaced Nenni as foreign minister. Relations between the leftist and moderate groupings in Italian politics deteriorated steadily thereafter. In large degree, this trend reflected the mounting diplomatic struggle, popularly termed the "cold war", between the western democracies and the Soviet bloc of E. European states, with Italian political parties and factions choosing sides according to their ideological orientation. Taking advantage of the divisions in anti-Fascist ranks, the extreme right, composed for the most part of former adherents of Mussolini and monarchists, employed increasingly bold tactics in its fight against the left and center. On May 1 an armed band of anti-Communists attacked a Communist-led parade at Greci, Sicily, killing eight persons. The massacre, together with disagreements in the Constituent Assembly on such government policies as increased taxation and dismissals of civil employees, precipitated another cabinet crisis, which extended from May 13 to May 31. De Gasperi resolved the crisis by forming a ministry consisting of Christian Democrats and nonparty specialists. For the first time since the re-establishment of democracy in Italy, the Communists and Socialists were excluded from the government. The new regime immediately began a purge of leftists from important public positions.

The period following the complete rupture of the anti-Fascist coalition was marked by bitter political strife in Italy, with the leftist opposition utilizing a wide variety of tactics, including mass demonstrations and general strikes, in its efforts to dislodge the De Gasperi cabinet. In the realm of foreign policy, the Communists and their left-wing Socialist allies were especially vehement in their denunciations of the United States and of De Gasperi's approval of the European Recovery Program (q.v.), the American plan for rehabilitation of the war-torn economies of Europe. Russian hostility to the Italian government was indicated when, on October 1, Italy's application for membership in the United Nations was vetoed by the Soviet delegate to the Security Council. In the same month the Italian Communist Party became a founding member of the Communist Information Bureau. This organization, popularly known as the Cominform and representative of the Communist parties of certain w. European and the Soviet bloc of states, was established to combat American influence and activities in Europe and to extend the power of the U.S.S.R. Throughout the remainder of 1947 repeated attempts by the antigovernment caucus in the Constituent Assembly to overthrow the De Gasperi cabinet ended in failure. Although the neo-Fascist movement increased its activity during this period, it gained little support among the Italian people.

The Constituent Assembly had meanwhile completed its primary task, the draft of a constitution for the republic. Approved on December 22, 1947, by a vote of 453 to 62, the document became effective on January 1, 1948. National elections for the new Italian parliament were postponed until April, 1948. The ensuing campaign was the bitterest and, in some respects, the most dramatic in Italian history. Coinciding with a general intensification of the "cold war" in the international arena, the contest repeatedly brought Italy to the verge of civil war. Displays of force became a central feature of the strategy of both camps. The Communist-led coalition, operating through the General Confederation of Labor, made frequent use of strikes as a political weapon. As part of its reprisals against the left, the government confiscated arms and ammunition from Communist partisans and conducted intimidatory military

demonstrations in various urban areas. On March 10 Pope Pius XII sanctioned anti-Communist activity by the Italian clergy. Less than a week later Premier De Gasperi accused the Soviet Union and the Cominform of directing the Communist bid for power in Italy. Reflecting American concern over possible developments in Italy, George C. Marshall, Secretary of State, warned, on March 19, that no aid would be extended that nation under the European Recovery Program in the event of a Communist victory. However, E.R.P. relief shipments to Italy were authorized on April 9.

Held on April 18 and 19, the elections resulted in an overwhelming victory for the Christian Democratic Party, which received more than 12,750,000 votes. This total, nearly 49% of all ballots cast, gave the Christian Democrats 307 seats in the Chamber of Deputies and 151 seats in the Senate. The Popular Front, the coalition of Communists and left-wing Socialists, polled slightly more than 8,000,000 votes and won 182 seats in the Chamber of Deputies. Senators elected by the Popular Front numbered 31. The right-wing Socialists elected 33 deputies, and the remaining 52 seats were distributed among minor parties. Only six deputies were elected by the Italian Social Movement, the neo-Fascist party.

The decisive mandate rendered by the Italian people in the general elections produced a marked reduction of political tension in Italy. Because of the relative strength displayed at the polls by the Communists, however, reconciliation of the differences which had divided the nation into two camps appeared unlikely. On May 11, Luigi Einaudi, the candidate of the Christian Democrats and right-wing Socialists, was elected president of the republic. De Gasperi, who was reappointed premier on the following day, announced his cabinet on May 23. In its composition, the new ministry differed little from its predecessor.

Supplies and credits made available under the E.R.P. had meanwhile begun to flow into Italy, creating favorable conditions for reconstruction of the national economy. Adhering to their policy of irreconcilable struggle against the E.R.P., the Italian Communists promoted, beginning about the middle of June, a widespread strike movement for higher wages. The movement culminated, on July 2, in a general 12-hour walkout. Within two weeks Italy was plunged into another grave crisis as the result of the attempted assassina-

Ewing Galloway

Above: Sheep and cart drivers on the Appian Way, oldest and most famous of the ancient Roman roads. Right: Women washing clothes at a stream in Calabria province, Italy.

tion, on July 14, of Palmiro Togliatti, head of the Communist Party. The General Confederation of Labor, charging the De Gasperi government with political responsibility for the crime, immediately called a nation-wide general strike to force the premier's resignation. During the next two days riotous demonstrations occurred in practically every city of Italy. By mobilizing more than 300,000 troops and police, the government succeeded in ending the strike on July 16.

In the year following the July disturbances, the Italian Popular Front confined its struggle against the Christian Democratic regime chiefly to the chambers of parliament. The principal object of Communist attacks during this period was the proposed North Atlantic

Treaty (q.v.), a defensive alliance of the United States, Canada, and ten western European nations. The leftist onslaughts on the proposed treaty met with some success in Italy, primarily among the right-wing Socialist leadership, which voted 8 to 7 against Italian participation. However, with the unanimous approval of his cabinet and a large majority of the Chamber of Deputies, De Gasperi affixed his signature to the North Atlantic Treaty at Washington, D.C., on April 4, 1949. The Soviet Union, in sharp protests to the Italian and "Big-Three" governments on July 20, maintained that Italy's adherence to the North Atlantic pact constituted a violation of the World War II peace treaty. On the following day the Chamber of Deputies ratified the pact by a vote of 323 to 160. Ratification was subsequently voted by the Senate on July 30. See NORTH ATLANTIC TREATY ORGANIZATION.

The "Big Four" meanwhile had failed to reach agreement on the disposition of Italy's prewar colonies in Africa, and the matter had been referred to the General Assembly of the United Nations. During the second half (April 5 to May 18) of its third session, the General Assembly considered an Anglo-Italian plan of disposition, but the plan failed to receive the required support of a two-thirds majority. The Assembly then voted to table the question until its fourth session, scheduled to open in September. A plan developed by the Political and Social Committee of the General Assembly was adopted (48 to 1) on November 21, with Ethiopia casting the negative ballot and nine members abstaining. Among salient features of the plan were provisions for granting independence to Somaliland after ten years as a U.N. Trust Territory under Italian administration; for granting independence to Libya by January 1, 1952; and for disposition of Eritrea on the basis of a report to be prepared by a special U.N. commission.

During the fiscal year ending June 30, 1949, Italy received grants totaling $498 million under the European Recovery Program. Many sectors of the national economy responded favorably to E.R.P. aid, but due to the depressed conditions in various rural areas, the stagnation and retrenchment prevalent in certain industries, and the deflationary policies of the De Gasperi government, large sections of the peasantry and working class remained destitute. In March, 1949, the number of jobless Italians totaled nearly 2,200,000. Persons on public relief during July numbered over 3,500,000. Toward the close of the year the landless peasantry in scattered sections of Italy began the forcible seizure of vacant lands.

In the spring of 1950, after study and debate extending over a year, the Parliament approved the first part of a program providing for the distribution of large estates among the landless peasantry. Additional legislation, adopted later in the year, expanded the land-distribution program. Unemployment became chronic in the textile industry during 1950, but general industrial activity increased, especially after the outbreak (June 25) of the Korean War. Despite the resultant improvement in the economic situation, the Communists and left-wing Socialists retained their following among the electorate. Municipal elections, held in N. Italy on May 27-28, 1951, indicated a substantial increase in the left-wing popular vote. However, left-wing administrations were driven from office in many of the northern cities by an anti-Red four-party coalition.

In the realm of foreign affairs, Italy continued to collaborate with the Western democracies after its ratification of the North Atlantic Treaty. The government, in its first contribution to the North Atlantic defense system against possible Soviet aggression, announced (July, 1950) that the Italian army would be built up to 250,000 men, the limit imposed by the World War II peace treaty. Further expansion of the military establishment was announced in December. As a result of Italian efforts to secure revision of the treaty, the United States, Great Britain, France, and eight other western countries waived (December, 1951) the clauses limiting Italian rearmament. The Soviet Union, which had refused to agree to such a revision unless Italy renounced membership in the North Atlantic Treaty Organization, was strongly critical of the action taken by the United States and its allies. However, full implementation of the rearmament program was rendered extremely difficult, despite substantial aid from the United States, due to a domestic economic situation marked by widespread inflation and unemployment. The International Bank approved (Oct. 11) a loan of $10 million for the development of s. Italy.

Nationwide local elections were completed in May, 1952. The Christian Democrats polled the largest single bloc of votes, but lost considerable strength as compared with their showing in the 1948 parliamentary elections. The Communists and procommunist Socialists received about 33 percent of the vote, a slight gain over 1948. The largest relative increase was registered by the Neofascists and Monarchists; their combined vote was close to 25 percent. On the basis of the results the ruling, middle-of-the-road Christian Democratic Party faced danger from both the right and left.

Industrial production increased slightly during 1952, and national petroleum and natural-gas resources, which promised to alleviate fuel shortage, were explored. In June the Parliament ratified the treaty (popularly known as the Schuman Plan) establishing the European Coal and Steel Community (q.v.). Plans were completed in the late summer to distribute about 20 percent of the large land holdings throughout the country to landless peasants. During the year the government made repeated requests to the United States for increased economic and military aid. By the end of 1952 Italy had less than six of the twelve divisions promised for the N.A.T.O. defense force.

The prewar fascists, previously barred by a constitutional provision from voting and holding public office, regained these rights upon expiration (Jan. 1, 1953) of the five-year limitation on punitive action against them. In an attempt to improve the effectiveness of the executive branch of the government, the Christian Democrats and their allies secured passage (March 29) of an electoral-reform bill ensuring the party in power of a working majority in parliament. The bill provides that the party or coalition of parties polling 50 percent or more of the popular vote will receive 65 percent of the seats in the Chamber of Deputies.

Parliamentary elections were held on June 7–8. The results of the voting, which was the closest in Italian history, reflected the trend established in the local elections of 1951–52. The four-party, center coalition failed by a small margin to obtain a popular majority. The Christian Democrats, emerging again as the strongest single party, polled 40 percent of the votes. The Communists were second (22.6 percent) and the parties of the right, which registered the biggest gains (12.7 percent as compared with 4.2 percent in 1948), were third.

Premier De Gasperi resigned following the elections. After attempts at forming a coalition cabinet failed, due to the opposition of the Social Democrats, De Gasperi announced (July 16) a cabinet composed only of Christian Democrats but dependent on the support of other parties. On July 28, after losing a vote of confidence, his government fell. The Christian Democratic leader Giuseppi Pella (1902–), former minister of the treasury, having won the benevolent neutrality of the Socialists and the support of the Monarchists, formed another all-Christian Democratic cabinet on Aug. 17.

Late in 1953 the question of the future status of the Free Territory of Trieste brought Italy and Yugoslavia to the verge of war. The British and U.S. governments announced (Oct. 8) they intended to withdraw their occupation forces from Zone A and transfer administrative authority to Italy. Both Yugoslavia and the Soviet Union expressed strong opposition to the projected move, and Italy and Yugoslavia deployed troop reinforcements along the frontiers of Zone A and Zone B. Tensions abated after the United States, Great Britain, and France agreed to work out a formula acceptable to both sides. Italian and Yugoslav reinforcements were withdrawn from the Trieste frontiers on Dec. 20. See also TRIESTE, FREE TERRITORY OF.

Premier Pella and his cabinet resigned on Jan. 5, 1954, because of opposition within their own party to the appointment of a Conservative as agriculture minister. Amintore Fanfani (1908–), a left-of-center Christian Democrat and former agriculture and interior minister, formed a new government on Jan. 18. The cabinet, which consisted of Christian Democrats and one Independent, fell a few days later, precipitating a prolonged crisis.

ITASCA, LAKE, a small lake of N.W. Minnesota, situated in a State park of the same name about 25 miles S.W. of Bemidji. The lake is sometimes referred to as the source of the Mississippi R., but geologists assert that many other lakes of the surrounding morainic region contribute to the headwaters of the Mississippi. Its area is 2 sq.m.

ITCH, name for several diseases or conditions in which itching (a tingling sensation of the skin which creates a desire to scratch) is a prominent symptom. The name "itch" is applied to several forms of dermatitis (q.v.), to barber's itch, and to the contagious mange of animals.

In man, itch, also called *scabies,* is often produced by a number of small parasites, known as *itch mites,* which burrow into and irritate the skin. The commonest of these is the female of *Sarcoptes scabiei,* a round, pearly-white arachnid, about 1/60 in. long, with pointed mouth parts. This mite burrows into sensitive folds of the skin, such as those found in the armpit and between the digits; it occasionally infects the smooth skin of the face. Treatment of this condition, which can be transmitted from person to person, consists of avoiding scratching, careful cleansing of the infested parts, and application of sulfur ointment. Among other organisms which cause itch are the chigger (q.v.) and the crab louse.

ITEA, genus of shrubs belonging to the family Escalloniaceae. The genus is native to temperate regions of Asia and North America. The shrubs grow as tall as 8 feet, and bear simple alternate leaves. The fragrant, white flowers, which are borne in simple racemes, are composed of a five-cleft calyx, five lanceolate petals, five short stamens, and a solitary pistil. The fruit is a many-seeded, septicidal capsule. The single North American species is the Virginia willow or sweet spire, *I. virginica.* It is a hardy, deciduous shrub which grows well in moist soil, flowering in summer and producing brilliant red leaves in fall. It is native to swamps and river basins of E. United States. The holly-leaved itea, *I. ilicifolia,* and the Yunnan itea, *I. yunnanensis,* are tender evergreen shrubs native to China. Evergreen iteas are cultivated in warmer regions of the United States.

ITHACA, city and county seat of Tompkins Co., N.Y., situated at the s. end of Cayuga Lake, 55 miles s.w. of Syracuse. It is served by two railroads and several air lines, and is the s. terminal of the New York State Barge Canal. Industries include the manufacture of clothing, clay products, leather goods, machine tools, office machinery, paper products, and scientific instruments. Primarily an educational center, the city is the site of Cornell University (q.v.); the New York State Colleges of Veterinary Medicine, Agriculture, Home Economics, and Labor and Industrial Relations; and Ithaca College, a coeducational school offering courses in music, drama, radio, business, physical education, and physiotherapy. The *American Agriculturist,* a leading farm publication, is published in Ithaca, and in the city are the main offices of the Grange League Federation, the largest farmers' buying and marketing co-operative in the northeastern United States; the State offices of the Farm Bureau Federation; and a Federal nutrition laboratory. Also located in Ithaca are the headquarters offices of several Federal and State agricultural agencies.

Lying in a hilly region overlooking Cayuga Lake, Ithaca and environs are famous for their scenic beauty. Three streams traverse the city, flowing through deep gorges, and the rapids and waterfalls are one of its distinctive features. The municipal park system covering 500 acres contains bird and wild-fowl sanctuaries and varied recreational facilities. Three State parks, Buttermilk

Falls, Robert H. Treman, and Taurghannock Falls, are situated within 10 m. of the city. Ithaca was founded about 1787. It became the county seat in 1818, was incorporated as a village in 1821, and chartered as a city in 1888. Pop. (1950) 29,257.

ITO, MARQUIS HIROBUMI (1841–1909), Japanese statesman, born in Choshu Province. He was appointed vice-minister of finance in 1869, and two years later visited the United States, where he studied the monetary system and prepared a report which resulted in the adoption of the decimal system of currency by Japan. He subsequently visited Europe on several occasions to study constitutional forms of government; in 1882, the year in which he became premier, he was commissioned by Emperor Matsuhito to prepare a constitution for Japan. In collaboration with the statesman Kimmochi Saionji, he completed this task, and the constitution was promulgated in February, 1889 (see JAPAN: *History*). Ito was again premier when the Chinese-Japanese War broke out in 1894, and after its victorious conclusion in the following year negotiated the Treaty of Shimonoseki, ending the war. He was created a marquis in 1895. He was designated premier again in 1898 and 1900; in 1902 he negotiated a military and commercial alliance with England known as the Anglo-Japanese Alliance. In 1904 he went to Korea as a special emissary of the Japanese emperor, and conducted the negotiations which led to the establishment of a Japanese protectorate over Korea. He served in the post of the resident-general of Korea from 1905 until 1909. While in Harbin on a diplomatic mission to Manchuria, he was assassinated by a Korean patriot.

ITONAMAN, a group of South American Indian tribes, sometimes classified as a distinct linguistic stock, living in N.E. Bolivia. The *Itonomas,* the most important tribe of the group, live on the banks of the Itonama River, a branch of the Guaporé River. The Itonamas are an agricultural people; they weave excellent cotton textiles from cotton raised in their own fields, and supplement their vegetable diet with fish caught from canoes of their own making.

ITURÆA or **ITUREA,** a country in the N.E. part of ancient Palestine, lying s. of Damascus. Considerable uncertainty exists regarding the exact location and limits of Ituræa. According to tradition its founders, seminomadic migrants from the Arabian Peninsula, were descendants of the Jewish patriarch Abraham's grandson Jetur. The Ituræans were fierce warriors, famed as archers. King Aristobulus I of Judæa conquered and annexed their country late in the 2nd century B.C. and forcibly converted them to Judaism. About 64 B.C. Judæa was conquered by the Roman general Pompey the Great. Under Roman domination Ituræa formed part of the dominions of the Judæan king Herod the Great, was included in 4 B.C. in the newly created domain of Philip the Tetrarch (d. 34 A.D.), and about the middle of the 1st century A.D. was incorporated into the Roman province of Syria. After subjugation of the country by Rome many Ituræans served in the Roman armies. The Roman statesman Marcus Cicero, in one of his orations, accused the triumvir Marcus Antonius of attempting to terrify the Roman Senate with Ituræan guards; Ituræan troops in the Roman armies are mentioned in inscriptions of the 1st and 2nd centuries A.D.

ITURBI, José (1895–   ), Spanish pianist and conductor, born in Valencia, and educated in Valencia, Barcelona, and Paris. From 1919 to 1923 he taught at the Geneva Conservatory. His American debut in 1928 with the Philadelphia Symphony Orchestra was well-received by critics, and he subsequently established a reputation as one of the leading pianists active in the U.S. Beginning in 1933, when he conducted fifteen concerts in Mexico City, Iturbi also became known as an orchestra conductor. From 1936 to 1944 he was regular conductor of the Rochester Philharmonic Orchestra. He appeared as guest conductor with many of the major orchestras of the U.S., Europe, and South America. He also appeared as an actor and pianist in several American motion pictures.

ITURBIDE, AGUSTÍN DE (1783–1824), Mexican soldier and emperor, born in Valladolid de Michoacán (now Morelia). In 1797 he joined the Spanish military forces in Mexico. He remained loyal to Spain after the outbreak (1810) of the Mexican war of independence and, distinguishing himself in the subsequent fighting, won advancement (1815) to the position of commander in chief in Guanajuato and Michoacán provinces. In 1820, following a few years in retirement, he was appointed to command the royalist troops assigned the task of quelling an insurrection led by the revolutionist Vicente Guerrero. Developments in Spain, especially a revolt portending liberalization of the Mexican governmental and social order, meanwhile had engendered revolutionary unrest among conservative groupings in Mexico. Iturbide was selected to lead the resultant conspiracy

José Iturbi

against Spanish authority. His initial overt act, taken after he had secretly won the confidence of the radical wing of the revolutionary movement, was promulgation (Feb. 24, 1821), jointly with Guerrero, of the document known in history as the Act of Iguala, which included provisions for the establishment of Mexico as a constitutional monarchy. Containing concessions to all sections of the population, the plan won broad popular support. Revolutionary forces under Iturbide's command imposed successive defeats on the royalists during the next few months, and on August 24 the Spanish viceroy signed the Treaty of Córdoba, a convention accepting the plan of Iguala and recognizing Mexican independence. A provisional government headed by Iturbide assumed power on September 27.

In February, 1822, the legislature of Spain rejected the Treaty of Córdoba; an army-supported minority of the Mexican constituent congress proclaimed Iturbide emperor as Agustín I on the following May 19. Essentially despotic, his regime soon incurred armed opposition from the republican movement. He was forced to abdicate on March 19, 1823, and exiled to Italy. Unaware that he had been outlawed and hopeful of regaining the support of his former followers, he returned to Mexico on July 15, 1824. He was immediately arrested by authorities of Tamaulipas, condemned as a traitor by the State legislature, and exe-

Ivan the Great (from an old print)

cuted on July 19. While in exile, Iturbide
wrote a *Statement of Some of the Principal
Events in the Public Life of Agustin de
Iturbide* (1824).

ITYLUS. See AEDON.

ITYS. See PHILOMELA.

ITZA, a tribe of Mayan Indians common in
Guatemala and in Yucatan, Mexico, until the
beginning of the 18th century. About this
time a Spanish expedition destroyed their
principal city (see CHICHEN-ITZA), temples,
and sacred books, and dispersed the remaining population. The Itzas comprised one of
the principal semi-independent Mayan states,
and, by civil war with the other states, were
in part responsible for the weakening of the
Mayan empire.

IULUS or **ASCANIUS,** in Roman legend the
son of the warrior Æneas. He succeeded his
father to the throne of Latinus, and was the
founder of the family of the Cæsars, and of
the city of Lavinium.

IVAN, name of a number of Russian grand
dukes and czars. The following are notable in
history.

1. IVAN III VASILIEVICH, called IVAN THE
GREAT (1440–1505), grand duke of Moscow
from 1462 until his death. He did much to
further the policy, initiated by his predecessors, of enhancing and strengthening the
hegemony of Moscow over other Russian
principalities. In 1470 he launched a war
against the republic of Novgorod, which he
conquered and annexed in 1478, thereby acquiring all of northern Russia from Lapland
to the Urals. In 1480, by refusing to make
the customary payment of tribute to the
Tatar Khan Ahmed, Ivan ended the subservience of the Muscovite rulers to the Tatars.
Subsequently, he further increased his domain by conquest, by purchases of territory,
and by exacting allegiance from weaker
princes. He invaded Lithuania in 1492 and
again in 1500, and forced Alexander, the ruler
of that country, to cede a score of Lithuanian
towns to him in 1503. Ivan also succeeded,
through his marriage in 1472 to Sophia, niece
of the last Byzantine emperor Constantine
XI Palæologus, in establishing himself
as the protector of the Orthodox Christian
Church. Soon after his marriage Ivan added
the two-headed eagle of the Byzantine es-
cutcheon to his own coat-of-arms and, modeling his regime on that of the autocratic
Byzantine rulers, drastically curtailed the
powers and privileges of the Russian aristocracy. Another of the outstanding accomplishments of his reign was the compilation
of the first Russian code of law.

2. IVAN IV VASILIEVICH, called IVAN THE
TERRIBLE (1530–84), grandson of Ivan III. He
was proclaimed grand duke of Moscow at the
age of three, upon the death of his father.
Ivan ruled until he was fourteen under the
successive regencies of his mother and of
various aristocrats; in 1544 he took over control of the state. Three years later he assumed
the title of czar, thereby becoming the first
Russian ruler to bear that designation. The
first thirteen years of Ivan's reign comprise
one of the greatest periods of internal reform,
external expansion, and centralization of state
power in the history of Russia. In 1550 Ivan
convoked the *Zemski Sobor,* the first national
representative assembly ever summoned by a
Russian ruler. In the same year he initiated
a comprehensive revision and modernization
of the Russian law code. Ivan conquered and
annexed the Tatar khanates of Kazan and
Astrakhan in 1552 and 1556, respectively,
bringing the Volga River within the borders
of Russia and ending the sway of the Tatars
over Russian territory. The reign of Ivan after 1560 is remarkable rather for repeated displays of erratic behavior and wanton brutality by the czar than for his statesmanship.
He surrounded himself with a select group
of noblemen whom he allowed to exercise
despotic power over his entire domain. In
1570 he ravaged the town of Novgorod and

ordered the slaying of thousands of its inhabitants, because they had been reported, on dubious authority, to be conspiring against him. Ten years later Ivan brought personal tragedy upon himself when, in a fit of insane anger, he struck and killed his eldest and favorite son. The sole achievement of Ivan's later years was the acquisition of Siberia in 1581, after that vast territory had been brought under Russian control by Ermak Timofeev, the Cossack hetman; see COSSACKS. Shortly before his death, Ivan, overcome with feelings of guilt and remorse, entered a religious order of hermits, taking the name of Jonah.

IVANOVO, formerly IVANOVO-VOZNESENSK, a city of Soviet Russia, situated in the Ivanov Industrial Area, about 200 m. by rail N.E. of Moscow. The city was founded in 1861, when two villages, 16th-century Ivanovo and more modern Voznesensk, were united. An agricultural school and a polytechnic institute are located in the city. Manufactures of linen and cotton textiles, iron, and chemicals are the principal industries. Pop., about 285,000.

IVES, CHARLES EDWARD (1874–   ), American composer, born in Danbury, Conn. He received his early musical education from his father and later studied music at Yale University. After his graduation, in 1898, he went into the insurance business, and music became his avocation. He composed many orchestral, vocal, and chamber works, which have been performed both in America and Europe. His music is for the most part unconventional in style, making use of polytonal harmonies and unusual rhythms. The second piano (*Concord*) sonata, is one of his most frequently performed compositions.

IVES, FREDERICK EUGENE (1856–1937), American inventor and scientist, born in Litchfield, Conn. He had little formal education, but at the age of eighteen became director of the photographic laboratory at Cornell University. He held this position until 1878, when he originated the first halftone photoengraving process. Ives was a pioneer in the development of color photography. His inventions include the first trichromatic halftone process printing plates; the halftone photogravure method, which anticipated modern rotogravure; and a single-objective variety of the binocular microscope. He is the author of *Autobiography of an Amateur Inventor* (1928).

IVORY, the opaque, creamy-white, hard, fine-grained, modified dentine which composes the upper incisor teeth (tusks) of elephants. Ivory is composed of curved layers of dentine, alternating in shade, which intersect one another; the resulting lozenge-shaped structure is highly elastic and finely grained. The layers of an elephant's tusk are deposited from the pulp, so that the innermost layer is the newest. The base of the tusk, which is imbedded in the skull, is filled with pulp at the widest part. The pulp cavity becomes progressively narrower toward the tip of the tusk, ending as a minute, threadlike channel.

Most commercial elephant ivory is obtained from the tusks of the African elephant, *Loxodonta africana;* see ELEPHANT. Elephants formerly roamed over all of Africa south of the northern desert region, but the encroachment of civilization has driven them into the interior. Central Africa, Uganda, and Mozambique are now the primary sources of ivory. Most of the ivory of the western half of Africa is hard, whereas that from the eastern half is soft. Hard ivory is relatively glassier in texture, more difficult to cut, and more susceptible to cracking than soft ivory. The largest ivory tusks are 9 feet long and weigh about 225 pounds. The value of ivory depends on the size and condition of the tusks. Standard commercial grades are based primarily on weight. The usual four grades are: (1) tusks weighing 60 pounds or more, (2) tusks weighing 40 to 60 pounds, (3) tusks weighing 20 to 40 pounds, and (4) tusks weighing less than 20 pounds. Less than one quarter of commercial ivory is obtained from freshly killed elephants; the remainder is obtained from collections made by natives from the carcasses of elephants which died natural deaths. The principal ivory-distributing markets of the world are the ports of Antwerp, London, and Liverpool; smaller markets exist in French, Portuguese, and United States ports.

Fossil ivory, called *odontolite,* is a blue variety found in small quantities in the frozen soils of northern Siberia. The ivory was produced by the extinct mammoths of the Pleistocene geological epoch; its blue color is due to saturation by metallic salts.

Tusks of several other animals, such as hippopotamuses, narwhals, sperm whales, and walruses, are commonly called ivory and have similar physical properties. As genuine ivory has become rarer and more expensive, numerous plastic substitutes for ivory have been developed; see PLASTICS. Several ivorylike vegetable parts are also used as imitation ivory; the ivory palm (q.v.), for example, produces large, white, hard seeds, called ivory

Metropolitan Museum of Art

"Christ in Majesty," an ivory plaque carved in Italy in second half of the 10th century

nuts, the endosperm of which is commonly known as *vegetable ivory*.

Carved ivory has been used for decorative purposes since the time of the ancient Egyptians; see IVORY CARVING. Small pieces of ivory are used for high-quality furniture inlays, chessmen, and small jewelry. Larger pieces of ivory are sometimes used in the manufacture of billiard balls, piano keys, and toilet articles.

IVORY-BILLED WOODPECKER or IVORY-BILL, a large, richly colored American woodpecker, *Campephilus principalis,* so called because of its ivory-colored beak. The bird was once common in cypress forests throughout S.E. United States, but is rapidly becoming extinct; a few of them may still be found in central Florida. The bird is about 20 in. long, satiny-black, with white-tipped wings, and with a white line on each side running from just below the eye along the neck to the middle of the back. The male has a bright red crest on its head; the female has a black crest. The bird has a powerful cry.

IVORY CARVING, the art of carving ivory for ornamental or useful purposes, practiced from prehistoric to modern times. The ivory most frequently used is obtained from the tusks of elephants, but other types of ivory or substitute material include the tusks, teeth, horns, and bones of other animals, and also vegetable ivory (q.v.) and synthetic ivories. The earliest ivory carvings were made in the Paleolithic age which ended about 8000 B.C. The Aurignacian period in the latter part of this age is also called the "ivory period" because Aurignacian man produced great numbers of ivory, bone, and horn carvings. Nude female figures are the most common subject of Aurignacian carvings; representations of animals, especially reindeer, occur most often in the subsequent Magdalenian period.

In Egypt, the art of ivory and bone carving was developed as early as the 1st and 2nd dynasties, from 3200 to 2780 B.C. Large numbers of carved figures of men and women and also carved combs, hairpins, and handles have been found in tombs of this and later periods. Objects found in Egyptian tombs of later date include carved ivory weapon hilts and furniture and caskets inlaid with ivory carvings. Mesopotamian ivories show strong Egyptian influence. They include a series of tablets carved with figures in low relief, made at Nineveh in the 10th century B.C.

The Minoans and later the ancient Greeks were noted for their ivory carvings. The Greeks were famous especially in the 5th century B.C. for their chryselephantine statues, often of heroic size, in which the flesh was represented in carved ivory and the hair and garments in sculptured gold. Among the Romans, particularly in late Imperial times, from the 3rd to the 5th century A.D., carved ivories were much in demand. A popular type was the consular diptych, a two-leaved tablet decorated with portraits and scenes commemorating the inauguration of a consul.

Ivory carving flourished under the Byzantine Empire from the 6th to the 15th century. Christian figures, symbols, and scenes were used to decorate ivory book covers, icons, pyxes or boxes, shrines, crosiers, crucifixes, door panels, and thrones.

In Europe during the reign of Charlemagne and his successors in the 9th and 10th centuries elaborately carved ivory book covers and altarpieces were produced. Gothic ivories from the 13th to the 15th century included objects of ecclesiastical use as in preceding periods. The most popular subject was the Virgin and Child, executed in the round or in relief.

In the Renaissance during the 15th and 16th centuries, ivory carving was not a popular art, but in the Baroque period in the 17th century it again came into vogue, especially in Germany and the Netherlands. The German craftsmen were known for richly ornamented ivory tankards, and in Flanders the sculptor François Duquesnoy achieved great fame for his realistic ivories of plump children engaged in bacchanals. France again became an important center in the 17th and 18th centuries with the establishment of an ivory-carving industry at Dieppe, and large numbers of crucifixes and other religious objects were produced. Subsequently the demand for ivories diminished, and did not increase substantially until the end of the 19th century. Ivory carvings then became popular once more, and are still in demand today. The supply of ivory from elephant tusks is limited, and vegetable and synthetic ivory are often used as substitutes.

Among the Moslems the art of ivory carving has long been used in creating elaborately patterned inlay work on furniture and woodwork. In the Far East the best-known ivories are those of India and Japan, and particularly of China. The Indians carved figures of their gods, and ornate caskets and chessmen. The Japanese netsukes, small carved ornaments used as part of a costume or placed on view in the home, are often made of ivory. The Chinese have traditionally esteemed ivory, and under the Empire artists were encouraged to work in this medium. The art still flourishes today and objects created include statuettes, chopsticks, fans, screens, toilet articles, and models of buildings and boats. The Chinese are world-famous for their ivory curiosities, particularly the concentric ivory balls carved one inside the other. In Eskimo, African, and North American Indian cultures, carving in ivory, horn, and bone has been practiced from the earliest times to the present day.

IVORY COAST (*Fr. Côte d'Ivoire*), Territory of French West Africa, bounded on the N. by French Sudan, on the E. by Niger Territory and by Gold Coast, British West Africa, on the S. by the Gulf of Guinea, and on the W. by Liberia and French Guinea. Abidjan (pop., about 46,000) is the administrative center and largest town of the Territory. Port Bouet, the port of Abidjan, is the principal seaport. Other important towns are Grand Bassam (pop., about 5700), Grand Lahou (pop., about 4400), and Bingerville (pop., about 1000). Area of Territory, 123,310 sq.m.; pop. (1952) 2,223,787, including 10,500 French.

The Territorial coast, about 315 m. long, is fringed by a number of large lagoons, but due to offlying shoals few of these indentations are accessible to shipping. Adjoining the coast is a low plain, with a general width of about 40 m. and demarcated on the N. by an extensive plateau. This region, averaging about 1000 ft. above sea level, contains mountainous outcroppings, with elevations over 2000 ft., and numerous valleys. The w. and N.w. regions are mountainous; some of the summits are over 5000 ft. Ivory Coast is traversed by several large rivers, including the Sassandra and Bandama. Except in the mountains and in parts of the plateau region, the climate is hot and humid, and rainfall is extremely heavy.

The principal products and exports of the Territory are coffee, timber, cacao, and palm kernels. Nonindustrial crops include rice, corn, millet, pineapples, and yams. Fishing, weaving, and pottery making are important occupations. Among the leading imports are textiles, metal products, and beverages. Communication facilities include more than 6000 m. of roads suitable for motor traffic, and a railway, 494 m. in length, connecting Abidjan with Bobo-Dioulasso (pop.., about 18,500), Upper Volta, near the N.E. border. There is also a railway line between Abidjan and Port-Bouet.

A large majority of the native inhabitants of Ivory Coast belong to various tribal groups of the Sudanic linguistic stock. Numerically, the chief groups are the Agni, Kru, and Baule, who dwell mainly in the coastal region and central interior, and the Mandigo and Mossi, who predominate in the N. Mohammedanism is the religion of several of the Mandigo tribes, but most of the natives are fetishists.

Ivory Coast, like all the Territories of French West Africa, is administered by a governor, an appointee of the French government. His management of Territorial affairs is subject to supervision by the governor general of French West Africa. Assisting the governor are a privy council, which includes the heads of the various administrative departments, and a general council composed of 27 Negroes and 18 Europeans, all of whom are elected. Two deputies represent the Territory in the National Assembly of France; it is represented in the Council of the Republic by three councilors and in the French Union Assembly by four councilors.

Portuguese explorers visited the region now known as Ivory Coast late in the 15th century. During the next two centuries European slave and ivory traders were active there. The French established a trading post on the coast near Abidjan in 1700. Additional settlements were founded by the French early in the 19th century, and in 1842, through a treaty arranged with native chieftains, they obtained tracts of territory in the coastal area. The French subsequently enlarged their coastal holdings. After penetrating the interior they encountered (1885) resistance from the Mandigos, who were subdued in the following year. The region was made a French protectorate in 1889, and during the next decade the boundaries with Liberia and Gold Coast were demarcated. Meanwhile (1893) Ivory Coast was constituted a colony. Numerous native uprisings occurred during the final decade of the 19th century and the first decade of the 20th. In 1919 the French established the N. portion of Ivory Coast as Upper Volta Colony; the latter was liquidated in 1933, and part of the region was returned to Ivory Coast. The colony was designated (1946) a Territory within the French Union under the terms of the constitution of the Fourth Republic. With the re-establishment (1948) of Upper Volta, Ivory Coast relinquished to it the region obtained in 1933.

IVORY PALM, common name of a shrub, *Phytelephas macrocarpa,* belonging to the Palm family, native to N. South America. The short, prostrate stem of the ivory palm produces a large tuft of light-green, pinnately compound leaves, which rise like an immense ostrich plume to a height of from 30 to 40 feet. The small, perfect flowers are borne on crowded spadices which arise from the center of the leaf cluster. The aggregate fruit, as large as a man's head, consists of six or more four-celled fruitlets, and contains numerous seeds, each the size of a hen's egg. The seeds, called *corozo nuts* or *ivory nuts,* contain a hard, white endosperm. The endosperm, commonly called *vegetable ivory,* is used extensively as a substitute for ivory in the manufacture of buttons and small trinkets. Another member of the palm family, *Coelococcus amicarum,* native to Polynesia, produces seeds which are a minor source of vegetable ivory.

IVRY-SUR-SEINE, a city of the department of Seine, France, forming a suburb of Paris. Machinery, musical instruments, confections, rubber goods, and oil products are the chief manufactures. Pop. (1947) 42,445.

IVY, common name applied to woody vines of the genus *Hedera,* belonging to the Ginseng family. The genus is native to temperate regions of the Old World. Two kinds of leaves are produced by ivy plants: during the climbing phase, the leaves produced have three to five distinct lobes, but during the flowering stage the leaves usually have three indistinct lobes or may even be lobeless. The flowers, which are borne in terminal umbels, have a five-parted calyx, five-parted corolla, five sta-

mens, and a single pistil. The fruit is a smooth berry which contains a poisonous glucoside. The plant is supported by tendrils which become attached to trees or bare walls, producing rootlets used to obtain moisture.

The English ivy, *H. helix,* is commonly cultivated in gardens of Europe and North America, and trained to cover masonry walls of buildings. It has small leaves which are usually dark-green. The African or Irish ivy, *H. canariensis,* is native to the coast and islands of N.W. Africa, and produces large, dark-green, lobed leaves. The Asiatic ivy, *H. colchica,* bears dark-green leaves which are usually faintly lobed or entirely lobeless. Both African and Asiatic ivy are regarded as varieties of *H. helix* by many botanists. Ivy is easily cultivated from cuttings. It protects the walls on which it is grown from the corrosive effects of weathering. Ivy has no destructive effect on stone or brick walls except when tendrils are established in fissures; expansion of tendrils will hasten the extension of the fissures.

Several plants of the Vine family are commonly called ivy. The American ivy or Virginia creeper, *Parthenocissus quinquefolia,* and the Boston or Japanese ivy, *P. tricuspidata,* are shrubby climbers which cling by tendrils. American ivy has long-petioled leaves composed of five leaflets; Boston ivy has three-lobed leaves. Both species of *Parthenocissus* grow readily from cuttings.

Ground ivy (q.v.) is a small, creeping member of the Mint family. German ivy, *Senecio mikanioides,* is a small creeping herb, native to South Africa, which belongs to the Thistle family. *Rhus toxicodendron,* commonly known as poison ivy (see SUMAC), is a member of the Cashew family.

IVY POISONING, inflammation of the skin caused by contact with poisonous sumac plants, such as poison ivy, poison oak, and poison sumac; see SUMAC. The extent of the inflammation depends on the degree of susceptibility of the victim and the extent of contact. Sensitivity to sumac poison is considered an allergy (q.v.) by most physicians, because many individuals may be unaffected by handling poisonous sumac plants while others may be affected by such slight contact as touching a shoe after walking through sumac plants, or standing in the path of smoke from burning sumac plants. Temporary reduction in sensitivity of many individuals is effected by intramuscular administration of large doses of an oleoresin obtained from sumac plants.

The skin in typical cases of ivy poisoning becomes red, swollen, and covered with many water blisters, associated with severe burning, tingling, or itching. The inflammation may be spread from an affected area of the body to other parts by dispersal of the watery, irritating contents of blisters. The inflammation usually lasts one to four weeks. Prevention of ivy poisoning after contact with the plants is most simply achieved by washing with strong soap. Chemicals such as potassium permanganate neutralize the poison. Soothing lotions such as boric acid solution or calamine lotion are used to allay the discomfort caused by itching. Present-day treatment of severe cases may include the administration of ACTH or cortisone.

IWO JIMA or **NAKA IWO,** sometimes Iwo; in English "Sulfur Island", largest island of the Volcano Islands, situated in the Pacific Ocean, about 710 miles s. of Tokyo, and belonging to Japan. About 5½ m. long and 2½ m. wide, it is volcanic in origin and mountainous. Mt. Suribachi (556 ft.) is the highest point on the island. During World War II the Japanese constructed three airfields and other military installations on Iwo Jima, transforming it into one of the strongest defense bastions in their outer-defense system. United States marines captured the island in March, 1945, after one of the bitterest and costliest battles of the war (see Iwo JIMA, BATTLE OF). Following the war Iwo Jima remained under U.S. occupation until completion of the peace agreement with Japan. Area, 8 sq.m.

IWO JIMA, BATTLE OF, battle of World War II, fought in 1945 on the island of Iwo Jima (q.v.) between invading United States marines and defending Japanese. Conquest of the island was considered vital by American military leaders because of important strategic considerations, including the necessity of a base, within range of industrial Japan, for U.S. medium bombers and rocket-firing escort fighters. United States aircraft made successive attacks on Iwo Jima from December, 1944, to February, 1945. On February 19, following an intensive bombardment by numerous units of the U.S. Fifth Fleet, the Fourth Marine Division, commanded by Maj. Gen. Clifton B. Cates, and the Fifth Marine Division, commanded by Maj. Gen. Keller E. Rockey, invaded the island. The Third Marine Division, commanded by Maj. Gen. G. B. Erskine, landed three days later. Although the pre-invasion assault had destroyed many of the Japanese shore defenses, the inland

Wide World Photo

Raising the American flag on Mt. Suribachi at the capture of Iwo Jima in World War II

fortifications were largely intact. The American marines were subjected to severe fire from these positions.

Mount Suribachi (556 ft.), the highest point on the island and an important defense position, was captured on February 23. The raising of the American flag over Mt. Suribachi was one of the notable episodes of World War II. By the 26th two of the Japanese airfields on the island were captured, but heavy fighting continued until March 17. American losses totaled 4189 killed and 15,-749 wounded. Japanese losses included 21,000 killed and 1259 prisoners.

I.W.W. See INDUSTRIAL WORKERS OF THE WORLD.

IXIA, genus of tender herbs, commonly called corn lilies, belonging to the Iris family. The genus is native to South Africa and is cultivated in warm temperate regions. The plant grows from a bulblike corm, producing narrow, sword-shaped leaves, and slender flower stalks. The small, funnel-shaped flowers have three petal-like sepals, three petals, three stamens, and a single, three-celled pistil. The fruit is a many-seeded loculicidal capsule. Cultivated corn lilies occur in a wide range of colors. *I. maculata,* which is yellow-flowered in the wild state, includes hybrids which bear white, pink, red, or lilac flowers.

I. viridiflora, which is hardy enough to be grown in gardens of N. United States, has striking, pale-green flowers with black throats. *I. columellaris* produces mauve and blue flowers; *I. lutea* produces rich-yellow flowers; and *I. speciosa* produces crimson flowers. Corn lilies planted in greenhouses in fall produce winter blossoms, and those planted in gardens in early spring produce summer blossoms.

IXION, in Greek legend, a king of the Lapithæ, father of Pirithoüs. He married Dia, daughter of Deïoneus, and later by treachery caused the death of his father-in-law. Zeus pardoned him, invited him to his table, and gave him immortality. He sought to seduce Hera, but was deceived by a cloud in her image, sent by Zeus, and by this became father of the centaurs. As punishment, he was fastened to a fiery wheel perpetually rolling through the air. Later writers transferred the scene of his punishment to Tartarus.

IXTACIHUATL or **IZTACCIHUATL,** extinct volcanic mountain of Mexico, located about 40 miles S.S.E. of Mexico City and 10 miles N. of Popocateptl (q.v.). It has three summits, the central one being the tallest (17,343 ft. above sea level). Its summits are constantly covered with snow, and from Mexico City the mountain resembles a shrouded figure; hence the Aztec name "white woman", and the Spanish name "the fat woman".

IXTLILXOCHITL II (1500?–50), Aztec chief of the confederated pueblo of Tezcuco or Texcoco. In 1516, upon the death of his father King Netzahualpilli, he disputed the right of his elder brother Tezcucan to the throne. When Montezuma II, Emperor of Mexico, sided with Tezcucan, Ixtlilxochitl secured the aid of the invading Spaniards under Hernando Cortes (q.v.), promising in return to assist them in conquering Mexico. By this means he gained the throne. Throughout his reign he supported the Spanish rulers of Mexico, losing thereby the favor of his own people.

IXTLILXOCHITL, FERNANDO DE ALVA CORTES (1568?–1648?), Mexican historian, a lineal descendant of Ixtlilxochitl II (q.v.), Aztec king of Tezcuco, born in Texcoco, and educated at the College of the Holy Cross, Santa Cruz. He was commissioned by the Spanish viceroy of Mexico to write a history of Mexico; the resulting work, *Historia Chichimeca,* comprised thirteen volumes and recounted Mexican history from ancient times to the Spanish conquest of the 16th century. This work is notable as the first complete history of Mexico written from the standpoint of a native Mexican patriot.

IZHEVSK, administrative center of the Udmursk Autonomous Area, Soviet Russia, located on the Izh R., about 190 miles S.E. of Kirov. Its industries include flour milling, sawmilling, brickmaking, and metal founding. Pop., about 175,000.

IZMIR, formerly SMYRNA, capital of the il of the same name, Turkey. The city is situated at the head of the Gulf of Smyrna; it is one of the chief seaports of the nation and is served by several railroads. Tobacco, figs, raisins, carpets, valonia, and silk are the chief exports. An important commercial center early in the first millennium B.C., the city was seized by the Ionians before the 7th century B.C. In that century it was devastated by the Lydians. Antigonus I of Macedonia restored the city in the 4th century B.C., and subsequently it was fortified and improved by Lysimachus, Macedonian general in the service of Alexander the Great. Smyrna was later conquered by the Romans. Early in the Christian era, a church of the new faith was founded by the Jews of Smyrna, which shortly became known as one of the "seven churches of Asia" (Revelations 2:8). In 155 A.D. the city was the scene of the martyrdom of St. Polycarp, Bishop of Smyrna. Smyrna was besieged several times by the Turks during the Middle Ages, held for a brief period in the 14th century by the Crusaders, and ravaged in 1402 by the Mongols under Tamerlane. After 1424 the city belonged to the Turks. The Greeks claimed Smyrna after World War I, and by the terms of the Treaty of Sèvres (1920), the administration of the city and its Ionian hinterland was assigned to Greece for five years. The Greek occupation was contested by the Turks, who seized Smyrna in 1922. By the provisions of the Treaty of Lausanne (1923), the city was awarded to Turkey. Agriculture is the principal industry of the il, which is fertile and well watered. The Gedis R. is the chief stream. Area, 4826 sq.m.; pop. (1950) 767,374. Pop. of city (1950) 230,508.

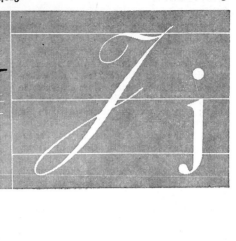

J, the tenth letter and seventh consonant in the English alphabet. It is the latest addition to English script, and has been inserted in the alphabet after I, from which it was developed, just as V and W follow U, the letter from which they arose. In form, J was originally merely a variation of I, arising in the 14th century in Provençal and Catalan manuscripts, in which, as a matter of fashion, the letter *i* was lengthened with a tail turned to the left (the form of the modern *j*). This device was used as an ornamental initial, and both characters were used interchangeably for either vowel or consonant. Initial I's, however, were often given a consonantal sound in English, with the vowel sounds for I usually occurring in the middle or at the ends of words; the initial J eventually became specialized functionally as well as formally to indicate the consonantal sound. Not until the middle of the 17th century did this usage become universal in English books; in the King James Bible of 1611, for example, the words *Jesus* and *judge* are invariably *Iesus* and *iudge*. When, long after the invention of printing, J and j thus became more than mere calligraphic variations of I and i (which in Latin could be either vowel or semivowel), the restriction of J to a consonantal function became a settled practice for any position in a word.

In English J has the composite sound of *d* + *zh*, as in *journal*. In French, on the other hand, the *zh* sound alone is given the letter, as in *jour*, while German has retained the original *y* sound of the Latin *i* consonant, as in *jahr*, and Spanish has introduced a new sound resembling a guttural *ch*, as in *Jerez*. In Middle English, before the differentiation of I and J, the combination *Gi* was sometimes used to represent the *dzh* combination, as in *Giews* for *Jews,* and in modern times the soft G is used for the same sound, as in *general.*

As an abbreviation, the capital J is used for personal names beginning with J, such as *John* and *Jane,* for Joule's equivalent, or the mechanical equivalent of heat (see JOULE, J. P.) in physics, for a variety of titles such as Judge and Justice, and in Old Testament criticism for any Jehovistic document included in one of the books of the Hexateuch (the oldest being designated as J^1, and the more recent as J^2, J^3, J^4, until the end of the series). As a symbol the capital or lower-case J is used to indicate the tenth in a class, order, group, or series, and occasionally to indicate ten, as a number or numeral. J was used in medieval Roman numerals for the number one, and was interchangeable with I (q.v.); this use survives in medical prescriptions, where a lower-case final J is used as a variant for *i* in numbers such as iij ($= 3$) or vij ($= 7$). The lower-case j is also sometimes used in mathematics (particularly in electrical engineering) as a symbol for the imaginary quantity $\sqrt{-1}$ (see IMAGINARY NUMBER).

JAAL GOAT. See IBEX.

JABESH-GILEAD, town of ancient Palestine, situated in the N. part of the Gilead region, about 20 miles S. of the Sea of Galilee. It is cited several times in the Old Testament. In the initial citation (Judges 21:8-14), the Benjamites, unable to secure wives elsewhere in Israel, dispatched a strong force against the town; only 400 virgins were spared in the ensuing massacre. Jabesh-gilead was later besieged by the Ammonite king Nahash. The inhabitants were offered the choice of slavery or the loss of their right eyes, but King Saul of Israel, responding to their appeals for help, annihilated the Ammonite troops (1 Samuel 11:1-11). After Saul and his three sons were killed in the battle on Mt. Gilboa their bodies were recovered from Bethshan by the men of Jabesh-gilead and given a decent burial (2 Samuel 4-5).

JABIRU. See WOOD IBIS; SADDLE-BILLED STORK.

JABORANDI. See PILOCARPINE.

JABOTINSKY, VLADIMIR EVGENEVICH (1880–1940), British Zionist-Revisionist leader, born in Odessa, Russia. As a young man he became active in Zionism and in 1903 was a delegate to the Sixth Zionist Congress at Basel, Switzerland. In 1915, while a war correspondent for a Russian newspaper, he organized in London the Jewish Legion, a military unit composed mainly of Jews expelled from Palestine by the Turks. With the consent of the British government, the legion participated in the Gallipoli campaign against Turkey. In 1917 he secured the creation of several Jewish regiments within the British army and, as a private in the first Judean regiment, served with distinction against the Turks in Palestine. During the anti-Jewish riots in Palestine in 1920 he formed and led the Jewish defensive organization called the Haganah. For his activities as leader of the Haganah, Jabotinsky was sentenced to fifteen years' hard labor by a British military tribunal. However, in response to protests from Jews and others in many countries, the sentence was withdrawn.

Jabotinsky was elected to the executive council of the World Zionist Organization in 1921, but he resigned in 1923, following the approval by Chaim Weizmann (q.v.) of the Winston Churchill White Paper of 1922, limiting Jewish development in Palestine. In that same year Jabotinsky formed and became president of the World Union of Zionist-Revisionists, a militant faction within the World Zionist Organization. In 1935, when the Revisionists were no longer allowed independent action within the Zionist organization, Jabotinsky assisted in founding in London the New Zionist Organization, a Revisionist group outside the World Zionist Organization. He was subsequently elected its president, holding that office until his death. See ISRAEL; PALESTINE; ZIONISM.

JACAMAR, common name of any of numerous species of tropical American birds in the family Galbulidae of the woodpecker order, especially those in the genus *Galbula*. The birds, which have long, sharp bills and long tails, are usually greenish gold above and reddish brown below, and have a white throat patch. The Jacamars nest in holes in which the female lays two glossy white eggs. The birds subsist chiefly on insects which they catch while in flight.

JAÇANA, common name of any tropical American bird in the family Jacanidae of the Tern order. They have extremely broad feet, long, thin toes tipped with sharp claws, and short tails, and are similar in appearance to rails. The birds have a leaf-shaped plate covering their foreheads, and a long sharp spur at the bend of each wing. They are 8 to 10 in. long. Jaçanas frequent marshes and quiet streams, making their way over the surface of the water in search of food by walking on pieces of floating vegetation. They subsist on insects, small shellfish, small frogs, and seeds. The birds usually nest on floating vegetation anchored near a shore; the female lays about four tan eggs. About twelve species of jaçanas are known.

The Mexican jaçana, *Jacana spinosa,* is the only one of these birds to be found in the U.S. It ranges from S. Texas to Central America, and is also found in Cuba and Haiti. This bird, which is 8½ in. long, is chiefly chestnut in color, with black head and neck and green wing feathers.

JACARANDA WOOD, timber of tropical American trees belonging to the genus *Jacaranda*. Jacaranda wood, also called *Brazilian rosewood,* is heavy, hard, and brown, and has a faint, roselike aroma. It is used extensively in cabinetmaking. Jacaranda trees belong to the Bignonia family. They have opposite pinnate leaves, and irregular blue flowers borne in panicles. Each flower has a five-cleft calyx, five-lobed corolla, two to four stamens, and a solitary pistil. The fruit is a dry, winged capsule.

JACARE. See CAYMAN.

JACINTH. See ZIRCON.

JACKAL, common name of an Old World wild dog, *Canis aureus,* common from S.E. Europe to India, and also throughout Africa. The animal is about the size of a fox, standing no more than 15 in. high at the shoulder. Its narrow head and pointed muzzle are also foxlike, but its other physical characteristics are similar to those of wolves. The jackal is grizzled tawny buff in color; the tip of the bushy tail is dark. The animal is cowardly, feeding on carrion, wounded animals, small poultry, and occasionally fruit; it hunts at night, sometimes in packs, more frequently in pairs, and habitually utters its cry, called the *pheal,* when hunting. During the day the jackal lives in holes in the ground; the young, usually six in a litter, grow to maturity within these burrows. Jackals commonly interbreed with domestic dogs, and may be tamed with little difficulty.

Jackal hunting is a popular sport among British and Dutch populations of Africa and India; a standardized set of rules, similar to those used in European fox hunts, has been adopted for this sport.

JACKASS, common name for any male ass (q.v.).

JACKDAW, or DAW, a European crow, *Corvus monedula.* The jackdaw is smaller than the common crow, attaining a maximum length of about 14 inches. It is black, with a whitish-gray neck and purplish wings and tail. It feeds on insects, worms, and snails. The jackdaw builds its nest in hollow trees and in buildings; the female lays about five bluish-white eggs which are usually speckled with brown. The bird is easily tamed, and has remarkable powers of mimicry; it can be taught to imitate the human voice. In the United States the names "jackdaw" and "starling" are frequently erroneously applied to the grackle (q.v.).

JACK-IN-THE-PULPIT, or INDIAN TURNIP, common name of a perennial herb, *Arisaema triphyllum,* belonging to the Arum family. The plant is native to moist woodlands of temperate North America. Jack-in-the-pulpit commonly has two leaves, each of which is divided into three pointed leaflets. The inflorescence, which is produced in late spring, is a spadix. A large, convoluted, green or purple spathe, sometimes flecked with white dots, arises from the base of the inflorescence and forms a pulpitlike canopy over the spadix. Small male flowers are borne at the upper end of the spadix and larger female flowers are borne at the lower end. Cross-pollination is assured in most jack-in-the-pulpits by the

The jackal

abortion of the male flowers of some spadices and the female flowers of others. Most pollination is effected by fungus gnats, particularly those which belong to the genus *Mycetophila.* The fruit, which ripens in late summer, is a small scarlet berry. The underground portion of the plant is a turnip-shaped, wrinkled, starchy corm which contains a bitter juice. The bitterness is due to the presence of needle-shaped crystals (*raphides*) of oxalic acid salts, such as calcium oxalate, CaC_2O_4, formerly used in medicine for treatment of amenorrhea and hemorrhage. The corm was formerly boiled by the Iroquois Indians and used as food.

JACK-MY-LANTERN. See FUNGI: *Poisonous Fungi.*

JACKS, common name of the numerous marine acanthopterygian fishes in the family Carangidae, found in all warm seas. Jacks are usually short, narrow, deep-bodied fishes with broadly forked tails. Many of them are valued as food.

The family includes the pilot fish, *Naucrates ductor,* which is about 1 ft. long. This fish, which is bluish gray, marked on the sides with five darker transverse bands, is often seen in the company of sharks, for which sailors once believed it acts as a pilot. The amberfishes or yellowtails are amber-tailed species comprising the genus *Seriola; S. dorsalis,* found off the coast of s. California, reaches a length of 3 ft. and is an excellent food fish. *S. dumerili,* found in tropical Atlantic waters, and *S. lalandi,* found from New Jersey to Brazil, are commonly called "amber jacks". The jurels are smaller fish constituting the genus *Paratractus; P. crysos,* the hardtail or runner, which is about 14 in. long, is found south of Cape Cod. The moonfishes, very short, deep, silvery fish, are contained in the genera *Vomer* and *Argyreiosus; V. setapinnis,* which is about 8 in. long, is found on the s. Atlantic and s. Pacific coasts of North America. The leather jack, *Oligoplites saurus,* is

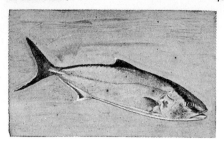

Amber jack (Seriola lalandi)

so called because of its leathery skin. See also
CREVALLÉ; POMPANO.

JACKSON, county seat of Jackson Co.,
Mich., situated on the Grand R., 75 miles w.
of Detroit. It maintains a municipal airport,
is served by four railroads, and is a railroad
division point, with extensive railroad repair
shops. The city is an important manufacturing
center, and the trading center and shipping
point of a fertile agricultural area. The chief
products of the surrounding region are cereal
grains, fruits, and vegetables; the principal industries in the city are the manufacture of
automobile and airplane parts and accessories,
radios, furniture, surgical appliances, sleeping
garments, lawn mowers, water heaters, grind-
ing wheels, air-conditioning equipment, space-
heating equipment, electric dishwashers,
candy, fruit extracts and flavorings, machine
tools, and forgings and castings.

Jackson is the center of a lake-resort region. Annual events there are a rose show and
the county fair. The city's parks include flower
gardens, a zoo, and picnicking facilities, and
the William and Matilda Sparks Foundation, a 465-acre park containing illuminated
cascades. The Foundation was the gift of William Sparks, a leading industrialist of the
city. On the outskirts of the city is the State
Prison of Southern Michigan, one of the largest walled prisons in the world. Jackson was
first settled in 1829, and became the county
seat in the same year. On July 6, 1854, the
Republican Party was founded at a convention held in Jackson. A bronze tablet, dedicated by President William H. Taft in 1910,
marks the site of the convention. Jackson was
chartered as a city in 1857. It was one of the
first cities of the U.S. to adopt (1914) the
city-manager form of government. Pop. (1950)
51,088.

JACKSON, capital and most populous city
of Mississippi, and county seat of Hinds
Co., situated on the Pearl R., about 42
miles E. of Vicksburg. It is an important
industrial, commercial, and cotton-shipping
center and is served by two railroads (operating nine lines), by three transcontinental
air lines, and by fifteen motor-truck lines.
Industry is highly diversified; chief among
the manufactures are lumber and lumber
products. Other leading industries are the
processing of cotton seed, poultry processing,
meat packing, and the manufacture of cement, asphalt tile, brick, clothing, dirt-mov-
ing equipment, farm implements, fertilizer,
fluorescent lamps, glass containers, lawn mowers, and television antennae. Petroleum producing, cotton and peanut growing, cattle
raising, and truck farming are major enterprises in the surrounding region.

Among points of interest in Jackson are a
number of imposing public buildings, including the State Capitol (known as the New
Capitol), constructed in 1903; the War Memorial Building (1939), housing the State
Hall of Fame and the collection of the State
Department of Archives and History; the
State Office Building; the County Court
House; and the Post Office and Federal Building. The Jackson Branch of the U.S. Waterways Experiment Station contains a 100-acre
scale model of the Mississippi R. system, including tributaries; it is used for experiments
designed to determine the effects of levee
and course changes in the system.

Noteworthy historic landmarks in the city
are the Old State Capitol (1842), scene of
the enactment (Jan. 10, 1861) of the Mississippi Ordinance of Secession; the Governor's Mansion (1842), a majestic edifice in
the ante-bellum architectural style; and the
City Hall, another ante-bellum edifice. Battlefield Park, a unit of the 720-acre municipal
park system, preserves the site of one of the
four battles fought in and around Jackson
during the Civil War.

The foremost educational and cultural in-
stitutions are Millsaps College (Methodist
Episcopal), founded in 1892; Belhaven College for women (Presbyterian), founded in
1894; Jackson College (1877), a school for
Negroes; the State Library; the State Museum; the Municipal Art Gallery; and the
Jackson Symphony Orchestra. A Veterans
Administration Hospital, the State Hospital
for the Insane, the Mississippi School for the
Deaf and Dumb, and the headquarters for the
Holly Springs, Homochitto, De Soto, and
Bienville national forests are located in the
city. An annual event in Jackson is the Mississippi Free State Fair.

The first settlement on the site of the present city was a trading post established by a French trader, Louis Le Fleur; the settlement was known as Le Fleur's Bluff. In 1821 it was selected as the site of the State capital and named in honor of Andrew Jackson, hero of the War of 1812. Jackson was chartered as a city in 1840. It suffered heavily during the Civil War, notably on July 17, 1863, when it was occupied and partially burned by Federal troops under Gen. William Tecumseh Sherman. Between 1900 and 1940 the population of Jackson increased from 7816 to 62,107. Pop. (1950) 98,271.

JACKSON, county seat of Madison Co., Tenn., situated on the South Fork of the Forked Deer R., 85 miles N.E. of Memphis. It is served by four railroads, and maintains a municipal airport. The city is the trading center and shipping point of a rich agricultural area, producing cotton, corn, fruit, and lumber. Industrial establishments in Jackson include railroad shops, planing mills, cotton mills, potteries, and factories manufacturing cotton bagging, furniture, store fixtures, and lumber products. The city is the site of Union University, founded in 1834, Lambuth College (1924), and Lane College for Negroes (1882). On the outskirts of Jackson are the West Tennessee Agricultural Experiment Station, and the State Forest Nursery, producing seedling trees for reforestation. Jackson was first settled about 1820, incorporated as a town and made the county seat in 1823, and chartered as a city in 1845. It was occupied alternately by Confederate and Federal forces during the Civil War, and in 1862 it served for a time as headquarters for Gen. Ulysses S. Grant after his advance into Tennessee. Pop. (1950) 30,207.

JACKSON, ABRAHAM VALENTINE WILLIAMS (1862-1937), American educator, born in New York City. After serving as instructor in Anglo-Saxon and Iranian languages, and adjunct professor of English language and literature, he was professor of Iranian at Columbia University, from 1895 to 1935. He wrote *A Hymn of Zoroaster* (1888), *An Avestan Grammar* (1892), *The Prophet of Ancient Iran* (1899), and *Researches in Manichaeism* (1931), and edited *A History of India* (9 vols., 1906-07).

JACKSON, ANDREW (1767-1845), American soldier and statesman, seventh President of the United States, born in Waxhaw, S.C., of Irish immigrant parents; he had little early schooling. At the age of thirteen he took part in a local skirmish of the Revolutionary War and was captured and im-

prisoned. By the following year, all the members of his immediate family had died, and he was left to find his own way in his native frontier region. In 1784 he began to study law at Salisbury, N.C., and was admitted to the bar there in 1787. The next year he moved to Nashville, and later became a leader in the new State of Tennessee. After helping to frame the State constitution, he served as a representative and senator in Congress, and from 1798 to 1804, as a judge of the State Supreme Court. For several years following, he worked as a planter, trader, and merchant.

When the War of 1812 began, Jackson, who had been elected a major general in the State militia ten years before, led 2500 volunteers in a march to New Orleans, but was ordered to return to Nashville after reaching Natchez, Miss. His subsequent campaign against the Creek Indians in Alabama culminated in a decisive victory at Horseshoe Bend on March 29, 1814, by virtue of which troops were made available for use against the British; his victory was thus an important factor in the later victory at New Orleans. On his own responsibility Jackson invaded Spanish Florida, stormed Pensacola, and drove out the British harbored there. He then marched to the defense of New Orleans, where on January 8, 1815, he overwhelmingly defeated the British, losing only seven men killed and six wounded; the

President Andrew Jackson

enemy's casualties totaled 2000 men killed, wounded, and captured. Jackson became the great military hero of the War of 1812, and was popularly called "Old Hickory".

In 1818, during the campaign against the Seminole Indians on the Florida border, Jackson, then a major general in the U.S. Army, exceeded orders, again captured Pensacola, and hanged two Englishmen who had been inciting the Indians against the United States. After the purchase of Florida by the United States, Jackson became the first governor of the Federal Territory of Florida but soon resigned. He next took public office in 1823, again as a U.S. senator. Nationally popular as a military hero, and admired in the West as a representative of the frontier and as a man of action, he was elected President in 1828, and re-elected in 1832.

In administration policy he followed a course between the extreme States' rights point of view and the doctrine of nullification (q.v.), urged by John Calhoun on the one hand, and the policy of a strongly centralized national government advocated by Henry Clay and John Adams (q.v.) on the other; his fundamental opposition to monopoly and the centralization of governmental power was demonstrated in his celebrated veto of the bill to recharter the Bank of the United States (See BANK AND BANKING). The charter question became the principal issue in his second election campaign, and when he defeated Clay, his opponent, he at once distributed the funds of the Bank of the United States among the State banks.

During his administration, Jackson dismissed large numbers of officials appointed in the previous administration, and replaced them with his political adherents. This system of rewarding friends and followers with political jobs became known as "the spoils system" (q.v.), and was the subject of heated public criticism. Jackson's practice of surrounding himself with an informal group of intimates who advised him directly on public policy was also much criticized, and the group was popularly and somewhat contemptuously called the "kitchen cabinet" (q.v.). Despite the widespread criticism which these policies evoked, Jackson's popularity and influence remained great, and constituted an important factor in the election of Martin Van Buren (q.v.), the Democratic candidate, in 1836. After the inauguration of Van Buren, Jackson retired to the Hermitage, his mansion near Nashville, Tenn., but continued to be an influence in national politics until the Whig candidate William Henry Harrison (q.v.) won the Presidency in 1840.

JACKSON, CHARLES THOMAS (1805-80), American scientist and physician, born in Plymouth, Mass., and educated at the Harvard Medical School and in Paris. After graduation from medical school he investigated cholera in Vienna during the epidemic of 1831, returning in 1832 to Boston to practice medicine. In 1836 he abandoned medicine to serve as State geologist of Maine, and later of Rhode Island and of New Hampshire. While exploring the southern shore of Lake Superior in 1844, he discovered deposits of mineral wealth. From 1847 to 1849 he was U.S. surveyor of mineral lands in Michigan. Jackson claimed credit for suggesting to the American inventor Samuel F. B. Morse the idea of the telegraph, and disputed with William T. Morton (q.v.) the discovery of surgical anesthesia. An investigating committee of the French Academy of Sciences ruled that both men should be credited with the discovery. Jackson's works include *Report on the Mineral Lands of the United States in Michigan* (1849), and *Manual of Etherization with a History of Its Discovery* (1863).

JACKSON, HELEN MARIA HUNT FISKE (1830-85), American novelist and poet, born in Amherst, Mass. After marrying William Sharpless Jackson, a banker in Colorado Springs, Colo., in 1857, she lived for some time in the West, where she became intensely interested in the Indians and worked actively to better conditions among them. Her *Century of Dishonor* (1881), was a sharp, documented criticism of the U.S. government for its treatment of the Indians. In 1882 she was appointed a special commissioner to investigate conditions among the Mission Indians of the State of California. Also on the Indian theme was her famous romance, *Ramona* (1884). Her other novels include *Mercy Philbrick's Choice* (1876) and *Hetty's Strange History* (1877). Her poems, which possess lyric power, are contained in the volumes *Verses* (1870) and *Sonnets and Lyrics* (1886).

JACKSON, ROBERT HOUGHWOUT (1892-), American jurist, born in Spring Creek, Pa., and educated at Albany (N.Y.) Law School. After practicing law for some years at Jamestown, N.Y., he became general counsel for the U.S. Bureau of Internal Revenue in 1934. He was assistant attorney general of the United States from 1936 to

1938, and distinguished himself by his able conduct of a number of prosecutions of major American corporations charged with violating the antitrust laws. In 1938-39 he served as solicitor general of the United States and in 1940-41 as U.S. attorney general. In 1941 President Franklin Roosevelt appointed him an associate justice of the U.S. Supreme Court. In 1945 he was granted a leave of absence from the Court to serve as chief U.S. prosecutor in the trials of the major Nazi war criminals, held at Nuremberg, Germany; see NUREMBERG TRIAL. His writings include *The Case Against the Nazi War Criminals* (1946), and *The Nürnberg Case* (1947).

JACKSON, THOMAS JONATHAN, commonly known as STONEWALL JACKSON (1824-63), American soldier and Confederate army general in the Civil War, born in Clarksburg, W.Va., and educated at the U.S. Military Academy. Following his graduation from West Point in 1846 he participated in the Mexican War. In 1851 he became an instructor at Virginia Military Institute and in the next year resigned from the U.S. Army. On the outbreak of the Civil War in 1861 he left V.M.I. to enter the Confederate service as a colonel. He was given the rank of brigadier general in that same year. Jackson earned his nickname at the first battle of Bull Run, where he stood firm against the Union forces, "like a stone wall", according to a colleague, General Barnard Bee. While in command of the Shenandoah Valley district in the spring of 1862 he executed a remarkable tactical maneuver against three Union armies then menacing Richmond. Immediately after driving back the army of General Nathaniel Prentiss Banks, which was advancing from the north, he turned and defeated the armies threatening to attack his rear ranks from the east and west.

Jackson subsequently took part, with General Robert E. Lee, in the defeat of General George B. McClellan in the Seven Days' Battle at Richmond. In August of 1862 he defeated the army of General John Pope in the second battle of Bull Run. He then crossed the Potomac into Maryland with Lee, who ordered him to capture Harpers Ferry. His task accomplished, Jackson learned that a surprise attack had been made on Lee by an overwhelming Union force and he managed to reach Antietam in time to save the Confederate commander in chief. Jackson commanded the right wing

Stonewall Jackson

of the victorious Confederate army in the battle of Fredericksburg at the end of 1862. During the Rappahannock campaign in the following spring, by launching a surprise attack on the rear columns of the Union army, Jackson prevented the threatened encirclement of the Confederate forces by the troops of General Joseph Hooker. However, while leading his forces to victory, Jackson was accidentally shot and fatally wounded by his own men.

General Jackson is generally considered by military authorities to have been an outstanding leader of men, a skilled tactician, and one of the ablest of the Confederate commanders.

JACKSON HOLE NATIONAL MONUMENT, a national monument in w. Wyoming, adjoining the E. boundary of Grand Teton National Park (q.v.). It was created in 1943 and embraces an area of 173,065 acres, or more than 400 sq.m., of the Jackson Hole valley, which lies a few miles w. of the Continental Divide, and is surrounded on all sides by mountain barriers. Within the monument area are lakes Jackson, Emma, Matilda, and Two Ocean, and the Snake R. and its headwaters. From the floor of Jackson Hole, which slopes from 7000 ft. above sea level in the N. portion to 6000 ft. at the s., exceptional views are afforded of the scenic Teton Range. Jackson

Hole was once a hunting ground for the Indians, and in the 19th century was an important base for British and American fur trappers and traders. It is now a refuge for big game and wild life of all kinds, including moose, mule deer, sage grouse, wild ducks, and geese; and is the winter home of one of the last great herds of elk in North America, numbering about 11,000.

JACKSONVILLE, county seat and port of entry of Duval Co., Fla., situated on the St. Johns R., 25 miles w. of its mouth on the Atlantic Ocean, and about 135 miles s. of Savannah, Ga. It is served by five railroads, coastwise and overseas steamship lines, and maintains a municipal airport, with service by major air lines. It is the second-largest city in population in the State, and the chief commercial and industrial center. The port of Jacksonville contains more than 70 piers, a number of drydocks, and 8 m. of developed water front, with extensive storage facilities for oil, fruit, lumber, and other products. The principal exports, both foreign and domestic, are naval stores, lumber, canned goods, citrus fruits, and iron and steel products; the leading imports are coffee, oil, and chemicals. Jacksonville contains approximately three hundred industrial establishments, the most important of which are shipbuilding yards, chemical plants, lumber and planing mills, pulp and paper mills, canneries, automobile-assembly plants, and factories manufacturing cigars, glass, and fertilizers. The city is the wholesale trading center of an area embracing a radius of about 150 m., with a population of more than a million persons. In addition, Jacksonville is a summer and winter vacation resort, with excellent recreational facilities. Several bathing beaches are situated in the vicinity, and the city maintains a park system of about 700 acres, with a municipal zoo, two municipal golf courses, a swimming pool, tennis courts, and baseball parks. The river and nearby lakes are abundantly stocked with fish, and facilities for yachting and boating are provided. A large U.S. naval air station is situated on the river 10 miles s. of Jacksonville.

The first settlement in the vicinity of Jacksonville was made by a colony of French Huguenots under René de Laudonnière in 1564. Fort Caroline, which they built upon a bluff above the river, was destroyed by a force from the Spanish settlement at St. Augustine in 1565. After the English had established their supremacy in Florida, permanent settlement of the site was made in 1816, and in 1822 a town was laid out and named in honor of Andrew Jackson, the first Territorial governor of Florida. It was incorporated in 1832. Jacksonville was occupied by Federal troops during the Civil War in order to control the operations of blockade runners on the St. Johns R. Pop. (1950) 204,517.

JACKSTONES or **JACKS,** a game played, usually by children, with a set of pebbles, or, more commonly, a set of metal objects each consisting of six small spokes radiating at equal angles from a common center. The number of jacks used in the game varies; five or six usually constitutes a set, but as many as twelve are sometimes used. In one form of the game the jacks are spread out on the playing surface; one of the jacks is tossed in the air and another jack is picked up before the tossed jack is caught. Only one hand is used. After all the jacks have been picked up individually in this manner, they are thrown out and picked up in pairs; they are then picked up in increasingly larger sets (threes, fours, fives) until all the jacks are picked up at one time. If a player touches any of the jacks other than the one or the set he is picking up, or if he fails to catch the jack tossed in the air, he loses his turn to the next player. The player who first succeeds in picking up all the jacks in the prescribed order wins the game. In another popular form of the game a ball is substituted for the jack that is tossed in the air. The ball must be caught after the first bounce. There are many variations of the game, the number and complexity of the variations depending only on the ingenuity and skill of the players.

Jackstones is of very ancient origin and was originally played with the knucklebones of a sheep; the game is still called "knucklebones" in England. An ancient form of the game, still used today, consists of throwing the bones up in the air and catching them, in a prescribed manner, on the back of the hand. A painting excavated at Pompeii represents various Greek goddesses engaged in playing this form of the game.

JACKSTRAWS, a game played with a set of sticks 4 to 6 inches long, made of ivory, bone, wood, or similar material. Between twenty and one hundred jackstraws are allowed to fall together in a loose heap. The first player then attempts to extricate one of the straws, using his fingers or a hooked instrument, without moving any other straw. If he succeeds, he attempts to remove another straw; if he disturbs a straw other than the one he is removing he loses his turn to the next player. The player who has removed the most straws at the end of the game is the winner. The original name of the game was jerkstraws. It was also called spillikins in England. In Germany it is known as *Federspiel,* and in France as *jonchets* or *honchets.*

JACOB, or ISRAEL (1837?-1690? B.C.) Biblical patriarch, son of Isaac and Rebekah. Jacob deprived his brother Esau of his father's blessing and his birthright by trickery. Jacob, while traveling, encountered an angel of God, and, when the angel refused to divulge his identity, wrestled with him. The angel finally prevailed over Jacob, after a night of wrestling, but confirmed Jacob as a prince of men, and changed his name to Israel. He worked for his uncle, Laban, for many years, and married Laban's daughters, Leah and Rachel. His wives and their handmaidens, Zilpah and Bilhah, bore him twelve sons who became the patriarchs of the twelve tribes of Israel. Leah bore Issachar, Judah, Levi, Reuben, Simeon, and Zebulun; Rachel bore Benjamin and Joseph; Zilpah bore Gad and Asher; and Bilhah bore Dan and Naphtali. The story of Jacob occurs in the Biblical book of Genesis, chapters 25 to 35. Many Biblical scholars believe that the story of Jacob was intended as a symbolic explanation for the tribal divisions of Israel rather than as the life story of a real person. See JEWS.

JACOBI, KARL GUSTAV JAKOB (1804-51), German mathematician, born in Potsdam, and educated at the University of Berlin. He lectured on mathematics at the University of Berlin until 1826, when he secured a similar position at the University of Königsberg, becoming professor of mathematics the following year; he held this chair until 1842, and then resumed his lectureship at the University of Berlin. Jacobi developed the theory of elliptic functions, and contributed to the theory of numbers, to analytical mechanics, and to the study of determinants, one of which, the functional determinant, bears his name. His writings include *Fundamenta Nova Theoriæ Functionum Ellipticarum* (1829), *De Formatione at Proprietatibus Determinantium* (1841-96), and *Gesammelte Werke* (1881-91).

JACOBINS, name given to the members of a radical French political club which played a controlling part in the French Revolution. It was founded in 1789 as the Society of Friends of the Constitution; the name "Jacobins" derives from the meeting place of the club, a former Jacobin monastery in Paris. The Revolutionary leaders Comte de Mirabeau and Maximilien Robespierre were early members of the club, and Robespierre subsequently became its principal figure. Although there were only 3000 members in Paris, the club had national scope through its control of 1200 related societies located throughout France. Its great political power resulted from the close organization of these affiliated groups and from the skillful hold on public opinion exercised by its leaders.

At its outset the club was in favor of a constitutional monarchy, but after the attempted escape from France of Louis XVI in 1791 the Jacobins, like most of the French people, turned against any form of royal rule. Simultaneously with the formation of the National Convention, the French ruling body from 1792 to 1795, the club reached the zenith of its power; it developed into so powerful a political party that no important action was undertaken by the Convention until the matter had first been discussed in the meetings of the Jacobins. Extremist elements of the group took control during this period, and they plunged the country into the Reign of Terror, a state policy of suppressing all opposition by violence. The Jacobins insisted on the death of the king, destroyed the moderate Girondist party, and incited the working class against the middle class. The club lost much of its power with the downfall of its leader Robespierre, and was finally banned by the Convention on November 11, 1794.

JACOBITE CHURCH, or OLD SYRIAN CHURCH, an independent Christian church in Syria, Iraq (Mesopotamia), and neighboring lands. It takes its name from Jacob Baradai, Bishop of Edessa, who in about 570 consolidated the Monophysites (q.v.) of that region into an organized church. It is in communion with the Coptic Church (see COPTS) but is not recognized as orthodox by the Greek churches (see ORTHODOX CHURCH), from which it differs only in minor matters of ritual. The hierarchy is headed by the Patriarch of Antioch, and consists of eight metropolitans, or archbishops, three bishops, and numerous monks (from whom the prelates are chosen) and priests. The metropolitan of Jerusalem, called the *Maphrian*, has nominal primacy after the Patriarch. The Patriarch and the Maphrian reside in the monastery of Zaferan, near Mardin. In a recent year the membership of the church numbered about 80,000.

JACOBITES, in English history, the name given to the adherents of the House of Stuart after the revolution of 1688, when James II was dethroned and exiled. After apparently accepting the change of dynasty, the Jacobites engaged for some years in minor, futile plots, then in 1715 John Erskine, Earl of Mar, and James Radcliffe, Earl of Derwentwater, led an uprising in Scotland and in the English Border country in favor of the *Old Pretender,* son of James II; see STUART, JAMES FRANCIS EDWARD. After an indecisive battle with the government forces at Sheriffmuir, the Jacobite forces surrendered at Preston, and the Old Pretender returned to exile in France. Seven noblemen were sentenced to death for their part in the revolt, but only Derwentwater and William Gordon, Viscount Kenmure, were executed.

The high point of the Jacobite movement was the second Jacobite rebellion, known as "The Forty-Five". In July, 1745, the *Young Pretender,* known also as Bonnie Prince Charlie (see STUART, CHARLES EDWARD), landed in Scotland, and in September entered Edinburgh with 2000 men. Jacobite forces won the battles of Prestonpans, Penrith, and Falkirk Moor, and invaded England as far as Derby. Jacobite sentiment was strong only in the Scottish Highlands, however; their forces retreated, and were completely defeated at the battle of Culloden. The revolt collapsed, and the Young Pretender fled to France. Among those executed for taking part in the rebellion were James Boyd, Earl of Kilmarnock; Arthur Elphinstone, Baron Balmerino; Simon Fraser, Baron Lovat; and Charles Radcliffe, brother of Derwentwater. Nearly a thousand others were condemned to death, but had their sentences commuted. With the crushing of "The Forty-Five", the political significance of the Jacobite movement ended; it survived only in local sentiment and as a theme in romantic literature. See STUART OR STEWART.

JACOBS, HELEN HULL (1908-), American tennis player and author, born in Globe, Ariz., and educated at the University of California and William and Mary College. She won her first major national tennis championships in 1932, taking both the U.S. women's singles and doubles titles, and repeated her success in singles play for the next three years, thereby becoming the first to win this championship in four successive years. In 1934 and 1935 she was on the winning women's national doubles team. She was Wimbledon singles champion in 1936 and for thirteen successive years was a member of the American Wightman Cup team; see TENNIS. During World War II she served as public relations officer of the U.S. Naval Training School, Bronx, N.Y., with the rank of lieutenant. Her writings include *Tennis* (1941), *By Your Leave, Sir* (1943), *Storm Against the Wind* (1944), and *Center Court* (1950).

JACOBS, WILLIAM WYMARK (1863-1943), English novelist and humorous writer, born in London. He was a contributor to *Pick-Me-Up* and other journals. His volume *Many Cargoes* (1896) established his reputation. In addition, he wrote *Captains All* (1905), *Salthaven* (1908), *Ship's Company* (1911), *The Castaways* (1916), *Deep Waters* (1919), and *Sea Whispers* (1926).

JACOB'S-LADDER, or GREEK VALERIAN, common name applied to perennial herbs of the genus *Polemonium,* belonging to the Phlox family. Plants of the genus have pinnate leaves which give the appearance of primitive ladders equipped with horizontal rungs. The blue, pale-blue, or white, bell-shaped flowers, borne in corymbs, have a five-lobed calyx, five-lobed corolla, five stamens, and a solitary pistil. The fruit is a three-celled loculicidal capsule. The American Jacob's-ladder or Greek valerian, *P. reptans,* which has pale blue flowers, is often called bluebell in E. United States. It is native to wooded areas of temperate North America. A blue-flowered species, *P. vanbruntiae,* is native to swampy areas of Eurasia and E. United States. Both species are occasionally cultivated in gardens.

JACOB'S PILLOW. See SCONE.

JACOPO DELLA QUERCIA. See QUERCIA, JACOPO DELLA.

JACQUEMART, JULES FERDINAND (1837-80), French etcher and illustrator, born in Paris. He first exhibited works in the Salon of Paris in 1861, and the *Gazette des Beaux-Arts* reproduced many of his best wood engravings and pen drawings. He etched 27 plates for the *Histoire de la Porcelaine* (1862) and 12 plates for the *Histoire de la*

Céramique (1873), both written by his father, Albert Jules Jacquemart (1808-73). Three of his water colors, "Japanese Art Objects", "Landscapes near Nice", and "Flowers", are in the Metropolitan Museum of Art, New York City. He copied many of the paintings by the great masters and also prepared 88 etchings for Joseph Florimond Loubat's *Medallic History of the United States of America* (1878), reproducing medal portraits of famous Americans, including George Washington, Horatio Gates, Anthony Wayne, Benjamin Franklin, and John Paul Jones.

JACQUERIE (from *Jacques Bonhomme*, derisive name applied by the nobility of France to the peasantry), in French history, an uprising of peasants in 1358, during the Hundred Years' War. Taking advantage of the revolutionary crisis precipitated by the English victory over France at Poitiers, the peasantry sought to even scores with their oppressors, particularly the nobility. The uprising, initiated by a minor clash between some peasants and soldiers late in May near Beauvais, swiftly spread to various parts of N.E. France. Supported by the burghers in some areas, the peasants sacked and burned numerous castles and killed a number of nobles. Royalist forces under King Charles II of Navarre, then captain general of Paris, decisively defeated an army of peasants on June 10 near Meaux, killing about 7000 and crushing the uprising. Sanguinary reprisals were inflicted on the peasantry in the ensuing period; according to some accounts about 20,000 were murdered in the course of two weeks.

JACUARU. See TEJU.

JADE, a compact, opaque, gem stone, ranging in color from dark green to almost white. The term is applied to specimens cut from the minerals jadeite and nephrite.

Jadeite, the less common and more highly prized of the two minerals, is a silicate of sodium and aluminum, usually containing some iron, calcium, and magnesium. It belongs to the pyroxene (q.v.) group of minerals. Jadeite crystallizes in the monoclinic system, but rarely occurs in distinct crystals and is usually found in fibrous, compact, massive aggregates. It has a hardness ranging from 6½ to 7 and a specific gravity ranging from 3.3 to 3.5; it is extremely tough and is difficult to break. The luster on fresh fracture is dull and waxlike, but polished jadeite has a vitreous luster. Jadeite occurs chiefly in eastern Asia in Upper Burma, and some is also found in

Metropolitan Museum of Art
Chinese jade ornament, K'ang Hsi period

sections of Tibet and of southern China.

Nephrite, which is a member of the amphibole group of minerals, is a silicate of calcium and magnesium, with a small amount of iron generally replacing part of the magnesium. It is a tough, compact variety of the mineral tremolite (q.v.) with hardness 6 and specific gravity 3.0. Polished nephrite has an oily luster. It occurs in Turkestan, Siberia, New Zealand, Alaska, and Silesia.

Jade was used in prehistoric times for weapons, utensils, and ornaments. A variety of jade called axstone is used by the natives of the South Sea Islands for making hatchets. Jade has always been prized by the Chinese and Japanese as the most precious of all stones, and the most beautiful specimens of carved jade in the form of ornamental pieces, such as vases, bowls, tablets, and statues, many of which are now museum pieces, were made in China. Jade is a highly valued gem stone used in rings, necklaces, earrings, and other articles of jewelry. See GEM.

JAEGER, or BOATSWAIN, common name for any large sea bird in the genus *Stercorarius* of the family Stercorariidae, which also contains the skua (q.v.). Jaegers are powerful fliers, and look somewhat like large gulls. They average seventeen to twenty-two inches in length. The birds are usually grayish brown or blackish above and white or light gray below. They have curved beaks, long, narrow wings, and webbed toes provided with long, sharp talons. Jaegers are noted for attacking slower and weaker sea birds, such as terns and gulls, in midair, forcing them to give up whatever food they have in their beaks. Jaegers feed on fish, on small rodents, and on the eggs and young of other birds. They nest in arctic regions on cliffs or plains; the female lays two or three spotted, dull-colored eggs in an unlined depression in the ground.

These species of jaeger winter in North America, where they are commonly known as "sea hawks", "robber gulls", and "teasers" because of their thieving habits. The pomarine jaeger, *Stercorarius pomarinus,* is common in the wintertime off the coasts of New England; the parasitic jaeger, *S. parasiticus,* is found throughout the U.S. in winter; and the long-tailed jaeger, *S. longicaudus,* is found on the Atlantic coast of the U.S.

JAEL. See DEBORAH.

JAÉN, capital of the province of the same name, Andalusia, Spain. The city is situated about 30 m. by rail S. of Lináres. After the Moorish invasion of Spain, the city, then known as *Jayyan,* became a leading trade center. It was fortified by the Moors, and the ancient citadel and walls erected by them still stand. Jaén is the seat of a Roman Catholic bishopric. Its cathedral dates from 1532. The Sierra Morena occupies the N. portion of the province; the Guadalquivir R. is the principal stream. The province contains rich mineral deposits, including lead, copper, salt, iron, and silver, which have been worked since early times. Mining is still the principal industry, and sheep raising, farming, and the manufacture of olive oil, textiles, and alcohol are other industries. Martos, Andujar Lináres, Ubeda (qq.v.), and the capital, are the chief towns. Area of province, 5209 sq.m.; pop. (1950) 765,697. Pop. of city (1950) 59,549.

JAFFA (anc. *Joppa*), an important seaport of Israel, situated on the Mediterranean coast, adjacent to Tel Aviv and about 50 m. by rail N.W. of Jerusalem. The harbor lacks docking facilities, and ships must be serviced by lighters. Oranges, grown extensively in the surrounding region, are the chief export. Corn, leather, and cotton are also important exports. Among the leading manufactures are furniture, soap, flour, and cement.

Jaffa is mentioned in the Old Testament as a seaport and border possession of the tribe of Dan. In antiquity it was besieged on different occasions by the Egyptians, Persians, and Greeks. During the Jewish War of 68 A.D., it was destroyed by the Roman emperor Vespasian. Christ's disciple Peter spent some time in Jaffa, and there restored Tabitha to life. Early in the Christian era the city became a bishopric of the Christian church. Jaffa was captured by the Crusaders in 1126 and again in 1191, and in each case it was reconquered by the Mohammedans. Confronted with the threat of another Crusade in 1345, the Mohammedans destroyed the town. About the beginning of the 18th century it was re-established as a seaport. British troops captured the city in 1917, during World War I, and from 1923 until 1948 it was part of the British-mandated territory of Palestine. By the terms of the United Nations partition plan of 1947, Jaffa was allocated to the Arabs, becoming a coastal outpost in Jewish territory. The city was attacked by Irgun Zwei Leumi forces in April, 1948, during the war between the Arab League and the Jews of Palestine, and all but about 15,000 of the Arab population fled. In later fighting the Jews completely occupied Jaffa, and the city was subsequently incorporated into the new state of Israel (q.v.). Pop., with Tel Aviv (1952 est.) 400,000.

JAFFNA, seaport and capital of Northern Province, Ceylon, situated on the Jaffna peninsula. As early as 204 B.C. it was inhabited by the Tamils, a Dravidian people. Several of the buildings in Jaffna date from the Portuguese and Dutch occupations in the 17th century. Palmyra fiber, tobacco, and rice are exported. Pop., about 63,000.

JAGELLON, name of the members of a dynasty which reigned in Lithuania, Poland, Hungary, and Bohemia. The name was derived from Jagello, the last of a line of hereditary grand dukes of Lithuania, who succeeded to his patrimonial possession in 1386 and changed his name to Ladislaus II. He was succeeded on the throne of Poland by six kings of his house, the last of whom, Sigismund II, died in 1572. Through a sister of the latter, the Jagellon dynasty continued on the Polish throne till 1668. See POLAND.

JAGUAR, a large cat, *Felis onca,* the most powerful of the American cats. It reaches a length of about six feet and stands two feet high at the shoulder. It is found from S. Texas through South America, and is especially abundant in the dense forests of Central America and Brazil. The jaguar is yellowish tan spotted with black. Its head and body are massive, and its legs are short and thick. The animal is an adept climber and an excellent swimmer; it feeds on arboreal, terrestrial, and aquatic animals. It rarely attacks man. It is extensively hunted in South America by professional hunters hired by ranchers to prevent depredations on their cattle.

JAHN, FRIEDRICH LUDWIG (1778-1852), Prussian patriot and teacher of gymnastics,

The jaguar

known as *Turnvater* ("Father of Gymnastics"), born in Lanz, and educated at the universities of Halle, Göttingen, and Greifswald. After the conquest and during the occupation of Prussia by the French during the Napoleonic Wars (see GERMANY: *History*), he determined to help bring about the emancipation of his country. Believing that the practice of gymnastics would result in a moral as well as physical regeneration of his disheartened compatriots, in 1811 he established an open-air athletic field, the *Turnplatz,* in Berlin. The courses in mass gymnastics he conducted there later formed the basis for the exercises of the German athletic clubs known as the *Turnvereine;* see GYMNASTICS. Upon the outbreak of the War of Liberation in 1813, he joined the Prussian army, and served as a battalion commander until the victorious conclusion of the war two years later. He was then appointed state teacher of gymnastics, and organized the *Burschenschaften,* student patriotic fraternities, which became famous for their liberal outlook and advocacy of the unification of Germany. Jahn's liberal views caused him to be arrested in 1819 by the Prussian government; upon gaining his release in 1825, he was forbidden to reside within ten miles of Berlin. He again attained prominence during the revolutionary uprisings of 1848, when he was elected to the German national parliament meeting at Frankfort on the Main to plan the unification of Germany. His writings include *Deutsches Volksthum* (1810), *Runenblätter* (1814), and *Selbstvertheidigung* (published posthumously, 1863).

JAIL. See PRISON.

JAIL FEVER. See TYPHUS.

JAINISM, a heterodox Hindu religion, concentrated for the most part in northern India, but also found throughout the western part of the Indian peninsula, particularly in the larger cities. Adherents of this religion are called Jains. Although totaling only about 1,430,000, they exert an influence in the Hindu community far out of proportion to their numbers; they are predominantly traders, and their wealth and authority has made their comparatively small sect one of the most important of living Indian religions.

Like Buddhism, to which it is in some respects analogous, and of which it is an important rival within the borders of India, Jainism made its early appeal as a protest against Brahmanism. Vardhamāna Jñātiputra Mahāvīra, the founder of Jainism, lived about the 6th century B.C., probably a little earlier than Gautama Buddha. Like the Buddhists, the Jains deny the divine origin and authority of the *Vedas* (see VEDA) and worship certain saints whom they call *jinas* and hold to be superior to the gods of the entire Hindu pantheon. Like their parent sect, the Brahmanical Hindus, on the other hand, the Jains admit the institution of caste, perform a group of forty essential rites called *samskaras* prescribed for the first three castes of Hindus, and recognize some of the minor deities of the Hindu pantheon.

These principles of faith are common to all classes of Jains, but some differences occur in the religious obligations of the religious and lay orders, called respectively the *Yatis* and the *S'râvakas.* The *Yatis* lead lives of silence, abstinence, and continence. They carry the Jainist reverence for animal life to its most extreme lengths; for example, the *Yati* wears a cloth over his mouth to prevent insects from flying into it, and carries a brush to sweep the place on which he is about to sit, to remove any living creature out of the way of danger. The secular *S'râvaka* must add to the observance of his religious and moral duties the practical worship of the saints and of his more pious brethren, the *Yatis.*

The most important Jainist sects, the *Digambara* and the *Svetambara,* have produced a vast body of religious literature in the Prakrit language, much of which has been lost or destroyed. The art of the Jains, consisting mainly of stupas and cave-temples elaborately decorated in carved stone, usually follows Buddhist models, but has a richness and fertility which represent one of the peaks of Indian art. Some sects, particularly the *Dhundia* and *Lunka,* which reject the worship of images, were responsible for the destruction of many works of art in the 12th century, and Mohammedan raids were responsible for the looting of many temples in northern India. To preserve their sacred places from desecration, the northern Jains early adopted Mohammedan styles in their architecture, and even included miniatures of Mohammedan tombs among their decorations.

JAIPUR, former princely state of India, now forming part of Rajasthan Union, Union of India. An upland plain, generally arid and sandy, occupies most of the Jaipur region; the terrain is hilly in the N., E., and W. Extensive tracts of the region are arable and irrigated, and farming is the principal occupation. Crops include corn, wheat, barley, cotton, tobacco, and sugar cane. Among manufacturing industries, largely confined to the former capital, Jaipur (q.v.), are pottery making, the weaving of textiles, and the production of enamel and metal wares. Marble quarrying, cobalt and copper mining, and the production of salt from saline Lake Sambhar are other industries. Jaipur state was founded in the 12th century by a Gwailor prince. In later times it was successively subject to the Mogul Empire and the Maratha Confederacy. The ruling maharajah recognized British paramountcy in 1818, and the state was subsequently included for administrative purposes in Jaipur Residency, a division of Rajputana Agency. Following the termination (1947) of British rule in India the state adhered to the newly formed Dominion (later Union) of India. On April 7, 1949, Jaipur and 17 other former princely states merged as Rajasthan Union. Area of former state, 15,610 sq.m.; pop. (1941) 3,040,-876.

JAIPUR, city of Rajasthan Union, Union of India, and former capital of Jaipur (q.v.), situated about 141 miles w. of Agra. It is an important railway junction and commercial center, with numerous trading establishments, bazaars, and banks. Industries include the manufacture of jewelry, textiles, gold enamel ware, brass products, carpets, and pottery. The only Indian city platted on the gridiron pattern, Jaipur is divided into rectangular blocks by broad intersecting avenues and streets. It is surrounded by a fortified wall, 20 ft. thick. Among points of interest are the vast palace of the maharajahs of Jaipur, an open-air astronomical observatory, and zoological gardens covering 70 acres. Several institutions of higher learning, including a free college and a school of art, are located in the city. Jaipur was founded in 1728. Pop. (1951) 291,130.

JALAPA or **XALAPA,** capital of the state of Veracruz, Mexico, situated on the slopes of the Sierra Madre Oriental, about 70 m. by rail N.W. of the city of Veracruz. Because of its cool and healthful climate Jalapa is a popular summer resort. The city has a Franciscan convent dating from 1556. In the fertile valleys of the surrounding region fruits, coffee, sugar cane, and tobacco are grown. The principal industrial products of Jalapa are cotton textiles, cigars, and chocolate. Pop., about 40,000.

JALISCO, a state of Mexico, bordering on the Pacific Ocean. It is traversed by the Sierra Madre Oriental. The principal river is the Rio Grande de Lerma and the largest of the many lakes in the state is the Chapala. Jalisco contains extensive forests, yielding palm oil and rubber. It has a diversified climate, which favors the cultivation of many crops. Corn, rice, sugar cane, wheat, cotton, beans, tobacco, and fruits are grown. The raising of livestock is also important, especially in the mountain areas. Silver, gold, bismuth, cinnabar, tin, iron, copper, and precious stones are mined. Among the leading manufacturing industries are smelting, tanning, sugar refining, and the manufacture of cotton goods, woolen textiles, and pottery. The capital Guadalajara (q.v.) and Ciudad Guzmán are the principal towns of the state. Area, 31,149 sq.m.; pop. (1950) 1,747,168.

JALUIT. See MARSHALL ISLANDS.

JAMAICA, island of the Greater Antilles of the West Indies, situated about 95 miles s. of Cuba, and constituting, with dependencies, a colony of the United Kingdom. Cayman Islands (q.v.), about 200 m. to the N.W., Turks and Caicos Islands (q.v.), about 400 m. to the N.E., and Pedro Cays and Morant Cays, comprising seven nearby guano islets, are the dependencies. Kingston (q.v.) is the capital and largest city of the colony. Other important communities are Spanish Town (pop., about 12,000), Montego Bay (about 11,500), Port Antonio (about 5500), Savanna-la-Mar (about 4000), Port Maria (about 3200), St. Ann's Bay (about 3100) and Falmouth (about 2600). The area of Jamaica is 4450 sq.m.; with dependencies, 4722 sq.m. Pop. of Jamaica (1950 est.) 1,416,987; with dependencies, about 1,429,000.

The largest island of the British West Indies, Jamaica has a maximum length from E. to w. of about 145 m.; its maximum width is about 49 m. Excluding several tracts of lowland in the s. coastal area, the terrain is extremely mountainous. The principal uplift, situated in the E. section of the island, is the Blue Mountains; Blue Mountain Peak (7388 ft.), the culminating elevation in this range, is the highest summit in the British West Indies. A series of lesser uplifts, with numerous transverse spurs, extends generally westward to the extremity of the island, surmounting an extensive tableland. Composed of white limestone, this upland is mainly a region of basins, valleys, and hills. Thermal springs occur in various areas. No other volcanic phenomena are apparent, but the island is subject to severe earthquakes. Many rivers, generally short torrential streams originating in the mountains, traverse the island. The coast line, about 500 m. long, is irregular, particularly in the s., and there are a number of excellent natural harbors, including the harbors of Kingston, St. Ann's Bay, Montego Bay, and Port Maria.

Tropical climatic conditions prevail in the coastal lowlands, the mean annual temperature in this region being almost 80° F., but oceanic winds frequently moderate the extremes of heat and humidity. Mean annual temperatures in the plateau and mountain areas range from about 73° F. at elevations below 3000 ft. to about 60° F. at the 5000-ft. level. The annual range of temperature in the plateau region is less than 10° F. Annual precipitation, averaging slightly more than 66 inches, is characterized by wide regional variations. Over 200 inches of rain are deposited annually in the N.E. section; in the vicinity of Kingston the average is about 32.5 inches. The months of maximum precipitation are May, June, October, and November. The island lies in a region occasionally visited by violent tropical hurricanes.

The Jamaican fauna, like that of the West Indies generally, includes highly diversified bird life. Autochthonous varieties are quite common, numbering over 40 according to some authorities. Parrots, humming birds, cuckoos, and green todies are especially abundant. There are no large indigenous quadrupeds or venomous reptiles. Luxuriant and remarkably diversified vegetation characterize the flora. More than 2000 species of flowering plants have been classified. Among indigenous trees are cedar, mahoe, mahogany, logwood, rosewood, ebony, palmetto palm, coco palm, and pimento (allspice). Such valuable trees and plants as the mango, breadfruit, cacao, banana, plantain, and coffee also flourish on the island, and these and many other varieties are widely cultivated.

The economy of Jamaica is predominantly agricultural. More than 1,000,000 acres were recently under cultivation or care, and of this total almost 550,000 acres were in pasturage. Sugar cane is the chief crop; the harvest in a recent year approximated 285,000 tons. Other leading crops are bananas, citrus fruits, tobacco, cacao, coffee, coconuts, corn, hay, peppers, ginger, mangoes, potatoes, yams, ochra, beans, eggplants, arrowroot, and allspice. Practically the entire world supply of the last-named product originates in Jamaica. The livestock population recently included about 300,000 goats, 150,500 hogs, and 248,500 cattle.

Rum distilling is the foremost manufacturing industry; output in a recent year exceeded 2,000,000 gallons. Among other industries are cigar making and the production of cocoa, logwood extract, matches, soap, condensed milk, and lard. Marble and bauxite are the principal mineral products. Catering to the tourist trade is another important occupation.

The foreign trade of the island in a recent year had an aggregate value of about £47,600,-000. Exports, consisting mainly of sugar, bananas, rum, cigars, cocoa, allspice, coffee, and citrus fruits, were valued at nearly £16,700,000.

Flour, textiles, motor vehicles, fish, paper, rice, machinery, petroleum products, fertilizers, and cement are the chief imports. The bulk of Jamaican foreign trade is transacted with the United Kingdom, Canada, and the United States.

The only railroad line on the island is 207 m. long; electric- and steam-tramway lines aggregate about 100 m. First-class highways total almost 2600 m., and there are over 2100 m. of secondary roads suitable for light automobile traffic. About 2600 m. of telegraph lines, 2800 m. of telephone lines, and 310 post offices are maintained.

Nearly 80 percent of the population of Jamaica consists of Negroes, largely descendants of African slaves. Persons of mixed Negroid-Caucasoid ancestry comprise the next-largest grouping (about 17 percent). In descending order of size other minorities are East Indians, whites, and Chinese.

Educational facilities recently included almost 700 public elementary schools, with about 186,000 enrolled pupils, 29 secondary schools, partly supported by governmental grants-in-aid, 4 vocational schools, 8 industrial schools, and 4 training colleges. The foremost institution of higher learning is the University College of the West Indies (chartered in 1949), an affiliate of London University, England.

Jamaica and Dependencies is governed according to the provisions of the constitution of 1944. Executive authority is vested in a captain general and governor-in-chief, an appointee of the British government. Legislative power is exercised by a bicameral legislature composed of a house of representatives, consisting of 32 members, and a legislative council consisting of 15 members. Members of the house are elected by universal suffrage; council members are appointed. The governor is assisted by a ten-member executive council, half of which is selected by the house and half by the governor; he is represented in the dependencies by commissioners. All citizens over 21 years of age are entitled to vote.

History. Members of the Arawak tribe, an important group of the Arawakan linguistic stock of American Indians, were the aboriginal inhabitants of Jamaica (Arawakan *Xaymaca*, "Isle of Springs"). The Genoese navigator Christopher Columbus discovered the island on May 3, 1494, during his second voyage to the New World. Columbus called it *St. Iago*, a name that endured for a relatively brief period. In June 1503, during his fourth voyage, he put in to Jamaica because of the unseaworthy condition of his vessel, and remained there slightly over a year while awaiting the arrival of a relief expedition.

Jamaica was formally incorporated as a Spanish colony in 1509. St. Iago de la Vego (modern Spanish Town), the first settlement and, for the ensuing 350 years, the capital, was founded about 1523. Colonization proceeded slowly under Spanish rule, and the Arawaks, subjected to merciless exploitation, were virtually exterminated. African slaves were imported to overcome the resultant labor shortage.

Jamaica was captured by a British naval force under Vice-Admiral William Penn in 1655, during the war between the Commonwealth and Spain. In 1661, after a period of military rule, civilian government, including a representative council, was instituted in Jamaica. Spain formally relinquished the island to Great Britain in 1676 under the provisions of the Treaty of Madrid. During the final decades of the 17th century growing numbers of British emigrants arrived, the sugar, cacao, and other agricultural and forest industries were rapidly expanded, and the consequent demand for plantation labor led to large-scale importation of Negro slaves. Jamaica soon became one of the world's principal slave-trading centers. In 1692 Port Royal, the chief Jamaican slave mart, was destroyed by an earthquake. Kingston was established on a nearby site in the same year.

Considerably more than 600,000 slaves were landed in Jamaica for transhipment and to fill domestic demands during the 18th century, a period of steady economic growth. At frequent intervals, especially between 1715 and 1738, bands of maroons (fugitive slaves), operating from hideouts in the interior, made armed attacks on coastal settlements, causing serious damage and casualties. In 1807, when the British government abolished the slave trade, the Jamaican slave population numbered over 319,000. The next quarter century was marked by the rise of a strong movement, both in Great Britain and among Jamaican Negroes, for emancipation. Particularly powerful after 1831, when a serious Negro insurrection took place on the island, the movement culminated (1833) in the Emancipation Act, Parliamentary legislation providing for the complete abolition of slavery after August 1, 1838. The Act made available nearly $30,-000,000 as compensation to the owners of the liberated slaves, who totaled about 309,000.

Large numbers of the freedmen abandoned the plantations, following emancipation, and

Pan Amer. World Air.; Can. Nat. Rys.

ON THE ISLAND OF JAMAICA

Above: Harvesting sugar cane, one of the principal crops of the island. Right: View of Port Maria, a seaport on the northern coast. Below: Native houses in a densely wooded forest in the interior.

took possession of unoccupied lands in the interior, gravely disrupting the economy. Labor shortages, bankrupt plantations, and declining trade resulted in a protracted economic crisis. Oppressive taxation, discriminatory acts by the courts, and land-exclusion measures ultimately caused widespread unrest among the Negroes. In October, 1865, a sanguinary insurrection occurred at Port Morant. Imposing martial law, the government speedily quelled the uprising and inflicted brutal reprisals on Negroes in many parts of the island. Following investigations by the home government, Jamaica was deprived (1866) of its legislative council and reduced to the status of a crown colony. Representative government was partially restored in 1884.

In January, 1907, an earthquake devastated Kingston, killing about 800 persons. Property in the w. part of the island was extensively damaged by a tropical hurricane in November, 1912. Under an Anglo-American agreement approved in September, 1940, the United States obtained a lease on various Jamaican areas and installations, including a fleet anchorage at Old Harbor Bay and the Port Royal dockyard. In 1944 the British government approved a new constitution granting a greater measure of self-rule to the colony. Another tropical hurricane swept across Jamaica in August, 1951. Approximately 30,000 persons were made homeless, casualties included 165 persons killed, and property with an estimated value of $50 million was destroyed.

JAMAICA BULLACE PLUM. See MELICOCCA.

JAMAICA PEPPER. See PIMENTO.

JAMES, name of two Apostles. **1.** JAMES THE GREATER, SAINT (d. about 44 A.D.), son of Zebedee and Salome, and brother of John. The brothers were called by Jesus (Mark 3) *Boanerges,* "Sons of Thunder", because of their zeal. According to tradition James preached Christianity in Spain, and then returned to Judea, where he was martyred by the sword under Herod Agrippa. He is venerated as the patron of Spain and Chile, and of druggists, pilgrims, and laborers. In art his emblems are the pilgrim's staff and shell and the sword. His feast is celebrated July 25. **2.** JAMES THE LESS, SAINT (d. about 62 A.D.), son of Alphæus, or Cleophas, called "the Less" or "the Little" to distinguish him from the son of Zebedee, who was of greater stature. By many authorities he is identified with James, "the brother of the Lord", who was bishop

of Jerusalem and author of the Epistle of James. They regard him as son of Mary of Cleophas, sister of Mary, and therefore cousin of Jesus. Other scholars consider the "brother of the Lord" to have been a different person, the son of Joseph by a former marriage or the son of Joseph and Mary after the birth of Jesus. James the Less is invoked as the patron of fullers and hatters; his emblems in art are a square rule, a halberd, and a fuller's club. His feast is celebrated May 1.

JAMES I (1208-76), King of Aragon, son of Pedro II, born in Montpellier, France. He succeeded his father to the throne of Aragon in 1213 and later became known as *El Conquistador* ("the Conqueror"), as a result of his conquest (1229-35) of the Balearic Islands and his capture of the city of Valencia from the Moors in 1238. James promulgated a new legal code in 1247, and settled outstanding differences between his kingdom and France by concluding the Treaty of Corbeil with Louis IX in 1258. The remaining years of his realm were spent in fighting the Moors, whom he attempted to drive from Spain.

JAMES II, called THE JUST (about 1260-1327), King of Aragon, grandson of James I and second son of Pedro III. James inherited the kingdom of Sicily from his father in 1285, and six years later, on the death of his elder brother Alfonso III of Aragon, resigned the Sicilian throne to become king of Aragon. Pope Nicholas IV recompensed James for relinquishing Sicily by extending his realm to include Corsica and Sardinia. In an effort to compose the differences between his house and the house of Anjou, James married, in 1295, Blanche, daughter of Charles of Anjou. In 1300 James founded the University of Lérida.

JAMES I (1566-1625), King of Great Britain from 1603 to 1625 and King of Scotland, as James VI, from 1567. He was the only son of Mary, Queen of Scots and of Henry Stuart, Lord Darnley. On the abdication of his mother in 1567, James was proclaimed King of Scotland, but the actual administration of the kingdom was conducted by a succession of regents until 1576, when James became nominal ruler. The boy king was little more than a puppet in the hands of political intriguers until 1581; in that year, with the aid of his favorites James Stewart, Earl of Arran, and Esmé Stuart, Duke of Lennox, James assumed actual rule of Scotland. In 1582 he was kidnaped by a group of Protestant nobles headed by William Ruthven, Earl of Gowrie; he was compelled to give up his favorites, and was held virtual prisoner until the following year, when he escaped.

In the following years, by intrigues and trickery, playing one influential house against another, James succeeded in reducing the power of the great Roman Catholic nobles. His marriage to Anne of Denmark in 1589 brought him for a time into close relationship with the Protestants, but after the Gowrie Conspiracy (1600) in which he killed John Ruthven, Earl of Gowrie and leader of the Protestant party, James repressed the Protestants as strongly as he had the Catholics. He succeeded in replacing the feudal power of the nobility with a strong central government, and, maintaining the divine right (q.v.) of kings, he enforced the superiority of the state over the church. See SCOTLAND: *History.*

In 1603 James succeeded Queen Elizabeth of England, becoming first ruler of Great Britain. In England his policy, based on divine right, antagonized the parliament and prepared the way for the Great Rebellion. He alienated the Nonconformists by his rudeness at the Hampton Court Conference in 1604, and his undue severity toward Roman Catholics gave rise to the Gunpowder Plot (q.v.) in 1605. He initiated the Ulster Settlement in 1607. James tried unsuccessfully to advance the cause of religious peace in Europe, giving his daughter Elizabeth in marriage to the elector palatine Frederick V, the leader of the German Protestants, and attempting to arrange a marriage between his son Charles and the Infanta of Spain, then the principal Catholic power. Due to the failure of his planning, England was drawn into the Thirty Years' War (q.v.). See GREAT BRITAIN: *History.*

James was the first king of England after Alfred to aspire to literary fame; he wrote a number of works in verse and in prose. Under his patronage a group of scholars prepared the Authorized Version of the Bible in English, called the King James Bible in his honor.

JAMES II (1633-1701), King of Great Britain from 1685 to 1688, second surviving son of Charles I and Henrietta Maria. He was created Duke of York in 1643, and at the Restoration, in 1660, his title was recognized and he was made lord high admiral of England. In 1659 he had married Anne Hyde, daughter of the Earl of Clarendon, and on her death in 1671 James made a public profession of his conversion to the Roman Catholic faith. In 1673 the English Parliament passed the Test Act, requiring all officials to subscribe to a declaration against transubstantiation and to receive the sacrament according to the rites of the Established Church, and James consequently resigned as lord high admiral. Shortly after, he married Mary Beatrice, daughter of Alfonso IV, Duke of Modena. In 1679 the House of Commons made an attempt to bar the succession of James to the throne by passing the Exclusion Bill; the attempt was defeated by the House of Lords.

On the death of his brother Charles II in 1685, James became king. In the same year he crushed the revolt of the dukes of Argyll and Monmouth, but alienated many supporters by his severe reprisals, especially by the "Bloody Assizes" conducted by George Jeffreys (q.v.). James attempted to win the support of the Dissenters and the Roman Catholics by issuing in 1687 the Declaration of Indulgence and a declaration of liberty of conscience. He underestimated the power of the Established Church, which by these acts was turned completely against him. The birth of his son (see STUART, JAMES FRANCIS EDWARD), seeming to insure a Roman Catholic succession, finally induced his opponents to invite his son-in-law, William of Orange, to take the British throne. William landed with an army at Tor Bay in November, 1688, and marched on London. He was hailed as a deliverer, and James, deserted by his troops, fled to France, where King Louis XIV gave him a pension and a home at St. Germain. In the following year, aided by a small body of French troops, James landed in Ireland in an attempt to regain his throne. He was defeated at the Battle of the Boyne, and returned to St. Germain, where he remained until his death. See GREAT BRITAIN: *History;* JACOBITES.

JAMES I (1394-1437), King of Scotland from 1406 to 1437, second son of Robert III, born in Dunfermline. About 1406 he was sent to France for safety from rebellious Scottish nobles, but the ship was seized by the English and James was carried to London. He became king on the death of his father the same year, but was detained a prisoner in England till 1423. He then returned to Scotland and was crowned in 1424. He married Jane Beaufort, daughter of the Earl of Somerset, niece of Richard II, and granddaughter of John of Gaunt. James crushed the Scottish noble house of Albany in 1425, and forced Alexander, the Lord of the Isles, to submit to royal authority in 1429. In the Scottish parliament he introduced the principle of representation, and for the first time caused parliamentary acts to be published in the language of the common people. He drew closer the bond of alliance with France, and gave his eldest daughter in marriage to the Dauphin. He was assassinated in 1437. He achieved renown as a poet with *The Kingis Quair*.

JAMES II (1430-60), King of Scotland, son of James I. He was crowned at the age of six years, shortly after his father's murder, but ruled under a regency until 1449, when he undertook to govern by himself. His efforts to promote social welfare were greatly obstructed by the nobles, and especially by the Douglases, one of whom, Earl William, who had entered into a treasonable bond with the earls of Crawford and Ross, was stabbed to death by the king. After the killing of the Earl of Douglas his friends made war on the king, but when the Douglas heir was attainted they abandoned their cause; their estates were then forfeited, and they were compelled to take refuge in England. James became entangled in the contest between the houses of York and Lancaster, and marched for England in 1460 at the head of an army. He besieged Roxburgh Castle, and was killed there by the bursting of a cannon.

JAMES III (1451-88), King of Scotland, son of James II, whom he succeeded in 1460. Until 1466 the government was carried on by his guardians. In retaliation for an invasion of the country by an English fleet, James started an invasion of England, but disaffected nobles revolted; they seized the king, and kept him prisoner in the castle of Edinburgh. Under James' brother Alexander, Duke of Albany, the English forces took Berwick and advanced to Edinburgh. James made peace with the English, thereby alienating his turbulent nobles, who rose in rebellion and induced James' son, the heir to the throne, to become their nominal head. The king was supported by the northern barons, and an encounter took place between the two Scottish forces at Sauchieburn, a mile from the famous field of Bannockburn. When the battle turned against the royalists, the king galloped from the field, but was thrown from his horse and was murdered by a soldier disguised as a priest.

JAMES IV (1473-1513), King of Scotland from 1488 to 1513, son of James III. He asserted the ecclesiastical independence of his kingdom. His romantic disposition induced him to support the cause of Perkin Warbeck, who claimed to be the duke of York, and to invade England in his behalf. However, in 1497 a truce for seven years was concluded between the two kingdoms, and in August, 1503, the Scottish king was married to Margaret, eldest daughter of Henry VII; this alliance led ultimately to the union of the crowns. In 1513 James invaded England, and was killed at the battle of Flodden Field.

JAMES V (1512-42), King of Scotland, son of James IV. When he ascended the throne the kingdom was torn by feuds between the English and French parties. In 1525 the Douglases made him a prisoner, keeping him until he made his escape in 1528. He renewed the commercial treaty between Scotland and the Netherlands, founded the College of Justice, and took measures to protect the peasantry, to whom he was known as the "gudeman of Ballangeich". Henry VIII of England tried to induce James to follow his ecclesiastical policy and to repudiate the authority of the papal see. James ignored Henry's invitation to a meeting at York in the autumn of 1541, and during the following year relations between the two countries became further strained. War broke out in 1542, and with the rout of a Scottish force at Solway Moss, James fell into a state of despondency and retired to Falkland Palace, where he died. He left one legitimate child, Mary, Queen of Scots, who was an infant a few days old at his death.

JAMES, HENRY (1843-1916), Anglo-American novelist, born in New York City, son of the theologian Henry James and brother of the psychologist-philosopher William James (qq.v.), educated in New York, London, Paris, and Geneva. In 1875 he settled permanently in England and returned to the U.S. only for short visits; in 1915 he became a British subject. While still in his early twenties he began to contribute short stories and articles to American periodicals. The novelist William Dean Howells (q.v) encouraged him and introduced his work to the magazine *The Atlantic Monthly*. His work is characterized by leisurely pacing and subtle delineation of character rather than by dramatic incidents or complicated plots. His major writings, highly sensitive examples of the objective psychological novel, describe the world of leisure and sophistication he grew to know intimately in Europe.

In his earlier popular novels he dealt with the impact of European culture on Americans traveling or living abroad. Examples of this phase, written between 1875 and 1881, are *Roderick Hudson, The American, Daisy Miller, Washington Square,* and *Portrait of a Lady.* Next he explored the types and manners of the English scene, in *The Tragic Muse, The Spoils of Poynton,* and *The Awkward Age,* all written in the 1890's. His last three great novels, written between 1901 and 1904, *The Wings of the Dove, The Ambassadors,* and *The Golden Bowl,* take up again the theme of contrast between American and European points of view. In general his later works are more complex and psychologically analytical than the earlier ones, and their characters and settings seem to exist only in the minds of the other characters.

James was a prolific writer, and one or more of his books was published every year until the end of his life. Among his many novels and books of essays are *French Poets and Novelists* (1878), *An International Episode* (1879), *The Author of Beltraffio* (1885), *The Bostonians* (1886), *The Princess Casamassima* (1886), *What Maisie Knew* (1897), *In the Cage* (1898), *The Soft Side* (1900), *The Sacred Fount* (1901), *The Better Sort* (1903), *The Finer Grain* (1910), *The Outcry* (1911); *Notes on Novelists, with Some Other Notes* (1914), and two autobiographical volumes, *A Small Boy and Others* (1913) and *Notes of a Son and Brother* (1914).

JAMES, JESSE (WOODSON) (1847-82), American outlaw, born in Clay County, Mo. His family was persecuted by its neighbors for being sympathetic to the Confederacy during the Civil War. James joined the guerrilla forces of rebel William Clarke Quantrill, and his activities soon earned him a reputation for reckless daring. He was outlawed because of these activities in 1866, and led a band of brigands from that time until his death. His exploits, both real and legendary, in bank and train robberies won him world-wide notoriety. In 1882, tempted by a reward of $10,000 offered by Governor Thomas Theodore Crittenden (1832-1909) of Missouri for James' capture, dead or alive, two members of his own band killed him in his home in St. Joseph, Mo. They surrendered themselves to the police, collected the reward, and were tried and sentenced to death, but later pardoned.

JAMES, WILLIAM (1842-1910), American philosopher and psychologist, born in New York City, son of the theologian Henry James and brother of the novelist Henry James (q.v.), and educated at Harvard University and the Harvard Medical School. In 1869, after having interrupted his studies to go to South America on an exploring expedition up the Amazon R. and to Germany to study psychology and philosophy, he received an M.D. degree at Harvard Medical School, and three years later he was appointed to its faculty. He taught anatomy and physiology until 1880; from 1880 to 1907 he taught psychology and philosophy.

His monumental book *The Principles of Psychology* (1890) established him as one of the most influential thinkers of his day. It advanced the principle of functionalism (q.v.) in psychology, thus removing psychology from its traditional place as a branch of philosophy and placing it among the laboratory sciences based on experimental method. In the next decade James applied his empirical methods of inquiry to questions of religion and philosophy. He studied the problems of the existence of God, of the immortality of the soul, and of free will (q.v.) as opposed to determinism (q.v.). His views were expounded in the lectures and essays published as *The Will to Believe and Other Essays in Popular Philosophy* (1897), *Human Immortality* (1898), *Talks to Teachers on Psychology and to Students on Some of Life's Ideals* (1899), and *The Varieties of Religious Experience* (1902). The last-named work was especially welcome to religious readers as it provided scientific justification for their beliefs.

Later lectures published as *Pragmatism: A New Name for Old Ways of Thinking* (1907) summed up his epoch-making theory of the method known as pragmatism (q.v.), a term first used by the physicist Charles S. Peirce (q.v.). James generalized the pragmatic method, developing it from a critique of the logical basis of the sciences into a critique of all experience. He maintained that the value of ideas is found only in terms of their usefulness or actual consequences. He was vehemently opposed to absolute conceptions and lectured polemically against monism (q.v.).

In *Essays in Radical Empiricism* (1912), he attacked the idea that the world can be explained in terms of a mystic force or scheme that determines the interrelation of things and events. He held that the interrelations, whether they serve to hold things together or apart, are just as real as the things themselves.

By the end of his life, James had become world famous as a philosopher and a psychologist. In both fields he functioned more as an originator of new thought than as a founder of dogmatic schools. His pragmatic philosophy was continued and developed by John Dewey (q.v.), and the later physics of Albert Einstein (q.v.) made his theories of interrelations appear prophetic.

JAMES BAY, the southern arm of Hudson Bay (q.v.), extending about 280 miles from N. to S. and about 150 miles from E. to W. James Bay contains a number of islands, the largest of which, Agomska, is 70 miles long. The bay is too shallow for navigation, except for a narrow channel leading to the mouth of the Moose R. at the S.W., where Moose Factory, one of the most important stations of the Hudson's Bay Company (q.v.), is located. James Bay received its name from Thomas James (q.v.), who explored it in 1631-32.

JAMES EDWARD, PRINCE, known as the OLD PRETENDER. See STUART, JAMES FRANCIS EDWARD.

JAMES, EPISTLE OF, the twentieth book of the New Testament, ascribed to the Apostle James, called "the Less", son of Alphæus, and "brother of the Lord". It is the first of the seven catholic epistles, so-called from being addressed to the entire Church, rather than to a specific group. The content of the epistle is distinctly homiletic in character, being composed of exhortations bearing on practical religious living.

JAMESON, JOHN FRANKLIN (1859–1937), American historian, born in Boston. He was professor of history at Brown University from 1888 to 1901, and professor and head of the department of history at the University of Chicago from 1901 to 1905. He was president of the American Historical Association, and was director of the department of historical research at the Carnegie Institution in Washington from 1905 to 1928. He became director of manuscripts at the Library of ·Congress in 1928. His works include *Privateering and Piracy* (1923) and *The American Revolution Considered as a Social Movement* (1926).

JAMESON, SIR LEANDER STARR (1853-1917), British physician and statesman, born in Edinburgh, and educated at London University. In 1878, because of ill-health, he went to South Africa and practiced medicine in Kimberley. He came into contact with Cecil Rhodes (q.v.) and assisted Rhodes in negotiations with South African natives, particularly the Matabele chief Lobengula, whom Jameson induced to grant concessions which led to the formation of the British South Africa Company. In 1891 the British government appointed Jameson administrator of Rhodesia.

In an unauthorized attempt to assist the Uitlanders, the British residents of the Transvaal and the Orange Free State, who were planning an uprising in Johannesburg against the Boer government, Jameson, on December 31, 1895, led a force of six hundred men in a raid into the Transvaal. The raid met with resistance at Krugersdorp and Doornkop; at the latter, after thirty-six hours of fighting and the loss of seventeen men killed and forty-nine wounded, Jameson surrendered to the Boers. Jameson was turned over to the British government for punishment, and was sentenced to ten months' imprisonment. He was released after eight months because of ill-health.

The so-called Jameson raid was one of the most important precipitating causes of the South African War. Jameson fought against the Boers in this war, and later became a member of the Cape Colony legislature in 1900 and served as prime minister from 1904 to 1908. He was created a baronet in 1911. See UNION OF SOUTH AFRICA.

JAMESON RAID. See JAMESON, SIR LEANDER STARR.

JAMES RIVER. See DAKOTA RIVER.

JAMES RIVER, the longest river of Virginia, formed at Iron Gate, Alleghany Co., by the union of the Jackson and Cowpasture rivers. It flows generally S.E. to Lynchburg, then N.E. to Scottsville, in central Virginia, where it turns S.E., passing Richmond and emptying into Chesapeake Bay through a broad, deep estuary. At its entrance to the bay is Hampton Roads (q.v.). The James R. is navigable to Richmond, about 120 m. from its mouth, for vessels up to 150 tons. The total length of the river is about 450 m. The falls at Richmond furnish abundant water power for the city's industries. Tributaries of the James are the Appomattox and the Chickahominy rivers. Jamestown, the first permanent English settlement in America, was founded on the banks of the James R. in 1607.

JAMESTOWN, a city of Chautauqua Co., N.Y., situated at the s. end of Chautauqua Lake, 70 miles s.w. of Buffalo. Jamestown is served by a railroad, and it maintains a municipal airport. The city is the trading center of a fertile agricultural region producing garden truck, grapes, fruit, and dairy products. Jamestown is noted for the manufacture of upholstered and case furniture, metal office furniture and equipment, and kitchen cabinets. Other manufactures are voting machines, washing machines, bank and library equipment, metal doors, building trim, automobile radiators, mattresses, mirrors, textiles, and dairy feed. The city is a summer resort, with numerous summer cottages lining the shores of Chautauqua Lake. The Chautauqua Institution (q.v.) is on the w. shore of the lake, 18 miles N.W. of Jamestown. Educational institutions in the city include a business college, and an extension school of Alfred University. Jamestown was first settled in 1810, incorporated as a village in 1827, and chartered as a city in 1886. Pop. (1950) 43,354.

JAMESTOWN, county seat of Stutsman Co., N.Dak., situated on the James R., 90 miles w. of Fargo. It has air-line service, is served by two railroads, and is a railroad division headquarters, with railroad repair shops. The city is the center and shipping point of a fertile farming, stock-raising, and dairying area. The principal industrial establishments are bottling works, and plants processing agricultural products. Jamestown is the site of Jamestown College (Presbyterian) and the State Hospital for the Insane. In the vicinity is Arrowwood National Wildlife Refuge, covering more than 16,000 acres and containing several lakes, frequented by many forms of water fowl and other wildlife. Jamestown was first settled in 1873 near the site of old Fort William H. Seward, a U.S. Army post established in 1872 and abandoned in 1877. It was chartered as a city in 1883. Pop. (1950) 10,697.

JAMESTOWN, a former village in what is now James City Co., Va., situated on Jamestown Island in the James R., about 32 m. from the river's mouth. It is part of the Colonial National Historical Park. Jamestown is the site of the first permanent English settlement in America, founded on May 14, 1607, by a small company under the leadership of Captain Christopher Newport (q.v.). Captain John Smith (q.v.) was also a member of the group. The original buildings of the settlement were destroyed

by fire in 1608 and the settlers' numbers were depleted by famine and disease in the winter of 1609-10. The survivors abandoned the settlement on June 7, 1610, but met the ship of Thomas West De La Warr (Lord Delaware) at the mouth of the river bringing supplies and about 150 new settlers, and returned to the village. The colony prospered, and was the capital of Virginia until 1699. In 1619 the first representative assembly in America was held there. In the same year, at Jamestown, the first Negro slaves were introduced into the original thirteen Colonies. In 1676 the village was burned by Nathaniel Bacon (see BACON'S REBELLION) and fire again destroyed several public buildings in 1698. The seat of government was moved from Jamestown to the Middle Plantations (now Williamsburg) in 1699, and the village was deserted. An area of about 21 acres on the island is separate from the national park and is owned by the Association for the Preservation of Virginia Antiquities. It contains several interesting remains, including an old church tower dating from 1639, the foundations of the State houses, ancient tombstones, statues of Pocahontas (q.v.) and John Smith, and the Hunt Memorial, honoring Rev. Robert Hunt, who celebrated the first Anglican communion in America at Jamestown in 1607. The Jamestown Archeological Laboratory and Museum contains relics unearthed by excavations carried on by the National Park Service.

JAMESTOWN WEED. See JIMSON WEED.

JAMI (1414-92), Persian poet, born near Herat, in Khurasan. Foremost among his works is a collection of seven poems entitled *Haft Aurang* ("Seven Thrones"). One of the poems in this series, the *Salāmān u Absāl,* is known in English through Edward FitzGerald's translation. His works are held in high esteem among the Persians, and some of the manuscripts of his poems are splendid specimens of Oriental calligraphy and illumination.

JAMMES, FRANCIS (1868-1938), French poet and novelist, born in Tournay. His prose was almost as poetic as his verse, and in both he was usually a chronicler of the countryside. *Feuilles dans le Vent* (1914) contained the best of his first-period poetry. His other volumes include *Œuvres de Francis Jammes* (1913), *Poèmes Mesurés* (1921), and *Quatrains* (4 vols., 1923-25). His novels and other prose include *Mémoires* (3 vols., 1921–23), *Cloches pour Deux Mariages* (1925),

Ma France Poetique (1926), *Cardinale Lâvigerie* (1928), and *Divine Douleur* (1928).

JAMMU, city of Kashmir (q.v.), located on the Tiwa R., about 90 miles s. of Srinagar and 16 m. by rail N.E. of Sialkot, West Punjab, Pakistan. It was the residence of the Rajput (see RAJPUTANA, UNION OF) dynasty until its conquest by the Sikhs under Ranjit Singh in 1819. Jammu became a British possession in 1846. A palace, a fort, a college, and a missionary hospital are located in the city. Pop., about 50,000.

JAMMU AND KASHMIR. See KASHMIR.

JANÁČEK, LEOŠ (1854-1928), Czech composer, born in Hukvaldy, Moravia, and educated at the Community of the Austin Friars in Brünn, at the Organ School in Prague, and at the Leipzig Conservatory. In 1882 he became conductor of the Philharmonic Society of Brünn, and in the same year founded the Brünn Organ School, where he taught until 1920, when the new Czechoslovakian state took over the school and he was appointed professor at the State Conservatory of Prague.

Public recognition was withheld from Janáček until very late in his life. His best-known opera, *Jenufa,* first produced in 1904, had no popular success until its performance in Prague in 1916, when the composer was 62. From this time onward, however, he rose steadily toward national prominence and honor. In his seventieth year, for example, Janáček was given the degree of Doctor of Philosophy by the Masaryk University.

Janáček spent much of his life in research on the folk melody and speech of his country. He believed that only through a detailed study of characteristic "speech-melodies" could the national life of Czechoslovakia be properly interpreted in music. His numerous theater, choral, and chamber works reflect his theories, deriving most of their stylistic features from folk material.

JANESVILLE, county seat of Rock Co., Wis., situated on the Rock R., 12 miles N. of the Illinois boundary and about 35 miles S.E. of Madison. It is served by two railroads, and is the trading center of an area producing tobacco, grain, and dairy products. In addition to large tobacco warehouses, industrial establishments in the city include factories manufacturing automobiles, automobile bodies, fountain pens, machinery, agricultural sprayers, insulation materials, woolen and cotton goods, awnings, thread, and metal fencing. Janesville is the site of the Wisconsin State School for the Blind, the oldest charitable institution in the State; it was established as a private institution in 1849, and the State assumed its operation in 1850. Janesville was settled in 1835 and incorporated as a city in 1853. It became the county seat in 1859. The city is named after an early settler, Henry F. Janes. Pop. (1950) 24,899.

JANET, PIERRE (1859-1947), French psychologist, born in Paris, and educated at the École Normale and the École de Médecine in Paris. From 1881 to 1898 he taught philosophy at the lycées of Chateauroux and Havre, at the Collège Rollin, and at the lycées Louis-le-Grand and Condorcet. His interest in neurology and psychology, which he studied under Jean Martin Charcot (q.v.), was already in evidence at this time, and from 1889 to 1898 he was director of the psychological laboratory of the Salpétrière in addition to his other duties. From 1898 to 1902 he lectured on psychology at the Sorbonne, and from 1897 taught psychology at the Collège de France where, from 1902 until his death, he served as professor of psychology. Janet did important pioneer work on the scientific treatment of neuroses and hysteria; his investigations of hypnosis (q.v.) as an aid to the understanding of the mind and the diagnosis of its disorders greatly influenced the early work of another pupil of Charcot, Sigmund Freud (q.v.). Among Janet's works are *Major Symptoms of Hysteria* (1908), *Les Névroses* (1909), and *Principles of Psychotherapy* (1923).

JANINA or **YANINA** (Gr. *Ioannina*), city of north Epirus, Greece, situated about 40 m. from the Mediterranean Sea. It is believed to have existed before the 11th century. During the early Middle Ages it was part of the Eastern Roman Empire. It was successively invaded by the Normans, Serbs, Macedonians, and Albanians. From 1431 until 1913 Janina was part of the Turkish Empire. The city was taken by Greece in 1913 during the First Balkan War and subsequently became the principal city of Grecian Epirus. During World War II, after the Axis victory in the Balkans in 1940-41, Janina was occupied by the Italian forces and incorporated within Albania (q.v). Goldsmithing, embroidering in silver and gold, and the manufacture of leather and silk goods and of colored linens are the principal occupations of the inhabitants. Pop., about 33,000.

JANIS, ELSIE, stage name of ELSIE BIER-BOWER (1889-   ), American variety performer, musical-comedy librettist, and composer, born in Columbus, Ohio. She scored her first major success as a variety entertainer in *When We Were Forty-One* (1905) at the New York Theater Roof Garden. She later appeared as a comedienne and singer in such variety revues as *The Vanderbilt Cup* (1906); *The Slim Princess* (1910); *A Star for a Night* (1911), which she wrote; *Miss Information* (1915); and *Miss 1917*. During World War I, in 1917 and 1918, she entertained troops of the American Expeditionary Force in France, gaining great popularity and becoming known as the "Darling of the A.E.F.". Subsequently, she wrote and starred in the variety reviews *Elsie Janis and Her Gang* (1919), *It's All Wrong* (1920), and *Puzzles of 1925*. She also composed more than fifty popular songs, wrote the scenario of the motion picture *Close Harmony* (1929), and appeared in several short films and the full-length motion picture *Women in War* (1940). Her writings include *Love Letters of an Actress* (1913) and the autobiography *So Far So Good* (1932).

JANIZARIES, or JANISSARIES, the regular standing army of the Ottoman Turks, formed by Sultan Orkhan in 1330. Orkhan had previously organized a regular paid army, but the Turcomans from which the organization was recruited were unsatisfactory soldiers. Orkhan adopted a system of troop procurement under which the children of Christian subjects were taken from their parents and trained as *yeni cheri* (Turkish, "new troops"). The Janizaries were led by an *aga,* who was held in reverential respect and who had the power of life or death over his soldiers. The Janizaries served as police during peacetime. In wartime they served on foot, and were noted for the wild impetuosity of their attacks. The bodyguard of the sultan was composed of selected Janizaries.

In the middle of the 15th century the Janizaries, who had been an orderly body of troops until that time, began the first of a long series of revolts. By the 17th century the organization had become completely corrupt, exacting tribute from each new sultan at his accession. In 1825 Sultan Mahmud II ordered his subjects to attack the mutinous Janizaries. Deserted by their aga and other officers, the soldiers were defeated, with a loss of 16,000 men. The organization was dissolved by proclamation

in 1826, and all opposition was put down by bloodshed. Thousands of Janizaries were killed, and more than 20,000 were banished.

JANSEN, CORNELIS, or (Lat.) CORNELIUS JANSENIUS (1585-1638), Dutch Roman Catholic theologian, founder of Jansenism, born in Acquoi, near Leerdam, and educated at the universities of Utrecht, Louvain, and Paris. During his school days he came in contact with the disciples of Michael Baius, and began a lifelong friendship with Jean Du Vergier de Hauranne, who later became abbot of St. Cyran and chaplain of the convent of Port Royal. In 1617 Jansen became head of the Dutch theological college of St. Pulcheria at Louvain, and in 1630 became professor of exegesis at the University of Louvain. He was made bishop of Ypres in 1636, and died of the plague just after he completed his great work the *Augustinus,* which was published two years after his death.

The main object of this work was to prove that the teachings of St. Augustine against the Pelagians on grace, free will, and predestination were directly opposed to the doctrines of the modern schools, especially those of the Jesuits. This work and the *Frequent Communion* (1643) of Antoine Arnauld contained the principal tenets of the Jansenist movement. They included denial of the orthodox Catholic doctrine of freedom of the will; refusal to admit the existence of sufficient grace, maintaining that all interior grace is irresistible; and denial of the dogma that Christ died for all mankind, holding that He died only for those predestined to salvation. The principal promoters of the movement were Du Vergier de Hauranne and Arnauld, and later Pasquier Quesnel (q.v.), who wrote *Moral Reflections on the New Testament* (1687-94), a work reproducing their teachings. Prominent among the defenders of the movement were the scholars and divines of the convent of Port Royal, and Blaise Pascal (q.v.).

The *Augustinus* was prohibited by a decree of the Inquisition in 1641, and in the following year was condemned in general terms by Pope Urban VIII. In 1705 Pope Clement XI issued the bull *Vineam Domini,* closing the convent of Port Royal, and in 1713, the bull *Unigenitus,* condemning 101 propositions in the *Moral Reflections* by Quesnel. Many of the Jansenists appealed from the decision of the pope to a general council, forming a party known as the Appellants; the remaining members of the movement, the Acceptants, accepted the pope's decision. A firm policy on the part of the papacy and the French state brought the Appellants into disfavor; many submitted, and the recusants were subjected to severe penalties. Jansenism declined in France, but survived in Febronianism and Gallicanism (qq.v.). A large number of Appellants emigrated to the Netherlands, where they formed a community with Utrecht as a center. This group is still in existence, being governed by the archbishop of Utrecht and the bishops of Haarlem and Deventer.

JANSENISM. See JANSEN, CORNELIS.

JANSSEN, PIERRE JULES CÉSAR (1824-1907), French astronomer, born in Paris. He was in charge of various scientific expeditions, including missions to Peru in 1857-1858 to determine the magnetic equator, to Italy in 1861 and 1864 to study the solar spectrum, and to the Azores in 1867 for magnetic and topographic studies, and various expeditions to study solar eclipses. In 1875 he was appointed director of the astrophysical observatory at Meudon, and in 1893 he established and became the director of the observatory on Mont Blanc. He wrote *Annales de l'Observatoire de Meudon* (1896), and collected a series of solar photographs published as *Atlas de Photographies Solaires* (1904).

JANUARIUS, SAINT, or SAN GENNARO (272?-305?), Christian martyr under the Roman emperor Diocletian. He was bishop of Beneventum, and the place of his martyrdom was Pozzuoli. His body is preserved at Naples, in the crypt of the cathedral, where are also separately preserved the head of the martyr, and two phials containing a substance, supposed to be blood, which liquefies when exhibited in May and September of each year.

JANUARY, the first month of the year in the Gregorian calendar, consisting of thirty-one days. The name is derived from the Roman deity Janus (q.v.) to whom the month was sacred. The Anglo-Saxons called January *Wulfmonath,* as the month during which hunger made the wolves bold enough to enter the villages. When the Gregorian calendar was adopted by English statute in 1752, the beginning of the year was changed from March 25 to January 1. Thus Dec. 31, 1750, was followed by Jan. 31, 1750, and March 24, 1750, was followed by March 25, 1751; but Dec. 31, 1752, was followed by Jan. 1, 1753, and March 24, 1753, was followed by March 25, 1753. See CALENDAR.

JANUS, an ancient Roman god. His name is derived from the same root as the Latin word *janua,* "a gate" or "opening". As the spirit of opening he was invoked at the beginning of all undertakings. He was also the god of the beginning of day, and of the beginning of the agricultural year, the first month of which, January, was dedicated to him. As the spirit of openings, Janus was the god under whose care were all *januæ,* or gates, in Rome, and the archway out of which the army marched to war and by which it returned. This archway, which in later times was replaced by a temple of Janus, had its gates open in time of war and closed in time of peace. The gates opened both ways, and the god of gates was himself represented by an image having two faces, looking both ways.

JAPAN, in Japanese *Dai* ("Great") *Nihon* or *Nippon* ("origin of light"), hence, LAND OF THE RISING SUN, an island empire off the coast of N.E. Asia, bounded on the N. by the Sea of Okhotsk, on the E. by the Pacific Ocean, on the S. by the Pacific Ocean and the East China Sea, and on the W. by the Sea of Japan. The Japanese islands extend in an irregular crescent from the island of Sakhalin (U.S.S.R.) to the island of Formosa (China). Japan proper consists chiefly of four large islands: Hokkaido, the northernmost; Honshu, the largest, and called the mainland; Shikoku; and Kyushu (qq.v.), the southernmost. In addition, the empire includes seven secondary islands and island groups: Awaji, Oki, Sado, Tsushima, Okinawa (qq.v.), Iki, and Ogasawarajima (see BONIN ISLANDS), and more than a thousand lesser adjacent islands. The total area of Japan is 143,667 sq.m., the four large islands comprising 141,011 sq.m., the secondary islands and island groups comprising 1976 sq.m., and the small adjacent islands accounting for the remainder of the area. Population of Japan proper (1950) 83,199,637.

The Kuril Islands (q.v.), N. of Hokkaido, and formerly included in Japan proper as Chishima, were occupied by the U.S.S.R. at the conclusion of World War II under an agreement concluded at the Yalta Conference (q.v.) in 1945. Until the unconditional surrender of Japan to the Allied powers on Sept. 2, 1945, the Japanese Empire controlled, in addition to present Japan and the Kuril Islands, an area of about 637,500

Ewing Galloway; Canadian Pacific Railway

Above: Theater Street in the city of Kobe, on the island of Honshu, Japan. Right: Japanese women in Nara deer park, Nara, Japan.

sq.m., including Korea, Formosa, the Pescadores, Karafuto (s. half of Sakhalin), Manchuria (Manchukuo), the leased territory of Kwantung (qq.v.), and the South Sea Mandated Territories, comprising the Marshall, Marianas (except Guam, a U.S. possession), and Caroline islands (qq.v.), which were made a Japanese mandate by the Treaty of Versailles in 1919, after World War I. For the disposition of these territories and others acquired by Japanese conquest during World War II, see *History,* below.

The largest city and capital of Japan is Tokyo (q.v.); the second-largest city and greatest industrial center is Osaka. Japan has many ports engaged in foreign trade; the most important, all on the island of Honshu, include Yokohama, Kobe, and Osaka (qq.v.) on the Pacific coast, and Niigata (q.v.) on the Sea of Japan. In addition to these five cities, other principal cities of Japan are Okayama, Kyoto, Nagoya, Fukuoka, Sendai,

Kawasaki, Sapporo, Amagasaki, Kumamoto, Hiroshima, Kanazawa, Yokosuka, Nagasaki, Shizuoka, Kure, Kagoshima, Hakodate, Sakai, Himeji, Gifu, Yawata, Kokura, Wakayama, Sasebo, Shimonoseki, Kokura, Omuta, Otaru, and Moji.

Physical Features. The islands of Japan are the projecting summits of a huge chain of mountains originally a part of the continent of Asia from which they were detached in the Cenozoic period (see GEOLOGY, SYSTEMATIC). The islands are, generally, long and narrow in shape, the main island, Honshu, measuring less than 200 m. at its greatest breadth; no part of Japan is more than 100 m. from the sea. The coastline of Japan is exceedingly long in proportion to the area of the islands, totaling, with the many bays and indentations, about 15,500 m. The greatest amount of indentation is on the Pacific coast, and is the result of the erosive action of the tides and severe coastal storms. The w. coast of Kyushu, on the East China Sea, is the most irregular portion of the Japanese coast. Few navigable inlets are found on the E. coast above Tokyo, but s. of Tokyo Bay are many of the best bays and harbors in Japan. Between Honshu, Shikoku, and Kyushu is the Inland Sea (q.v.), dotted with islands and connected with the Pacific Ocean and the Sea of Japan (see JAPAN, SEA OF) by four narrow straits through which oceanic storms rarely pass. The w. coast of the islands of Japan, on the almost tideless Sea of Japan, is relatively straight, and measures less than 3000 m.; the only conspicuous indentations in the coast line are Wakasa and Toyama bays in Honshu.

Topographically, Japan is a rugged land of high mountains and deep valleys, with many small plains. The alternating sequence of mountain and valley, and the rocky soil account for the fact that only about 13% of Japan is arable land. Because of the prevailing climatic conditions, particularly strong winds and heavy rains, the Japanese landscape has become rounded and smooth, with gentle inclines. Few mountains have permanent caps of snow, and remarkably luxuriant vegetation and many forests cover the mountain slopes, except in the few regions where craggy, shattered peaks are found.

Though Japan is abundantly watered, every valley having a stream, there are no long navigable rivers. The larger Jananese rivers vary in size from swollen freshets during the spring thaw or the summer rainy season to small streams during dry weather. Successions of rapids and shallows are so common that only boats with extremely shallow draft can navigate. The longest river in Japan is the Ishikari (q.v.) on Hokkaido, which is 227 m. long; other large rivers on Hokkaido are the Teshio and the Tokachi. The important rivers of Honshu include the Shinano, Tone, Kitakami, Tenryu, and Mogami. The Yoshino is the longest river in Shikoku. The many Japanese lakes are noted for their scenic beauty. Some are located in the river valleys, but the majority are mountain lakes and many are summer resorts. The largest lake in Japan is Biwa (q.v.), on Honshu, which is 40 m. long by 7 m. wide. One of the highest lakes is Chuzenji, on Honshu, which is 4375 ft. above sea level. Among other large lakes are Hakone, Inawashiro, Suwa, and Shoji.

The Japanese plains lie chiefly along the lower courses of the principal rivers, on plateaus along the lowest slopes of mountain ranges, and on lowlands along the seacoast. The most extensive plains are in Hokkaido: along the Ishikari R. in the w. part of the island (480,000 acres), along the Tokachi R. in the s.e. (744,000 acres), and around the cities of Nemuro and Kushiro on the E. central shore (1,229,000 acres). Honshu has five large plains; that of Kinai contains the cities of Kobe, Kyoto, and Osaka, and the plain of Kwanto is the site of Tokyo. The plain of Tsukushi is the most important level area in Kyushu.

The mountains of Japan are the most conspicuous feature of the topography. Mountain ranges extend across the islands from N. to S., the main chains sending off smaller ranges which branch out laterally or run parallel to the parent range, and frequently descend to the coast, where they form bays and harbors. In the N., the island of Hokkaido is marked by a volcanic range which descends from the Kurils and merges in the s.w. part of the island with a chain branching from Cape Soya on the N.W. tip. These mountains branch into two lines near Volcano Bay, on the s.w. coast, and reappear on the island of Honshu in two parallel ranges. The minor range, situated entirely in the N.E., separates the valley of the Kitakami R. from the Pacific Ocean. The other, and main, range continues toward the s.w. until it meets a mass of intersecting ridges which enclose the plateau of the Shinano R., and forms a belt of mountains, the highest in Japan, across the widest part of the island. The highest peak, 12,395 ft., is Mt. Fujiyama (q.v.), near Yokohama, which, because of its beauty, is one of the favorite themes of Japanese decorative art. One of the subsidiary chains in the central mountain mass is called the Japanese Alps because of the grandeur of the landscape; six peaks of the so-called Alps are more than 9000 ft. high, and one, Mt. Ontake (10,450 ft.), is the second-highest mountain in Japan. Farther s. is another chain of high peaks, Mt. Kaigane (10,330 ft.) being the highest. The islands of Shikoku and Kyushu are dotted with mountain ranges, though none contains any peak higher than Ishizuchi-san (7727 ft.) on Shikoku. Volcanoes are common in the Japanese mountains; about 200 volcanoes are known, about 50 of them still active. They are found principally in three ranges: the chain which descends into Hokkaido from the Kurils; the range in central Honshu of which Fujiyama, itself a volcano, is a part; and a volcanic range in Kyushu which contains Asosan. Among the volcanoes which have erupted disastrously during the past century are Asamayama, Bandai-san, and Sakurajima. Thermal springs and volcanic areas emitting gases are exceedingly numerous.

Earthquakes are frequent in Japan; a survey made during a recent period showed that seismic disturbances, mostly of a minor nature, occurred more than three times a day. Geological research has shown that, possibly under the continous impact of these disturbances, the w. coast of the Japanese islands is settling, while the Pacific coast is rising. The E. coast is frequently subject to quakes affecting large areas and usually accompanied by tidal waves; these shocks seem to begin at the bottom of the ocean near the N.E. coast of Honshu, where a gigantic crater is thought to exist more than 5 m. below the surface. The most disastrous earthquake in Japanese history occurred in 1923 in Segami Bay, near Tokyo and Yokohama, in which more than 91,000 persons were killed (see EARTHQUAKES, MEMORABLE).

Climate. The Japanese islands extend through approximately 20 degrees of latitude (about 25° N. to 45° N.), and climatic conditions vary widely. Average temperatures range from about 41° F. in Nemuro (Hokkaido) to about 61° F. in Okinawa. Short summers and severe long winters characterize Hokkaido and the N. part of Honshu. The severity of the winters is due in great part to N.W. winds blowing from Siberia and the cold Oyashio, or Okhotsk, current which flows southward into the Sea of Japan. To the s. and E. of this region the winters are considerably moderated by the influence of the warm Kuroshio, or Japan, current. In Shikoku, Kyushu, and s. Honshu the summers are hot and humid, almost subtropical, while the winters are mild with comparatively little snow. Japan lies in the path of the s.w. monsoons which add considerably to the oppressive humidity of the summers. Rainfall averages about 62 inches a year, and is particularly heavy during June and September, the latter being the wettest month. From June to October tropical cyclones, called typhoons (Jap. *tai-fu,* "great wind") occur and cause great damage, especially to shipping.

Flora and Fauna. The great variety and luxuriance of Japanese flora is due mainly to the heat and moisture of Japanese summers. Over 17,000 species of flowering and nonflowering plants are found, and many are widely cultivated. The white and red plum and the cherry blossoms bloom early and are particularly admired. The Japanese hills are colorful with azaleas in April, and the tree peony, one of the most popular cultivated flowers, blossoms at the beginning of May. The lotus blooms in August, and in November the blooming of the chrysanthemum, the national flower of Japan, is the occasion of one of the greatest of the numerous Japanese flower festivals. Other flowers include the pimpernel, bluebell, gladiolus, and many varieties of lily. Few wild flowers are found, the small area of arable land permitting little space for uncultivated vegetation in the plains.

The predominant variety of Japanese tree is the conifer; a common species is the sugi, or Japanese cedar, which sometimes attains a height of 150 ft. Other evergreens include the larch, spruce, and many varieties of fir. In Kyushu, Shikoku, and s. Honshu subtropical trees such as the bamboo, camphor tree, and banyan are found, and the tea plant and wax tree are cultivated. In central and N. Honshu the trees are those of the temperate zone, such as the beech, willow, horse chestnut, and many conifers. Lacquer and mulberry trees are cultivated extensively, and the cypress, yew, box, holly, and myrtle are plentiful. In Hokkaido the vegetation is subarctic, and similar to that of s. Siberia. Spruce, larch, and northern fir are the most common trees, and some forests

Ewing Galloway

An itinerant fish peddler on a street in Tokyo, Japan

contain alders, poplars, and beeches. The most common Japanese fruit is the orange.

The diversity of Japanese vegetation, the rugged topography, and the scarcity of land available for nonutilitarian cultivation have resulted in a unique kind of landscape gardening. Japanese gardens attempt to reproduce in miniature a stylization of natural landscapes. A characteristic of these gardens is the dwarf tree, such as the cherry or plum, which, through skillful pruning, is kept as low as 12 in.

Though not so varied as the flora, the Japanese fauna includes at least 140 species of mammals, 450 species of birds, and a wide variety of reptiles, batrachians, and fish. The most prevalent and only primate mammal is the red-faced monkey, the Japanese macaque, found throughout Honshu and eaten as a delicacy. The 32 carnivora include the red bear, black bear, and brown bear. Foxes are found throughout Japan, as is the badger, sometimes called the bamboo bear. Other fur-bearing animals include the marten, Japanese mink, otter, weasel, and several varieties of seal. Rodents are numerous and include squirrels, flying squirrels, hares, rabbits, rats, and mice, though the common house mouse is not found. Many varieties of

bat exist; insectivores include the Japanese mole and shrew mouse. Of the two species of deer, the most common is the small Japanese deer which has a spotted white coat in summer and a brown coat in winter.

The sparrow, house swallow, and thrush are the commonest Japanese birds. Water birds comprise almost 25% of the known species, and include the crane, heron, swan, duck, cormorant, stork, and albatross. Song birds are numerous, the bullfinch and two varieties of nightingale being the best known. Among other common birds are the robin, cuckoo, woodpecker, pheasant, and pigeon.

The coastal waters of Japan teem with fish, which are caught in enormous quantities for use as daily food or for canning, and also for fertilizer. Among the edible varieties are the tai, or Japanese porgy, the herring, mackerel, cod, and tuna. The northern rivers contain salmon and trout.

Production and Industry. Japan is primarily an agricultural country. Of the comparatively small acreage available for cultivation, more than half (about 7,420,000 acres) is devoted to rice fields; the remainder (about 5,923,000 acres) is planted chiefly to other cereals, such as wheat, barley, and rye. Rice is the staple of the Japanese diet;

in a recent year the rice crop amounted to about 9,435,000 metric tons. However, production of rice is insufficient for domestic consumption, and considerable quantities must be imported.

The arable area is divided into small farms averaging about 2 acres each; almost 2,000,000 farmers work less than 1 acre. The land is tilled intensively, but largely with primitive methods. Until recent years about 40% of the cultivated land was owned by great landlords and leased to tenant farmers. In Dec., 1945, the headquarters of the Allied occupation forces ordered land reforms to prevent absentee landlordism and to divide the great estates among the peasants.

The cultivation of tea plants is a minor agricultural endeavor; about 100,000 acres were planted to tea before World War II. Important fruit crops are peaches, oranges, tangerines, plums, persimmons, pears, grapes, and apples. More than half of Japan's total area is covered with forests, and lumber industries are important. Fishing is one of the most important Japanese industries, fish being a food staple equal to rice. Many Japanese are engaged in fishing and related activities, such as fish canning and oyster cultivation for food and pearls. In a recent year the fish catch amounted to more than 3,500,000 metric tons. The mineral resources of Japan proper are varied but limited in quantity. Coal, gold, and copper are the leading minerals. The last-named, however, is the only metal found in quantities more than sufficient for domestic needs.

During the first three decades of the 20th century, Japan became one of the most important producers of consumer goods in the world. Textiles are the most important manufactured product, followed by machinery, chemicals, food products, paper, and pottery. Before World War II about 75% of all silk exports in the world came from Japan, about 30% of all farms raising silkworms. The Japanese rayon industry was one of the largest in the world, producing about 25,000,000 lbs. of rayon filament yarn a month. During the 1930's Japanese industries concentrated on producing war materials, particularly iron and steel, machinery, munitions, and airplanes. Following World War II, the Far Eastern Commission, which controlled Allied policy for the Japanese occupation, set restrictions on eventual iron and steel manufacture, after war damage had been repaired. The production of ingot steel was limited to 3,500,000 tons annually (compared with a capacity of 12,000,000 tons) and 2,000,000 tons of pig iron (compared with 3,000,000 tons). The Commission also began rehabilitation of the textile industry, which had been largely neglected by emphasis on war manufactures.

Before and during World War II the entire Japanese economy was controlled by about a dozen wealthy families, called the *Zaibatsu* ("wealth cliques") collectively. The greatest of these families were the Mitsui, Mitsubishi, Sumitomo, Yasuda, and Fuji (or Nakajima), who owned 255 separate corporations capitalized at considerably more than four billion dollars and controlling most of the coal, steam-engine, pulp, aluminum, and airplane industries of Japan. These immense family trusts were dissolved in 1945-46 by order of the occupation authorities.

Commerce. Prior to World War II Japan was ranked as the fifth nation in world trade. In 1939 Japanese exports amounted to over $928,500,000, and imports totaled over $757,775,000. Most Japanese exports went to territories controlled by the Empire, such as Manchuria and occupied China. Trade balance with other countries, such as the U.S. and Great Britain, was unfavorable; imports from the U.S., for example, exceeded exports to that country by more than $70,000,000. Allied occupation authorities permitted a resumption of foreign trade by private enterprises in 1946. In a recent year imports amounted to about $1,995,000,000, and exports to about $1,355,000,000. About 40% of Japan's imports, mainly food and fertilizers, came from the U.S. In addition to textiles, which make up the bulk of exports, exported manufactured goods include radios, radio tubes, bicycles, phonographs, and electric-light bulbs.

Communications. Japanese railway mileage amounted to about 15,250 m. before World War II. The highway system includes about 620,700 m. of roads, of which about 121,000 m. can be used by motor vehicles. The greatest progress in communications in the seabound country was in shipping, and the Japanese merchant marine comprised (in 1939) over 4000 ships of more than 100 gross tons, some 1180 being over 1000 gross tons. Shipping suffered extremely heavy losses during the war; in a recent year the merchant marine included 1587 vessels of more than 100 gross tons, with a combined gross tonnage of 2,787,163. Shipbuilding restrictions imposed by the Far Eastern Commission allowed construction of 650,000 gross tons of shipping annually, as opposed to a 1,900,000-ton capacity. About 1,256,000 telephones were in use during a recent year.

People, Language, and Religion. The modern Japanese are essentially a Mongolian race, similar to the Chinese and Koreans, although slightly smaller in stature; the average height of a Japanese male is 5 ft. 3½ in., and that of a female, 4 ft. 10½ in. General physical characteristics include prominent cheekbones, straight black hair, slanted eyes, and sparse facial hair on males. Ethnologically, the Japanese can be divided into three distinct types, apart from the Mongol type found throughout the islands. In the N. is an Ainu (q.v.) type, descendants of a people considered by ethnologists to be aborigines. A Manchu-Korean type, characterized by comparatively tall stature and fine features, is found in the regions nearest Korea. In central and E. Japan is found a Malay or Polynesian type, with round faces, short necks and head, prominent chins, and small, well-knit bodies. See RACES OF MANKIND.

The language spoken in Japan is an agglutinative tongue which has been greatly influenced by the Chinese language and is written in ideographs (see JAPANESE LANGUAGE). Religious freedom was first guaranteed by the constitution of 1889. The principal religious faiths are: Shinto (q.v.), a cult based on ancestor and nature worship, with 85 sects and about 56,000,000 followers in a recent year; Buddhism, with almost 100 denominations and about 37,000,000 adherents; and Christianity, including the Roman Catholic, Greek Orthodox, and Protestant faiths, with about 370,000 followers. During the 1930's Shintoism was made a state religion, stressing worship of the emperor as a divinity and the racial superiority of the Japanese; all Japanese, regardless of their religious affiliation, were forced to worship at state Shinto shrines. In 1946 the Allied occupation authorities ordered Shinto disestablished and reduced it to the level of a sect. On Jan. 1, 1946, Emperor Hirohito (q.v.) renounced all claim to divinity. The constitution promulgated in 1947 re-established absolute freedom of religion and ended state support of Shinto.

Education. Elementary education was made compulsory for all children for four years by an educational code in 1872, and the compulsory period was later extended to nine years, six of elementary school and three of middle schools, tuition being free. Beyond the age of fifteen education is optional, with a three-year high-school course available. More than 21,000 elementary schools and about 15,000 middle and high schools were maintained by the state in a recent year. Technical, commercial, and vocational schools are also maintained. Japan has seven imperial universities, located in Tokyo, Kyoto, Sendai, Fukuoka, Sapporo, Osaka, and Nagoya. The largest and oldest (1877) is the Tokyo Imperial University. There is a total of more than 400 colleges and universities; many of these institutions are coeducational. Japan's educational system is the most highly developed in Asia. Under postwar U.S. supervision the educational system was simplified and ultranationalistic indoctrination was eliminated from the curriculum. The illiteracy rate is less than 10 percent for the entire nation, and English, as the chief commercial language, is a required course of study in secondary schools. In a recent year about 19,160,000 students were enrolled in all educational institutions. Of this number, more than 11,419,000 attended elementary schools, about 7,320,000 were in middle and upper secondary schools, and more than 420,000 were enrolled in colleges and universities.

Government. Japan is governed according to the provisions of the Constitution of 1947. Under the terms of this document, which was formulated under the guidance of the Allied Occupation authorities after World War II, the emperor is the symbol of the state. Executive power is vested in a cabinet, which is headed by a prime minister. The cabinet is chosen by the national legislature (Diet) from among its own members and is responsible to it. The Diet, the supreme organ of state power, is a bicameral body, elected by universal suffrage and consisting of the House of Representatives (lower house) and the House of Councilors (upper house). Lower house members, totaling 466, are elected for a term not to exceed four years. Upper house members, totaling 250, are elected for six-year terms; elections for one half the membership are held every three years. One hundred councilors are elected at large, the others from the prefectural districts. Decisions by the House of Councilors may be vetoed by the lower house, which also retains control over legislation dealing with treaties and fiscal matters.

Judicial authority is vested in the Supreme Court, the members of which are appointed by the cabinet. The justices enjoy life tenure, subject to the approval of the voters in the first general election after their appointment, and every ten years thereafter. Otherwise they

Ewing Galloway; Canadian Pacific Railway

Above: Mount Fuji seen from the bay. This famous landmark is the most sacred mountain in Japan. Right: Scene on the shore of Lake Chūzenji, a popular Japanese resort.

must retire. Between 1889, when the first modern Japanese constitution was promulgated, and the end of World War II in 1945, the supreme and executive power in Japan was officially designated as resident in the sacred and inviolable person of the emperor, called the *Dai Nippon Teikoku Tenno* ("Imperial Son of Heaven of Great Japan"). The throne is hereditary and descended only in the male line; in default of a direct male heir, an emperor may be chosen only from four princely families equal in rank to the imperial house. The present emperor, Hirohito, succeeded to the throne in 1926, and was said to be the 124th of his line. Legislative power was accorded to a two-house legislature, the Diet, including a House of Peers (composed of hereditary peers, distinguished commoners nominated by the emperor, and a limited number of elective seats) and a House of Representatives elected by male citizens over 25. Cabinet ministers were responsible to the emperor and appointed by him.

History. The earliest extant records of Japanese history are contained in two semi-mythical chronicles, the Kojiki and the Nihongi, purporting to deal with events from about the 7th century B.C. to about the 8th century A.D. These chronicles and other collections of legends were made the basis of an official history of Japan which was written in the late 19th century under Imperial direction, and which dates the founding of the Japanese Empire exactly from Feb. 11, 660 B.C., the supposed date of the accession of Jimmu Tenno, the first emperor of Japan. Archeological and historical research have shown that the Ainus, a tribal people concerning whose origins nothing is known, were the earliest inhabitants of the Japanese archipelago. They populated all the Japanese islands about the 9th or 8th centuries B.C. During this period, invading peoples from central Asia, Korea, and from Polynesia and Malaysia to the S. of Japan, began expeditions of conquest to the islands. Gradually the Ainus were forced to the N. and E. portions of Honshu by the invaders. Jimmu, according to the chronicles, seems to have lived between 711 and 585 B.C. After having established his rule in Kyushu, Jimmu led his forces northward, crossed the Inland Sea, and extended his domains to Yamato, a province in central Honshu which gave its name to the Imperial house and, eventually, to all of ancient Japan. The Mikado, the Yamato chieftain, consolidated his power by making a primitive form of Shinto the general religion and, thus, a political instrument. By about the beginning of the Christian era, Japan was gripped by a rude feudal system, headed by the Yamato Mikado. A large number of clans, called *uji,* each with its own clan god, ruled the separate domains. Of these clans, the most important were the Omi, claiming divine descent, and the Muraji, claiming descent from nobles of the pre-Yamato era. The rule of the Imperial clan, regarded as the head clan, was more nominal than actual, though its clan god, in early Shinto, was worshiped nationally.

About 360 A.D. the empress Jingo, a legendary ruler who came to be considered a goddess, took over the government at the death of her husband, the emperor Chuai. The warrior empress, having fitted out an army, invaded and conquered a portion of Korea. Korean culture, greatly influenced by adja-

cent China, had already advanced to a comparatively high level. During the next several centuries intercourse between Japan and Korea considerably stimulated the developing civilization of the islands. Chinese writing, literature, and philosophy became popular at the court of Yamato and several of the feudal courts in Kyushu. About the beginning of the 5th century A.D. the Chinese script was officially decreed the alphabet of Japan. In 430 the Imperial court appointed its first historiographers, and records acquired a degree of exactitude. The most important event of the period was the importation of Buddhism. About 552 A.D. the king of Pakche, in S.W. Korea, sent Buddhist priests to Japan, together with religious images, Buddhist scriptures, and calendars and methods of keeping time. The Koreans drove out the Japanese invaders about 562, but the imported culture was already strongly rooted in the archipelago. An Imperial edict in 621 made Buddhism the official religion of Japan.

Some years earlier, in 604, the first Japanese constitution had been drafted, its seventeen articles strongly influenced by the centralized government of China. Eight boards or departments of state were established, and a new order of nobility, in nine ranks was created. A great council, the Dajo-Kwan, superintended the boards and ruled the realm through local governors sent out from the capital. Nara in Yamato became the fixed capital in 710; in 794 Kyoto was made the Imperial residence and, with few interruptions, remained the capital until 1869. During this period the emperors began to withdraw from public life. Delegating the affairs of government to subordinates, they went into seclusion and, in time, came to be regarded as abstractions in the national life rather than its directors. The retirement of the emperors was accompanied by the rise of great military lords.

About the 9th century Japanese armies extended the power of the Empire in every direction, subduing the Ainus in N. Honshu and bringing all of Shikoku and Kyushu into the Yamato orbit of influence. The rise of great military lords in the provinces was concomitant with the growing power of other princes and clan heads in court and civil life, and the seclusion of the emperors enabled both the military and civil lords to acquire various degrees of domination over the government. In 858 the Fujiwara clan, who became princes of the Imperial house,

Wide World Photo

Japanese artisans painting designs on silk fabrics from which kimonos will be made

became masters of Japan, maintaining their power for the next three centuries. In that year a Fujiwara prince, Yoshifusa (804-72) became regent for his grandson, the emperor Seiwa, then less than a year old. The Fujiwara monopolized most of the court and administrative offices. In 880 Fujiwara Mototsune (836-91) became the first official civil dictator (*kwampaku*). The greatest of the Fujiwara leaders was Michinaga (966-1027), whose five daughters married successive emperors, and who was *kwampaku* for about 30 years (998-1027).

The period of Fujiwara dictatorship was marked by a great flowering of Japanese culture, and by the growth of a civilization greatly influenced but not dominated by the Chinese civilization which had been its fountainhead. The dictatorship of Michinaga is regarded as the classical age of Japanese literature (q.v.). The character of the government also changed under the Fujiwara ascendancy. The centralized administration,

which became rife with corruption, weakened, and a medieval feudal system slowly took its place. Great nobles acquired large, hereditary estates as tax-free emoluments for their official positions. Most peasants were only too willing to attach their lands to such estates in order to escape the heavy burden of taxes on the public lands which had been meted out to them. Thus, great private estates became characteristic of land ownership throughout the Empire.

Clans became predominant in their chosen fields, such as the administration of religious rites or the cultivation of learning. Military commands were always given to the Taira and the Minamoto clans, both of which had been founded by Imperial princes. The Taira warriors acquired their military renown and power in the s.w.; the Minamoto in the E. and N. By the 11th century, when Japan entered a comparatively peaceful era in its home islands, both great military clans initiated efforts to extend their power to the court itself, dominated by the Fujiwara, and a struggle for control of Japan ensued. In 1156 a civil war began between the forces of two rival emperors and, after a second war, in 1160, the Taira ousted the Fujiwara and seized control of Japan. Conflict between the Minamoto and the Taira inevitably resulted. The Taira leader, Kiyomori (1118-81), was named prime minister in 1167 and, modeling his policies on those of the Fujiwara, married his daughter to an Imperial prince, their infant son becoming emperor in 1180. On the death of Kiyomori (1181), the Minamoto leader, Yoritomo (1147-99), led an uprising of clans from E. Japan and the Taira were driven from the capital. The civil war endured four years, ending with the naval battle of Dan no Ura (1185), near present Shimonoseki on the Inland Sea. Yoritomo became the leader of Japan, ending the era of Imperial administration and inaugurating a military dictatorship which ruled Japan for the next seven centuries.

Stressing the almost complete division between the civil and military phases of government, Minamoto Yoritomo established a separate, military capital at Kamakura, on Tokyo Bay. From that time forward Japanese feudalism developed until it was stronger than the Imperial administration had ever been. Under the Imperial system (604-1185), the provincial governors had been charged with both the collection of revenue and the repression of crime. When Yoritomo became the military ruler of the E., he had the emperor appoint him to a rank equal to high constable. Thus, while Imperial officials continued to collect revenue, the Minamoto leader superintended the maintenance of order and repression of crime. He established boards of military magistrates throughout the Empire, and their impartial justice was an important factor in strengthening the Minamoto regime. His constables, who were, in effect, military governors, became prominent in provincial administration, and he appointed stewards on the large, private estates to collect taxes for military funds. In 1192 Yoritomo was appointed to the office of *Seiidaishogun* ("barbarian-subduing great general"), usually shortened to *shogun* (q.v.), the military commander in chief. Through his military network, Yoritomo was already the virtual ruler of Japan and his shogunate made him titular leader as well. Imperial officers in charge of revenue left Kyoto for Kamakura, and the emperor and court were left entirely

dependent on the shogun. Kamakura became the true court and government, while Kyoto remained a titular court, without power.

In 1219 the Hojo clan, by means of a series of conspiracies and murders which eliminated Minamoto heirs and their supporters, became the military rulers of Japan. No Hojo ever became shogun; instead, the clan prevailed on the emperor to appoint figurehead shoguns, sometimes small children, while a Hojo leader governed as the *shikken*, or regent, with the actual power. For over a century the Hojo maintained their rule. In 1274 and again in 1281 the Mongols, then in control of China and Korea, attempted to invade Japan, each time unsuccessfully. The invasions were a serious drain on Hojo resources and, unable to reward their vassals for their support during the invasions, the Hojo shikkens were faced by increasing revolt at the beginning of the 14th century. In 1333 an able emperor, Daigo II (reigned 1318-39), led a rebellion which was climaxed in 1333 with the capture of Kamakura and the downfall of the Hojo. For the next two years Daigo tried to restore the Imperial administration. One of his vassals, Ashikaga Takauji (1305-58), revolted in 1335 and, driving Daigo from Kyoto, set up his own candidate for emperor. Daigo and his supporters fled to Yoshina, a region s. of Nara in N.E. Shikoku, and established a rival court. For the next fifty-six years civil war between Daigo and his successors and the emperors controlled by the Ashikaga, who became shoguns, ravaged Japan. At length, in 1392, an Ashikaga envoy persuaded the true emperor at Yoshino, to abdicate and relinquish the sacred Imperial regalia (mirror, crystal ball, and sword). With their nominees acknowledged as rightful emperors, the Ashikaga shoguns felt empowered to advance Japanese feudalism by making the military magistracies, which had been established by Yoritomo, hereditary in the families of their own nominees. This development was the beginning of a class of feudal lords known as *daimios* or *daimyos*. In general, the period of Ashikaga ascendancy was one of great refinement of manners, of great art and literary endeavor, and, notably, of the development of Buddhism as a political force. In the first half of the 16th century Buddhist clerics became so wealthy and powerful that they became one of the great forces in the state. Buddhist abbots and monks, clad in armor and bearing weapons, often turned the tide of medieval battles with their strong organizations and fortified monasteries. Local wars among feudal lords became common by the 16th century, which is still known in Japanese history as the "Epoch of a Warring Country."

Three great contemporary war lords finally established order in the strife-torn Empire. Nobunaga (1534-82), a Taira general, broke the power of the monasteries between 1568 and 1571, destroying Buddhism as a political force. Hideyoshi (1536-98), a follower of Nobunaga, united all of Japan under his rule, as civil dictator, in 1590. Using his power to its greatest extent, the dictator marked out the boundaries of all feudal fiefs and appointed his own nominees, or daimios, without referring his choices to the emperor. In 1603 the successor to Hideyoshi, Tokugawa Iyeyasu (1542-1616), became the first of the Tokugawa shoguns who ruled Japan for the succeeding two-and-a-half centuries. Iyeyasu made Edo (later Tokyo) his capital. In a comparatively short time the city became the greatest in the Empire, developing culturally and economically as well as politically. Iyeyasu brought the feudal organization which had been planned by Hideyoshi to fulfillment. The daimios and administrators, as well as the emperor and his court, were put under the strict control of the shogunate. Social classes became rigidly stratified. The form of feudalism established by Iyeyasu and succeeding Tokugawa shoguns endured until the end of the feudal period in the late 19th century.

Another result of Tokugawa domination was the imposed isolation of Japan from the western world. The first Europeans to visit Japan were Portugese traders who had landed on an island near Kyushu about 1542. St. Francis Xavier, the celebrated Jesuit missionary, had brought Christianity to Japan in 1549. During the remainder of the century about 300,000 Japanese were converted to Catholicism, despite disapproval and persecution by Hideyoshi. Portuguese, Spanish, and Dutch traders visited Japan more and more frequently. The shoguns became convinced that the introduction of Christianity was designed to serve as a preliminary to European conquest. In 1612 Christians became subject to official persecution and various massacres occurred. Spaniards were refused permission to land in Japan after 1624 and a series of edicts in the next decade forbade travel to and from Europe, prohibiting even the building of large ships. The only Europeans permitted to remain in Japan were a small group of Dutch traders restricted to the artificial island of Deshima in the harbor of Nagasaki, and continually subjected to indignities and limitations on their activities. During the succeeding two centuries the forms of Japanese feudalism remained static. *Bushido* (q.v.), the code of the feudal warriors, became the standard of conduct for the great lords and the lesser nobility, the professional warriors called *samurai* (q.v.). Japanese culture, closed to outside influence, grew inward and received intensive development resulting in extreme nationalism.

During the 18th century, however, new social and economic conditions in the islands began to indicate the inevitable collapse of rigid feudalism. A large, wealthy merchant class rose in such strength as to equal the warriors in influence. At that time, too, the fundamentally agricultural economy of Japan entered a decline, characterized by frequent rebellions of peasants who resented their poverty-stricken status as landless tenants.

The awakening consciousness of Japan to the outside world was formally evidenced in 1720 when Tokugawa Yoshimune, then shogun, repealed the proscription on European books and study. By the early 19th century visits from Europeans, mostly traders and explorers, became comparatively frequent, though the ban was still officially in force. The United States was particularly anxious to make a treaty of friendship and, if possible, one of commerce with Japan. One of the major factors on which this American policy was compounded was the circumstance of the shipwrecking of American whaling ships on the Japanese coast. In 1852 the American government appointed Commodore Matthew Calbraith Perry (q.v.) to head a formal mission, with a squadron of naval ships, to the emperor of Japan. After almost a year of negotiations, Perry and representatives of the emperor signed a treaty (Mar. 31, 1854) establishing trade relations between the U.S. and Japan. In 1860 a Japanese embassy was sent to the U.S., and two years later Japanese trade missions visited European capitals to negotiate formal agreements.

The opening of Japan was due more to the show of superior force by western nations than to an actual desire for foreign relations on the part of Japanese leaders. The Japanese war lords, equipped with medieval weapons and trained in small-scale warfare, were dismayed by western military equipment and dared not, at first, resist. Nevertheless, a militant antiforeign faction immediately developed and attacks on foreign traders became common occurrences in the 1860's. The leaders of the antiforeign movement were the great clans which had always resented Tokugawa rule from Edo. They rallied around the emperor at Kyoto and, with Imperial support, initiated military and naval attacks on foreign ships in Japanese harbors. The antiforeign movement was short-lived, ending in 1864, but it resulted in the decline of the shogunate and the restoration of Imperial administration. In 1867 the last shogun, Hitotsubashi Yoshinobu, resigned and the emperor, Mutsuhito, regained the position of actual head of the government, with the support of the s.w. clans. Mutsuhito took the name of Meiji ("Enlightened Government") to designate himself and his reign. The Imperial capital was transferred to Edo, renamed Tokyo ("Eastern Capital"). In 1869 the lords of the great Choshu, Hizen, Satsuma, and Tosa clans surrendered their feudal fiefs to the emperor and, after a succession of such surrenders by other clans, an Imperial decree in 1871 abolished all fiefs and created centrally-administered prefectures in their stead. The suppression of the feudal system marked the political ascendancy of the upper middle classes led by trading families.

Under the direction of such farsighted statesmen as Tomomi Iwakura and Toshimichi Okubo the Japanese remained untouched by the European imperialism which, at the time, was engulfing other Asiatic countries and, by concerted imitation of western civilization in all its aspects, set out to make Japan itself a world power (see FAR EASTERN QUESTION). French officers were engaged to remodel the army, British seamen reorganized the navy, and Dutch engineers supervised new construction in the islands. Japanese were sent abroad to analyze foreign governments and to select their best features for duplication in Japan. A new penal code was modeled on that of France, and a ministry of education was established (1871) to develop a system of universal education based on that of the U.S. Universal military service was decreed in 1872 and four years later the samurai class of professional warriors was abolished by decree. These far-reaching changes were not accomplished without protest from the war lords. In 1877, resentful of the treatment accorded the samurai, General Saigo Takamori, a leader of the Sat-

suma clan, led a samurai revolt against, as he put it, the emperor's "evil advisers". The so-called Satsuma Rebellion was put down in less than a year by the modernized Imperial army and marked the final repression of the medieval warriors as an organized class.

The Japanese political system, developed along European and, particularly, German lines, became full-grown during the 1880-90 decade. In 1881 the emperor promised formally to establish a national legislature and in 1884, preparing for an upper house, he created a peerage with five orders of nobility. A cabinet modeled on that of Germany was organized in 1885 with Marquis Hirobumi Ito (q.v.) as the first prime minister, and a privy council was created in 1888, both being responsible to the emperor. The new constitution, drafted by Marquis Ito after constitutional research in Europe and the U.S., was promulgated in 1889. A two-house Diet was designed to have a house of peers of 363 members, and a 463-member lower house elected by citizens paying direct annual taxes of not less than 15 yen. The emperor's powers were carefully safeguarded; he was permitted to issue decrees as laws, and only he could decide on war or the cessation of war. Moreover, the lower house could be dissolved and the upper prorogued by Imperial decree. Rapid industrialization, under government direction, accompanied this concentrated political growth. By 1890 Japan had about 200 steam factories. The first railway had begun operations in 1872 and mileage was continually added thereafter. By 1893 the construction of steamships totaled 15,000 tons, and steamship construction increased steadily thereafter; control of strategic industries, such as communications, shipbuilding, and munitions, was retained by the government. Even when great commercial trusts, such as those of the Mitsui and Mitsubishi, took over direction of such industries, leaders of the Japanese state kept essential control.

The Empire also began to organize its policies on an international scale. In 1879 Japan had taken over the islands of the Ryukyu archipelago, designating them the prefecture of Okinawa. The struggle for control of Korea became the next step in Japanese expansion. Conflict with China in Korea resulted in the Sino-Japanese War (1894-95), in which the modernized Japanese forces completely and easily defeated the Chinese army and navy. By the terms of the Treaty of Shimonoseki in April, 1895, China gave Japan Formosa, the Pescadores, and a large monetary indemnity. The treaty had originally awarded the Liaotung peninsula (s. Manchuria) to Japan, in addition; but intervention by Russia, France, and Germany forced Japan to accept an additional indemnity instead.

The decisive Japanese triumph indicated to the world that a new, great power was rising in the East. As a preliminary to negotiating full equality with the great powers, Japan, in 1890, had completely revised its criminal, civil, and commercial law codes on Western models. Thus, the Empire was in a position to demand the revocation of extraterritoriality (q.v.) clauses from its treaties. By 1899 all the great powers had signed treaties abandoning extraterritoriality in Japan. The U.S. and Great Britain, the first nations to do so (1894), were given the freedom of the entire Empire for trade.

In pursuing its interests in Korea, Japan inevitably conflicted with Russia. Resentment against Russia was already high because that country had been the principal agent in depriving Japan of the Liaotung peninsula after the Chinese war. The two countries signed a treaty pledging the independence of Korea in 1898, but allowing Japanese commercial interests to predominate. In 1900, following the Boxer Rebellion (see BOXERS) in China, Russia occupied Manchuria and, from bases there, began to penetrate N. Korea. In 1904, after repeated attempts to negotiate the matter had failed, Japan broke off diplomatic relations with Russia and attacked Russian-leased Port Arthur in s. Manchuria, beginning the Russo-Japanese War (q.v.). Japan won its second modern war in less than eighteen months. The peace treaty, mediated by U.S. President Theodore Roosevelt, was signed in Portsmouth, New Hampshire, on Sept. 5, 1905. Japan was awarded the lease (to 1923, later extended to 1997) of the Liaotung peninsula, including the Kwantung territory, and the s. half of Sakhalin, thereafter known as Karafuto. Moreover, Russia acknowledged the paramount interest of Japan in Korea. Five years later (1910) Korea, called Chosen, was formally annexed to Japan. (See KOREA; RUSSIA; MANCHURIA. Details of Sino-Japanese relations from the end of the 19th century to the present will be found under CHINA.)

The status of Japan as an acknowledged world power had been evidenced also in 1905, with the signing of the Anglo-Japanese Alliance (q.v.). The signatories guaranteed to respect each other's territorial rights in India and E. Asia. When the treaty was renewed in 1911 (for ten years), a new clause specified that neither Britain nor Japan would be obligated to go to war with a nation with which one of the signatories had signed an arbitration treaty. This clause was required by Great Britain, then negotiating an arbitration treaty with the U.S. Japanese-American relations had for some years been strained by difficulties over Japanese emigration to the United States. Thousands of Japanese had settled in the States of California, Oregon, and Washington, and the American residents of these States demanded their exclusion by legislation similar to the Chinese Exclusion Acts of 1882, 1892, and 1902. This agitation was led by American labor unions, resenting the fact that Japanese laborers were willing to work for less wages and longer hours than those called for by American labor policies. Formal protests against the treatment of Japanese in Pacific-coast States were delivered by the Japanese ambassador in Washington (1906), and, after a series of negotiations, Japan and the U.S. concluded a so-called "gentleman's agreement" in 1908. By this extralegal agreement, confirmed in 1911, Japan consented to withhold passports from laborers, and the U.S. Department of State promised to disapprove anti-Japanese legislation. The problem, however, was never fully resolved and was a contributing factor to anti-American feeling in Japan, which increased in the following three decades.

In Japan, popular resentment against the unsatisfactory negotiations with the U.S. was a major factor in the fall of a ministry headed by Count Gombei Yamamoto in 1914. Criticism of the government, and particularly of the *Genro,* or "elder statesmen", who were the confidential advisers of the emperor, had been evident since the Russo-Japanese War, which had been very costly. Several attempts were made by Japanese political parties to destroy the influence of the Genro, but Emperor Yoshihito (q.v.), who as Taisho ("Great Righteousness") succeeded his father Mutsuhito in 1912, allowed Genro influence to prevail. Moreover, political parties then exercised little actual influence, only 1,500,000 out of a population of more than 50,000,000 being enfranchised. An added factor in popular discontent with the government was the heavy taxation necessary to maintain the army and navy. In 1912 alone the naval program included the building of eight armored cruisers and eight battleships.

In Aug., 1914, following the outbreak of World War I, Japan sent an ultimatum to Germany, demanding the evacuation of the German-leased territory of Kiaochow (q.v.) in N.E. China. When Germany refused to comply, Japan entered the war on the side of the Allies. The fortress of Tsingtao, on Kiaochow Bay, was attacked by Japanese and British warships and a landing force of 50,000 Japanese troops. The fortress capitulated after an eleven-week siege and was occupied by Japan. During the same period Japanese troops occupied the German-held Marshall, Caroline, and Marianas islands in the Pacific Ocean. In 1915 the Empire submitted the Twenty-One Demands to China, calling for industrial, railway, and mining privileges, and a promise that China would not lease or give any coastal territory to a nation other than Japan. These demands, which were quickly granted, were the first statement of the Japanese policy of domination over China and the Far East. A year later (1916) China ceded commercial rights in Inner Mongolia and s. Manchuria to Japan.

As a result of the World War I peace settlement, Japan received the Pacific islands which it had occupied during World War I as mandates from the League of Nations, the Empire having become a charter member of that organization. The territory of Kiaochow was also awarded to Japan, but the Empire restored Kiaochow to China in 1922 as a result of an agreement, the Shantung Treaty, made during the Washington Conference (q.v.) in 1922. This conference also resulted in the replacement of the Anglo-Japanese Alliance by the Four-Power Treaty, by which Japan, France, Great Britain, and the U.S. pledged themselves to respect one another's territories in the Pacific Ocean and to consult if their territorial rights were threatened. The Nine-Power Treaty (Belgium, the British Empire, the Netherlands, Portugal, Japan, France, Italy, China, and the U.S.) bound the signatories to respect the territorial integrity and sovereignty of China. An additional treaty between Great Britain, the U.S., and Japan dealt with naval disarmament on a 5-5-3 ratio, respectively, the Japanese navy being limited to 315,000 tons of capital ships (see DISARMAMENT).

Sino-Japanese relations following the Shantung and Nine-Power treaties were friendly; Japan was almost conciliatory, though the Empire continued to regard its interests, particularly in commerce, as paramount in China. Russo-Japanese relations, which had become strained after the Russian Revolution in 1917 and the subsequent invasion of Siberia and N. Sakhalin (1918) by the Japanese, became more amicable after Japan recognized the Soviet Union in 1925. This less aggressive attitude on the part of Japan was due in great part to events within Japan proper. In 1923 a great earthquake devastated Yokohama, Tokyo, and other cities, occasioning losses estimated at a billion dollars. The resulting economic and physical havoc was a major factor in Japan's change of policy. Another factor was a surge of political liberalism stimulated by the victory of the democratic states in World War I. This liberalism was evidenced by the increasing influence of the two leading Japanese political parties: the Seiyukai, a moderate party, representing landowning and commercial interests; and the Minseito, or Democratic Party, representing, chiefly, urban interests. Beginning with 1919 the government was assailed with increasing demands for universal suffrage, an issue which occasioned rioting in the cities. To placate these demands the government, in 1919, passed a reform act doubling the electorate (to 3,000,000); but the universal suffrage issue became more intense until it was granted by a 1925 bill, increasing the electorate to 14,000,000. Reflecting the rising interest in popular government, the political trend during the 1920-30 decade was toward party cabinets and away from oligarchic rule by the "elder statesmen", the nobility, and military leaders. This movement was short-lived, lasting only until about 1932, when totalitarianism became the trend of Japanese government.

Hirohito (q.v.), adopting *Showa* ("Light and Peace") as the official designation for his reign, succeeded as emperor in 1926. One year later Gen. Baron Gi-ichi Tanaka (q.v.) became prime minister, and declared the resumption of an aggressive policy in China. The impelling factor in this change of policy lay in the expansion in Japanese industry which began with the declaration of World War I in 1914 and was then continuing at a great pace, requiring new markets for the increased output.

Japan had played only a minor military

Canadian Pacific Railway; Ewing Galloway

Left: Japanese woman at work in a flooded rice field. Right: A Japanese farmer and his wife working a treadmill by which water is pumped from a ditch to a rice field.

role during World War I, devoting itself instead to shipping, foreign trade, and to replacing Germany as a commercial power in the Far East. The trade balances Japan acquired during the war were used to expand industrial capacity. In 1915 Japanese exports amounted to about $316,200,000; in 1922 exports rose to over $818,700,000. By 1929 the value of manufactured products alone was almost $3,900,000,000. A tremendous factor in this industrial expansion was the available labor supply in the Japanese islands. The population of Japan had been about 35,000,000 in 1872; in 1930 it was about 65,000,000. During a single 5-year period (1920-25), the population increased by almost 4,000,000 and by 1930 the rate of increase was about 1,000,000 a year. Overpopulation, moreover, resulted in a supply of workers willing to work for exceedingly low wages. The low standard of living, and a high standard of industrial efficiency, comparable to European or American standards, enabled Japanese industrialists to keep prices low. Textiles were the leading manufactured product during the industrial expansion of the 1920's, but the change to aggression in foreign policy was reflected in an increase in heavy industry. By 1937 the chemical, machinery, and metal industries accounted for 60% of the total value of all manufactures. Moreover, conditions in industry became a contributing factor to the growth of military rule. The international economic crises which began in 1929 was strongly evident in Japan, resulting in severe losses to farmers and industrial unemployment. The situation gave the great industrialists a reason for supporting military aggression which would supply new markets.

In the late 1920's Japan, in effect, gained domination of the administrative and economic affairs of Manchuria. The Chinese, however, increasingly resented Japanese interference in what was, technically, part of China. On Sept. 18, 1931, the Japanese army in Kwantung, claiming that an explosion on the Japanese-owned South Manchuria Railroad had been caused by Chinese saboteurs, seized the arsenals of Mukden and of several neighboring cities. Chinese troops were forced to withdraw from the area. Entirely without official sanction by the Japanese government, the Kwantung army extended its operations into all of Manchuria and, in about five months, was in possession of the entire region. Manchuria was then reestablished as an independent state, Manchukuo, controlled by Japan through a puppet ruler, Henry Pu-Yi (see Hsuan T'ung), who was made regent and later (1934) emperor.

All pretense of party government in Japan was abandoned as a result of the occupation of Manchuria. Admiral Viscount Makoto Saito formed a so-called national cabinet composed, chiefly, of men who belonged to no party. The international repercussions of the Manchurian incident resulted in an inquiry by a League of Nations commission, acting by authority of the Kellogg-Briand Pact (q.v.). When, in 1933, the League Assembly requested that Japan cease hostilities in China, Japan instead announced its withdrawal from the League, to take effect in 1935. To consolidate its gains in China, Japan landed troops in Shanghai to quell an effective Chinese boycott of Japanese goods. In the N. the Japanese Manchurian army occupied and annexed the province of Jehol, and threatened to occupy the cities of Peiping and Tientsin. Unable to resist the superior Japanese forces, China, in May, 1933, recognized the Japanese conquest by signing a truce.

The acquisition of Manchuria at once eased the economic crises within Japan proper by supplying a market for Japanese goods. Moreover, the independent action of the army evidenced the power of the military leaders as the controlling element in Japanese politics. Military expenditures in 1935 were more than 50% of the national budget and increased each following year. The cabinet, chosen in Feb., 1937, had to be approved by the army before it could take office. In its foreign relations Japan isolated itself from the U.S. and the European democracies. In 1936 the Empire signed an anti-communist pact with Nazi Germany and, one year later, a similar pact with Fascist Italy. The establishment of almost

complete military rule, with the co-operation of the Zaibatsu, made aggression and expansion the avowed policy of the Empire.

On July 7, 1937, a Chinese patrol clashed with Japanese troops on the Marco Polo Bridge near Peiping. Using the incident as a pretext to begin hostilities, the Japanese army in Manchukuo moved troops into the area, precipitating another Sino-Japanese War, never actually declared. A Japanese force quickly overran N. China. By the end of 1937 the Japanese navy had completed a blockade of almost the entire Chinese coast. The army advanced into E. and S. China throughout 1937 and 1938, capturing, successively, Shanghai, Soochow, Nanking, Tsingtao, Canton, and Hankow, and forcing the Chinese army into the w. A Japanese force occupied the island of Hainan. Protests by foreign governments concerning property owned by their nationals and mistreatment, by Japanese troops, of foreigners resident in China, were, in effect, ignored by the Empire. By the end of 1938 the war reached a virtual stalemate. The Japanese army was checked by the mountains of central China, behind which the Kuomintang government of Chiang Kai-shek directed a guerrilla warfare against the invaders.

Japan, meanwhile, was subjected to controlled war economy. In 1937 a cabinet headed by Prince Fumimaro Konoye (q.v.) relegated the entire conduct of the war, without government interference, to military and naval leaders. To eliminate criticism of the military regime the cabinet authorized the arrest of the liberals, radicals, and leaders of organized groups, such as labor unions, which were hostile to the authoritarian rule by the military. In 1938 the Konoye cabinet had the National Mobilization Bill enacted, providing a legal basis for almost entire state control of capital, industry, and labor.

The beginning of World War II in Europe, in Sept., 1939, gave Japan new opportunity for aggression in S.E. Asia. These aggressive acts were prefaced by a series of diplomatic arrangements. In Sept., 1940, the Empire concluded a tripartite alliance with Germany and Italy, the so-called Rome-Berlin Axis, pledging mutual and total aid for a period of ten years. Japan considered, however, that a 1939 neutrality pact between Germany and the Soviet Union had released the Empire from any obligation incurred by the 1936 anti-Communist alliance. In Sept., 1941, therefore, Japan signed a neutrality pact with the Soviet Union, thus protecting the

N. border of Manchuria. A year before, with the consent of the German-sponsored Vichy government of France, Japanese forces occupied French Indochina (see INDOCHINA, ASSOCIATED STATES OF). At the same time Japan tried to obtain economic and political footholds in the Netherlands East Indies.

These acts, in Indochina and the East Indies, contributed to increasing hostility between Japan and the United States. The protection of American property in E. Asia had been a source of friction since the Japanese invasion of China in 1937. Continued protests from Joseph Clark Grew, then U.S. ambassador to Japan, were fruitless. In October, 1941, Gen. Hideki Tojo (q.v.), who was militantly anti-American, became the Japanese premier and minister of war. After vain attempts to negotiate and several exchanges of notes, the U.S., on Nov. 26, 1941, presented a tentative agreement to Saburo Kurusu, then Japanese Ambassador to the U.S. The agreement called for the withdrawal of Japanese troops from China and Indochina, guarantees of territorial integrity in the Far East, support of the Kuomintang government of China, and nonaggression pacts with governments concerned in the Pacific area.

On Dec. 7, 1941, without warning and while negotiations between American and Japanese diplomats were still in progress, Japanese carrier-based airplanes attacked Pearl Harbor, the main American naval base in the Pacific. Simultaneous attacks were launched by the Japanese army, navy, and air force against the Philippine Islands, Guam, Wake Island, Midway Island, Hong Kong, British Malaya, and Siam (qq.v.). On Dec. 8 the U.S. Congress declared war on Japan, as did all the Allied powers with the exception of the U.S.S.R. For a detailed analysis of the military and naval conflict in the Asiatic and Pacific theaters of war, see WORLD WAR II.

For about a year following the successful surprise attacks, Japan maintained the offensive in S.E. Asia and the islands of the South Pacific. The Empire designated E. Asia and its environs as the "Greater East Asia Co-Prosperity Sphere" and made effective propaganda of the slogan "Asia for the Asiatics". Moreover, nationalistic elements in many of the countries of E. Asia gave tacit and, in some cases, active support to the Japanese, because they saw an apparent way to free themselves from Western imperialism. In December, 1941, Japan invaded Siam, forcing the government to conclude a treaty of alliance. Japanese troops occupied Burma, British Malaya, Borneo, Hong Kong, and the Netherlands East Indies. By May, 1942, the Philippines were in Japanese hands. Striking toward Australia and New Zealand, Japanese forces landed in New Guinea, New Britain, and the Solomon Islands. A Japanese task force invaded the North American continent, occupying Attu, Agattu, and Miska in the Aleutian Islands off the Alaskan coast. Ultimately, however, the war became a naval struggle for control of the vast expanses of the Pacific Ocean. Allied operations against the Japanese were conducted almost entirely by U.S. forces.

The tide of battle began to change in 1942, when an Allied naval and air force defeated a Japanese invasion fleet in the Battle of the Coral Sea (q.v.) between New Guinea and the Solomon Islands. A month later an even larger Japanese fleet was defeated in the Battle of Midway (q.v.). Using combined operations of military, naval, and air units under the command of Gen. Douglas MacArthur (q.v.), Allied forces fought northward from island to island in the South Pacific, invading and driving out the Japanese. In July, 1944, after the fall of Saipan, a major Japanese base in the Marianas Islands, the Japanese leaders realized that Japan had lost the war. Tojo was forced to resign, weakening the hold of the military oligarchy. In Nov., 1944, the U.S. began a series of major air raids over Japan by B-29 bombers based on Saipan. In early 1945 an air base even closer to Japan (750 m.) was acquired with the conquest, after a fierce battle, of Iwo Jima (q.v.). During the same period Allied forces under Admiral Lord Louis Mountbatten (q.v.) defeated the Japanese armies in S.E. Asia. In the next four months (May-Aug.) bombing attacks devastated Japanese communications, industry, and what was left of the navy. These attacks were climaxed on Aug. 6 by the dropping of the first atomic bomb (see ATOMIC ENERGY) on the city of Hiroshima (q.v.). Two days later (Aug. 8) the Soviet Union declared war on Japan, and on Aug. 9 a second atomic bomb was dropped on Nagasaki. Russian forces invaded Manchuria, Korea, and Karafuto. By the terms of the Potsdam Declaration (q.v.) the Allied powers had agreed that only unconditional surrender would be acceptable from the Japanese government. On Aug. 14 Japan accepted the Allied terms, signing the formal surrender aboard the U.S. battleship *Missouri* in Tokyo Bay on Sept. 2. Ten days later the Japanese commanders in s.e. Asia formally surrendered to the British at Singapore.

The U.S. army was designated, by the Allied powers, as the army of occupation in the Japanese home islands. Japan was stripped of its empire. Inner Mongolia, Manchuria, Formosa, and Hainan were returned to China. The U.S.S.R. was awarded the Kuril Islands and Karafuto, and the control of Outer Mongolia; Port Arthur and the South Manchurian Railway were placed under the joint control of the U.S.S.R. and China. All the former Japanese mandated islands in the South Pacific were occupied by the U.S. under a United Nations trusteeship.

On Aug. 11, 1945, following the Japanese offer of unconditional surrender, Gen. Douglas MacArthur (q.v.) was appointed Supreme Commander of the Allied Powers occupying Japan. Representatives of China, the U.S.S.R., and the British Empire were named to an Allied Council for Japan, sitting in Tokyo, to assist MacArthur. Broad questions of occupation policy became the province of the Far Eastern Commission, sitting in Washington, D.C., representing the United States, the United Kingdom, the U.S.S.R., Australia, Canada, China, France, India, the Netherlands, New Zealand, and the Philippines.

The American occupation of the Japanese islands was in no way resisted. The demilitarization of Japan was at once put into effect, and, by Dec., 1945, the Japanese army, navy, and air force in the islands were disarmed and demobilized. The objectives of the occupation policy were declared to be, basically, the democratization of the Japanese government and the re-establishment of a peacetime industrial economy sufficient for the Japanese population. The Supreme Commander for the Allied Powers (SCAP), Gen. MacArthur, was directed to exercise his authority through the emperor and existing government machinery as far as possible. Among other Allied objectives were the dissolution of the great industrial and banking trusts, the assets of which were seized in 1946 and later liquidated through the SCAP. A program of land reform, designed to give the tenants of the great, private estates an opportunity to purchase the land they worked, was in operation by 1947, and an education program along democratic lines was organized. Women were

given the franchise in the first postwar Japanese general election in April, 1946, and 38 women were elected to the Japanese Diet. The 1946 Diet was elected to approve a new constitution, which was written in that year and put into effect in May, 1947. By its terms, the emperor became merely a symbol of state, without important political powers. The peerage and privy council were abolished. The Diet, reconstituted with the House of Councilors as the upper house and the House of Representatives as the lower, was made the highest state body, with the cabinet responsible to it. A Bill of Rights, similar to that embodied in the American Constitution, was included in the constitution. Among other activities of SCAP was the organization of procedure for trying war criminals, including statesmen such as Tojo.

The rehabilitation of the Japanese economy was more difficult than the reorganization of the government. The scarcity of food had to be offset by imports from the Allied powers, and from the U.S. in particular. Severe bombings during the war had almost nullified Japanese industrial capacity. By the beginning of 1949 aid to Japan was costing the U.S. more than $1,000,000 a day.

Beginning in May work stoppages took place in various Japanese industries, notably coal mining. The government accused the Communist Party, which had polled 3,000,000 votes in a recent national election, of instigating the strike movement for political purposes. SCAP concurred in this view, and subsequently the government launched a large-scale investigation of Communist activities. Gen. MacArthur's labor policies were sharply criticized (June, 1949) by the Soviet member of the Allied Control Council. In his reply, Gen. MacArthur accused the U.S.S.R. of fomenting disorder in Japan through the Communist Party and of "callous indifference" in repatriating Japanese prisoners of war. For the next year communism and repatriation were dominant issues in national politics. The Soviet Union announced in April, 1950, that, excluding about 10,000 war criminals, all prisoners (94,973) had been returned to Japan, but according to Japanese records over 300,000 prisoners were still in Soviet custody. At SCAP's direction the government decreed (June 6) that the top leaders of the Communist Party could not hold public office and banned (June 24) the chief Communist publication. The government's anti-Red campaign was intensified after the outbreak (June 25) of the Korean War.

Burton Holmes

Ainu tribesmen on the northern island of Hokkaido, Japan

Allied negotiations during 1950 relative to a Japanese peace treaty were marked by basic differences between the United States and the Soviet Union on several issues, especially whether Red China should participate in the drafting of the document. On May 18 the American Republican statesman John Foster Dulles, adviser to the U.S. secretary of state, was named to prepare the terms of the treaty. More than a year of consultations and negotiations with and among the Allied powers, Japan, and the Far Eastern nations which had fought against Japan culminated (July 12, 1951) in the publication of the draft treaty. The U.S.S.R., which had been consulted also, criticized the document, maintaining it was conducive to the resurgence of Japanese militarism. On July 20 the U.S. government invited fifty-four countries to attend the peace conference. Invitations were not extended to Nationalist China or Communist China.

The peace conference opened in San Francisco, Calif., on Sept. 4. Of the nations invited, the Indian Union, Burma, and Yugoslavia refused to attend. During the conference discussion was limited to the previously prepared treaty text, a procedure which nullified Soviet attempts to reopen negotiations on its various provisions. Forty-nine countries, including Japan, signed the treaty on Sept. 8; the U.S.S.R., Czechoslovakia, and Poland refused to do so.

By the terms of the treaty Japan renounced all claims to Korea, Formosa, the Kuriles, Sakhalin, and former mandated islands and relinquished any special rights and interests in China and Korea; the right of Japan to defend itself and enter into collective-security arrangements was recognized; Japan accepted the validity of reparations claims, to be paid in goods and services in view of the country's insufficient financial resources.

Later on Sept. 8 the United States and Japan signed a bilateral agreement providing for the

Canadian Pacific Railway

Pagoda in Nara, Japan, built in 1462

land. Recognizing the importance of the Chinese market, the United States granted (Oct. 1, 1951) Japan the right to carry on limited trade with Communist China.

On April 28, 1952, the Japanese peace treaty became effective and full sovereignty was restored to Japan. By the terms of the Japanese-American treaty of 1951 U.S. troops remained in Japan as security forces. The Japanese government concluded treaties of peace or renewed diplomatic relations during 1952 with Nationalist China, Burma, the Union of India, and Yugoslavia. It suspended negotiations with the Republic of the Philippines on reparations on Feb. 13, taking the position that Filipino demands were excessive. The Allied Council for Japan, of which the U.S.S.R. had been a member, was disbanded on April 23. Inasmuch as the U.S.S.R. had not signed the peace treaty with Japan, the Soviet mission continued to function. On May 6 the Japanese government, finding this situation intolerable, requested the Soviet representatives to leave the country. The request was rejected by the U.S.S.R. On Sept. 18 the Soviet Union vetoed a U.N. Security Council resolution approving admission of Japan to the United Nations.

The question of rearmament was widely debated throughout 1952. The government was reluctant to commit itself in favor of rebuilding the country's defenses, mainly because of economic difficulties, legal obstacles (in the Japanese constitution of 1947 war is renounced "forever"), and the widespread fear among the populace of the resurgence of militarism. However, steps were taken to expand the National Police Reserve and the Coast Guard.

After heated debate the Diet approved (July 21) a bill to suppress the activities of subversive groups, including the communists, whose demonstrations on May 1, 1952, had been particularly violent. In general elections on Oct. 1, the first since the end of the occupation, Premier Shigeru Yoshida's Liberal Party lost strength but retained its majority in the Diet. The communists lost all of their 22 seats, and the socialists, who openly opposed rearmament, made important gains. Yoshida was again named premier.

On Mar. 14, 1953, Premier Yoshida, after losing a vote of confidence on proposals for increased centralization of the school system and the police force, scheduled new elections. The electorate went to the polls in April and again returned the Liberals to power. Yoshida was renamed premier on May 19, but his government's position in the Diet was made

maintenance of U.S. military bases and armed forces in and around Japan to protect the disarmed country from aggression or from large-scale internal disturbances.

Meanwhile, Gen. MacArthur had been relieved of his post as SCAP on April 11. Lt. Gen. Matthew Bunker Ridgway, then commander of the U.N. forces in Korea, succeeded him. On June 30 the United States had terminated economic aid to Japan, but the detrimental effect of this action on the Japanese economy was largely offset by American military procurement orders for the Korean War. The country's chief economic problem stemmed mainly from the wartime loss of overseas markets, especially the Chinese main-

tenuous by the emergence of an anti-Liberal coalition of the opposition parties. During the year Japan completed trade agreements with Pakistan, West Germany, Nationalist China, and the U.S.S.R. Trade with Communist China, in items approved by the United States, increased from $700,000 in 1952 to $3 million in the first seven months of 1953. The Chinese Communists began (Mar. 23) the release of approximately 30,000 Japanese interned in China during World War II. On April 2 Japan and the United States signed a ten-year treaty of friendship, commerce, and navigation. The Philippines government granted amnesty on June 27 to 113 Japanese war criminals. Japan agreed (June 29) to pay reparations to the Philippines.

During 1953 the U.S. government, seeking further to safeguard the country against possible communist aggression, actively encouraged Japan to rearm. On Aug. 6 the two countries signed a military-aid treaty which contained provision for the manufacture of Japanese arms according to American specifications. In a joint statement (Sept. 27) Premier Yoshida and Mamoru Shigemitsu, Progressive Party leader, officially recommended that Japan rearm for self-defense and that the constitution be amended accordingly.

On Dec. 24, the United States restored to Japanese control the Amami Is. (pop., about 213,000), situated between Okinawa and Japan. The ten islands were the first of the Japanese territories lost in World War II to be returned to Japan.

JAPANESE ART AND ARCHITECTURE, that work produced in Japan from the 6th century A.D. to the present. At first strongly and repeatedly influenced by the arts of China, the Japanese rapidly assimilated the lessons learned from the Chinese and developed their own forms and techniques. In painting, architecture, and the other arts, with few exceptions, the Japanese have always preferred working in light materials such as wood, paper, and silk to obtain the light, spacious, and naturalistic effects for which they are known. Although they also made use of stone and bronze, most of their production has been in nondurable materials; nevertheless, a great number of early works have been preserved through diligent care.

Architecture. Throughout its long historical continuity from the 6th century to the present day, the basic structure in Japanese architecture has been a skeleton framework of timbers carrying a peaked roof or series of roofs. As in related Chinese and Korean architecture, the principal building material is wood; stone, a secondary material, is often used for foundations, stairways, and terraces. The most distinctive external feature is the roof, gabled or hipped, with a concave-curved sweep and wide eaves turned up at the corners. The bracketed skeleton framework which supports it is mortised or halved into round or square posts spaced at regular intervals so that the walls, which often are made of paper, serve only as screens against the weather and for privacy.

Although the main tradition of Japanese architecture begins with the adoption of Buddhism as the state religion in the 6th century, a few vestiges of pre-Buddhist indigenous architecture survive. One example, the Imperial Ise Shrine, a plain white wood structure thatched in bark, built before the 4th century, exists today because it has been rebuilt in exact replica every twenty years since it was first erected. Buddhism, imported by Korean monks from China, brought with it the building styles of the contemporary Chinese Six dynasties and, later, of the T'ang dynasty. Extant examples of Chinese style carried to Japan include the pagoda and temple hall at Horyiuji (early 7th century), which are believed to be the oldest wooden buildings in the world; and the monasteries, much rebuilt, at Horyiuji, Nara, and Osaka. Japanese modification and simplification of the style are seen in the Yakushiji pagoda near Nara (7th century), and in small temples such as Todaiji and Yakushiji. Much of the subsequent history of Japanese architecture may be traced in terms of successively waxing and waning influence from China, and also in the special demands of various religious sects. A large number of castles, palaces, and temples, both Buddhist and Shinto, have survived. Notable among them are the 11th-century temple of Howodo near Uji-Yamada, the 12th-century pagoda of the Kofukiji at Nara, the 15th-century Kinkauji and Ginkakuji palace pavilions at Kyoto, elements of the 16th-century castles in Nishi Hongwanji, Kyoto, and the elaborate 17th-century mausoleums at Nikko and the Nijo palace in Kyoto.

The style of the present-day typical dwelling house began to take form in the Fujiwara and Kamakara periods, from 889 to 1335, with the development of a new domestic and palace architecture. The interior of the new buildings was better lighted; two other innovations were the *tokonoma,* a recess for the display of paintings and orna-

Art Institute of Chicago

JAPANESE PAINTING

Above: Section of a painted folding screen, attributed to the 17th-century court painter Kano Tanyu. Left: "Woman with a Hand Mirror," by Hashimoto Goyo.

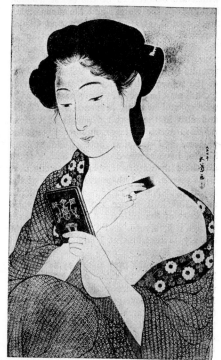

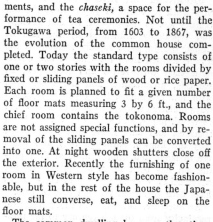

ments, and the *chaseki,* a space for the performance of tea ceremonies. Not until the Tokugawa period, from 1603 to 1867, was the evolution of the common house completed. Today the standard type consists of one or two stories with the rooms divided by fixed or sliding panels of wood or rice paper. Each room is planned to fit a given number of floor mats measuring 3 by 6 ft., and the chief room contains the tokonoma. Rooms are not assigned special functions, and by removal of the sliding panels can be converted into one. At night wooden shutters close off the exterior. Recently the furnishing of one room in Western style has become fashionable, but in the rest of the house the Japanese still converse, eat, and sleep on the floor mats.

The common dwelling house, rather than the monumental examples of Japanese architecture, has had a direct influence on modern Western architecture. Although more often working in steel and concrete than in wood and tile, Western architects in recent years have admired and emulated Japanese integration of structure and garden, and the general tendency toward low-lying horizontal proportions, spaciousness, and cleanness of line. Reciprocally, the Japanese since the late 19th century have extensively followed Western styles in the design of nonresidential buildings. Modern ferroconcrete and glass structures are common for Japanese factories, department stores, and public buildings.

Painting and Sculpture. Japanese civilized art began at the end of the 6th century with the introduction of Buddhism from Korea, after the conquest of that country by the Japanese empress Suiko in 593. The Suiko bronze Buddhas were like the 5th century Korean Buddhas. One of the major works of the Suiko period is a large wood carving of a Kwannon (goddess of mercy) in contemplation, in the temple of Chuguji. In the 7th century, attempts were made to discard the clumsier features of the primitive models and achieve more graceful and delicate effects. Many statuettes of bodhisattvas date from this period, depicting the Buddhist conception of a being who has advanced so far in wisdom and insight, and in the renunciation of fleshly ties, as to be on the point of entrance into Nirvana and salvation. One example is the standing Buddha, Yakushi Niorai, symbol of Buddha as the great soul physician, the most sacred altarpiece of the Yakushiji temple in Nara.

In 708 copper was discovered in Japan in large quantities, making possible the casting of bronze images of large size. The style of this bronze work was a synthesis of the new Greco-Buddhist ideals, coming from India through China, and the gentle quality of the statuettes. New delicacy of feeling, remarkable finish, and great dignity and grace mark this work. A supreme example of the new group of large bronze deities is the Black Bronze Trinity at Yakushiji (about 720).

The end of the 8th century witnessed the degeneration of Greco-Buddhist art in Japan. Mystical Buddhist art was introduced into Japan from China, where the T'ang period flourished in the 8th century. The priest and saint Kobo visited China in 804-06 and brought hundreds of paintings back to Japan. In the 9th century, a new style developed, combining late T'ang elements with the overdecorative forms of the old Nara style. Painting was often regarded as a branch of calligraphy. In sculpture there was a twofold tendency: a strength in portraiture and in militant types, and an effeminacy in carved Buddhas and bodhisattvas. The Engi era (901-22) represented the highest development of Japanese civilization. Kanaoka and Eshin Sozu formed the Kose school of painting; Eshin painted "Amida's Paradise", rep-

Art Institute of Chicago

"Evening Rain at Massaki," print by Ichiryusai Hiroshige

17th-century Japanese statuette of Brahma

resenting gracious figures of childlike innocence.

Tobo Sojo, working in the late 11th and early 12th century, marked the beginning of secular art in Japan as opposed to the previous religious forms in sculpture and painting. He employed black and white instead of color in his painting, and gave to art a new flexible line of great motion. A noteworthy example is his large scroll painting "Battle of the Bulls". The other chief innovator in painting, Takanobu, made popular the representation of every-day types of Japanese countenance, and infused a new realism into all subjects. He also made many fine portraits. Japan's cultural contact with China was broken after the fall of the Northern Sung dynasty in 1127. Her new art developed a unique individuality, depicting crowded scenes of street pageantry, of

fairs and temple courts, of dramatic groupings, and scenes of violent action. Nobuzane used sweeping and powerful line work for his greatest painting, a panoramic account, in nine wide scrolls, of the life of Michizane, minister of Engi. Exuberant genre pictures became typical. Sculpture was a subordinate art in the Fujiwara period, particularly after the introduction of mystic Buddhist painting, when sculpture turned to portraiture. This period may be summed up as one of historical painting and portrait sculpture. With the breakup of the Fujiwara oligarchy in the 12th century the last trace of the early Chinese T'ang influence disappeared.

During the feudal age of Kamakura, Japan developed her dominant art, national in form and content. From 1378 to 1428 the great bulk of original T'ang and Sung paintings was imported from China. The Sung culture was a gospel of nature idealization and of the divinity of art. Japanese art responded to the new Chinese stimulus with a large force of fine painters educated at well-established schools. Noami and Soga Shubun, painters of the 15th century, were great landscapists, and followed the tradition of imitating Chinese landscapes. Classicism was as rampant in this renaissance as in the contemporary one of Italy, Japan paying homage to China as Italy did to Greece. Sesshu, who worked during this period, was one of the greatest of all Japanese painters. His works included religious, historical, symbolical, and biographical subjects; he portrayed the crowded life of the people in cities, and painted scenes of palaces, temples, farms, and mountain valleys. He was a supreme landscape artist, working in a style characterized by a vigorous line full of short, dramatic accents and yet continuously interwoven.

During the 16th century the Kano school was developed. Its leading figure, Kano Motonobu, returned to Japanese influences. About 1510 the first fabrication of decorated porcelains in the new Ming fashion was introduced from China into Japan. Kano Yeitoku, with his use of rich, glazed color in painting, was an exponent of the most brilliant school of secular art Asia ever produced. It was characterized mainly by a sumptuously decorative mural art.

The Tokugawa dynasty of Shoguns lasted from 1600 to 1868. The two main streams of art in the Tokugawa period were the aristocratic and the plebian. Representative of the aristocratic art was the 17-century painter Kano Tanyu, a court painter who created a great eclectic school, making transcripts of old masterpieces, both Chinese and Japanese. He also made many studies of nature, severe and dignified in style. The Korin school (1661-1716) produced the foremost painters of tree and flower forms, and also designers for manufactured articles, such as Koyetsu, a great lacquerer and adapter of nature designs to fine pottery. Representative of plebeian art was the 18th-century painter Maruyama Okyo. His subjects were taken chiefly from the scenery and animal life of his native Kyoto. He also designed for silk weavers and bronze casters, embroiderers, fine lacquerers and potters in Kyoto, which had been the center of fine art manufacturers since the days of Fujiwara. Okyo's greatest screen represents a storm dragon arising from a rocky coast, against which the tortured waves leap and boil in foam.

The Ukiyoye school (17th-19th centuries) of Japanese painting was foremost among those which took Japanese life for its motive. It represented the art of the common people of Japan's largest city, Yedo (the former name of Tokyo). The school was founded by Iwasa Matabei, whose contemporary scenes and figures correspond to the genre paintings of the West. The Ukiyoye school is famous for originating and developing the Japanese color print, first used by Hishikawa Moronobu. The outlines of his prints were stamped from a wood block and the color applied afterward with a brush. His pupil Kiyonobu began to apply both outline and color from blocks. Haranobu (q.v.) increased the number of blocks to complete the design with background and atmosphere. He is generally considered the founder of the polychrome wood-block print. Shunsho portrayed a large variety of actors in character. Kiyonaga pictured the festive life of Yedo, its processions, ceremonies and music parties on houseboats. The most popular and versatile of Japanese print masters, Hokusai (q.v.) produced many landscape masterpieces and witty figure sketches. Immensely prolific, he was the dominant figure of Ukiyoye. Hiroshige (q.v.), the second best-known print master of the school, excelled in rendering scenes of sleet, snow, rain, and other atmospheric effects. The work of the last-named two artists had a considerable influence on Western art dating from about 1860. See IMPRESSIONISM.

JAPANESE BEETLE, an insect pest, *Popillia japonica,* in the Scarab family, accidentally introduced into New Jersey from Japan in 1916 and now widespread over E. United States. The adult is about ½ in. long, and is iridescent green with tan wing covers; its body is broad and thick. It attacks the foliage of a wide variety of plants and also eats fruits, causing widespread destruction. The Japanese beetle is most common in July and August, at which time the female lays its eggs 5 to 6 in. below the surface of the ground. The white grubs feed on the roots of grasses until fall, when they descend a foot or more underground and hibernate. They emerge from hibernation in midspring and pupate in June after attaining a length of slightly less than 1 in. D.D.T. sprays are useful in controlling the adult; the soil may be grub-proofed with chlordane, D.D.T., aldrin, or dieldrin. Parasitic wasps, largely responsible for the control of the insect in Japan, were imported into the United States in the 1920's. Now established in American beetle-infested areas, the wasps are contributing to the reduction of the beetle population by preying upon the grubs. The grubs are also subject to certain diseases, caused by bacteria, fungi, nematodes, and viruses. Most important for biological control are milky disease, caused by *Bacillus popilliae,* and a virus infection, called blue disease. See ENTOMOLOGY, ECONOMIC.

JAPANESE LANGUAGE, the language of the Japanese people. It belongs structurally to the Ural-Altaic family, and delights in long involved sentences. The verbs, which carry untranslatable honorific endings, come at the close of the clause. Grammatical gender is unrecognized; case is indicated by separable particles; there are no articles; prepositions follow the words they govern. The language, though difficult to master, is easily pronounced and musical. The introduction of Chinese civilization in the 6th century was followed by a wholesale absorption of Chinese words and characters, but the language remained grammatically unchanged. The revolution of 1868 caused the language to become more Chinese in vocabulary than ever, from the necessity of coining new scientific terms. Many European words were also transferred directly into the Japanese language.

JAPANESE LITERATURE, the literature of the Japanese people from about the beginning of the 8th century to the present. Japanese literature may be divided into four principal periods: the archaic period, the classic period, the dark age, and the modern period.

Archaic Period (about 8th to 9th century A.D.). The earliest Japanese literature was written either in the archaic Japanese language (q.v.), which was set down in Chinese characters, or in the Chinese language itself. The principal work of this period was written in the first-mentioned manner. It was the *Kojiki* ("Record of Ancient Matters"), a compilation made in 712 of the myths, hymns, and prayers of Shinto (q.v.), the native religion of Japan. The *Kojiki,* often called the Japanese Bible and perhaps the most influential book ever produced in Japan, tells the story of the creation of the world according to Shinto, and of the divine origin of the Japanese imperial family; the belief in the divinity of the imperial family was generally held in Japan until it was officially abolished in 1946 (see HIROHITO). A second important collection of religious material was the *Nihongi* ("Chronicles of Japan"), finished in 720; this work was written in Chinese.

The Classic Period (about the 9th to the 12th century). During this period religious and scholarly literature was under the influence of Chinese civilization and was written chiefly in Chinese. Verse and fiction, however, were written in Japanese. Among the notable works of the classic period, in which literary life centered principally in Kyoto, then the capital of Japan, were the *Kokinshu* (905), a collection of poetry; the poems of Tsurayuki (early 10th century), who was also the author of the travel journal *Tosa Nikki* (935); and two prose works of the 11th century which are valuable as sources of information on the life of the period, the romance *Genji Monogatari* ("The Tale of Genji", 2 vols., first published in English 1935), and the volume of sketches *Makura no Zoshi* ("Pillow Sketches") by Sei Shonagon, a lady of the imperial court. The two traditional Japanese verse forms originated at this time; these were the *hokku,* consisting of three unrhymed lines containing respectively five, seven, and five syllables, and the *tanka,* consisting of five lines containing respectively five, seven, five, seven, and seven syllables.

The Dark Age (12th to 17th century). Historically this period is characterized by strife between the various feudal lords of Japan (see JAPAN: *History*); the constant warfare that ravaged the country was inimical to literary development. The period is notable, however, for the creation of the Japanese drama, the *nogaku,* or Nō drama (q.v.); and for a number of prose works, including the *Hojoki* (about 1212), a book of meditations by the priest Kamono Chomei, and the volume of essays *Tsurezure Gusa* (about 1345) by Kenko-Boshi.

The Modern Period (about the beginning of 17th century to the present). The modern period in Japanese literature has been principally one of imitation of the literature of other countries. From 1603 to 1867, the period during which the shoguns or military governors of the Tokugawa family ruled Japan, a renewed Chinese influence was the most important factor in Japanese literature. The principal literary works of the Tokugawa era were translations from Chinese literature or were modeled upon Chinese works. They were written chiefly by a group of writers known as *kangakusha* or Chinese scholars and included books on philosophy, history, and morals. In the succeeding era, the Meiji or the reign of Emperor Mutsuhito (1867–1912), the people of Japan became intensely interested in the culture of the Occident, and Japanese literature consisted largely of translations of the works of European and American writers, including Shakespeare, Dante, Calderon, Byron, Goethe, Emerson, and Daudet; or of Japanese books by writers strongly under the influence of Western ideas and literary forms. So strong was this influence that in the latter part of this period Japanese poets abandoned the traditional forms of Japanese verse, the *tanka* and the *hokku,* in favor of the free verse (q.v.) in use at the time by European and American poets. In the succeeding era, the Taisho or reign of Emperor Yoshihito (1912-26), interest turned from western Europe and America to Russia. The works of Russian writers such as Pushkin, Gogol, Turgenev, and Chekhov were translated and widely read, and Japanese authors wrote numerous novels in which they sought to express through Japanese characters and settings the melancholy characteristic of much Russian literature. Among the best-known Japanese authors of the 20th century were the novelists Yayoi Nogami (*The Sea-god Ship*), Natsume Soseki (*I Am a Cat*), and Morita Sohei (*Sooty Smoke*); the dramatist Kurata Hyakuzo (*The Priest and His Disciples*); and the essayist and poet Matsura Hajime (*The Pure White Light of Literature*). The Showa era or the reign of Emperor Hirohito (1926-) has not to date been productive of literature of significance.

JAPANESE SPANIEL, a toy dog which reputedly originated in China many centuries ago and was later introduced into Japan, where it was the pet of royalty and the nobility, and developed its present characteristics. Several specimens were presented to the American Commodore Matthew Perry as a sign of esteem when he was negotiating (1853) a trade treaty with Japan. The dog was imported into the United States in large numbers at the beginning of the 20th century. The Japanese spaniel has a broad skull, the front of which is round; a flat face; prominent, dark, and lustrous eyes, set wide apart; small v-shaped ears; a short nose; and a silky coat. The tail is covered with a profusion of long hair; from its root the tail curves naturally to one side and rises upward over the dog's back to fall on the opposite side. The dog is either black and white or red and white in color; it weighs about seven pounds. The Japanese spaniel is intelligent, clean, and sturdy. Its loyalty and affection make it an excellent pet.

Japanese spaniel

JAPAN, SEA OF, an arm of the Pacific Ocean, lying between Japan on the E. and Korea and Maritime Territory, Russian S.F.S.R. on the w. Tatary Gulf and Tatar Strait connect it with the Sea of Okhotsk to the N.; on the N.E. it is connected to the Sea of Okhotsk by Soya Strait. Tsugaru Strait and the Inland Sea link it with the Pacific Ocean to the E. Korea Strait, on the s.w., connects it with the East China Sea. Area, about 405,000 sq.m.

JAPHETIDES, or JAPHETIC PEOPLES, in ethnology, a loose designation for the Caucasian peoples of Europe and certain parts of Asia, supposed to be descended from Japheth, a son of the Biblical patriarch Noah (compare HAMITES; SEMITES). In comparative linguistics, the term is used in a stricter sense to denote an important group of non-Indo-European languages spoken in west Asia and in Europe. Among the dead languages in this group are Etruscan and Minoan; modern Japhetic languages include Basque and Chechen (qq.v.).

JAPURÁ, a tributary of the Amazon, rising in the Andes Mts. of s.w. Colombia and flowing through N.W. Brazil, where it is joined by several branches. In its course through Colombia it is called the Caquetá. The Japurá is navigable for about half of its 1750-mile length.

JAQUES-DALCROZE, ÉMILE (1862–1950), Swiss composer and teacher, born in Vienna, and educated in Paris and at the Geneva Conservatoire. He became a professor of harmony at the Conservatoire in 1892, and developed a system of musical training designed to "create by the help of rhythm a rapid and regular current of communication between brain and body, and to make feeling for rhythm a physical experience." In 1915 he founded the Institut Jaques-Dalcroze in Geneva for the teaching and further development of this system, which became known as "Dalcroze Eurhythmics", and has since been taught in music schools all over the world. Jaques-Dalcroze was also an active composer; his works include several operas, two violin concertos, three string quartets, piano pieces, and many songs. His literary works include *Méthode Jaques-Dalcroze* (1907-14) and *Rhythm, Music and Education* (1921).

JARRAH, common name of two trees belonging to the genus *Eucalyptus* (q.v.). The common jarrah, *E. marginata,* is a tall tree native to s.w. Australia. The trunk of the tree is very straight, and yields lumber up to 40 feet long and 24 inches wide. Jarrah wood, which is hard and heavy, resembles red mahogany. It is not adapted to general use in building or cabinetmaking, however, because it breaks easily. The lack of strength is due to frequent blisters of resin occurring in the sapwood and to relative lack of fiber elements. Well-seasoned jarrah timber is used for telegraph poles, piles, and railroad ties, especially in tropical countries infested with termites, to which jarrah wood is resistant.

JASHER, BOOK OF, one of the lost books of the Hebrews. Most scholars adopt the conjecture of the Syriac and Arabic translators that the Book of Jasher was a collection of national ballads. Some held it to be a composition of the age of Solomon, and a work of Nathan and Gad. In the 12th to the 14th centuries no less than three works professing to be the lost Book of Jasher were produced; and in 1751 another forgery, traced to a London printer, created some excitement. It claimed to have been translated from Hebrew by "Alcuin of Britain", and was reprinted in 1829.

JASMINE, or JESSAMINE, common names applied to plants of the genera *Jasminum,* true jasmine, and *Gelsemium,* false jasmine, which belong to closely related families of the Gentian order. The true jasmines, which belong to the Olive family, are a genus of shrubs and climbing plants, including about 100 species, most of which are native to tropical regions of the Old World. The salver-shaped jasmine flower has a five or eight-cleft calyx, five- or eight-lobed corolla, two stamens, and a solitary pistil. The fruit is a two-lobed berry. The common white jasmine, *J. officinale,* is native to s. Asia, and naturalized in s. Europe. It is a tall climbing plant, usually 6 to 10 feet high, bearing pinnate leaves and fragrant white flowers. Spanish jasmine, *J. grandiflorum,* is a bushy shrub, native to the East Indies, which bears white flowers flecked with pink. Arabian jasmine, *J. sambac,* is a white-flowered climbing plant, native to India, which grows about 6 feet high. Flowers of all three species contain an essential oil, called *oil of jasmine,* which is used in making perfumes. White, Spanish, and Arabian jasmine, as well as several other members of the genus, are cultivated throughout the tropical and warm temperate regions of the world.

The false jasmine genus, which belongs to the Logania family, contains two Asiatic and one North American species. The latter is the yellow or Carolina jasmine, *G. sempervirens,* the State flower of South Carolina. Yellow jasmine has fragrant yellow flowers with a five-parted calyx, five-lobed, funnel-shaped corolla, five stamens with arrowhead-shaped anthers, and a solitary pistil. The fruit is a two-celled, septicidal capsule. The roots, which contain a crystalline alkaloid called *gelsemine,* $C_{20}H_{22}N_2O_2$, were formerly used in medicine as an antispasmodic and diaphoretic.

JASON, in Greek mythology, the son of King Æson of Iolus, and nephew of Pelias, usurper of Æson's throne. Jason was prom-

ised the throne by his uncle if he could recover the Golden Fleece (q.v.) of the ram that had carried away Pelias' children Phrixus and Helle. He sailed in search of the Golden Fleece with a crew of heroes in the ship Argo, and had a series of adventures comprising one of the oldest and most famous of Greek legends; see ARGONAUTS. With the aid of the sorceress Medea (q.v.) whom he married, Jason secured the fleece and returned to live at Corinth. He later left Medea in order to marry Glauce, daughter of Creon, king of Corinth; but the marriage was prevented by Medea, who killed her own children by Jason and made Glauce a gift of magic garments which burned her to death when she wore them. In the most popular version of the legend, Jason, overwhelmed by grief, committed suicide. Jason's treatment of Medea and Medea's revenge comprise the motive and climax in the tragedy *Medea* by the ancient dramatist Euripides.

JASPER, an opaque, cryptocrystalline variety of quartz (q.v.). The mineral takes a high polish and is used as a gem stone. It is usually stained by impurities and occurs in various colors, such as red, green, yellow, and blue. When the colors are arranged in bands, the mineral is called riband jasper; a variety containing alternating bands of red and green is known as Siberian jasper. Mottled yellow or brown varieties of jasper are called Egyptian jasper. Agate jasper is intermediate in structure between true jasper and chalcedony (q.v.). Inclusions of red jasper occur in heliotrope (q.v.).

The jasper mentioned in the Bible as one of the stones in the breastplate of the high priest (Ex. 28:20) and as the foundation of the wall of the New Jerusalem (Rev. 21:18) is believed to have been a dark-green, opalescent stone. The jaspis of the ancients was a partially translucent stone, probably containing some chalcedony and chrysoprase. Many medicinal values were attributed to jasper, and as late as the beginning of the seventeenth century it was believed that this stone, if worn about the neck, had powers to strengthen the stomach.

JASPER WARE, a form of terra cotta or porcelain bisque in delicate shades and embossed with white, invented by Josiah Wedgwood (q.v.) at his Burslem potteries in England about 1773. The cameo-like effects obtainable in this ware are well suited to the neoclassic designs of the fine pottery produced in the Wedgwood kilns.

JASSY (Rom. *Iaşi*), capital of the department of Iaşi, Romania, situated on the Bahlui R., about 10 miles w. of the Prut R. The city is an important commercial center. Jassy was founded before the 14th century and from 1565 until 1857 was the capital of the principality of Moldavia (q.v.). It was successively burned by the Tatars and Turks in the 16th century and by the Russians in the 17th. In 1643 the first book to be printed in Romania was published in Jassy. The peace of Jassy concluded the second Russo-Turkish War, in 1792. During World War I Jassy replaced Bucharest as the capital of Romania. The city is the seat of the metropolitan of Moldavia and Suceava and of a Roman Catholic archbishopric. Noteworthy points of interest include a cathedral, two 15th-century churches, a library housing the chief records of Romanian history, and the most important Romanian university, established in 1860. Pop. (1948 prelim.) 94,075.

JASTROW, MORRIS, JR. (1861-1921), American Orientalist, born in Warsaw, Poland, and educated at the University of Pennsylvania and the universities of Leipzig and Paris. He was professor of Semitic languages and librarian at the University of Pennsylvania from 1892 until his death, and special editor of *Webster's New International Dictionary* in 1910. Among his works are *The Study of Religion* (1901), *The Book of Job* (1920), and *The Song of Songs* (1921).

JATS, the largest and most industrious agricultural caste of N.W. India, numbering over 8,000,000 in a recent year, and living mainly in the Punjab, Rajasthan, and Uttar Pradesh. Many ethnologists and historians have identified the Jats with the ancient Getæ, a supposition which, though conjectural, is not directly contradicted by any of the available historical evidence about them; in their own traditions, their origin is ascribed to a small group (usually restricted to three clans) which settled fairly recently in their present area from an original home somewhere on the Indus R. As they are known today, the Jats are an Indo-Aryan people of dark skin and strong, well-built physique, and have gained prominence in India not only as cultivators, but also as soldiers and athletes. The majority are Hindus.

JAUNDICE, or ICTERUS, a symptom of several body disorders, manifesting itself in yellowness of the skin and eyeballs, and in darkening of the urine. In severe cases the feces are clay-colored. The symptom is due to the presence of bile pigments in the blood and body tissues of the diseased individual. Three types of conditions produce jaundice: obstruction of the common bile duct; hemolysis; and poisoning or infection of the liver.

Obstructive jaundice is produced by obstruction of the duct which normally carries bile from the liver and gall bladder into the intestine. Such obstruction may be due to gallstones, to tumors, to internal swelling because of inflammation, or to constriction. The bile, unable to pass out through normal channels, builds up pressure and bursts out of the liver tissues into the blood stream. *Hemolytic jaundice* is brought on by any condition which destroys red blood cells, converting their hemoglobin (q.v.) into bile pigments. Transfusion of incompatible blood and snake bite are among the many causative agents of such conditions. *Toxic* or *infectious jaundice* is produced by a number of poisons, such as arsenic and mercury, and by diseases, such as infectious hepatitis and yellow fever, which attack the liver (q.v.).

Newborn infants frequently have a mild form of jaundice which lasts only a day or two. See also RH FACTOR.

JAUNPUR, city in the United Provinces, Union of India, situated on the Gumti R., 34 miles N.W. of Benares. Perfume and papier-mâché are manufactured in Jaunpur, which is also a fairly important trading center. The city was formerly the capital of an ancient Mohammedan kingdom; it possesses the mosques of Atala Musjid (1408), Dariba, Lal Darwaza, and Jamma Musjid, as well as the ruins of the fort of Feroze Shah and the Jinjiri Musjid mosques. Other antiquities are the baths of Ibrahim Shah, a 16th-century gateway, and a 16th-century bridge over the Gumti, built by the Mogul ruler Munim Khan. Pop., about 45,000.

JAUREGG, JULIUS WAGNER VON. See WAGNER VON JAUREGG, JULIUS.

JAVA, one of the islands of the Malay Archipelago (q.v.), bounded on the N. by the Java Sea, on the E. by Bali Strait, on the S. by the Indian Ocean, and on the W. by Sunda Strait, and forming part of the Republic of Indonesia. Java was formerly an administrative division with Madura (q.v.) of the Netherlands Indies (q.v.), and after World War II was briefly under the partial jurisdiction and control of the Indonesian Republic (see REPUBLIC OF INDONESIA), an independent state proclaimed in August, 1945, and of the Kingdom of the Netherlands. In 1950, following conclusion of the Indonesian war against the Dutch, the island became, in its entirety, a part of the Indonesian Republic. See *History* section of this article.

Java extends in a generally E. and W. direction for a distance of about 605 m. The maximum width of the island, which lies about midway between the fifth and tenth parallels of south latitude, is about 127 m. Batavia (q.v.), properly Jakarta, is the largest city of Java and capital of the Republic. Other important cities are Jokyakarta, Bandoeng, Semarang, Surabaya, Cheribon, Kediri (qq.v.), Pekalongan, Soekaboemi, Malang, and Surakarta. The area of Java is 48,830 sq.m. The island is the most densely populated region of the world, with a population of about 48,000,000.

Java is traversed from E. to W. by a volcanic mountain chain. This longitudinal uplift has approximately 110 volcanic centers, including about 35 active craters. Semeru (12,060 ft.), situated in the E. portion of the island, is the highest volcano and one of the most active. A number of summits up to nearly 11,000 ft. are situated in E. Java. In the central section of the island the maximum elevation is Slamat (11,400 ft.). Elevations in W. Java are generally lower, rarely exceeding 5700 ft. Besides Semeru, the most active volcanoes of Java include Bromo, Kawah Ijen, Kelut, Lamongan, Merapi, Papandayang, and Tangkuhan Prau. Mount Kloet, a mud volcano which caused the death of 550 persons during an eruption in 1919, has had a "safety-valve" tunnel built in its side. Java has been the scene of a number of other disastrous volcanic eruptions, notably that of Mount Ringghit in 1686, when about 10,000 lives were lost, and that of Papandayang in 1772, when about 3000 persons were killed. A low coastal plain, with a maximum width of about 40 m., adjoins the central mountain chain on the N. The S. portion of the island is occupied by a series of limestone ridges, which form a precipitous coastal escarpment. With few exceptions, the rivers of Java are swift, narrow, and shallow. The Solo R., about 335 m. in length, is the largest stream. Other important rivers are the Tarum, the Manuk, and the Brantas. The best natural harbors of Java are situated on the N. coast of the island.

Temperatures as high as 99°F. occur at midday in the coastal and lowland regions of Java, and the relative humidity often exceeds 80%. During the rainy season, extending from November to April, ocean breezes and frequent thunderstorms exercise a cooling influence. At elevations above 2000 ft. temperate climatic conditions prevail, and temperatures as low as 27°F. occur at extreme elevations. The mean annual precipitation is about 80 inches. Wide regional variations occur, however, with extremes ranging from an annual maximum of about 166 inches at Buitenzorg to an annual minimum of about 35 inches at Assembagus.

The vegetation of Java is luxuriant, particularly along the lower slopes of the central mountain chain and on the coastal plain. In addition to a broad variety of plants, numerous species of trees, including palms, bamboo, acacia, rubber, and teak, abound in this zone, which is confined largely to the area below 1700 ft. The teak forests, one of the most valuable natural resources of Java, are extensive. Among the trees common to the higher slopes of the central uplift are the magnolia, rasamala, oak, elm, laurel, maple, and chestnut. Stands of timber occupy approximately 7,627,000 acres, or about 23% of the total surface of the island. Java also has a numerous and diversified fauna. Noteworthy quadrupeds are the one-horned rhinoceros, tiger, leopard, banteng (wild ox), wild pig, lemur, and several species of ape. The island is the habitat of more than 400 species of birds, including the red jungle fowl (*Gallus gallus*), the green peacock, two species of parrot, the swift (*Collocalia*), 10 species of pigeon, 2 species of cuckoo, and 11 species of heron. Among the reptilian fauna are the great python (*Python reticulatus*), cobra, a species of adder, and the crocodile. Specimens of the last-named animal sometimes attain 30 ft. in length. The coastal and inland waters teem with fish, including many edible varieties. Crabs, crayfish, and lobsters are numerous.

The economy of Java is predominantly agrarian. Under normal conditions, lands under cultivation total about 22,000,000 acres. Of this total, about 2,500,000 acres are divided among foreign-controlled plantations, which produce chiefly for the export markets. The remainder consists mainly of small-scale holdings, operated by native peasants. Irrigation figures significantly in farming operations on the island. About 8,345,000 acres were under irrigation in a recent year. Rice, grown largely for domestic consumption, is the principal food crop.

Netherlands Information Bureau

ON THE ISLAND OF JAVA

Above: Thatched huts in a village in western Java. Right: An Indonesian merchant carrying straw baskets on a street in Batavia. Below: Scene in a town market place in western Java.

Netherlands Information Bureau

Javanese dancing girls, trained from childhood as professional performers

Other leading crops of the native farms are corn, cassava, soybeans, sweet potatoes, capsicum, peanuts, bananas, citrus fruits, mangos, tea, coffee, coconuts, kapok, and tobacco. Sugar cane, rubber, tea, tobacco, coffee, and cinchona bark (the source of quinine) are the leading crops of the plantations. The output of quinine normally approximates more than 90% of the world supply.

Several hundred manufacturing plants were established in Java between 1935 and 1942. Prior to this development, manufacturing activity centered chiefly in home enterprises, such as weaving and the manufacture of men's hats and rattan products. Large-scale manufacturing industries on the island include food processing, tire making, automobile assembling, shipbuilding, brewing, and the manufacture of shoes, textiles, clothing, paper, tobacco products, soap, wood products, drugs, and chemicals. Productive mineral deposits on Java include petroleum, manganese ore, gold, silver, salt, sulfur, and coal.

All major points on the island are reached by railway lines. The mileage of the railway network, including urban systems, totals about 3300. Java also has an extensive network of highways. The island is serviced regularly by freight and passenger vessels operating from all parts of the world. International and intra-island connections are provided by air-transport systems.

The native population of Java is composed largely of two distinct racial types. Sundanese, a minority grouping of the Arabic linguistic stock, inhabit the extreme w. portion of the island. The rest of the native population is composed predominantly of Indonesians, a people of obscure racial origin. In the view of some authorities, the Indonesians are an admixture of Polynesians and Malays (qq.v.). Mohammedanism is the religious faith of the overwhelming majority of the Javanese.

History. The earliest Javanese civilization of which there is record was Hindu, probably introduced about the 1st century A.D. Archeological evidence of Hindu culture dates from about the middle of the 8th century. Little is known of Javanese political developments prior to the 13th century, but after 1293 there are records of several kingdoms, including that of Majapahit, which endured until overthrown in 1520 by the Moslems. As a consequence of the fall of Majapahit and of the Moslem conquest of India, Mohammedanism gradually became the religious faith of the Javanese people. Portuguese traders visited the island early in the 16th century. Toward the close of that century, Dutch traders broke the Portuguese commercial monopoly in Java. The Dutch swiftly enlarged their sphere of influence (see EAST INDIA COMPANY), and by 1755 they controlled a large portion of the island. In 1811, during the Napoleonic Wars in Europe, a French expeditionary force expelled the Dutch. The French were driven out later that year by the British, who remained in Java until 1816, when the island was returned to Dutch sovereignty. Between 1825 and 1830 Dutch authority in Java was unsuccessfully challenged by a Javanese rebellion. Thereafter, the island remained under the rule of the Netherlands until the Japanese occupation, begun in February, 1942, during World War II.

In August, 1945, shortly after the surrender of Japanese forces on the island, native insurgents under the leadership of Dr. Achmed Soekarno seized control of parts of Java and proclaimed establishment of the Republic of Indonesia. On behalf of the Netherlands government, Allied military forces, mainly Indian troops of the British army, attempted to crush the rebellion. Severe

GROWING RICE IN JAVA

Below: A terraced rice field in which each section is dammed to hold the great amount of water necessary for the culture of rice. Right: Women harvesting rice. Only the top of the plant is removed; the remaining strawlike stem is left lying on the ground.

Netherlands Information Bureau

The common American blue jay

fighting continued until November 15, 1946, when the governments of the Netherlands and the Indonesian Republic reached agreement on peace conditions. Among other things, the agreement provided for the establishment, by January 1, 1949, of the United States of Indonesia, a sovereign confederation of Indonesian states. The Indonesian Republic, consisting of Sumatra, Java, and Madura, was tentatively recognized as one of the component states of the proposed confederation. The remainder of Java remained under the control of the Netherlands government. Subsequent disagreements between the leaders of the Indonesian Republic and the Dutch government led to a resumption of hostilities in Java and Sumatra, in July, 1947. In the course of the fighting, which was terminated on August 4, 1947, through the intervention of the United Nations, Dutch troops occupied much of the island, leaving only part of Middle Java and of West Java under Indonesian control. (For later developments, see REPUBLIC OF INDONESIA.)

JAVA MAN. See MAN, ANCIENT; HOMINIDAE.

JAVA SPARROW, RICEBIRD, or **PADDY,** a bird, *Munia oryzivora,* of the Weaverbird family, native to Java and commonly kept as a cage bird in other parts of the world. The bird is about seven inches long. The body is greenish blue above and pink below. The head is black, the cheeks are white, and the large, conical bill is pink. A narrow edging of red surrounds the eye. The rump and tail are black. The Java sparrow has been transported to Asia and Africa, where it has become wild and, to some extent, a

pest in rice and other grain fields, devouring large quantities of grain.

JAVELIN, a long, light spear, used in hunting and warfare by the ancients. In a Roman legion each man in the first and second lines was equipped with two javelins, about 6¾ ft. long. In action the legionary hurled one javelin at the enemy at the onset of battle, and retained the other for defense against cavalry.

The javelin is used in modern track and field sports; javelin throwing was incorporated into modern Olympic games in 1908. Javelins for this purpose are slightly over 8½ ft. long, and are made of wood tipped with steel points. The world's record for throwing the javelin was made in 1938 by the Finnish athlete Yrjo Nikkanen who threw it a distance of 258 ft., 2⅜ in.

JAWS. See SKULL.

JAY, common name for any bird in the subfamily Garrulinae of the Crow family, found in temperate and warm regions throughout the world. Jays are smaller and more brightly colored than crows; many of them have crests. Jays eat the eggs and young of other birds, and also large insects, seeds, nuts, small amphibians, and invertebrates.

The common European jay, or jay bird, is *Garrulus glandarius,* about 14 in. long. It is chiefly tan in color, with a black and white crest. The blue jay, or common American jay, *Cyanocitta cristata,* found throughout eastern U.S. from the Great Plains to the Atlantic coast, is 11½ to 12 in. long, and has a large crest. It is grayish blue above and white below. Its tail is bright blue; its wings are bright blue banded with black and spotted with white. An irregular circle of black rings its neck and lower throat. The Canada jay, whisky-jack, moose bird, or camp robber, *Perisoreus canadensis,* is a crestless jay of N. North America, found as far south as New York. This bird, which is known for stealing food from hunters' camps, is about 12 in. long; it is dirty gray in general body color, with a white forehead. Other crestless jays include the California jay, *Aphelocoma californica,* and the piñon bird, *Cyanocephalus cyanocephalus,* of western U.S.

JAY, JOHN (1745-1829), American statesman and jurist, first Chief Justice of the Supreme Court of the United States, born in New York City. He was educated at King's College (now Columbia University),

New York City, and was admitted to the bar in 1768. Allied to prosperous merchant families by birth and marriage, he represented the point of view of the merchants in protesting English restrictions on the commercial activities of the colonies. He was elected to the first and second Continental Congresses in 1774 and 1775, respectively, and although at first opposed to independence from England, he energetically supported the colonies, following the adoption of the Declaration of Independence. He drafted the constitution of New York State, and was appointed chief justice of the State in 1777. In the following year he was again elected to the Continental Congress and was chosen its president. In 1779 he was sent to Spain to seek aid for, and diplomatic recognition of, the Confederation of the United States. He joined Benjamin Franklin (q.v.) in Paris in 1782, and later was one of the American commissioners who negotiated peace with England after the Americans had been victorious in the Revolutionary War.

From 1784 to 1789 he served as secretary for foreign affairs; the general ineffectiveness of the Confederation government led him to become a proponent of a strong national government, endowed with powers adequate to the execution of its tasks. In collaboration with Alexander Hamilton and James Madison (qq.v.), Jay wrote the notable series of articles known as *The Federalist,* which urged ratification of the U.S. Constitution, following its adoption by the Continental Congress. After the establishment of the Federal government, President George Washington appointed him chief justice of the Supreme Court. In 1794, when war with England threatened over unsettled controversies, Jay was appointed by Washington to negotiate a settlement. He went to England and concluded an agreement known as Jay's Treaty (q.v.). Much resentment against the treaty was expressed in the United States on the ground that it allied the young nation with its former oppressor, England, against the French Revolution (q.v.).

On his return from England Jay discovered to his surprise that he had meanwhile been elected governor of New York State. He thereupon resigned from the Supreme Court, and served as governor from 1795 to 1801; he was then offered his former position as chief justice of the U.S. Supreme Court, but declined in order to retire from public life.

JAY'S TREATY, name given in the United States to the treaty negotiated in 1794 by the American statesman and jurist John Jay (q.v.), disposing of outstanding differences between the United States and Great Britain. The popular designation reflected in part the attitude of large numbers of Americans, who were highly critical of the pact's provisions and wished, by calling the treaty "Jay's", to dissociate themselves from it.

The differences which the treaty was intended to settle arose from violations and nonobservance by Great Britain of the Treaty of Paris (1783), terminating the American Revolutionary War. Jay's Treaty provided for evacuation by the British of forts and fur posts on the northern border of the United States, and for the appointment of arbitration commissions to define the northeastern and northwestern boundaries of the United States. It also provided for compensation by Great Britain for damage done to American shippers, and for the payment by Americans of debts due British merchants. By the terms of the treaty severe restrictions were placed on American trade with the British West Indies, and the British were allowed to trade with the United States on a most-favored-nation

Metropolitan Museum of Art

John Jay (from painting by Gilbert Stuart)

basis. No provision was made in the treaty for compensation to Americans for slaves previously stolen from them by the British. The treaty also failed to provide a solution for the irritating British practices of searching American vessels on the high seas and impressing American seamen (see IMPRESSMENT), which were contributing factors to the subsequent outbreak of the War of 1812 (q.v.).

An intense political struggle took place in the United States over Jay's Treaty. In the leadership of those opposed to the treaty, were the Republicans, who were sympathetic to the revolutionary democratic French republic regarded by them as a friendly power, and then at war with England, the recent foe of American freedom. Jay was burned in effigy in many parts of the country; Alexander Hamilton (q.v.) was stoned while speaking in favor of the treaty in New York City; and even George Washington did not escape vilification. In favor of the treaty were merchants eager to take advantage of the opportunities for trade provided for in the pact, the Federalists (see FEDERALIST PARTY), and Washington, James Madison, and other statesmen who regarded the terms of the treaty as the best that could be obtained in the circumstances. Owing largely to Washington's influence the treaty was ratified by the Senate in a secret session on June 24, 1795.

JAZYGES, an ancient tribe of the group called Sarmatians (q.v.), originally occupying the shores of the Black Sea and the Sea of Azov. In the 1st century A.D. they moved westward, and a detached body of them settled as far west as the region between the Tisza and Danube rivers in the center of modern Hungary, where they first came into contact with the Romans. Though at first friendly to Rome, they began to struggle against Roman authority during the reign of Domitian (q.v.), and were eventually subdued by Marcus Aurelius (q.v.). Later, under Hungarian kings, the Jazyges maintained an independent military organization, and retained a certain amount of autonomy for their region. Even in modern times the names for the people and the area survive in Hungary, and a body of Magyars numbering about 70,000 still claim distinction as Jazygian.

JAZZ, a form of American music characterized by intense personal emotional expression, with emphasis on rhythmic drive and improvisation (q.v.). A prime element

of jazz is the use of improvised solos. As in all improvisation, the personal creative element is highly important; however, unlike the undisciplined improvisation of primitive folk music, jazz improvisation is strongly modified by the musical background of the individual musician and his favored style of playing. Traditional definitions emphasize the element of syncopation in jazz. While important, it is far more obvious as a dominant element in ragtime (see below), an early form of jazz, than in present-day jazz music. As jazz developed, it became more concerned with rhythmic contrast than with simple syncopation, and as it became more popular in America and subsequently throughout the world, the meaning of the term "jazz" was expanded to take in such other segments of American music as "symphonic jazz", "dance music", and "swing"; all of these are variants from the main stream of the jazz tradition itself. Properly speaking, there is no such entity as a jazz song or tune; there are melodies which lend themselves well to jazz treatment, but the primary essential of improvisation by the musicians themselves keeps any composer from saying correctly that he is writing a jazz song, suite, or symphony.

The origin of the word has been associated with an old Creole verb meaning "to speed up"; however, inasmuch as jazz in its early days was closely associated with the brothels of late 19th-century New Orleans, the opinion held by most authorities that the word is of vulgar origin seems correct. The source material from which jazz springs is still a subject of great controversy among critics and musicians. Negro work songs, blues, spirituals, and hymns lent themselves most easily to jazz adaptation, as did many of the rhythmic patterns of African music brought over by the slaves. All of these factors were distilled through the traditional New Orleans marching band.

Bands were included in all New Orleans processionals, whether for weddings, funerals, or festivals. Competition between the bands for prestige was enormous, and gradually a tradition of musical competition developed. Bands marched to a funeral playing slow laments, but returned playing popular quadrilles in quick-step time. The use of the quadrille was fortunate in that the structure of this dance form brought from Paris allowed for "breaks" or pauses in which the individual musicians could play short solos. From such a quadrille

Metronome

JAZZ IN AMERICA

Above: Paul Whiteman and his band appearing in "Rhapsody in Blue," motion picture based on the life of George Gershwin.
Right: Lionel Hampton (right), famous band leader in the jazz field, with his drummer.

(*Get Out of Here*) came the famed ragtime song *Tiger Rag*.

As time went on, the bands evolved a definite style of playing called jazz, which in its more conservative popular form was known as ragtime (as in *Maple Leaf Rag* by the Negro pianist Scott Joplin). Good musicians were not only in demand for bands and dances, but also in Storeyville, the enormous brothel district of New Orleans, where pianists played ragtime (literally "ragged time") characterized by a powerfully rhythmic left hand; this style started a tradition which was followed by such well-known jazz pianists as Thomas "Fats" Waller, James P. Johnson, and Edward Kennedy "Duke" Ellington.

Jazz music at this time was almost completely a Negro creation. A few white men at the turn of the century, such as Jack Pappa Laine, played what became known as "New Orleans" jazz, but the main figures were such Negro musicians as the trumpet players Buddy Bolden and Joe "King" Oliver and the pianist Jelly Roll Morton. These men not only dominated the musicians around them but set a tradition which has influenced jazz and all its variants to this day. Some sociologists look upon jazz as primarily Negro "protest" music. Actually, since it was a gainful source of employment, the primacy of Negroes in jazz is due largely to the means for fame and fortune it offered them.

Before World War I some jazz musicians had begun to drift out of New Orleans, working their way north on the river boats which plied the Mississippi. These little river-boat bands were the first jazz influence upon such white musicians as the trumpeter Bix Beiderbecke and the pianist Hoaglund Howard "Hoagy" Carmichael.

Louis Armstrong, probably more responsible for the present jazz tradition than any other musician, after hearing Oliver play in New Orleans, joined Fate Marable's band on the river boats, and in 1922 joined Oliver in Chicago. He was one of the many musicians who emigrated from New Orleans after the shutting down of Storeyville by the U.S. Navy in 1917, during World War I. In Chicago, which had by now become a center for the jazz idiom, Armstrong's fame and influence among musicians grew enormously, and he very quickly became the pre-eminent figure in jazz, noted for his ability to play with power, simplicity, and lyric creativeness. His playing strongly influenced that of a young Chicago Negro pianist named Earl Hines. As a result of the "trumpet style" (phrases of single notes as opposed to the two-handed chords used by most ragtime exponents) which Hines developed, a com-

pletely new tradition of piano playing ensued, and is still felt today in the playing of Teddy Wilson, Art Tatum, and Jess Stacy, and even so far afield as the straight dance music played by Eddie Duchin.

At the same time, white musicians were attempting to emulate what they heard on Chicago's South Side. The group known as the Original Dixieland Five, then working in Chicago, was called to New York City in 1917 to play at Riesenweber's Cafe; this occasion was the first time a jazz band appeared at a fashionable place of entertainment. A group of Chicago high-school students who won fame as the Austin High Gang, including Dave Tough on the drums, Jimmy MacPartland on trumpet, and Frank Teschmaker playing clarinet, became widely known as the prime advocates of the "Chi-

JAZZ IN AMERICA

Below: Famous jazz personalities at a jam session led by Eddie Condon (with guitar). They are, from left to right (standing), Pee-Wee Russell, Sidney Bechet, Wild Bill Davison, Max Kaminsky, and Fred Ohms.
Left: Louis Armstrong, for many years regarded as the most creative jazz musician.

Metronome

Metronome; Joe Glaser, Inc.

JAZZ IN AMERICA

*Above: "Duke" Ellington (at right) and two
of his saxophonists making a recording with
his band. Right: Sidney Catlett at drums.*

cago style". Teschmaker is generally credited
with having been the mentor of noted swing-
band leader Benny Goodman. Bix Beiderbecke, while still a young student in Chicago,
had started to play with the group later
known as the Wolverines; he founded a
style and a cult that persists today. His
melodic playing was a softer, more restrained
variant of the Oliver-Armstrong tradition of
jazz.

The Chicago style itself was similar to
that of New Orleans music in that it ac-
cented two beats of every measure, but was
nervously explosive and lacked the more
easily flowing power of expression possessed
by the New Orleans bands. It is today a
dying force in jazz, though occasional small
units affect its style and the Bob Crosby
band (1935-1942) built a national reputation
on a big-band version of the original five-
man style. Surviving is a form of piano

playing known as boogiewoogie, first popularized by a group of Chicago Negro pianists
in the middle nineteen-twenties. Boogiewoogie utilizes a figured bass (often of eight
notes to the measure) repeated over and
over again with great strength, and may be
used to play any song, though it is generally
used in conjunction with the blues.

Throughout the first twenty-five years of
the developments in jazz, the instruments
used were primarily trumpet, trombone, clarinet, tuba or bass, banjo, piano, and drums.
Orchestral arrangements were sketchy, confined for the most part to "traditional"
figures that the musicians had heard other
bands use. These figures, known as "riffs"
if repeated, were used not only in their

original context but transposed to other songs at the musicians' pleasure. A famous example is the song *In the Mood* (1938) which was originally a figure in *Tar Paper Stomp* as performed by Wingy Manone in the late nineteen-twenties.

Up until this time musicians played either New Orleans marches or the blues. Contrary to popular impression, the blues are not ordinary popular songs, but rather a traditional harmonic framework. When a leader says to a band, "Play the blues", he means specifically four bars of the key chord, four bars of the key a fourth below the key, two bars of the key a fifth above, and two bars of the key chord again. Over and over again this format (tonic, subdominant, dominant, and tonic) has been used as the background to tens of thousands of melodies. It is probably derived from the plagal cadence of the 16th century, but it has become the basis of all jazz improvisational playing. The curious fact is that, according to this rule, *Basin Street Blues* and the first part of *St. Louis Blues* are not blues at all but merely popular songs.

With the movement up the river, the success of the Dixieland Five, and the awakening of interest in jazz in Chicago, academic musicians started to listen to jazz, and to derive many ideas from its experiments and successes. Such composers as the Frenchman Darius Milhaud and the Russian Igor Stravinsky borrowed not only jazz ideas of rhythm, but also use of mutes, blendings, and voicings of instruments. Milhaud's *Creation of the World* (1923) antedated George Gershwin's *Rhapsody in Blue* as presented by Paul Whiteman at New York's Town Hall in 1924, and was built on many of the same ideas. The resounding success of Gershwin's *Rhapsody* started a school of writing known as "symphonic jazz". These works properly speaking have nothing to do with jazz; Gershwin was a fine creator of popular songs, but never properly a jazz musician. At the same time Whiteman, by then the best-known bandleader in the country, hired many jazz musicians to work in his orchestra, including the trombonist Tommy Dorsey and his brother Jimmy playing saxophone, the violinist Joe Venuti, and the trumpeter Bix Beiderbecke. The tradition started here continued with huge orchestras in theater pits and later on the radio by Fred Waring, Nathanial Shilkret, Meredith Willson, Andre Kostelanetz, and Morton Gould. These orchestras, while deriving a great deal of their inspiration from jazz proper, played only dance music or elaborately arranged symphonic jazz.

Up until this time, jazz (or "hot jazz" as it was being called to distinguish it from "sweet music", the dance music played by Wayne King, Guy Lombardo, and their followers) had been performed by small units. The impact of Whiteman, however, had its effect; Negro bands became larger and began to include more instruments. The saxophone, never used in New Orleans and early Chicago days, now became the trade-mark of jazz. Brass sections of four, five, and six men became common, while the size of the bands increased from six to twelve men. Complex orchestral arrangements added to the repertoire made the music more palatable to sophisticated ears, but tended to reduce in importance the essential improvisational element which jazz had to contribute to music. Bands led by such men as Fletcher Henderson, Earl Hines, Claude Hopkins, and Don Redman set the musical tone of the period. Chicago-style jazz was still heard, but was considered raw, unrefined, and even old-fashioned; Louis Armstrong, however, was still regarded as the most creative musician in the field.

During the first years of the economic depression of the nineteen-thirties, all jazz except dance music suffered financially, and very little pure jazz was played. However, Duke Ellington, a young Washington, D.C., pianist who had first gained notice in the mid-twenties, made a series of phonograph records which again shaped the course of jazz and even symphonic music in America. Ellington, by this time firmly established at the Cotton Club, a New York City night club, made a series of phonograph arrangements which not only utilized the most sophisticated ideas of scoring then known in the jazz field, but wrote for his orchestra in such fashion that improvised solos by his musicians became an intrinsic part of the score itself. The Ellington band was from its beginning (1927), and for twenty years remained, a unique performing unit in the jazz field. Arguments are legion among critics as to whether Ellington's music can properly be called jazz or whether it is actually symphonic music with a strong rhythmic emphasis. When Ellington toured Europe in the early nineteen-thirties, he was given a reception never before accorded any American musician. Critics hailed him as "the most creative force in music", and he gave performances before such high-ranking persons as the Prince of Wales and King Gustaf V of Sweden.

Throughout the period of this big-band development, the only well-known white bands paying attention to jazz were those headed by Isham Jones and the Glen Gray Casa Loma band, an outgrowth of a Detroit orchestra headed by Jean Goldkette in the late nineteen-twenties. These two units were concerned mostly with arranged instrumental music and did not integrate individual solos within the general framework of the score in the manner of Fletcher Henderson or Duke Ellington.

In 1935 Benny Goodman, with a drummer named Gene Krupa, moved from Chicago to New York and organized a band which toured the country playing in a style essentially similar to that of the Fletcher Henderson band, but with less solo virtuosity and more precision. The tour was a complete failure until the band played at the Palomar Ballroom in Los Angeles, Calif., to the most riotous success ever known to jazz.

From this event grew the so-called swing era, with its exhibitionistic "jitterbug" dancing. Swing as opposed to jazz was the use of a big band playing arranged melodies, with the occasional use of jazz soloists. As the bands led by Goodman, the Dorsey Brothers, Bunny Berigan, Harry James, Artie Shaw, Glenn Miller, and Woody Herman became more popular they played less pure jazz, and became better disciplined versions of the "sweet music" bands which had followed the Whiteman success in the early nineteen-twenties; all these swing bands, however, included smaller jazz units, such as the Benny Goodman Sextet, the Artie Shaw Gramercy Five, and the Woody Herman Wood Choppers.

During the early years of World War II, because of the lack of manpower, few changes in personnel were made in the bands, and jazz forms remained static. In 1944, however, a group of musicians in New York City started a form of jazz known as "be bop". As opposed to swing, this form was a return to small groups and much improvised-solo playing, with the arranging confined to unison ideas for the melodic instruments. Unlike early jazz bands, these units, led by such men as trumpeter Dizzy Gillespie and alto saxophonist Charlie Parker, incorporated into their playing much of the tradition of formal European classical music, such as that of Stravinsky. Rhythm sections, instead of being content to play an even four bars to the measure, utilized extreme variations, while the soloists used harmonies of a far more complex nature than even those of the Ellington band. In addition, tempos were speeded up and a great deal more technical facility was required of musicians. Like swing, the "be bop" influence was not without its cultism. Shell-rimmed eyeglasses, berets, and an air of pronounced intellectualism replaced the exhibitionism of the jitterbugs.

With a return to small-group musical activity, the essential factor of improvisation in American jazz was restored. However the addition of scoring and harmonic complexities acquired from formal European music led some critics to believe that a new synthesis composed of the formal European classical tradition and of the unique experiments in improvisation backed by rhythm (the fundamental characteristics of jazz) might in the future be the path of much American music.

JEANNE D'ARC. See JOAN OF ARC.

JEANNETTE, a city of Westmoreland Co., Pa., situated about 25 m. by rail S.E. of Pittsburgh. It is surrounded by an agricultural and coal-mining area, and in the vicinity are natural-gas fields. The city is noted for the manufacture of glass. The principal products of the industrial establishments in Jeannette are bottles, lamps, jars, lenses, window glass, tableware, marine and submarine equipment, cement, rubber goods, heating systems, iron pipe fittings, and power-plant equipment. Jeannette was founded in 1888 and incorporated as a borough in 1889, in which year the first glassworks was established there. It was incorporated as a city in 1938. Pop. (1950) 16,172.

JEANNETTE EXPEDITION. See ARCTIC EXPLORATION.

JEAN PAUL. See RICHTER, JEAN PAUL FRIEDRICH.

JEANS, SIR JAMES HOPWOOD (1877-1946), English astronomer and mathematician, born in London, and educated at Trinity College, Cambridge University. Jeans was professor of applied mathematics at Princeton University from 1905 to 1909, lecturer in applied mathematics at Cambridge from 1910 to 1912, lecturer at Oxford in 1922, and research associate at the Mt. Wilson Observatory in 1923. He was secretary of the Royal Society from 1919 to 1929. He is best known for his work in cosmogony (q.v.), and for his researches on the kinetics and radiations of gases. Jeans was knighted in 1928, and was awarded the Order of Merit in 1939. His technical works include *The Dynamical Theory of Gases* (1904), *Radiation and the Quantum Theory* (1914), *Problems and Cosmogony and Stellar Dynamics* (1919), and *Eos, or the Wider Aspects of Cosmogony* (1928). He also wrote books for the layman, such as *The Universe Around Us* (1929), *The Stars in Their Courses* (1931), *Through Space and Time* (1934), *Science and Music* (1937), and *The Growth of Physical Science* (published posthumously in 1948).

JEBB, SIR RICHARD CLAVERHOUSE (1841-1905), Scottish Greek scholar, born in Dundee, and educated at St. Columba's College, Dublin, the Charterhouse School, London, and Trinity College, Cambridge University. In 1875 he became professor of Greek at the University of Glasgow and in 1889 was made regius professor of Greek at Cambridge. He was president of the Society for the Promotion of Hellenic Studies from 1891 to 1905, and after 1891 was a member of Parliament from the University of Cambridge. In 1892 he was Turnbull lecturer at Johns Hopkins University in Baltimore, Md. His works include *The Characters of Theophrastus* (1870-1909), *Attic Orators* (1893), *Homer* (1887), *A Complete Edition of Sophocles* (1883-1903), *Bacchylides* (1905), and the *Rhetoric* of Aristotle (1909).

JEDDA. See JIDDA.

JEFFERIES, RICHARD (1848-87), English author, born near Swindon, Wiltshire. He is known for the descriptions of nature in his stories *The Gamekeeper at Home* (1877), *Wild Life in a Southern County* (1879), *Wood Magic* (1881), *Life of the Fields* (1884), and *After London* (1885).

JEFFERS, (JOHN) ROBINSON (1887-   ), American poet, born in Pittsburgh, Pa., and educated at Occidental College, Calif., and at the University of Southern California Medical School. His works have a strongly naturalistic setting, in which man is at the mercy of the forces of the universe. One of his recurring themes, variously symbolized, is man's desire for self-destruction; another is Jeffers' disdain of society. His poetic works include *Tamar and Other Poems* (1924), *The Women at Point Sur* (1927), *Cawdor, and Other Poems* (1928), *Dear Judas* (1929), *Descent to the Dead* (1931), *Thurso's Landing* (1932), *Solstice* (1935), *Such Counsels You Gave to Me* (1937), and *The Double Axe* (1948). He is the author of a nota-

ble English adaptation (1946) of *Medea* by the ancient Greek dramatist Euripides (q.v.).

JEFFERSON, JOSEPH (1829-1905), American actor, fourth of a directly descended line of actors, born in Philadephia, and privately educated. He made his first stage appearance at the age of three, as Cora's child in *Pizarro*, by August Friedrich Ferdinand von Kotzebue. For many years he underwent the hard training of a strolling actor, and then played with Laura Keene's company in New York City, where in 1858 he created the part of Asa Trenchard in *Our American Cousin*, by Tom Taylor. In 1865 he visited London, and played for the first time the title role in *Rip Van Winkle,* by Dion Boucicault; thereafter his name was especially identified with this character, and also with that of Bob Acres in *The Rivals*, by Richard Brinsley Sheridan. Jefferson attained distinction as a landscape painter, and wrote an *Autobiography* (1890).

JEFFERSON, THOMAS (1743-1826), third President of the United States, born in Shadwell, Virginia. His father, Peter Jefferson, was a planter in Goochland (now Albemarle) County, then a frontier territory in the Blue Ridge Mountains; his mother was Jane Randolph, a member of a prominent and aristocratic Virginia family. Thomas Jefferson was the third child and oldest son of a family of ten children. He was educated at William and Mary College, and in 1767 was admitted to the Virginia bar, subsequently becoming a successful lawyer. He was elected to the Virginia House of Burgesses in 1769, and, for the next six years, was a member of every assembly and convention of the Colony.

In the Virginia convention of 1774, Jefferson submitted resolutions which, although they were not adopted at the time, were published in pamphlet form as *A Summary View of the Rights of America* and earned him a place among the foremost advocates of revolution. He was elected to the Continental Congress in 1775 and again in 1776. In the latter body, when Richard Henry Lee moved that the Colonies declare their independence of England, Jefferson was elected chairman of a committee of five to prepare a draft of the declaration. His colleagues were Benjamin Franklin, John Adams, Roger Sherman, and Robert R. Livingston; at their request, Jefferson wrote the draft of the Declaration of Independence (q.v.), which was submitted to the Congress and adopted, essentially in its original form.

After the adoption of the Declaration, Jef-

Virginia State Chamber of Commerce

Above: Monticello, home of President Thomas Jefferson near Charlottesville, Virginia. Right: A portrait of Thomas Jefferson (engraving after a painting by Gilbert Stuart).

ferson resigned from the Congress and entered the Virginia legislature, devoting himself to reforming the laws of the State. Among the reforms largely due to his influence were the abolition of entail and primogeniture (q.v.), and the guarantee of freedom of religion by the disestablishment of the State church. In 1779 Jefferson succeeded Patrick Henry as governor of Virginia, and served until 1781; during his terms the State was the battleground of the British and American Revolutionary armies. In 1783 he was elected to the United States Congress, in which he drafted a plan for the government of the Northwest Territory (q.v.), and secured the adoption of the decimal system of coinage. In 1784 he was sent to France to join the commercial mission of Benjamin Franklin and John Adams, and in the following year he succeeded Franklin as minister to France.

Jefferson returned to America in 1789 and in the next year became secretary of state in Washington's cabinet. There the conflict between Jefferson and Alexander Hamilton over the constitutional powers of the Federal

government resulted in the formation of two political factions, one of which developed into the Federalist Party (q.v.), headed by Hamilton and devoted to the formation of a strong central government, and the other into a States' rights party (see DEMOCRATIC PARTY), headed by Jefferson. The conflict came to a head over the adoption of a bill to establish a national bank. Jefferson held the measure to be unconstitutional; Washington agreed with Hamilton's view that the bill was within the "implied powers" granted to the Federal government by the constitution. Jefferson tried several times to resign in the interests of cabinet harmony; Washington finally accepted his resignation on the last day of 1793. Jefferson retired to the home he had designed and built at Monticello, near Charlottesville, Virginia, where, for the next three years, he devoted his time to farming.

In 1796 Jefferson was elected Vice-President of the United States, serving from 1797 to 1801. During his term he consistently opposed the assumption of power by the Federal government, and in particular the passage of the Alien and Sedition Acts (q.v.). With James Madison he formulated and secured the passage of the Kentucky Resolutions and the Virginia Resolutions (qq.v.), which gave rise to the doctrine of States' Rights (q.v.).

In the Presidential election of 1800, Jefferson and Aaron Burr were tied in electoral votes, and the election was thrown into the House of Representatives. Through the influence of his political opponent, Alexander Hamilton, who judged Jefferson's integrity to be preferable to Burr's ambition, Jefferson was elected. He was re-elected by a large majority in 1804. His conduct in office was marked by absence of pomp and ceremony, and a disregard of social distinctions, which has since become known as "Jeffersonian simplicity". The great achievement of his administration was the negotiation of the Louisiana Purchase (q.v.). He dispatched the Lewis and Clark Expedition (q.v.) to explore the territories to the west, initiating the expansion of the country to the Pacific Ocean, and sent naval expeditions against the pirates of Tripoli, ensuring the safety of American commerce in the Mediterranean Sea. In the later years of his administration, troubles with France and England, then engaged in the Napoleonic Wars, led to his advocating the passage of the Embargo Acts (q.v.). Although the resistance of the New England ship owners made the enforcement of the Acts impossible, Jefferson claimed that if the Acts had been observed, the United States would have achieved its rights on the high seas without recourse to the War of 1812. Other notable events of his administration were the attack on the American ship *Chesapeake* (q.v.) by the British

warship *Leopard*, the prohibition of the importation of slaves, the trial of Aaron Burr for treason, and the definition of treason by the Supreme Court.

At the end of his second term Jefferson retired to Monticello. There during his remaining years he entertained prominent persons from all over the world, who called on him to consult on questions of government and economics. During this period his wide interests and great influence were exercised in such diverse fields as the betterment of agriculture, continued efforts in the reform of the State laws of Virginia, and the development of better systems of education; he regarded his foundation of the University of Virginia in 1819 as the crowning achievement of his career. He became known as the "Sage of Monticello"; so many personages visited him, and the demands on his hospitality were so great, that he died bankrupt. Among the many monuments to his memory are the Jefferson Memorial at Washington, D.C., a replica of his home at Monticello, containing a sixteen-foot standing statue of him by Rudolph Evans, and the "Shrine of Democracy" designed by Gutzon Borglum, with heads of Washington, Jefferson, Lincoln, and Theodore Roosevelt carved in heroic size on the granite face of Mount Rushmore, South Dakota.

JEFFERSON CITY, capital of Missouri and county seat of Cole Co., situated on the Missouri R. at the center of the State, about 115 m. by rail w.s.w. of St. Louis. It is served by two railroads and maintains a municipal airport. Fruit, dairy products, livestock, and zinc, coal, and limestone, are products of the surrounding area. In the city are extensive railroad shops, breweries, printing and publishing plants, and factories manufacturing shoes and work clothing. Jefferson City is the site of Lincoln University for Negroes, founded in 1866 by members of two Negro Civil War regiments following their discharge from the Union Army; it was made a State institution in 1879. The city is also the site of the State Penitentiary, and a national cemetery established in 1867. The State Capitol, completed in 1918, is built of Carthage marble on a bluff overlooking the river, and contains excellent murals and other interior decorations. Other notable buildings are the States Museum, with historical exhibits, and the Supreme Court Building, housing one of the finest law libraries in United States. The site of the present city was chosen in 1821 to be the capital of the State, and in 1822 the town was laid out and officially named City of Jefferson. The first State House was built in 1826. Jefferson City became the county seat in 1828 and was chartered as a city in 1839. Pop. (1950) 25,099.

JEFFERSON RIVER, a river of Montana, and one of the three rivers which unite to form the Missouri R. It rises in the Red Rock lakes, in Beaverhead Co., and flows N.E. for about 150 m. to its confluence with the Madison and Gallatin rivers at Three Forks.

JEFFREY, FRANCIS, LORD JEFFREY (1773–1850), Scottish literary critic and jurist, born in Edinburgh, and educated at Glasgow and Oxford universities. In association with the English author Sydney Smith (q.v.) and others, he founded the *Edinburgh Review* (q.v.), a literary periodical, in 1802. Jeffrey was editor and literary critic of the *Review* until 1829, and became famous for his trenchant style and caustic treatment of the works of such poets as William Wordsworth, John Keats, and Percy Shelley. He also proved to be an able and eloquent barrister, and in 1830 was appointed lord advocate. Four years later he was created Lord Jeffrey and was appointed judge of the Court of Session. He served in that capacity until his death.

JEFFREYS, GEORGE, 1st BARON JEFFREYS OF WEM (1648-89), English jurist, born in Acton Park, Denbighshire, and educated at St. Peter's College, known as Westminster School. After attending Cambridge University for a year, he entered the Inner Temple, London, to study law, and was called to the bar in 1668. Jeffreys' brilliant eloquence soon won him a large private practice, in which he continued after being appointed, in 1671, sergeant-at-law of the City of London. He won the favor of influential courtiers, and was employed in confidential legal business for King Charles II. In 1677 he was knighted and in the following year was appointed solicitor general to the Duke of York (later James II). Jeffreys rapidly advanced to higher appointments; he became chief justice of Chester in 1680, a baronet in 1681, lord chief justice of England in 1682, and a member of the king's privy council the following year.

Jeffreys was an able and upright judge in civil cases, and had few superiors in the clarity with which he expressed his decisions. He was also responsible for stamping out such abuses as the systematic kidnaping practiced by the municipal authorities of Bristol, and the legal frauds committed by London lawyers. However, his conduct of criminal trials, particularly of those involving treason, was so outstandingly brutal, even for his period, that he earned the sobriquet of "the Hanging Judge". In 1683 he presided at the trials of the conspirators in the Rye House Plot (q.v.), to kill Charles II and the Duke of York. His conduct toward the accused, especially toward Lord William Russell and Algernon Sidney (q.v.), was regarded as so unscrupulously unjust that he became infamous throughout England.

In 1685 James II raised Jeffreys to the peerage, creating him Baron Jeffreys of Wem, the first chief justice to be so honored during his tenure of office. Later in the same year, Jeffreys toured the western part of England, conducting a series of trials of men charged with complicity in a rebellion against James II, led by the Duke of Monmouth; see ENGLAND: *History*. Because he conducted these trials with ruthless disregard for legal procedure, they became known as the "bloody assizes". Hundreds were condemned to death, 320 being actually executed, and over 800 persons were condemned to deportation and sold as slaves in the British West Indies. James II appointed him lord chancellor of England and keeper of the great seal. In the following years Jeffreys upheld the king in his most tyrannical assertions of authority, and, when James II fled the country in December, 1688, during the Glorious Revolution (q.v.), Jeffreys also attempted to escape, disguised as a seaman. He was recognized and arrested, and imprisoned in the Tower of London, where he died four months later.

JEFFREYS, HAROLD (1891–   ), British geophysicist, born in Birtley, Durham, and educated at Armstrong College, Newcastle, and at St. John's College, Cambridge University. A fellow of St. John's College after 1914, he became (1946) Plumian professor of astronomy and experimental philosophy at Cambridge University. One of the world's leading authorities on geophysics (q.v.), Jeffreys made notable contributions to the theory of cosmogony (q.v.). His writings include *The Earth: Its Origin, History, and Physical Constitution* (1924), *Operational Methods in Mathematical Physics* (1927), *Cartesian Tensors* (1931), *Earthquakes and Mountains* (1935), *Methods of Mathematical Physics* (with B. Jeffreys, 1946), and numerous papers for scientific journals.

JEFFRIES, JAMES J. (1875–1953), American pugilist, born in Carroll, Ohio. He entered the professional ring in 1896. On June 9, 1899, he fought the British pugilist Robert Fitzsimmons (1862–1917), then heavyweight champion of the world, in Coney Island, N.Y., and knocked him out in the eleventh round, winning the title. Jeffries successfully defended his crown on five occasions during the next five years. In each bout except the first, which resulted in a decision over Tom Sharkey, he won by a knockout. He retired undefeated in 1905. Attempting a comeback in 1910, he met the American world champion Jack Johnson on July 4 at Reno, Nev. Johnson knocked him out in the fifteenth round.

JEFFRIES, ZAY (1888–   ), American metallurgical engineer, born in Willow Lake, S. Dak., and educated at the South Dakota School of Mines and at Harvard University. After serving as instructor (1911–16) and as assistant professor (1916–17) at the Case School of Applied Science, he left the teaching profession to enter private industry as a metallurgical engineer. Until his retirement in 1949 he contributed greatly to the advancement of the science of metallurgy (q.v.) ; he is best known for metallurgical developments in the electric-light and aluminum industries. He is coauthor of *The Science of Metals* (1924) and *The Aluminum Industry* (1930).

JEHOASH. See JOASH.

JEHOL, province of N.E. China. The capital is Chengteh (q.v.), formerly the summer residence of the rulers of the Manchu dynasty. In 1933 Jehol was taken by the Japanese and incorporated within the puppet state of Manchukuo. During the civil war between the Chinese Nationalist and Communist forces following World War II, Jehol was occupied by the Communists. See CHINA; MANCHURIA. Area, 74,297 sq.m.; pop. (1952 est.) 6,110,000.

JEHOSHAPHAT (d. 851? B.C.), King of Judah (875–51 B.C.), and son and successor of Asa. Jehoshaphat allied himself with Israel against the Syrians and joined Ahab, King of Israel, in a military expedition to Ramoth Gilead. He later renewed the alliance with Ahab's son and successor, Ahaziah, and joined Ahaziah's brother and successor, Jehoram, in a war against the Moabites. Jehoshaphat was succeeded by his oldest son, Jehoram (d. 844? B.C.).

JEHOSHAPHAT, VALLEY OF, traditional name of the Kidron wadi, a deep ravine lying between Jerusalem and the Mount of Olives, in Jordan-occupied Palestine. Scholars have been unable to determine why or when the name was applied to the ravine. It is the site of a Jewish and Moslem cemetery. According to Joel 3, containing the only Scriptural citation, the Valley of Jehoshaphat is the place in which Jehovah will pass judgment against the enemies of His people.

JEHOVAH, name of the God of the Hebrew people, as transliterated from the Massoretic Hebrew text. The word consists of the consonants JHVH or JHWH, with the vowels of a separate word, AdOnAI (Lord). What its original vowels were is a matter of speculation, for, because of a peculiar interpretation of such texts as Ex. 20:7 and Lev. 24:11, the name came to be regarded as too sacred for expression; the scribes in reading substituted "Lord." The evidence of the Greek Church fathers shows the forms *Jabe* and *Jaô* to be traditional, as well as the shortened Hebrew forms of the word *Jah* (Ps. 68:4, etc.) and *Jahu* (in proper names). It indicates that the name was originally spoken *Jahweh* or *Yahwe*. Etymologically, it is a third person singular, imperfect, probably of the verb *hawah* (or *hajah*), signifying "to be". The older interpreters explain the verb in a metaphysical and abstract sense; the "I am" is "He who is", the absolutely existent.

JEHOVIST. See ELOHIST AND YAHWIST.

JEHU (d. 816? B.C.), King of Israel (843?–16? B.C.), son of Jehoshaphat. Jehu was originally a soldier of Ahab, King of Israel, and rose to the rank of general under Ahab's son, Jehoram. Ahab's wife, Jezebel, introduced the worship of Baal into Israel and instigated persecution of Hebrew prophets, and so Jehu slew her, and killed King Jehoram of Israel and King Ahaziah of Judah. He was anointed King of Israel by the prophet Elijah, and controlled the kingdom of Judah. He paid tribute to the Assyrian king, Shalmaneser III, and fought Hazael, King of Damascus. He was succeeded at his death by his son, Jehoahaz (d. 800? B.C.).

JEHUDA, BEN SAMUEL. See JUDAH HA-LEVI.

JEJUNUM. See INTESTINE.

JEKYLL AND HYDE, contrary dispositions or personalities in a person, in one part good, the other bad, as exemplified by Robert Louis Stevenson in *The Strange Case of Dr. Jekyll and Mr. Hyde* (1886). In Stevenson's story, Dr. Jekyll, a man of high ideals, transforms himself at will by a drug into Mr. Hyde, a misshapen dwarf of debased and evil nature. An antidote, which habitually has restored him to his former character, finally fails and the base nature rules.

JELLICOE, JOHN RUSHWORTH, 1st EARL JELLICOE (1859–1935), British naval officer, born in Southampton. He received an appointment as a naval cadet in 1872 and was commissioned a sub-lieutenant in 1880. After service (1882) in the war in Egypt he studied at the Royal Naval College, specializing in gunnery. Alternate periods of duty at sea and ashore followed, and by 1897 he had attained the rank of captain. In 1898, as commander of H.M.S. *Centurion*, he was sent to China. While leading one of the units of the international force sent against Peking during the Boxer Rebellion (1900) he suffered severe wounds. He was made a Commander of the Bath for his services on this expedition.

In the decade preceding the outbreak of World War I Jellicoe advanced (1907) to the rank of rear admiral and served in various leading posts, including those of director of naval ordnance (1905–07), lord commissioner of the admiralty and controller of the navy (1908–09), commander of the Atlantic fleet, with the rank of vice admiral (1910–11), and second sea lord of the admiralty (1912–14). He was appointed acting admiral and commander in chief of the British Grand Fleet on the start of hostilities with Germany. In this position Jellicoe directed (1916) British naval forces at the Battle of Jutland (see JUTLAND, BATTLE OF) and inflicted a serious defeat on the German High Seas Fleet. He supervised British antisubmarine operations after November, 1917, when he became first sea lord and chief of naval staff. Following the war he was promoted (1919) to the rank of admiral of the fleet and appointed (1920) governor general of New Zealand. He retired from this position in 1924. Among honors conferred on Jellicoe for his war services were membership in the Order of Merit and elevation to the peerage as Viscount Jellicoe of Scapa. In 1925 he was created an earl. His writings include *The Grand Fleet, 1914–16: Its Creation, Development, and Work* (1919) and *The Submarine Peril; the Admiralty Policy in 1917* (1934).

JELLIFFE, SMITH ELY (1866–1945), American neurologist and psychoanalyst, born in Brooklyn, N.Y., and educated at the Brooklyn Polytechnic Institute and Columbia University. He taught at the College of Physicians and Surgeons of Columbia University from 1903 to 1907, and from the latter year until 1912 was clinical professor of mental diseases at Fordham University. From 1911 until his death he was adjunct professor of diseases of the mind and nervous system at the New York Post Graduate Hospital and Medical School.

Jelliffe's career covered a wide range of interests and specialties; in his earlier work he wrote on such diverse subjects as botany, chemistry, and materia medica; after turning to neurology in his later years he embraced the theory and practice of psychoanalysis (q.v.), and was one of the pioneer psychoanalysts in the United States as well as one of the most effective propagandists among physicians and psychiatrists for psychoanalytic doctrine. In 1913, with William Alanson White (q.v.), he founded the *Psychoanalytic Review*, of which he was subsequently coeditor; other periodicals which he served in an editorial capacity were the New York *Journal of Nervous and Mental Diseases,* the *Medical News,* and the New York *Medical Journal.* His most important editorial work, also done in collaboration with White, was the "Nervous and Mental Disease Monograph Series", founded in 1907, of which twenty-two volumes appeared. He also collaborated with White on a textbook, *Diseases of the Nervous System* (1915).

JELLYFISH or **MEDUSA,** common name for any of the chiefly marine species of free-swimming coelenterate animals constituting the class Scyphozoa. They are found in most temperate and cold waters of the world. The animals are transparent and disk-shaped or bell-shaped. Water constitutes almost 96% of their body weight, so that if left to dry in the sun they virtually disappear in a short time. In structure they resemble the hydromedusa state of the Hydrozoa (q.v.), differing chiefly in the absence of the velum. Unlike most hydrozoans, scyphozoans pass through a very minute polyp stage during which they are anchored at the ocean bottom; some species never show an alternation of generations. The chief order of jellyfish is Discomedusæ, which contains the large red species, *Cyanea arctica,* common off the N. Atlantic coast of the U.S. This species attains a diameter of 7½ ft. and a tentacle length of 120 ft. Jellyfish are dried, flavored, and used as food in the Orient.

JENA, city of Thuringia, East Germany, situated on the Saale R., about 56 m. by rail s.w. of Leipzig and 12 m. by rail s.e. of Weimar. It was chartered in the 13th century and in 1423 was transferred from the control of Meissen to that of Saxony. Jena is the site of a famous university, founded by the

Jellyfish of the genus Chrysaora. The disk is about 12 inches in diameter.

elector John Frederick of Saxony in 1558. Between 1758 and 1828 Johann Gottlieb Fichte, Georg Wilhelm Friedrich Hegel, Friedrich Wilhelm Joseph von Schelling, Johann Christoph Friedrich von Schiller, and August Wilhelm von Schlegel taught at Jena. Johann Wolfgang von Goethe wrote *Hermann und Dorothea* in the ducal palace, later destroyed and replaced by several new university buildings. Other notable points of interest are the Schwarzer Bär hotel, where Martin Luther lived after his flight from the castle of Wartburg, and the church of St. Michael, dating from the 15th century. North of the city is the plain on which Napoleon defeated the Prussians in 1806, during the Napoleonic Wars. The celebrated Zeiss optical works are situated in Jena. Other industrial establishments are machine shops, printing shops, and plants manufacturing scientific instruments and chemicals. Following World War II Jena was included within the Soviet Zone of Occupation. Pop. (1946) 82,722.

JENGHIZ KHAN. See GENGHIS KHAN.

JENKINS' EAR, WAR OF, in English history, name given to the military conflict, begun in 1739, between Great Britain and Spain. The war developed from British attempts to circumvent the Treaty of Utrecht (see UTRECHT, TREATY OF), which terminated the War of the Spanish Succession (1701–14). Under the commercial provisions of this treaty British trade with Spanish colonies in America was seriously restricted; many British merchants consequently resorted to smuggling. In 1731 Robert Jenkins, a British smuggler in command of the brig *Rebecca,* was seized by the crew of a Spanish coast guard vessel and compelled to surrender his cargo. The commander of the Spanish boat then cut off one of Jenkins' ears. Immediately upon his return to England Jenkins vainly appealed to the British crown for redress. The incident received little attention at the time, but subsequent outrages against British seamen engendered widespread anti-Spanish sentiment in Great Britain. Ultimately the Jenkins affair was extensively exploited in the public press by critics and opponents of Prime Minister Robert Walpole's conciliatory policy toward Spain. The affair was hotly debated in Parliament in 1738, and in the following year, confronted by an implacable opposition, Walpole was obliged to declare war against Spain.

Hostilities were confined to the New World. In November, 1739, a British squadron attacked Porto Bello (Puerto Bello) in the Spanish viceroyalty of New Granada. The next year British naval forces attacked Cartagena and captured Chagres. American colonial troops under General James Edward Oglethorpe attempted to take St. Augustine, Florida, then a Spanish possession, but were repulsed. In 1741 another British squadron, commanded by Commodore George Anson, began raiding operations along the w. coast of South America and against Spanish commerce in the Pacific Ocean. Meanwhile (1740) the desultory struggle had become part of the general European conflict known in history as the War of the Austrian Succession (see SUCCESSION WARS; see also KING GEORGE'S WAR).

JENKS, JEREMIAH WHIPPLE (1856-1929), American economist and educator, born in St. Clair, Mich. From 1891 until 1912 he was professor of political economy and politics at Cornell University. He then joined the faculty of New York University, as research professor of government and public administration, and served also as director of the division of Oriental commerce and politics after 1917. In 1913 he founded the Far Eastern Bureau and was its director until 1921. After 1918 he was a member of the High Commission of Nicaragua and director of the Pacific Railways and the National Bank of Nicaragua. His writings include *Business and the Government* (1917), *Jesus' Principles of Living* (with C. F. Kent, 1920), *Great American Issues* (with J. H. Hammond, 1921), and *We and Our Government* (with R. D. Smith, 1922).

JENNER, EDWARD (1749-1832), English physician, born in Berkeley, Gloucestershire, and educated privately by several physicians, including the celebrated John Hunter (q.v.), and in St. George's Hospital. Jenner is known for his discovery of the principles of vaccination (q.v.), considered the basis of the modern science of immunology; see IMMUNITY. Having observed that people infected with cowpox were immune to smallpox, a much severer disease, Jenner in 1796 injected a young boy with cowpox; six weeks later attempts to produce smallpox in the boy were unsuccessful. In 1798 Jenner published his discovery in *An Inquiry into the Cause and Effect of the Variolæ Vaccinæ.* Vaccination against smallpox met with great opposition among the medical profession, but enough principal physicians and surgeons of England were convinced by Jenner's arguments to establish the practice. Jenner received parliamentary grants totaling about $150,000 for his discovery.

JENNINGS, HERBERT SPENCER (1868-1947), American scientist, born in Tonica, Illinois, and educated at Harvard University and the universities of Michigan and Jena (Germany). Jennings was director of the zoological laboratories at Johns Hopkins University from 1910 to 1938. His researches, in the fields of physiology, genetics, and animal psychology, were made chiefly on microorganisms. His books include *Contribu-

tions to the Study of the Behavior of Lower Organisms* (1904), in which he first applied the phrase "trial and error", which was later much used by behaviorist psychologists, to animal psychology; *The Universe and Life* (1933); and *Genetic Variations in Relation to Evolution* (1935).

JENNINGS, HUGH AMBROSE (1870-1928), American professional baseball player, born in Pittston, Pa. He began his professional baseball career in 1890 and subsequently played in the American Association, the National League, and the American League. He became famous as shortstop with the Baltimore team (the "Orioles") of the National League. From 1907 to 1920 he was manager of the Detroit team of the American League; during this period the team won three American League pennants. From 1920 to 1925 Jennings was a coach for the New York team of the National League. During his career he played in 1264 games and had a batting average of .314; he was a noted baserunner, succeeding three times in stealing more than sixty bases in a season. Jennings was appointed to the Baseball Hall of Fame (q.v.) in 1945.

JENSEN, JOHANNES VILHELM (1873-1950), Danish author, born in Farsø, Jutland, and educated at the University of Copenhagen. He was awarded the Nobel Prize for literature in 1944. His writings are notable for their profound understanding and sympathetic portrayal of the plain people of his own and other countries; these qualities are most apparent in *Himmerlandshistorier* (3 vols., 1898-1910), a collection of folk tales of the people of Himmerland, his native province. Jensen was also deeply interested in the theory of evolution, and in a series of six novels published from 1909 to 1920, expounded his view of the development of mankind from savagery to lofty intellectual aspiration. These novels, *Det Tabte Land, Bræen, Cimbrernes Tog, Norne Gæst, Skibet,* and *Christopher Columbus,* were combined into two volumes under the title *Den Lange Rejse,* in 1938, after they had been translated into English under the title *The Long Journey* (3 vols., 1922-24). Among his other writings are a collection of lyric verse *Digte* (1906); the historical novel *Kongens Fald* (1899-1902); the short-story collection *Exotiske Noveller* (1907-09); and a volume of essays *Dyrenes Forvandling* (1927).

JEPHTHAH, one of the Judges of Israel, an illegitimate son of Gilead. Before going into battle against the Ammonites he vowed

Jerboa (Jaculus orientalis)

to make a burnt offering of the first thing that came forth from his house on his return. The Ammonites were defeated, and as the conqueror drew near his house at Mizpeh there came forth to meet him his daughter with a procession of maidens to celebrate his return. On being told of her father's vow the maiden asked for two months in which to bewail her fate, and then returned to her father, who, according to the Scriptures, "did unto her his vow". Jephthah next subdued the tribe of Ephraim. He judged Israel for six years.

JEPSON, WILLIS LINN (1867-1947), American botanist, born in Vacaville, Calif., and educated at the University of California and Cornell University, and in England and Germany. He was made professor of botany at the University of California in 1919. Jepson is best known for his extensive investigations in the taxonomy and geographic distribution of plants in w. United States, particularly in California. He also conducted botanical expeditions to various parts of the world, including Alaska, Syria, and Palestine. Among his writings are *Flora of Western Middle California* (1901), *The Trees of California* (1909), *The Silva of California* (1910), *A Flora of the Economic Plants of California* (1924), and *An Illustrated Manual of the Flowering Plants of California* (1925).

JERASH. See GERASA.

JERBA or **DJERBA** (anc. *Meninx*), island in the Mediterranean Sea, situated in the Gulf of Gabés, off the coast of Tunisia, and forming part of Tunisia. The terrain is flat and arid, but the soil is arable; wells are the principal source of water. Olives, dates, and figs are the chief crops. Besides farming, occupations include sponge fishing, pottery making, and the manufacture of silk-and-wool cloth and olive oil. Haumpt-es-suk (pop., about 3000) on the N. side of the island, is the administrative center. In ancient Greek and Roman legend the island is the home of the Lotus-eaters. As *Meninx,* it was a Roman possession, and during the Middle Ages it was taken successively by the Normans of Sicily, the Spanish, and the Turks. In 1881 Jerba, together with the mainland of Tunisia, was occupied by the French. Area, 425 sq.m.; pop., about 35,000.

JERBOA, common name for any of the Old World jumping rodents in the family Dipodidæ, found especially in the arid regions of Africa and central Asia. These animals have short front limbs and long hind limbs on which they leap about. They are about 6 in. long from the head to the rump, and have hind legs about 4 in. long. They are sandy above and white below, often with the tip of the tail black. Some species have large, broad ears. *Jaculus jaculus* is a common N. African species.

JEREMIAH or **JEREMIAS,** one of the Books of the Bible, in the Old Testament. The Book tells of the times and teachings of the prophet Jeremiah, who was born in Anathoh, near Jerusalem. He is believed to have been born about 650 B.C., as the Book describes his first coming into public notice about 625 B.C., at the time of the adoption of the Deuteronomic code (see DEUTERONOMY) in the reign of King Josiah of Judah. The Book describes the prophet as strongly supporting the introduction of the code, which re-emphasized the importance of Yahweh-worship in the Temple at Jerusalem, and repeated numerous Mosaic religious laws. After telling of the death of Josiah and the reaction of the people against his religious reforms, the Book describes Jeremiah as becoming a prophet of doom, warning of the destruction of the Temple and ascribing the victories of Babylon over Judah to Yahweh's displeasure with the wickedness of his people. According to the Book, this position made the prophet exceedingly unpopular; and some scholars think that he suffered considerable persecution. The Book ends with the fulfillment of Jeremiah's prophecies, the destruction of the Temple (586 B.C.), the downfall of Judah, and the beginning of the Babylonian Exile. The prophet is described as fleeing to Egypt, and as dying there about a year later.

The Book of Jeremiah is believed by most critics to be a composite production; and contains narrative, prophecy, poetry, and psalms. Its frequent references to later events indicates that the Book was not compiled until the third century B.C., more than 300 years after Jeremiah died. The compilations are thought to have been intended to describe religious and political conditions immediately prior to the destruction of the Judean kingdom in such a way as to give consolation and religious inspiration to the Jewish community in Jerusalem during the later periods of Persian and Greek domination; see JEWS: *History*. Its implication for readers at the time of compilation was that freedom could be regained by adhering to God's commandments and observing religious ritual, rather than by warfare.

JEREZ or **JEREZ DE LA FRONTERA,** formerly XERES, city of Cadiz Province, Spain, situated near the Guadalete R., about 13 miles N.E. of Cadiz. It is the center of a fertile agricultural and livestock-raising region; wine grapes, fruit, and grain are the chief crops. Sherry wine, a product for which the city was formerly famous, is named for Jerez. Points of interest in the city include a 15th-century church, a Moorish castle, remnants of medieval walls, and immense *bodegas* ("wine cellars"). The ancient Romans colonized the site of Jerez, and early in the 8th century the settlement was seized by the Moslems. According to some historians it was the scene of the defeat (711) inflicted on the Visigoths by an army of Moors under the Moslem general Tariq (d. about 720). The Moors were expelled from Jerez in 1264 by Spanish forces under Alfonso X, King of Castile and Leon. Pop. (1950) 107,040.

JERICHO (Ar. *Erīha*), village of Jordan-occupied Palestine, situated about 17 miles E.N.E. of Jerusalem, near the site of an important ancient city of the same name. Modern Jericho is a vacation resort, frequented by wealthy Arab residents of Jerusalem. Bananas, figs, and oranges are grown in the surrounding region. Among points of interest is a medieval castle, built reputedly by the Crusaders. Extensive ruins, including massive, winding double walls, are in the vicinity. Excavated early in the 20th century, these walls are generally identified as the fortifications of original Jericho, a city of Canaan. In the first Biblical reference to Jericho (Joshua 2), the Hebrew leader Joshua dispatched two spies to the Canaanite city from Shittim, the place of encampment of the Israelites. Subsequently besieged by the Israelites, Jericho fell after its walls were leveled by the seven trumpet-blowing priests (Joshua 6). All of the inhabitants were massacred, and the city was cursed by Joshua and destroyed.

According to 1 Kings 16 Jericho was rebuilt, about 500 years later, during the reign (875–853 B.C.) of the Israelite king Ahab, by the Bethelite Hiel. The city is mentioned in later books of the Old Testament, notably (2 Kings 25) as the scene of the defeat (586 B.C.) of Zedekiah last king of Judah, by the Chaldeans under King Nebuchadrezzar. During the reign (37–4 B.C.) of the Judean ruler Herod the Great Jericho was the winter capital of the kingdom; its fortifications were strengthened, and several palaces, an amphitheatre, and other imposing structures were built. After Herod's death, which occurred in the city, it was destroyed by rebellious slaves. Later rebuilt on a nearby site, the city figured prominently in the life of Jesus Christ. According to Matthew 20:30, for example, it was there that He restored sight to the two blind men. Jesus passed through Jericho on His last journey to Jerusalem (Luke 19). The city was razed by the Romans under Vespasian during his campaign (66 A.D.) against the Jews. Its site was later occupied and settled by the Crusaders, who were expelled in turn by the Moslems. British forces captured the modern village in February, 1918, during World War II. By the terms of the United Nations partition plan for Palestine (1947), Jericho was allocated to Arab control. Pop. (1950 est.) 5000.

JERITZA, MARIA (real name MARIE JEDLITZKA) (about 1887-), Austrian operatic soprano, born in Brünn, Austria, and educated in Brünn and Olmütz. She made her debut at the Vienna Volksoper in 1912, as Elisabeth in *Tannhäuser* and in 1913 was engaged by the Vienna Hofoper, where she became famous for her interpretations of roles in the operas of Richard Wagner and Giacomo Puccini. On November 17, 1921, she made her American debut at the Metropolitan Opera House in New York City, in the American premier of Erich Wolfgang Korngold's opera *The Dead City*. She remained with the Metropolitan until 1932, and appeared in many American premiers, including those of Leoš Janáček's *Jenufa*, Puccini's *Turandot*, Korngold's *Violanta*, and Richard Strauss's *Ægyptische Helena*. She also appeared as guest artist with the Los Angeles and San Francisco opera companies and at Convent Garden in London, and gave many concert recitals. Some of her other roles were those of *Carmen, Ariadne, Santuzza, Thais,* and *Sieglinde.*

JEROBOAM, name of two early kings of Israel. **1.** JEROBOAM I (d. 912? B.C.), first king of the Kingdom of Judah, and member of the tribe of Ephraim. He led an unsuccessful plot against the life of Solomon and fled to Egypt, remaining there until Solomon's death. He returned to Palestine to lead a revolt against Solomon's son and successor, Rehoboam, and about 933 B.C. succeeded in establishing himself as king of the ten northern tribes of Israel; this kingdom, with Shechem as its capital, was thereafter known as Judah. He set up shrines at Dan and Bethel to discourage his subjects from making pilgrimages to Jerusalem in the kingdom of Israel. Biblical accounts accuse him of favoring animal worship. He was succeeded at his death by his son Nadab. **2.** JEROBOAM II (d. 744? B.C.), King of Israel (785?–44? B.C.), son of Joash (q.v.). During his reign Jeroboam recovered the lost provinces of Ammon and Moab from Damascus. His reign was outwardly successful and prosperous, but he was denounced by the prophets Amos and Hosea for contributing to the ultimate doom of Israel. Jeroboam, considered the last of the powerful kings of Israel, was succeeded at his death by his son Zechariah.

JEROME, SAINT, or (Lat.) EUSEBIUS HIERONYMUS SOPHRONIUS (340?-420), born in Stridon, on the confines of Dalmatia and Pannonia. In 379 he was ordained a priest, and then spent three years in Constantinople with Gregory of Nazianzus. In 382 he went to Rome, where he became secretary to Pope Damasus and gained much influence. Many persons placed themselves under his spiritual direction, including a noble Roman widow named Paula and her daughter Eustochium, both of whom followed him to the Holy Land in 385. He fixed his residence at Bethlehem in 386, Paula having founded there four convents, three for nuns and one for monks, the latter of which was governed by Jerome himself. Here Jerome pursued his literary labors, accomplishing his most important work, the translation of the Bible into the common, or vulgar, tongue; see VULGATE. He engaged in controversy not only with the heretics Jovinian, Vigilantius, and the Pelagians, but also with Tyrannius Rufinus and St. Augustine. His conflict with the Pelagians rendering his life insecure at Bethlehem, he was compelled to go into concealment for about two years; he died soon after his return. His feast is celebrated September 30.

JEROME, JEROME KLAPKA (1859-1927), English humorist and playwright, born in Walsall, Staffordshire, and educated at Marylebone Grammar School, London. In his early years he was employed successively as a railroad clerk, a teacher, an actor, and a journalist. From 1892 to 1897 he was co-editor of the periodical *The Idler* and simultaneously, from 1893 to 1897, he was editor of the weekly *To-Day*. His first two humorous books, *Idle Thoughts of an Idle Fellow* and *Three Men in a Boat* (both 1889), won immediate success. His *Three Men on the Bummel* (1900) was a sequel to the latter work. His first success in the field of drama was *The Passing of the Third Floor Back* (1908), which has been revived several times. Other plays include *Barbara* (1886), *Miss Hobbs* (1899), *Fanny and the Servant Problem* (1908), and *The Great Gamble* (1914).

JEROME, WILLIAM TRAVERS (1859-1934), American lawyer, born in New York City, and educated at Columbia Law School. He was appointed assistant district attorney of New York County in 1888. Because he regarded them as corrupt, he became an opponent of Tammany Hall (see TAMMANY SOCIETY) in New York City and of the city administrations it controlled. In 1890 he became active in the reform organization called the Municipal League, and in 1893 he was appointed assistant counsel to the Lexow Investigating Committee, empowered by the New York State legislature to investigate both corruption in the municipal government of New York City and the alleged protection of vice by the city police force. In 1894 Jerome was the campaign manager for the successful anti-Tammany mayoralty candidate William L. Strong, and was appointed judge of the Court of Special Sessions in the same year. In the election of 1901, in which the Tammany candidates were defeated, Jerome was elected district attorney of New York County; he was re-elected in 1905. He sponsored a law against gambling which was passed by the New York State legislature, and eliminated police protection of vice and crime in New York City. In his second administration he conducted the prosecution of Harry K. Thaw for the murder of the notable architect Stanford White (q.v.). In 1909 he returned to private practice.

JEROME OF PRAGUE (1360?-1416), Bohemian religious reformer, born in Prague. He studied for some time at Oxford University, at which he became converted to the unorthodox doctrines of the theologian

John Wycliffe (q.v.). On returning to Prague in 1407, he became an associate of the religious reformer John Huss (q.v.), and joined him in preaching against the abuses of the hierarchy of the Catholic Church and the profligacy of the clergy. When Huss was denounced by the Council of Constance (1414-18) and was arrested, Jerome hastened to Constance to defend him, but, on learning that he, too, would be condemned for his preaching, he attempted to return to Prague. He was arrested at Hirschau in Bavaria and was returned to Constance. At first he recanted his views, but later withdrew his recantation and was burned at the stake as a heretic.

JERSEY, the largest and southernmost of the Channel Islands, situated in the English Channel, about 15 miles w. of the coast of Manche Department, France, and about 17 miles s.e. of Guernsey (q.v.), and constituting a semiautonomous bailiwick of the United Kingdom. Generally oblong, it is about 10 m. long and from 4 to 6¼ m. wide. Precipitous rocky headlands, with elevations up to 500 ft., a deeply indented coast, and an interior tableland broken by numerous valleys are the outstanding physical features. Climatic conditions are equable, the highest and lowest recorded temperatures being 89° F. and 31° F. respectively. Precipitation averages about 25 inches annually.

The raising of Jersey cattle, a breed originated on the island, the cultivation of potatoes, tomatoes, fruits, and flowers, fishing, and catering to tourists are the principal occupations. In a recent year nearly 1200 head of cattle, about 18,200 tons of tomatoes, and over 39,250 tons of potatoes were shipped from the island. Foodstuffs, building materials, and fuel comprise the most important imports.

Among points of interest in Jersey are numerous megaliths, an 11th-century church, and two ruined medieval castles. An excellent highway system is maintained. Cargo and passenger steamships operate on regular schedules between the island and Guernsey, St. Malo, France, and points in England. The island is also linked to Great Britain and France by air-transport lines.

Educational facilities include a primary-school system, with about 4600 enrolled pupils, various private schools, with about 1700 enrolled pupils, and two public schools, namely Jersey College, for boys, and Victoria College, for girls. Enrolled students in the two last-named institutions recently numbered

about 7300. The Anglican Church is the predominant religious denomination, but there are Roman Catholic and other Protestant congregations. French is the official language; the language in common use by the people is English.

St. Helier (q.v.), a seaport on the s. coast, is the administrative center and largest town. Other towns include St. Aubin, Gorey, and St. Brelade.

Legislative and executive power in Jersey is vested in the Assembly of the States. This body consists of 12 senators, 12 constables, and 12 deputies, all of whom are elected by universal suffrage; the lieutenant governor and commander in chief, the attorney general, the solicitor general, and the dean of Jersey, all crown appointees, who have the right to speak but not to vote; and the bailiff, also a crown appointee, who may dissent and is entitled to cast a deciding vote. The lieutenant governor is empowered to veto certain types of legislation. Assembly of the States legislation designed to remain effective permanently must have the approval of the King in Council. Executive power is exercised by committees appointed by the Assembly of the States. The highest judicial body is the Royal Court, composed of the bailiff and 12 jurats. To become effective, acts of the British Parliament must be registered in the records of the Royal Court. For the history of Jersey, see CHANNEL ISLANDS. Area of island, 45 sq.m.; pop. (1952) 55,888.

JERSEY CITY, county seat of Hudson Co., N.J., situated on a peninsula bounded on the e. by Upper New York Bay and the Hudson R. and on the w. by Newark Bay and the Hackensack R.; and lying opposite the s. end of Manhattan Island, with which it is connected by ferries and by several tunnels. It is served by eight railroads, and by overseas and coastwise steamships. The extensive commerce carried on at the city's eleven miles of waterfront is part of the shipping trade of the Port of New York. Jersey City is the second-largest city in the State and one of the leading manufacturing centers on the Atlantic Coast. Industrial establishments, several of which produce products with world-known trade names, include railroad shops, foundry and machine shops, and factories manufacturing soap, perfume, lead pencils, cans and containers, electrical machinery, patent medicines, packed meats, macaroni, cheese, chemicals, gypsum, paints, varnishes, steel, cigarettes, and antiseptics. The city is the site of St. Peter's College

(Roman Catholic), established in 1872, and a State teachers college, established in 1929.

Most of Jersey City lies on a low and swampy area, but an extension of the Palisades (q.v.) runs through the city from N. to S.; the residential section of the city is largely centered on this height. Among the interesting structures in Jersey City is a huge electric clock, measuring 50 ft. in diameter, on one of the Colgate-Palmolive-Peet factories along the Hudson river front. The minute hand of the clock weighs more than a ton and moves 31 inches a minute.

The region was first settled by the Dutch and was part of the patroonship of Pavonia, granted to Michael Pauw in 1630. The site of the present city was known as Powles Hook (Paulus Hoeck), and was first settled in 1633. A highway between New York and Philadelphia was built through the settlement in 1764, and in the same year a ferry to New York was established. During the Revolutionary War the British took the American fort at Powles Hook in 1776 and occupied it until 1779, when it was retaken by the Americans under Major Henry ("Light-Horse Harry") Lee. In 1804 a town was laid out at Powles Hook by a private corporation, and in 1820 it was incorporated as the City of Jersey, a part of Bergen township. It was reincorporated as a separate town in 1838, made the county seat in 1840, and chartered as a city in 1855. Pop. (1950) 299,017.

JERUSALEM, city of central Palestine, situated on a plateau between the valley of Kidron on the E. and the valley of Hinnom on the S. and W. It lies 15 miles W. of the N. extremity of the Dead Sea, 33 miles E. of the Mediterranean Ocean, and 54 m. by rail S.E. of Jaffa. The heart of present-day Jerusalem is the "Old City", a one-square-mile area enclosed by ancient walls and divided into Christian, Jewish, Mohammedan, and Armenian sections. The Christian section, in the N.W., contains the New Gate, shares the Jaffa Gate with the Armenian section on the S., and shares with the Mohammedan section the Damascus Gate, N.W. of which is located the Tomb of Christ. The Mohammedan section, in the N.E. portion of the Old City, contains Herod's Gate, St. Stephen's Gate, and the Golden Gate, E. of which is located the Mount of Olives and the Garden of Gethsemane. The Jewish section, occupying the S. portion, contains the Zion Gate, S. of which is Mt. Zion and the Tomb of David. Chiefly N.W. of the Old City

walls is New Jerusalem, which has developed since the middle of the 19th century; it extends over the surrounding hills into garden suburbs and then desert, and its broad avenues, modern apartments and office buildings are in contrast to the narrow, twisting streets and alleys, and meager dwellings of the Old City. The population of the New City (1951 est.) is 150,000; that of the Old City is about 27,500, including about 2500 Jews.

The Old City is sacred to Christians as the site of Christ's last days on earth; it is sacred to Jews as the historic symbol of the Jewish homeland and the capital of the first Jewish kingdom; and it is sacred to Mohammedans as the site of Mohammed's ascent into heaven. The notable structures of the Old City are the Christian Church of the Holy Sepulchre, built over the tomb of Christ; the Jewish Wailing Wall, the remnant of the great temple built by Herod; and the Mohammedan Dome of the Rock, better known as the Mosque of Omar, built upon the site where Mohammed is said to have ascended to heaven. In New Jerusalem are several hospitals, educational institutions, missions and monasteries. The Hebrew University, opened in 1925, is located E. of the city on Mt. Scopus.

Little is known of the history of Jerusalem prior to the time of David other than it was a place of some importance long before the Hebrew occupation. According to the Old Testament, when David became king over all of Israel, he decided to make Jerusalem his residence and the capital of his country. The new king brought to his capital the ark of Jehovah from its obscurity at Kirjath-Jearim, and installed it in a new temple (2 Sam. 6; 1 Chron. 11:4-9); built a royal palace and a number of other buildings (Neh. 3:16); and strengthened the city's fortifications. David's son Solomon continued the development of Jerusalem. He built a city wall and many buildings on a scale of magnificence previously unknown to Israel. Solomon's principal buildings were a new temple and a new royal palace, encircled by a wall. The palace, built on successive terraces, consisted of a house constructed of cedar beams and pillars brought from the forests of Lebanon, the dimensions of which were 50 cubits wide, 100 cubits long, and 30 cubits high; the throne hall; the palace proper or royal apartments; the apartments of the Queen of Sheba; and the prison (1 Kings 7:1-12;

Ewing Galloway

Thousands of pilgrims visiting the walled city of Jerusalem at Easter time

Jer. 32:2; Neh. 3:25-27). The courts and buildings of the temple were constructed on a level above the palace. The main building of the temple was considered of great beauty, but was comparatively small, being only 20 cubits wide and 60 cubits long, exclusive of the porch and the side chambers. The temple was built of cedar and of stone (1 Kings 6:3-6), and was surrounded by a court in which were contained the altar of burnt offerings and a reservoir (1 Kings 7:9-12, 23-47).

Jerusalem continued to expand after Solomon's reign, until about 933 B.C., when the northern tribes of Israel seceded from the rule of the house of David, after which the city's importance diminished greatly. Not until the reigns of Uzziah and his son Jotham (2 Chron. 26 and 27), some two centuries later, did the city begin to regain its previous status. Between this period and the rise of the powerful Maccabee family (see MACCABEES), about six centuries later, the history of Jerusalem is that of the Jews

(q.v.); see also PALESTINE. Under the Maccabees Jerusalem entered upon an unprecedented era of prosperity. It was the holy city of Judaism and the great pilgrim shrine of the Jewish world.

The capture of Jerusalem by the Romans under Gnæus Pompeuis Magnus in 65 B.C. resulted in no serious material disaster to the city. Its greatest prosperity was attained under Herod the Great (q.v.). Besides a complete reconstruction of the Temple on a scale truly magnificent, involving the expenditure of vast sums of money, he built the Xystus, an open place surrounded by a gallery; his own great palace, on the w. side of the city; and a large reservoir, hippodrome, and theater. In addition to these works many minor improvements were made, including the general strengthening of the fortifications. In 70 A.D., during the rebellion of Jews against Roman authority, the Romans, under Emperor Titus, captured and razed the city; only a few remnants of the w. fortifications were left standing. With this event the history of ancient Jerusalem came to a close.

The Roman emperor Hadrian visited the city, largely in ruins, about 130 A.D. and began its reconstruction. The desperate rebellion of the Jews against the Romans under Bar Cocheba (q.v.) between the years 132 and 135 led the emperor to make it a pagan city and he prohibited all Jews from entering it. The new city was called Ælia Capitolina. The wall with which Hadrian encircled it was, in general, on the line of the old wall, except on the s., where it left a large portion of the old city outside of the enclosure. Little is known of the city from the time of Hadrian to the time of Constantine the Great (q.v.). The pagan population was gradually supplemented by Christians. With the recognition of Christianity as the religion of the Empire, pilgrims began to flock to Jerusalem to visit the holy places. The church of the Holy Sepulchre (see HOLY SEPULCHRE) was built at the order of Emperor Constantine. Other buildings of like character were subsequently built, and Jerusalem became a Christian city, and a place of pilgrimage for religious devotees from all quarters of Christendom. Among the noteworthy buildings belonging to this period are the church of St. Stephen, N. of the city, built by the Byzantine empress Eudocia, who also rebuilt the ancient s. wall; and the great church of St. Mary on the temple hill, built by the Byzantine emperor Justinian.

The Christian city, after being captured by the Persians under Khosrau II (q.v.) in 614, but recovered by Emperor Heraclius in 628, was taken in 637 by the Moslems under the caliph Omar. The Christians were treated leniently by the Moslems. A mosque, The Dome of the Rock, was erected over the rock which, in all probability, was the altar place of Solomon's temple. When the Egyptian Fatimite caliphs became rulers of Jerusalem in 969, the condition of the Christian population became more precarious. The Seljuk Turks conquered the city in 1077, and their maltreatment of Christians was one of the causes of the Crusades (q.v.). In 1099 the Crusaders, under Godfrey of Bouillon, gained possession of the city, and slaughtered many of its inhabitants. Jerusalem became once more a Christian city, and the capital of the so-called Latin Kingdom (q.v.), until its capture in 1187 by the Moslem leader Saladin (q.v.).

The contemporary history of Jerusalem is closely connected with that of Palestine and of the new state of Israel (qq.v.). Jerusalem was the site of some of the most bitter fighting between the Jews and the Arabs in the conflict over partition of Palestine. The General Assembly of the United Nations, in its original partition plan of Nov. 29, 1947, proposed to establish Jerusalem and its environs as an international enclave, some 280 sq.m. in area. The objective was to assure free access for all religious groups to the holy places of the city. However, in the spring of 1948, during the war over partition between the Jews and the Arab League, the opposing armies of Israel and of Trans-Jordan seized Jerusalem, with Israel occupying the w. portion of the city, the modern residential and business sections, and Trans-Jordan occupying the E. portion, including the Old City. In addition, the Israeli forces held a corridor to Jerusalem extending from Tel Aviv on the coast. In the armistice signed on April 3, 1949, between Israel and Trans-Jordan, both sides recognized the other's holdings in Jerusalem. The Israel government proposed the internationalization of the Old City; however, Trans-Jordan refused consent to this proposal unless the rest of the city were placed under international administration. In 1950 the New City was made the capital of Israel.

JERUSALEM ARTICHOKE. See ARTICHOKE, JERUSALEM.

JERVIS BAY, a bay on the coast of New South Wales, Australia, 90 miles S.S.E. of Sydney. It is 10 to 12 m. long and has one of the finest harbors in the world. An area of 28 sq.m., including the excellent harbor on the s. side of the bay, were ceded by New South Wales and incorporated within the Australian Capital Territory (q.v.) in 1915 for the establishment of a port to be connected by rail with Canberra (q.v.).

JESPERSEN, JENS OTTO HARRY (1860-1943), Danish philologist and grammarian, born in Randers, and educated at the University of Copenhagen. In 1893 he became professor of English language and literature at the University of Copenhagen, and except for a year (1909-10) as lecturer at Columbia University in New York City, he taught there until his death. Jespersen's early studies dealt mainly with phonetics; his first major work, *Fonetik* (1897–99), was the first complete presentation of phonetics in Danish and still remains a classic in the field. Later in his career he turned to the study of grammar, particularly English grammar, on scientific principles. In his last period he formulated a general philosophy of language which reflects the contributions of modern linguistic science. Among his writings are *Growth and Structure of the English Language* (1905) and *Language, Its Nature, Development and Origin* (1922). See GRAMMAR: *History of Grammar.*

JESSAMINE. See JASMINE.

JESSE TREE or **TREE OF JESSE,** in decorative art, a representation of the genealogical tree of Jesus Christ, showing his descent from "the root of Jesse", father of David, king of Israel, as recounted in the Old Testament in the Book of Isaiah 11:1. The Jesse tree has long been a frequent motif in stained-glass church windows, called Jesse windows. The tree is shown springing from the recumbent figure of Jesse. In the branches are figures from the royal line of David as described in the Old Testament, and figures of Jesus or of the Virgin and Child appear at the top. Notable examples of Jesse windows occur in the cathedral at Chartres, France, and at Wells Cathedral, England. Sculptured representations of the Jesse tree are set over a number of the doorways of the French Gothic cathedrals of Amiens and Laon.

JESSE WINDOW. See JESSE TREE.

JESTBOOK, a once popular literary genre, comprising a collection of jokes and anecdotes, some satirizing contemporary institutions and others developed from folklore. Jestbooks were especially popular in Italy during the 15th century. During the following two centuries they also became popular in other European countries. The earliest of these jestbooks were written in Latin and were known as *facetiæ.* Notable among the early Italian collections was the *Liber Facetiarum* written by the Italian humanist scholar (see HUMANISM) Giovanni Francesco Poggio Bracciolini (see POGGIO BRACCIOLINI). This work was a collection of satires, sometimes coarse, on the monks and secular orders of the Church of the period, and many of his jokes found their way into the anecdotal literature of Italy, France, Germany, and England. Jestbooks began to flourish in England in the 16th century and included such early collections of vernacular verse as *The Merry Gests of the Widow Edith* (1525). A notable early English jestbook in prose was *The Hundred Merry Tales* (1526). Jestbooks continued to be popular in England for two hundred years, their vogue culminating in the middle of the 18th century. Authorship of many of these collections was attributed by publishers to well-known persons in order to enhance the sales value of the jestbooks. A notable example was *Joe Miller's Jests, or Wit's Vade Mecum* (1739), in which only three of the jokes had been coined by Joseph Miller, a contemporary popular comedian. At a later date, after jestbooks had ceased to have a popular vogue, jokes and anecdotes of the same type were included in novels of manners; the first example of this development was *Sayings and Doings* (1824-28) by Theodore Edward Hook. The older English jests were collected and edited by the literary historian William Carew Hazlitt (q.v.) under the title *Shakespeare Jest-Books* (3 vols., 1864).

JESUITS or **SOCIETY OF JESUS,** a religious order of men in the Roman Catholic Church, founded by Ignatius of Loyola (see LOYOLA) in 1534, and confirmed by Pope Paul III in 1540. The motto of the order is *Ad Majorem Dei Gloriam,* "To the greater glory of God", and its object is the spread of the Church by preaching and teaching.

The time of preparation required of a candidate for membership in the order is considerably longer than that required for the secular priesthood or for membership in other religious orders: after two years in seclusion and prayer as a *novice,* the candidate takes simple vows of poverty, chastity, and obedience, and becomes a *scholastic;* he then spends two years of study in review of classical subjects, and three years studying philosophy, mathematics, and the physical sciences; five years of teaching in Jesuit colleges follow, and, after four years' study of theology and another year of retirement and prayer, the candidate takes solemn vows and is ordained a priest, becoming a *coadjutor* or *professed.* In addition to the usual vows of poverty, chastity, and obedience, the coadjutors take a special vow to go wherever the pope may send them, and a vow renouncing all ecclesiastical honors. The order is governed by a *general,* residing at Rome, who is elected for life by the general Congregation of the order, consisting of representatives of the various provinces.

The original aim of Ignatius of Loyola in forming his band was to make a pilgrimage to the Holy Land to convert the Mohammedans; all access to the Holy Land was barred, however, by the outbreak of war with the Turks, and the members of the order submitted to the pope a constitution which bound them to go as missionaries to any place the pope might direct. After the constitution was approved, Loyola was elected the first general of the order.

The development of the order was rapid. Its members took leading parts in the Counter Reformation (see REFORMATION; CHURCH HISTORY), establishing schools and colleges throughout Europe. For a hundred and fifty years they were the leaders in European education; by 1640 they had more than five hundred colleges, located in nearly every important city in Europe. In the mission field the expansion of the order was equally great. Missions were established by Francis Xavier in India and Japan, and the order spread to the interior of China and the coast of Africa. Letters from the Jesuit missionaries in Canada, containing ethnological, historical, and scientific information, were published as the *Jesuit Relations,* and form a valuable and unique source of information concerning the aboriginal tribes of that country. The most famous work of the Jesuit missionaries in the New World, however, was the establishment in South America of a Christian Commonwealth, known as the *Reductions of Paraguay.* There for almost two hundred years they conducted a communal nation of native Indians, founding thirty-two villages with a total population of about 160,000; they taught the Indians agriculture, mechanical arts, and commerce, and trained a small army for defense of the settlements.

The history of the Jesuit order has been marked by a steadily increasing prejudice against it, especially in Catholic countries. Their devotion to the papacy called forth opposition from nationalistic rulers and leaders, and their zeal for ecclesiastical reform antagonized the clergy. At one time or another the order has been expelled from every country in Europe, and in 1773 a coalition of powers under Bourbon influence induced Pope Clement XIV to issue a brief suppressing the order. In Prussia and Russia, however, Frederick the Great and Catherine the Great refused to give the brief the publication necessary to make it effective, and in those countries the order survived in local organizations until in 1814 Pope Pius VII re-established the Jesuits on a world-wide basis. Political and religious opposition also revived; since the re-establishment of the order, it has been free from

attack only in Denmark, Sweden, England, and the United States.

In a recent year the order had a membership of approximately 26,000, of which about one fifth was in the United States. In the U.S. alone, the order maintained twenty-three colleges and universities, five seismological stations, and three radio broadcasting stations.

JESUITS' BARK. See CINCHONA.

JESUP, MORRIS KETCHUM (1830-1908), American banker and philanthropist, born in Westport, Conn. He entered the banking business in New York City in 1852 and retired from it thirty years later. During his business career, he was an active member of several religious institutions, including the New York City Mission and Tract Society, of which he was president from 1881 to 1903, and for which he financed the construction of the DeWitt Memorial Church in New York City. He was a founder of the Young Men's Christian Association (q.v.) in the United States, and in 1872 became president of the association. His financial contributions to the advancement of science were distributed principally through the Museum of Natural History in New York City, which he helped to found in 1869 and of which he was president from 1881 until his death. Jesup donated about two million dollars to encourage research through the museum; notable in this connection were his contributions to the Arctic expeditions conducted by the explorer Robert Edwin Peary (q.v.) and to the Jesup North Pacific Expedition (1897-1903), planned by the anthropologist Franz Boas (q.v.) to investigate archeological remains in the extreme northwestern areas of the North American continent; the Jesup Expedition discovered archeological proofs of the connections between Asiatic and American aborigines. Jesup was also a generous contributor to the National Association of Audubon Societies.

JESUS, son of Sirach Eleazer. See ECCLESIASTICUS.

JESUS CHRIST (between 8 and 4 B.C.– about 29 A.D.), the central figure of Christianity (q.v.), born in Bethlehem in Judea. He was legally the son of Joseph, a carpenter of Nazareth, but is believed by the great majority of Christians to be the incarnate son of God, and to have been divinely conceived by Mary, Joseph's wife. The name Jesus is a Greek rendering of the Hebrew name Joshua or *Yehoshua* (literally, "Jehovah is deliverance"). Christ, or Christos, is

Jesus Christ preaching the Sermon on the Mount

the Greek translation of the Hebrew *Messiah* ("Anointed"), signifying that Jesus was regarded by his early followers as the promised deliverer of Israel, and by later Christian doctrine as the redeemer of all mankind. The chronology of the Christian Era is reckoned from a 6th-century computation of His death, which is now recognized as being from four to eight years in error.

The four canonical Gospels (q.v.) are the principal sources of information concerning the life of Jesus. Except for a group of disciples, He was almost forgotten after his death until, with the increasing importance of Christianity, He became a figure of legend. Jesus Himself wrote nothing, and no original writings by His disciples are extant. Hebrew literature contains few references to the Master, though His existence is there authenticated. Several Roman historians, notably Publius Cornelius Tacitus and Suetonius Tranquilus, use the word "Christos" in describing Roman persecution of the primitive sect. Biblical scholars doubt that the Gospels were written before the late 1st century A.D. The accounts on which they were based were presumably written

shortly after the death of Jesus, in order to facilitate the spreading of the Christian faith throughout the ancient world. Edited and elaborated, these first accounts were later developed into the Gospels in their present form.

Three of the Gospels, Matthew, Mark, and Luke, are considered to be based upon a single one of these early accounts, and are called the Synoptic Gospels because they tell essentially the same story. In Biblical criticism, this assumed Synoptic document is called "Q" and the common elements of the three Gospels are called the "Q strain". Mark was the first and simplest written Gospel, incorporating the Q document, oral traditions, and, possibly, an earlier version of the Mark Gospel called Ur-Mark (Ger. *ur,* "primitive"). Matthew and Luke were new versions, based on Q, a collection of Jesus's sayings in Aramaic, and on Mark. The version of John is considered much later than the first three, and is termed *Christological,* i.e., more concerned with doctrine and theology than its predecessors.

The scantiness of historical source material, and its relative unreliability, has produced many expositions of the life of Jesus, varying in detail, and based on differing interpretations of available records. The Gospels say that Jesus was both the Son of God and the son of Joseph, his legal father. Jesus is described as a scion of the royal House of David, but, in the genealogy given in Luke and Matthew, Joseph and not Mary is the descendant of David. The doctrine of the virgin birth is based upon the Luke account and has been an article of faith since Apostolic times. Matthew and Luke record the birth of Jesus at Bethlehem, where Joseph and Mary had gone to comply with the Roman edict of registration for tax lists. Matthew alone describes the flight into Egypt, when Joseph and Mary took the Child Jesus out of reach of King Herod, warned against what he considered a potential usurper. Only Luke relates the compliance of Joseph and Mary with the Jewish Law requiring circumcision and presentation of the firstborn son at the Temple in Jerusalem, and describes the pilgrimage to the Temple for the Passover feast. Nothing is told in the Gospels concerning Jesus from the time He was twelve to the time He began His public ministry, about eighteen years later.

All four Gospels give the major part of their space to the public ministry. The three Synoptic Gospels describe it as having taken place entirely in little more than a year; the Gospel of John gives the time as three years. None of the Gospels, however, state that Jesus attempted to found a new religion; they all describe him as a minister preaching repentance for sin in Israel. This concept is stated in simple terms in Matthew. When a Canaanite woman asks Jesus to heal her daughter, He replies, "I am not sent but unto the lost sheep of the house of Israel" (Matt. 15:24).

The account of the public ministry is generally the same in the three Synoptic Gospels; they do not disagree, but each supplies details not present in the other two. Each version, including John, describes the baptism of Jesus in the Jordan River by John the Baptist; after the baptism Jesus retired to the neighboring wilderness for a period of fasting and meditation. In Matthew and Luke this period is given as forty days, and both versions use the same apocryphal details to describe the temptations brought forth by the devil to dissuade Jesus from fulfillment of His mission. Following this period of what was, according to Biblical scholars, ritual preparation, Jesus returned to the scene of His baptism and then, accompanied by several of John's disciples, traveled into Galilee. He visited His home in Nazareth and then made Capernaum His place of residence. There He began the organization of a formal following, beginning with Simon, Andrew, and John, who had come with Him from the baptism, and, later, James, the brother of John. As His followers increased, He selected twelve of His disciples (see APOSTLE) to work more closely with Him in his preaching mission.

Using Capernaum as a base, Jesus made tours of the neighboring towns and villages, proclaiming the advent of the kingdom of God as had the Israelite prophets before Him. When the wounded in body and spirit asked help from Him, He sought to heal them with the power of faith. He stressed the infinite love of God for the lowest and meanest of mankind, and promised pardon and eternal life in Heaven to the most hardened sinners, provided their repentence was sincere. His emphasis on moral sincerity rather than Jewish ritual incurred the enmity of the Pharisees (q.v.). In the view of the Jewish leaders, Jesus preached not the word of God, but His own, which to them was heresy.

However, His popularity with the Judean populace increased. Without His intention, He came to be viewed as a political leader and, eventually, the enthusiasm of the people led them to make an unsuccessful attempt to force Him, as the long-awaited Messiah, into a political revolution against Rome. In answer, in the synagogue at Capernaum, Jesus delivered a discourse on the "Bread of Life" (John 6) to demonstrate the irreconcilable opposition of His doctrine with the material ambitions of the people. The discourse, emphasizing the spiritual and communion with God, bewildered His audience, which awaited practical political counsel. Many of Jesus' followers left Him, and his influence in Galilee came to an end. Leaving Galilee, Jesus thenceforth divided his time into periods of travel and preaching, and periods of retirement in Bethany and Ephraim, where He taught His disciples and prepared them to carry on His work. His discourses and the miracles He performed were greeted with such popular fervor that Jesus became suspect as a potential rebel against Jewish civil and religious authority, and hence incurred the enmity of Jewish leaders.

On the approach of the Passover, Jesus traveled to Jerusalem for the last time. On the Sunday of Passover week He entered the city in the midst of a large gathering, with a demonstration of enthusiasm that alarmed the Jerusalem authorities. The first three days of the week were given to discourses containing in exact terms His Messianic claims. He criticized the priests and denounced the scribes and Pharisees for their formalism. Moreover, He drove from the court of the Temple the traders and money changers who, by long-established custom, had been permitted to transact business in the outer court, declaring that they had made His house "a den of thieves".

Meanwhile, the priests and scribes sought to have Him put to death, and Judas Iscariot (q.v.), one of the disciples, agreed to help them. On Thursday Jesus ate the Passover supper with his disciples, and during the meal referred to His imminent death as a sacrifice for the sins of mankind. In blessing the unleavened bread and wine during the Passover services, He called the bread His body and the wine His blood, "which shall be shed for many", a ritual which has been repeated by Christians in services of worship since that time and which has become one of the most important sacraments in the Christian church; see LORD'S SUPPER. After the meal Jesus and His disciples went to an olive grove, called Gethsemane, where, according to Matthew, Mark, and John, Jesus said that He would rise again after His death. Then the Master retired for prayer and meditation. He was arrested at Gethsemane by the Jewish authorities, led to Him by Judas, His betrayer.

Jesus was brought before Annas, a former High Priest, for examination and was taken to a meeting of the Sanhedrin, the supreme council of the Jews. The High Priest, Caiaphas, placed Jesus under oath and asked Him directly whether He conceived Himself to be "Christ, Son of the Blessed". Upon His positive affirmation, described in all four Gospels, Jesus was condemned for blasphemy, which, according to the Jewish Law, required the death penalty. Because the Roman procurator was the only authority with the right to inflict capital punishment, Jesus was on Friday morning led before Pontius Pilate, the Roman procurator, for formal condemnation. When Pilate asked Him if He were King of the Jews, Jesus replied, "Thou sayest it"; the Gospels relate that Pilate tried several expedients to save Jesus, but left the decision to the people, whom he wished to satisfy. Disappointed at the failure of Jesus to become the Messiah they had hoped for, a political leader against Rome, the Jerusalem populace turned against Him and insisted on His death. At length Pilate ordered the "King of the Jews" to be executed as a rebel against Rome. (The actual role of Pilate has been much debated by many historians; the early Church tended to place the major blame on the Jews, and to deal less harshly with Pilate, who was noted for his ruthlessness.) Jesus was taken to Golgotha, the place of execution, and there crucified, the Roman punishment for political offenders and criminals. Late in the day His body was taken down from the cross, and, because of the approach of the Sabbath, when burial was not permitted, was hastily laid in a nearby tomb belonging to Joseph of Arimathea.

Early on the following Sunday, several of the women disciples, going to the tomb to take the body and give it burial, found that the stone door had been opened and the sepulcher was empty. One or two young men clothed in white garments, or two angels, announced to them that Christ was risen. Later, on the same day, according to the Gospels, Jesus appeared to the women and to others of the disciples in various places in Jerusalem. The disciples did not doubt that they had again seen and heard the Master Whom they had known and followed during His ministry in Galilee and Judea.

The resurrection of Jesus became one of the most compelling doctrines of the Christian religion. By rising from the dead, Jesus gave man hope of a life after death in the Kingdom of Heaven. According to the Gospels, Jesus devoted Himself, in the post-resurrection period, to further instruction of His disciples in matters pertaining to the spiritual Kingdom of God. He laid on them the specific commission of going throughout the world as His representatives and bringing all men into His following. Finally, by a company of disciples whom He had led out of Jerusalem to Bethany, He was seen to ascend into the heavens. These doctrines, both those He pronounced and those concerning Him, came to be principal tenets of Christianity; see CHURCH HISTORY.

JESUS COLLEGE, a college of Cambridge University, England, founded in 1496 by John Alcock, bishop of Ely, on the site of the 12th-century Benedictine convent of

Saint Radigund. The buildings of the college, comprising the original convent and church and various subsequently-erected structures, are among the handsomest in Cambridge. The faculty of the college consists of a master, twelve fellows, and thirty-four scholars; the master and one of the fellows are appointed by the bishop of Ely. A large proportion of the student body, almost 300 in a recent year, pursues the courses of study under scholarships granted by the college. For a description of the courses of study and degrees offered, see CAMBRIDGE UNIVERSITY. Among distinguished graduates of Jesus College are Archbishop Thomas Cranmer, Bishop Edward Fox, the historian John Strype, and the authors Laurence Sterne and Samuel Taylor Coleridge.

JESUS COLLEGE, a college of Oxford University, England, founded in 1571 under a charter granted by Queen Elizabeth, by Dr. Hugh ap Rice, or Price, treasurer of the see of St. David's, Wales. Later the queen added to the original grant a gift of part of the land on which the college now stands and of timber from the royal forests, and assumed the title of founder of the college. Jesus College was originally intended to serve exclusively as an institution for Welshmen studying at Oxford, and it still restricts a number of its scholarships to natives of Wales. For a description of the courses given, and degrees offered, see OXFORD UNIVERSITY. The college buildings, erected chiefly in the 16th and 17th centuries, later fell into disrepair and were restored in the latter part of the 19th century. The library, built in 1674, has valuable collections of rare books and manuscripts, particularly those connected with the history and literature of Wales; and also has an extensive collection

of Celtic works. The faculty consists of a master, twelve fellows, and thirty scholars; in a recent year, about 175 students were enrolled.

JET, a hard, compact, deep-black variety of lignite (q.v.) or brown coal. It has a hardness ranging from 2 to 2.5 and a specific gravity ranging from 1.1 to 1.4. It is easily cut and carved and takes a high polish, and is used in making ornaments and inexpensive jewelry. The most important center for production of jet and manufacture of jet articles is Whitby, England. Pennsylvania anthracite coal is often used in place of jet; other substitutes are black, cryptocrystalline varieties of quartz, black glass, and black Bakelite and other plastics.

JET PROPULSION. See AIRPLANE.

JEVONS, WILLIAM STANLEY (1835-82), English economist, philosopher, and mathematician, born in Liverpool, and educated at University College in London. He is known for his work in the mathematical analysis of logic and for the development of the theory of marginal utility in economics. He opposed trade unions because he did not believe they could achieve their ends; instead he supported the idea of worker's co-operatives. Among his writings are *Pure Logic* (1864), *Elementary Lessons in Logic* (1870), *The Theory of Political Economy* (1871), *Principles of Science* (1874), and *The State in Relation to Labour* (1882).

JEWEL CAVE NATIONAL MONUMENT, a national monument in w. South Dakota, established in 1908. It covers an area of 1275 acres in Custer Co., about 14 miles w. of the town of Custer, and contains Jewel Cave, the subterranean limestone chambers of which are noted for their stalactite growths and calcite crystal formations.